ROUTLEDGE HANDBOOK OF RISK MANAGEMENT AND THE LAW

In today's highly globalized and regulated economy, private and public organizations face myriad complex laws and regulations. A process designed to detect and prevent regulatory compliance failures is vital. However, such an effective process cannot succeed without development and maintenance of a strong compliance and legal risk management culture.

This wide-ranging handbook pulls together work from experts across universities and industries around the world in a variety of key disciplines such as law, management, and business ethics. It provides an all-inclusive resource, specifying what needs to be known and what needs to be further pursued in these developing areas. With no such single text currently available, the book fills a gap in our current understanding of legal risk management, regulatory compliance, and ethics, offering the potential to advance research efforts and enhance our approaches to effective legal risk management practices.

Edited by an expert on legal risk management, this book is an essential reference for students, researchers, and professionals with an interest in business law, risk management, strategic management, and business ethics.

Virginia A. Suveiu, Esq., counsels on legal risk management, regulatory compliance, and commercial law matters and has held several related positions, including Chief Safeguard Officer and Of Counsel. She is an arbitrator for the Financial Industry Regulatory Authority. She served on the editorial board of the National Contract Management Association's *Contract Management Magazine*. She is affiliated with and has been invited to speak to several professional organizations on issues related to business law. She is an active member of the State Bar of California and admitted to the US District Court, Central District of California. She has held numerous positions in academia, including as founding dean and professor, and currently is an instructor and content developer for the University of California, Irvine, where she was given the Distinguished Instructor Award.

ROUTLEDGE HANDBOOK OF RISK MANAGEMENT AND THE LAW

Edited by Virginia A. Suveiu

Routledge
Taylor & Francis Group
NEW YORK AND LONDON

Cover image: © Getty Images

First published 2023
by Routledge
605 Third Avenue, New York, NY 10158

and by Routledge
4 Park Square, Milton Park, Abingdon, Oxon, OX14 4RN

Routledge is an imprint of the Taylor & Francis Group, an informa business

Library of Congress Cataloging-in-Publication Data
Names: Suveiu, Virginia A., editor.
Title: Routledge handbook of risk management and the law / edited by Virginia A. Suveiu.
Description: New York, NY : Routledge, 2023. | Includes bibliographical references and index.
Identifiers: LCCN 2022038543 (print) | LCCN 2022038544 (ebook) | ISBN 9780815364382 (hardback) | ISBN 9781032349725 (paperback) | ISBN 9781351107242 (ebook)
Subjects: LCSH: Corporate governance—Law and legislation—United States. | Risk management—Law and legislation—United States.
Classification: LCC KF1422 .R68 2023 (print) | LCC KF1422 (ebook) | DDC 346.73/0664—dc23/eng/20220930
LC record available at https://lccn.loc.gov/2022038543
LC ebook record available at https://lccn.loc.gov/2022038544

ISBN: 978-0-8153-6438-2 (hbk)
ISBN: 978-1-032-34972-5 (pbk)
ISBN: 978-1-351-10724-2 (ebk)

DOI: 10.4324/9781351107242

Typeset in Bembo
by Apex CoVantage, LLC

Access the Support Material: www.routledge.com/9780815364382

Dedicated to the memory of Edward Velasquez, CPCM

CONTENTS

THE EDITOR

Virginia A. Suveiu, Esq., counsels on legal risk management, regulatory compliance, and commercial law matters and has held several related positions, including Chief Safeguard Officer and Of Counsel. She is an arbitrator for the Financial Industry Regulatory Authority. She served on the editorial board of the National Contract Management Association's *Contract Management Magazine*. She is affiliated with and has been invited to speak to several professional organizations on issues related to business law. She is an active member of the State Bar of California and admitted to the US District Court, Central District of California. She has held numerous positions in academia, including as founding dean and professor, and currently is an instructor and content developer for the University of California, Irvine, where she was given the Distinguished Instructor Award.

CONTRIBUTORS

Amber Baylor, Director of Environmental Compliance, South Orange County Wastewater Authority.

Amber Baylor is a published environmental scientist with over 11 years of management experience solving water quality and regulatory matters for drinking water and wastewater treatment plants. Ms. Baylor has an extensive knowledge in water quality science that she utilizes in step with operations to achieve environmental compliance. Ms. Baylor is well versed in NPDES and waste discharge compliance related to recycled water, ocean discharge, storm water, and biosolids management. Ms. Baylor has also held many leadership roles in industry working groups. Ms. Baylor has a B.A. in Biology from Lindsey Wilson College and an M.S. in Environmental Science and Policy from Johns Hopkins University. She is currently enrolled in the M.P.A. program at the Price School at the University of Southern California.

LaSharnda Beckwith, President and Chief Executive Officer, Lutheran Social Services of Southern California.

Dr. LaSharnda Beckwith is a passionate and energetic leader who loves to empower others to imagine what is possible. She is a world traveler and international speaker, author, and executive who delivers results. Dr. Beckwith retired from the Army and Air Force Exchange Service as the Vice President of Eastern Region. She worked for AAFES for 26 years and took the knowledge and skills she learned there to her own organization, Beckwith Leadership Consulting Group. As the CEO of Beckwith Leadership Consulting Group, she and her team, train, develop and provide executive coaching to individuals and organizations. Concurrent with her leadership training consultancy, Dr. Beckwith is also in higher education as a chief academic officer at a local university. This adds to her training in the area of the most current research and applications.

Dr. Beckwith has also been a chair and dean in higher education and currently works at a local university building programs that will prepare learners for the future. In this space, she is able to benefit from the most current research and applications industry.

In her spare time, Dr. Beckwith can be found writing. She has published four books and she is a monthly contributor to *Wordsmith Journal Magazine*, where she writes a column titled "Power of Positive Faith." She also blogs at http://www.LaSharndaBeckwith.wp.com.

Her 4 books are: *When You're Happy With You*; *It's Your Life; Own It. No Blame, No Excuses*; *You Call That Love? This is Love*; and *Passionate and Purposeful Leadership*.

Dr. Beckwith holds a Doctorate of Philosophy in Organization and Management with a specialization in Leadership. She has an MBA with Distinction and a Masters of Arts in Business Management with a minor in Human Resource Development. Her undergraduate degree is in Business also.

Shepard "Shep" G. Bentley, Principal, Bentley Biomedical

Shep Bentley is a regulatory affairs professional, founder of Bentley Biomedical, who leads a team with diverse talents, qualifications and cultural backgrounds to enable unconventional results at competitive rates. A student of literature, law and medicine with a knack for languages and debating, he has a passion for championing to regulators new ideas and approaches to the age-old problems of health care. He and his team are resourceful, perpetually inquisitive and dissatisfied with the more burdensome approaches to portraying safety and effectiveness to the government. Their combined education spans the range of life sciences through the doctoral level. He retired from the reserve of the U.S. Marine Corps as a Lieutenant Colonel in 2005, after having served in Iraq. He is dedicated to the advancement of the life sciences.

Jessie Castro, MBA, Manager (Contracts)-Sensor Programs.

Mr. Castro is a seasoned contracting professional, who works for one of the largest aerospace and defense contractors in the world. His experience spans the entire contract life cycle, from negotiation, pre-award, award, post-award, to close out. He provides expert support in the areas of Research and Development (R&D) for Emerging Technologies, including, but not limited to Defense Space Security. His current technology focus lies in Data Sciences & Analytics Technologies (i.e. Virtual Environments, Immersive Design), R&D for Support & Analytics, Flight Science, Technology Materials, Manufacturing, and Technology. Areas of focus also involve research, early product development of various technologies for commercial, defense, space and cyber applications, supplier diversity engagement for small businesses with promising capabilities. Other areas of support include but are not limited to working with data analytics, sourcing material, additive manufacturing technologies, composites, and international suppliers.

Peter Coffee, MBA, Vice President for Strategic Research, Salesforce.

In his capacity as VP for Strategic Research at Salesforce, Mr. Coffee interacts with IT managers, software developers and policymakers in the global community to learn more about their requirements and promote broader understanding of the capabilities of cloud computing in creating and building customer companies.

John Joseph Drudi, Esq., Counsel, Kinsale Insurance Company, Richmond, VA.

Mr. Drudi is licensed as an attorney in California, the District of Columbia, Maryland, and Virginia. He holds several other professional certifications and designations in the field of risk management and insurance, including the Chartered Property Casualty Underwriter (CPCU) designation, Associates in Insurance Accounting and Finance (AIAF), Associates in Insurance Regulation and Compliance (ARC), Associates in Risk Management (ARM), Associates in Marine Insurance Management (AMIM), Associates in Risk Management for Public Entities (ARM-P), Associates in Enterprise Risk Management (ARM-E), Associate in Insurance Regulatory Compliance (AIRC), IRMI certified Energy Risk and Insurance Specialist (ERIS), and IRMI Transportation Risk and Insurance Professional (TRIP). He is certified by Insurance Institutes in Managing Cyber Risk. Certified in Marine Insurance by Lloyd's Maritime Academy. He is a licensed insurance producer in the State of Virginia for Property/Casualty, Life and Health, and Title Insurance. He is a licensed insurance adjuster in Connecticut, Delaware, Florida, Idaho, Kentucky, Louisiana, Michigan, New Hampshire, New Mexico, New York, North Carolina, Oklahoma, Oregon, Rhode Island, South Carolina, Texas, Vermont, West Virginia, and Wyoming. He is admitted in the following federal courts: United States Supreme Court; United States Court of Appeals for the Federal Circuit; United States Court of Claims; United States Court of Appeals for the Ninth Circuit; United States Court of Appeals for the Fourth Circuit; United States District Court for the Northern, Southern, Eastern, and Central Districts of California; United States District Court for the Eastern and Western Districts of Virginia; United States District Court for the District of Columbia; United States District Court for the District of Maryland. He is a member of the Chartered Property Casualty Underwriter Society, the Phi Beta Kappa Alumni Association, the California State Bar, the District of Columbia Bar, the Maryland State Bar, and the Virginia State Bar (construction, real estate, and litigation sections). Mr. Drudi earned a B.A. from the University of Massachusetts at Amherst (Cum Laude, Phi Beta Kappa) and a J.D. from the University of San Diego Law School (Cum Laude), where he was a member of the San Diego Law Review.

Tim East, MS, Executive Director, Corporate Risk Management, Walt Disney Company.

Tim East was honored as the recipient of the 2021 Bill McIntyre Leadership Award, which recognizes visionary leaders who demonstrate a commitment to construction risk management through creativity, service, mentoring, and education.

For more than 30 years, Mr. East has provided vision and guidance to Disney as it has expanded in California, Florida, Japan, and France, as well as greenfield developments in New York City, India, Hong Kong, and Shanghai. His guidance has ensured that construction risk exposures and the interfaces among early works, construction, fit-out works, the defect liability period, and operations are treated effectively and as consistently as possible regardless of time zone.

He served as chair of the California Coalition on Worker's Compensation from 2000 to 2014. He currently leads the board and oversees the management of the California Self-Insurers' Security Fund, a 501(c)(6) mutual benefit corporation of over 350 member companies. The Security Fund's purpose is to ensure that injured workers receive payment of workers compensation benefits if a private self-insured employer defaults on its workers compensation benefit obligations.

Mr. East is an instructor for business ethics at The Master's College and guest lectures at the University of Southern California's Marshall School of Business Administration and at California State University College of Business and Economics.

His contributions have been recognized with awards, including the ARM Distinguished Graduate Award, the Christy Award from the Risk and Insurance Management Society, and Worker's Compensation Professional of the Year.

Tom Fox, Esq., The Compliance Evangelist™.

Tom Fox is the Compliance Evangelist™ and the Voice of Compliance. He is literally the guy who wrote the book on compliance with his seminal one volume book *The Compliance Handbook* (2nd edition) published in June 2021. Additionally, Mr. Fox has authored 19 books on business leadership, compliance and ethics and corporate governance, including the international best-sellers *Lessons Learned on Compliance and Ethics* and *Best Practices Under the FCPA and Bribery Act* as well as his award-winning series *Fox on Compliance*.

He is the Voice of Compliance, having founded the only podcast network in compliance, the award-winning Compliance Podcast Network. He is also a member of the C-Suite Radio Network. Mr. Fox writes and speaks nationally and internationally on a wide variety of topics, ranging from FCPA compliance, indemnities and other forms of risk management for a worldwide energy practice, tax issues faced by multi-national US companies, insurance coverage issues and protection of trade secrets.

He has practiced law in Houston for 25 years. He is now assisting companies with FCPA compliance, risk management and international transactions. He was most recently the General Counsel at Drilling Controls, Inc., a worldwide oilfield manufacturing and service company. He was previously

Division Counsel with Halliburton Energy Services, Inc. where he supported Halliburton's software division and its downhole division, which included the logging, directional drilling and drill bit business units.

Mr. Fox attended undergraduate school at the University of Texas, graduate school at Michigan State University and law school at the University of Michigan.

Chris Guzelian, Esq., Assistant Professor Finance and Economics, Texas State University.

Professor Guzelian is co-editor and co-author of *The Legal Risk Management Handbook*. He has worked professionally as a tenured business, constitutional, and criminal law professor, deputy district attorney, military intelligence analyst (civilian), U.S. bankruptcy court staff attorney, general counsel of a veteran-owned business (for a decade), and Dean of the only accredited Orthodox Christian university (University of St. Katherine). He externed as a water resources economist. He holds a J.D. from Stanford University Law School, and B.A. and M.A. degrees in Economics from the University of Colorado at Boulder.

Linda Harris, MA, The National Center for American Indian Enterprise Development (NCAIED) – Arizona Minority Business Development Agency (AZ MBDA) Export Center, US Department of Commerce.

Ms. Harris is a seasoned business development manager and procurement specialist. She provides business development services to generate increased financing and contract opportunities, and greater access to global markets. She promotes and secures new opportunities for minority-owned enterprises that have resulted in increased revenues for their clients.

Todd Haugh, Esq., Associate Professor of Business Law and Ethics, Indiana University - Kelley School of Business.

Professor Haugh is an Associate Professor of Business Law and Ethics and Arthur M. Weimer Faculty Fellow in Business Law at Indiana University's Kelley School of Business. His scholarship focuses on white collar and corporate crime, business and behavioral ethics, and federal sentencing policy. His work has appeared in top law and business journals, including the *Northwestern University Law Review*, *Notre Dame Law Review*, *Vanderbilt Law Review*, and the *MIT-Sloan Management Review*. Professor Haugh's expertise relating to the burgeoning field of behavioral compliance has led to frequent speaking and consulting engagements with major U.S. companies and ethics organizations. He is also regularly quoted in national news publications such as the *New York Times*, *Wall Street Journal*, *Forbes*, *Bloomberg News*, and *USA Today*.

A graduate of the University of Illinois College of Law and Brown University, Professor Haugh has extensive professional experience as a white collar criminal defense attorney, a federal law clerk, and a member of the general counsel's office of the United States Sentencing Commission. In 2011, he was chosen as one of four Supreme Court Fellows of the Supreme Court of the United States to study the administrative machinery of the federal judiciary.

Claudiu Jipescu-Munteanu, Esq., Partner, Dentons.

Claudiu Munteanu-Jipescu is an experienced lawyer with over 20 years of experience in the areas of corporate M&A, energy and PPP Infrastructure. He advises local and international clients in relation to group structuring, joint ventures, distressed companies takeover, shareholders agreements and investment regulation and has significant experience in mergers and acquisitions. He advises local and international clients on complex regulatory, contractual and corporate matters, and is also highly specialized in renewable energy. He has led a large number of wind and solar energy projects, acting both on the buyers and sellers side, as well as oil and gas projects. In addition, he is experienced in private-public partnerships (PPP), public procurement and concessions, having worked on several privatization projects that required dealing with the Romanian public authorities. As part of his membership in AmCham's (American Chamber of Commerce in Romania) Energy & Environment Committee, Claudiu has been involved in lobbying activity with respect to the energy legislation.

He has also led a large number of M&A projects, acting both on the buyers and sellers side. He worked in several significant infrastructure projects (PPP and Concessions), as well as in privatization projects that required dealings with joint ventures between foreign companies and the Romanian state.

Cynthia Fascenelli Kirkeby, Founder and CVO, Adaptifyed.

Ms. Kirkeby is a serial entrepreneur. She is Founder of Seasonally Fresh, Inc. (voted "Most Fundable Company" by Tech Coast Angels); Founder and CVO at Adaptifyed, Inc.; Founder of Covert Ink™ by Inkable Arts; and CVO of IMPRINT Adtech. She has numerous publications and patents, and given honors and awards, including AI Med Shark Tank Finalist 2019, Defense TechConnect Abstract Finalist 2019, and Panelist | Speaker – Defense Advanced Research Projects Agency (DARPA)/BTO 2019 Neurotechnology, among several others.

Jeff Koller, Esq., Associate General Counsel, Veritext.

Mr. Koller career evolved from being a private practitioner litigating cases throughout southern California to being the Associate General Counsel at Veritext Legal Solutions. He regularly provided consultation and specific issue responses on a wide array of legal topics involving business operations, expansion and the litigation discovery process. From March through September 2020, he actively trained clients on the intricacies and means to take their litigation practice to a virtual platform. The necessary evolution in the legal practice was overnight due to the pandemic.

Patricia Lee-Gulley, Esq., Partner, Gordon Rees.

Patricia Lee-Gulley is a partner in the Orange County office and has been with Gordon & Rees since 1998. Her active litigation practice focuses primarily on products liability, complex/mass tort litigation, premises liability, business/commercial litigation and employment litigation for the firm's Southern California offices. Ms. Lee-Gulley's litigation practice is supplemented with her industry experience and background in both manufacturing and business, including operations, processes, safety and human resources. Ms. Lee-Gulley has also served as national counsel for a major corporation and has served as local counsel for various out-of-state corporations.

Ms. Lee-Gulley is AV-Preeminent rated by Martindale-Hubbell; a Top Attorney for litigation by the OC Register Metro Magazine; and Superb rated by Avvo.com.

Marius Măgureanu, Esq., Partner, Măgureanu, Bourdenet & Asociații S.C.A.

Mr. Măgureanu is a Romanian licensed attorney, having acquired experience as a senior attorney from 2005 to 2014 and as partner in a regional law firm from 2014 to 2016, where he was involved in numerous transactions and acted as lead legal counsel in projects involving cross-border project finance, real estate, commercial law, corporate law, competition law and capital markets.

In addition, he used to act as a member of the Real Estate and Construction Practice Group, the Competition Practice Group and the Banking and Finance Practice Group. He has acted as speaker on corporate law and real estate law at events in Romania and Austria, such as the Austrian Economic Chambers (WKÖ) and the Akademie für Recht und Steuer (ARS).

He also conducts seminar workshops on topics such as competition law and on the fight against corruption and money laundering. Between 2005 and 2009, he co-edited a number of publications in Romania, Austria and worldwide.

Laura McNamire, Esq., Regional Director, Financial Industry Regulatory Authority (FINRA).

Ms. McNamire is Regional Director at the West Region Office of FINRA. She earned her JD at Pepperdine University School of Law.

Kevin Meredith, MBA, Founder, 4th Sector Innovations.

With over 20 years of experience in a diverse set of program and functional positions, Mr. Meredith most recently transitioned out of chief of staff, strategy development and program management roles. He has BS/MS degrees in engineering from the Industrial and Systems Department at the Rochester Institute of Technology (RIT) and an MBA in Entrepreneurship at Pepperdine University. Prior to 4th Sector Innovations, he was Enterprise Innovation Cell Leader at Boeing, among other leadership positions.

Lauren Miller, PhD.

Dr. Miller is a lecturer at the University of Miami, and a legal author and researcher.

Kristine A. Hayes Munson, MBA, CISM, PMP, CIA, Vice President, IT Risk & Compliance, State Street.

Ms. Munson is an experienced IT executive leading divisional information security, risk, compliance and business continuity programs, creating an information security aware culture, ensuring adherence to published standards, regulatory controls and best practices, and delivering multi-million dollar cross-functional team projects impacting internal and external clients. She is a professional/academic project management instructor presenting experience-based academic classes, seminars, and presentations focusing on project management and leadership internationally.

Cynthia Patton, Esq., General Counsel, Verily Life Sciences.

Ms. Patton served as SVP and chief compliance officer for Amgen's global privacy, trade and healthcare compliance organizations from October 2012 through July 2020. She joined Amgen in 2005, and was a VP in the law department with responsibility for commercial legal activities in the US. Prior to that, she served as the lead commercial lawyer for both the oncology and inflammation business units.

Before joining Amgen, she spent seven years as general counsel of SCAN Health Plan, a California HMO. Prior to SCAN, she served as assistant GC and worked in law firms specializing in healthcare, corporate and securities law. Dedicated to giving back, she serves as Chair of the Amgen Foundation and is the executive sponsor for two employee research groups. She is also the executive sponsor for Amgen's Career Discovery Program. She serves as a board member for the Ethics and Compliance Initiative, Martin Luther King, Jr. Community Hospital in Los Angeles, the Los Angeles Music Center, Vassar College, Wildwood School, and The National Association for Law Placement Foundation. She previously served as board chair of Watts Healthcare.

She has been honored with the 2019 ECI Carol R. Marshall Award for Innovation in Corporate Ethics as well as recognized by BlackDoctor.org and The George Washington University Milken Institute School of Public Health as one of the 2019 Top Blacks in Healthcare. She was named one of 2018's Most Influential Black Lawyers by *Savoy Magazine* and honored by the Black Women Lawyers Association of LA with the Corporate Excellence Award in 2018. In addition, Black Enterprise selected her for inclusion in the 2017 Black Enterprise Most Powerful Executives in Corporate America feature. Ms. Patton received her JD from George Washington University and her bachelor's degree from Vassar College.

Roger Philips, MS, Principal at Philips Associates.

Professor Philips is a senior consultant to management in international business development, education, and engineering. He has held executive positions in the software industry, and built and managed worldwide sales and support divisions for two software firms, earning the President's Award for Export Excellence. He is co-editor of the book *Business in Contemporary China*, and the book *Global*

Enterprise: The Theory & Practice of International Business, as well as author of the book *Guide to Software Export*. He is an adjunct professor of international business at Concordia University, Irvine.

James N. Phillips Jr., JNP Associates.

Dr. Phillips is a former government contracting officer who has served in the Department of Defense and Department of Veterans Affairs. He is an author who has been published in NCMA's *Contract Management*, DAU's *Defense Acquisition, Federal Management, Government CIO, Journal of Healthcare Contracting*, and *The Lean Post*. Dr. Phillips holds numerous business-related degrees and certifications.

Don J. Polden, Dean Emeritus, Professor of Law, Santa Clara University.

Professor Polden served as Dean of Santa Clara University School of Law from 2003 to 2013. In addition to his service as dean, he is a well-known scholar in the areas of employment law and legal education and has practiced law, principally in the areas of federal antitrust law and employment law, in the federal and state courts. He is co-author (with U.S. District Court Judge Mark Bennett) *of Employment Relationships: Law and Practice*. He also is the author of several law review articles on topics of federal antitrust and securities law and legal education and he is a contributing writer on employment law and business topics to *Huffington Post*. Previously to being appointed as Santa Clara Law's Dean, he served as Dean and Professor of Law at the University of Memphis (1993 through 2003).

At Santa Clara University School of Law, Dean Emeritus and Professor, he was instrumental in developing the curriculum for leadership education, a movement that is growing in significance in American legal education. He also served as chair of the American Bar Association's Standards Review Committee during the ABA's revisions to the accreditation policies for American legal education. He was elected to membership in the American Law Institute in 1992, selected for membership in the College of Labor and Employment Lawyers and serves as chair of the Advisory Board of the Institute of Sports Law and Ethics. He also continues his work on leadership education for lawyers and law students with several national organizations including the Center for Creative Leadership.

During his service as Dean, the School of Law completed its first major capital campaign (which included 43 newly endowed student scholarships), initiated the second major campaign emphasizing funding for the new law school building (a project coming to a very successful conclusion soon!), hired almost a third of its full time faculty (including several "junior" faculty members who have developed into national stars!), was initiated into the national Order of the COIF (the Phi Beta Kappa of legal education), secured the gift and launched the annual Katharine & George Alexander Prize, launched the tremendously successful annual Jerry Kasner Estate Planning Seminar, and grew the summer international programs to ten with addition of programs in Munich, The Hague and San Jose, Costa Rica.

Melissa Rorie, Senior Research Manager, OMNI Institute.

Dr. Melissa Rorie received her Ph.D. from the University of Maryland, College Park in 2013. Her research interests lie primarily in the field of corporate compliance, but also include theory testing and research methodology. She is currently involved in a variety of projects that examine theoretical explanations for corporate compliance and beyond-compliance behavior, the prevention of corporate noncompliance, and the use of Monte Carlo Simulations as well as other quantitative methods. She has edited two books, including the *Handbook of White-Collar Crime* (2019) and the book (with Benjamin van Rooij) *Measuring Compliance: Assessing Corporate Crime and Misconduct Prevention* (2022). Her research has also been published in Oxford Handbooks and Edgar Elgar readers as well as a variety of peer-reviewed journals, including: *Crime, Law and Social Change*; *Criminology & Public Policy*; *Criminal Justice Studies*; *Law & Policy*; *The International Journal of Law, Crime, and Social*

Justice; *Journal of Criminal Law and Criminology*; the *UNLV Gaming Research and Review Journal*; and *Theoretical Criminology*. She received her Ph.D. from the University of Maryland, College Park in 2013.

Joyce Segelken, Esq., Litigation Supervisor, Chubb Insurance Company.

Ms. Segelken has been with Chubb for over 25 years, and manages a team of adjusters in southern California core offices responding to severe claims and coverage issues. Prior to joining Chubb, she was a claims attorney at Nationwide Insurance. She received her BA from UC Irvine and JD from Loyola Law School.

Don Shannon, PMP, CPCM, CFCM, and National Contract Management Association (NCMA) Fellow, Certified Professional Contract Manager.

Mr. Shannon is a retired U.S. Air Force officer (1966 through 1990) with an additional 30 years' experience as a business owner, contracts manager, and project manager at Boeing, Martin Marietta, ABB, and others. He is self-employed as a veteran-owned small business providing business and consulting services to emerging small businesses in the government contracting sector. He has published numerous articles in *Contract Management* Magazine and is a frequent presenter at conferences and seminars where he teaches diverse government contracting topics including risk management, project management, and contract administration. He is a volunteer mentor with the New Mexico PTAC. He holds multiple certifications including Project Management Professional, Certified Federal Contracts Manager, Certified Professional Contracts Manager, and Certified Cost Technician.

Noah Smith, Esq., Counsel at Verizon.

Prior to becoming Counsel at Verizon, Noah Smith was a Senior Associate at The Volkov Law Group, where devised and executed litigation strategy; led clients through federal investigations while conducting internal investigations, and identified compliance and policy risks. He also was a Judicial Law Clerk to Judge Malachy Mannion, US District Court in Scranton, Pennsylvania, and served as a Law Clerk at the DOJ and Library of Congress. He earned his JD cum laude from Georgetown University Law Center.

Matt Stankiewicz, Esq., Partner, The Volkov Law Group.

Mr. Stankiewicz is a partner at the Volkov Law Group, a boutique law firm, specializing in anti-bribery and corruption controls and compliance programs. His areas of expertise include global anti-corruption compliance, FCPA, export controls, KYC procedures, AML/BSA regulations, OFAC sanctions, as well as privacy compliance. He received his JD from Seton Hall University School of Law, where he was a Dean's Scholar and Riccio Law Scholar.

Christyne Vachon, Esq., President and Founder, TerraNyx.

Ms. Vachon is a strategic consultant in law and business with several years of in-house counsel experience serving as general counsel, CCO and other for early stage and established companies. She is a former law professor and attorney with primary experience in governance, securities and corporate law. With in-house experience, she has managed employment, compliance, intellectual property, M & A, antitrust, privacy, immigration and other issues relevant to tech companies and regulated entities. She has international experience, managing international contracts and transactions. She has served on the boards of many for-profit and not-for-profit companies.

Silvia Van Dusen, SHRM- SCP, Executive Vice President, Chief Human Resources Officer, LinQuest.

Ms. Van Dusen is an experienced Human Capital Executive with a demonstrated history of developing and leading high performance team. She is skilled in HR Strategy, Culture Building, Career Development, HR Consulting, HR Strategy Development, Talent Management, and high level benefit and compensation design. Prior to her current role, she was Vice President of Human Resources at LISI Aerospace. She holds a Master's degree in Industrial and Organizational Psychology.

Michael Volkov, Esq., CEO, The Volkov Law Group.

Michael Volkov specializes in ethics and compliance, white collar defense, government investigations and internal investigations. Mr. Volkov devotes a significant portion of his practice to anti-corruption compliance and defense. He regularly assists clients on FCPA, UK Bribery Act, AML, OFAC, Export-Import, Securities Fraud, and other issues.

Mr. Volkov has extensive trial experience, and has developed a problem-solving approach to serve client needs. He has extensive contacts in the federal government and on Capitol Hill. Given his broad government experience, he represents clients in federal and state court, before the Justice Department and other federal agencies, and on Capitol Hill.

Prior to launching his own law firm, Mr. Volkov was a partner at LeClairRyan (2012–2013); Mayer Brown (2010–2012), Dickinson Wright (2008–2010); Deputy Assistant Attorney General in the Department of Justice (2008); Chief Counsel, Subcommittee on Crime, Terrorism and Homeland Security, House Judiciary Committee (2005–2008); and Counsel, Senate Judiciary Committee (2003–2005); Assistant US Attorney, United States Attorney's Office for the District of Columbia (1989–2005); and a Trial Attorney, Antitrust Division, United States Department of Justice (1985–1989).

Marcia Narine Weldon, Esq., Lecturer in Law, School of Law, University of Miami.

Marcia Narine Weldon has thirty years of legal experience in a variety of settings. She spent several years in-house as the Vice President and Deputy General Counsel, as well as the Vice President, Global Compliance and Business Standards, and Chief Privacy Officer of Ryder, a publicly traded, multinational Fortune 500 company. She oversaw the company's global compliance, business ethics, privacy, government relations, environmental compliance, enterprise risk management, corporate responsibility, and labor and employment legal programs. She also served as the head of human resources for one of the company's two divisions before being tasked with developing the compliance, enterprise risk management, corporate social responsibility, and privacy programs from scratch. Prior to joining Ryder, she worked as labor and employment associate at Morgan Lewis in Miami, a commercial litigator at Cleary Gottlieb in New York, and clerked for the Supreme Court of New Jersey. She currently serves as the co-chair of the governance committee of the Women's Fund of Miami-Dade and as a business coach for social entrepreneurs through Radical Partners.

She has spoken on ESG matters on panels for the American Bar Association and other organizations.

She is also the Director of the Transactional Skills Program and Faculty Coordinator of the Business Compliance and Sustainability concentration at the University of Miami School of Law; founder of Illuminating Wisdom, an executive coaching, business strategy, and corporate training firm; general counsel of MDO Partners; and the general counsel of a sustainable startup. She teaches regulatory compliance, corporate governance, and sustainability; business and human rights; transactional lawyering; and business associations. She has written several law review articles and blogs every two weeks on compliance and ESG matters for the Business Law Professor Blog. Additionally, she has been interviewed by or featured in the New York Times, Wall Street Journal, NPR, the Guardian, Verge, Forbes, Agenda (Financial Times), and other news outlets around the world on compliance and corporate governance. Within the ESG sphere, she specializes in business and human rights and has traveled to Pakistan, Democratic Republic of Congo, Guatemala, the UK, and Cuba to research and speak on corporate obligations for human rights impacts. Additionally, she regularly attends the United Nations Forum on Business and Human Rights in Geneva, Switzerland.

In May 2011, she testified before the House Financial Services Committee in Congress on the unintended impact of Dodd-Frank Financial Reform on corporate compliance programs. In 2012, the Secretary of Labor appointed her to the Whistleblower Protection Advisory Committee, where she served for five years. She also served on the Miami-Dade Commission on Ethics and Public Trust from 2014–2017. She earned her law degree, cum laude, from Harvard Law School, and her undergraduate degree, cum laude, in political science and psychology from Columbia University. She has been admitted to the bars of New York, New Jersey, Florida and the United States Supreme Court. Most important, she's the proud mother of an artist.

Philip Wood, CBE, QC (Hon), MA (Oxford), LLD (Hon, Lund), Former Partner, Allen Overy.

Philip Wood is an expert in world comparative financial law, insolvency, and financial regulation and on law firm information systems. He is a PRIME Finance Expert (arbitration), and frequent speaker.

In 2019, he published nine stand-alone books in the revised series Law and Practice of International Finance via Sweet & Maxwell, London. These books cover international loans and bonds, world insolvency and restructuring, comparative security interests and title finance, derivatives, the regulation of international finance and banking, sovereign and bank bankruptcies, set-off and netting, securitizations, project finance, intercreditor agreements, clearing systems, conflict of laws (including governing law and forum) and many other subjects. Two of the books have summaries of the relevant law in all the jurisdictions of the world (321 of them), perhaps the first time that this has been done. The books cover world legal data, structures, practice and negotiation.

He has been awarded two honors by the Queen for law services, CBE and QC (Hon). His university textbook of 2008 on financial law has been translated into Chinese, Japanese and Korean.

In 2016, he published *The Fall of the Priests and the Rise of the Lawyers*, a book for the general reader. This work has been described as "a ground-breaking philosophical book of our time". He has a BA from Cape Town University and an MA in English literature from Oxford. He was a triple prize-winner in his Law Society qualifying exams.

He has lectured at more than 60 universities world-wide in all regions of the world, including, the United States, South America, Africa, Europe, India, China, Central and South-East Asia, Australia and elsewhere. He devised the World Universities Comparative Law Project involving over 70 universities. He published *Maps of World Financial Law* in 2008.

FOREWORD

Melissa Rorie

Corporate noncompliance has the potential to cause incredible damage to consumers, competitors, the environment, governments, and the public more generally. Recent cases such as Wells Fargo's repeated violations (including the creation of as many as 3.5 million unapproved bank accounts; Cheslow, 2019) or car manufacturers' emissions scandals (the violation by Volkswagen alone is estimated to have caused about 60 premature deaths in the United States and about 1,200 premature deaths across Europe; Barrett et al., 2015; Chossière et al., 2017) demonstrate the major financial and physical impacts of even one case of corporate noncompliance.

Importantly, most cases of corporate noncompliance do not arise from a deliberate attempt to victimize citizens, and we need to recognize that these actions have the potential to hurt the corporations themselves. We have seen corporations in recent years receiving tough sanctions from legal authorities. As one example, in addition to millions of dollars in penalties, in February 2018 the US Federal Reserve put a cap on Wells Fargo's ability to grow their assets until the company corrected the causes behind widespread consumer abuses. Informally, the company has been experiencing trouble financially since the violations became publicly known (Moyer, 2019). Even when a company is not subject to legal sanctions, we have seen intense public criticism result in costly corrective actions; Starbucks shut down its US stores for a day to train employees on racial biases after a highly publicized wrongful arrest of two black customers at their store in Philadelphia. The day of training was estimated to have cost Starbucks $16.7 million in lost revenue (Pontefract, 2018). Thus, it is often in the corporation's best interest—as well as the interest of society—to engage in proactive compliance strategies.

It's not surprising, then, that the compliance industry has grown and become increasingly professionalized since the early 1980s. With enhanced legal sanctions against corporations (e.g., the US Federal Sentencing Guidelines in 1992, the passage of Sarbanes-Oxley in 2002), new regulatory rules, the rise of transnational corporate structures, the global financial crisis of 2008, the collective efforts of compliance professionals and scholars, and an increased risk of cybersecurity issues, compliance personnel have become increasingly important in businesses around the world (Martin, 2015; Tsingou, 2018). Concomitant with an increased reliance on compliance professionals, businesses and other stakeholders have heightened their expectations about compliance personnel's training and expertise. Hiring efforts in the compliance domain—across all occupations and industries—increasingly require professional certifications and training as a condition for employment. Perhaps as a result, there are more professional organizations for compliance professionals than ever before (e.g., the Ethics and Compliance Officers Association, Association of Insurance Compliance Professionals, Society of

Corporate Compliance and Ethics, National Contract Management Association, National Society of Compliance Professionals). These groups provide networking opportunities within the industry and increased education, training, and formal certifications to further the reputation of the field as a whole.

Paralleling the rise in the compliance industry is increased scholarly attention on the subject. Across many disciplines, academic scholars are attempting to explain why corporations might lag behind regulatory expectations or exceed them. Studies of business compliance include those under the "risk management" paradigm, but also those labeled as studies of "corporate crime", "business ethics", "corporate social responsibility/irresponsibility", "behavioral ethics", "regulatory governance", and so forth. There have also been some efforts by academics to bring their research to compliance professionals (e.g., through organizations like ComplianceNet, New York University's Program on Corporate Compliance and Enforcement, Temple University's Center for Compliance and Ethics). However, despite this seeming proliferation of scholarship, I believe that knowledge building has been hindered because business compliance scholars are often engaged in niche research within their own disciplines and are either unaware of, or unable to collaborate with, scholars studying similar topics in other disciplines.

In addition, researchers are often studying these processes in isolation from compliance practitioners. I, myself, have met resistance from regulators as a result of my association with a criminal justice department—I have been told that regulatory authorities, although they value the type of research I do, are afraid of being the ones on the "autopsy table". Compliance professionals within corporations have paid lip service to the desire for participating in research but also have concerns about making corporate data available to an external researcher and being under scrutiny. Thus, we have an issue whereby experts in researching compliance using rigorous methods are unable to interact with the people promoting compliance in practice.

This book—along with professional networks like ComplianceNet that seek to bring together scholars and practitioners so they can learn from one another—has a great potential to encourage more translational approaches to research. In "translational research", research results are moved from the research setting into real-world applications. A key component of the strategy is the recognition that research subjects are not only consumers of research that is imposed on them from the ivory tower but are also active participants; they are encouraged to work with the researcher in identifying what needs to be done to answer the questions of import to them. I encourage readers to use this book as a starting point, in which legal issues and practical considerations are considered at length. From there, I also encourage students of compliance to think beyond the legal scholars and practitioners highlighted here and consider how social scientists like myself can help them identify and systematically study compliance questions in need of answers.

Thus, I see this book as an incredibly important first step forward. It incorporates expertise on compliance from a variety of perspectives and is meant to be used by practitioners and researchers from many different fields. As such, the book has the potential to serve as a starting point from which to begin a dialogue across professions and disciplines. In seeking broader lessons for compliance, irrespective of industry or jurisdiction, this book helps identify common ground for many different stakeholders, encourages us to get out of our silos, provokes a much-needed dialog, and suggests future research needs—all for the betterment of society.

References

Barrett, S. R. H., Speth, R. L., Eastham, S. D., Dedoussi, I. C., Ashok, A., Malina, R., and Keith, D. W. (2015). Impact of the Volkswagen emissions control defeat device on US public health. *Environmental Research Letters, 10*(11), 114005.

Cheslow, Daniela. (March 12, 2019). CEO says Wells Fargo has transformed after scandals; Lawmakers are skeptical. *NPR News*. www.npr.org/2019/03/12/702501160/ceo-says-wells-fargo-has-transformed-after-scandals-lawmakers-are-skeptical.

Chossière, G., P., Malina, R., Ashok, A., Dedoussi, I. C., Eastham, S. D., Speth, R. L., and Barrett, S. R. H. (2017). Public health impacts of excess NO_x emissions from Volkswagen diesel passenger vehicles in Germany. *Environmental Research Letters, 12*(3), 034014.

Martin, Susan Lorde. 2015. Compliance officers: More jobs, more responsibility, more liability. *Notre Dame Journal of Law, Ethics & Public Policy*, *29*, 169–198.

Moyer, Liz. (January 15, 2019). Wells Fargo will operate under Fed's growth cap through the end of this year, CEO says. *CNBC*. www.cnbc.com/2019/01/14/wells-fargo-earnings-q4-2018.html.

Pontefract, Dan. (June 1, 2018). "Did the Starbucks Racial-Bias Training Plan Work?" *Forbes*. www.forbes.com/sites/danpontefract/2018/06/01/did-the-starbucks-racial-bias-training-plan-work/#1691063d591e.

Tsingou, Eleni. 2018. New governors on the block: The rise of anti–money laundering professionals. *Crime, Law, and Social Change*, *69*, 191–205.

ACKNOWLEDGEMENTS

I am grateful to my parents, and to so many colleagues, students and friends, who have been a part of this work, providing support and gold nuggets of wisdom all along the way.

I would like to highlight:

The remarkable contributors to this handbook (please see "List of Contributors" section).

The incredible team at Routledge, especially: Brianna Ascher, Emma Morley, Siobhàn Poole, Marie Louise Roberts (Apex CoVantage), and Nicola Sharpe.

My colleagues at UC Irvine, in particular: Gina Cho, Ian Gibson, Angela Jeantet, Missy Pitman, and Laani Watanabe.

The academics, professionals and researchers I've had the privilege to interact with, especially:

Virginia Abadessa, Orange County Transportation Authority
Dan Alfonzo, CPCM
Betsy Berkhemer-Credaire, CEO
Judith Berman, PhD
Professor Ethan Bernstein, Harvard Business School
Kahni Bizub, CPA
Celine Bourgoin, UNAVCO
Kathleen Boyle, CEO at Verify
Cristian Calugarita, Honeywell Aerospace
Kraig Conrad, CEO at National Contract Management Association
Jo Ellen Chatham, PhD, Director at Center of Civics Education, Concordia University
Barry Draskovich, Vice President at Parker Aerospace
Rafael Durand, Esq.
Jack Dhuwalia, MBA, ASQ Quality Manager
Bill Edwards, CFE
Brenda Eways
Laura Fay, BTS Boston
Professor David Feldman, UC Irvine
Michael Fischetti, former Executive Director at National Contract Management Association
Professor Catherine Fisk, UC Berkeley
Laura Fleming, Esq.
Cathy Finnie, Stantec
Jeannine Ford, Experian

Var Fox, Executive Vice President at Judicate West
Geeta Ghai, CPCU
Maurice Gilbert, Conselium Compliance Search
Bob Godlasky
Angela Goodwin, Avanade
Kanika Goyal, People Matters
Janet Grondin, CEO at Stellar Solutions
Cheryl Guyatt, CPCU
Larry Haas, MBA
Julie Ann Hernandez, MSHSA, CPHRM
Thad Hoffmaster
Thi Hagenbuechle, MBA
Arina Hooks, CMLDP
Debra Hunter-Bonner, EJD
Colleen Johnston, AECOM
Professor John Paul Jones, University of Richmond
Joyce Kaufman, PhD
Jack Kelly, CEO at The Compliance Search Group
Dan King, President and CEO at American Association of University Administrators
Craig Lavrenz
Kendall Lockhart, Founder of Me+U
Jahnavi Lokre, COO at Diality
Thomas Lotts, New York Life
Elizabeth Loufti, BetterWork Media Group
Dean Timothy D. Lytton, Georgia State University
Laurel Mann, CFP
Carol Marinello, Executive Vice President at Loar Group
Stefanie Mazer and Alain Mazer
June McLaughlin, Esq.
Marlo Naber Mole
Don Neff, President at LJP Construction Services
Jackie Osborne, Safran Cabin
Tommi (Trudy R.) Papson, former FDA Consumer Safety Officer-Investigator
Professor Barry Posner, Santa Clara University
Dean Michelle Rahman, University of Richmond
Mima Ransom and Dale Ransom
L. Song Richardson, President at Colorado College
Ruxandra Risko, MBA
Neil Sahota, IBM Master Inventor
Ty Smith, MBV, D.H.L., Retired Navy SEAL
Professor Andy Spalding, University of Richmond
Jason Starr, CEO at Dillistone Group
Fredrick Carl Stegmann, Jr.
Professor Ann Southworth, UC Irvine
Professor Jonathan Stubbs, University of Richmond
Richard Susskind, President at Society for Computers and Law
Nancy M. Thevenin, Esq., FCIArb
Matteo Tonnello, The Conference Board
Mark Treston, Chief Academic Officer

Paul Valencia, Founding Managing Partner at Redmount Mergers & Acquisitions
Professor Benjamin van Rooji, University of Amsterdam
Kim Walker, MS, RAC (US & EU), FRAPS
Matthew Whalley, Ernst and Young

And, to the professionals at: National Contract Management Association; Project Management Institute; National Center for State Courts; Risk Management Association; American Society for Quality; Orange County Regulatory Affairs; Regulatory Affairs Professional Society; International Risk Management Institute; The Institutes Risk and Insurance Knowledge Group; Risk & Insurance Management Society; Women in Defense; and The British Standards Institution.

INTRODUCTION

Patricia Lee-Gulley and Virginia A. Suveiu

This text is appropriate for law school instruction, undergraduate and graduate programs, schools of continuing education, international studies, and other academic programs of interest to legal, risk, and compliance professionals. Businesspeople of all types, across all industries worldwide, should find significant value in these pages.

Private and public organizations face a complex myriad of operational laws and regulations in a globalized and regulated economy. Traditionally, mainly public companies in the financial services industry were focused on such issues. Nowadays, regulatory compliance protocols have become a critical factor in the welfare of every organization. Regulatory compliance hits at different levels regardless of business size, from sole practitioners, small businesses, and entrepreneurs to government agencies, nonprofit organizations, and Fortune 500s. Adding to the mix, the prominence of "unicorns" continues to accelerate in the corporate world, creating cultural changes steeped in the excitement of hyper-innovation. In a world where only the deftest players survive, risk management and compliance can be a bedrock foundation from which innovation may safely grow. Regardless of type or level, culture or size, organizations nowadays need to promote sustained cultures of compliance and legal risk management wherein all stakeholders are properly educated, proactive, and agile participants. Successful detection and prevention demands business intelligence and collaboration far more than maintenance of basic protocols.

This book is useful and accessible to the widest possible audience of academics and practitioners. It gleans timeless, thought-provoking insights from contributors across an array of industries and professional experiences. With an intentionally broad view, the pervasiveness of contemporary legal risk management, regulatory compliance, and ethics issues comes to light in vibrant, real-world examples.

At the time of this printing, the body of scholarship in one volume available to those in risk-related professions is severely lacking. There is currently no other reference that provides a high-level, comprehensive view of legal risk management, compliance and ethics, leaving this compendium a uniquely convenient "one-stop shop." It will serve as an enduring primer for ongoing scholarly attention to legal risk management, regulatory compliance, and ethics.

Focus is on guiding principles that are not specific to any particular jurisdiction but are helpful to all. The broad view of critical areas of interest is intended to promote great flexibility for evolving interpretations and novel applications of precepts well into the future.

Lessons fall into three broad themes: solutions-oriented classroom training, workshops and seminars, and academic progress.

DOI: 10.4324/9781351107242-1

Increasingly, working professionals seek real-world classroom instruction for real-world solutions. Organizations of all sizes are recognizing risk management and compliance are integral to success in their respective industries. For instance, micro-learning, the gold standard for Fortune 1000 companies, has been adapted to train legal, finance, and operations professionals with shorter attention spans and who are incessantly bombarded with information.

Trade association workshops and seminars have provided industrious students with practical, but piecemeal, insights on risk management and compliance for years, as the subjects were not taught at the higher institutions. Today, business students and working professionals want to learn these disciplines, including their application, thoroughly in the classroom and immediately apply that knowledge in the working environment.

This handbook is the "academic" book for the classroom, as well as a definitive reference guide in the workplace. From both academic and practitioner points of view, it will shape dialog on risk management and the law for years to come, on pressing issues that will include the changing practice of law, including the introduction of AI; the increase of standardization, in recognition that risk and compliance are coming into their own, unrealistic demands for immediate solutions and how this leads to more negative risk, as well as what standardization will bring: more ethical dilemmas, disputes, and interpretations.

The book is organized into the following parts:

Part I: What Are Risk Management, Regulatory Compliance, and Ethics?
Part II: Contract Risk Management and Insurance Considerations
Part III: Corporate Compliance and Ethics Challenges
Part IV: Cyber, Data Risks, and Technological Considerations
Part V: Best Practices Emerging from Lessons Learned

PART I

What Are Risk Management, Regulatory Compliance, and Ethics?

1

OPERATIONAL RISK MANAGEMENT

Tim East

As civilization emerged in various parts of the world, so did the community's experience of loss and the recognition that the causes and consequences had to be managed. In the first millennium BC the mariners of Rhodes expanded commerce across the Mediterranean, with trade from Egypt to the Middle East and as far as Spain. Storms were common, and to maintain fairness they established laws to deal with the loss of ships: if cargo was thrown overboard to save a ship, the loss was distributed evenly both to those who lost cargo and those whose shipments were saved.[1] These laws were widely adopted by the Romans and in some places can be found in maritime law to this very day.[2]

The history of risk and how we have managed it closely parallels growth in the complexity of commerce and trade. There is a direct relationship between population growth, the accumulation of wealth and risk; as the former two increase, so does risk in both breadth and potential impact.[3]

If we look carefully, every civilization made informal risk assessments for individual, family and communal decisions. Where to locate a village or town: High on a defensible bluff, or in the valley closer to the fields? Near a source of water? Or perhaps a little more distant, to avoid diseases associated with wetlands? What materials to use or avoid in building? Should resources be used for defense and economic activity? Shall we submit to a powerful lord or maintain our independence? All involve significant risks, potential benefits and often the very life of the community itself.

Risk and Insurance

The expansion of trade pushed the growth of insurance contracts. Early evidence appears in Italy in the 13th century, and in Genoa contracts for insuring trade as a separate agreement from the exchange itself were created in due course. Financing a loss was the primary focus.

After the Great London Fire of 1666 destroyed over 13,000 homes, Edward Lloyd opened his coffee house where merchants, ship owners and investors gathered to exchange information on upcoming shipments of cargo, ships, destinations and their captains. Representatives of wealthy investors would scrutinize the details and sign their names and how much of a risk they would accept beneath the heading—and the profession of "underwriting" was born.

1. Emmett J. Vaughn, *Risk Management*, Wiley & Sons, 1997.
2. R. Benedict, The historical positions of the Rhodian law, *Yale Law Journal*, Is. 4, pp. 223–242, 1909.
3. Emmett Vaughan and Therese Vaughan, *Essentials of Risk Management and Insurance*, Wiley & Sons, 2001, 2nd ed.

DOI: 10.4324/9781351107242-3

In another example from maritime history, the expansion of commercial shipping and naval fleets in the 1700s far outstripped the available seamen and officers to crew them. Gangs lurked to kidnap idle men into service, and due to both physical dangers and poor health, many never returned. Although ships and cargo were insured, efforts to deal with this economic impact were unaddressed and society wasn't compensated for the loss of young male lives.

This reflects one of the downsides to linking risk management solely to insurance. Viewed as insurance alone, risk is merely paying premiums and funding losses when there are claims. If a loss could not be quantified in these terms, it was likely neither covered nor properly recognized, despite the reality that many losses that are very real to individuals and society cannot be measured by money alone.

Another side effect of linking risk to insurance was the singular focus on gathering information and data to determine probabilities and premiums. Abraham De Moivre, in his 16th-century text on the subject of chance and probabilities, described that an expected outcome was simply the product of the probability of loss times the number of units at risk.[4]

This formulation was the foundation for most insurance pricing, but the overemphasis on a purely mathematical approach has three clear deficits:

- It reduces risk assessment and management to merely the quantification of a loss in terms of money and transfer.
- This focus on premiums, losses and deductibles alone tended to delay the development of better methods for risk avoidance, prevention and mitigation.
- It fails to address the impacts that are difficult to measure and quantify, such as the impact on an organization's reputation or effects on other stakeholders.

Over time, insurance companies and mutual associations recognized the value of a broader perspective and explored prevention and mitigation efforts. From small beginnings, they developed large and sophisticated engineering functions that studied fire prevention, formed firefighting companies and gave birth to the industrial safety movement. Whether from profit incentives or more noble motives, insurance providers gradually became invested in both mitigating risk—reducing the probability and severity of a loss—and distributing the financial loss among their shareholders or members.

Thus the global insurance industry matured alongside commerce, trade, industrialization and complex economies, and risk management in a nascent form grew as well. When risk transfer and redistribution was combined with risk reduction, insurance played an important role in supporting modern industry and its expansion.

The Emergence of Risk Management in the Modern Era

The industrial age reached its zenith shortly after WWII. As nations gradually recovered from the global cataclysm, they encountered a permanent shift in both opportunity and risk. The world had been transformed by two world wars into a global network of commerce, economies, languages, exports and imports. As the complexity of multinational enterprises increased, the risks from natural, political, operational, financial and human factors increased exponentially in both frequency and potential severity.

Business executives and managers gradually realized that a more robust and comprehensive system of understanding risk and addressing it was needed to support growing worldwide investments. In

4. Abraham de Moivre, *The Doctrine of Chances: Or, a Method of Calculating the Probability of Events in Play*, Pearson, 1718.

the 1950s and the decades that followed, the study of risk *management* gradually emerged out of commercial insurance, financial management and industrial safety to take its own distinct place in business schools and commercial organizations.

An early work in this direction was penned by Russell Gallagher, the risk manager at the Philco Company (a pioneer in electronics). In an article for the *Harvard Business Review* titled "Risk Management: A New Phase of Cost Control", Gallagher asserted that insurance should be one tool among many in a more scientific and broader approach to risk management. This was further advanced by Dr. Wayne Snider of the University of Pennsylvania; in a speech in 1955 he suggested that the professional "insurance manager" should be recognized as a "risk manager".[5] Insurance managers, those who primarily focused on buying policies and presenting claims for recovery, faced the reality of adapting to this change or being left behind.

Over time, corporations, private enterprises, nonprofit entities and government agencies embraced the new concept, and those who practiced the trade adopted the new moniker and broader mandate. Risk management as a profession became more disciplined in practice, no longer satisfied with deciding how much insurance to buy or how large a deductible should be chosen, but to measurement of risk and often the hard question of whether to buy insurance at all.[6]

Defining Terms: What Is Risk?

As the new profession and its scope took shape, it was difficult to state clearly the very definition of *risk*. Risk is a concept so simple and self-evident that in its essence, most people understand it.[7] Although they may find difficulty in putting it into words, risk usually receives a negative connotation and is stripped of its upside possibilities—an outcome that is *better* than expected. Risk is also expressed in casual ways, such as "he took a *calculated* risk" (that is rarely actually calculated), or someone was involved in some "risky business".

However, a technical definition that can be applied broadly across the spectrum of organizations, and be sustained over time, was far more difficult to put down on paper.

Nearly all definitions for *risk* include some shared strands of thought. There is the concept of an objective, goal or expectation—a state that is desired or sought for. Following this, most definitions include an event or series of events that occur and intervene—although this could also include a "nonevent" that was expected and *didn't* occur, further complicating the task of finding a definition. For economy of words, one may consider the fact that something *didn't* happen an "event" as well—a non-occurrence being a type of event—and keep moving.

Attached to these two anchors—the desired state and the intervening event—a definition of risk needs some expression of *probability* or *variance* attached to the event: the likelihood that it will or will not occur.

Finally, any full definition of risk will naturally lead to describing the result or outcome. This is usually expressed as a *loss*, unfavorable *impact* or negative *consequence*. At this point, however, battle lines were drawn: some practitioners insisted that the outcome may be favorable or unfavorable, positive or negative, and that both should be considered equally. This debate is reflected in the note to the ISO Guide 73:2009 definition of risk, which has adopted both positive and negative outcomes.

Others strongly object to this and see a clear dividing line. In normal use, no one speaks of an unexpected profit as risk. Outcomes of a risk that are positive or favorable to an organization's goals were called *speculative* risks and should not be included in the scope of defining risks to be managed.

5. H. Felix Kloman, Rethinking risk management, *The Geneva Papers on Risk and Insurance*, vol. 17, Is. 64, pp. 299–313, 1992.
6. Emmett Vaughan and Therese Vaughan, *Essentials of Risk Management and Insurance*, Wiley & Sons, 2001, 2nd ed.
7. Emmett Vaughan and Therese Vaughan, *Essentials of Risk Management and Insurance*, Wiley & Sons, 2001, 2nd ed.

These are *pure* risks, those with only two possible outcomes: "loss" or "no loss". The latter is neutral, neither favorable nor unfavorable, while the loss is always a negative event.

This controversy is not to be dismissed lightly; if positive outcomes and gains are included in the definition of risk, the scope of practice is enlarged accordingly. This changes the entire field of risk management and cuts some important ties back to insurance, where profiting is definitely out of bounds. For introductory purposes in this handbook, both views are presented and the reader may continue the debate, while the discussion on operational risk management will primarily focus on unfavorable or negative outcomes.

With this in view, the reader should consider and review some of the current definitions of risk; these are illustrative examples but by no means exhaustive:

- Robert Mehr and Bob Hedges adopted a viewpoint very much from an insurance perspective in their textbook *Risk Management, Concepts and Applications*, stating that risk "may be defined as the possibility that losses will be greater than is normal, expected or usual".[8]
- James Athearn in his 1977 text *Risk and Insurance* embraced a definition similar to Mehr and Hedges that was both simple and basic:

  Risk is the possibility of an unfavorable deviation from expectations; that is, the occurrence of an undesirable contingency. It is the possibility that something we do not want to happen will happen or that something we want to happen will fail to do so. Such an occurrence is commonly referred to as a loss.[9]

- While recognizing that no definition is "correct," Robert Williams and Bob Heins take the position in *Risk Management and Insurance* that risk is "the variation in the outcomes that could occur over a specified period in a given situation . . . the greater the variation, the greater the risk."[10]
- In a similar vein, but more succinctly, the co-authors of a popular text on risk management, Emmett and Therese Vaughn, define risk as "a condition in which there is a possibility of an adverse deviations from a desired outcome that is expected and hoped for)".[11]
- The American Law Institute (ALI) defines risk management as

  the processes that an organization uses to identify, assess, prioritize, avoid, prevent, monitor, mitigate, reduce, share, transfer, and to whatever extent still necessary or appropriate, accept, the risks the organization faces in achieving its strategy and business objectives. Each organization should seek to manage risk in a manner that it deems appropriate given its particular attributes and circumstances.[12]

The variations on these themes abound, and these few examples do not even begin to describe the number attempts to improve the definitions of *risk*. While nearly all contain the essential element included above, authors and professional argue vehemently about nuanced emphasis and subtle distinctions over dozens of definitions of *risk*.

8. Robert I. Mehr and Bob A. Hedges, *Risk Management: Concepts and Applications*, Irwin, 1974.
9. James L. Athearn, *Risk and Insurance*, West, 1977.
10. C. Arthur Williams and Richard M. Heins, *Risk Management and Insurance*, McGraw-Hill, 1989, 6th ed.
11. Emmett Vaughan and Therese Vaughan, *Essentials of Risk Management and Insurance*, Wiley & Sons, 2001, 2nd ed.
12. www.ali.org.

Related Terms and Concepts

Further complicating this debate is that the definition of *risk* is further refined and expressed in terms of uncertainty, probability, hazard, peril, value, exposure and chance. These are often defined by words that refer to the same concepts in their definition, creating in some cases a valid objection of circular reasoning. So it is important to be familiar with these terms and concepts that are used in risk definitions:

While *risk* is a condition that exists in the real world, *uncertainty* is a state of mind;[13] it is how an individual estimates their risk or perceives the likelihood of its occurrence. One may have correctly identified a risk but inaccurately arrived at different estimates in their assessment of the risk and thus their degree of certainty.

For example, will it rain on the day of a major outdoor event? One may have studied the historical data and current weather forecasts and have high uncertainty on the probability and amount of rain; their mind is unsettled on the prospects. Another individual may have ignored data, relied on their subjective experience and hold high confidence that it will not rain. The risk remains the same, but the individuals experience different degrees of uncertainty; some authors label this *subjective* risk.[14]

Probability is the long-term relative frequency of the event, typically expressed in mathematical terms; "chance" is the more informal word. Probabilities may be determined by experimentation or estimated based on data.[15] In some cases, probabilities are developed by modeling or simulation in order to develop a more reliable value to use in forecasting.

A *hazard* is a condition that also exists in the real world that either creates or increases the probability or chance of a loss.[16] For example, in all cases gasoline is considered a hazardous substance due to its flammability and vapor; properly contained in my car's fuel tank, its hazard is relatively low. If it is poorly stored in an unvented cabinet, or leaking across my garage floor, its hazard has dramatically increased the probability and potential severity of a loss.

A commonly misused term is "peril", or the *cause* of the loss, often used synonymously with "source of loss". Perils include such common events as fire, windstorm, rising waters or lawsuits brought by aggrieved parties.

Value or *exposure* can have many meanings, but for the purpose of defining and assessing risk, these are the object or subject of the risk. The words are used in risk management as nouns as opposed to verbs. Most definitions of *risk* contained an objective or goal that may or may not be attained, and the "value" or "exposure unit" is the thing that embodies that objective. An automobile usually has value; it may vary from an old car in poor repair to a European luxury car in mint condition. Both cars are *exposed* to the peril of fire, but the *value* exposed to loss will vary considerably.

Exposure may also be used to describe the *degree* to which an organization is vulnerable to a loss; a manufacturer of fireworks has a *high exposure* to the peril of explosion, while an ordinary manufacturing company might have a risk but a *lower exposure*.

13. James L. Athearn, *Risk and Insurance*, West, 1977.
14. George Rejda, *Principles of Risk Management and Insurance*, Addison Wesley, 2003, 8th ed.
15. George Rejda, *Principles of Risk Management and Insurance*, Addison Wesley, 2003, 8th ed.
16. Emmett Vaughan and Therese Vaughan, *Essentials of Risk Management and Insurance*, Wiley & Sons, 2001, 2nd ed.

Defining Risk in the International Standards

No discussion of defining *risk* would be complete without considering the two major risk management standards that have been developed over in the past two decades. More will follow on the origin and impact of the risk management standards, but at this point how they define *risk* should be reviewed.

In their 2004 *Enterprise Risk Management—Integrated Framework Executive Summary*, the Committee of Sponsoring Organizations of the Treadway Commission (COSO) described risk as "events can have negative impact, positive impact, or both. Events with a negative impact represent *risks*, which can prevent value creation or erode existing value".[17] This definition appears to both consider positive outcomes and then exclude them from the definition of risk, but with limited comment on uncertainty, probability or the measurement of the outcome other than the event's effect on value. While the COSO Framework considers uncertainty and quantification, the core definition itself is ambiguous.

The International Organization for Standardization (ISO) developed the *ISO 31000 Standard for Risk Management* and published it in 2009 (it was revised in 2018).[18] In this framework, *risk* is simply the "effect of uncertainty on objectives, and an *effect* is a positive or negative deviation from what is expected". This definition has been debated and discussed extensively; it is attractive for its simplicity, and yet challenged in how it can include positive outcomes as a "risk", as well as how the standard can be applied universally across diverse and complex organizations.

Crafting a Useful Definition

Several comments can be made on all this word-wrestling and arguments over the definition of risk and the various terms associated with it. On the one hand, this is a worthy effort: words do have explicit meanings—the precise definition of a term—as well as connotations, which are the emotional components that influence how we interpret and act on words. These are important and can affect how organizational partners and key stakeholders respond.

It is vitally important to communicate risk clearly to stakeholders. But at the same time, students of risk management and practitioners should not get overwrought with the debate over definitions. The essential components of the definitions of risk are what must be understood, and these can be readily grasped by every level of an organization.

- Individuals and organizations have *goals* and *objectives*.
- We live in a world that presents us with *opportunities* to pursue these.
- We organize in our minds and actions with *expectations* toward these goals.
- *Events* can occur, or fail to occur, that promote or interfere with attaining the goals.
- There is *uncertainty* about the *frequency* of the events and the *severity* of their impacts.

The expressions in italics are the key words in defining risk, and the task is to adopt a coherent definition—or craft one around these—that may be understood and embraced by those we must influence. The primary goal is to effectively communicate risk across an organization so that it may be recognized and managed, and there are many definitions that will do.

Enterprise Risk Management (ERM)

As the study and practice of risk management matured in the late 1980s, different related spheres of risk were growing as well. In addition to traditional operational risk was financial risk, which had

17. *Enterprise Risk Management—Integrated Framework Executive Summary*, the Committee of Sponsoring Organizations of the Treadway Commission (COSO), https://www.coso.org/SitePages/Guidance-on-Enterprise-Risk-Management.aspx?web=1, describes the 2004 version along with updates.
18. www.iso.org.

been the subject of emerging management techniques and study since the 1970s.[19] Political risks from failed states, terrorism and foreign regulations that virtually confiscated a company's assets abounded; these were the subject of a completely different set of practitioners. The explosion of tort and securities litigation, as well as increased regulation, fueled compliance and legal risk management. Unfortunately, each set of risks grew in its own silo, as did the mindset of those who managed them. They occupied their own space in government organizations, businesses and nonprofit entities, each with their own terminology. It was clear that a more comprehensive approach was needed in order to pull together all risks into a coherent management system.

Felix Kloman, a consultant and publisher of *Risk Management Reports* for over 33 years, saw the problems in 1992 and suggested that risk management "should be a holistic endeavor, one that looks at *all* risks and their inter-relationships including primary, secondary and tertiary effects" (emphasis in the original).[20]

Although the term *holistic* faded from common use, the concept gradually gained wider acceptance as enterprise risk management (ERM), and it now has widespread global acceptance by that name.

Yet ERM today reflects Kloman's desire for a holistic approach. ERM seeks to influence a corporate culture and develop risk management systems that deal with uncertainties across all risks in a thorough and systematic way.[21]

As opposed to a fragmented approach to risk where each business unit and risk owner is making individual decisions about risks, rewards and risk treatment, ERM seeks to push this both higher in the organization and down to the operational decision makers

At the top of the organization, ERM does not endorse centralizing decisions at the board or executive level; that would needlessly delay and choke the organization's ability to act. Rather, the board of directors effect the ERM strategy across the organization and set the overall risk appetite. They then empower leaders and require them to identify potential events that may affect the entity, and to then manage risks within its risk appetite.[22]

ERM should seek to give all involved a broad view of the total risk picture; executives establish the entity's risk appetite and strategic direction, and then operational managers and leaders consider the total picture in terms of both opportunities and risks.[23] All managers are accountable for their decisions, but ultimately, they should make better and more optimal decisions on business opportunities and the risks that come along with them.

ERM is not without its challengers in theory and difficulties in implementation. It is not a panacea or one-size-fits-all solution, nor should anyone involved think that it is going to be an easy or fast process. ERM will not be easily cost justified on some kind of return on investment or other profit measure, as financial measurements alone cannot quantify every risk or forecast in dollar terms all the benefits.[24] What is the precise value of the lawsuit that is *never* filed or the scandal that didn't occur? Neither can be readily quantified.

19. Georges Dionne, Risk management: History, definition and critique, *Risk Management and Insurance Review*, 2013, vol. 16, September, Is. 2, pp. 147–166.
20. H. Felix Kloman, Rethinking risk management, *The Geneva Papers on Risk and Insurance*, vol. 17, Is. 64, pp. 299–313, 1992.
21. Jean-Paul Louisot and Christopher Ketcham, *Enterprise-Wide Risk Management: Developing and Implementing*, American Institute for Chartered Property Casualty Underwriters/Insurance Institute of America, pp. 1–19, 2009.
22. *Ibid.*, at 17.
23. Jean-Paul Louisot and Christopher Ketcham, *Enterprise-Wide Risk Management: Developing and Implementing*, American Institute for Chartered Property Casualty Underwriters/Insurance Institute of America, pp. 1–19, 2009.
24. Jim Negus, 10 common ERM challenges, *Risk Management Magazine*, March 2010.

ERM is definitely not a program that is implemented and runs without further adjustment; it should be a living and growing practice that permeates every space of an organization. When done right, it becomes a lasting change in the way an entity thinks about and considers risk, and leaders choose to consider not only the risks they are taking in their own world but how these might compound, affect or reduce the risk faced by the entire enterprise.

Development of Risk Management Standards

The further advancement of risk management took a significant step forward in the first two decades of the 21st century with the development of risk management standards. To understand the standards it is necessary to go back to their origin stories: past is prelude to the present.

As is so often the case, the source was compelled by crisis. In the late 1970s a series of scandals in the fields of accounting, finance and financial reporting, along with significant loss events in traditional risk management, revealed the need for more comprehensive approaches to managing these risks that could be applied globally.

It is an unfortunate fact that so many "advances" in risk management are reactions to events rather than carefully developed strategies that anticipate the loss. Risk management should be proactive as opposed to reactive. Continuous processes of risk assessment, measurement and mitigation should be the norm instead of cycles of complacency followed by overreactions and course corrections made in a panic.

But as a result of these scandals, over 400 companies based in the United States admitting to making questionable and sometimes unlawful payments to foreign governments, officials and political parties. In one of the larger cases, involving the aircraft manufacturer and defense contractor Lockheed Martin, over $22 million in bribes had been paid to foreign officials in completing a large transaction for the sale of fighter jets, with total payouts to representative of multiple nations of well over $200 million.

Hearings were held by Congress and executives were compelled to testify publicly. Although individual explanations varied, they generally claimed that such payments were necessary to secure agreements or simply in the ordinary cost of business overseas. Almost as serious as the payments themselves were the accounting practices that misclassified or disguised the payments.

After conducting hearings and listening to lengthy testimony, Congress passed the Foreign Corrupt Practices Act (FCPA), and it was signed into law by President Jimmy Carter in 1977. This was clearly an appropriate response, but it should have been pursued far earlier.

Yet further accounting scandals wreaked havoc on banks, businesses and investors even after the FCPA went into effect into the 1980s. In response to the growing financial scandals, five professional associations from the financial reporting, audit and accounting fields formed the National Commission on Fraudulent Financial Reporting, commonly named after its first chair, James C. Treadway Jr., the former commissioner of the US Securities and Exchange Commission. This became its common name: the "Treadway Commission".

Beginning their work and studying the various scandals and their sources, the Commission published their report in 1987, and afterward COSO was formed to continue to study the issues that had been raised in the report.

A clear goal of this effort was to move risk management into a more proactive position of identifying threats in advance. Alongside this, COSO was to develop a system of internal controls that would detect and prevent financial fraud. It gradually evolved to include a broader perspective that addressed a wider array of risks, and grew in scope to include risk identification, assessment, treatment and monitoring controls. These had application far beyond financial reporting and accounting.

This may have occurred as a result of another emerging crisis. At the same time as the Treadway Commission's work was in progress, a liability insurance crisis developed in the United States. This appeared, at the time, to put the availability of commercial insurance for risk transfer into doubt. From 1984 to 1987, premiums for general liability increased from about $6.5 billion to approximately $19.5 billion, and coverage terms and conditions that had generally been included policies for decades were dramatically changed to the insurer's advantage.

COSO addressed the issues of financial accounting, reporting and audit and published in 1992 the *Internal Control—Integrated Framework* to help businesses and other entities assess and enhance their internal control systems.[25] This was the source of the most significant effort for a comprehensive risk management system up to that date.

The COSO authors and future members of the Committee did not publish their work and retire. Increased concerns and focus on the broader issues of risk management made it clear that "a more robust framework was needed". COSO pursued this starting in 2001; they updated it significantly in 2004 and published *Enterprise Risk Management—Integrated Framework* to expand and incorporate their work on internal controls.

The Framework divides ERM in three dimensions. Objectives are organized into strategic, operations, reporting and compliance categories, applied to the entity level, division, business and subsidiary units. The components of the RM *Framework* reflect the risk processes:

- Objective setting
- Event identification
- Risk assessment
- Risk response
- Control activities
- Information and communication
- Monitoring.[26]

The COSO Framework continued to address new risks, emerging technologies and changes in the commercial environment, with the most recent revision published in 2017.

The International Organization for Standardization (ISO)

In 1946 representatives of 25 countries met in London and created a new organization to meet the demand for standards in various areas of engineering, manufacturing and similar industries. Their goal was to coordinate and attempt to unify practices and systems within a particular industry across international borders. The ISO (the acronym is always the same, regardless of language) develops and publishes consensus standards that are pursued only in response to market needs, and they are independent of government regulators and agencies. Their work is prodigious: the ISO has published over 22,000 international standards covering subjects from calibrating medical devices to formats to record dates and times consistently.

The ISO 31000 Risk Management Standard

In response to the continued industry interest in defining risk and how it should be managed, the ISO began the development of a risk management standard in the early 2000s. To avoid the need to start from scratch, a work that had already been developed was used as a foundation. Published by a joint committee of representatives from New Zealand and Australia in 1995, the AS/NZS 4360

25. *Ibid.*, at 17.
26. *Ibid.*, at 17.

Risk Management standard was revised in 1999 and again in 2004. At that point the AS/NZS Committee desired to support an international standard, and the work was picked up and moved forward by the ISO.

Engaging academics and professionals working in the field, the ISO published the 31000 Standard in 2009 for the implementation of risk management principles. In addition to being compatible with the COSO ERM Framework, the Standard included two key companion publications: The Guide 73 *Risk Management—Vocabulary—Guidelines for Use in Standards* to provide consistent terminology, and the *ISO/IEC 31010:2019* standard for risk assessment techniques.[27]

The ISO 31000 Standard and its sister guides provided a defined and coherent system or "framework" for implementing risk management within an organization, while allowing an entity to define and describe its own risk architecture, strategy and protocols. Although the Standard is not without its detractors, it clearly represented an advance in defining terms and providing a structure for managing risk. It also sets out the conceptual basis and scope of ERM, providing a strategy for making risk management a part of a company's culture and improving the ability of managers to identify, treat and monitor the risks they face.

As opposed to a set of rigid standards or oft-changing lists of specific methods, the ISO Standards are framed up as principles. One group of authors, writing from the viewpoint of project management risks, stated that "the ISO principles have the potential to be the basis for our shared understanding of best practice, and to catalyze the professionalism of project management".[28]

As with its COSO counterpart, the 31000 Standard has continued to be the subject of expansion and updating, the most recent in early 2018, placing a greater emphasis on the involvement of executive leadership and integrating risk management from corporate governance down to how risk is managed at all levels.

Implementation of the Standards

How broadly and how well have the COSO Framework, ERM and the ISO 31000 Standard been embraced and adopted by organizations? These are now widely accepted, with the ISO framework growing more popular in its use and impact.

An important development occurred in June of 2018, when the Risk and Insurance Management Society (RIMS), based in the United States, encouraged all countries to adopt the revised 2018 31000 Standard as their national standard for ERM and risk management practice, including making it the American standard.[29] As the largest of organization of risk professionals, this was a significant endorsement.

While verbal endorsement and praise of the standards are widespread, actual implementation is a major undertaking that meets resistance, and actual adoption of risk management standards is not always consistent.

The challenges to implementing standardized risk management systems are daunting. The ordinary obstacles to any change across an organization will come first, and then the specific problems that are unique to risk management. Finally, some practitioners and academic authors argue that the standards are in themselves flawed and should be either scrapped or re-engineered to fit each organization, and the latter approach is probably closer to the truth.

27. www.iso.org/standard/72140.html.
28. A. Olechowski et al., The professionalization of risk management: What role can the ISO 31000 risk management principles play? *International Journal of Risk Management*, vol. 34, pp. 1568–1578, 2016.
29. Lucy Hook, *RIMS Urges Countries to Adopt Updated ISO 31000:18 as National Standard*, Corporate and Risk Insurance, Key Media, June 6, 2018.

Common Organizational Challenges

In the first case, organizational change is always hard. Once established, all human endeavors resist change and prefer to maintain the status quo. Even entrepreneurial start-ups in today's high-tech world that claim to value change and innovation will vigorously resist attempts to introduce order, discipline and systems—which are a form of change—into their workplaces.

Further, as a society and on an individual level, we have an optimism bias. Although many will recognize the possibility that bad events will (theoretically) occur, the majority will act and believe that they won't happen in the near term, won't happen to them, or won't be as bad. This fundamental tendency will work against the efforts to establish ERM, and this bias will be further augmented if a business unit or the organization as a whole has not suffered a significant loss or catastrophic event.

If no serious losses have been experienced recently, executives will often assume that this is evidence against change. They conclude that they have been successful at managing risk, or the perils and hazards that impact others won't occur to them (perhaps for a variety of idiosyncratic reasons). Often, when asked to consider that combinations of adverse events might occur simultaneously or that redundancies may fail, they will dismiss these arguments and maintain their current course.

Unique Risk Management Obstacles

Specific to risk management are the unique challenges to the language of risk, identification of exposures, measurement of probabilities and the quantification of future loss events. Each one is a daunting task for an executive or business unit leader to devote a significant amount of time, attention and resources to.

The language of risk is often arcane and unique to the professionals, engineers and academics in the field, and must often be translated or simplified in implementing ERM. Monte Carlo simulations, Poisson and Bayesian distributions, actuarial methods (of which there are dozens), coefficients of variance and catastrophe models based on deterministic and probabilistic analysis—and all of these are common tools of the trade—are a completely foreign language to most business executives. Risk professionals must carefully consider their language and communication skills, and the best result will be obtained by carefully considering the audience well before any presentation.

It is not simply the language of risk itself but a respectful consideration for attention spans that will determine the engagement level of an executive. While not accusing the average business leader of having a diagnosable disorder, the reality is that they face on a daily basis a deluge of demands, decisions and strategic debates in the here and now of a rapidly changing economy. Asking them to focus on the wide array of possible loss exposures and identify those most salient risks, and then discuss the probabilities and severity of the impact, may push them beyond their time/attention capacity. If brevity is the soul of wit, it well may be the heart of any executive-level ERM presentation, and it may be better to break up ERM implementation into multiple sessions and digestible surveys, summaries and recaps where slow progress over time builds and supports sustainable corporate change.

And this is a critical issue in the implementation of any ERM effort: the goal is not a process or program, but effecting a change in corporate culture that considers risk management a core value seeks to assess risk at the start of any new endeavor and integrates risk management as an ongoing part of every business activity. A strange paradox can been seen: ERM can be "implemented" as a program, documented, defined and consistently applied, and yet be ineffective in practice when it is pushed aside for the next big corporate initiative.

On the other hand, ERM might be introduced as fit for each business unit, and gradually permeate the organization's thinking and behavior. Although it might not be as well documented or rigidly applied in the same way to every part of the organization, it is effective because it has grown organically; risk identification, measurement and management have become part of the corporate culture and value system.

Implementing the Standards in Managing Risk

Regarding the standards themselves, and the issue of whether they are fatally flawed or useful tools, heated rhetoric can be found on both sides of this debate. For the risk management professional, it's important to be aware and understand the issues, and then to apply the many useful concept, strategies and structures in the standards to their unique organization.

In this process of using the standards, the risk practitioner first needs to recognize the limitations of risk assessment, and especially risk measurement. As ERM grew out of financial and accounting practices, proponents believed that with sufficient data and information, any loss exposure can be the subject of a probability and loss distribution; with the high volume of reliable data on credit defaults, interest rates, options pricing and equity markets, this is often true of financial risks.

But the view of risk is pulled back to consider the world more broadly: data becomes more scarce and quantification much more difficult. Strategic, operational, technological and environmental risk—and there are many more existing and emerging risk categories than can be easily named—all of these must be identified and assessed in the ERM process. When one considers then the broader array of interrelated risks an organization might be exposed to, precise quantification is often impossible. These are risks and events with consequences that can literally destroy an organization's value—not to mention its very survival.

Can we quantify the probability that an executive or well-known representative of the company will molest a minor? That a celebrity endorsing their products will overdose? Or an employee will post a devastating photo or crude bit of humor online, and it will circulate around the globe before anyone can respond? What is the chance that a low-level team of engineers will decide to save 30 cents on a minor part and cause dozens of fatal accidents? Further compounding the risk, how will the organization respond? So often today, it is not entirely the event itself but the delayed, flawed and ill-conceived reaction that turns a manageable event into a crisis that threatens the organization.

Effective ERM, as guided by the international standards and supporting literature, can and should be used to identify risks, approximate their frequency and range of severity, and admit that these estimates may well be subjective. After risks have been identified, the critical task of treating these risks to mitigate their consequences and monitor for change can begin. But an attempt to measure them in a mathematical way that can be added and modeled in the same manner as an investment portfolio is not realistically achievable.

An effective risk-management program should ordinarily include the following:

1. Setting the organization's risk appetite and risk tolerance, and determining the organization's risk capacity;
2. Identifying risks;
3. Assessing risks;
4. Prioritizing risks;
5. Validating risk assessments;
6. Monitoring risks;
7. Designing, selecting, and if appropriate, implementing risk responses;
8. Assessing and accepting residual risk;
9. Ensuring that mechanisms are in place to promote ongoing communication of risk-relevant information to the appropriate executives and other organizational actors;
10. Creating, promoting and retaining an appropriate risk culture;
11. Hiring, sufficiently and appropriately compensating, and supporting qualified risk managers, including, if appropriate or required, a chief risk officer;
12. On a scheduled and an ongoing basis, as appropriate, monitoring and reviewing both the outputs and the elements of the program to assess its efficacy and to improve it;

13. Establishing appropriate governance structures for the organization's risk-management framework and risk-management program within the organization;
14. Coordinating risk-management activities with those of other internal control functions;
15. Integrating and embedding risk management throughout the organization, including into its strategy and business-objectives planning; and
16. Committing the appropriate resources, leadership, and support to risk management.

Expansion of Risk Management: Opportunities and Threats

The role of risk and risk management in the global community of businesses, governments and non-profit organizations is at a historic inflection point. Various crisis have roiled through the past two decades, raising the profile and public awareness of risk. The dot-com collapse was followed in short order by the Enron and WorldCom financial scandals—and the September 11th attacks. Before these could even be properly comprehended, natural catastrophes of unprecedented loss occurred—the 2004 Indian Ocean earthquake and tsunami are estimated to have killed over 230,000 people, and were shortly followed by Hurricane Katrina in the United States—which revealed that the impact of natural disasters can be increased significantly by the poor planning, inadequate preparation and failures in crisis management during and after an event.

The Tohoku earthquake in Japan in 2011—which was one of the five strongest earthquakes ever recorded—was combined with a tsunami and nuclear meltdown all in the same event.

Suffice to say, risk and risk management are publicly viewed and debated in a way never seen before. This is good news: rising awareness and recognition of the need to manage risk has provided support and energy to its study, practice and implementation. At the same time, this can be negative, as risk is misunderstood or mishandled for political purposes or poorly communicated in traditional and social media. Three conclusions can be made:

1. *Take advantage to extend the study, practice and influence of risk management.* The maturing of the profession and emergence of global standards and frameworks for risk management, combined with the public concern and awareness described above, provide a historic opportunity to advance the extension, application and resulting benefits of effective risk management systems.
2. *Strive to avoid the cycle of crisis and reaction, followed by apathy.* Unfortunately, the history of risk and our response to it repeats a chronic cycle of "unforeseen" events that are followed by frenetic activity, questionable responses and a gradual decline in public awareness. Many of these crises are labeled by some as not only unforeseen but *unforeseeable*, a truly questionable and unfortunate conclusion.
3. *Communicate risk clearly and accurately.* A by-product of the hyper-reaction to natural or human-made events with 24/7 news coverage and ensuing panels of "experts" often feeds the public's fear, worry and understanding of a risk. As a result, individuals worry excessively about risks that are actually low (e.g., shark attack, asbestos in school rooms) and appear unconcerned about significant perils (e.g., air pollution, drug addiction). Academic and risk professionals should make every effort to understand, inform and communicate risk accurately and clearly to every stakeholder and policy maker.

The Future of Risk Management

A lengthy discussion on the definition of risk was included earlier in this chapter; that was certainly necessary to set a foundation. But as we consider the future of risk and the risk management profession, perhaps we should step back and ask even bigger questions: What is the role of risk in society, and what is our purpose? Is understanding risk simply a business function, or does it play a significant role in our culture? Who do we serve—not only in an organizational structure but in communities, societies, nations and the human experience?

Within organizations there has been a gradual shift from viewing risk management as an *activity* to that of a *shared value*. Risk is seen not just as insurance or safety rules; it's about caring for people, for the customer, for employees, and for communities. There is a growing recognition that we need to give people better reasons for how they act. In today's world, individuals conduct themselves not out of obedience to rules or conformity to regulations but out of a sincere concern for the lives and health of their families and co-workers, and for themselves. Given a proper context and communication, these motives are sustainable and have deeper persistence in changing risk awareness and conduct.

At a larger level it can be argued that risk management can transform lives. A significant factor that separates developed nations and functional economies from the failed states that litter the globe is, in fact, risk management. High risk, uncertainty and the inability to manage these cause capital to flee—along with industry, jobs, educational institutions and hope. Although political, historical and systemic factors may be more visible and overwhelming, the inability of corrupt governments and oligarchies to provide a sovereign space where risk can be managed and commerce nurtured makes the reversal of these conditions truly impossible.

Felix Kloman perhaps went even further. In comments presented to the World Insurance Congress in 1991, he stated that

> the real objective of risk management is to reduce fear of the unknown and the unexpected, and to create confidence in the future. It is certainly not simply the technical understanding of risk nor making financial provisions for alleviating the pain of loss. . . . If risk management can contribute to the larger goal of creating new confidence—reducing fear—it will be important to all of us both individually and in the organizations and political structures in which we participate.[30]

There are few endeavors, careers or professions that offer such an opportunity and purpose to serve; may all who practice the study and management of risk be committed to such a goal.

30. H. Felix Kloman, Rethinking risk management, *The Geneva Papers on Risk and Insurance*, vol. 17, Is. 64, pp. 299–313, 1992.

2

COMPLIANCE, CORPORATE GOVERNANCE, AND CORPORATE SOCIAL RESPONSIBILITY

Part I—The Interplay Between the Company, the Stakeholder, and the Regulators

Marcia Weldon and Lauren Miller

Introduction

It is no longer enough to comply with the law—companies must also consider their social license to operate and their responsibility to the communities in which they operate. The community members, employees, government officials, and those affected by the corporate activities—the stakeholders—must grant a social license because they believe that the business cares about more than the bottom line.[1] Corporate social responsibility (CSR) activities often add legitimacy to projects or companies that local communities oppose. Companies memorialize their CSR commitments in annual reports, codes of conduct,[2] and philanthropic activities and in turn, require those in their supply chains to act responsibly. Stakeholders and shareholders then scrutinize these commitments and take action based upon adherence to these commitments. They act through investment, divestment, boycott, or litigation.

This chapter will first discuss how compliance and corporate social responsibility relate to each other, and how they increasingly overlap through various environmental, social, and governance (ESG) regulations and guidelines. We will provide examples of instances in which companies have failed to earn or retain their social licenses and where CSR codes have been used against companies in litigation. In Chapter 3, we will examine the corporate governance aspects of CSR and how shareholder demands and regulation are shaping board action.

What Is Compliance?

Firms today must comply with a myriad of domestic and in some cases, international laws. An effective compliance program aims to prevent and detect violations of the law that may lead to civil

1. For more on the history of the term "social license," see Joel Gehman, Lianne M. Lefsrud and Stewart Fast, *Social License to Operate: Legitimacy by Another Name?*, Wiley Online Library (June 15, 2017), https://onlinelibrary.wiley.com/doi/full/10.1111/capa.12218.
2. These codes of conduct are part of what Scott Killingsworth has called the "privatization of compliance." Scott Killingsworth and Bryan Cave, The Privatization of Compliance (2014), http://root.bryancavemedia.com/marketing/downloads/The_Privatization_of_Compliance_29_May_2014.pdf.

DOI: 10.4324/9781351107242-4

or criminal liability. After a spate of scandals over the past 20 years, firms of all sizes have dedicated increased focus to compliance. In the United States, firms use the Federal Sentencing Guidelines for Organizational Defendants[3] ("Sentencing Guidelines") as a template. Companies that develop programs based on these Sentencing Guidelines benefit through lower fines and penalties for criminal conduct. The US Sentencing Commission first promulgated the Sentencing Guidelines after the enactment of the Sentencing Reform Act of 1984, which ushered in an era of mitigation for organizations that have developed effective compliance programs and, when possible, self-disclosed and cooperated with authorities.

The Sentencing Guidelines list seven requirements at a minimum, for an effective compliance program. First, the company must exercise due diligence and develop standards and procedures to prevent and detect criminal conduct. Companies must also promote an ethical corporate culture. Typically, companies accomplish this through a code of ethical conduct. Second, the board must have knowledge about and oversee the program. Top management must ensure that the program is effective, and specific high-level personnel must have responsibility for managing the program on a day-to-day basis. Ideally, the individual with the day-to-day responsibility, often a compliance officer or general counsel, must have the authority and ability to report directly to the board or subcommittee at least annually regarding the compliance program's effectiveness and, as needed, if there is a suspicion of criminal conduct. Third, the company must use reasonable efforts to exclude bad actors from positions of power and influence in the organization and ensure that those who engage in illegal activities or unethical conduct are not in the managerial ranks. Fourth, the company must communicate standards and procedures through training of personnel throughout the organization and must communicate the role of individuals who are responsible for managing the compliance program. Fifth, the company must put practices into place to monitor and audit criminal conduct. It must also evaluate the program on a regular basis and have a publicized system for reporting known or suspected wrongdoing and seeking guidance without retaliation on how to address it. Commonly, this includes instituting an anonymous hotline, where legally permitted. Sixth, the company must promote and enforce its program through appropriate incentives and discipline when warranted. Finally, when a company detects criminal conduct, it must take steps to respond and prevent similar conduct which may necessitate modifying the program. Good compliance programs are thus both proactive and reactive. Their main focus is ensuring compliance with the law and mitigations of fines and penalties in the event of a violation of the law.

In April 2019, the Department of Justice established guidelines[4] for federal prosecutors to determine whether a company's compliance program is "effective." Accordingly, in addition to reviewing the Sentencing Guidelines, compliance practitioners should evaluate their own programs based upon the three guiding principles outlined in the DOJ guidance: (1) Is the corporation's compliance program well designed? (2) Is the program being applied earnestly and in good faith? and (3) Does the corporation's compliance program work in practice? Compliance officers working for multinational firms must also keep abreast of a number of regulatory schemes and standards as regulators increasingly work together for cross-border prosecutions.

Optimally, compliance professionals help to prevent violation of law and mitigate risk through integrating compliance into the business operations. To help operationalize and internationalize compliance, practitioners should have a working knowledge of the following in addition to local law: the Committee of Sponsoring Organizations of the Treadway Commission (COSO) Framework

3. Chapter 8, United States Sentencing Commission (2016), www.ussc.gov/guidelines/2015-guidelines-manual/2015-chapter-8.
4. US Dep't of Justice, Criminal Division, Evaluation of Corporate Compliance Programs, at 1 (2019), www.justice.gov/criminal-fraud/page/file/937501/download.

(addressing enterprise risk management);[5] the Securities and Exchange Commission/Department of Justice, A Resource Guide to the US Foreign Corrupt Practices Act;[6] the UK Bribery Act of 2010, Guidance;[7] and the OECD Good Practice Guidance on Internal Controls, Ethics, and Compliance.[8] Other helpful resources include ISO 196000:2014 (revised by ISO 37301:2021), which provides guidelines for compliance management systems, and ISO 37001:2016, which addresses bribery and corruption and provides for a certification process.[9]

From Compliance to Corporate Social Responsibility to Responsible Business Conduct

As discussed above, compliance with law is the baseline. Successful companies also have a social license[10] to operate, which they gain through "the broad acceptance of [their] activities by society or the local community [because] [w]ithout this approval, a business may not be able to carry on its activities without incurring serious delays and costs."[11] More importantly,

> social license can never be self-awarded, it requires that an activity enjoys sufficient trust and legitimacy, and has the consent of those affected. Business cannot determine how much prevention or mitigation it should engage in to meet environmental or social risk—stakeholders and rights-holders have to be involved for thresholds of due diligence to be legitimate (sometimes even if these are clearly determined in law).[12]

Companies must thus act legally and ethically.

Organizations often use corporate social responsibility (CSR) programs to gain and retain this social license to operate. The Harvard Kennedy School of Government defines corporate responsibility as

> not only what companies do with their profits but also how they make them. It goes beyond philanthropy and compliance and addresses how companies manage the economic, social,

5. See Committee of Sponsoring Organizations of the Treadway Commission (COSO), Thought Leadership in ERM Demystifying Sustainability Risk 5 (May 2013).
6. Criminal Div. of the US Dep't of Justice and the Enforcement Div. of the US SEC, FCPA, A Resource Guide to the US Foreign Corrupt Practices Act (November 14, 2012), www.sec.gov/spotlight/fcpa/fcpa-resource-guide.pdf. See also Spotlight on Foreign Corrupt Practices Act, US SEC, www.sec.gov/spotlight/foreign-corrupt-practices-act.shtml; Foreign Corrupt Practices Act, US Dep't of Justice (February 3, 2017), www.justice.gov/criminal-fraud/foreign-corrupt-practices-act.
7. Bribery Act 2010, c. 23, § 9 (UK), www.legislation.gov.uk/ukpga/2010/23/section/9.
8. OECD 2010.
9. See Crescenzi, ISO 37001 Certification: Understanding and navigating the process, *Compliance & Ethics Professional* 36 (August 2018).
10. See John G. Ruggie, UN Special Representative of the Secretary-General on the Issue of Human Rights and Transnational Corporations and Other Business Enterprises, *Protect, Respect and Remedy: A Framework for Business and Human Rights*, ¶ 54, Human Rights Council, UN Doc. A/HRC/8/5 (April 7, 2008), www.reports-and-materials.org/Ruggie-report-7-Apr-2008.pdf. Author and executive director of the Institute for Human Rights and Business John Morrison prefers the term "social license" and argues that legal and political licenses are dependent upon the social license and that it goes beyond a concept of corporate social responsibility. John Morrison, *The Social License: How to Keep Your Organization Legitimate* (2014).
11. Kathleen Wilburn and Ralph Wilburn, Achieving social license to operate using stakeholder theory. *Journal of International Business Ethics* (2011), 4, 3–16, www.researchgate.net/publication/284663470_Achieving_social_license_to_operate_using_stakeholder_theory.
12. John Morrison, Business and society: defining the "social license", *The Guardian* (2014), www.theguardian.com/sustainable-business/2014/sep/29/social-licence-operate-shell-bp-business-leaders.

> and environmental impacts, as well as relationships in all key spheres of influence: the workplace, the marketplace, the supply chain, community, and the public policy realm.[13]

Complicating matters further, some organizations and countries use the term "sustainability" rather than CSR. Often called the triple bottom line—people, planet, profit—sustainability is a key factor in integrated reporting: public disclosure of financial and nonfinancial performance.[14] According to the UN World Commission on Environment and Development, "sustainable development is development that meets the needs of the present without compromising the ability of future generations to meet their own needs."[15] This chapter will use the terms CSR, sustainability, or responsible business conduct depending on the term used in the legislation or policies discussed.

The United States government and the Organisation for Economic Co-operation and Development (OECD) no longer use the term CSR, however. Instead they use the term "responsible business conduct" (RBC). The OECD, an organization consisting of 34 democratic nations and 70 nonmembers, differentiates responsible business conduct from CSR, explaining that

> businesses should make a positive contribution to economic, environmental, and social progress with a view to achieving sustainable development and have a responsibility to avoid and address the adverse impact of the operations. The concept of CSR is often associated with philanthropic corporate conduct extra to business operations. RBC goes beyond this to emphasize integration of responsible practices within internal operations and throughout business relationships and supply chains.[16]

The OECD has advised that RBC is an integral part of the business function which must integrate with corporate governance, procurement, finance, and other departments, while CSR is often considered an "add-on."

Unfortunately, companies have often relied on CSR initiatives as a public relations tool even as they failed to live up to their own commitments. For example, a number of companies had conducted CSR audits shortly before the tragic 2013 Rana Plaza collapse in Bangladesh, in which over 1,100 people died.[17] Large multinational companies performed audits, discovered safety issues, and yet continued to use those factories. Other companies involved in scandals were at the top of any number of CSR indices. Volkswagen used to be number one in the Dow Jones Sustainability Index even as it rigged emissions, forcing it to pay billions in fines as executives faced jail sentences.[18] Enron was embroiled in a major accounting scandal even while it received CSR awards.[19]

13. Beth Kytle and John Gerald Ruggie, *Corporate Social Responsibility as Risk Management: A Model for Multinationals* (2005), https://sites.hks.harvard.edu/m-rcbg/CSRI/publications/workingpaper_10_kytle_ruggie.pdf.
14. About Sustainability Reporting, Global Reporting Initiative, www.globalreporting.org/information/sustainability-reporting/Pages/default.aspx.
15. UN World Commission on Environment and Development: "Sustainable development is development that meets the needs of the present without compromising the ability of future generations to meet their own needs."
16. Roel Nieuwenkamp, CSR is dead! What's next? *OECD Insights Blog* (2016), http://oecdinsights.org/2016/01/22/2016-csr-is-dead-whats-next/.
17. Dave Jamieson and Emran Hossain, Deadly flaws in safety inspection programs Bangladesh collapse shows safety audit shortcomings, www.huffingtonpost.com/2013/05/04/bangladesh-collapse-safety-audit_n_3211091.html.
18. Haw Yan Man, François Vetri and David Guarino, Volkswagen AG to be removed from the Dow Jones Sustainability Indices, S&P Dow Jones Indices (2015), www.sustainability-indices.com/images/150929-statement-vw-exclusion_vdef.pdf; www.bloomberg.com/news/articles/2017-12-06/vw-executive-sentenced-to-7-years-in-prison-for-diesel-role.
19. Ken Silverstein, Enron, ethics and today's corporate values, *Forbes* (2013), www.forbes.com/sites/kensilverstein/2013/05/14/enron-ethics-and-todays-corporate-values/#182324a5ab81.

Nomenclature aside, governments have been reluctant to rigorously legislate either CSR or responsible business conduct. Instead, states have relied on shareholders and stakeholders to motivate good corporate citizenship, typically through due diligence disclosure regimes. Some of these regimes are merely voluntary or use a comply or explain approach, and some are regulatory requirements, albeit in most cases with minimal financial downside for noncompliance. In some cases, these regulations merely require disclosure of a companies' efforts or lack thereof to prevent human rights and environmental harms. In other cases, laws require affirmative conduct in addition to disclosure. Often, the governments do not provide a private right of action or financial penalties. Instead, they choose to rely on public or commercial pressure through "naming and shaming" under the theory that reputational damage can have financial consequences. A description of some of these voluntary and binding rules and frameworks follows.

Voluntary CSR/RBC Reporting Mechanisms

OECD Guidelines for Multinational Enterprises

Responsible business conduct, according to the OECD, requires preventing the risks in the first place and addressing the negative impacts when they occur, particularly in foreign jurisdictions. To aid its member states, the OECD established its Guidelines for Multinational Enterprises ("OECD Guidelines") in 1976.[20] The nonbinding OECD Guidelines have a significant influence on member states' decisions to regulate responsible business conduct, particularly in the areas of human rights, the environment, bribery, fair labor, consumer impact, and corporate governance.

Significantly, the OECD Guidelines provide the only international corporate responsibility mechanism with a built-in grievance mechanism known as national contact points (NCPs). NCPs are agencies established by governments to promote and implement the OECD Guidelines. They also provide for a mediation platform to resolve issues between community members and companies.[21] However, critics complain that there are no consequences for failing to comply and that companies often demand strict confidentiality in mediations. Further, there are no global standards for NCPs. Accordingly, some believe that the OECD process provides the veneer of responsible business conduct without a true access to remedy.[22]

Notwithstanding any shortcomings in the OECD Guidelines, they do facilitate comprehensive due diligence by covering all types of business relationships including suppliers, franchisees, licensees, joint ventures, investors, clients, contractors, customers, consultants, advisors, or any state or nonstate actor linked to the products or services that the business provides. Further, the OECD Guidelines require companies to use the results of their preventive, risk-based diligence efforts to address actual or potential adverse impacts related to their business enterprises. Because they helped develop them, most countries with ESG reporting requirements allow the use of the OECD Guidelines as an acceptable due diligence platform.

Global Reporting Initiative

In 1997, the Coalition for Environmentally Responsible economics (CERES) and the United Nations Environment Programme (UNEP) launched the most comprehensive objective sustainability

20. OECD Guidelines for Multinational Enterprises (2011), http://mneguidelines.oecd.org/guidelines/.
21. OCED (2018), Structures and Procedures of National Contact Points for the OECD Guidelines for Multinational Enterprises, http://mneguidelines.oecd.org/Structures-and-procedures-of-NCPs-for-the-OECD-guidelines-for-multinational-enterprises.pdf.
22. Narine Weldon, Marcia, From Kansas to the Congo: Why naming and shaming corporations through Dodd-Frank's corporate governance disclosure won't solve a human rights crisis (March 5, 2013), 25 U.L. Rev. 351 (2012/2013), https://ssrn.com/abstract=2228737.

framework to report on ESG factors.[23] The Global Reporting Initiative (GRI) is now considered the gold standard for sustainability reporting. GRI reports require companies to examine operational, governance, human rights, labor, environmental, property, consumer, and community involvement and development practices. GRI also partners with the OECD, the UN Global Compact, and the International Standards Organization (ISO).[24] GRI claims that of the world's largest 50 corporations, 93% report on their sustainability performance, and 82% use the GRI standards.[25] GRI has almost 50,000 reports from over 12,000 organizations in its database from all over the world, with over 30,000 reports following all GRI standards.[26] Thirty-five countries have used the GRI standards to develop their own sustainability reporting requirements.

The UN Global Compact

Founded in 1999, the UN Global Compact (the "Compact") is the world's largest corporate sustainability initiative.[27] The Compact supports companies that do business responsibly in accordance with ten specific principles on human rights, labor, the environment, anticorruption, and companies that focus on advancing broader societal goals such as the United Nations Sustainable Development Goals.[28] As of August 2018, the UN Compact had 12,000 signatories in over 160 countries, including 9,000 companies and 3,000 nonbusiness participants.[29] Approximately 500 of the participants are US-based. Signatories must complete a Communication on Progress in their annual reports or separate sustainability reports and are subject to expulsion for failing to do so.[30] The Compact, however, has no legal force. Instead, it complements other voluntary initiatives and assists companies in complying with regulatory requirements for sustainability reporting.

Although the Compact has no enforcement mechanism, it is considered to be a mandatory disclosure framework. The Compact expels those who do not indicate progress for two years in a row and publishes their names on the website.[31] Moreover, not every firm has access to Compact membership. The Compact excludes certain participants such as tobacco companies, reasoning that tobacco products conflict with the UN's goals regarding public health. Other companies that cannot join the Compact include those subject to a UN sanction, those that derive revenue from production of certain weapons such as land mines and cluster bombs, and those listed on the UN ineligible vendor list for ethical reasons.[32]

ISO 26000:2010

Some companies that rely on the OECD Guidelines also use ISO 26000:2010 to assist in ascertaining their social responsibility because the standards complement each other. ISO developed its standard

23. GRI's history, Global Reporting Initiative, www.globalreporting.org/information/about-gri/gri-history/Pages/GRIs history.aspx.
24. GRI and sustainability reporting, Global Reporting Initiative, www.globalreporting.org/information/sustainability-reporting/Pages/gri-standards.aspx.
25. Jose Luis Blasco et al., *The Road Ahead: The KPMG Survey of Corporate Responsibility Reporting 2017*, https://home.kpmg.com/content/dam/kpmg/campaigns/csr/pdf/CSR_Reporting_2017.pdf.
26. SDD–GRI Database, http://database.globalreporting.org/.
27. UN Global Compact, www.unglobalcompact.org/.
28. United Nations, Sustainable Development Goals, www.un.org/sustainabledevelopment/sustainable-development-goals/.
29. UN Global Compact, www.unglobalcompact.org.
30. UN Global Compact, Create and submit your CoP, www.unglobalcompact.org/participation/report/cop/create-and-submit.
31. UN Global Compact, The Communication on Progress (CoP) in Brief, www.unglobalcompact.org/participation/report/cop; UN Global Compact, Delisted Participants, www.unglobalcompact.org/participation/report/cop/create-and-submit/expelled.
32. UN Global Contact, *Frequently Asked Questions*, www.unglobalcompact.org/about/faq.

through consultation with experts from 90 countries and 40 international organizations working with six stakeholder groups including consumers, government, industry, labor, nongovernmental organizations (NGOs), academics, and others. Notably, ISO uses the term "social responsibility" rather than "corporate social responsibility" because the standard applies to organizations regardless of size or location. ISO provides guidance on the

> responsibility of an organization for the impacts of its decisions and activities on society and the environment, through transparent and ethical behaviour that: contributes to sustainable development, including health and the welfare of society; takes into account the expectations of stakeholders; is in compliance with applicable law and consistent with international norms of behaviour; and is integrated throughout the organization and practised in its relationships.[33]

ISO and OECD overlap but have some differences in focus. The OECD Guidelines provide guidance on human rights, labor relations, environment, bribery and anticorruption, consumer interests, technology, competition, and taxation. ISO 26000 provides guidance on organizational governance, human rights, labor practices, the environment, fair operating practices, consumer issues, and community involvement and development. Within these seven subjects, ISO includes detailed guidance on 37 issues for social responsibility.[34] However, although organizations cannot use ISO 26000:2010 for certification, many firms develop their sustainability reports using ISO standards nonetheless. Notably, while the OECD Guidelines have a dispute resolution mechanism, ISO relies on disclosure and public scrutiny.[35]

The UN Guiding Principles on Business and Human Rights

In 2011, the United Nations Human Rights Council unanimously approved of the "Guiding Principles on Business and Human Rights: Implementing the United Nations 'Protect, Respect and Remedy' Framework" (GPs).[36] The 31 GPs are voluntary and nonbinding, however, the OECD and others adopted recommendations adding human rights components to their own guidelines. The GPs require companies to develop a policy statement on human rights and embed that policy in operational policies and procedures. Companies must perform due diligence within their supply chains and provide a remedy for impacted stakeholders. This remedy must be a legitimate, transparent, accessible, predictable, and equitable mechanism for aggrieved individuals.

The GPs apply to all states and all business enterprises regardless of size, sector, location, or structure, and a number of companies use the language of the GPs in their sustainability filings. Although they do not bind businesses, they do bind states and states are therefore required to develop National Action Plans (NAPs) to promote responsible business conduct for those that operate in their jurisdictions. As of June 2019, 21 countries including the United States had completed NAPs, while

33. Practical Overview of the Linkages Between ISO 26000:2010, Guidance on Social Responsibility and OECD Guidelines for Multinational Enterprises (2011), http://iso26000.info/wp-content/uploads/2017/02/ISO-26000_and_OECD_Guidelines_MNE_PPO_v1.pdf.
34. Practical Overview of the Linkages Between ISO 26000:2010, Guidance on Social Responsibility and OECD Guidelines for Multinational Enterprises 8 (2011), http://iso26000.info/wp-content/uploads/2017/02/ISO-26000_and_OECD_Guidelines_MNE_PPO_v1.pdf.
35. Practical Overview of the Linkages Between ISO 26000:2010, Guidance on Social Responsibility and OECD Guidelines for Multinational Enterprises 9 (2011), http://iso26000.info/wp-content/uploads/2017/02/ISO-26000_and_OECD_Guidelines_MNE_PPO_v1.pdf.
36. United Nations, Guiding Principles on Business and Human Rights (2011), www.ohchr.org/Documents/Publications/GuidingPrinciplesBusinessHR_EN.pdf.

23 countries had plans "in progress." The United States' NAP, released in 2016, includes (1) a peer review process to enhance access to remedy through the OECD complaint process; (2) stronger enforcement of existing laws related to forced labor and convict labor; (3) a best practices list related to sustainability that the government will use in the procurement process; (4) the designation of "labor compliance advisors" for federal contractors; and (5) more support for voluntary reporting on responsible business conduct by publicly recognizing the effort of compliant companies.[37] Apart from the NAPs, the GP's due diligence framework has had an impact on a number of regulations related to ESG, including US and EU conflict minerals legislation, discussed in more detail below.[38]

Sustainability Accounting Standards Board

The nonprofit Sustainability Accounting Standards Board (SASB) is the most recent entrant into the CSR arena. SASB aims to develop standards for publicly traded companies in the United States in 11 sectors from 79 industries so that they can disclose material sustainability information to investors and the public.[39] SASB expects companies to use its standards when filing Forms 8-K,10-K, 20-F, and 40-F with the Securities Exchange Commission.

SASB examines 30 topics on five broad subjects: (1) environment, including environmental impacts, that may affect a company's financial condition or operating performance; (2) social capital, related to the contribution to society and the social license to operate; (3) human capital, addressing labor relations, health, and safety; (4) business model and innovation, addressing the integration of ESG factors and product innovation; and (5) leadership and governance, related to regulatory compliance, risk management, conflicts of interest, anticompetitive behavior, bribery, and other aspects that could create liability or result in the removal of the social license to operate.[40] SASB, which focuses on publicly traded companies and materiality, and GRI, which has a broader scope, have different foci but complement each other rather than compete.[41] Many sophisticated firms have adopted both to deal with the large number of global disclosure regimes. We will address those in more detail below.

US Regulations on Corporate Social Responsibility Disclosures

The Dodd-Frank Conflict Minerals Act

In 2010, the US Congress passed a sweeping and controversial disclosure act. The Dodd-Frank Conflict Minerals Act[42] requires US issuers to disclose their use of "conflict minerals" if the minerals are necessary to the functionality or the production of a product. Section 1502 of Dodd-Frank specifically requires that affected companies using gold, tin, tungsten, and tantalum determine whether those materials came from the Democratic Republic of Congo or adjoining countries through a

37. US Dep't of State, Responsible Business Conduct: First National Action Plan for the United States of America (December 16, 2016), www.state.gov/documents/organization/265918.pdf.
38. The Center for Human Rights and Global Justice, Panel Discussion of John Ruggie's *Just Business: Multinational Corporations and Human Rights*, at New York University School of Law, YouTube (May 4, 2013), www.youtube.com/watch?v=_UjdBGg0Fd0
39. SASB, View the Standards, www.sasb.org; SASB, About the SASB, www.sasb.org/about-the-sasb/.
40. SASB, Sustainability Framework, www.sasb.org/approach/sustainability-framework/.
41. Tim Mohin and Jean Rogers, How to approach corporate sustainability reporting in 2017, *GreenBiz* (March 16, 2017), www.greenbiz.com/article/how-approach-corporate-sustainability-reporting-2017/?dm_i=4J5,4UZ3L,83POPQ,IDRI5,1.
42. Dodd-Frank Wall Street Reform and Consumer Protection Act of 2010, Pub. L. No. 111–203, 124 Stat. 1376 (H.R. 4173 § 1502(a)) [hereinafter "Dodd-Frank"]; 15 U.S.C. § 78m.

reasonable country of origin inquiry. The rule requires companies to report publicly through Form SD each year providing a description of the due diligence process, the products manufactured or contracted to be manufactured that are not "DRC conflict free," the name of the independent auditor, the country from where the minerals were sourced, and the efforts used to determine which mine produced the minerals.[43]

The conflict minerals rule has been the subject of a number of court challenges, and in 2015, a federal appellate court found that the disclosure requirements violated the First Amendment.[44] Members of the House of Representatives have sought to repeal the conflict minerals rule in the Financial Choice Act,[45] however, the Senate has not passed the bill as of the time of this writing. In April 2017, the SEC's division of corporate finance indicated that it would not recommend enforcement against companies that fail to comply with the requirement to file a conflict minerals report, although it still would expect companies to file their Form SD.[46] Even so, regardless of whether the conflict minerals rule survives legislative challenge, several large companies will likely continue to file the disclosures. In June 2018, the Investor Alliance for Human Rights, which consists of nearly 50 investor groups with $1.2 trillion in assets under management, issued a statement urging companies to continue to disclose.[47]

The California Transparency in Supply Chain Act

As of 2012, retailers or manufacturers that do business in California and have annual worldwide gross receipts exceeding $100 million must comply with the California Transparency in Supply Chain Act of 2010.[48] This act requires that certain companies disclose the extent of their efforts, if any, to ensure that the goods they sell are not produced by slaves, coerced labor, or those who been the victims of human trafficking. Companies must disclose at a minimum what actions they are taking in the following five areas: verification of their supply chains to evaluate and address risks on human trafficking and slavery; auditing of suppliers to evaluate their compliance with company standards; requiring certification from direct suppliers that they are complying with the laws regarding slavery and human trafficking in the countries in which they do business; maintaining internal accountability standards for employees and contractors who fail to meet company standards; and providing training to employees and management with direct responsibility for supply chain management risk mitigation regarding slavery.

As with the Dodd-Frank conflict minerals rule, there is no private right of action. The Attorney General instead has exclusive authority to enforce the rules and may file a civil action for injunctive relief. Companies that do not comply must disclose on their company's website. In addition, a number of watchdog groups such as Know the Chain[49] and others publish information on those companies that do not comply. California has the world's seventh largest economy and the country's

43. 15 U.S.C. § 78m(p)(1)(A)(i)–(ii).
44. *Nat'l Ass'n of Mfrs. v. SEC*, No. 13-5252 (D.C. Cir. August 8, 2015), www.cadc.uscourts.gov/internet/opinions.nsf/7677C9E435244EC985257EA50054F3D4/$file/13-5252-1568402.pdf.
45. H.R.10—Financial CHOICE Act of 2017 (amended June 8, 2017), www.congress.gov/bill/115th-congress/house-bill/10.
46. *Updated Statement on the Effect of the Court of Appeals Decision on the Conflict Minerals Rule*, US SEC,www.sec.gov/news/public-statement/corpfin-updated-statement-court-decision-conflict-minerals-rule.
47. Investor Alliance for Human Rights, Investor Expectations on Conflict Mineral Reporting, https://investorsforhumanrights.org/sites/default/files/attachments/2018-06/InvestorExpectationsConflictMineralReporting_5.31.18_FINAL.pdf.
48. Kamala D. Harris, Att'y Gen. Cal. Dep't of Justice, The California Transparency in Supply Chains Act (2015), https://oag.ca.gov/sites/all/files/agweb/pdfs/sb657/resource-guide.pdf.
49. KnowTheChain, https://knowthechain.org/.

largest consumer base, and thus provides a model for other states and/or countries wishing to enact similar disclosure laws.

Federal Acquisition Regulation

The US federal government is the largest procurer of goods and services in the world. In 2012, President Obama enacted Executive Order 13627 and supplemented it in 2015 with a new Order, "Ending Trafficking In Persons."[50] Those subject to the law must not destroy, conceal, confiscate, or deny an employee access to his or her identity or immigration documents; use misleading or fraudulent practices while recruiting or offering an employee a job; use recruiters who do not comply with local labor laws; charge employees recruitment fees; provide or arrange substandard or unsafe housing; or if required by law or contract, fail to provide an employment contract, recruitment agreement, or similar work paper in writing in the employee's native language prior to the employee departing from his or her country of origin.

The rule also institutes transportation requirements.

The rule also establishes additional requirements for contracts (other than commercially available contracts), including those in which any portion of a contract for which the estimated value of the supplies acquired, or the services required to be performed outside the United States, exceeds $500,000. For these contracts, contractors must develop a compliance plan applicable to the portions of a contract performed outside the United States. The final rule states that contractors should maintain the compliance plan during the performance of the contract and that the compliance plan include an employee awareness program, the process for employees to report trafficking violations, and recruitment housing plans. Contractors and subcontractors must also certify that they are not engaged in trafficking-related activities. Contractors that fail the requirements of the rule may be subject to penalties including but not limited to a requirement that the contractor remove employees from the performance of the contract, termination of subcontracts, suspension of contract payments until the contractor take appropriate remedial action, retraction of the award fee, declining to exercise available options of the contract, termination of the contract for default, and suspension or debarment from government contracting.[51]

As with most compliance regimes, the due diligence required for these contracts is a risk-based business decision requiring analysis of the risks inherent in each particular situation. Companies should not take a one-size-fits-all approach and instead should conduct due diligence based on the size and complexity of the particular contract. Government contractors and subcontractors must *proactively* assess the nature of their current activities to ensure their compliance programs meet the needs of their business to conform to these requirements.

International Regulations on Corporate Social Responsibility Disclosures

European Union Non-financial Disclosure Laws

In 2014, the European Union passed a non-financial disclosure law known as Directive 2014/95/EU.[52] Beginning in 2018, an estimated 6,000 companies must include nonfinancial statements with

50. Conny Rijken, Federal Acquisition Regulation; Ending Trafficking in Persons, Fed. Reg. (January 29, 2015) (effective March 2, 2015), www.federalregister.gov/documents/2015/01/29/2015-01524/federal-acquisition-regulation-ending-trafficking-in-persons.
51. *Ibid.*
52. European Commission, Non-financial reporting, https://ec.europa.eu/info/business-economy-euro/company-reporting-and-auditing/company-reporting/non-financial-reporting_en.

their annual reports. The Directive aims to assist consumers, investors, policy makers, and other stakeholders in evaluating large public-interest companies with more than 500 employees including listed companies, banks, and insurance companies on their non-financial performance. The Directive specifically requires large companies to report on the policies that they have implemented related to environmental protection, social responsibility and treatment of employees, human rights, bribery/anticorruption, and diversity on company boards. For each of the aforementioned subjects, companies must disclose a description of their business model, the policies pursued including their due diligence processes, the outcome of the due diligence, the risks related to the operations including business relationships products or services which may cause adverse impact, how the company will manage the risk, and the nonfinancial key performance indicators relevance the business. Companies that fail to provide a disclosure must explain why they have not done so.

The Directive applies to member states, however, each member state can define its own requirements, meaning that fines can range from the thousands to millions and may apply to individuals or companies.[53] Twenty-seven countries include some penalty for noncompliance, however, Estonia, the Netherlands, and Spain do not mention any specific financial penalties. The United Kingdom assesses penalties on a case-by-case basis, while Germany assesses fines up to the amount whichever is the highest of: €10 million, or 5% of the total annual turnover of the company, or twice the amount of the profits' gains or losses avoided due to the breach. Portugal, on the other hand, issues fines from €50 to €1,500 on responsible persons, while Latvia issues fines of up to $1 million. Ireland's law even imposes a prison sentence of up to six months. Accordingly, companies operating in more than one jurisdiction must keep abreast of the varying requirements.

Fortunately for transnational organizations, the EU allows flexibility in reporting, although most countries require an independent audit firm to verify the existence of a non-financial report. Companies may either issue a separate sustainability report or reference them in management reports or in annual reports and may produce statements based on the guidance from the UN Global Compact, the OECD Guidelines for Multinational Enterprises, or ISO 26000:2010.[54]

The UK Modern Slavery Act of 2015

The UK Modern Slavery Act of 2015[55] requires organizations to prepare and publish an annual slavery and human rights statement. Provision 54 applies to commercial organizations that supply goods or services in the UK with a global annual turnover of more than £36 million. These firms must disclose the steps they are taking to address modern slavery in their supply chains, and if they are not taking any action, they must disclose that fact. Firms may link to a public statement on the homepage of their website, and the statement must have sign-off by senior executives or the Board of Directors. Like the California Act discussed above, the UK Act does not require a firm to take any positive steps to eradicate slavery in the supply chain. Instead, the UK government relies on the "name and shame" principle, meaning that in theory, consumers or other businesses will pressure organizations that failed to take action to eradicate slavery in their supply chains. The guidance document from the UK government[56] suggests that policy statements must be written in plain English and provide

53. CSR Europe and GRI, Member State Implementation of Directive 2014/95/EU (2017), www.globalreporting.org/resourcelibrary/NFRpublication%20online_version.pdf.
54. European Commission, Non-financial reporting, https://ec.europa.eu/info/business-economy-euro/company-reporting-and-auditing/company-reporting/non-financial-reporting_en.
55. Legislation.gov.uk, Modern Slavery Act 2015, www.legislation.gov.uk/ukpga/2015/30/contents/enacted.
56. Rt Hon Amber Rudd MP, Transparency in Supply Chains etc. A practical guide. Guidance issued under section 54(9) of the Modern Slavery Act 2015, https://assets.publishing.service.gov.uk/government/uploads/system/uploads/attachment_data/file/649906/Transparency_in_Supply_Chains_A_Practical_Guide_2017.pdf.

links to the organizations' publications, documents, or policies, including the steps that the company is taking or plans to take to address modern slavery. The guidance also recommends reporting on operational governance, remediation, and training by country; however, the law only requires that the company publicly post what it is or is not doing.

Similar to many of the disclosure laws discussed in this chapter, there is no private right of action under the UK Act; however, the Secretary of State may apply to the UK's High Court for an injunction against an organization that failed to comply with the requirements, and failure to comply with the injunction may lead to an unlimited fine. Notably, the UK Act applies regardless of the company's geographic location; therefore, overseas businesses that provide goods or services within the UK must also comply.

France's Duty of Vigilance Law

In 2017, France enacted its own duty of care law,[57] which both resembles and differs from the UK Modern Slavery Act. Although both laws have at their core the principle of due diligence, France's law covers a much broader swath of issues than the UK law because it includes both human rights and environmental concerns. French lawmakers were inspired by two events: the promulgation of the UN Guiding Principles in 2011 and the 2013 Rana Plaza disaster. The law requires large French companies to establish and implement vigilance plans. These plans must explain the measures to both identify *and* prevent human rights and environmental risks resulting from their activities as well as the activities of the companies that they control and their subcontractors. Specifically, the plan must cover a mapping that identifies, analyzes, and ranks risks; an assessment of the company's subsidiaries, subcontractors, or suppliers; measures to mitigate risks or prevent serious violations; an alert mechanism that collects potential or actual risks, developed with the trade unions; and a monitoring scheme to follow up on the implemented measures and assess their efficiency. The French government expects companies to develop action plans and consultation with civil society organizations.

The French law only applies to French companies with over 5,000 employees in France or with 10,000 worldwide, including through subsidiaries. Accordingly, the French law covers far fewer companies than the UK Act. Unlike the UK Act, private citizens have standing to seek an injunction to compel the publication of a report. Noncompliant companies are also subject to *astreintes* or injunctive fines payable on a daily or per-event basis until the company complies. Companies also face civil liability to remedy the damage that "the execution of these obligations could have prevented."[58] As of the time of this writing, no penalties have been imposed. In contrast, the UK law does not specify a penalty amount and focuses on risk to reputation.

The Commonwealth Modern Slavery Act

In November 2018, the Australian government established a modern slavery act of its own.[59] The law requires Australia's largest businesses (and those that operate in Australia) with revenue of over

57. Pierre Lequiller, *Rapport dinformation déposé par la délégation de lAssemblée nationale pour l'Union européenne sur les comptes rendus des missions des missi dominici sur le suivi de la Conférence intergouvernementale* (2007). Available at www.assemblee-nationale.fr/14/pdf/ta/ta0924.pdf; Texte adopt n 924—Proposition de loi, adopte dfinitivement, par l'Assemble nationale, dans les conditions prevues l'article 45, alina 4, de la Constitution, relative au devoir de vigilance des socits mres et des entreprises donneuses d'ordre, Assemble nationale ~ Les deputs, le vote de la loi, le Parlement franais(2017), www.assemblee-nationale.fr/14/ta/ta0924.asp (August 10, 2018).
58. Stéphane Brabant and Elsa Savourey, France's corporate duty of vigilance law: A closer look at the penalties faced by companies, *Revue Internationale de la Compliance et de L'éthique des Affaires* (2017), www.business-humanrights.org/sites/default/files/documents/French%20Corporate%20Duty%20of%20Vigilance%20Law%20-%20Penalties%20-%20Int%25271%20Rev.Compl_.%20%26%20Bus.%20Ethics_.pdf.
59. Commonwealth of Australia, Fact Sheet: Modern Slavery Reporting Requirement (2017), www.homeaffairs.gov.au/consultations/Documents/modern-slavery/modern-slavery-reporting-requirement.pdf.

US$100 million to publish an annual statement of the steps they are taking to address modern slavery in their supply chains. Specifically, companies must disclose information about their structure, potential risks of modern slavery in their supply chains, the actions they have taken to assess and address these risks, and assessment mechanisms to measure effectiveness and remedial actions.[60] The government estimates that the law will impact 3,000 companies, and has announced that it will post reports in a central, publicly available repository and establish a business engagement unit to assist organizations with compliance. Like the UK Modern Slavery Act, the act has no listed financial penalties. However, the Australian government hopes to "foster a 'race to the top' culture that will ensure Australia is a regional and world leader in tackling modern slavery in supply chains."[61]

European Union Conflict Minerals Rule

Entered into force on January 1, 2021, the European Union Conflict Minerals Rule applies across the European Union regarding disclosure on conflict minerals.[62] This law will cover more than the analogous US Dodd-Frank rule discussed above and will require certifications for importers of tin, tungsten, tantalum, and gold; third-party audits for refiners and smelters; and information on due diligence measures by downstream companies. The law applies beyond the Democratic Republic of Congo and defines conflict areas as those in a state of armed conflict; fragile post-conflict areas; areas with weak or nonexistent governance and security, such as failed states; and any state with a widespread or systematic violation of international law including human rights abuses.[63] European Union importers will have to identify and address the actual potential risks linked to conflict-affected areas or high-risk areas during the due diligence of their supply chains. Metal importers, smelters, refineries, and manufacturers of consumer products must ensure that revenues for the minerals they use are not funding conflicts.

A Binding Treaty on Business and Human Rights?

In July 2018, the UN working group on business and human rights finally released a draft treaty on business and human rights.[64] The United States, the EU, and Russia, among others rejected the idea from its first proposal in 2014. Unlike other instruments, this treaty would bind businesses of a transnational character including any for-profit economic activity. Notably, the draft treaty does not apply to companies whose business sector activities occur exclusively within its own borders, and

60. Commonwealth of Australia, Modern Slavery in Supply Chains Reporting Requirement, *Public Consultation Paper and Regulation Impact Statement* (2017), www.homeaffairs.gov.au/consultations/Documents/modern-slavery/modern-slavery-supply-chains-reporting-requirement-public-consultation-paper.pdf.
61. Gareth Hutchens and Ben Doherty, Modern slavery bill welcomed, but no penalties for breaching act, *The Guardian* (2018), www.theguardian.com/australia-news/2018/jun/28/modern-slavery-bill-welcomed-but-no-penalties-for-breaching-act.
62. Regulation (EU) 2017/821 of the European Parliament and of the Council of May 17, 2017, laying down supply chain due diligence obligations for Union importers of tin, tantalum and tungsten, their ores, and gold originating from conflict-affected and high-risk areas, 130 OECD Due Diligence Guidance for Responsible Supply Chains of Minerals from Conflict-Affected and High-Risk Areas 31–60 (2011), https://eur-lex.europa.eu/legal-content/EN/TXT/HTML/?uri=OJ:L:2017:130:FULL&from=EN.
63. Conflict Minerals Regulation explained, Social protection statistics—unemployment benefits—Statistics Explained (2017), http://ec.europa.eu/trade/policy/in-focus/conflict-minerals-regulation/regulation-explained/.
64. Legally Binding Instrument to Regulate, in International Human Rights law, the Activities of Transnational Corporations and other Business Enterprises UNHCR (July 17, 2018), www.ohchr.org/Documents/HRBodies/HRCouncil/WGTransCorp/Session3/DraftLBI.pdf. Updated: https://www.ohchr.org/sites/default/files/LBI3rdDRAFT.pdf.

those companies of course can affect human rights. Among other things, the draft treaty requires specific mechanisms for due diligence including monitoring and preventing adverse human rights impacts and those of subsidiaries; identifying and assessing actual potential violations, including environmental and human rights policies, as well as their risk outcome indicators; conducting pre- and post-environmental human rights impact assessments; integrating the findings of those assessments into business operations; including specific requirements and contractual relationships which involve transnational business; holding meaningful consultations with potentially affected groups; and, when appropriate, providing financial guarantees such as insurance funds to cover potential costs of compensation.[65]

As with the nonbinding UN GPs, the draft treaty proposes that businesses must provide remedies and cooperate in enforcement. Failure to comply with the diligence duties will result in liability and compensation in accordance with the treaty. The treaty also contemplates that states will mandate human rights diligence by businesses and provide victims with access to judicial remedies. The draft also proposes international monitoring. Nonetheless, without the support of the United States and the EU, this treaty's adoption is unlikely.

What Happens When a Company Fails to Live Up to Its CSR Commitment?

Although organizations generally have no legal obligations to issue a CSR or sustainability report to the public other than the disclosures discussed above, many companies devote several pages of their websites to showcasing their commitments to the environment and human rights. The rise of these reports predated the disclosure regime we have discussed in this chapter, but the spate of new laws and voluntary initiatives accelerated the proliferation. CSR reports are not legally binding, but they can lead to legal trouble or ethical scandals. In this section, we will discuss some recent examples.

The Chocolate Cases

Chocolate companies have been the targets of NGOs for years because many of the world's favorite chocolatiers have been accused of using child labor in their supply chains. In 2001, eight large chocolate companies signed the Harkin-Engel Protocol, in which manufacturers developed a certification program using the International Cocoa Verification Board.[66] Notwithstanding the Harkin-Engel Protocol, the child slavery problem persists, particularly in states with extreme poverty that depend on the cocoa multinationals, such as Mars and Hershey's. This led to several lawsuits filed in 2015 and 2017 under state unfair competition, consumer protection, and false advertising laws in California and more recently, Massachusetts.

There is no private right of action under the California Transparency in Supply Chain Act; therefore, in 2015 plaintiffs used another route, filing suit in California under unfair competition and false advertising laws against the Hershey Company, Mars, and Nestlé. The suits alleged, among other things, that "in violation of California law, Hershey's, Mars and Nestle failed to disclose that their

65. Julianne Hughes Jennett, Peter Hood and Alison Berthet, UN treaty on business and human rights: Working Group publishes draft instrument: Focus on Regulation (2018), www.hlregulation.com/2018/07/26/un-treaty-on-business-and-human-rights-working-group-publishes-draft-instrument/.
66. See Chocolate Manufacturers Association, Protocol for the Growing and Processing of Cocoa Beans and Their Derivative Products in a Manner that Complies with ILO Convention 182 Concerning the Prohibition and Immediate Action for the Elimination of the Worst Forms of Child Labor (September 19, 2001), www.harkin.senate.gov/documents/pdf/HarkinEngelProtocol.pdf; International Cocoa Verification Board, Considerations in Setting Future Directions for Eliminating WFCL and FAL in the Cocoa Sector, www.verite.org/sites/default/files/images/Considerations_in_Setting_Future_Directions_for_Eliminating_WFCL_and_FAL_in_the_Cocoa_Sector.pdf.

suppliers in the Ivory Coast relied on child laborers and profited from the child labor that supplies the chocolate sold to American consumers."[67] Although Hershey's 2016 CSR report claimed that it was the country's most trusted chocolate maker, it had already acknowledged that it had not yet met its "voluntary commitment" to reach 100% certified/sustainable cocoa and sugar by 2020, falling short by 40%.[68] In the litigation, plaintiffs pointed out that only 36% of Mars' cocoa was certified in accordance with the protocol.

In litigation, the chocolate companies argued, among other things, that California law does not mandate disclosures at the point of sale, and if it did require disclosure of labor practices, that disclosure would violate the First Amendment of the US Constitution. Defendants also contended that plaintiffs did not claim that they purchased chocolate containing cocoa harvested by slaves, nor could they because consumers cannot trace the chocolate to particular farms that used child labor.[69] Although the courts in the separate chocolate cases stated that the labor practices were unacceptable, plaintiffs lost those cases because the courts found that these companies had no legal duty to disclose on their labels that African child slaves might have been involved in manufacturing their cocoa. In the Mars case, the court noted that in compliance with the California Transparency in Supply Chain Act, information about the company's efforts to combat slavery and child labor practices was on the company website, and that plaintiff had access to that disclosure. The court concluded that the company had no legal obligation to add that information to its packaging. In June 2018, the Ninth Circuit Court of Appeals upheld the dismissal of the claims in the Mars cases.[70]

In 2018, the same law firm filed a similar class action lawsuit[71] against Hershey in Massachusetts. This claim alleged unjust enrichment in violation of that state's consumer protection law. According to plaintiffs, "much of the world's chocolate is quite literally brought to us by the back-breaking labor of children, in many cases under conditions of slavery." Moreover, they claimed,

> Hershey's material omissions and failure to disclose at the point of sale [are] all the more appalling considering that Hershey's Corporate Social Responsibility Report state[s] that "Hershey has zero tolerance for the worst forms of child labor in its supply chain." But Hershey does not live up to its own ideals.[72]

The plaintiffs aim to use Hershey's zero-tolerance statements against it.

In 2019, a Massachusetts federal judge ruled on the class action suits against Nestlé, Hershey, and Mars.[73] These proposed class actions claimed that the three companies deceived customers by not disclosing on their labels that their chocolate may have been made using slave and child labor.[74] Although the judge recognized that the use of slave and child labor in cocoa production is reprehensible and tragic, she ultimately dismissed the lawsuits.[75] The court ruled that the lack of disclosure by these companies was not an omission likely to deceive or influence customers because it would not be reasonable

67. *Hodsdon v. Mars, Inc.*, 891 F.3d 857 (9th Cir. 2018); *Dana v. Hershey Co*, 180 F. Supp. 3d 652 (N.D. Cal. 2016).
68. The Hershey Company, Shared Goodness: 2016 Corporate Social Responsibility Report 39–41 (2016), www.thehersheycompany.com/content/dam/corporate-us/documents/csr-reports/2016-hershey-csr-report-detail.pdf.
69. *Ibid.*
70. *Hodsdon v. Mars, Inc.*, 891 F.3d 857 (9th Cir. 2018).
71. *Tomasella v. Hershey Co.*, 2018 WL 1051865 (D. Mass.).
72. *Ibid.*
73. Mike Curley, Nestle, Hershey, Mars get child labor labeling suit tossed, *Law360* (January 30, 2019), www.law360.com/articles/1123699/nestle-hershey-mars-get-child-labor-labeling-suit-tossed.
74. *Ibid.*
75. *Ibid.*

for a consumer to affirmatively form a preconception about the use of slave or child labor based on a company's silence regarding its labor practices.[76] Additionally, as opposed to alleging that Nestlé, Hershey, or Mars violated state law by using slave or child labor, plaintiffs only alleged that these companies violated the Massachusetts Consumer Protection Act by failing to disclose their use of slave or child labor; however, plaintiffs did not identify any common law or statutory authority requiring such a disclosure.[77] Further, these companies have indicated that slave and child labor is likely occurring in their supply chain by providing information on their websites.[78] Because Nestlé, Hershey, and Mars have made this information available, the court found that the absence of this information on the packaging itself was not a cause of injury to the customers.[79] Nonetheless, these companies publicly remain committed to eradicating the use of forced labor from their supply chain.[80]

Ethics and Compliance Scandals

Companies with strong CSR policies are understandable targets for litigants when the firms do not live up to their promises. Similarly, when a company that prides itself on its ethical culture becomes embroiled in a scandal, regulators and the general public subject it to heightened scrutiny. From sales misconduct and wrongful termination to data breaches and insider trading, no two corporate scandals are alike. The resulting effects on each company have been significant, whether it be resignation of top executives, decrease in share value, or financial penalties. One commonality among each corporate scandal is the wide-reaching influence on the local and global population. Notably, the scandals that occurred in recent years are at odds with almost every company's respective Code of Ethics or Corporate Social Responsibility Report. As these companies seek to overcome challenges that the scandals have caused and rebuild their brands, firms have created rebranding initiatives in furtherance of this goal. Some examples of the biggest corporate scandals follow.

Wells Fargo

Prosecutors and regulators allege that, among other things, from 2011 to mid-2016, Wells Fargo employees created more than 1.5 million fake bank accounts and produced half a million unauthorized credit card applications in response to unrealistic sales goals.[81] The company was thereafter ordered to pay $185 million in fines to both the city and federal regulators, which represents the largest penalty ever levied by the Consumer Financial Protection Bureau.[82] In 2017, Wells Fargo admitted that it charged up to 570,000 auto loan customers for unnecessary car insurance, and 20,000 of those consumers had their cars wrongfully repossessed resulting in part from these unwanted insurance charges; the bank said that it would pay $80 million in remediation.[83] The

76. *Ibid.*
77. *Ibid.*
78. *Ibid.*
79. *Ibid.*
80. *Ibid.*
81. Casey Wilson, 5 shameful corporate scandals that won't go away in 2018, *Wall Street Examiner* (October 19, 2017), http://wallstreetexaminer.com/2017/10/5-shameful-corporate-scandals-wont-go-away-2018/; Donna Borak, Danielle Wiener-Bronner, and Jackie Wattles, The Fed drops the hammer on Wells Fargo, *CNN Money* (February 3, 2018), https://money.cnn.com/2018/02/02/news/companies/wells-fargo-federal-reserve/index.html?iid=EL.
82. Casey Wilson, 5 shameful corporate scandals that won't go away in 2018, *Wall Street Examiner* (October 19, 2017), http://wallstreetexaminer.com/2017/10/5-shameful-corporate-scandals-wont-go-away-2018/.
83. Donna Borak, Danielle Wiener-Bronner, and Jackie Wattles, The Fed drops the hammer on Wells Fargo, *CNN Money* (February 3, 2018), https://money.cnn.com/2018/02/02/news/companies/wells-fargo-

company's problems only deepened that same year when an outside review discovered an additional 1.4 million fraudulent accounts, thus totaling as many as 3.5 million accounts created without customers' knowledge.[84] Wells Fargo announced that it has paid or identified $10.7 million in customer compensation linked with this investigation, which includes $7 million in refunds as well as $3.7 million in the complaints process and mediation.[85] A class-action lawsuit also resulted in another $142 million in compensation for customers.[86] As part of the settlement, the bank will implement changes to its sales practices and internal oversight; however, as of the time of this writing, Wells Fargo continues to face federal and state investigations, lawsuits, and congressional inquiries as a consequence of this scandal.[87]

Further, regaining the trust of Wells Fargo employees has proved to be a challenge.[88] In 2016, nearly half a dozen workers told CNNMoney that they were fired as a result of using the company's ethics hotline in an attempt to stop the fake account problem.[89] In 2017, Wells Fargo was forced to rehire and pay $5.4 million to a whistleblower who was terminated after calling the bank's hotline to report suspected fraud.[90] The company currently faces numerous lawsuits from workers who claim that they protested sales misbehavior.[91] In addition, Wells Fargo is facing state law whistleblower actions filed with the Labor Department that allege retaliation.[92] To restore trust with customers, the company launched a multimillion-dollar television, radio, and print advertising campaign.[93] Moreover, Wells Fargo has also released a rebranding initiative that focuses on the company's commitment to its vision and values, as well as the bank's emphasis on its goals.[94]

In 2018, the Federal Reserve penalized Wells Fargo with unprecedented sanctions because of the company's widespread consumer abuses.[95] These sanctions are intended to prevent the bank from growing larger than it was at the end of 2017, until regulators are satisfied that the company has

federal-reserve/index.html?iid=EL; Lucinda Shen, The 10 biggest business scandals of 2017, *Fortune* (December 31, 2017), http://fortune.com/2017/12/31/biggest-corporate-scandals-misconduct-2017-pr/.

84. Bloomberg, The Wells Fargo fake accounts scandal just got a lot worse, *Fortune* (August 31, 2017), http://fortune.com/2017/08/31/wells-fargo-increases-fake-account-estimate/; Donna Borak, Danielle Wiener-Bronner, and Jackie Wattles, The Fed drops the hammer on Wells Fargo, *CNN Money* (February 3, 2018), https://money.cnn.com/2018/02/02/news/companies/wells-fargo-federal-reserve/index.html?iid=EL.
85. Bloomberg, The Wells Fargo fake accounts scandal just got a lot worse, *Fortune* (August 31, 2017), http://fortune.com/2017/08/31/wells-fargo-increases-fake-account-estimate/.
86. Nerd Wallet, How to check if Wells Fargo owes you money, ABC 15 (September 5, 2017), www.abc15.com/money/consumer/dont-waste-your-money/wells-fargo-refunded-3-7-million-owed-money.
87. Casey Wilson, 5 shameful corporate scandals that won't go away in 2018, *Wall Street Examiner* (October 19, 2017), http://wallstreetexaminer.com/2017/10/5-shameful-corporate-scandals-wont-go-away-2018/; Donna Borak, Danielle Wiener-Bronner, and Jackie Wattles, The Fed drops the hammer on Wells Fargo, *CNN Money* (February 3, 2018), https://money.cnn.com/2018/02/02/news/companies/wells-fargo-federal-reserve/index.html?iid=EL.
88. Matt Egan, Wells Fargo's ethics hotline calls are on the rise, *CNN Money* (June 19, 2018), http://money.cnn.com/2018/06/19/news/companies/wells-fargo-ethics-hotline/index.html.
89. *Ibid.*
90. *Ibid.*
91. *Ibid.*
92. *Ibid.*
93. *Ibid.*
94. Wells Fargo, Committed to our Vision and Values and Focused on our Goals (March 2018), www08.wellsfargomedia.com/assets/pdf/about/investor-relations/presentations/2018/committed-and-focused.pdf.
95. Donna Borak, Danielle Wiener-Bronner, and Jackie Wattles, The Fed drops the hammer on Wells Fargo, *CNN Money* (February 3, 2018), https://money.cnn.com/2018/02/02/news/companies/wells-fargo-federal-reserve/index.html?iid=EL; Matt Egan, Wells Fargo's ethics hotline calls are on the rise, *CNN Money* (June 19, 2018), http://money.cnn.com/2018/06/19/news/companies/wells-fargo-ethics-hotline/index.html.

cleaned up its act.[96] According to a Federal Reserve official, this is the first instance in which the institution has imposed a cap on the entire assets of a financial institution.[97] Wells Fargo has agreed to the conditions represented in a consent decree, which requires the company to submit detailed plans of what it has done and what it intends to do to fix the board of directors; additionally, the company must turn in a broader explanation of how it will improve internal controls and its risk management.[98] By September 30, 2018, Wells Fargo had to retain a third party to assess how the bank is implementing these plans, however, concerns remain for its slow remedial process.[99]

Even today, Wells Fargo still struggles to put its scandals in the past. In August 2018, the company announced that it had erroneously foreclosed on hundreds of homes over a five-year period.[100] Despite the criticism directed at Wells Fargo for its past scandals, which resulted in a change of CEOs and a drop in stock price, the media have barely reacted to this announcement and the company's stock price has been unaffected for the most part.[101] Although this scandal had a tangible impact on the hundreds who lost their homes, it was far less widespread than the fake accounts problem that had an effect on millions of customers.[102] As a result of this scandal, the bank has set aside $8 million to compensate the homeowners who were harmed, which is relatively low in comparison to the high regulatory costs of prior scandals.[103] Further, Wells Fargo has apologized to affected customers for the mistaken foreclosures.[104] Overall, Wells Fargo's myriad of scandals has negatively affected its reputation, placed it under heightened scrutiny from regulators, and impacted its bottom line as the company has struggled to win back its customer base with promises of transparency and reform; despite this, the bank admits it will take time to repair the company and remains optimistic at the prospect of ultimately building a better Wells Fargo.[105]

96. Matt Egan, Wells Fargo's ethics hotline calls are on the rise, *CNN Money* (June 19, 2018), http://money.cnn.com/2018/06/19/news/companies/wells-fargo-ethics-hotline/index.html; Donna Borak, Danielle Wiener-Bronner, and Jackie Wattles, The Fed drops the hammer on Wells Fargo, CNN *Money* (February 3, 2018), https://money.cnn.com/2018/02/02/news/companies/wells-fargo-federal-reserve/index.html?iid=EL.
97. Donna Borak, Danielle Wiener-Bronner, and Jackie Wattles, The Fed drops the hammer on Wells Fargo, *CNN Money* (February 3, 2018), https://money.cnn.com/2018/02/02/news/companies/wells-fargo-federal-reserve/index.html?iid=EL.
98. Donna Borak, Danielle Wiener-Bronner, and Jackie Wattles, The Fed drops the hammer on Wells Fargo, *CNN Money* (February 3, 2018), https://money.cnn.com/2018/02/02/news/companies/wells-fargo-federal-reserve/index.html?iid=EL.
99. *Ibid.*, See also, Zacks Equity Research, *Wells Fargo's (WFC) Slow Remedial Moves Might Prompt Sanctions* (September 1, 2021), https://www.nasdaq.com/articles/wells-fargos-wfc-slow-remedial-moves-might-prompt-sanctions-2021-09-01.
100. Victoria Finkle, Bankshot Wells Fargo was hit with more scandal. But does anyone care?, *American Banker* (August 13, 2018), www.americanbanker.com/opinion/wells-fargo-was-hit-with-more-scandal-but-does-anyone-care.
101. Victoria Finkle, Bankshot Wells Fargo was hit with more scandal. But does anyone care?, *American Banker* (August 13, 2018), www.americanbanker.com/opinion/wells-fargo-was-hit-with-more-scandal-but-does-anyone-care; Donna Borak, Danielle Wiener-Bronner, and Jackie Wattles, The Fed drops the hammer on Wells Fargo, *CNN Money* (February 3, 2018), https://money.cnn.com/2018/02/02/news/companies/wells-fargo-federal-reserve/index.html?iid=EL.
102. Victoria Finkle, Bankshot Wells Fargo was hit with more scandal. But does anyone care?, *American Banker* (August 13, 2018), www.americanbanker.com/opinion/wells-fargo-was-hit-with-more-scandal-but-does-anyone-care.
103. *Ibid.*
104. *Ibid.*
105. Matt Egan, Wells Fargo's ethics hotline calls are on the rise, *CNN Money* (June 19, 2018), http://money.cnn.com/2018/06/19/news/companies/wells-fargo-ethics-hotline/index.html; Lucinda Shen, The 10 biggest business scandals of 2017, *Fortune* (December 31, 2017), http://fortune.com/2017/12/31/biggest-corporate-scandals-misconduct-2017-pr/; Donna Borak, Danielle Wiener-Bronner, and Jackie Wattles, The Fed drops the hammer on Wells Fargo, *CNN Money* (February 3, 2018), https://money.cnn.com/2018/02/02/news/companies/wells-fargo-federal-reserve/index.html?iid=EL.

Uber

In 2017, ride-hailing company Uber suffered from a series of public relations nightmares.[106] Uber does not have a Code of Conduct, but its 2017 Community Guidelines indicate that drivers may lose their access to customers for failing to comply with the law, including laws against harassment, discrimination, sexual misconduct, and fraud; even so, Uber may have failed to heed its own standards in 2017.[107] In January, thousands of protests broke out at airports across the United States after President Donald Trump signed a travel ban related to certain Muslim-majority countries.[108] To the disappointment of protestors, former Uber CEO and former member of Trump's Economic Advisory Council Travis Kalanick ordered his staff to continue driving during a taxi driver protest.[109] As a result, customers were upset about the company's ties to President Trump and accused Uber of attempting to profit off of the taxi protest.[110] Customers took to Twitter to express their dismay with the company, and the #DeleteUber movement was born.[111] The #DeleteUber hashtag led to the loss of 200,000 customers in one weekend and ultimately to Kalanick's resignation from the council.[112]

In February, former Uber employee Susan Fowler alleged a culture of sexual harassment and gender discrimination, and the hashtag #DeleteUber started trending again on Twitter.[113] Later that month, the self-driving car company Waymo sued Uber and alleged that Uber used stolen technology to further its own autonomous-car development; however, Uber denied the claims.[114] In May, the Justice Department exposed a criminal investigation into Uber's alleged use of software known as "Greyball," which is used to avoid regulators in geographic areas where it has illegal operations.[115] In November, it was revealed that Uber was hacked and the personal data of 57 million users was put at risk; the stolen data included the names, emails, and phone numbers of 50 million riders globally in addition to the US drivers' license numbers of 7 million people.[116] Although this data breach

106. Casey Wilson, 5 shameful corporate scandals that won't go away in 2018, *Wall Street Examiner* (October 19, 2017), http://wallstreetexaminer.com/2017/10/5-shameful-corporate-scandals-wont-go-away-2018/.
107. Uber, Uber Community Guidelines, www.uber.com/legal/community-guidelines/us-en/.
108. Casey Wilson, 5 shameful corporate scandals that won't go away in 2018, *Wall Street Examiner* (October 19, 2017), http://wallstreetexaminer.com/2017/10/5-shameful-corporate-scandals-wont-go-away-2018/.
109. *Ibid.*
110. Avery Hartmans, The 17 biggest tech scandals of 2017, *Business Insider* (December 30, 2018), www.businessinsider.com/biggest-tech-scandals-2017-12; Casey Wilson, 5 shameful corporate scandals that won't go away in 2018, *Wall Street Examiner* (October 19, 2017), http://wallstreetexaminer.com/2017/10/5-shameful-corporate-scandals-wont-go-away-2018/.
111. Casey Wilson, 5 shameful corporate scandals that won't go away in 2018 *Wall Street Examiner* (October 19, 2017), http://wallstreetexaminer.com/2017/10/5-shameful-corporate-scandals-wont-go-away-2018/.
112. Avery Hartmans, The 17 biggest tech scandals of 2017, *Business Insider* (December 30, 2018), www.businessinsider.com/biggest-tech-scandals-2017-12; Casey Wilson, 5 shameful corporate scandals that won't go away in 2018, *Wall Street Examiner* (October 19, 2017), http://wallstreetexaminer.com/2017/10/5-shameful-corporate-scandals-wont-go-away-2018/.
113. Avery Hartmans, The 17 biggest tech scandals of 2017, Business Insider (December 30, 2018), www.businessinsider.com/biggest-tech-scandals-2017-12; Casey Wilson, 5 shameful corporate scandals that won't go away in 2018, *Wall Street Examiner* (October 19, 2017), http://wallstreetexaminer.com/2017/10/5-shameful-corporate-scandals-wont-go-away-2018/; Lucinda Shen, The 10 biggest business scandals of 2017, *Fortune* (December 31, 2017), http://fortune.com/2017/12/31/biggest-corporate-scandals-misconduct-2017-pr/.
114. Avery Hartmans, The 17 biggest tech scandals of 2017, *Business Insider* (December 30, 2018), www.businessinsider.com/biggest-tech-scandals-2017-12.
115. Lucinda Shen, The 10 biggest business scandals of 2017, *Fortune* (December 31, 2017), http://fortune.com/2017/12/31/biggest-corporate-scandals-misconduct-2017-pr/.
116. Lucinda Shen, The 10 biggest business scandals of 2017, *Fortune* (December 31, 2017), http://fortune.com/2017/12/31/biggest-corporate-scandals-misconduct-2017-pr/; Avery Hartmans, The 17 biggest tech scandals of 2017, *Business Insider* (December 30, 2018), www.businessinsider.com/biggest-tech-scandals-2017-12.

occurred in 2016, it was not made public until almost a year later when the company published a blog post about the incident.[117] Further, Uber paid hackers $100,000 to conceal this cyberattack.[118] In December, additional questionable business practices were revealed when a letter was unsealed that contained allegations that the company had internal teams that bugged hotels, infiltrated sensitive WhatsApp groups, and obtained trade secrets from the company's competitors.[119]

Overall, Uber's challenging year had numerous impacts on the company. By May, at least half a million users deleted their existing Uber accounts, which caused a loss in market share and a significant decrease in company value.[120] Additionally, the company suffered from a series of high-profile resignations including its Vice President for Product and Growth Ed Baker, company President Jeff Jones, and Head of Communications Policy Rachel Whetstone.[121] These events led to the ouster of Uber founder and former CEO Travis Kalanick; other top executives also resigned or were forced out due to an investor revolt.[122] Further, over 20 employees were fired following an internal investigation into misconduct in the workplace, which included sexual harassment.[123] As of the time of this writing, Uber announced plans to go public.[124] If it does so, it will be required to have a code of ethics for the senior executive and senior financial officers under Sarbanes-Oxley Rule 406.[125]

Google

Employees also hold companies responsible for failing to live up to the ideals expressed in a code of ethics. In August 2018, over 1,000 Google employees signed a letter protesting the company's secret work on a censored version of its search engine for China.[126] Employees indicated that the company's apparent willingness to act in accordance with China's censorship requirements raises moral and ethical issues.[127] In this letter, employees address their concern that they do not have the information required to make ethically informed decisions about their work, projects, and employment.[128] They demand more transparency in order to understand the ethical consequences of their work. They

117. *Ibid.*
118. Avery Hartmans, The 17 biggest tech scandals of 2017, *Business Insider* (December 30, 2018), www.businessinsider.com/biggest-tech-scandals-2017-12.
119. *Ibid.*
120. Casey Wilson, 5 shameful corporate scandals that won't go away in 2018, *Wall Street Examiner* (October 19, 2017), http://wallstreetexaminer.com/2017/10/5-shameful-corporate-scandals-wont-go-away-2018/; Lucinda Shen, The 10 biggest business scandals of 2017, *Fortune* (December 31, 2017), http://fortune.com/2017/12/31/biggest-corporate-scandals-misconduct-2017-pr/; Avery Hartmans, The 17 biggest tech scandals of 2017, *Business Insider* (December 30, 2018), www.businessinsider.com/biggest-tech-scandals-2017-12.
121. Casey Wilson, 5 shameful corporate scandals that won't go away in 2018, *Wall Street Examiner* (October 19, 2017), http://wallstreetexaminer.com/2017/10/5-shameful-corporate-scandals-wont-go-away-2018/.
122. Lucinda Shen, The 10 biggest business scandals of 2017, *Fortune* (December 31, 2017), http://fortune.com/2017/12/31/biggest-corporate-scandals-misconduct-2017-pr/; Avery Hartmans, The 17 biggest tech scandals of 2017, *Business Insider* (December 30, 2018), www.businessinsider.com/biggest-tech-scandals-2017-12.
123. Avery Hartmans, The 17 biggest tech scandals of 2017, *Business Insider* (December 30, 2018), www.businessinsider.com/biggest-tech-scandals-2017-12.
124. Casey Wilson, 5 shameful corporate scandals that won't go away in 2018, *Wall Street Examiner* (October 19, 2017), http://wallstreetexaminer.com/2017/10/5-shameful-corporate-scandals-wont-go-away-2018/.
125. 17 C.F.R. § 229.406 (Item 406) Code of ethics, www.law.cornell.edu/cfr/text/17/229.406.
126. Kate Conger and Daisuke Wakabayashi, Google employees protest secret work on censored search engine for China, *New York Times* (August 16, 2018), www.nytimes.com/2018/08/16/technology/google-employees-protest-search-censored-china.html.
127. *Ibid.*
128. *Ibid.*

also request implementation of an ethics review structure, appointment of external representatives, proposition of a clear plan for transparency, and publication of an ethical evaluation of controversial projects.[129]

The company's participation in this project surfaced eight years after Google publicly withdrew from China in protest of both censorship and government hijacking.[130] In 2010, Google discovered that Chinese hackers attacked the company's corporate infrastructure as a means of gaining access to the Gmail accounts of human rights activists, which prompted the company to remove its search engine from the country.[131] Further, Google objected to China's censorship, political speech, and internet communications.[132] Although Google's flagship services are not available in China, the company has maintained a prominent presence in the country.[133] Charles Mok, who is a member of the Hong Kong Legislative Council, acknowledged the possibility that the company is facing intense pressure to introduce more of its products in China.[134] He also recognized that Google would lend legitimacy to government censorship as a result of introducing a censored search product in China, which is precisely what employees fear today.[135]

Yet, Google's current controversial project is not the only project that has been developed largely in secret.[136] The company's desire to bring search back to China came about amid reports that Google was working on a search application that restricts content that is banned by Beijing, China, known internally as Dragonfly.[137] Dragonfly sparked outrage between employees due to their concern that they had been contributing to a project that would assist China in withholding information from its citizens.[138] As a result of these secret projects, employees demand more transparency as well as commitment to clear and open processes so that they are aware of what they are building.[139]

Further, this is not the first instance that Google's employees have voiced their desire for changes to strategy.[140] In April 2018, employees spoke out against the company's participation in a Pentagon program that uses artificial intelligence to improve weaponry.[141] Hundreds of employees at the company have advocated for their leadership to be more transparent about its ethics and its use of artificial intelligence.[142] In June 2018, Google said it would not renew its contract with the Pentagon for the artificial intelligence work.[143] The company thereafter revealed a series of ethical principles concerning its use of artificial intelligence.[144] In those principles, Google made a public commitment to only use artificial intelligence in socially beneficial ways that would not cause harm.[145] Moreover, the company promised to advance its capabilities in accord with human rights law.[146] Some Google

129. *Ibid.*
130. *Ibid.*
131. *Ibid.*
132. *Ibid.*
133. *Ibid.*
134. *Ibid.*
135. *Ibid.*
136. *Ibid.*
137. *Ibid.*
138. *Ibid.*
139. *Ibid.*
140. *Ibid.*
141. *Ibid.*
142. *Ibid.*
143. *Ibid.*
144. *Ibid.*
145. *Ibid.*
146. *Ibid.*

employees have acknowledged their concern that the company's involvement in helping China censor the free flow of information will contradict the company's new principles.[147]

In comparison to other major technology companies, Google has historically been more receptive to concerns of its employees and more transparent about its future projects as well as its inner workings by inviting questions from its workers and encouraging internal debate.[148] Google's Code of Ethics states that the company values freedom of expression:

> Google is committed to advancing privacy and freedom of expression for our users around the world. Where user privacy and freedom of expression face government challenges, we seek to implement internationally recognized standards that respect those rights as we develop products, do business in diverse markets, and respond to government requests to access user information or remove user content.[149]

Employees will no doubt hold the company accountable to its Code.

Conclusion

Companies face scrutiny from regulators monitoring their compliance with law and from members of internal and external communities monitoring compliance with the social license. Responsible business conduct now means more than earning money for shareholders—it also means keeping commitments to stakeholders.

147. *Ibid.*
148. *Ibid.*
149. Alphabet, Google Code of Conduct, https://abc.xyz/investor/other/google-code-of-conduct.html.

3

COMPLIANCE, CORPORATE GOVERNANCE, AND CORPORATE SOCIAL RESPONSIBILITY

Part II—The Interplay Between the Company, the Stakeholder, and Shareholders

Marcia Weldon and Christyne Vachon

Introducing the Role of the Board of Directors

Whether a corporation or a limited liability company (LLC), a for-profit business evaluates compliance decisions at the board and executive suite level balancing many competing concepts. Depending on the industry, as mentioned in Chapter 2, a company may face many regulations and rules that require a greater or lesser degree of oversight. In addition, the company many have an industry or a history that makes fulfilling the obligations of the social license more or less organic to the organization. Of course, the degree to which that line or aspect of the business financially supports the company will dictate the level of attention the company allocates to compliance. However, it holds true, as well, that a company may allocate great resources to oversight of one aspect of its business that props up a small portion of the bottom line, yet, if upon compliance failure, may cause resounding negative impacts across the whole company, affecting the other business lines and the company's social license. This is when the company may want to reevaluate whether that business line is worth the resources for compliance versus what it brings to the company's bottom line.

In addition, the size of a company greatly effects whether management opts for a formal, informal, or any CSR policy. To some, corporate social responsibility and the social licensure distills down into what role the business plays in society.[1] Alone, this may not be at the top of a Board's agenda.[2] Yet, there are powerful financial and reputational reasons. Ultimately, the Board is responsible for managing the company's operations to increase profits and decrease risk.

As mentioned in Chapter 2, parties that have an interest in the company and its business actions are referred to as "stakeholders." Stakeholders have a large or small, direct or indirect stake in the

1. Dennis T. Whalen, Stephen L. Brown, Claudia H. Allen, Susan M. Angele, and David A. Brown, *ESG, Strategy, and the Long View* (KPMG) (2017), https://boardleadership.kpmg.us/relevant-topics/articles/2017/09/esg-strategy-and-the-long-view.html?utm_source=google&utm_medium=cpc&mid=m-00002771&utm_campaign=c-00054825&cid=c-00054825&gclid=EAIaIQobChMIuvzGqdqI3AIVh4izCh0EXgVGEAAYASAAEgLlufD_BwE.
2. Paul Hohnen, *Corporate Social Responsibility: An Implementation Guide for Business* (IISD) (2007), www.iisd.org/pdf/2007/csr_guide.pdf.

DOI: 10.4324/9781351107242-5

business. The most commonly recognized stakeholders are the various classes of shareholders. Others include employees; the communities in which the company does business; local, state and federal governments; the environment, international organizations; regulators; vendors; consumers; and suppliers. Based upon the concept of the social license, non–shareholder stakeholders gamble that companies work to lessen or prevent adverse environmental and social impacts related to the business operations to fulfill the social license.[3]

Many have attributed short-term thinking by Boards and management to the profit maximization directive. Short-term thinking has led to increased exploitation by business and approaches described as unsustainable. Yet, Larry Fink, CEO of Blackrock, encourages companies to pursue long-term thinking, instead. In his 2018 annual letter, Fink stated,

> To prosper over time, every company must not only deliver financial performance, but also show how it makes a positive contribution to society. . . . Companies must benefit all of their stakeholders, including shareholders, employees, customers, and the communities in which they operate.[4]

Sustainability concerns are now a going concern and, consequently, a regular business governance and compliance topic as companies consider the impact on the bottom line and their social license.[5] Sustainability relates to a business' own successful sustainability and other stakeholder issues such as human rights, labor management, environmental damage and risk, consumer safety, and product testing.[6] A company's sustainability policy will help it develop a response to the stakeholder concerns and proactive risk management.[7]

> Properly understood, CSR should be seen as the way that firms—working with those most affected by their decisions (often called "stakeholders")—can develop innovative and economically viable products, processes and services within core business processes, resulting in improved environmental protection and social conditions.[8]

Should It Be the Board?

While the Board of Directors (or, for instance, a Board of Managers in an LLC) is ultimately responsible for the company's success or failure, management oversees the day-to-day operations. Both owe fiduciary duties to the company and shareholders. How companies manage sustainability concerns varies based on a variety of factors. However, one overarching issue is whether responsibility for the sustainability should be with the Board—to decide how to comply with legal sustainability requirements, which sustainability measures not legally required should be implemented, to what degree, and whether and how to publicly report, among other things. Traditionally, responsibility for social and environmental concerns falls within the managerial and operational functions of a company.

3. Sarah Altschuller, *Corporate Social Responsibility and the Role of the Board of Directors* (June 21, 2011), www.businessinsider.com/corporate-social-responsibility-and-the-role-of-the-board-of-directors-2011-6.
4. Larry Fink, *Larry Fink's Annual Letter to CEOs: A Sense of Purpose* (2017), www.wlrk.com/docs/BlackRocks LarryFinkTheNewConscienceofWallStreetBarrons.pdf.
5. David M. Silk, David A. Katz, Sabastian V. Niles and Carmen X.W. Lu, *Wachtell Lipton Discusses Boards' Role in Sustainability and Corporate Social Responsibility* (July 3, 2018).
6. *Ibid.*
7. Sarah Altschuller, *Corporate Social Responsibility and the Role of the Board of Directors* (June 21, 2011), www.businessinsider.com/corporate-social-responsibility-and-the-role-of-the-board-of-directors-2011-6.
8. Paul Hohnen, *Corporate Social Responsibility: An Implementation Guide for Business* (IISD) (2007), www.iisd.org/pdf/2007/csr_guide.pdf.

Consequently, the argument is that it is inefficient for the Board to supervise.[9] Further, another argument against the Board's responsibility for sustainability proposes that it detracts from the primary focus of the Board, profit maximization, by prioritizing the concerns of other stakeholders over those of shareholders.[10] On the other hand, as shareholders have argued, sustainability issues have impacts on the company's strategy, reputation, investment strategy, and brand name.[11] With this broad impact, sustainability management should fall under the responsibility of the Board. A Board can provide the necessary "tone at the top" to fulfill the social license. Investors and other stakeholders gather information from the Board about how the company identifies sustainability issues, priorities, and approaches. In fact, given the mainstream concerns of sustainability issues, absence of Board responsibility may raise a red flag for shareholders and regulators.[12]

Instead, a constructive and necessary approach to sustainability treats the Board and management as working collaboratively, instead of management functioning without Board support or the Board mandating management buy-in.[13] These matters have the potential to greatly impact the company's reputation and whether it actually engages in responsible conduct. Through this approach, the company's sustainability program, whether voluntary or otherwise, evolves through well-informed and responsive policies that have buy-in from the Board and management with oversight systems, training and enforcement.[14] The Board and management should work together to identify which sustainability concerns are most likely triggered by the company's operations, relevant risks and those that have greater impacts for the company's business, including key stakeholders. Following this determination, together the Board and management should determine responsive policies, implementation steps, and compliance assessment procedures.[15]

With sustainability issues mainstreamed, company success short-term and long-term depends on the Board and management working together effectively on CSR. Consequently, the company should regularly review and prioritize sustainability issues, how to approach each, and the overall effectiveness of the collaboration between the Board and management.[16] As Wachtell-Lipton's team clearly identified:

> As the public conversation on the role of companies in addressing [CSR] issues continues to evolve, boards should consider how their risk oversight role specifically applies to various [CSR]-related risks. In large part, the board's function in overseeing management's identification and assessment of material [CSR]-related risks, such as supply chain disruptions, energy sources and alternatives, labor practices, and environmental impacts, involves both issue-specific and company-specific application of general risk oversight practices. However, as the public and investors scrutinize how companies address [CSR] issues, the board,

9. Stu Dalheim, Mike Lombardo, and Aditi Mohapatra, *Board Oversight of Environmental and Social Issues: An Analysis of Corporate North American Practices* (Calvert Investments) (2010), http://plusweb.org/Portals/0/DandO%20Material%202011/Board%20Oversight%20of%20Env%20&%20Social%20Issues.pdf.
10. *Ibid.*
11. *Ibid.*
12. *Ibid.*
13. David M. Silk, David A. Katz, Sabastian V. Niles and Carmen X.W. Lu, *Wachtell Lipton Discusses Boards' Role in Sustainability and Corporate Social Responsibility* (July 3, 2018).
14. Sarah Altschuller, *Corporate Social Responsibility and the Role of the Board of Directors* (June 21, 2011), www.businessinsider.com/corporate-social-responsibility-and-the-role-of-the-board-of-directors-2011-6.
15. David M. Silk, David A. Katz, Sabastian V. Niles and Carmen X.W. Lu, *Wachtell Lipton Discusses Boards' Role in Sustainability and Corporate Social Responsibility* (July 3, 2018). "In addition, companies should determine how best to integrate important risks and opportunities related to these areas into strategic and operational planning, crisis preparedness and risk management, corporate governance, investor and stakeholder communications, budgets, resource allocation and incentive structures." *Ibid.*
16. *Ibid.*

working with management, should make a particular effort to ensure that its risk oversight role is satisfied with regards to various [CSR] risks. As part of this process, management should identify whether there are any emerging [CSR] issues or trends that could materially impact the company's ability to create long-term sustainable value and decide how best to allocate corporate resources towards managing the most critical [CSR] risks.[17]

What the Board Should Consider

Although it may seem rather logical, increasingly, directors identify reputational risk as one of the top risk concerns for their companies.[18] Reputational risk boils down to the perception that companies are participants in our society, more and more like human beings. Consequently, the Board needs to factor into its decisions that the public desires, under the social licensure concept, that companies act as conscious citizens in operations and will judge the company according to its sustainability impacts. Therefore, as the public will do too, the Board should evaluate the company's short-term and long-term interests in contributing to fix societal problem versus remaining silent or adding to the problems.[19] Particularly in certain industries, effective and robust CSR programs will have definitive impacts on the company's financials. When a company fails to recognize sustainability issues or implement an adequate response, the impact on the company may range from financial to non-financial. Examples of these impacts include:

- Decreased sales;
- Exposure to, often unanticipated, law suits;
- Increased regulatory fees/fines;
- Failure to obtain necessary financing at various stages in a company's life;
- Community disenfranchisement;
- Low employee morale; and
- Service provider opposition.

Negative exposure such as this, even if a one-off event, has the potential to cause long-lasting harm to a company. Consequently, this type of "reputational harm can impair a company's capacity to leverage relationships with key public and private stakeholders and to implement short- and long-term business strategies."[20] And, taking it to the next level beyond mere risk avoidance, a company may opt to implement or build a more robust CSR program to gain a competitive edge over other companies in a company's industry.[21] In this context, the Board recognizes the reputational value of the social license.

Indeed, more and more, the Board needs to ensure implementation of a program that considers how the public perceives the company on key CSR matters, such as environmental impacts, labor,

17. *Ibid.*
18. Sarah Altschuller, *Corporate Social Responsibility and the Role of the Board of Directors* (June 21, 2011), www.businessinsider.com/corporate-social-responsibility-and-the-role-of-the-board-of-directors-2011-6. "It is no surprise, therefore, that 54 percent of the directors surveyed in a 2009 study by accounting firm Eisner identified reputational risk as a key risk area for their companies." *Ibid.*
19. Paul Hohnen, *Corporate Social Responsibility: An Implementation Guide for Business* (IISD) (2007), www.iisd.org/pdf/2007/csr_guide.pdf.
20. Sarah Altschuller, *Corporate Social Responsibility and the Role of the Board of Directors* (June 21, 2011), www.businessinsider.com/corporate-social-responsibility-and-the-role-of-the-board-of-directors-2011-6.
21. David M. Silk, David A. Katz, Sabastian V. Niles and Carmen X.W. Lu, *Wachtell Lipton Discusses Boards' Role in Sustainability and Corporate Social Responsibility* (July 3, 2018).

human rights, consumer health, product safety, investment priorities, and others.[22] Each industry has its leading matters. For instance, in the extraction industry, labor and environment lead the charge, with sexual exploitation not far behind. In the pharmaceutical industry, product safety and labor issues lead the charge.

To be expected, this is not a stagnant process, and the CSR program should not be either. Boards of public companies need to follow these trends closely as more and more investors, particularly the institutional investors, make CSR a priority in their investments.[23] As the public's focus on CSR shifts, as a company's operations change, as a company's sources of funding change or change thinking, the company needs to continually evaluate and determine through oversight how responsive the company's current program is and its appetite for risk.[24] The Board should understand how management is dealing with investors' interest on and requests for CSR-related steps. For instance, investors may request the company report on its methods of dealing with a key CSR issue and ask for progress reports.[25] Smaller, non-public companies may expect this as well from funding sources, such as private equity.

As public and investor scrutiny increases, the company's social license implicates the Board's risk oversight more and more. Ultimately, one of the key considerations for the Board's oversight is identification of CSR risks and implementation of appropriate response management. This oversight may involve an issue-by-issue approach as well as a systemic company program to address risk management practices.[26] Such identified risks may be whether labor issues exist that may disrupt the supply chain or whether alternative energy sources exist that have a smaller footprint. The Board should be asking about and continually evaluating the CSR issues and trends happening outside the company and what is the company doing. This requires staying informed and having adequate resources to accomplish the tasks.[27]

Setting up the company's sustainability program, the Board must consider more than just a creating a policy. With only a policy, the company faces a greater risk—failure to comply with its own policy. The Board's risk analysis and decision to implement a CSR response should go further to include how to ensure compliance with any policy and continual evaluation of the policy and related programs. To start, key to this equation is education of every director on the Board and senior management on an ongoing basis—education of (1) what CSR is, (2) what is going on at the company, and (3) what is going on outside the company. Having this information is only half the battle; getting it is the second half.

Clearly, not every Board director or senior manager of the company is or should be a CSR guru. However, to properly fulfill fiduciary responsibilities, every director should educate herself about the key CSR issues faced by the company, be able to explain the issues, including implications for risk management, and know the issues are being appropriately managed. This will also affect Board (and Committee) composition—considering the knowledge and experience that equips a director or committee member to best serve the issue. Additionally, the Board's choice of key company personnel will require personnel to similarly understand and be well-versed in company CSR concerns. These personnel must have adequate resources, a clear direct or indirect method of reporting, and appropriate enforcement mechanisms. Consistent with what should be a collaborative relationship between the Board and upper management on the CSR program, the Board should identify the best methods to communicate with employees and receive information. The Board should consider

22. *Ibid.*
23. *Ibid.*
24. *Ibid.*
25. *Ibid.*
26. *Ibid.*
27. *Ibid.*

the amount of resources to allocate to CSR program, areas of focus, whether to add a Board Committee, and whether to hire a CSR officer. In fact, in companies with high resources the Board and senior management designate specialized in-house experts and developing self-sustaining programs to improve capacity of the company's CSR program.[28]

With a knowledge base, the Board and management can construct a policy and program that suits their company's situation. When creating the policy, the Board should consider that for every policy measure implemented, there needs to be a corresponding allocation of resources for implementation, enforcement, and oversight. The often-used approach is for a Board to approve a policy that emphasizes monitoring and review of business operations and internal systems. That is an important part of a CSR program but not the whole. As the Board increases its understanding of CSR, it will learn that this is just the start.[29]

The Board needs to factor into oversight creation of a method to ensure that the CSR program on an ongoing basis addresses risk management concerns and, consequently, integrates the CSR company concerns into overall company operations and strategic planning. To properly implement a CSR program, large or small, a Board must understand that a CSR program is so much more than an attempt at philanthropy or marketing strategy, as discussed above. In addition, multiple times a year, the Board should be evaluating their program for competitive advantages, risk management, and company durability over the long-term.[30] With "[b]usiness opinion polls and corporate behavior both show[ing] increased levels of understanding of the link between responsible business and good business," investors are sitting up and taking note.[31] Increasingly, investors search out investment opportunities with business strategies that take into account sustainability concerns and the recognition of the value of the social license.[32] Not too surprisingly, CSR concerns must now be an integral part of the business model. Boards must plan accordingly.

Further, the Board should decide whether it will be responsible for ongoing oversight of the CSR program or whether it will be management. Best practices dictate that the Board should proactively claim oversight of the CSR program. To satisfy the governance requirements that fiduciary duties necessitate, the Board will have to create a robust plan for fulfillment of the oversight function.[33] Consistent with other governance challenges, the Board's plan will provide a method to implement its decisions starting at a boots-on-the-ground level. "As high-profile examples like Massey Energy

28. *Ibid.*
29. Stu Dalheim, Mike Lombardo, Aditi Mohapatra, *Board Oversight of Environmental and Social Issues: An Analysis of Corporate North American Practices* (Calvert Investments) (2010), http://plusweb.org/Portals/0/DandO%20 Material%202011/Board%20Oversight%20of%20Env%20&%20Social%20Issues.pdf. "Fewer than half of these committees require their directors to monitor and make forward-looking recommendations about sustainability trends, strategies, or targets; only about a quarter are responsible for environmental and social risk management; and even smaller numbers involve boards in oversight of corporate responsibility-related stakeholder engagement, incident readiness, or reporting. In terms of specific issues referenced in the S&P 100 committee charters, the environment is mentioned most frequently, with community relations, health and safety, and diversity also appearing often, but human rights receiving less attention." *Ibid.*
30. *Ibid.*
31. Paul Hohnen, *Corporate Social Responsibility: An Implementation Guide for Business* (IISD) (2007), www.iisd.org/pdf/2007/csr_guide.pdf. "In part, the problem stems from definitional issues, and a perception in some quarters that CSR is more about philanthropy, rather than 'doing business' and responding to shareholder interests." *Ibid.*
32. *Ibid.* "In addition to building trust with the community and giving firms an edge in attracting good customers and employees, acting responsibly towards workers and others in society can help build value for firms and their shareholders." *Ibid.*
33. Stu Dalheim, Mike Lombardo, Aditi Mohapatra, *Board Oversight of Environmental and Social Issues: An Analysis of Corporate North American Practices* (Calvert Investments) (2010), http://plusweb.org/Portals/0/DandO%20 Material%202011/Board%20Oversight%20of%20Env%20&%20Social%20Issues.pdf.

and BP demonstrate, some companies have experienced disasters related to employee safety and environmental protection, despite having board committees responsible for these issues."[34]

In 2010, Calvert Asset Management and the Corporate Library reviewed the committee charters of S&P 100 firms to determine corporate board's oversight approach to environmental and social concerns.[35] One element of a formalized CSR program the Board should consider is whether to delegate implementation and oversight of the CSR program to a currently existing Committee, such as Audit, or designate a new Committee which only has this responsibility. The Board should ensure that the Committee(s) and its directives are identified in a manual and formalize the process—the frequency, method, and content—of the briefings to the Board from the Committee(s).

Committees are a positive step but, like a policy, creation is half the battle. Where's the plan that ensures that oversight actually occurs at the Committee level? For instance, Calvert's 2010 study shows the low level of substantive oversight functionality the Committees pursued. It showed that only 65% of S&P 100 companies' Boards had Committees with some amount of responsibility for oversight of the CSR program. Of those Board Committees, only 27% (18 of 65) periodically review the CSR program's method of identifying and prioritizing the company's CSR concerns and corresponding approaches to manage the identified concerns or actually provide ongoing monitoring and oversight of the company's risk management plans.

Even if identification, prioritizing, and management of CSR concerns occurs on the Committee level, something needs to happen to the findings. The 2010 study found that only 8% (5 of 65) of the S&P 100 companies' Committees evaluate and are consulted related to CSR impacts of important decisions in business operations. The takeaway is that the Board must develop a strategic plan that is a proper part of business operations and create guidelines related to creation of a Committee (or Committees), arming it with a plan and resources. Furthermore, the plan should recognize the need for the company to use the Committee's discoveries in business operations, with which, as the 2010 study found, "board responsibility for corporate responsibility does not extend to true strategic planning and risk management."[36]

In another 2010 study, data for 2,939 Russell 3000 companies showed 8% of companies reviewed had a Board committee titled with a "corporate responsibility-related word" in its name. In fact, some of the companies had more than one relevant committee.[37] The study showed that 17% of the

34. *Ibid.*
35. *Ibid.* In this report, the authors refer to social and environmental issues as "corporate responsibility" and "sustainability."
36. Sarah Altschuller, *Corporate Social Responsibility and the Role of the Board of Directors* (June 21, 2011), www.businessinsider.com/corporate-social-responsibility-and-the-role-of-the-board-of-directors-2011-6.
37. Stu Dalheim, Mike Lombardo, Aditi Mohapatra, *Board Oversight of Environmental and Social Issues: An Analysis of Corporate North American Practices* (Calvert Investments) (2010). http://plusweb.org/Portals/0/DandO%20Material%202011/Board%20Oversight%20of%20Env%20&%20Social%20Issues.pdf ("11 companies have two such committees and one company, Occidental Petroleum, had three"). "Committees containing the following terms were included in our data set: Social Responsibility (or related phrases such as Sustainability or Corporate Responsibility), Diversity, Environment, Ethics, Nuclear, Public Policy (and related formulations such as Public Affairs or Public Issues), Quality, Safety, Shareholder Relations (and similar terms such as Investor Relations and Shareholder Value). We decided to exclude from our data set Human Resources and Compensation committees without other sustainability-related words in their names, since many of them are likely to focus primarily on compensation policy and recruitment for high-level executives. We also created a 'Miscellaneous' category to capture committees containing less-frequently-seen words that are not in the list above, but that did suggest a social or environmental aspect to the committee's work (for example, words as 'disclosure,' 'charitable giving,' and 'labor'). Finally, the 'Multi-Issue—Other' category includes both some committees tasked with evaluating several specific issues (e.g., 'Disclosure and Ethics') and some whose names suggest a broader corporate responsibility mandate (e.g., 'Public Policy and Corporate Responsibility'). As shown in the table to the right, the most common type of committee in the data set has a general name such as Social Responsibility Committee. Other common, and similarly broadly-named, committees include Public Policy Committees and committees using the three words Safety, Health and Environment (in some order). Committees focused on one CSR-related issue (e.g., Diversity, Quality) are less common." *Ibid.*

committees identified were essential Board committees, such as Audit, Corporate Governance, or Compensation. In that case, the CSR-related term had been added to the Committee name, such as "Governance, Nominating and Social Responsibility Committee" or "Audit and Public Policy Committee."[38] The study showed that larger companies (versus smaller) in the Russell 3000 sub-indices tended to have a committee with a name that suggested CSR oversight. "Specifically, 18% of the companies in the Russell 1000 have a corporate responsibility–related committee, while only 4% of the Russell 2000 companies have such a committee."[39]

Again, in the study that analyzed S&P Small Cap, they determined that the size of the companies relates to whether the companies have CSR-related committee(s). "Only 4% of the S&P Small Cap companies studied have a [CSR-related] committee . . . and only 9% of the S&P Mid Cap companies do. However, 28% of the S&P 500 companies have a [CSR-related] committee." As suggested by the authors of the study, larger companies may have a higher number due to the increased level of scrutiny received by these companies. Yet, often, the larger companies implement governance practices that become common across businesses soon thereafter.[40] The process starts somewhere and grows. This is important information of which the Board needs to stay informed.

Putting the issue of naming the Committee aside, over all, the Board should also consider that when assigning CSR oversight to a Committee, whether it is better to assign to a preexisting Committee, such as Governance, or to create a new Committee. For instance, assigning CSR oversight to a preexisting, highly level Committee may bring the issue more attention. Yet, assigning CSR oversight to a preexisting Committee may overburden an already burdened Committee and, consequently, decrease the amount of resources (including focus) the CSR program receives from the Committee and, therefore, the company.[41]

What's Going on Outside the Company Is an Essential Ingredient to Any CSR Program

Remarkably, even Boards of companies with robust CSR policies and internal systems fail to stay informed, and make related modifications internally, to the events going on outside the Company. This boils down to a CSR program that implements a policy and system and monitors compliance with that policy and system, but nothing further. This is compliance with the existing standard set forth by the Company. This is a massive failing by the Board to implement an adequate CSR program and provide oversight. In the study of the S&P 100, the authors found that "less than 50 percent of the boards surveyed (30 of 65) monitor and provide recommendations on CSR trends and developments." If stakeholders' concerns change, what then?[42] An adequate oversight mechanism requires the Board to be able to continually evaluate the world outside the current

38. *Ibid.* "The remaining 83% were other types of committees with corporate responsibility-related names (e.g., the Safety, Health and Environment Committee or the Corporate Responsibility Committee)." *Ibid.*
39. *Ibid.*
40. *Ibid.* "However, in general, it is clear that larger companies are more likely to have committees with names that more broadly address sustainability issues, such as Social Responsibility or Public Policy. The smaller companies are more likely to have committees with a more specific focus, such as Quality or Ethics." *Ibid.*
41. *Ibid.* "The sector with the most sustainability-related committees is the Consumer, Non-Cyclical sector. Of the 246 companies in this portion of our study, 22% are in the Consumer, Non-Cyclical sector. Other sectors with a high proportion of the companies studied are Financials and Utilities, as shown in the following chart. (The Bloomberg classification system was used for our sector analysis.)"
42. Sarah Altschuller, *Corporate Social Responsibility and the Role of the Board of Directors* (June 21, 2011), www.businessinsider.com/corporate-social-responsibility-and-the-role-of-the-board-of-directors-2011-6.

system—the expectations of the company's stakeholders.[43] The Board understand that from day 1, "[u]nderstanding key developments and trends is an integral component of effective long-term strategy development and can help ensure that companies have the capacity to respond to concerns when they arise." If the Board treats the CSR program as part of the business strategy, like monitoring industry equipment updates and consumer preferences, the Board must regularly conduct its fiduciary diligence to identify changes in stakeholder expectations and anticipate future evolutions in CSR. "CSR-focused stakeholders frequently expect companies to go 'beyond compliance' with existing legal and regulatory standards. At the same time, their expectations are often predictive of the future content of such standards."[44]

Additionally, to successfully implement a CSR program, the Board needs to ensure it receives adequate information. Consequently, the Board may want to ensure it obtains frequent briefings from management and external parties on the identified sustainability priorities.[45] These reports should, among other things, evaluate issues posing material risks to the company. For example, and tying in the Committee development concept from above, one trend that has existed suggests companies in industries that have commonly received high scrutiny for their negative approaches to the environment and labor (utilities, raw materials, and energy) will more likely have Board committees with naming that pulls in CSR-related terms and, therefore, have focused that Committee's task on the key issues. Companies from industries that have received less scrutiny for CSR-related matters (communication, financial, and tech) are less likely to have Committees designated for CSR-related issues, focusing exclusively on the concerns.[46] This information may be important for companies. Consequently, the Board may want regular briefings on relevant topics.[47]

Interacting With Funding Sources: A Key Stakeholder

Ultimately, the Board focuses on the bottom line, particularly in public companies, to make the shareholders happy. The Board's primary duties are to the company and the shareholders, and the effort a Board, management, and a company exerts to implement a robust CSR program requires

43. *Ibid.*
44. *Ibid.*
45. David M. Silk, David A. Katz, Sabastian V. Niles and Carmen X.W. Lu, *Wachtell Lipton Discusses Boards' Role in Sustainability and Corporate Social Responsibility* (July 3, 2018).
46. Stu Dalheim, Mike Lombardo, Aditi Mohapatra, *Board Oversight of Environmental and Social Issues: An Analysis of Corporate North American Practices* (Calvert Investments) (2010), http://plusweb.org/Portals/0/DandO%20 Material%202011/Board%20Oversight%20of%20Env%20&%20Social%20Issues.pdf. "For example, more than one-third (34%, or 33 of 96) of the companies in the Utilities sector in the Russell 3000 have a committee with a corporate responsibility-related word in the name. Similarly, one quarter (25%, or 28 of 111) of the Russell 3000 companies in the Basic Materials sector have such a committee. In contrast, only 5% (or 31 of 605) of the Russell 3000 companies in the Financial sector have a corporate responsibility-related committee." *Ibid.* "As might be expected, the prevalence of committees in different subject-matter areas also varies greatly with the sector of the company. For example, the chart below shows that the companies with committees addressing Safety, Health & Environment are often those in the Basic Materials and Energy sectors. Not surprisingly [*sic*], special board committees dedicated to Nuclear issues are found in the Utilities sector. Consistent with their need to preserve their public image and customer-facing focus, Consumer Cyclical companies are most likely to have a broad committee dedicated to Diversity issues or Social Responsibility issues in general." *Ibid.*
47. David M. Silk, David A. Katz, Sabastian V. Niles and Carmen X.W. Lu, *Wachtell Lipton Discusses Boards' Role in Sustainability and Corporate Social Responsibility* (July 3, 2018).

a noticeable allocation of resources. What do the investors have to say about CSR? Shareholders have different methods of influencing company and Board activity. In public companies, the Rule 14a-8 proposal allows shareholders to try to influence the matters acted on by the Board and management.[48] These proposals may cover a variety of issues. The types of shareholders filing proposals varies. Shareholder proposals, however, are indicative of where the primary interests of the primary stakeholder lie for public companies. Examining recent proposals provides a glimpse into shareholder concerns. For example,

> [s]ince 2010, there have been more proposals about social issues than concerning the environment, but the long-term trend shows growth in sustainable governance. This year [2018] marks a drop in social resolutions, and a convergence between the environment and governance.[49]

In a recent study by Proxy Preview that analyzed shareholder proposals filed in early 2018, just over half of the shareholder proposals related to "[c]limate change, corporate political activity and sustainability".[50] This is similar to 2017. Another third of the early-2018 proposals splits evenly between human rights, board diversity, decent work, and workplace diversity. "Resolutions on health issues, board oversight, proposals from conservatives and a few miscellaneous subjects account for the final 16 percent."[51] As of February 16, 2018, the 2018 Proxy Preview identified 429 shareholder resolutions on social, environmental, and other sustainability issues.[52]

In the 2018 proxy season, the number of requests from investors in public companies for sustainability reporting increased.[53] In 2018, a few interesting reporting requests occurred. The shareholder request pending in early 2018 at Amazon.com related to a report on CSR impact risk management and, specifically, referenced the broad impact of Amazon on American society.[54] Also, in early 2018 Tesla Motors experienced its first shareholder request—asking the company to use CSR metrics, as discussed above, in its financial reporting.[55] As Proxy Preview stated in its 2018 review:

> In a big shift, this year there are 18 resolutions seeking reports on links between a variety of issues and executive compensation, reflecting many of the issues raised in this report—drug pricing, executive diversity, sustainability in general, cybersecurity and data privacy, fossil fuel reserves accounting and risky financial practices.[56]

It is full steam ahead with shareholders echoing the American public's interest in companies participating as social citizens in the marketplace. They will determine the best forum for this

48. Cam Hoang, Gary Tygesson, and Violet Richardson, *Shareholder Proposals: Strategies and Tactics* (Dorsey & Whitney LLP), www.dorsey.com/newsresources/events/videos/2016/10/~/media/0ee87bda7cc84b59824d6c786cff39b5.ashx.
49. Heidi Welsh and Michael Passoff, *Proxy Preview: Helping Shareholders Vote Their Values* (2018), https://vimeo.com/259236161.
50. *Ibid.*
51. *Ibid.*
52. *Ibid.* (review of the proposals as of February 16, 2018).
53. *Ibid.*
54. *Ibid.* This proposal request faced an SEC challenge. *Ibid.*
55. *Ibid.*
56. *Ibid.*

communication—website, public filings, and so forth. What are the Company's competitors doing or not doing, as the following examples illustrate? The Board and management will learn from what is going on around it, and not just on its bottom line.[57] There is definitely not a one-size-fits-all approach to pursuing social responsibility.[58]

57. David M. Silk, David A. Katz, Sabastian V. Niles and Carmen X.W. Lu, *Wachtell Lipton Discusses Boards' Role in Sustainability and Corporate Social Responsibility* (July 3, 2018). "In some cases, companies will embrace appropriate public reporting on specific ESG issues over acceptable timeframes. Companies will also have to deal with pressure to set—and disclose—specific goals and targets. When constructively avoiding premature, immaterial or duplicative disclosures, or those that involve unwarranted time, effort or cost, it is prudent to also recognize that a complete lack of transparency is unlikely to be a sustainable approach over the long term. In the current environment, disclosure of the right kind may be viewed as an opportunity instead of just as a cost." *Ibid.* See also: Mandatory ESG reporting gains momentum, https://www.blackrock.com/corporate/investor-relations/larry-fink-ceo-letter?cid=ppc:blk:ll:na:ol:goog:na:v1:bhv:tl&gclid=3cc7673bf3fb15edb3e806cba9056a96&gclsrc=3p.ds, explaining that, for instance, in early 2022, the CEO of BlackRock, Larry Fink, published a letter delineating the greater importance of ESG in its investment strategy, reflecting greater demands of ESG inclusion in overall business strategy.
58. *Ibid.*

4

UNDERSTANDING AND MANAGING BEHAVIORAL ETHICS RISK

Todd Haugh

Introduction

"Governance, risk management, and compliance are in vogue."[1] That is how the leading governance, risk management, and compliance (GRC) textbook describes these three overlapping corporate functions. Whether something as staid as GRC can ever be in vogue is debatable—after all, the purpose of risk management and compliance is often to *lessen* the effects of trendy or superficial governance and business practices. But it is true that these functions have become more visible, and therefore arguably more important, than in the past. Fueled by corporate scandals beginning in the 1960s and intensifying in the early and mid-2000s, risk management and compliance have taken on more prominent roles in corporate America. Indeed, it would be hard to find a sizable company that does not commit a significant amount of resources to addressing business risk and regulatory compliance, a claim that could hardly be made a few decades earlier.

On the whole, this is a good thing given the laudable goals of risk management and compliance. Risk management is aimed at identifying, analyzing, and planning for various risks the company faces, all with the intention of mitigating them so business can function more effectively. The goal of compliance is to make sure the company is following applicable laws and norms. The two functions overlap in substance and form: noncompliance, either by individual employees or on the organizational level, creates risk; and both compliance and risk can be managed by targeted organizational processes. Thus, a company that puts in place processes to lessen compliance failures will consequently lesson its "conduct risk," which ultimately leads to more effective corporate governance.[2]

The nature of this relationship has led some to suggest that risk management and compliance have overtaken corporate governance within companies—the R and C have swallowed the G, as it were. Again, whether that is accurate is debatable, this much is clear: if a company has not been paying attention to GRC, and especially to risk caused by compliance failures, it had better start. That is

1. Geoffrey P. Miller, The Law of Governance, Risk Management, and Compliance 1 (2017).
2. Conduct risk can be defined as "unethical business practices, individual behaviors, and organizational behaviors that have led to outcomes that have harmed either individual players or the financial system." Deloitte, *Conduct Risk: Improving Culture Across the Enterprise*, Wall St. J. (May 14, 2018), http://deloitte.wsj.com/riskandcompliance/2018/05/14/conduct-risk-improving-culture-across-the-enterprise/. See also Tom Butler et al., *A Systematic Approach for Managing and Supervising Conduct Culture and Risk*, Governance, Risk & Compliance Tech Center, at 2–3 (2017), www.grctc.com/wp-content/uploads/2017/08/GRCTC-Conduct-Risk-2017-_-Final.pdf.

DOI: 10.4324/9781351107242-6

because everyone else is—employees, directors, investors, regulators, and even competitors—essentially every stakeholder that has the power to impact the company.

But saying that governance, risk management, and compliance are important or even in vogue only goes so far. What corporate leaders truly care about is how to *manage* these functions effectively. Unfortunately, there has been a long-standing lack of guidance in this area. If GRC began its rise to current prominence in the 1960s, then there has been roughly a half century of trying to determine "what works and what hurts" without much resolution.[3] Reasons for this abound—regulators, corporate leaders, and third-party providers are all to blame—but the fact remains that GRC's increased importance has not resulted in a corresponding increase in its efficacy. We seem to have more and fancier corporate tools and metrics these days, but little understanding of how best to use them.

With that in mind, this chapter suggests a new GRC paradigm, one organized around the concept of *behavioral ethics risk management*. This approach, which works inside out from compliance to governance, offers a better way to understand the risks associated with compliance failures and how to combat them to improve corporate governance. What this paradigm does better than existing notions of GRC is to focus on what is at the heart of these related functions: individual ethical decision-making. Drawing from the fields of behavioral ethics, criminology, and network theory, this chapter will explain how individual unethical decisions are made, how that leads to compliance failures, and how those failures may spread throughout a company.[4] This discussion will highlight how risk emanating from unethical employee decision-making, if left unaddressed, may result in significant risk to the firm.

Once this newly understood risk is identified and explored, the chapter turns to how best to mitigate it. A series of risk assessment and compliance strategies are offered, ones that properly focus on the decision-making processes of individual employees, as opposed to the command and control–oriented tools of traditional corporate compliance and governance. Again, the idea is to move past accepted practices, even those that are considered current "best practices," to focus on reducing individual unethical decisions, the precursors to unethical behavior and corporate wrongdoing. By employing these strategies, companies may reduce their conduct risk and allow for more efficient and effective operations—the overarching goal of all companies' GRC efforts.[5]

Behavioral Ethics Risk: What It Is and How It Spreads

GRC and Its Ethical Decision-Making Core

As an initial matter, it is helpful to consider the relationship between corporate governance, risk management, and compliance—the three aspects of GRC. As others have pointed out, these functions

3. *See* Linda Klebe Trevino et al., *Managing Ethics and Legal Compliance: What Works and What Hurts*, 41 CAL. MGMT. REV. 131 (1999) (exploring efficacy of deterrence-based compliance programs in Fortune 1000 firms).
4. The ideas in this chapter come from three of my recent articles. See e.g., Todd Haugh, *The Criminalization of Compliance*, 92 NOTRE DAME L. REV. 1215 (2017); Todd Haugh, *Nudging Corporate Compliance*, 54 AM. BUS. L.J. 683 (2017); Todd Haugh, *The Power Few of Corporate Compliance*, 53 GA. L. REV. 129 (2019).
5. I am mindful that offering this new GRC paradigm can sound both grandiose and pedestrian at the same time. On the one hand, theories of ethical decision-making go back a long way, at least as far as Aristotle, so it is hard to claim novelty here. And because companies are legal fictions that can only act through their agents, it may seem obvious that everything within a company originates from the decision-making of individuals. The insight I hope to provide by using the paradigm of behavioral ethics risk comes from bringing theory and practice from divergent fields together and refocusing GRC on what matters—individual ethical decision-making. Understanding how ethical decision-making occurs, how it creates small-bore and systemic risk, and how it can be targeted to increase compliance and mitigate conduct risk are topics many in corporate governance and compliance ignore.

are distinct within corporations, yet they clearly overlap in ways that are more than "simpl[e] matters of definition."[6]

The most straightforward way to conceptualize the relationship is as a set of concentric circles, with compliance at the center, risk management as the second ring, and corporate governance as the third. This structuring recognizes that each function occupies a distinct definitional and substantive role in a company, but that all serve a common purpose; that is, to ensure the company is effectively managed to meet its welfare enhancing goals. It also recognizes that the compliance function is central to GRC. This makes sense, as noncompliance by members of an organization creates risk that must be managed if effective governance is to be achieved. Figure 4.1 provides the basic definitions of each component.[7]

Because compliance is central to GRC efforts, it is important to understand in more detail what the function entails. Although compliance is a broad concept, it can be thought of as having two primary purposes. The first is deterring violations of law, which may be criminal or civil in nature. On the criminal side, compliance programs are aimed at preventing violations of state and federal law, as well as regulatory violations that may be criminally enforced. In addition, compliance programs attempt to prevent tort-based violations of purely civil law. Put another way, compliance programs attempt to deter all aspects of unlawful employee behavior, which reduces the risk that the company will be held responsible under broad respondeat superior legal liability.[8]

The second purpose of compliance is to generate positive behavioral norms within the company. Internal corporate norms, which are expressed by the company through rules, guidance, and mores, are important because they fill the gaps left by more formal legal mechanisms. Norm generation and enforcement is often considered the "ethical culture" aspect of compliance, and a majority of companies see creating an ethical culture as the larger goal of their compliance programs.[9] The hope is that through these efforts all employees will share a common belief about the company's "purpose (i.e., mission, strategy, and goals) . . . [and] the necessary means to achieve it (i.e., systems, structure, and processes)."[10]

Governance	Processes by which decisions relative to risk management and compliance are made within their organizations.
Risk Management	Processes by which risk is identified, analyzed, and included in strategic planning, and either mitigated or accepted as inherent in necessary company conduct.
Compliance	Processes by which an organization polices its own behavior to ensure legal and normative conformity.
EDM	Individual ethical decision making.

Figure 4.1 GRC relationship and component definitions.

6. Miller, *supra* note 1, at 3.
7. Definitions adopted from Miller, *supra* note 1, at 2–3.
8. *See* Harvey L. Pitt and Karl A. Groskaufmanis, *Minimizing Corporate Civil and Criminal Liability: A Second Look at Corporate Codes of Conduct*, 78 Geo. L.J. 1559, 1570–74 (1990).
9. Sean J. Griffith, *Corporate Governance in an Era of Compliance*, 57 Wm. & Mary L. Rev. 2075, 2093–94, n.73 (2016).
10. Caterina Bulgarella, *Predicting Risk: A Strategic Culture Framework for the C-Suite*, SAI Global, at 10, https://m.comms.saiglobal.com/res/saiglob_mkt_prod1/SAI_Global_Strategic_Culture_Framework_Report_April2018.pdf.

In order to achieve these two purposes, compliance simultaneously operates on multiple levels within a company. Education and training, one level, is essentially "policy-setting" by the company to its employees. The company explains what the applicable laws and corporate policies are and how employees (and other stakeholders) should comply with them. Monitoring, another level, ensures that those corporate policies are understood and followed, and that any violations are quickly identified. Enforcement, a third level, attempts to deter future violations by punishing wrongdoers. Often this means a reprimand, but termination is common for ethical transgressions. Legal violations by employees, however, may result in a range of more serious sanctions for both the individual and the company. These types of compliance violations in particular create significant conduct risk for firms.[11]

It should be obvious from the above that much of compliance—and therefore much of risk management and corporate governance—turns on individual employee behavior. If directors, managers, and lower-level employees act in a law-abiding and ethical manner, the company will likely avoid legal liability and significant compliance-based disruption of its business practices. This means that companies intent on creating effective compliance programs must develop the "skill [of] predicting human behavior."[12] But behavior is predicated on individual decision-making, in this instance ethical decision-making. Thus, the core of compliance, and in turn much of GRC, is dependent on individual ethical decision-making.

Behavioral Ethics Theory and Practice

This concept, that individual ethical decision-making is at the heart of the concentric functions of GRC, is likely to be edifying for many companies. Yet even for those organizations that have already come around to this view, there is often scant understanding of how employees make ethical decisions, and even less understanding of how to incorporate that information into GRC practices. Luckily, the field of behavioral ethics—and the behavioral science behind it—provides significant insights, laying the foundation for the behavioral ethics risk management paradigm.

The Behavioral Ethics Field and Its Central Findings

Likely because it is a still-emerging field, there is no standard definition of behavioral ethics. Early proponents broadly characterized it as the "scientific approach for studying perceptions of how we ought to treat one another . . . and how such perceptions influence behavior."[13] While that was a useful start because it made clear that ethical behavior could be studied systematically, to really understand what behavioral ethics is, it is necessary to take a more practical approach. Thus, a better way to define the field is the "aim[] to understand how even well-intentioned people can sometimes behave unethically."[14] Going a step farther, and more closely linking behavior and decision-making, behavioral ethics can be defined as the study of the "systematic and predictable ways in which individuals make ethical decisions and judge the ethical decisions of others."[15]

11. For example, Siemens A.G. reported spending more than $1 billion solely related to the government's inquiry into the payment of foreign bribes by individual executives. The reputational and operational costs were much higher. See Peter J. Henning, *The Mounting Costs of Internal Investigations*, N.Y. Times (March 5, 2012), http://dealbook.nytimes.com/2012/03/05/the-mounting-costs-of-internal-investigations/?_r=0.
12. Donald Langevoort, *Behavioral Ethics, Behavioral Compliance*, in Research Handbook on Corporate Crime and Financial Misdealing [1] (Jennifer Arlen, ed., 2016) (hereinafter *Behavioral Compliance*).
13. Robert Folger, *Deonance: Behavioral Ethics and Moral Obligation*, in Behavioral Business Ethics 125 (David De Cremer and Ann E. Tenbrunsel, eds., 2012).
14. Jason Dana et al., *Ethical Immunity: How People Violate Their Own Moral Standards Without Feeling They Are Doing So*, in Behavioral Business Ethics 202 (David De Cremer and Ann E. Tenbrunsel, eds., 2012).
15. Max H. Brazerman and Francesca Gino, *Behavioral Ethics: Toward a Deeper Understanding of Moral Judgment and Dishonesty*, 8 Ann. Rev. Law Soc. Sci. 85, 90 (2012).

These last two definitions hint at the central findings of the many studies conducted under the behavioral ethics umbrella. That is, "cognitive heuristics, psychological tendencies, social and organizational pressures, and even seemingly irrelevant situational factors can make it more likely that good people will do bad things."[16] In plain terms, behavioral ethics research tells us that while most people are moral individuals intent on doing right, we are not as ethical as we think we are. Another way to consider this finding is that ethical decision-making and behavior are *limited* in a significant way. Most people will make moral decisions in line with their ethical beliefs, but only up to a point. Because of cognitive obstacles, which may be exacerbated by external factors, many people will be blind to their own unethical conduct—they engage in unethical acts without even realizing it, acts that they would condemn upon further reflection. As one leader in the field put it, we are ethical, but "only boundedly so."[17]

The Decision-Making Theory Underlying Behavioral Ethics

The findings of behavioral ethics provide a critical understanding of individual ethical decision-making, but left open is the question of how. How does the ethical decision-making process operate so that it falls prey to these cognitive obstacles, which leads to us to commit unethical behavior?

For the answer, it is necessary to consider dual process theory, or the notion that "human thought processes are subserved by two distinct mechanisms."[18] Put simply, the theory suggests that we make decisions through two separate minds sharing space in our single brain. Jonathan Evans and Keith Frankish provide a concise summary:

> These theories come in different forms, but all agree in positing two distinct processing mechanisms for a given task, which employ different procedures and may yield different, sometimes conflicting, results. Typically, one of the processes is characterized as fast, effortless, automatic, non-conscience, inflexible, heavily contextualized, and undemanding of working memory, and the other as slow, effortful, controlled, conscious, flexible, decontextualized, and demanding of working memory.[19]

To add a bit more context, the fast or intuitive process, now generally referred to as System 1, is "evolutionally old, and shared with most higher animals."[20] Because it operates by associative memory, it is governed by habit and therefore difficult to control or modify. System 1 thinking may not seem like thinking at all because so much happens through it all at once. The speed and ease in which this thinking system operates means that "most of the work of associative thinking is silent, hidden from our conscious selves."[21]

In contrast, the slower reasoning process, or System 2, is evolutionally recent, typical to humans and likely only the most advanced primates. System 2 is "serial, effortful, and deliberately controlled," subject to logic and rules—it is engaged whenever we use thought in an organized manner.[22] The

16. Robert Prentice, Behavioral Ethics: Can It Help Lawyers (and Others) Be Their Best Selves?, 29 Notre Dame J.L. Ethics & Pub. Pol'y 35, 36 (2015).
17. *Ibid.*
18. Lauri Järvilehto, The Nature and Function of Intuitive Thought and Decision Making 24 (2015) (internal citation omitted).
19. Jonathan St. B. T. Evans and Keith Frankish, In Two Minds: Dual Processes and Beyond 1 (2009).
20. Järvilehto, *supra* note 18, at 25.
21. Daniel Kahneman, Thinking, Fast and Slow 52 (2011).
22. Daniel Kahneman, *Maps of Bounded Rationality: Psychology for Behavioral Economics*, 93 Am. Econ. Rev. 1449, 1451 (2003).

effort that this type of thinking requires is significant, but it is how the brain carefully addresses new tasks when there are no easy associations to make. System 2 thinking, unlike its more automatic counterpart, gives us the "experience of agency, autonomy, and volition."[23]

Based on these descriptions it is tempting to view System 2 as superior, but that is not entirely accurate. Because System 1 thinking is associative and not constrained by working memory, it is virtually effortless and therefore highly efficient. In fact, because it can process several streams of information at once, System 1 is uniquely suited for making the vast majority of our daily decisions, everything from walking and talking to driving a car and brushing one's teeth.

But for more important decisions, System 2 thinking is required to ensure a thoughtful, and potentially more accurate, outcome. The difficulty is that because of the greater cognitive load required to employ System 2, it is easily overwhelmed. This results in a series of cognitive limitations that "typically manifest as the inability to focus attention."[24] The cause of these limitations is that effortful mental processes disrupt each other, while effortless ones do not. Thus, System 1 thinking tends to proliferate when we are under significant cognitive load, which is anytime we are facing non-routine decisions.

This last point is important because it reveals the perceived versus actual relationship between our dual systems of thinking. While most of us believe that we make decisions carefully and deliberately, the behavioral research demonstrates that can only be true for a small subset of decisions. There simply is not enough mental energy to give every decision the treatment it requires. Instead of making most decisions through the reflective system, studies show that System 1 is the dominant mode of thinking. As such, the most we can hope for is that System 2 operates as a watchful monitor, kicking in when really important mental tasks arise or when it is needed to correct a decision-making error.[25] But that necessarily means that some decisions, even important ones, will slip through the cracks and be made subject to biases and heuristics based on quick associations and limited cognitive processes.

Dual System Thinking and Ethical Decision-Making

Although dual system theory was developed independent of questions related to ethical decision-making, it serves as the foundation for the central findings of behavioral ethics—that individual ethical decision-making is bounded, even when we intend to behave ethically. Behavioral ethics researchers believe that self-interest is associated with System 1, the automatic thinking system. A majority of researchers also believe that individuals approach ethical decisions in a way that "grants System 1 the leading role," causing us to initially "prefer outcomes that benefit ourselves."[26] In other words, making unethical decisions, or at least ones that preference our own well-being over others, is likely our default decision-making condition.

But as we know from dual system theory, that is not the end of the story. Once System 2 has been activated, prompting thoughtful reflection, people often do "choose to behave in an ethically

23. Pelle Guldborg Hansen and Andreas Maaloe Jespersen, *Nudge and the Manipulation of Choice: A Framework for the Responsible Use of the Nudge Approach to Behaviour Change in Public Policy*, 4 Eur. J. Risk Reg. 3, 13 (2013).
24. Järvilehto, *supra* note 18, at 26.
25. Kahneman, *supra* note 21, at 44 ("One of the main functions of System 2 is to monitor and control thoughts and actions 'suggested' by System 1, allowing some to be expressed directly in behavior and suppressing or modifying others.").
26. Yuval Feldman, *Behavioral Ethics Meets Behavioral Law and Economics*, in The Oxford Handbook of Behavioral Economics and the Law 8 (Eyal Zamir and Doron Teichman, eds., 2014); Minette Drumwright et al., *Behavioral Ethics and Teaching Ethical Decision Making*, 13 Decision Sci. J. Innovative Educ. 431, 433 (2015); Nicholas Epley and Eugene M. Caruso, *Egocentric Ethics*, 17 Soc. Just. Res. 171, 179 (2004).

appropriate manner."[27] Just as in other decision-making contexts, behavioral ethics researchers have found that System 2 can act as a watchful *ethical* monitor, jumping in to control the automatic self-interest each of us possess. This monitoring function appears to work best when cognitive load is low and individuals are able to fully consider the ethical ramifications of a decision—these are the conditions in which we are most likely to act in a way consistent with our morals.[28] However, when cognitive load is high, the automatic system may supplant the reflective, increasing the chance that individuals will act according to their less ethical self-interests.

Rationalizations as the Link Between Unethical Decision-Making and Unethical Behavior

The central findings of behavioral ethics, as well as the decision-making science underlying it, have significant ramifications for companies trying to predict and mitigate the conduct risk generated by its employees. Increasing System 2 thinking related to ethical decisions would seem to be an obvious path toward increasing GRC effectiveness. Unfortunately, however, the story is a bit more complicated. That is because System 2 thinking itself is part of the cause of unethical and illegal acts in business.

To understand this, we have to turn to those researchers even more steeped in the study of unethical behavior than behavioral ethicists: criminologists. As far back as the 1930s, criminologists studying white collar and organizational crime have theorized how offenders move from unethical decision-making to unethical behavior.

In his classic study of embezzlers, criminologist Donald Cressey found that three conditions are necessary for a white collar crime to occur. First, an individual must possess a non-shareable financial problem, that is, a problem the person feels cannot be solved by revealing it to others.[29] Second, the individual must believe that the problem can be solved in secret by violating a trust.[30] Trust, of course, is essential to the operation of all organizations: the entire principal-agent or employer-employee relationship is built upon it. Third, the individual must verbalize the relationship between the non-shareable problem and the unethical or illegal solution in "language that lets him look on trust violation as something other than trust violation."[31] Put another way, the individual conducts an internal dialogue that "reasons" the trust violation as acceptable. The paradigmatic example is a bank teller convincing himself that he is only "borrowing" the embezzled funds and will pay them back.[32]

This last step, what criminologists call "verbalizations," has been called as "the crux of the problem" of white-collar and corporate crime.[33] Criminologists do not view verbalizations as simple, after-the-fact excuses that offenders use to relieve their culpability upon being caught. Instead, they see verbalizations as "vocabularies of motive," words and phrases used by offenders that label unethical

27. Feldman, *supra* note 26, at 8. But see David G. Rand et al., *Spontaneous Giving and Calculated Greed*, 489 Nature 427 (2012) (finding that cooperation is intuitive and automatic, possibly because cooperative heuristics are developed in daily life where cooperation is typically advantageous).
28. Don A. Moore and George Loewenstein, *Self-Interest, Automaticity, and the Psychology of Conflict of Interest*, 17 Soc. Just. Res. 189, 193 (2004).
29. Donald R. Cressey, *The Respectable Criminal*, 3 Criminologica 13, 14–15 (1965). While this sounds sophisticated, it usually is not; the problem could be anything from gambling debts to business losses, anything that matters from "the psychological perspective of the potential offender."
30. Mark M. Lanier and Stuart Henry, Essential Criminology 168 (3rd ed. 2004).
31. Cressey, *supra* note 29, at 15.
32. *Ibid.*
33. *Ibid.*

behavior as appropriate.[34] Importantly, this means that an offender's rationalizations are created *before* the unethical or illegal behavior occurs. "The rationalization is [the offender's] motivation"—it not only justifies his behavior to others, but it makes the behavior intelligible, and therefore actionable, to himself.[35] Thus, rationalizations permit behavior to proceed that would otherwise be unacceptable to an offender.[36]

The concept of rationalizations is so powerful—and so critical to understanding unethical and illegal employee acts—because it provides the bridge between individual ethical decision-making and unethical behavior. Behavioral ethics research suggests that we default toward unethical decision-making, and therefore unethical action, because we are driven by self-interested System 1 thinking. At the same time, criminological research tells us that we come up with ways to convince ourselves—consciously and subconsciously—that we are acting ethically.[37] This is System 2 thinking justifying our System 1 conclusions. Essentially, we have developed a mechanism to accommodate the countervailing aspects of living in a "hyper-social" world that rewards self-interested behavior but also social cooperation.[38] That mechanism is to rationalize—redefining how we look at our own behavior so as to square our self-perception as a "good person" with the self-interested unethical or illegal behavior we are contemplating.[39] In a way, rationalizations trick the System 2 reflective thinking process that would otherwise intervene to contain the "automaticity of self-interest."[40] This is not a product of intentional amorality for most people; instead, they are blind to the "correction their mind applies as it weighs ethical concerns against other motives."[41]

The Spread of Unethical Behavioral Within Organizations

Admittedly, this does not paint a very rosy picture for corporate compliance or a company's larger GRC efforts. If the behavioral ethics and criminological research suggest that both System 1 and System 2 are feeding unethical decision-making and behavior, companies would appear to be fighting an uphill battle against employee wrongdoing and the risk it creates. Unfortunately, the picture gets worse before it gets better. That is because behavioral ethics research also suggests that unethical behavior can spread easily within companies through social and organizational networks, ratcheting up the conduct risk companies face.

We have long known that social and organizational ties can have significant impacts on ethical behavior. But only recently have we come to understand the behavioral mechanisms behind those impacts. One group of researchers coalescing around Francesca Gino has published a series of studies addressing whether being exposed to the unethical behavior of others with which you have

34. *Ibid.*
35. Donald R. Cressey, *Other People's Money: A Study in the Social Psychology of Embezzlement* 94, 95 (1973).
36. The definitional examples are drawn from Paul Michael Klenowski, "Other People's Money": An Empirical Examination of the Motivational Differences Between Male and Female White Collar Offenders 56, 67 (May 2008) (unpublished Ph.D. dissertation, Indiana University of Pennsylvania) (on file with author) (internal citations omitted).
37. Feldman, *supra* note 26, at 7, 17.
38. Elizabeth Kolbert, *That's What You Think: Why Reason and Evidence Won't Change Our Minds*, New Yorker, at 66 (February 27, 2017) (citing Hugo Mercier and Dan Sperber, The Enigma of Reason: A New Theory of Human Understanding [2017]).
39. Vikas Anad et al., *Business as Usual: The Acceptance and Perpetuation of Corruption in Organizations*, 18 Acad. Mgmt. Exec. 39, 40–43 (2004).
40. Feldman, *supra* note 26, at 3, 7 (calling the "automaticity of self-interest" one of behavioral ethics basic tenets).
41. Bulgarella, *supra* note 10, at 7.

an association increases dishonesty.[42] Gino and her colleagues found that student participants who observed other students from the same school cheat on a task were much more likely to cheat themselves. This was not the case when the participants observed cheating from non-affiliated students.[43] Another study found that when student participants felt "psychologically close" to cheating students, the participants cheated in higher numbers themselves and viewed selfish behavior as "less unethical or wrong."[44] Taken together, these and other studies suggest that "people copy the behavior of in-group members," using that behavior to justify and rationalize their own unethical conduct.[45]

These findings take on special significance when considering the natural networks—social and organizational—within companies. If close connections and in-group dynamics influence unethical behavior, that means individuals who are joined by psychological closeness, even if slight, may be more prone to commit violations of laws or norms when others around them are doing so.[46] And when these individuals are linked in a network, the number and harm of those violations increases. In other words, individual wrongdoing can be "contagious," spreading quickly through an organizational network in unexpected ways.[47]

Sociologist and network theorist Mark Granovetter's study of how riots occur supports this proposition. Granovetter posited that potential rioters—the persons in a crowd milling around and witnessing the group's actions—have a "threshold" for joining.[48] This threshold differs for each participant based on their own ethical decision-making, that is, the level at which their mind allows potential bad behavior to be operationalized. Granovetter created a model that assigned 100 potential rioters a number from 0 to 99, which corresponded to their individual thresholds—the person with the zero threshold would begin rioting all on his own, the person with the 1 threshold would see that and join in, and on and on until the last person joined. This model suggested that riots would "grow like wildfire, eventually sucking in even people with very high [individual] thresholds."[49] But the model also suggested that if just one person early on had a slightly higher threshold, say a 6 instead of a 4, the riot would end before it gained momentum because the next threshold would never be reached.

This simple model led Granovetter to better understand actual riot behavior, in which the "equilibrium number of rioters" did not build uniformly, but rather appeared to jump up drastically at a certain point.[50] He modeled that riot size would increase by a factor of seven after crossing a seemingly arbitrary point—an explosion more than a wildfire. Granovetter suggested that this phenomenon was caused by the relationships between the active and potential rioters—he believed friendships were lowering individual thresholds to joining the riot. Accordingly, if some number of people in the crowd were friends with those rioting, the overall number of riot participants would skyrocket along with the harm caused. Granovetter called this the "bandwagon" effect.[51]

42. See e.g., Francesca Gino, Shahar Ayal and Dan Ariely, *Contagion and Differentiation in Unethical Behavior: The Effect of One Bad Apple on the Barrel*, 20 Psychol. Sci. 393 (2009); Francesca Gino and Adam D. Galinsky, *Vicarious Dishonesty: When Psychological Closeness Creates Distance from One's Moral Compass*, 119 Org. Behav. & Hum. Decision Processes 15 (2012).
43. Gino, Ayal and Ariely, *supra* note 42, at 396–97.
44. Gino and Galinsky, *supra* note 42, at 23.
45. Cilea Moore and Francesca Gino, *Ethically Adrift: How Others Pull Our Moral Compass from True North, and How We Can Fix It*, 22 Res. Org. Behav. 53, 57 (2013).
46. Gino and Galinsky, *supra* note 42, at 23. *See also*, Kristin Smith-Crowe and Danielle E. Warren, *The Emotion-Evoked Collective Corruption Model: The Role of Emotion in the Spread of Corruption Within Organizations*, 25 Org. Sci. 1124, 1165 (2014) (study providing a model showing how corruption might spread through emotion even to a well-intentioned and morally engaged population).
47. Gino, Ayal and Ariely, *supra* note 42, at 398.
48. Mark Granovetter, *Threshold Models of Collective Behavior*, 83 J. Soc. 1420, 1422 (1978).
49. Mark Buchanan, *Nexus: Small Worlds and the Groundbreaking Science of Networks* 107 (2002).
50. Granovetter, *supra* note 48, at 1428.
51. *Ibid.* at 1429 (describing two factors that have a role in changing the effects of threshold distributions, including "social structure").

This finding is consistent with behavioral ethics research. Granovetter's modeling shows how individual ethical decision-making, as influenced by relationship, creates significant conduct risk. When there is an in-group relationship between a wrongdoer and others in the group, the others' thresholds to unethical behavior are lowered. And if one or more of the wrongdoers is an important part of a network of related individuals, they possess an outsized ability to lower many thresholds all at once. This spreads bad behavior in an unpredictable and highly volatile manner—it becomes contagious. Thus, a company's social and organizational network—and who within it is making unethical decisions and committing unethical acts—can greatly impact the ethicality of the *entire* organization. This is how a few individual unethical decisions can translate into systemic behavioral ethics risk for a company.

Behavioral Ethics Risk: Managing a New Paradigm

The above offers a more accurate—and arguably more challenging—paradigm of GRC, one that is organized around individual unethical decision-making. This is the root cause of compliance failures and the driver of significant conduct risk facing companies. It begs the question: how can business leaders manage this newly identified risk?

The short answer is that behavioral ethics risk can be managed through the same means by which it originates. By understanding, targeting, and even harnessing the ethical decision-making processes occurring at the individual employee level, companies can increase compliance and build ethical culture. That is to say, they can increase GRC from the inside out, helping employees understand and adapt their own ethical decision-making to foster positive behavior. As individual ethical transgressions are lessened, so is the spread of bad conduct, allowing ethical culture to grow organically within the organization—all of which lessens behavioral ethics risk. While there are no quick fixes, the following offers a series of strategies companies can employ as part of their GRC efforts.

Assessing Individual Employees' Behavioral Ethics Risk

Companies can begin managing behavioral ethics risk at the hiring process by screening for it. While many companies look at past employment history, bankruptcies, and criminal violations in order to identify potential wrongdoers, these are imperfect indicators of individual ethical decision-making. Instead, companies can explicitly screen for propensity to make ethical decisions. For example, prospective or probationary employees can be asked to take the Defining Issues Test, which questions respondents on how they would address a series of moral vignettes, providing an ethicality assessment based on the principle of justice.[52] Another assessment, the Mach IV, determines a person's propensity toward Machiavellian-type behavior, or the lack of concern with conventional morality.[53] These diagnostic tools have been around for years and are well validated, yet they have not been widely used in business to identify conduct risk.

And more recently, a scale measuring rule orientation and behavior has been developed by researchers.[54] This tool may be particularly useful for companies because it assesses how an individual considers rules—whether rules should be followed in a rigid manner or are subject to exception. In other words, there is now a diagnostic that measures our feelings about rules and our propensity to rationalize rule breaking—essentially, what a person's threshold to unethical or illegal behavior might

52. *See* Kelly Richmond Pope, *Measuring the Ethical Propensity of Accounting Students: Mach IV Versus DIT*, 3 J. Acad. Ethics 89, 89–90 (2005).
53. *Ibid.* at 90.
54. *See* Adam Fine, et al., *Rule Orientation and Behavior: Development and Validation of a Scale Measuring Individual Acceptance of Rule Violation*, 22 Psychol. Pub. Pol'y & Law 314, 323 (2016).

be.[55] While companies must be careful how they collect and use diagnostic information, these assessments offer a baseline of individual behavioral ethics risk, a critical compliance metric.

Early-stage employees can be assessed for ethical decision-making in other ways. For example, Goldman Sachs invites its analyst interns seeking full-time employment to attend a rigorous training and orientation program.[56] Goldman personnel warn the analysts repeatedly that cheating on skills tests is not tolerated. In one test, which is not particularly difficult, interns are told they cannot conduct outside research yet are given access to computers with internet connections. Recently, Goldman dismissed 20 interns from the program for Googling answers, which was intentionally monitored by the firm. The true test was whether an intern could make an ethical decision in a highly competitive environment. Dismissing the violators not only eliminates future conduct risk emanating from the rule violators, but it also helps to build a culture of honesty by signaling firm values.[57]

Identifying and Monitoring Employees Posing Heightened Behavioral Ethics Risk

Once an employee joins a company, efforts can be directed at identifying and monitoring problematic ethical decision-making. Companies should start by identifying those individuals in the company's network who possess outsized ethical influence. These are the employees that by virtue of their position in the company's social or organizational hierarchy are "connectors"—those "prolific few who tie an entire . . . [organizational] network together."[58] As explained above, these employees have the ability to generate significant conduct risk and spread it throughout the firm.

How are these employees identified? The company's org chart is a useful starting point because it provides a sense of professional reach, but it only goes so far in showing ethical influence. As seen with the Wells Fargo fake accounts scandal, the CEO was not the origin or driver of the unethical behavior.[59] The true influencers were a few regional managers connected to the head of the community banking division; they were the "hubs" of the network through which behavioral compliance risk spread. Accordingly, compliance personnel need to identify those in the company who are the true catalysts of potentially unethical behavior. While most of the rhetoric regarding corporate culture focuses on "tone at the top," that may not be where the most significant behavioral ethics risk lies.

After it is determined who in the organization is an ethical influencer, they should be assessed for individual behavioral compliance risk. The diagnostic tools discussed earlier would provide one data point, but assessing risk is dynamic and multifaceted. Fortunately, conducting risk assessments as part of the GRC function is familiar to most companies. However, companies must keep in mind that they are trying to identify ethical decision-making risk, not the more familiar business process and enterprise risk.[60]

55. *Ibid.* at 315.
56. Julia La Roche, *This Is How the Goldman Sachs Analysts Who Got Fired Were Cheating*, Bus. Insider, October 19, 2015, www.businessinsider.com/goldman-sachs-analysts-fired-for-cheating-2015-10.
57. *See* John C. Hollwitz and Donna R. Pawlowski, *The Development of a Structured Ethical Integrity Interview for Pre-employment Screening*, 34 J. Bus. Comm. 203, 214–16 (1997) (outlining procedures for structured pre-employment ethics interviews).
58. Buchanan, *supra* note 49, at 114.
59. *See* Sales Practices Investigation Report, Independent Directors of the Board of Wells Fargo and Company 50 (April 10, 2017), www08.wellsfargomedia.com/assets/pdf/about/investor-relations/presentations/2017/board-report.pdf.
60. For a good discussion of corporate approaches to identifying legal, regulatory, and compliance risk, see generally, Robert C. Bird and Stephan Kim Park, *Turning Corporate Compliance into Competitive Advantage*, 19 U. Penn. J. Bus. L. 285 (2017).

One company taking the correct approach is Morgan Stanley, which now asks its risk and compliance officers to evaluate "material risk-takers."[61] For example, a trader who frequently hits trading limits, misses compliance trainings, or fails to take mandatory holidays imposed to uncover fraud would raise concern. Once identified, such an employee would be monitored for risk-taking behavior, and how they manage it would factor into promotion and compensation decisions. This could lead to bonus reductions or even termination for cause.

Ideally, however, a behavioral risk evaluation would consider many other factors that impact ethical decision-making, and do so more prospectively. Behavioral ethics research has demonstrated that factors related to stress and depleted mental resources cause ethical decision-making shortcuts, so assessments should consider if employees are under such strain—caused either by personal issues or company pressures.[62] Another evaluative tool is to identify employees who regularly rationalize. While this may be more difficult to objectively monitor, one way to assess the propensity to rationalize is to hold employee roundtables in which rule breaking and ethical dilemmas are discussed. Fairly quickly, employees will offer a host of rationalizations justifying various behaviors. Parsons, an international engineering company, hosts an internal website where it poses hypothetical ethics problems and asks employees to vote on how they should be resolved; the responses indicate what rationalizations are being employed by individuals and groups.[63] Finally, although counterintuitive, employees engaged in creative tasks are at heightened ethical risk.[64] Compliance personnel should assess business units and job categories where creativity is expected and add that to the behavioral risk assessment schedule. Specific behavioral risk factors will vary depending on an individual's place in an industry, a company, a business unit, and a sub-group—and will change over time—but thoughtful compliance professionals should be able to craft a behavioral risk matrix that considers many of these factors.[65]

For the employees who do exhibit heightened behavioral ethics risk, and even more so for those that are also ethical influencers, the company should allocate disproportionate compliance resources toward them. Such employees should receive more training, more monitoring, and be subject to more investigative inquiries. Put simply, compliance officers should be on a first-name basis with these employees. In addition, compliance tools should be tailored to these high-risk employees. Although it is framed as a management practice, global equipment and engineering consulting firm Barry-Wehmiller provides individualized ethics and compliance programing to its employees.[66] The company's CEO meets with each employee to understand their values, interests, goals, and personal and professional challenges. Employees are then slotted into an appropriate level of the firm's ethical leadership training curriculum.

61. Olivia Oran, *Wells Fargo Scandal Reignites Debate about Big Bank Culture*, REUTERS, September 28, 2016, www.reuters.com/article/us-wells-fargo-accounts-culture-analysis/wells-fargo-scandal-reignites-debate-about-big-bank-culture-idUSKCN11Y1S1.
62. *See* Francesca Gino, et al., *Unable to Resist Temptations: How Self-Control Depletion Promotes Unethical Behavior*, 115 ORG. BEHAVIOR & HUMAN DEC. MAKING PROCESSES 191 (2001). This, of course, requires companies to be introspective and honest about the pressures and incentives it is placing on employees.
63. See Scott Killingsworth, *Modeling the Message: Communicating Compliance through Organizational Values and Culture*, 25 GEO. J. LEGAL ETHICS 983 (2012).
64. Francesca Gino and Dan Ariely, *The Dark Side of Creativity: Original Thinkers Can Be More Dishonest*, 102 J. PERSONALITY & SOC. PSYCHOL. 445 (2012).
65. *See* ROGER MILES, CONDUCT RISK MANAGEMENT: USING A BEHAVIORAL APPROACH TO PROTECT YOUR BOARD AND FINANCIAL SERVICES BUSINESS 37, 161 (2015) (explaining reference points that inform risk profile and listing five factors that increase conduct risk).
66. *See* BOB CHAPMAN AND RAJ SISODIA, EVERYBODY MATTERS: THE EXTRAORDINARY POWER OF CARING FOR YOUR PEOPLE LIKE FAMILY 213–23 (2015) (explaining company's employee-centered approach to business).

Mitigating Behavioral Ethics Risk

Regardless of an employee's ethical risk profile, every company's compliance program should be looking for opportunities to increase employee ethical decision-making and behavior. While most companies' programs attempt to educate and train employees on legal doctrines and company rules, this ignores the System 1 process that dominates ethical decision-making. It is simply unrealistic to expect employees to memorize a litany of complex rules, identify when those rules apply in complex and fast-moving factual situations, and then harness their reflective thinking system to properly follow them—not to mention also guarding against System 2 motivated reasoning.

A more fruitful approach is to aim compliance interventions at the inflection points where decision-making becomes behavior. Not only is this approach more consistent with behavioral theory, it recognizes the practicalities of "what actually happens" with employee thinking.[67] The idea is that companies must "frame [their] training around . . . specific, risky job tasks" to ensure unethical employee decision-making is properly targeted.[68] Doing otherwise "pushes all of the 'transfer' work to the employee," and transfer is the critical step in the application of learned knowledge.[69]

For example, Broadcat, a start-up compliance provider, uses a series of checklists for its clients that are task specific and direct employee action. One called "Going Overseas on a Business Trip?" contains checkboxes for things such as getting company preapprovals for gifts and entertainment, securing computer files before travel, and carrying an ethics helpline phone number.[70] Although the checklist is simple and easy to understand, it is grounded in sophisticated behavioral science—it is a "precommitment device" for avoiding conduct risk. By committing to the company's antibribery provisions, and then being reminded of them while undertaking the task of overseas travel, employees are less likely to engage in risk-creating behavior when the temptation is highest.

A host of these types of "behavioral ethics nudges" are available to be integrated into existing compliance programs.[71] Probably the most ubiquitous example is asking employees to read and affirm an ethics-focused certification before they engage in behavior that poses compliance risk; for example, filling out expense reports, transferring client funds, or meeting with government officials. Studies show that reminding employees of morality before they act reduces dishonesty, likely because it prompts deeper System 2 reflection regarding the ethics surrounding the task.[72] This type of "just-in-time" compliance nudge was first used in the insurance business but is now considered standard practice in many companies. International Paper uses a similar strategy; instead of certifications, though, the company provides all employees with a wallet card containing ethics-related questions.[73] As employees consider business decisions, they will be reminded of the questions and more fully contemplate their ethical obligations.

Companies may also consider using more sophisticated behavioral strategies. JPMorgan uses proprietary software to monitor the email and telephone communications of its traders to ensure they "adhere to 'personal trading rules' and risk limits."[74] While this type of monitoring has been part of

67. Miles, *supra* note 65, at 63.
68. Ricardo Pellefone, *Keeping Compliance Simple*, www.thebroadcat.com/downloads.
69. *Ibid.* See also Susan Ambrose et al., How Learning Works: 7 Research-Based Principles for Smart Teaching (2010).
70. *Ibid.*
71. Haugh, *Nudging*, *supra* note 4, at 710–15 (discussing a number of nudges being used in business to increase employee ethicality).
72. *See* Dan Ariely, *The Honest Truth About Dishonesty* 39–53 (2012) (explaining the impact of asking participants to recall moral standard before engaging in behavior).
73. Francesca Gino, Lisa D. Ordonez and David Welsh, *How Unethical Behavior Becomes Habit*, Harv. Bus. Rev., September 4, 2014, https://hbr.org/2014/09/how-unethical-behavior-becomes-habit.
74. Portia Crowe, *JP Morgan Is Working on a New Employee Surveillance Program*, Bus. Insider, April 8, 2015, www.businessinsider.com/jpmorgans-employee-surveillance-program-2015-4.

corporate compliance and risk management for years, JPMorgan's efforts are noteworthy because the bank's software algorithms attempt to predict unethical or illegal trading behavior and stop it before it occurs. Such "predictive monitoring" uses a series of alerts to nudge traders, and alert compliance staff, if they are about to violate a company or legal rule.[75]

Finally, not all behavioral ethics risk management strategies are aimed at intervening to stop unethical behavior; just as important is fostering ethical acts. Research shows that compliance messaging is more effective when it demonstrates that ethical behaviors are widely engaged in and supported.[76] The reason is likely related to how individuals rationalize their conduct. Positive compliance messaging of this type combats the notion that ethical decision-making is an isolated act, therefore bad behavior is somehow normal.[77] That means companies need to share genuine stories of their ethics and compliance successes, conveying the message that the majority of the company is committed to making ethical decisions.

One way to do this that takes advantage of network theory is to leverage ethical employees who are hubs of influence as compliance ambassadors. This can take many forms. One is that they can be asked to identify gaps in compliance and "bring those issues back to HQ, with suggestions on how to fix them."[78] This not only helps compliance officers who cannot anticipate every possible compliance risk, but it also strengthens in-group ethical behavior.[79] Another behavioral-focused approach is to ask these ambassadors to simply talk about ethics and compliance with their co-workers, including temptations and pressures that may cause ethical decision-making lapses. When System 1 biases and heuristics or System 2 rationalizations arise, they should be drawn out and explored. The goal is for the ambassador, possibly with the help of compliance personnel, to raise "conscious awareness [of] certain patterns of self-exculpatory reasoning, and to flag them as suspicious."[80] That way, employees will be less likely to use bounded ethical decision-making in the future.

Conclusion

The goal of this chapter has been to outline key insights from research in behavioral ethics, criminology, and network theory to provide a new paradigm through which to consider corporate governance, risk management, and compliance. By focusing on the core driver of compliance failures, individual unethical decision-making, the GRC functions at companies can be better understood and improved upon. A behavioral ethics risk management approach is best positioned to achieve the overarching goal of all companies' GRC efforts—the reduction of conduct risk to allow for more efficient and effective business operation.

75. Hugh Son, *JPMorgan Algorithm Knows You're a Rogue Employee Before You Do*, Bloomberg, April 5, 2015, www.bloomberg.com/news/articles/2015-04-08/jpmorgan-algorithm-knows-you-re-a-rogue-employee-before-you-do.
76. *See* Robert B. Cialdini et al., *Managing Social Norms for Persuasive Impact*, 1 Soc. Influence 3, 11–12 (2006); Lynn S. Paine, *Managing for Organizational Integrity*, 72 Harv. Bus. Rev. 106, 111 (1994) (explaining that "[e]mployees may rebel against programs that stress penalties" and view compliance programs that do not address root causes of misconduct skeptically).
77. *See* James William Coleman, *The Criminal Elite* 197 (5th ed. 2002) (describing the claim of relative acceptability/normality rationalization).
78. Richard Bistrong, *Are Your Sales Teams Compliance Ambassadors?*, FCPABlog, February 24, 2016, www.fcpablog.com/blog/2016/2/24/richard-bistrong-are-your-sales-teams-compliance-ambassadors.html.
79. Linda Klebe Trevino et al., *(Un)ethical Behavior in Organizations*, 65 Ann. R. Psychol. 635, 643 (2014); Gino, Ayal and Ariely, *supra* note 42, at 393.
80. Joseph Heath, *Business Ethics and Moral Motivation: A Criminological Perspective*, 83 J. Bus. Ethics 595, 611 (2008).

5 DECONSTRUCTING RISK

Practical Understanding and Perspectives

Kevin Meredith

Context, Principles and Actively Managing Risk

Dreams are being pursued and realized every second of every day. Some of these dreams may be simply small, and others may appear to be too big to understand. Some of them are dismissed for the wrong reason, and others that never live up to their potential while receiving too much attention. Some of these dreams will seem to have the tiniest of ambition, and some will be so bold and massive that the idea alone forces history to yield to its influence.

And at the very same time, other people's dreams are raining down the debris of their destruction—or perhaps even worse, dreams that were never given the opportunity to realize their true potential. What is the buzzword from one generation is now the disparaging punchline of a meme. This is the world that most people actively try to forget, especially when it is their own ideas and efforts that are crashing down.

American writer, publisher, artist and philosopher Elbert Green Hubbard said that "The line between failure and success is so fine . . . that we are often on the line and do not know it."

The same could be said about risk and opportunity.

A more direct example to explore risk and opportunity can be found when Hubbard's generic "line" is replaced with a high-wire tightrope.

A high-wire tightrope comprises braided rope or metal connecting two points elevated at least 20 feet above the ground. The skill of funambulism, tightrope walking, dates to ancient Greece. Its popularity peaked in the period spanning the 1850s to the mid-1900s in the circus, except for a few spectacles with skyscrapers and global landmarks.

The circus was the most popular spectator event of the day. From custom-built arenas to traveling tent cities, the circus entertained people with peculiar and spectacular feats. Each subsequent act would amaze live audiences as one performance after another would outdo its predecessors from the beginning to the end of the show. The high-wire acts were often the pinnacle of the experience.

Cornelius Sullivan was born in Australia the day after Christmas 1899. Less than 20 years later he performed a seemingly impossible feat that no person in history is known to have ever previously accomplished: a full somersault on the tightwire. Within five years, Con Calleano (as his stage name) took hold, and he was employed by Ringling Bros. and Barnum & Bailey Combined Circus in the United States. Ultimately, he was the star performer of Ringling Bros. where he received a salary of

DOI: 10.4324/9781351107242-7

three quarters of a million dollars per year in today's dollars and billing as "The Australian Wizard of the Wire."[1]

Most of the 21st century has seen the spotlight in high wire shift from the big top to seemingly ever more demanding media events at spectacular natural and man-made locations around the world. One of the most famous modern tightrope walkers is Nik Wallenda. He is known as the "King of the High Wire" and the holder of 11 Guinness World Records related to his craft. In 2012 he became the first person to cross over the entire width of Niagara Falls, and a year later he became the first person to walk across the Grand Canyon on a tightrope. He was also part of a 25-foot high-wire act team in 2001 that broke the record for the tallest four-person pyramid walk on a tightrope.

What can we learn from these thrill seekers and acrobats?

They achieved the highest acclaim of their profession through a lifetime commitment to furthering their individual skills. No single magnificent act was accomplished without relentless preparation and prior demonstrated performance.

No matter how famous or wealthy they are, the entirety or themselves remained intensely focused into the pursuit of their craft.

They were in the family business, and both were exposed to the roots of their craft at a very early age.

While these factors are certainly shared by Con and Nik, it is all best summed up by Nik in his own words, as he recalled one of the hardest moments in his career. In 2017 Nik Wallenda and members of his family fell practicing for a performance similar to the record-holding four-person pyramid. Some of them crashed more than 20 feet to the venue's floor. (*Note*: They do not train or perform with a safety net because they do not want to practice with a false sense of protection.) The next day Nik was back on the wire, and he addressed the crowd about the fall:

> What you have to understand is this is our passion. This isn't a job to us, this is our life. My great-grandfather said, "Life is on the wire, everything else is just waiting." I can tell you I feel no greater peace than when I'm on that wire. . . . Through tragedy we always say. . . . I've said my entire life, the Wallendas continue on through triumph and tragedy."[2]

In a more abstract way, the wire itself can constructively inform the understanding of risk and opportunity. The rope and wire that is used in tightrope performances is almost always braided, and its total diameter is usually between 0.75 and 1 inch. There is not a single monolithic wire or fiber, but rather it comprises sub-bundles of wires and fibers (strands), which can in turn be made up of numerous yarns that can comprise hundreds of individual fibers.

> *Did you know?* "Twisted ropes are built up in three steps. First, fibers are gathered and spun into yarns. A number of these yarns are then formed into strands by twisting. The strands are then twisted together to lay the rope. The twist of the yarn is opposite to that of the strand, and that in turn is opposite to that of the rope. It is this counter-twist, introduced with each successive operation, which holds the final rope together as a stable, unified object."[3]

1. Mark Valentine St Leon biography article, "Colleano, Con (Cornelius) (1899–1973)", [1] This article was published in *Australian Dictionary of Biography*, Volume 13, (MUP), 1993
2. www.bradenton.com/news/local/article132123984.html
3. https://en.wikipedia.org/wiki/Rope

Any single fiber or yarn is never as strong as the entirety of the braided rope or wire. The tightrope pioneers discussed above used their understanding, practice, experience and focus to effectively shift the mental interpretation of the rope's diameter. They are absolutely in the present and aware of their reality, but they have developed a level of mastery that has the mental equivalent of using a much wider rope.

On the other hand, if the average person on the street to were asked to climb up a 20-foot pole and walk across a rope to another pole 20 feet away, they would likely use their mental models to make the actual diameter feel skinnier. The lack of practice and experience would likely enhance fear and doubt. This could produce a potentially insurmountable barrier to the individual's ability to achieve the desired outcome. And for about 5% of the population that suffers from acrophobia (the fear of heights),[4] the thought of just going up the pole would be enough to make the task seem impossible—regardless of the rope's thickness.

While they might seem unrelated, almost everything that is needed to understand and manage risks and opportunities has been touched on with the community "Nestled in the Shadows of the Mountains," the aerialists performing their craft and the rope that is the medium of their high-wire magic. Such abstractions will be referenced throughout the chapters of this textbook from a diverse range of perspectives. That being said, it is important to shift attention to some of the more grounded and foundational aspects of risk: the vocabulary, definitions and other basics concerning risks and opportunities.

Terms

The first is risk itself.

Risk—the assessed potential detriment to objectives.

Assessed is used here to demonstrate that risk is calculated. A calculation must include a minimum of two variables (likelihood and consequence) to be meaningful. This is covered in more detail in the following section.

Potential is used to capture the fact that risk is future leaning and recognition that even with strong empirical data, chance plays a role and there is uncertainty around the ultimate assessment of detriment.

Detriment is used to show that the impact of a risk works against a given objective or set of objectives. It also shows a causal relationship exists.

Objectives are used to define the desired outcome or outcomes that are being pursued. It is from this baseline that both risks and opportunities deviate above and below expectations, respectively.

This is not the standard definition found in most dictionaries and established international standards. The *Oxford English Dictionary* defines risk as "the possibility of something bad happening at some time in the future; a situation that could be dangerous or have a bad result."[5] The main problem with this definition is that one cannot sufficiently understand risk by simply understanding the "possibility" of something "bad" in the future. Again, there must be at least two variables to meaningfully define risk, and this definition only accounts for one. The other concern is that the term "bad" is subjective and lacks nuance or insight as to which specific part of the risk is "bad."

4. Misiewicz Z, Hiekkalinna T, Paunio T, et al. A genome-wide screen for acrophobia susceptibility loci in a Finnish isolate. *Sci Rep*. 2016;6:39345. Published 2016 Dec 20. doi:10.1038/srep39345
5. www.oxfordlearnersdictionaries.com/us/definition/english/risk_1

The International Organization for Standardization (ISO) defines risk as the "effect of uncertainty on objectives."[6]

The concerns with ISO's definition in the ISO 31000 standard are:

1. In practical terms, risk is not only created by uncertainty. There are empirical data that predict when and where a risk will be realized. There is always uncertainty around such a prediction, but this uncertainty is not the equivalent of risk itself. It is a component of it. A detailed explanation as to why this is insufficient is laid out in the next section.
2. ISO also suggests that risk is synonymous with "chance" by suggesting risk can be positive or negative. This stance overreaches what risk is and obfuscates any need to make a distinction between risks and opportunities. There is agreement that chance is always present with the potential to impact risks and opportunities, but that does not mean that they are synonymous.
3. The definition requires three footnotes to support the definition. This could lead one to conclude that the definition is insufficient if it requires so many supplemental clarifiers.

"Note 1 to entry: An effect is a deviation from the expected. It can be positive, negative or both, and can address, create or result in opportunities and threats.

Note 2 to entry: Objectives can have different aspects and categories, and can be applied at different levels.

Note 3 to entry: Risk is usually expressed in terms of *risk sources* (3.4), potential *events* (3.5), their *consequences* (3.6) and their *likelihood* (3.7)."[7]

Opportunity—the assessed potential benefit to objectives.

Assessed is used here to reiterate that opportunity is calculated. A calculation must include a minimum of two variables (likelihood and consequence) to be meaningful. This is covered in more detail in the following section.

Potential is used to capture the fact that opportunity is future leaning and a recognition that even with strong empirical data, chance plays a role and there is uncertainty around the ultimate assessment of benefit.

Benefit is used to show that the impact of a risk works against a given objective or set of objectives. It also shows a causal relationship exists.

Objectives are used to define the desired outcome or outcomes that are being pursued. It is from this baseline that both risks and opportunities deviate above and below expectations, respectively.

Risk and Opportunity Management

ISO defines risk management as "coordinated activities to direct and control an organization with regard to risk."[8]

It is important to note here that there are often multiple forms of risk and opportunity management that exist in nearly every organization. The first is a formal system aligned with the expectations of ISO and other systems that has very defined expectations for what constitutes compliance and a healthy risk and opportunity management system. At the same time, there is a second type of risk and opportunity management that is frequently misunderstood. These are the informal processes

6. www.iso.org/obp/ui/#iso:std:iso:31000:ed-2:v1:en
7. www.iso.org/obp/ui/#iso:std:iso:31000:ed-2:v1:en
8. www.iso.org/obp/ui/#iso:std:iso:31000:ed-2:v1:en:term:3.1

that employees utilize and are frequently more prevalent in organizational cultures that have a "do as I say not as I do" leadership. This is like the shadowy, lurking figure in the background when everyone has their attention on the main action. There is a good chance that this approach is operating with good intention, although it can lead to derelict and cumulative backsliding that creates its own significant risks.

Additional definitions will be included throughout the text and defined inline.

With a requisite foundation in place, the following section is designed to start building the structure to secure that the current understanding of risks and opportunities can be applied in everyday activities. Only from there would one be able to protect core investments with the solid bones of vital principles and pursue new growth to enhance it through active management insights.

The following list comprises six principles that have been informed through years of practical, hands-on experience understanding and managing risks, opportunities and the relationships between them. This is not an academic collection. It has been informed and applies regardless of sector, industry and organization motive. This collection is called the "Six Secrets of Risk," and represents six simple principles to more effectively understand, manage and prevent risks from negatively impacting desired outcomes.

Secrets of Risk

RISK IS MULTIVARIATE

It is impossible to talk about risk in any meaningful way using a single dimension of evaluation.

Simply knowing that something will happen with no understanding of or relationship to the impact's magnitude is insufficient to know anything meaningful about the risk being faced.

Using historical data and the widely acknowledged understanding of life on earth, anyone who reads this book can predict with very high confidence (not 100% but really, really, really close) that they, and everyone else they know, will die at some point in the future. There are zero confirmed cases of an individual that has escaped this reality.

(*Note*: That does not mean that it has not happened, because the absence of evidence is not the same thing as evidence of absence.)

Life insurance is one way to demonstrate this. As people age, they have increased risk factors for death. The older someone is, the more expensive the life insurance policy. In general, a $1 million life insurance plan's monthly cost for an individual who is 65 years old will be exponentially higher compared to the cost for someone who is 25 years old. Life insurance plans also see dramatically different pricing based on assessed health (lower health equals higher rates), the individual's gender (woman pay about one-third less), lifestyle choices (smokers can pay 200% more than nonsmokers) and many other considerations.

Simply knowing that someone is expected to die is insufficient, though.

The insurance companies build their business by obsessively understanding risk factors of the individuals they insure and minimizing their own financial risk by adjusting the monthly premiums to participate in their insurance programs. The insurance companies want you to live. They continuously strive to improve predictions on who they insure so they minimize the payouts. The more people who pay in without ever having to disburse funds for claims, the better their financial position. (*Note*: It has also been reported that fewer than 2% of term policies ever result in a death claim, which certainly helps ensure the coffers are filled.)[9]

This is where there is greatest alignment between the insurance providers and the individuals being insured exists: they both do better when the insured are alive and do not seek a claim.

9. www.huffpost.com/entry/the-life-insurance-indust_b_1937246

The insurance companies can only fully calculate risk to themselves when they look at the consequence of payouts. In this case, the consequence is paying out a $1 million claim. It is a relatively straightforward impact.

However, this is where things diverge from the insured individual's perspective. There are many more immediate and long-term consequences that remain for the survivors of the insured. Were they single or married? Did they have children? If so, how many? Did they have long-term obligations (e.g., mortgage debt)? What was their contribution to society? And what opportunity costs to society are now lost?

It is only when one assesses such impacts and the likelihood of occurrence concurrently that one can meaningfully understand and manage risk.

A natural next question would be to see if there are other dimensions in addition to likelihood and consequence. Does it matter if something has a high likelihood of occurrence and consequence but there is only a small sliver of time in which the conditions for both can exist?

From an absolute perspective, does not it matter if someone were to die today compared to some point further into the future? In a year? In ten years? In 50 years? The ending is the same; everyone should be able to agree that there is all practical likelihood that death is the outcome.

Yet, the impact or consequence of any individual's death is absolutely dependent on when, and possibly how, an individual dies.

For example, it could be argued that a new parent with a growing family would be much more impacted if today was "their day" compared to the same thing happening 50 years from now. The impact cascades to other components of the system at different rates depending on context and relationships.

Currently, astrophysics predicts with high certainty that the future of Earth and its solar system is likely to follow devastating future that is shared by hundreds of billions of others. The likelihood of a catastrophic end to our billions of years of stability will go away. On the human time frame, this is nearly an unfathomable point in the future.

The most informed scientific guess on the age of the human species is about 300,000 years.[10] Of that, the previous 10,000 years have coalesced in the major epochs of civilizations rising and falling. And the last 200 years have demonstrated what humans are capable to produce in a short period of time.

Yet, all of these significant milestones in the progress of humanity are simply rounding errors to the estimated 4.5-billion-year-old Earth or 14-billion-year-old universe. If an advanced lifeform visited every 300,000 years, there is a good chance (99.997857%) that they would not have even known about human evolution. Time and timing matter immensely.

More generally, if the time frame is not considered, a meaningful discussion about risk—and perhaps more importantly risk management—is not possible. The conditions must be within a relevant period of time to result in the expected outcome. Without this dimension, actions taken to mitigate risk or accelerate opportunity will be less likely to produce the intended outcome.

In certain circumstances it might be beneficial to consider additional variables based on a given set of common influences in a particular discipline, industry or organization When this is considered, the advice of legendary football coach of the New York Giants, Bill Parcells should be applied: "I don't look at a problem and put variables in there that don't affect it." Only the most essential variables should be added as a standard evaluation of risk.

10. Eleanor M. L. Scerri, Mark G. Thomas, Andrea Manica, Philipp Gunz, Jay T Stock, Chris Stringer, Matt Grove, Huw S. Groucutt, Axel Timmermann, G. Philip Rightmire, Francesco d'Errico (August 1, 2018). Did Our Species Evolve in Subdivided Populations across Africa, and Why Does It Matter? Trends in Ecology & Evolution 33 (8): 582–594.

RISK IS RELATIONAL

In the last few decades there have amazing breakthroughs in our understanding of living organisms. One of the most revealing is the relationship between mycelium and trees. Mycelium is part of a fungus comprising a network of very fine, hairlike structures that surround and integrate with tree roots.

This previously unknown, and still not fully understood, underground network connects entire forests and has the ability to communicate and redistribute resources (nutrients such as water, nitrogen, carbon and minerals) to the collective benefit of the broader ecosystem.

A study from Suzanne Simard concerning a Canadian forest was able to show that an established tree had mycelium connectivity and, based on microsatellite DNA analysis, it had relationships to 47 other trees.[11] And the mycelium supports not a single species of trees but an entire forest. There is a symbiotic relationship between the fungi and the trees that is collectively beneficial to a broader set of stakeholders. This illustrates how relationships can be vital to those that are not even aware of them and that the scalability of networks of relationships is exponential.

Paul Stamets is a mycologist who is seen by many as the leader of the field across many different domains and disciplines. His TED talk has been viewed nearly 7 million times. It is in this storied forum that he attests the largest living organism in the world, a one-cell-thick mycelium mat in Oregon in an old-growth forest, is estimated to be 2,000 years old and covers an area of 2,200 acres.[12] One can only imagine the web of relationships required to sustain such a diverse, dynamic network for such a protracted period of time.

To fully understand risk, one must have a deep appreciation of both obvious and seemingly invisible relationships.

There must be causality between at least one other factor for a risk to be realized. Many times, there are multiple factors that act as contributing causes and root causes.

All risks have a relationship to multiple factors (as described in secret 1 above). That is not what is being said here. The major point here is that nothing—not even risk—exists in a complete vacuum or isolated island.

Furthermore, because risk is relational, it can accumulate. This accumulation can occur linearly, like links in a chain, or nonlinearly, like nodes in a network.

There is one additional way to use the rope analogy when developing a mental model about risk that builds on the tightrope construction from earlier in the chapter, with a minor twist.

It can be beneficial to consider each fiber as the most basic form of risk. Each individual fiber can take on many shapes. The thickness and shape of an individual fiber is dependent on three variables (impact, likelihood, and time). Keeping track of all the individual fibers can be difficult because they are so numerous. That being said, the effort required to alter an individual fiber is relatively low.

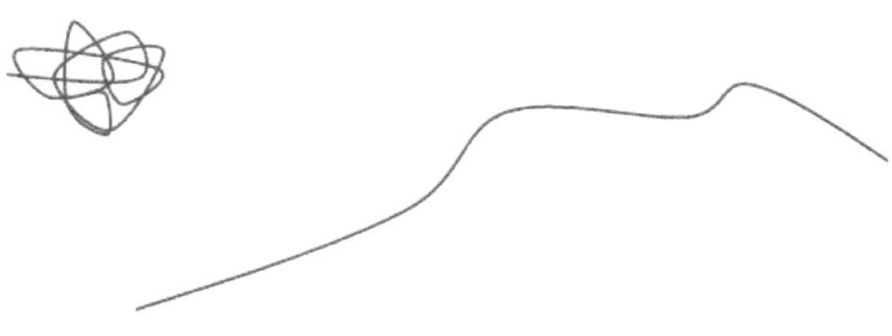

Figure 5.1 That being said, the effort required to alter an individual fiber is relatively low.

11. www.zoology.ubc.ca/bdg/pdfs_bdg/2015%20Spring/Simard%20et%20al.%202012.pdf
12. www.ted.com/talks/paul_stamets_6_ways_mushrooms_can_save_the_world#t-446084 (9:50 seconds in)

Multiple fibers can form into a yarn that represents greater risk. That is, a composite set of fibers (risks) form a bigger risk. The number of fibers and the way the yarn is formed impacts its strength and influences the options available to ultimately mitigate its impact. There are typically fewer individual yarns compared to the quantity of individual fibers, however, they require more effort to alter. It is much more difficult to separate an individual fiber from a yarn than it is when it is a separate entity. It also takes more resources to significantly alter threads with greater profiles when all other factors remain constant.

Figure 5.2 It also takes more resources to significantly alter threads with greater profiles when all other factors remain constant.

Multiple yarns can be used to make ropes and fabrics, both of which represent greater risk. Ropes are in the same form as yarn and are made in a similar fashion as when fibers are made into yarns. The number of strings of yarn and the way the rope is formed impacts the strength and influences the options available to ultimately mitigate its impact. There are typically fewer individual ropes compared to individual yarns and fibers, however, they require more effort to alter. Likewise, it is even more difficult to separate an individual fiber from a rope than it is a yarn or a separate entity. It also takes more resources to significantly alter ropes to prevent risks from being realized in ropes with larger profiles when all other factors remain constant.

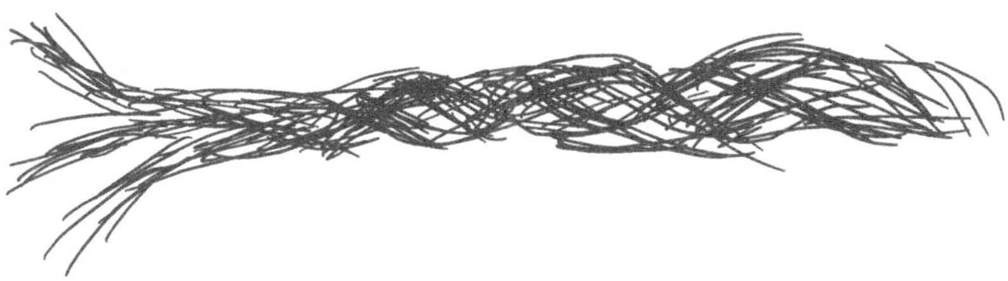

Figure 5.3 It also takes more resources to significantly alter ropes to prevent risks from being realized in ropes with larger profiles when all other factors remain constant.

Textiles are the most advanced composition of fibers and are formed by interlacing yarns together. This represents the most complex type of risk. Having deep knowledge of the system as well as the pedigree of each yarn and fiber helps ensure that the impact of each cause and risk is understood when it is more deeply integrated. There are typically the fewest textiles in a portfolio of risk compared to the building components. It takes more resources to mitigate textile risk, as it has the most modes of failure and uses.

Figure 5.4 It takes more resources to mitigate textile risk, as it has the most modes of failure and uses.

The strength of cause and effect can be at the fiber, yarn, rope or fabric. The more dense or the higher the "weight," the stronger the relationship between cause and effect. For example, a ship docked at the terminal requires a thick rope to hold it in place. One single fiber or yarn would most likely be insufficient at maintaining the ship at port.

RISK ACCUMULATES

The likelihood of a risk being realized must take cumulative impacts into account when there is more than one source or contributor to cause. Let's say that the goal is to flip a "head" on a coin and then immediately roll a "four" on a die (finally, a non-morbid use of the word). The probability of flipping a "head" on a fair coin and then immediately rolling a "four" on a fair die are two related outcomes for our goal, however, the result of one has no direct influence on the result of the other (independence). The probability of flipping a "head" is 1 out of 2, or 50% (it will either be a head or tail), and the probability of rolling a "four" is 1 in 6, or 16%.

The cumulative probability that one will achieve the desired outcome of a "head" and "four" is 1 out 12, or 8.3%. However, the goal is not just to have any order of achieving a "head" on the coin and a "four" on the die, but to get a "head" and then roll a "four" on the first roll. In this scenario, one must accomplish both in sequence, meaning if one flips a head but does not roll a four, the player needs to start the whole sequence over.

Now let's say that someone just did the experiment and it took 40 attempts. It is important to know that this is within the confines of a deterministic system, which means that the likelihood that an outcome will result beyond heads and tails on the coin and one through six on the die are inconsequentially small. Please note, there are "known unknowns" and "unknown unknowns" that prevent us from saying that such possibilities do not exist.

> "I just tried this experiment, and it took me two tries. Your math is wrong." Well, this is called probability theory, and it needs to be applied across a meaningful set of data. Probability and statistics are approximations of reality. In order for them to be optimally insightful, the right conditions must be applied, and their limitations must be understood.

A single or series of *dependent* factors can realize risk, such as when B can only occur if A happens first. Please note that A may or may not necessarily cause B to happen, but without A happening, B could not.

A series of *independent* factors can also realize risk, if B can occur regardless of any relationship to A, yet A contributes to the overall risk by influencing composite likelihood or significance.

The ability to understand dependent and independent relationships and their impact on complexity is important if one really is interested in managing risks and opportunities.

Can you catch and throw a single ball six consecutive times without dropping it?

How about two balls?

How about three? Or 11?

In each of these scenarios, there are the same exact basic principles (the physics don't change) acting on the system. Yet many people (not you, of course) would struggle to thrive at the three-ball juggling progression of this exercise.

Why? What changes when we go from a single ball to two balls to three balls? Is it simply three times as hard to juggle one ball as it is to juggle three?

Is it complicated or complexity that is a major contributor to risk and the ability to juggle?

It is not simply a linear progression as one adds each additional unit and total quantity of items being juggled, because there are multiple elements that have dynamic relationships.

One specific reason for this is risk stack-up.

The individual juggling has the least demanding task when simply tossing and catching a single ball to oneself. There is only one object and two primary tasks to accomplish (toss and catch). Now when an additional ball is added, there is one additional step of transferring one ball from one hand to the other as well as an additional constraint of increased pressure from shorter time cycles per related task. Correspondingly, there is less time to make adjustments to errors, and the impact accumulated errors grows. Can one accurately model and predict when and how these errors will progress for every person that tries to juggle for the first time?

> FYI: By some estimates, only about 15% of the general population can juggle at least three balls, just one out of a million people can juggle six balls, and the world record for juggling is 11 balls!

This principle is called tolerance stack-up in engineering. The basic principle is that each component of an assembly or system that integrates together has the potential to introduce minor errors that accumulate variation and can ultimately impact form, fit and function. In most cases it holds true that the higher the accuracy, the lower the impact of tolerance stacking. In reality, it is often more costly to process a component with higher tolerance. The tighter the accepted tolerance, the more likely the accumulated errors that impact the final assembly. That being said, there are limits on how loose tolerance can be too. If there is too much tolerance, there is greater opportunity for loose fittings and premature failure to occur.

Stack-up is not free. There are vast differences in the architecture, engineering, and construction (AEC) and the aerospace industries with respect to tolerance stack-up. Aerospace is defined by very high tolerances with very highly skilled and specialized workers. Construction-engineering firms drive a bunch of over-engineered solutions because they have the ultimate responsibility. The architect's designs are translated by engineers to ensure the project can be produced to given constraints and requirements. Construction contractors are paid to produce it. Almost all use various trades to complete the project, many of which are subcontracted out. There is a high rate of variability in the quality of works that are done because many works use low-skilled workers. As a result, there is a penalty because things that are over-designed and overbuilt cost more. They also use more natural resources than are actually required. Big variability in quality of the work is mitigated by the over-engineering and overbuilding.

This vicious cycle is manifested in many different ways but exists in some form in every sector of the economy—for profit, nonprofit and government. Over-regulation is an example of government de-risking its responsibility. Over-regulation can actually drag down performance and hinder progress. It can also protect entire populations of innocent stakeholders from significant negative externalities.

With risk, the stack-up or accumulation can occur following many different pathways (linear, nonlinear, regressive, progressive, incremental and catastrophic). Risk can also scale with cascading effects similar to an avalanche that gets bigger and more forceful as it progresses down the mountainside.

It is the multitudes of these pathways and inability to completely characterize them that contributes to the connection between complexity and risk.

RISK IS CORRELATED WITH COMPLEXITY

Complexity is a seemingly straightforward concept that is often condensed to being the opposite of simplicity. When one places these two on opposite sides of a seesaw, there is often a failure to appreciate how difficult it can be to accurately define complexity. More importantly, there is an increased chance that the wrong decisions will be made because management is unaware that complexity requires specific actions to reduce risk that are unique to this domain.

And while the relationships between words are being explored, the distinction between complicated and complex is important. Far too often these words are used interchangeably. Complex and complicated are not synonyms.

Very simple things can be complicated.

If there are two people that have three children—two girls and one boy—and each of their children has the desire to have three of their own children, ultimately the original two people are the proud grandparents of six grandchildren, with each child producing grandchildren. How many grandchildren are there, and how many are from each parent?

OK, that is a trick question. There is not enough information to fully answer that question.

The real point here is that this is actually a very simple math problem in which the answer is directly provided in the question.

$$3 \text{ children} \times 2 \text{ grandchildren per child} = 6 \text{ grandchildren}$$

It is the wording of the question that makes this complicated, primarily because there is a lot of superfluous information here that makes the question complicated. The wording of the problem forces you to expend more mental energy than should be required to do a simple arithmetic problem ($3 \times 2 = 6$) because it is overly complicated, not because it is complex.

Very simple things can be complicated at the unit level, yet the same is not necessarily true for complexity. While the component parts can be very simple, it is their relationships, interactions and other contributors that yield complexity. To help leaders distinguish between the two, it is suggested that they realign their mental maps to associate complicated as a synonym for confusing predictability than it is for the commonly attributed complexity.

One way to look at complexity is outlined by evolutionary biologist Richard Dawkins. In *The Blind Watchmaker*,[13] he asserts that there are multiple conditions that are required to properly define complexity in the natural world:

1. Heterogeneity and "many partedness"—"A car is heterogeneous: unlike a blancmange, almost any portion of the car is different from other portions." And, "Two halves of any two cars do not make a whole and functioning car."
2. Probability and intent—"A complex thing is something whose constituent parts are arranged in a way that is unlikely to have arisen by chance alone." "Hitting upon the lucky number that opens the bank's safe is the equivalent . . . of hurling scrap metal around at random and happening to assemble a Boeing 747. Of all the millions of unique and, with hindsight equally improbable, positions of the combination lock, only one opens the lock. Similarly, of all the millions of unique and, with hindsight equally improbable, arrangements of a heap of junk, only one (or very few) will fly. The uniqueness of the arrangement that flies, or that opens the safe, is nothing to do with hindsight. It is specified in advance."
3. Hierarchy and relationships—"If we wish to understand how a machine or living body works, we look to its component parts and ask how they interact with each other. If there is a complex thing that we do not yet understand, we can come to understand it in terms of simpler parts that we do already understand. . . . We peel our way down the hierarchy, until we reach units so simple that, for everyday purposes, we no longer feel the need to ask questions about them."

13. Richard Dawkins, *The Blind Watchmaker*, 1986.

In the *Harvard Business Review*'s "Learning to Live With Complexity",[14] the authors link the physical and electronic networks and systems that have become increasingly interconnected over recent decades to higher complexity and risk globally. These systems are "imbued with features that may operate in patterned ways but whose interactions are continually changing." Like Dawkins, the authors also provide a list of three features that should be considered to understand if something is complex.

1. *Multiplicity*, referring to the number of potentially interacting elements.
2. *Interdependence*, relating to how connected those elements are.
3. *Diversity*, having to do with the degree of their heterogeneity.

The greater the multiplicity, interdependence and diversity, the greater the complexity.

Author Larry Haas, an expert in helping organizations navigate change when they face challenges has a helpful heuristic to help understand identify complexity and risk. In his book *SOS to ROI* he introduces the "Complexity Monster" as a construct to describe significant role that complexity plays in creating risks. If it can be accurately modeled with sustained, predictive accuracy over time, there is a good chance it is not complex. Complex systems are very difficult to model because of many of the factors identified above. Additionally, as noted in secret 1 above, time and timing are significant contributors to understanding and managing risk in any dynamic system.

Last, essayist Nassim Nicholas Taleb has created a series of paradigm-shifting works with his collections of essays. In his best-selling book *The Black Swan*, Taleb connects complexity, fragility and our connectedness as breeding grounds for future significant risks to be realized in expected and unforeseen ways. And unlike the premise of the title *HBR* article above, which suggests the future must succumb to complexity as an indefinite sidekick, Taleb rings a much stronger warning bell to the future if institutions and societies do not take more active steps to dismantle systemic risks by deliberately reducing complexity.

For example, when another shape is considered as a *dodecahedron* (3D polygon with 12 sides), the formula for the area of a 12-sided shape is equal to the total of each individual side's area. In this case, each surface is in the shape of a trapezoid which is calculated by the following formula: $1/2(b_1 + b_2) \times h$.

This is a regular dodecahedron, which means all the faces are the same size and shape. Once the area of one side is calculated, it simply has to be multiplied by 12.

Before that can be accomplished, there is an additional step to take. It is unlikely that the height of the trapezoid will be provided. One still has to calculate the height by drawing a vertical reference line connecting the two parallel sides together to form a right triangle. Once that is accomplished, trigonometric functions can be applied to calculate the height of the trapezoid.

All these additional steps increase the potential risk that the wrong calculation will result. Adding the dimension of time or the desire to predict the influence of each vector arrow contributing to the risk could be enough to push the example on the right from simply a complicated problem to a complex one. In either case, it is hard to argue that the simple cause on the left is easier to understand and therefore manage compared to the figure at the right.

RISK IS CONTEXTUAL

There is a bustling small city that is growing its regional presence and in the heart of its historic downtown. This could be any city, but for illustration purposes Ontario, California, is chosen. On the main strip, there are several banks that support the financial needs of local residents and businesses.

14. https://hbr.org/2011/09/learning-to-live-with-complexity

One of these financial institutions is Bank of America (BoA). It is unlikely that there were more than a few hundred thousand dollars in the vault at any given time (individual bank locations typically keep enough cash to cover its transaction needs; the FDIC cash reserve requirement that resulted from the Great Depression only exists at a composite corporate level). In this case, BoA maintains about $100,000 cash on hand.

Now compare that to a bank down the street that is owned by Citizen's Business Bank, a regional financial institution primarily focused on supporting small businesses. Their vault is exactly the same make and size and handles the same volume of transactions as BoA up the street, so they also keep about $100,000 of cash in the vault.

The world's most prolific bank vault robber is casing both banks, unbeknownst to local authorities or bank management. The robber is facing the same outcome (payday if not caught and jail time if caught), regardless of the bank chosen.

All things equal, which bank is facing a greater risk? Is there enough information provided?

Without knowing specifics, it is likely that a large financial institution that is one of the largest banks in one of the largest economies of the world is quite likely to hold many times more resources under management compared to a regional bank.

The regional bank may also face higher cascading risks if their vault was the recipient of the heist. One of the drivers of commercial banking usage is the confidence that your money is safe. The impact to reputation and potential future lost business would likely be more significant for a smaller bank compared to a large institution.

It is only when contextual realities are considered that proper understanding and management of risk can occur. The same quantitative properties of a given risk may have different assessment outcomes based on perspectives and circumstances of a given set of stakeholders.

Note: For those that can't stand the suspense of not knowing, at the time of this writing BoA has $564 billion in assets under management, and Citizens Business Bank has $13 billion).

> We have converted an old bank vault into an executive conference center at one of our innovation and entrepreneurship collectives that was originally built as a bank. Unfortunately, we did not find any hidden caches of riches when we converted the space . . . but we did learn a lot about vaults in the process. In fact, we learned more than we ever thought we would have to about the design and construction of bank vaults. Some potentially interesting facts: bank vaults are the first thing built and then the rest of the bank is built around it. In the case of our vault, a major driver of this is because the vault door (which ours still has the BoA asset tracking tag on it) is virtually impossible to install once all the rest of walls, doorways and ceilings are constructed. We also learned that the geometry of doors, particularly the interface between the door and frame, has evolved over time. Our door is a plug door that was designed to keep an airtight seal when the door is closed. Last, the acoustics are awful in an empty vault. We used professional sound proofing to stop the sound from incessantly echoing on the vault walls. It probably would have been cheaper to line the walls with stacks of money to do the job!

Risk and all components used to calculate risk are contextual, even when highest degrees of objectivity are applied. The likelihood and consequence are both contextual. They are different for one company or organization than they are for any other company or industry.

As Taleb postulates in *The Black Swan*, an event depends on the observer. What may be a Black Swan surprise for one stakeholder is not a Black Swan surprise for a stakeholder that orchestrated the event. Understanding vulnerability should be a higher priority so that risk practitioners can "turn the Black Swans white".

A good place to start is understanding requirements and the distinction between errors, defects and failures (EDF). Each of these elements can be used to enhance the ability for people and organizations to manage risk more objectively and appropriately.

Requirements establish the range of acceptable parameters impacting form, fit and function of a given offering for a defined use and life cycle. Requirements are specified in advance based on desired final properties and expectations of performance. Producers try to establish processes to identify and act against errors, defects and failures. A lack of conformance to requirements is directly related to a lack of quality. Key performance characteristics are tested using verification and validation processes. Verification efforts ensure the offering conforms to design, whereas validation ensures the offering conforms to the expectation's functionality.

Not all EDFs are created equal and therefore have to be understood in context. In certain high-performance industries like aerospace, the form, fit and function are all vital and tightly coupled. EDF imperfections to the surface of a jet, whether they be form or fit, will have performance impacts on the vehicle's core functionality of flying. In contrast, a clothing company in the textile industry may take the function of a T-shirt (a short-sleeved garment that covers the torso with holes for the arms, neck and waist) to be granted and they focus more of their effort on the form and fit. EDF imperfections to the design of an abstract pattern on a T-shirt may or may not be consequential and would certainly not impact the functionality of the T-shirt for the end consumer.

The best scenario is to understand the contributing and causal factors that could generate errors, defects and failures in advance to prevent their occurrence. This is what most business processes try to accomplish. In the event that this cannot be achieved, the producer is incentivized to identify errors, defects and failures at their closest point of origin. It is much more costly and potentially dangerous when errors, defects, and failures make it out into the public domain. There is also increased exposure to risk as these "escapes" occur. Establishing clear requirements is the starting point to identify EDF.

> One example of an escape is a product recall. This is when the producer has sold a product or service that it already has. One of the most expensive product recalls ever occurred in 2016, in which Takata airbags—which are used by nearly all of the world's largest automobile manufacturers—had defective components that could cause bodily harm to people in the vehicle if the airbag was deployed. This recall cost at least $26 billion,[15] without factoring in reputational damage to Takata and the automotive companies that utilized their product.

One of the most culturally understood manifestations of an error in the United States is associated with baseball. Major League Baseball (MLB) states that "A fielder is given an error if, in the judgment of the official scorer, he fails to convert an out on a play that an average fielder should have made."[16]

Does this mean that every player in baseball is perfect except for those moments? Absolutely not. There are many other ways in which players make mistakes that are not formally tracked in one of the most stats-obsessed sports on the planet.

The sport of baseball is made up of batters (offense) and fielders (defense). The definition above only covers half of the sport! Even though a batter certainly has a relationship to a fielder being able to "convert an out on a play that an average fielder should have made" because they hit the ball, the batter does not intend to make the fielder make an error. The batter is trying to get on base and

15. www.statista.com/topics/3798/product-recalls-in-the-united-states/
16. www.mlb.com/glossary/standard-stats/error#:~:text=A%20fielder%20is%20given%20an,average%20fielder%20should%20have%20made.&text=A%20batter%20does%20not%20necessarily,to%20be%20given%20an%20error.

ultimately score a "run" by crossing home plate. There is no formal accounting of errors on the offensive half of baseball, an activity dominated by the act of batting in which the greatest players of all time average just over one successful hit out of three tries and the average of all players over the history of MLB dating all the way back to 1894 is closer to one in four (.263).

In most organizations this level of performance would have devastating impacts on goals and objectives. What if the employees and leaders in every organization only successfully completed their desired outcome once out of every three or four attempts?

Imagine how much more risk would be in the world if everything performed at similar rates of success. What if the correct meal was received just once out of every three or four orders? What if someone's mouth refused to chew for seven or eight bites out of every ten? What if a car would only stop once out of every three or four times the brakes are applied? What if a traffic signal only worked properly once out of every three or four times the lights changed? This might seem like an absurd premise, yet risk management activities in some organizations achieve this level of performance or worse.

In science, statistics and research, there is a much higher standard, burden of proof or level of acceptable uncertainty. It is widely accepted that a threshold of 95% confidence is used to evaluate statistical significance. This means that a study's authors are only willing to live with an acceptable level of 5% that the outcome of their study was the result of chance or randomness alone. It is also important to note that a study is typically an approximation using a representative sample of the broader population being studied. The 5% acceptance of chance provides some room for such approximations to be accurate without being exact. Additionally, in such studies there is typically an expected level of rigor to identify and mitigate the most common types of that could result.

There are four possibilities that can result from any study. There are two ways to be correct and two ways to introduce errors (Table 5.1).

The scenarios in which to be correct are (1) when researchers think there is a relationship and there really is one and (2) when researchers conclude there is no relationship when there really is not one.

A false positive (Type I error, alpha error) occurs when a researcher thinks they detected a relationship when one does not really exist. A false negative (Type II error, beta error) occurs when a researcher thinks they did not detect a relationship when one really does exist.

Even with this higher threshold for acceptability and more comprehensive understanding of error, there are some very unsatisfactory levels of performance. Risk is contextual. Whether one believes that performance levels of one in three or 95 out of 100 are acceptable is based on the accepted norms of the business, sport, industry and society at large, and is therefore contextual. Risk and risk management require individuals, organizations and institutions to honor this reality.

Defects

Defects are the manifestation of errors and other factors that result in outcomes that are beyond the established range of acceptability. As stated above, the most common way to create a baseline of acceptability is by establishing requirements that define the ranges of acceptability for form, fit and

Table 5.1 There Are Two Ways to Be Correct and Two Ways to Introduce Errors

	Association	*No association*
Reject null hypothesis	Correct	Type I error
Fail to reject null hypothesis	Type II error	Correct

function. Defects are often identified during inspection and testing when being compared to a given set of requirements.

One powerful way to develop and utilize processes that help identify and eliminate defects is six sigma (6σ). Six sigma is a capability that aims to eliminate variation. The basic premise is that as variation is reduced, defects will be reduced, and operational performance will be enhanced. Six sigma gets its name from the number of standard deviations from an average value in which defects will be measured. The higher the number of sigmas, the fewer the number of defects that can be expected.

The most widely utilized distribution is a normal, or bell, curve. The qualities of a given population that is being approximated are represented by the sample's data. This approximation is described by statistics with great emphasis placed on the average (the peak of the curve) and the deviation away from the average (how spread out the curve is).

Frequently, the normal curve is described in terms of three sigma. The three represents three standard deviations from the average. Three sigma is said to account for 99.7% of the area under the curve. This is the equivalent of 66,800 errors per million opportunities.

Similarly, in six sigma, the six represents six standard deviations from the average. Six sigma is said to account for 99.9999% of the area under the curve. This equivalent to 3.4 defects per million opportunities.

While the difference between three sigma and six sigma might seem tiny, its cumulative effect really becomes evident at scale. At three sigma, about 140 million out of 2.1 trillion text messages sent annually[17] would never reach their intended recipient, whereas only about 7 million would not make it with six sigma.

The industry standard for high-demand web applications is five "9s" (99.999%) of server uptime. This equates to five minutes and 19 seconds of downtime per year. Those that reach six sigma cut that down to just 31.6 seconds per year. If the other opposite was chosen and three sigma was accepted, there would be massive negative global impact through lost engagements and missed potential customers. Going back to the baseball analogy above, it is hard to imagine the impact to an e-commerce site if one out of every three or four visits returned a "404—This page cannot be found" error.

Defects can be conforming or nonconforming. Conforming defects are things that do not affect form, fit or function. Nonconforming defects (nonconformances) are defects in adhering to the processes used to create the process and that impact form, fit or function or other defined requirements.

Like errors above, not all defects are created equal. Defects are contextual.

> *Note*: It is also recommended that progressive risk management systems support the ability to support the tracking and elimination of near misses. Near misses are situations in which an error or defect is in the process of producing an error, defect or failure, or realizing a risk that does not materialize. They have the potential to cause an undesirable consequence but ultimately do not at that moment in time.

Failures occur when the product or service does not adequately satisfy the intent of use under expected conditions. Engineers use a tool called Failure Modes and Effects Analysis (FMEA) to predict and prevent failure modes. FMEA was developed and utilized extensively by the National Aeronautics and Space Administration (NASA) in the 1960s. Since that time it has expanded to become an important engineering, design and investigatory tool for critical and diverse industries around the world.

Failures are identified as the loss of a function under stated conditions.

17. www.ctia.org/news/report-2020-annual-survey-highlights

Errors may or may not lead to defects, yet all defects are the result of error. Similarly, defects may or may not lead to failures, yet all failures are the result of some form of deficiency or defect. All other things being equal, an individual error has lower impact than an individual defect, which has lower impact than a failure. Risk can be introduced and increase in all these scenarios.

Heuristics, Bias and Culture

Over seemingly countless generations of evolution, selective pressures have helped humans develop pretty amazing cognitive abilities. Most of this brain power is supporting people without even having awareness that it is happening.

A critical ability that has helped enable this part of the virtuous cycle is that humans are amazing pattern recognizers. We are particularly keen when the sensory input is core to human experience (such as reproduction and survival). The euphoria of starting a new relationship. Hearing a baby cry. Recognizing faces. The list can go on and on.

Sometimes this system sometimes gets a little too ambitious and tries to make patterns where they don't actually exist. This happens whenever someone reacts to stimuli that is not actually what it is thought to be—a stick on the ground that is processed as a snake, thinking that clouds take on the shapes of animals, or "seeing" a visual pattern or trend in statistical quality control graphs when there is no mathematical significance.

There is also bias in our interpretation of the world based on macro and micro familiarity. Most of human evolution occurred with a progressive understanding of the world. This includes our understanding of things that move at the types of speeds most common on Earth over periods of human life spans. Over this time we have developed heuristics, mental shortcuts, to process information and make decisions more quickly. While heuristics can ease the mental load, reduce energy demands of the brain and increase the speed to act, they do not exist without penalty. These approximations are estimates of reality and are therefore imperfect.

Similarly, some forms of bias are believed to be generationally wired in to our evolutionary past. A bias is a disproportionate inclination toward or away from something. An area of ever-increasing understanding surrounds cognitive bias, which are "systematic patterns of deviation from norm and or rationality in judgment."[18]

Cognitive biases can be explicit and implicit, meaning that sometimes they are applied intentionally and other times they seem to be initiated with no direct intent (and even sometimes overriding rational thought).

Biases are not inherently bad.

Hammers are not inherently bad.

To drive a nail into a piece of wood, a hammer works great. Sometimes the hammer misses the nail and the operator's fingers that are supporting the nail get smashed. Even if the operator curses the tool, this does not make the hammer bad. It demonstrates that it is not the perfect tool for the job because the risk of injury was realized. Just like when the hammer smashes the worker's fingers, biases too can result in undesirable outcomes.

Such biases do not stop within the confines of individuals. So too do the organizations, institutions, and societies that people construct, operate, and exist within. The collection of accepted individually shared beliefs, behaviors and norms are the basis of culture. As a result, the culture of a given organization has a direct influence from individual and collective bias, both of which directly influence decision-making in risk management activities.

18. https://en.wikipedia.org/wiki/List_of_cognitive_biases

One of the most important books ever written about risk and certainly the one that has struck deepest into the vein of cultural pervasiveness is Nassim Nicholas Taleb's *The Black Swan: The Impact of the Highly Improbable.* While there is no shortage of great content throughout the book, its major tenets are defined by the impact of outliers and the difficulty of predicting them because of increased complexity throughout the world.

An outlier in the scientific and research fields is often treated as an anomaly. When a study is developed and performed on a given topic, researchers collect and analyze data. During the data analysis the researchers determine the distribution of the data that most appropriately fits the samples. The notion of heuristics and models was discussed earlier. Distributions are models with specific parameters and properties. The most widely used is the normal distribution described by the normal curve (also discussed in the "Errors, Defects and Failures" section above). Many distributions are sensitive to outliers, especially the normal distribution. This effect is amplified when the sample size is small because of the outlier's greater influence on averages and standard deviation. To remedy this, a widely accepted practice to deal with outliers is to lop them off and exclude them from the data set. The researchers then go on to justify their action in a footnote or other mechanism.

Taleb suggests that this biased mindset helps create conditions for the impact of outliers to produce disproportionate impacts when certain risks are realized, the events that people did not think, or failed to allow themselves to believe, could ever occur.

Furthermore, this vicious cycle deepens when the bias caused by convenience over truth is allowed to exist. One of the most common manifestations of this bias is hindsight bias, a lack of rigor in understanding the real reasons why something happens versus the most readily available explanation created.

Hindsight bias is a major contributor here. As was stated above, humans are amazing pattern-recognizing beings, and sometimes we see patterns when they don't exist. Hindsight bias occurs when the cause and effect of something are prescribed ad hoc to have occurred based on information that is pieced together after the event. "Hindsight is 20/20" is often used to describe how it is so apparently easy to see the contributing causes to an event with perfect vision looking back. In reality, our biases lead us to believe that it is 20/20 when it is really much worse.

In the United States there is a term called "Monday morning quarterbacking." In American football, the quarterback is the player who is the offensive team's on-field leader and the one that initiates the call to action on each play (often they choose the play in the best interest of the team as well). National Football League games are traditionally played on Sundays. This provides for countless conversations to occur Monday mornings with pundits, friends and colleagues about what the quarterback or team should have done differently or better.

This same issue certainly arises within just about every organization that is performing risk management activities. There is a very high likelihood that if an organization or institution has a formal risk management system, there are unsanctioned processes and individuals performing in the shadows. These are the informal processes that employees and managers utilize with good intention (mostly) that augment or supplement the formal processes. The source of this dark or gray suite of operations is often subtle and directly linked to the culture of the organization. These shadow activities occur most frequently when the formal system is deemed too onerous by practitioners compared to the assessed consequence of using alternative means.

There is another principle that can be more nefarious here as well. In human resource management there is a principle called equity theory, in which employers and employees seek balance between the inputs and outputs of work. When either side feels out of balance, formal and informal activities can ensue. When an employee feels inequities associated with their work and compensation, they can use formal processes (meet with management or HR to address concerns). Often, if these pathways do not yield the sought remedy, the employee will begin to make the corrections consciously and unconsciously. In practice, this can manifest itself in many different attitudes and behaviors (not working as much or as hard). Sometimes this can result in illegal activities such as embezzlement and theft. Regardless of the outcome, the underground activities the informal processes take are estimated to have a disproportionately high lack of accounting for the financial impact on an organization.

Note: *The Black Swan* fits into the broader *Incerto* series. While none of these had the impact of *The Black Swan*, each of the works in the *Incerto* collection are valuable contributors to push risk practitioners to develop a more comprehensive understanding of core aspects of their job including chance, uncertainty and decision-making.

Endlessly Seek Truth Over Convenience

Out of the pan and into the fire—

If you are engaging in illegal or even unethical behavior, this is crucial. If you commit a crime and own up to it, there are typically fewer penalties than if you try to cover it up. Richard Nixon did not leave office because he authorized the activity but because he obstructed justice and. . . . While this is certainly a super-simplified view of the events, that is what history does. It boils down the details to the fundamental items.

Risk analysis and management should be seen the same way. If you compound the risk with the wrong activities, you have to be willing to accept the consequences. This is the start of a vicious cycle. One bad decision leads to another until the situation spirals out of control.

One of the best ways to overcome bias is to introduce an alternative heuristic that is a better (more rational) shortcut for the risk management goals.

Objectivity and enhanced decision-making are the most compelling ways to achieve this. The first step is to encourage the entire organization to identify irrationality and all forms of bias whenever observed. Next, encourage employees to openly discuss negative and positive biases that they observe. Then, establish actionable measures to proliferate data-driven decision-making. Then, ensure the right incentives are in place to encourage alternatives to undesirable bias and to further desirable ones. Finally, allocate resources and take appropriate action to reinforce the previous two steps.

RISK HAS SIMULPLANEITY

Jim Fortune is one of the world's leading experts in the vertical transportation industry (primarily elevators and lifts, depending on location) for super-tall structures. Through his decades of experience, he has helped people and goods efficiently transit throughout some of the most iconic and tallest buildings ever built. This impressive list includes the two tallest buildings in Hong Kong (International Finance Center, International Commerce Center), the iconic Taipei 101 and the current world's tallest building, the Burj Khalifa. He also supported the world's next tallest tower, the Jeddah Tower in Saudi Arabia.

Until recently, the Taipei 101 that Fortune supported had the fastest lifts ever created, with speeds of 38.8 miles per hour. The vertical transportation system could go from the lobby to roof, some 1,670 feet, in just 30 seconds. And while the speeds of elevators are now reaching even faster velocities, it is not today's most pressing design consideration.

As the buildings get taller and the number of people within each building increases, it becomes increasingly difficult to safely evacuate all occupants in the event of an emergency. This was made evident by the events of September 11 at the World Trade Center's Twin Towers, in which the deaths of an estimated 200 of the total 1,140 victims are believed to have perished in the worst passenger elevator disaster ever.[19] It took One World Trade Center and Two World Trade Center 102 and 56 minutes to catastrophically fail after the initial triggering events, respectively.

In response, Fortune developed a new approach to evacuating mega-tall structures that aims to set the international standard for mass evacuation events and be accomplished within the first 60 minutes. His invention, the "Lifeboat" Emergency Elevator Evacuation Operation is described in a Council of Tall Buildings and Urban Habitat (CTBUH) paper,[20] in which he describes the implementation in a forthcoming project that is pushing the limits of mega-tall buildings.

A requisite number of lifts within a building should be designated as "lifeboats," in which the elevator is designed to be operated by emergency responders continuously throughout a total evacuation event. These lifeboats have unique capabilities that are activated in the event of an emergency that help expedite the evacuation of all occupants faster and more inclusively (lifeboats can supporting occupants who are not able to use stairways). A key feature is that all lifeboat lifts are "equipped to operate continuously on the building emergency generator on standby power, in case normal power is lost." Each lift also a set of car-top closed-circuit television cameras and lights and performs test runs prior to lifeboat operations commencing. To aid the operations, there are on-board paging, firefighters' sound–powered phone jacks, an intercom system, attendant operations (constant pressure door close and hall call bypass buttons), refuge floor special arrival/loading lanterns, and crowd detectors. When designing the system for the "next tallest building of the world," Fortune was able to demonstrate the mega-tall building can be completely emptied within 54 minutes.

This is an amazing contribution toward reducing major components of risk in not only a groundbreaking structure, but to the AEC industries as a whole.

Much like elevators connect occupants to various levels and functions within a building, it can be helpful to think of risk in terms of planes of influence. Each identified plane can have influence directly on the risk and indirectly on other layers. Layers do not require direct awareness by the risk holder to create influence.

When a risk is influenced by multiple planes at the same time, this is called simulplaneity.

Each plane is synonymous with the floors of a building. In many buildings, entire floors or collections of floors have a shared capability or functionality. In *Fortune*'s "the world's next tallest building" example, the building comprises the following basic functionality by floor (Table 5.2).

In this heuristic, each risk is the equivalent to being the entire high-rise building. Each floor or groupings of floors by shared function represents a plane of influence on the risk. Each plane of influence is defined by hierarchical relationships and or a stated purpose. There are activities, relationships and objectives that occur on each floor as well as those that exist between floors.

> "One person's ceiling is another's floor."

Not everything that happens on every floor of the building directly impacts everything else on the remaining floors, but it can. There are many components and infrastructure that are shared and integrated into the system, such as water, electricity and air handling. There are also discrete relationships that can have a range of influence on a risk; for example, a major event or a fire on a residential floor. The fire may be isolated to a single unit, impact the entire floor, the immediate floors surrounding it

19. www.911memorial.org/connect/blog/elevator-motor-symbolizes-disaster-world-trade-center-site#:~:text=At%208%3A46%20a.m.%2C%20on,the%20World%20Trade%20Center%20site
20. https://global.ctbuh.org/resources/papers/download/2388-elevator-designs-for-the-kingdom-tower.pdf

Table 5.2 Fortune's "the World's Next Tallest Building" Example

Floors	*Purposes*
>168	Empty spire
168 (682 m)	*Tuned mass damper*
158–167	Building control machines
157 (637 m)	Observation deck, outdoor balcony
155–156	Hotel, restaurants
154	*Four Seasons Hotel*
144–153	Hotel rooms
141–143	Building control machines
140	Hotel rooms, refuge area
127–139	Hotel rooms
125–126	Hotel sky lobby
115–124	Hotel rooms
114	Building control machines, refuge area
104–113	Residence
103	Residence, refuge area
94–102	Residence
93	Residential sky lobby
90–92	Building control machines
89	Refuge area
80–88	Offices
79	Refuge area
67–78	Offices
65–66	Sky lobby
64	Refuge area
51–63	Offices
48–50	Building control machines
47	Refuge area
35–46	Offices
33–34	Sky lobby
29–32	Building control machines
18–28	Offices
16–17	Building control machines
6–15	Offices
3–5	Building control machines
2	Shopping mall
1	Office lobby, serviced hotel lobby
B1	Observatory entrance, shops and restaurants
B2	Parking, building control machines

or even possibly the entire building. Understanding and stopping the spread or propagation of impact is known as containment. If the fire is prevented from spreading from the originating unit, the lower the impact to other parts of the building.

"If a tree falls in the forest . . ."

An evil villain is about to engage a reign of domination on the world after years of preparation isolated on a remote tropical island somewhere. The villain has learned from every other incompetent villain that has ever tried to accomplish global domination. The new plan is ready to execute with six sigma confidence. Is the current world order at greater risk?

It is hard to argue that it is not. Just because people do not know about a risk does not mean that it is not present.

This would be the equivalent of "Officer, I did not know what the speed limit was" as an excuse when a driver is pulled over for speeding. "Ignorance is no excuse for the law" and is not an acceptable position to take managing risk.

It is important that this is not confused with an expectation of omniscience to apply systems methodologies in order to more effectively understand and manage risk. To the contrary, it is a recognition that nobody or no organization knows everything. Said another way, nobody knows anything about the future with complete certainty. False omniscience is the result when they, and the organizations they support, enable such thinking. This can be a dangerous and fine line to walk when being overly dependent subject matter experts that are insufficiently balanced.

There will be influences and impacts to risk management efforts that will not be known. Processes and specific efforts need to be developed to prepare organizations for impacts caused by the unknown.

These last two points, ignorance and omniscience, place boundaries on behaviors and attitudes that will be explored in more detail in secret 6 below. It helps provide two important insights in the fight against risks hampering stated objectives.

The focus of this work is to provide the reader with a practical guide to understand and manage risk and not to espouse esoteric deep philosophical debates. That being said, this section is a good place to equip risk management practitioners with some important ways to respond when members of an organization do not share such values.

A "classic" philosophical question to ponder is "If a tree falls in the forest and no one is around to hear it, does it make a sound?" This is where science (primarily physics in this case), reason and accumulated objectivity thrive. The first problem with this postulation is how human-centric it is. Is there any reason to suggest that humans are the only beings in a forest that could hear a tree fall? Absolutely not. So one that cannot hear could observe animals in the forest that did hear and react to the tree falling. Even if we get beyond that, we can filter out the noise produced by this experience from a risk perspective. As we stated in secret 1, risk requires likelihood and impact. In this case, the impact is a physical manifestation that creates the greatest contribution to sound waves created. We can also look at likelihood part of the risk calculation. One cannot say with 100% certainty that the next tree that falls in a forest will produce a sound; however, have there ever been any objectively verified accounts of a tree falling to earth and it did not make a sound? With all things equal, one would have to ask why this tree falling would be different. How many billions or trillions of trees have been cut down or fallen? How many of them were reported to not produce any sound? The likelihood that the next one would is say, 1 in 3 trillion, or 0.0000000333%. Again, this does not guarantee the next one will not make a sound, but the likelihood is this occurrence is much closer to zero (not being the first tree to make a sound) than 1 (the first tree to not make a sound).

Aside from a plan from the evil villain above to place all forests in giant vacuums where sound waves cannot propagate or employing an antigravity machine where trees cannot fall, there is no meaningful reason to debate such postulations in application. Not every question that can be asked deserves the same rigor in responding as all others. It is these same paths of logic, or lack thereof, that reinforce heuristics and mindsets that can ultimately create systemic and existential risk.

Not all risks are as static as a high-rise building. Such buildings are of a discrete form and essentially stationary. Aside from the sometimes noticeable sway occupants feel on upper floors, it is really the activities in and around the building that are the most dynamic. An understanding of an entire system is required if the building heuristic above is to remain relevant.

One way to use systems principles was already touched on above: the allocation of specific floors and groups of floors based on gross functionality (residential, lobby, hotel, shopping, etc.). Additional understanding is likely required to fully understand effectiveness of supporting these gross functions, because the people in each section are not monolithic.

Stakeholder analysis allows practitioners to dig deeper in their understanding of the needs and activities of people in each area of gross functionality. In the case of the residential areas of the building, some of the likely stakeholders are residents, facilities and maintenance personnel, property managers, visitors or guests, and so forth. Once the stakeholders are identified, their needs and activities should be understood. What do residents do and expect? Just a bed to sleep? The ability to prepare meals? Do they leave for the day to go to work? Do they work from home? And so on. A similar line of exploration should be repeated for the other major stakeholders on the residential floor and all subsequent gross functional areas.

A different way to characterize the building is by discrete function. In this approach the practitioner is trying to identify discrete activities that are shared by key stakeholders throughout the entire building. For example, there are many ways to for people to receive nourishment in the building: self-prepared meals, delivery, sit-down restaurant, vending machines and so on.

Another discrete function that is important is communications. This would cover how people and equipment communicate within the building and out to the world beyond. These types of communication systems are often management by information technology (IT) teams. One of the tools they use to understand system interactions are system diagrams. One type of diagram that has been used in various capacities within this space for decades is the Open Systems Interconnection (OSI) model. This model has been used for so long because it helps identify critical components of communication function without the need to specify detailed structure or individual components to be effective. There are seven layers in the OSI model (physical, data link, network, transport, session, presentation and application). Errors, defects, failures and risk can occur in and between layers. And while the details of this model are well beyond the scope of this section, they provide a relatively straightforward example of how system models can be used to support the understand of discrete functions. Notice consistency in the OSI model to the floors in a building or the planes of influence in risk management.

It is also helpful to illustrate how complexity quickly ensues as a number of discrete functions are required to be performed within a broader system.

A simplified heuristic that can be helpful to understand the effects of simulplaneity can be found with a "big circle, little circle" model. In its baseline use there are only two types of influence on risk: those beyond direct control (big circle) and those within direct control (little circle). This simplified model distills the numerous floors and layers of the previous examples down to just two: beyond direct control and within direct control. They both exist in perpetuity for a given endeavor. The relative sizing and influence of each is dynamic. Great effort is required to understand these influences over time and to ensure the most important aspects of each are perpetually understood and managed as appropriate. When an organization excels at managing risks within the little circle with little or no understanding of big-circle influences, they can optimize locally while increasing risks globally. Likewise, if an organization only focuses on problems out of their control, they are likely to face higher risks being realized that could have been directly managed and avoided.

The model can be enhanced slightly if a third dimension is considered in addition to the big and little circles; namely, the impact of influence that can happen at the interface between big and little circles. It is here that the small circles can try to influence big circles. This is often where lobbyists reside. They try to negotiate greater influence by the small circle on the big circle. There are many legalities and ethical considerations that can yield their own risks in this dimension of the model. There is also a bit of a paradox in that often it is larger organizations and institutions that have the resources to "incentivize" the big circle to alter its influence in support of the little circle growing, which in turn increases the likelihood that a small circle becomes a big circle to another entity.

Risk can be meaningfully categorized in many different ways and on many different planes of influence. The perspective or perspectives that are chosen to understand and manage risk should be correlated to contextual realities. It is important that risk management practitioners utilize a systems mindset.

RISK AND OPPORTUNITY DUALITY

In the beginning of time the universe was in chaos. It was here that two forces joined in a dynamic relationship that would be inexorably linked for eternity. This linkage did not produce a new entity, however, it provided a new way to connect the future. Ultimately the two forces established balance in the cosmic egg which led the way to the birth of Pangu, the first human. The dynamic relationship between and within the two forces are what we now call yin and yang.

Like many mythologies, this ancient Chinese story may not have actually occurred, yet the powerful principle of dynamic balance represented by yin and yang is one of the most apt ways to think about the relationship between risks and opportunities.

One of the most influential artists and activists of a generation was Adam Yauch of the Beastie Boys. It was on the band's 1992 classic album, *Check Your Head*, that Yauch interjects: "My fear was just a shadow. And then a voice spoke in my head . . . and she said 'Dark is not the opposite of light. It's the absence of light.' And I thought to myself, 'She knows what she is talking about.' And for a moment I knew what it was all about."

Similar to the relationship between light and dark, and yin and yang, the relationship between risk and opportunity is not simply defined by opposites.

Risk and opportunity are not antonyms.

Risk and opportunity are part of something that cannot be described by either alone, while each of them remain conceptually distinct.

> Within every risk lies opportunity.
> Within every opportunity lies risk.
> And one cannot ever exist without the presence of the other.

This principle is called duality. It exists whenever two things are inseparable while remaining conceptually distinct.

Oftentimes organizations will have defined procedures that define risk management and opportunity management as two discrete processes. In practice, there is often much more focus put on the risk management side than the opportunity management component. It is almost as if they convince themselves that risks are real and require more attention and opportunities reside in the "shadows" described by Yauch above. Said another way, risk management is the cake and opportunity management is the icing.

This management paradigm must dramatically shift if there an expectation to meaningful enhance performance levels and capabilities for risk and opportunity management. Only when one actively manages risks and opportunities with respect of duality can this shift occur.

Risks and opportunities are present under the same conditions. Whenever there is a risk, there is an opportunity and vice versa. Risks and opportunities both face uncertainty. When we are evaluating risks and opportunities, we use the same multivariate principle provided above to evaluate them (requiring both the likelihood of occurrence and the magnitude of the impact at a minimum).

NOTE: There is a relatively new notion that seems to be in vogue right now that risk is not positive or negative. This is not the required shift in mindset that is required. Simply by stating that risk and opportunities are synonymous with chance alone is moving things in the wrong direction of progress.

It is important for any risk and opportunity management effort to live within the realities of the system and maintain diligence in not succumbing to the fantasy of convenience. This is often seen with respect to risks and opportunities associated with innovation and entrepreneurship.

When most of the world's non-pedestrian transportation was dominated by horse and buggy, two emerging industries were just prodding to find paths of viability. In 1903 Orville and Wilbur Wright flew the first motor-driven airplane. And five years later, Henry Ford developed mass assembly of the Model T. These were two events that would drastically shift the trajectories of transportation forever. How many people in the world sitting on their horses and wagons in the early 20th century would have been able to image the dramatic and rapid shifts that were headed their way?

How many of the companies that dominated the horse-and-buggy paradigm grew as big as even the smallest players in the automotive and aerospace industries by the middle of the century? How many of them even exist today?

It does not seem unfathomable that the discussions and decision based on personal incredulity to dismiss the potential impact of the emerging transportation industries played a role in their demise. If they did realize there was a potential risk, how many of them doubled down and worked harder? How many of them saw it as an opportunity?

Yet one cannot simply point the finger at the horse-and-buggy paradigm as a unique place. It was estimated by Credit Suisse[21] in 2017 that the average age of a company listed on the S&P 500 index has reduced to just 20 years, down from 60 years in the 1950s. How many current company leaders facing existential risks are falling back into the similar pitfalls as the buggy producers of the early 1900s?

The impact of not doing anything is too rarely or properly evaluated when managing risks. The risk of not trying is different than the risk of doing nothing. Making a deliberate choice not to take action is different than making excuses that cover your rationale for not trying.

A risk that should be on every single risk chart, but rarely is, is the risk of the status quo. Many organizations have processes implemented to eliminate variability and enhance stability. There are certainly operational efficiencies that can occur with this approach. However, when this is not kept in balance, the paths for future opportunities narrow. There is an opportunity cost when innovation and entrepreneurial endeavors are passed up. The cumulative effect of this opportunity cost over time will increase existential risk to the organizations over time.

The Risk of the Status Quo Should Be on Every Risk Chart

Risks and opportunities also exist in a dynamic system. As a result, there are fluctuations in the proportionality between risks and opportunities. Sometimes risks have a greater influence or require more resources, and sometimes opportunities are greater. There is no requirement that risks and opportunities have constant and universal proportionality. The contextual and simulplaneity principles are at the heart of this.

RISK AND OPPORTUNITY ARE COLLECTIVELY BOUNDLESS

For all practical intents, risk is boundless. That is to say, "there are effectively an endless number of ways in which risk can negatively impact a desired outcome." Harkening back to secret 5, with only slight modifications the same can be said of opportunities in the other direction, "there are effectively an endless number of ways in which opportunity can positively impact a desired outcome."

21. https://plus.credit-suisse.com/rpc4/ravDocView?docid=V6y0SB2AF-WEr1ce

This can be postulated with confidence because of the earlier explored other secrets and the fact that nearly all endeavors that can feasibly be considered are part of dynamic systems.

The Earth is spinning at a perceptively normal rate of one revolution per day. For a sphere the size of Earth, that is approximately 1,000 mph at the equator. The daily cycles of day and night are the most common shared reminder of this regular rotation. Furthermore, Earth is not spinning in place within our solar system. The earth makes a regular trip around the sun at a speed of 67,000 mph. While harder to observe, significant differences from one day to the next are still perceptible by most people throughout the course of the 365 days it takes to orbit the sun (namely, in seasonal changes). Next, our solar system is part of the Milky Way galaxy, in which Earth (and the solar system) are moving at a staggering 515,000 miles per hour. The Milky Way is one of many galaxies that are thought to be rotating with the Virgo Supercluster, and relative to the cosmic microwave background is moving at 1,340,000 mph.[22]

> FYI: Elon Musk once said that this train of thought "Makes it clear that you can only sense acceleration, not velocity." While trying to avoid initiating beef with Mr. Musk, his conclusion is not quite accurate. It is believed that universe is expanding at an accelerating rate and we do not feel that. In addition, we can sense velocity relative to motion. When driving in at constant speed and direction, (velocity) passengers can still "sense" velocity by observing a signpost up ahead appearing to get closer as the vehicle proceeds.

Most of our journey through the cosmos is not even perceived because humanity and life on earth exists in fractions of fractions of fractions compared to the time frames and scale of the cosmos. In these slivers of time of our existence and understanding, things have been pretty stable (consistent from one frame of reference to the next) even while constantly changing. There are key points in which life on Earth, the Earth as a whole and all of its immediate neighbors in the cosmos underwent massive and dramatic changes over similar periods of reference. If those events were to happen today, much of our unawareness of the constant change happening around us would be drastically different.

As one zooms back to the existence that most of humanity has more direct experience with, the relevance to risk and opportunity management becomes more clear.

The ability for humans and the constructs they create (technology, business, organizations, institutions, systems, etc.) to understand the relationship between the realities around them and the impact of change are vital to survival and risk management. It is not resource responsible (and possibly not even feasible) to properly perceive all sensory inputs constantly all the time. People do not process all stimuli. Much of it gets filtered out as noise, and most of the time these systems work pretty reliably for the resources required to utilize them. There are conscious and unconscious filters that prioritize the allocation of precious resources.

As illustrated previously, the mechanisms that have allowed people to thrive are not infallible. The impact of intentional and unintended bias and other shortcuts people use trade off resource optimization for accuracy. It is important that risk and opportunity practitioners be aware of the most influential forms of error-generating thoughts, behaviors and actions that impact their desired outcomes.

How likely is it that a police officer would let a driver go without a ticket after being pulled over for driving at excessive speeds just because the driver explained to the officer calmly, "Oh, I'm sorry, officer. I didn't know what the speed was." Ignorance is no excuse for the law.

And just like ignorance is no excuse for the law, it is no excuse for risk professionals and the organizations they support to hide behind. It is the responsibility of the organization and the practitioners

22. www.businessinsider.com/earth-screaming-through-space-nasa-animated-video-2019-10

to manage the organization's risk activities to understand the greatest and most likely risk that can have the greatest contribution in preventing the organization from realizing its desired outcomes.

A form of ignorance directly tied to hubris and intelligence is the argument of personal incredulity. The basis of this form of ignorance is summarized by someone not believing that something could possibly be the way others suggest simply because someone cannot understand, or refuses to try to understand with any sincerity/diligence, a given topic and therefore it must not be true, unlikely or based on a flaw.

There's another phrase that says "Ignorance is bliss."

At the core of this phrase is the notion that life is much more simple (and happier) when minor things like reality, facts and the accumulated knowledge base are taken out of the equation. Using the "little circle, big circle" example above, in the "ignorance is bliss" mindset everything is pushed from the small circle to the big circle. "If we don't think about "it" or understand "it," we don't have to worry about "it" or expend effort and resources to control "it." This is an invitation to abdicate responsibility, increase risk and initiate a vicious cycle.

It is better to live in the harshness of reality than in the convenience of fantasy.

This sentiment is wonderfully captured by Zach de la Rocha, who said, "If ignorance is bliss. Then knock the smile off my face. . . . If we don't action now. We'll settle for nothing later."

When people and organizations live in fantasy, they are more likely to get the smile knocked off their face without being prepared for their response to certain risks that should have been completely beyond immediate control. That being said, living in reality is not enough. Mike Tyson, one of the greatest heavyweight boxers of all time, said "Everyone has a plan until they get punched in the mouth." It is at this point that plans and strategy move aside and the rush of survival kicks in. Awareness, preparation and capability are all important. They need to be dynamically nurtured and adapt to realities within and around the organizations actively working to reduce or mitigate the impact of risk.

This provides us with a connection point to another important trap that can occur: the omniscience fallacy.

The omniscience fallacy can be seen as a bookend on the opposite side of the collection housing the volumes of ignorance titles on a bookcase. It is here that the musings of too many subject matter experts and seasoned risk professionals capture a disproportionate and unwarranted amount of overconfidence in their ability to understand and predict events and impacting the future. They believe, and even worse, the leaders and coworkers within their organization believe, that they possess the ability to see more than they actually can. Experts play can play important roles, and in some instances they are vital. Their value is not being highlighted as a broad concern. It is when they are not required to demonstrate their vast insights with evidence applied to the existing conditions at hand where this becomes most dangerous.

> It is the authors' contention that "truth," or at least a highly representative and robust approximation of truth, lies at the nexus of subject matter experts, crowd wisdom and artificial intelligence. The place these three circles overlap is the most desirable region for understanding and insight. That being said, great diligence is required to ensure understanding and awareness of bias in all three circles are understood and controlled for as appropriate.

Another derivation of the omniscience fallacy is the "not invented here" syndrome. The source of this shortcoming straddles the fence between arrogance and ignorance. Those afflicted with this ailment rely on the notion that "nobody else could possibly understand what we do as well as me or us, and therefore any solution that is not developed by us is could never be sufficient." The way to counter this claim is to demonstrate successful implementations of adaptive reuse, in which another company or industry has utilized the solution in a similar way that it is being proposed for the organization's risk or challenge.

The final trap covered is more of an operational construct on the daily work that is performed by individuals and teams. It hits particularly hard in large organizations and situations in which there are a lot of interfaces/transition points and when a significant amount of time can pass between one task and the next. When the work that is expected to be completed and have requisite quality parameters is allowed to progress through the system, it is called traveled work.

In many manufacturing-heavy industries, there are work instructions that remain with the component, sub-assembly or assembly being produced. These work instructions not only provide the instructions of the steps that are needed but also the pedigree of the widget that is ultimately produced. This is colloquially known as a "traveler." Typically, a number of engineering disciplines have collaborated to produce the traveler (and other important reference documents/artifacts), and the production team is able to complete the manufacturing as directed in the traveler. When work is performed out of sequence, it increases risk. There is risk that the work can be permanently overlooked and never performed. There is the risk that other production efforts cannot be completed until the previous work is complete. There is the risk that making the appropriate change can damage another component that is typically not present when the work is performed in-sequence. The list goes on and on.

While its origins and name are certainly connected to them, traveled risk is not limited to the production or manufacturing environments. Traveled risk can occur whenever work is allowed to proceed without the satisfying previously identified expectations of quality and completeness. Such actions have discrete and cumulative impacts that not only impact risks and opportunities but productivity as well. Constant care and management is needed to stay focused and satisfactorily finish work products before moving on to the next ones. Avoid the appeal of checking a box, false progress and "new," as they can motivate the wrong behaviors, override commitments made and increase traveled risk.

As daunting as it may seem, the notion that risks and opportunities are collectively boundless can be incredibly freeing, especially to those that pursue opportunity and manage risk as a profession. First, nobody knows everything about anything (a few exceptional people might get close, but just like risk, knowledge is part of a dynamic interdisciplinary system). This opens the path to acknowledge that risk practitioners don't have to know everything, because they *can't*! Furthermore, not all risks and opportunities are created equal, which means practitioners are not simultaneously facing an infinite barrage of every conceivable risk in perpetuity. Secret 6 and the other five secrets provide insights to think about risks and opportunities in ways that can enhance any individual's or organization's risk and opportunity knowledge base.

Knowing is not enough. Knowledge without action is apathy. And apathy is one of the most dangerous forms of waste.

That is why it is vital to move to the next section and explore some additional perspectives components that support an organization's ability to appropriately manage risks and opportunities. Just like the six secrets shared above are not definitive, there is no expectation that the upcoming aspects of risk and opportunity management constitute a comprehensive treatise or a flawless collection of everything that is or ever could be expected within the discipline. It is simply a push to get more out of the precious resources and limited time to make the greatest contribution.

Final Thoughts

All of this does not necessarily mean that all risk is greater the longer something is in a dynamic system but rather the conditions that produce more frequent, more significant or that open up different combinations of pathways of risks. As mentioned in secret 1 earlier, it is also important to consider time and timing.

If the sun follows the same life cycle as other predicted and observed stars, we can be pretty certain that our entire solar system will cease to be what we know it to be. In about 1 billion years the sun will be 10% brighter. It is expected that in about 5 or 6 billion years the sun will reach the end of its life of expansion after growing to 100 times its current size. This will ensure life on Earth and likely Earth itself will be destroyed to such a degree that it might not ever be known to ever have existed. It will then shrink and become a white dwarf, where it is expected to remain for 100 billion years!

What about an active mission to travel through the Milky Way to find other suitable places for humans to live? The journey across the Milky Way would take a few billion years using technology available today and using spacecraft speeds that have already been sent on cosmic missions.

If there were scientific breakthroughs that allowed us to travel at the speed of light, this journey would still take 200,000 years. This is approximately how long *Homo sapiens* (humans) are thought to have been evolving on Earth.

It is estimated that there are hundreds of billions (possibly trillions) of other galaxies. Think of the time it would take to make the journeys and the number of journeys that could be required.

So what?

These time frames are so beyond the human frame of reference that they become great fodder for science fiction of the far future or swept away into the invisibility of problems for others to worry about.

Most of the readers of this text will likely be supporting organizational risk mitigation efforts in a business or government agency. Where will such organizations exist in 105 billion years? A few billion years? Two hundred thousand years? One hundred years? Ten years? Next year? Next fiscal quarter?

What are the individual and collective risks that really matter? Are today's organizations taking meaningful action to reduce risk and pursue opportunity or are they operating in the noise of the normal?

Are they, in the words of Bill Garno, "bobbing like a cork in the water that thinks the movement is its own doing? Or are they leveraging the constraints of reality and actively charting the course and taking action on the best way to get their destination?"

How many of the risks, immediate and cumulative, at the present moment can preclude our collective ability to prevent their occurrence?

At its core, management is a series of administration of coordinated activities in pursuit of a desired outcome. As a discipline, management has only been rigorously studied since the 1900s. It was at this time that Frederick Winslow Taylor established "scientific management." Much of this focus was on efficiency and process, which ultimately created the knowledge base of industrial and systems engineering as discrete disciplines of their own.

Management theories have come and gone over the last 150 years, yet they have all collectively contributed to practices widely employed today. They also set the context for furthering theories that will bring organizations into the future. This includes the branching of sub-disciplines of management, like risk and opportunity management.

There are many reputable and well-established organizations and institutions around the world that have developed standards, methods and approaches to risk and opportunity management. While these have appeal, it is beyond the confines of this text to evaluate and unify these approaches. This text is designed to provide a broad perspective of risk and opportunity for practitioners and leaders to enhance knowledge and ultimately effectiveness of the entire discipline in application.

6

FOSTERING DIALOG ABOUT THE FUTURE OF LAW AS RISK AND COMPLIANCE ARE COMING INTO THEIR OWN

Virginia A. Suveiu

The main point of this chapter, and the handbook overall, is to underline the importance of fostering dialog with different voices from across academia and industry (representing various organizations and positions). More study is needed, and it is essential to have professional associations like National Contract Management Association, and other groups like ComplianceNet and the Reading Group on Private Governance,[1] involved in this dialog. This dialog will better inform how stakeholders will handle risk in their organizations as new careers in compliance, ethics and risk management arise to fulfill need.

I have been fortunate in my career so far to have one foot in academia and the other in industry, as an attorney, handling matters relating to ethics, risk and compliance. And, by holding this dual role, I have heard criticism from multiple sides, such as: "We hate lawyers! They just complicate the matter to make more money." Or, "Academics are stuck in their ivory towers and have no clue as to how the real world works." Thus, dialog is vital to help to eliminate misconceptions and to find solutions. I have found the following three main topics as critical in fostering this dialog; so, this chapter is divided into three parts:

1. Bias in decision-making
2. Ethics as the basis of decision-making
3. How risk and compliance are coming into their own

In each of these aforementioned topics, the common characteristic linking them is the necessity of being proactive. Therefore, handling risk and uncertainty cannot mean do nothing until you actually know. By then, it is often too late to build what is needed to have to respond to that situation. Risk is often characterized by uncertainty in potential events and consequences or a combination of these. Uncertainty is the state, even partial, of deficiency of information related to, understanding or knowledge of, an event, its consequence or likelihood.[2]

1. See, e.g., ComplianceNet Convenors Benjamin van Rooij and Yuval Feldman, https://www.law.uci.edu/events/2017-18/s2018/compliance-net.html; and, Reading Group on Private Governance, organized by Dean Timothy D. Lytton, Georgia State University College of Law.
2. See, e.g., *A Guide to the Project Management Body of Knowledge (PMBOK® Guide)*, 2021, 7th ed. While the PMBOK generally describes uncertainty as a lack of total certainty, it is difficult, if not impossible, to fully grasp the concept of uncertainty.

DOI: 10.4324/9781351107242-8

Moreover, all three of these above considerations are now more important than ever in handling the risk and uncertainty in the post-pandemic new normal, and these considerations equip organizations to now be better prepared to manage lingering and emerging risks, such as:[3]

- *Heightened regulatory, socio-economic and political uncertainties that complicate risk analysis*: legal/risk/ethics/compliance professionals[4] assess and manage organizational risks in an environment where fast and proactive responses are necessary to ensure success.
- *Clash of efficiency and ethics in new technological applications and privacy risks*: organizations can create new capabilities and value through technological advancements like quantum, artificial intelligence (AI), and the increasing use of big data as well as more advanced analytics. Yet, growth in these technologies continues to outpace clear regulatory, privacy and ethical rules, often leaving organizations struggling to balance current value against the potential of doing irreparable damage to themselves as well as to others.
- *Increase in use of third parties escalates complexity of compliance*: as discussed throughout this handbook, more organizations partner with third-party providers to work on projects. Due to recent regulatory developments (such as the California Privacy Rights Act), these relationships have exposed organizations to additional risk as these third parties operate within critical organization functions.
- *Rising social awareness leads to challenging stakeholder demands*: organizations are additionally pushed to do more than just increase shareholder value. Although the consequences of getting it wrong are steep, significant opportunities exist for organizations that can successfully navigate these new demands.

Organizations that aim to be successful in the long term must establish and maintain an ethical culture of compliance to handle risk successfully, with the help of the relevant professionals, considering the needs and expectations of interested parties. Compliance is therefore not only the basis, but also a significant opportunity, for a successful and sustainable organization. Organizations are increasingly realizing that by applying values and appropriate compliance management, they can safeguard their integrity and avoid or minimize noncompliance as well as negative risk exposure.[5]

Bias in Decision-Making

A key component causing error in judgment, thereby exposing an organization to risk, is the impact of bias on the process overall.[6] Bias is an inclination to present a partial perspective, often accompanied by a refusal to consider the possible merits of alternative points of view.[7]

3. For instance, as discussed generally in Chief Economists Outlook, Centre for the New Economy and Society, *World Economic Forum* (May 2022), https://www3.weforum.org/docs/WEF_Chief_Economists_Outlook_May_2022.pdf: there are increasingly more changes to deal with, especially in technology, over the next decade than have been seen in the last 50 years.
4. As explained further in this chapter, given the ever-developing professions in legal, risk, ethics and compliance, various titles and duties exist, depending on the need of the given organization. For the sake of brevity and clarity, in the rest of this chapter, the term "compliance professional" will be used.
5. See generally, ISO 37301:2021 Compliance management systems replaces ISO 19600:2014 because it emphasizes the value of an effective and efficient compliance management system for any organization, and value, not only in mitigating negative risk but also in finding opportunity (positive risk) as viewing compliance as a return on investment, https://www.iso.org/standard/75080.html.
6. For instance, it is instructive to see the US Federal Government's General Accountability Office (GAO) Bid Protest Annual Report to Congress for FY 2016, https://www.gao.gov/assets/gao-17-314sp.pdf. Essentially, federal government contracts are subject to protest if an unsuccessful offeror believes that the contract was awarded in violation of statute or regulation. The denying or sustaining of a protest can, unfortunately, include built-in biases, as discussed in this report.
7. For a good explanation in general on biases people hold, see Christopher Dwyer, *12 Common Biases That Affect How We Make Everyday Decisions* (September 2018), www.psychologytoday.com/us/blog/thoughts-thinking/201809/12-common-biases-affect-how-we-make-everyday-decisions.

A common response in organizations to ethics and compliance training designed to mitigate such risk is pushback. For instance, a typical response is something like: "our standard procedures already cover all we need to know and we haven't had problems before, so we're fine." Such a response is reactive, based on an assumption of past perceived success. This inhibits an organization's ultimate growth. The best risk management is a focus on better decision-making by recognizing bias exists in the first place and must be mitigated accordingly.

Biases have significant legal, political, financial, social and ethical implications. Even the appearance of bias can be detrimental; for instance, the (FINRA) Code of Arbitration Procedure provides specifically that "[t]he arbitrators should avoid even the appearance of impropriety," in order to minimize risk.[8]

Mitigation of bias is one of the most important tasks in the overall risk management process and is often overlooked. A reduction in bias allows for a better alignment to legal requirements; while it creates an objective, transparent and fair decision process.[9] How can the law help contain bias? For an example, while the Federal Acquisition Regulation (FAR) does not directly address bias, it does provide a framework of the solicitation and proposal evaluation process.[10] This framework provides a process and accompanying requirements that contain bias by defining rules and forcing evaluators to include justifications for their decisions. An illustrative example is found in the following case *Rotech Health Care, Inc.*, where the protestor alleged the proposal's past performance was not treated fairly as the awardee's past performance examples were all less in dollar value than the anticipated contract award. The Government Accountability Office (GAO) sustained this claim that indeed it was past performance and should have been similar in size, scope and complexity in order to merit the rating provided to the awardee.[11]

Another example relating to bias and legal matters—in particular, machine learning (ML) models—runs the risk of incorporating bias or unfairness into their outcomes. This bias is typically driven by the quality of the underlying data used to train or calibrate the model, which is often built using sensitive drivers/attributes, such as: age, gender, nationality, religion, race, language, culture, marital status, economic condition and zip code.[12] One example of how machine learning bias has occurred comes from the field of facial recognition. Due to the current lack of diversity in datasets used to train facial recognition software, models are prone to misidentification, especially among women and people of color. As an example of this, a system developed by IBM "was found to have misidentified gender in up to 7% of lighter-skinned females, up to 12% of darker-skinned males, and up to 35% of darker-skinned females."[13]

8. Under the FINRA Code of Arbitration Procedure, Part IV Appointment, Disqualification and Authority of Arbitrators, https://www.finra.org/arbitration-mediation/printable-code-arbitration-procedure-12000#IV, the following should be taken into account: any existing or past financial, business, professional, family, social, or other relationships or circumstances with any party, any party's representative, or anyone who the arbitrator is told may be a witness in the proceeding, that are likely to affect impartiality or might reasonably create an appearance of partiality or bias.
9. See, e.g., further the *US Federal Government's General Accountability Office (GAO) Bid Protest Annual Report to Congress for FY 2016*, https://www.gao.gov/assets/gao-17-314sp.pdf. As discussed, the denying or sustaining of a protest can, unfortunately, include built-in biases, as discussed in this report.
10. See FAR subparts 15.101-1 and 15.305, https://www.ecfr.gov/current/title-48/chapter-1/subchapter-C/part-15?toc=1.
11. *Rotech Health Care, Inc.* (B-413024 et al.), https://www.gao.gov/products/b-413024,b-413024.2,b-413024.3. The evaluator did not provide documentation to support its finding that the past performance was similar or relevant to the solicitation.
12. Kevin D. Oden, *Increasing Fairness in Machine Learning Models: Best Practices for Overcoming Algorithmic Bias*, Risk Management Association, 2020, https://www.rmahq.org/blogs/2020/increasing-fairness-in-machine-learning-models-best-practices-for-overcoming-algorithmic-bias/?gmssopc=1.
13. *Ibid.*

To mitigate the negative impact of this bias (which is risk exposure), Microsoft and Amazon are reportedly distancing themselves from the facial recognition market until "stronger regulations [are] put in place to govern the ethical use of facial recognition technology," while IBM plans on exiting the business altogether.[14]

Another example regards how best to achieve board diversity in the hopes of mitigating negative impact and risk exposure due to bias.[15] The importance of the board on the corporation cannot be overstated, as they set the tone for the entire organization. For instance, in 2018, Women on Boards was signed into law to help ensure equitable gender representation on California corporate boards,[16] although a criticism is that this law has yet to meet the goal of getting more women of color on boards.[17]

There are different views in regards to how to best achieve board diversity. For instance, the concept of "tokenism," as discussed in general next, provides one viewpoint:

> The primary risk to higher female board representation occurs when companies, in an effort to appear more gender-balanced, recruit underqualified directors. This practice, referred to as tokenism, is similar to the risk of appointing outside directors with the sole purpose of satisfying perceived external demand for diversity.[18]

While another view is as follows:

> There are thousands of well-qualified women candidates who would bring outstanding experience as well as different perspectives that shareholders deserve. Any company that selects a non-qualified woman is doing itself and its shareholders an incredible disservice. Enlightened companies with women on their boards realize the competitive advantages. Boards have to reach outside their immediate networks to find women candidates who would bring specific experience that the board needs. This has been the most frequent pushback from companies that simply want to maintain the status quo. They're not thinking about their shareholders, nor their bottom line.[19]

It is further argued that board diversity is helpful not only to mitigate bias but to also improve corporate governance overall, thereby minimizing exposure to risk.[20] For instance:

> Women tend to ask questions, not stay silent if they see better ways of finding solutions. Shareholders want directors to ask questions. Women do their homework in order to be

14. *Ibid.*
15. Based on editor interview with Betsy Berkhemer-Credaire, author of *The Board Game: How Smart Women Become Corporate Directors*, Angel City Press (2013), August 7, 2019.
16. SB-826 Corporations: boards of directors, Approved by Governor (September 30, 2018), https://leginfo.legislature.ca.gov/faces/billTextClient.xhtml?bill_id=201720180SB826.
17. Women of Color Underrepresented in Silicon Valley, *Silicon Valley Business Journal*, https://www.bizjournals.com/sanjose/news/2021/12/09/women-of-color-underrepresented-in-silicon-valley.html.
18. David Larcker and Brian Tayan, *Corporate Governance Matters: A Closer Look at Organizational Choices and Their Consequences*, Pearson, 2016, 2nd ed., p. 140.
19. Editor interview with Betsy Berkhemer-Credaire, author of *The Board Game: How Smart Women Become Corporate Directors*, Angel City Press (2013), August 7, 2019.
20. Although, as mentioned, there are differing viewpoints as well. In David Larcker and Brian Tayan, *Corporate Governance Matters: A Closer Look at Organizational Choices and Their Consequences*, Pearson, 2016, 2nd ed., p. 140, goes on to state: "Evidence is inconclusive about whether female board representation improves corporate performance." While, in the editor interview with Betsy Berkhemer-Credaire, author of *The Board Game: How Smart Women Become Corporate Directors*, Angel City Press (2013), August 7, 2019, argues: "Of course, there may never be a direct causal effect, but research says profitability, productivity and workforce engagement do improve. All aspects of company performance (including the increased benefits for women employees seeing women role models on the board) contribute to better performance."

prepared. That's also why having three women on a board is better for asking questions and backing each other up.[21]

Various measures have been taken in recent years to improve board diversity, especially by more visible companies such as those included in the S&P 500. Goldman Sachs recently announced a new policy stating they will not underwrite the IPOs of firms having only white male board members.[22]

Continued dialog will eventually lead to better results overall towards handling bias. Further dialog topics can include: (1) revising specific board membership policies and the selection process to increase their relevance and (2) critically assessing how, why, where and when all groups add value in today's governance ecosystem.

The bottom line is to encourage diverse voices as part of the deliberation process and make the intentional effort to address their bias as part of their participation.[23]

Bias also is a problem as it relates to misconceptions of the roles of risk, ethics and compliance in an organization. For instance, a survey of more than 160 CEOs and directors of North American public and private companies revealed that directors and boards have varying views and priorities regarding regulatory compliance. One question in the survey asked what impact an unexpected regulatory problem would have on their overall evaluation. Of the CEOs and directors surveyed, 54.7% of directors stated it would have a "moderately negative impact," whereas only 42.3% of CEOs stated the same. Interestingly, and perhaps unsurprisingly, another question asked what impact missed forecasts of revenues/earnings would have, and 58.7% of directors answered it would have a "moderately negative impact," whereas 69.1% of CEOs stated the same.[24]

Such statistics begin to paint a picture of the lack of understanding and appreciation on the part of some leaders of the key role compliance professionals play in not just curbing or avoiding entirely unexpected regulatory problems, but also the role they play in adding to the organization's bottom line. Furthermore, this lack of understanding and appreciation of their roles in mitigating risk, unfortunately, flows down to other areas of the organization.

Consider the topic of job descriptions for a moment. Recent research in the UK[25] concluded that poorly defined job descriptions drive staff turnover. Specifically, 58% of human resources (HR) managers believe that poor job descriptions directly contribute to weak candidate pools, which exacerbates the problem of poor candidate fit. Further, 79% of HR managers responded that actually getting good job descriptions from management is difficult and time-consuming. The question then arises: does management actually understand what the organization needs? Or, is it a better question to state: is this problem due to lack of mitigating bias in part?

Some have concluded (and in some corners, there is growing advocacy for this notion) that in order to simultaneously solve the problems of increased costs, growing transactional complexity,

21. Betsy Berkhemer-Credaire, *The Board Game: How Smart Women Become Corporate Directors*, Angel City Press, 2013, p. 250.
22. See, e.g., Goldman to Refuse IPOs If All Directors Are White, Straight Men, *Bloomberg* (January 2020), https://www.bloomberg.com/news/articles/2020-01-24/goldman-rule-adds-to-death-knell-of-the-all-white-male-board#xj4y7vzkg.
23. For an in-depth discussion, see: Eliminating Implicit Bias: First Step, Admit You Have It, *American Bar Association* (June 2017), https://www.americanbar.org/news/abanews/publications/youraba/2017/july-2017/the-first-step-to-eliminating-implicit-bias--admit-you-have-it-/.
24. Stanford University, Center for Leadership Development and Research, Stanford Graduate School of Business, Rock Center for Corporate Governance & The Miles Group, "2013 Survey on CEO Performance Evaluations" (2013), https://www.gsb.stanford.edu/faculty-research/publications/2013-ceo-performance-evaluation-survey.
25. Hay Group: Poor Job Descriptions Drive Staff Turnover, https://www.consultancy.uk/news/2240/hay-group-poor-job-descriptions-drive-staff-turnover.

dangers of noncompliance and poor candidate fit, technology is the only solution, and it can even completely replace the compliance professionals currently doing the work. Such a misguided conclusion is dangerous to automatically leap to. If one does not understand the role of the compliance professional, how can one claim to have found the compliance professional's replacement?

Ethics as the Basis of Decision-Making

Unfortunately, due to the fact that there is not sufficient risk mitigation of bias, the subject of ethics is often given short shrift. That is, what is lacking in many organizations is an understanding that strong compliance and ethics (C&E) are truly necessary. Again, going back to the "if it ain't broke, don't fix it" bias, if an organization starts with the assumption that it is already sufficiently ethical, this blinds them to all sorts of risk. It also does not follow that such an assumption directly leads to the conclusion that the organization is indeed ethical.

First, Some Definitions

What is compliance? It can be defined as conforming to relevant laws, regulations, policies, codes of conduct, ethics, standards, procedures and contractual obligations. The compliance function consists of efforts organizations undertake to ensure that employees and others associated with the firm do not violate applicable rules, regulations or norms.[26]

We then get to risk. You may be rather surprised to find that the International Organization for Standardization (ISO) views risk as neither positive nor negative; instead, risk is the effect of uncertainty on an organization's ability to meet its objectives. Further, the Contract Management Body of Knowledge (CMBOK) discusses uncertainty and risk in contract management. With uncertainty, in essence, there is no background information whatsoever; however, this is not the same as an unknown risk.[27]

Understanding behavioral ethics can strengthen an organization's risk management and compliance program.[28] For instance, the US Federal Sentencing Guidelines for Organizations and the FAR present standards and requirements for C&E programs, including: the need for a compliance and ethics officer; a "Code of Conduct" and policies and procedures to set behavioral standards; effective periodic training and communications about those standards; a hotline or some other type of communication mechanism to raise concerns about perceived misconduct confidentially or anonymously; and protection from retaliation for those raising concerns. FAR 3.1002 also states that elements of an ethics and compliance program should be "suitable to the size of the company and extent of its involvement in government contracting." What is most important is that the entity assess its own situation and implement a program that enables it to answer in the affirmative three fundamental questions as cited in the guidelines: (1) Is the corporation's compliance program well designed? (2) Is the program being applied earnestly and in good faith? and (3) Does the corporation's compliance program work in practice?

Therefore, being proactive is key: every entity should conduct an ethics and compliance risk assessment. The results of the risk assessment steer the focus of resources to high-risk areas. Also vital

26. See generally, Geoffrey P. Miller, "The Compliance Function: An Overview," New York University Law and Economics Working Papers (2014): Paper 393, https://papers.ssrn.com/sol3/papers.cfm?abstract_id=2527621.
27. See generally, *Contract Management Body of Knowledge (CMBOK),* National Contract Management Association, 2019, 6th ed. Moreover, while the PMBOK describes uncertainty as a lack of total certainty, it is difficult, if not impossible, to fully grasp the concept of uncertainty.
28. See generally, *Corporate Law for Good People,* Adi Libson, January 2020, https://corpgov.law.harvard.edu/2020/01/15/corporate-law-for-good-people/.

is whether the risk assessment is modified over time to take into account lessons learned from compliance failures—either internal or observed at other organizations in the same industry or region.

Behavioral ethics is a well-known field of social science which also brings to light, as well as analyzes and challenges, the assumption (due to various biases) that an entity or individual may not be as ethical as believed. Behavioral C&E (which is less well known) attempts to use behavioral ethics insights to develop and maintain effective compliance programs.

The more general aspect of behavioral C&E is the above-mentioned overarching finding that we are not as ethical as we think. One of the greatest challenges to having effective C&E programs in organizations is often more about the "will" than the "way," based on the assumption that "we have this and we had better focus our limited resources elsewhere." Or, it could also be fear on the part of the organization to admit in any way that they are not in some way ethical (therefore, noncompliant) and subject themselves to potential legal liability.

For instance, an interesting case in point: almost every major regulatory regime relies upon the essential principle of law enforcement policy that, by establishing incentives for self-policing, companies are more likely to adopt effective compliance programs. This premise depends on the certainty that the protections afforded by the attorney-client privilege and related privileges are available. So, if that certainty is lacking, then it is less likely that the organization would be in the position to adopt an ethical and effective compliance program. As demonstrated in *Barko*,[29] the US District Court judge issued an order which alarmed industry and the legal community, as it granted a motion to compel (which in their eyes threatened to destabilize attorney-client privilege). In this particular case, during discovery, internal documents were sought (such as audits and inspections), which were privileged. The appellate court later vacated the lower court's decision.

Regarding the risk of exposure to enforcement liability: research relating to bias, in particular, "motivated blindness"—which derives from a psychological concept which describes the tendency for people to easily miss information that contradicts what is in their own best interest—is relevant to distinct elements of a C&E program, such as: resolution of conflict of interest issues and decisions involving possible investigations of and discipline for violations of legal or ethical standards. For example, this research underscores the importance of the Sentencing Guidelines'[30] expectation that organizations discipline employees not only for engaging in wrongful conduct but also "for failing to take reasonable steps to prevent or detect" wrongdoing by others—something relatively few companies do well (and some don't do at all).

Other helpful considerations for effective measures to be taken by organizations, based on ISO Compliance Management standards, include:[31]

- Build and/or expand on the supervisory accountability into their policies;
- Be an example: speak forcefully to the issue(s) in C&E training and other communications for managers;
- Have appropriate discipline and notification that discipline occurred; and,
- Have relevant stakeholders take these requirements into account in their audits and controls of investigative and disciplinary records.

A further consideration regarding improving ethics by including stakeholders in the conversation is: as compliance evolves into its own, the question then becomes, when does following through with compliance and ethics duties tread into the unauthorized practice of law (UPL)?

29. *United States ex rel. Barko v. Halliburton Co.*, No. 1:05-CV-1276 (D.D.C. March 6, 2014).
30. US Sentencing Guidelines, 2021 Manual Annotated, https://www.ussc.gov/guidelines/2021-guidelines-manual-annotated.
31. Based on the new ISO 37301:2021 Compliance management systems, https://www.iso.org/standard/75080.html.

An example of this conundrum includes contracting professionals (who tended to work more on the business side of the procurement) now, in certain circumstances, must keep track of potential antitrust violations (a legal consideration), as they are considered to be particularly well situated to spot, analyze and directly report on illegal antitrust conspiracies, such as: price fixing, bid rigging and allocation.[32] Is this a potential example of UPL?

In order to be able to help answer that question, it would be instructive to look at some relevant definitions. Most states in the US have defined law practice, as well as its unauthorized variants, in statutes and case law. Most such definitions extend to the selection and preparation of documents.[33] For instance,

> The practice of law does not include the design, creation, publication, distribution, display or sale, including publication, distribution, display or sale by means of an internet website, of written materials, books, forms, computer software, or similar products clearly and conspicuously state that the products are not a substitute for the advice of an attorney.[34]

As discussed throughout this handbook, compliance has evolved over the past decades from being a "watchdog" function—charged with seeking out misconduct—to including an important advisory and counseling element. There is a gray area as to whether this can potentially tread into UPL. As with other aspects of the compliance function, there is no "one-size-fits-all" formula for how compliance-related advice should be provided, or by whom. The identity of the person providing such advice and the mechanism through which it is provided necessarily depends on the facts and circumstances of each organization.[35] Again, the issue arises whether such advice can potentially tread into UPL. Next are some considerations that might shed more light:

- To use attorney-client privilege in a compliance setting, the Chief Compliance Officer (CCO), along with others acting on their behalf, must be acting in "professional legal capacity," as opposed to their day-to-day business capacity. The following have been considered by some courts: whether CCO/compliance reports to Legal or attends Legal's meetings; whether CCO/compliance indicates to others that they are acting in a legal capacity; whether CCO/compliance was explicitly instructed to assist an attorney in providing legal advice; and the extent of the authorizing attorney's oversight regarding the CCO/compliance.[36]

32. For example, see, Kathryn B. Kushner, Does Something Seem Fishy? Tips for Spotting the Red Flags of Antitrust Crimes and Collusion in Contracting, National Contract Management Association, *Contract Management Magazine* (December 2020). Explaining that contracting is a ripe ground where antitrust crimes occur and that contracting professionals are encouraged to help the US Government (namely, the Procurement Collusion Strike Force) uncover such illegal conspiracies.
33. See, for instance, Ray Worthy Campbell, Rethinking regulation and innovation in the US legal services market, *NYU Journal of Law & Business*, vol. 9, Fall 2012, Is. 1, https://heinonline.org/HOL/LandingPage?handle=hein.journals/nyujolbu9&div=4&id=&page=, explains that the popularity of class actions against alleged UPL violators has made the business risk related to UPL greater than ever before.
34. See, for instance: *UPL Committee v. Parsons Tech. Inc.*, 1999 Westlaw 47235 (N.D. Tex. January 22, 1999), vacated, 179 F.3d 956 (5th Cir. 1999). In this particular case, the Texas UPL Committee sued two manufacturers of software that helped people prepare wills and other documents and was granted summary judgment by the court.
35. Based on editor interview with Celine de Bourgoin, Contract Manager, UNAVCO, July 22, 2019. Furthermore, compliance-related advice is useful only if it is credible. Organizations should seek to reward employees or agents who reach out in good faith to seek such advice. Accordingly, organizations should not retaliate or punish employees or agents who, in good faith, act in reliance on such advice if the advice given proves to be mistaken.
36. For a good discussion, see: Doug Gallagher and Manasi Raveendran, Attorney-Client Privilege for In-House Counsel, *American Bar Association* (Nov/Dec 2017), https://www.americanbar.org/groups/intellectual_property_law/publications/landslide/2017-18/november-december/attorney-client-privilege-inhouse-counsel/.

- The basis for the attorney-client privilege is the principle that clients and attorneys should be able to communicate in a free and frank manner.[37] The privilege belongs to the client and is a protection provided by various statutes and common law for certain communications between the client and the client's attorney to encourage full disclosure of info between the client and attorney.
- For attorney-client privilege to apply, in general, (1) the communication must be between client and attorney (i.e., an individual having a law degree and bar membership, and acting as an attorney for the client) or an agent of an attorney (e.g., tax accountant, patent agent, expert); (2) the communication must be made by the client and contain confidential information; (3) the communication must be made outside the presence of a nonprivileged third party; (4) the communication must be made for the purpose of securing legal advice; and 5) the privilege has not otherwise been waived. Privileged communications can be written or oral, but only communications between or among "privileged" persons are protected.[38]
- What is typically not protected under the privilege: (1) underlying facts of a matter are always discoverable. For example, if a corporation initiates an investigation into when the first public disclosure of an invention occurred, the factual results of the investigation are not privileged, whereas the legal advice by the lawyer on the impact of the investigation and recommended course of action might be privileged; (2) client communications not involving a lawyer (or non-lawyer acting as an agent for a lawyer); (3) cannot be used to facilitate or conceal a crime or fraud, such as perjury and witness tampering.

How Risk and Compliance Are Coming Into Their Own

In addition to the aforementioned, it is helpful to also look at Professor Juran's *Quality Control Handbook* because Juran was at the forefront in pinpointing how an emerging area (in that case, quality management) came into its own as a separate profession, and how that emerging area was vital to organizations' overall success. Juran's book is a good model to review as it relates to understanding what is happening now as risk and compliance come into their own.[39]

Let's start first with a brief history:[40]

Compliance 1.0 (late 1990s–early 2000s): an era described as having heavy-handed enforcement with a "bulldog" mentality, which left the legacy that all CCOs and compliance professionals must be attorneys in order to adequately protect the organization. In that era, risk management processes reflected the enforcement tactics by government agencies, thus, primarily were based on fear, which leads to bad communication and poor productivity overall.

Compliance 2.0 (today): still in the toddler stage as it relates to specific separation of titles, departments and responsibilities (discussed later regarding uneven job descriptions and duties); Board of Directors are disconnected in many instances and there is a need for buy-in from all stakeholders to improve risk mitigation and lead to better productivity. This also includes necessary recognition by the board and upper level management of the return on investment (ROI) due to an effective compliance and ethics culture. Thus, the compliance professional also needs to be an educator and have excellent communication skills to convey this message, with the support from management. Overall,

37. See, *Upjohn Co. v. United States*, 449 U.S. 383, 389 (1981).
38. Note: Work product doctrine, which is a close relative of attorney-client privilege, can work together with attorney-client privilege to help keep certain communications out of the reach of opposing counsel during litigation.
39. See in general, Joseph A. DeFeo, *Juran's Quality Handbook*, American Society for Quality, 2016, 7th ed.
40. Based on Editor interview with Maurice Gilbert, Partner at Conselium Compliance, October 30, 2020.

there is a greater need for compliance professionals who are not all attorneys, as attorneys are often seen as inflexible and unable to fully meet needs.

Another important aspect in Compliance 2.0 relates to the need for standardization. For example, the Contract Management Standard (CMS) of the National Contract Management Association (NCMA) was accredited in April 2019 by the Board of Standards Review of the American National Standards Institute (ANSI) as an American National Standard. Consistent application of such professional standards enables successful application of related risk and compliance duties across diverse industries and diverse organizations.

Important to add to this discussion as compliance is coming into its own is the simultaneous evolution of the legal profession.

As discussed, the difficulty of enforcing the "practice of law" restriction stems from the fact that no one, it seems, has adequately defined what is meant by "practice of law."[41] This opens the door to these new positions in compliance and compliance-related fields.

Permissible legal services that are not the "practice of law" exist, as there are law-related products and services that do not constitute the practice of law[42] as well as nonlawyers who have begun dispensing legal services from multidisciplinary firms in the guise of consulting services.[43]

It is instructive to view job descriptions to see the concomitant evolution of both the legal profession and compliance profession, as they further define themselves. Job descriptions are helpful as well because they demonstrate the direct need that is sought by the organization for the job candidate to fill. Increasingly, job titles and job descriptions may mix or separate the functions of legal, risk, ethics and compliance, depending on several factors, including regulations affecting their particular industry, size of the organization and other relevant considerations. The uneven nature of such job titles and accompanying job duties described, can include: advising management on matters of legal and ethical problems, risk management and overseeing compliance training as a "Legal Risk Compliance Manager."[44]

As can be seen from the need described in various job duties, the compliance function should play an advisory and consultative role in organizational decision-making. When an organization is considering important questions regarding its future, it is often well-advised to give a compliance officer a voice in the decision process. Depending on the facts and circumstances, it may be appropriate for a compliance officer to be involved in a wide range of strategic decisions. Compliance should thus be integrated into institutional design so that compliance officers can offer their advice early on in the decision-making process and help the organization avoid problems down the line.

It is also clear that Legal needs to do more than the "day job" to identify, manage and mitigate legal risks. Some organizations apply a narrow definition in which legal risks are solely those arising

41. A blue ribbon ABA task force labored to craft such a definition (see, for instance, ABA Task Force on the Model Definition of the Practice of Law, Board of Governors Resolution, www.americanbar.org/groups/professional_responsibility/task_force_model_definition_practice_law.html). Also, state definitions tend to be circular, describing the practice of law as "what lawyers do." (see, e.g., NEB. CT. R. section 3-1001, providing a "General Definition": the practice of law or to practice law is the application of legal principles and judgment re: to the circumstances or objectives of another entity or person which require the knowledge, judgment and skill of a person trained as a lawyer).
42. See e.g., Thomas D. Morgan, On the Declining Importance of Legal Institutions, MICH ST. L REV, http://ssrn.com/abstract=2007273, discussing the lawyers' monopoly over the delivery of legal services has eroded.
43. See generally, Paul D. Paton, Multidisciplinary Practice Redux: Globalization, Core Values, and Reviving the MDP Debate in America, 78 Fordham L. Rev. 2193 (2010) and John Leubsdorf, Legal Ethics Falls Apart, 57 Buffalo L. Rev. 959, 1042 (2009).
44. Based on a summary of keyword searches "legal," "risk," "compliance" and "ethics" by Editor on LinkedIn from August 1, 2022 to August 31, 2022.

from Legal's operations, such as resourcing decisions (in-house v. use of law firms v. other third parties) and the quality of the advice provided by Legal and the conduct of its lawyers. Such a definition fails to take into account the many other risks that an organization faces which have a legal component, for instance, financial crime, procurement or IP. Such underlying activities may be owned by other parts of the business. For instance, the Program Manager may handle contract and procurement matters.[45] Yet to deny Legal responsibility for managing the legal risk inherent in those activities does not make sense and could result in responsibilities falling through the gap between Legal and Compliance. Hence, many organizations apply a broad definition of legal risk which encompasses any risk faced by the business which has a legal component.[46] Of more importance than definition is identifying the risks, legal and otherwise, than the organization faces and establishing an effective framework for their management so that responsibility can be allocated among Legal, Compliance and other functional areas.

Moreover, the role of the General Counsel (GC) and of the Chief Legal Officer (CLO) looks very different these days than just 10 years ago, having gone from a position of largely exclusively providing legal expertise to now playing a key role in business strategy and overseeing a much broader scope of responsibilities. As the role of the GC/CLO has evolved, so too has the organizational structure. It is now common to see Legal, Operations, Privacy, Compliance and Ethics all reporting up to this role, with cross functional dotted lines to IT Security and ERM departments.[47]

And yet, another example relating to the uneven job titles and duties relates to the Chief Compliance Officer (CCO) and Legal Counsel, sometimes considered by some organizations as an interchangeable role, is in general responsible for overseeing all ongoing activities related to the development, implementation and maintenance of organization's compliance program and helping to ensure firm compliance with applicable rules and regulations.[48]

Typically, the GC typically has a role in interacting with regulators, although more often than not specifically in relation to legal risk only. In large regulated organizations that separate ownership of legal risk, regulatory risk and compliance risk into different teams, this may be less frequent as interaction is shared between the GC, the CCO and the CRO. In smaller or less regulated organizations, all three areas may be within the Legal department under the overall responsibility of the GC

45. CMBOK describing various stakeholders in contract management, including Legal, Finance and Program Management, p. 4.
46. In the past, GCs and organizations have typically not considered legal risk as a category in its own right and it has been subsumed within other risks rather than being explicitly identified in risk management frameworks managed by Operational Risk, Compliance or Internal Audit. This may have been the case for financial services because Basel II defined legal risk as being a part of operational risk. Another reason for this lack of identification of legal risk in its own right could be because of its comparative lower profile when compared to other risks arising from financial crime, conduct and duty of care, IT and cyber, which can have a much larger impact on the viability or capital adequacy of an organization. However, the level of fines and increased enforcement over recent years has driven significant changes in the profile of legal risk in those organizations and peer group companies.
47. See generally, Legal GRC: The New Role of General Counsel and Chief Legal Officers, 2020, *Exterro*, https://www.exterro.com/resources/the-new-role-general-counsel-and-chief-legal-officers-must-play.
48. See generally, The Privatization of Compliance, white paper RAND Symposium presented on May 28, 2014, Scott Killingsworth, http://compliancestrategists.com/pro/wp-content/uploads/2013/10/The-Privatization-of-Compliance-final-29-May-2014-Killingsworth.pdf. Or, you may also see something like: the Chief Legal and Risk Officer will play a pivotal role in the organization. They will ensure the company operates within the law at all times and offer counsel on legal and risk related issues. They will be an effective guardian of the organization and facilitate business development strategies while adding value to the current executive team. As a senior executive of the corporation, they act as a strategic business partner focused on understanding the overall business strategy and ensuring the legal department actions and deliverables are aligned by providing advice, oversight and engaging in numerous areas, including: ethics, privacy, transparency, regulatory and governmental changes and compliance. They are also a member of the crisis management team.

or may be shared with the Program Manager. The extent of interaction by the GC with regulators (and how proactive this is) will be dictated in large part by how regulated the industry is in which the organization operates. Keeping abreast of emerging regulations which carry legal risk is essential, including those regulations which primarily relate to operations, as is also demonstrated by the job duties described earlier. A good approach should include some narrative around interactions with regulators and what this means for the organization.[49]

This debate of what should be under Legal and what should be under Compliance is necessary, and continued dialog between academia and industry is salutary here. As discussed, some view that Compliance has always been a separate and distinct profession. The skill set required is different from that of an attorney, and yet, that skill set nicely complements an attorney's work. In compliance, essentially, you are at the heart of where an organization's stakeholders intersect, such as: law; regulatory; quality; public policy; risk management; technology; business; operations; project management; etc., and, to be successful, you must wear those multiple hats simultaneously to achieve the ultimate goal of full compliance for your organization.

"I believe that the compliance profession will continue to grow and develop; however, not necessarily solely intertwined with the legal profession. Compliance will only deepen its relevance into corporations and other regulated entities, as well as into third-party agencies as they relate to lobbying and public policy."[50]

So, as a relatively new specialty that is emerging,[51] compliance is needed to meet the evolving demands brought on by economic, technological, business and political changes, as well as to keep stakeholders resilient in times of crisis.

So, as compliance is coming into its own, does this mean that compliance professionals can, or should, practice law?

For example, the California Paraprofessional Program Working Group is charged with developing recommendations for consideration by the Board of Trustees for the creation of a paraprofessional licensure/certification program for non-attorneys to increase access to legal services in California. In carrying out this charge, the working group hoped to balance the dual goals of ensuring public protection and increasing access to legal services.[52]

The impetus is that legal services provided by attorneys are far too expensive and inaccessible, and there is not enough competition to drive this price down for those needing the services. In most states, only lawyers licensed by their respective states can give legal advice, as well as hold an economic interest in law firms. This is controversial in the legal community, with critics stating that such changes can diminish the value and standards of legal services and the professional in general.[53]

49. See generally, Melissa L. Rorie, Sally S. Simpson, Mark A. Cohen, and Michael P. Vandenbergh, Examining procedural justice and legitimacy in corporate offending and beyond-compliance behavior: The efficacy of direct and indirect regulatory interactions, *Law & Policy*, vol. 40, Is. 2, April 2018.
50. Editor interview with Debra Hunter-Bonner, Compliance Manager at a major utilities company, April 2021, emphasizing that compliance has always been a separate profession. Furthermore: "Given this distinction between Compliance and Legal, in order to be a successful compliance professional, it would be ideal to have at least 10 years or more experience in the business/corporate world, and have a fundamental understanding of contracts."
51. Harvard Law School, The Practice, "The Emergence of Compliance, A New Profession?" (2016), https://thepractice.law.harvard.edu/article/the-emergence-of-compliance/.
52. California Paraprofessional Program Working Group, www.calbar.ca.gov/About-Us/Who-We-Are/Committees/California-Paraprofessional-Program-Working-Group.
53. See generally, "Legal Advice is Often Unaffordable," www.usatoday.com/story/opinion/2020/09/17/lawyers-expensive-competition-innovation-increase-access-gorsuch-column/5817467002. Moreover, other viewpoints voice that opposition to programs like the paraprofessional license is rooted in nothing more than turf warfare waged by attorneys, who are afraid of losing business and prestige as a new professional category emerges.

So, by 2017, adverse court opinions, legislative criticism, and advocacy by certain bar leaders led to the passage of the State Bar Act of 2017, separating the regulatory and trade association functions. The new California Lawyers Association (CLA) took the trade association functions, while the State Bar kept regulatory functions.[54] This de-unification brought fundamental changes,[55] and since de-unification, "attorneys" became "licensees," paving the way for the proposed paraprofessional license, as well as opening the door for future dialog as to whether or not non-attorney compliance professionals should be allowed to practice law in some way.

The proposed paraprofessional license would allow non-lawyers to provide legal services to the public without oversight by an attorney, including court representation of these clients, with the exception of jury trials.

Concern about this proposed program includes that it would fail to accomplish the primary edict of the State Bar-public protection. For instance, on June 5, 2020, the Washington Supreme Court announced that it suspended the state's LLLT (limited license legal technician) program (similar to the paraprofessional license proposal). Chief Justice Debra L. Stephens stated "the program was an innovative attempt to increase access to legal services . . . [yet] a majority of the court determined that the LLLT program is not an effective way to meet these needs . . ."[56]

Conclusion (Or, Rather, Only the Beginning)

The moment is propitious for continued dialog about the future of law as risk and compliance are coming into their own. While lawyers may have some influence over the ways their business clients voluntarily comply,[57] due to technological advances, an increasingly globalized world and accompanying complex transactions, the demand for compliance professionals cannot be denied, as they carry specialized skillsets with broad responsibilities meeting a growing need. The compliance professional should not be at all marginalized; rather, embraced as a welcome partner to assist with the health of the organization and eventually in helping to positively influence public policy overall.[58] The goal of this chapter is to provide further food for thought, and I look forward to more discussion from academia and industry alike.

54. "The State Bar Takes Significant Step Towards Sweeping Changes," Nikki Presley Milibrand, Chair of OCBA Task Force, www.ocbar.org, July 2020.
55. Such as, starting with substantially reducing attorney members of the State Bar governing body and ultimately eliminating all trustee elections in favor of appointments only.
56. See, ABA Journal, Washington Supreme Court Sunsets Limited License Program for Non-Lawyers, June 6, 2020. Moreover, the 2022 licensing fee bill, Assembly Bill 2958, is, as of this printing, awaiting a vote by the California Senate, so the proposed paraprofessional license program is on hold.
57. For further relevant discussion, see, Ben Heineman, *The General Counsel as Lawyer-Statesman*, https://corpgov.law.harvard.edu/2010/09/05/the-general-counsel-as-lawyer-statesman/.
58. Editor is grateful to Professor David Feldman, Ph.D., Social and Behavioral Sciences, Water UC Irvine, for inspiring this point.

PART II

Contract Risk Management and Insurance Considerations

7
INSURANCE
A Look Inside the Claims Department

Joyce Segelken

"If there were no losses, there would be no premiums" goes an old insurance proverb. Indeed, it is risk that drives insurance and the handling of those risks by claims departments that makes or breaks an insurance company. Risk in the property and casualty insurance world is losses, both expense and indemnity, that result in exposure to the insurance carrier. It is the likelihood, whether foreseeable or not, that an insured event will occur, requiring the insurer to pay a claim. Any risk management strategy includes the placement of risk with the corresponding insurance policy. It is important to understand the inner workings of insurance to fully comprehend risk transfer and to manage and contain the exposure once insurance is implicated by an event that leads to a claim. This chapter will explore what types of claims are covered under casualty liability insurance, provide an understanding of the claim process once a claim is submitted to the claim department of an insurance company, and inform on what can be expected from the handling claim professional.

Commercial General and Personal Liability Policies Cover Specific Risks

Almost every individual and every industry and business whether small or large is subject to risk of some kind or another, be it the risk of flood or fire, crime, injury to an employee subject to worker's compensation regulations, or professional errors and omissions. This chapter focuses on commercial general liability and personal liability policies and the specific risks covered by those policies.

The insuring agreement of a commercial general liability policy promises its insureds that the insurer or insurance company will cover bodily injury and property damage caused by an occurrence, as well as personal injury or advertising injury caused by an offense which the insured is legally obligated to pay, that takes place within the policy period, subject to policy exclusions. The definitions of key words within the insuring agreement are important to determining whether damages will be covered by a general liability policy. For instance, "bodily injury" typically means physical injury, sickness or disease sustained by a person, including resulting death, humiliation, mental anguish, mental injury or shock at any time.[1] "Property damage" means physical injury to tangible property, including all resulting loss of use of that property, or loss of use of tangible property that is not physically injured as defined within a general liability policy.[2] In order for the bodily injury or property

1. For instance, see Insurance Services Office, *Verisk*, https://products.iso.com/productcenter/.
2. *Ibid.*

DOI: 10.4324/9781351107242-10

damage to be covered, it must be caused by an "occurrence" which means an accident, including continuous or repeated exposure to substantially the same general harmful conditions.[3] As an example, if a customer inside an insured's store stumbles over the manager's sleeping dog as he attempts to reach a display and breaks his arm, the general liability policy will respond with coverage for the claim for injury-related damages, as the broken arm would qualify as bodily injury that is accidental or caused by an occurrence for which the store owner is arguably liable.

Commercial general liability policies provide liability coverage for other types of damages as well under the definitions of "personal injury" and "advertising injury" caused by an offense. Definitions of personal injury and advertising injury will vary from company to company and the definitions have evolved over the years, but typically "personal injury" will cover injury, other than bodily injury, property damage or advertising injury caused by an offense of:

a. False arrest, false detention or false imprisonment;
b. Malicious prosecution;
c. Wrongful entry into, wrongful eviction of a person from or other violation of a person's right of private occupancy of a dwelling . . . that such person occupies, if committed by or on behalf of its landlord, lessor or owner; or
d. Electronic, oral, written or other publication of material that:
    (1) Libels or slanders a person or organization; or
    (2) Violates a person's right of privacy. (ISO Properties, Inc.,)[4]

Back to our insured shopkeeper. If one of her customers comes into the store and manages to step around the dog but in his irritation at almost tripping on the dog, he kicks the dog in anger before leaving, thus infuriating the shopkeeper to the point where the shopkeeper writes to the customer's boss and complains that your employee is a dog hater and is abusive to animals and should be fired, and word of this gets back to the employee/store customer, then the customer makes a claim for damages based on libel against the insured shopkeeper stating that the letter to his boss caused him damages for emotional distress and lost wages, such damages would be covered as personal injury caused by one of the offenses listed under the definition for the publication of material that libels or slanders someone.

> "Advertising injury" generally means injury, other than bodily injury, property damages or personal injury, sustained by a person or organization and caused by an offense of infringing, in that particular part of your advertisement about your goods, products or services upon their:
>
> a. Copyrighted advertising, or
> b. Registered collective mark, registered service mark or other registered trademarked name, slogan, symbol or title.[5]

Claims under the advertising injury coverage are less common in today's market, as the intent behind what an insurance company is willing to cover as "advertising" injury has narrowed and exclusions to preclude coverage for intellectual property type claims abound. However, if our shopkeeper sees a nice advertising layout on the internet and decides to rework it into her own marketing material plying her wares to potential customers, and the copyright owner of the advertising calls her up to

3. *Ibid.*
4. *Ibid.*
5. *Ibid.*

demand compensation, it just may pay off to submit that demand to the general liability insurance company as a claim under the advertising injury coverage of the policy.

Personal liability policies vary in scope of coverage from the basic to the more high end comprehensive policies available for added cost but are meant to provide individual protection over home, rental or auto for bodily injury and property damage caused by an occurrence as well as generally some form of personal injury type coverage.

Once the insuring agreement of a policy has been reviewed for potential coverage, an analysis of the policy exclusions must follow. It is possible for the insuring agreement to be met yet coverage be denied based on a policy exclusion. All insurance policies include pages of exclusions meant to narrow the scope of coverage. A commercial general liability policy will have exclusions that apply to the bodily injury and property damage portion of the policy, as well as special exclusions that apply to the personal injury and advertising sections and exclusions that apply to the policy as a whole. Some more commonly applied exclusions may be the intentional acts exclusion which limits or precludes coverage for damages caused with intent. Another is the employer's liability exclusion which makes it clear any injury to an insured's employee or an employment-related grievance by an insured's employee has no place being covered under a general liability policy. Others may be meant to limit long-term property damage to coverage under a single policy term. If our poor shopkeeper had lied to the customer's boss and made up the story of the dog kicking, an exclusion for intentional falsehoods would preclude that commercial personal injury coverage. Similarly, personal lines policies have exclusions meant to narrow coverage to what is intended by the industry.

Mention should be made of commercial excess umbrella policies and personal umbrella policies, as these policies with additional limits of insurance are becoming increasingly important to protect against risk of exposure in excess of the available primary policy limits, as well as to protect personal wealth management. Available policy limits, such as a $1 million limit on a general liability policy, have not increased in decades and are no longer adequate against today's exposure. A commercial excess umbrella policy will provide two types of coverage: typically, a follow form excess portion to a scheduled underlying policy over a required underlying limit, and an umbrella portion that applies under certain circumstances offering its own insuring agreement and policy definitions and exclusions. It is important for insureds to be aware of their excess and umbrella coverages and also to make sure the required underlying limits are in place to avoid a gap in coverage.

Claim Process

Insurance policies including liability coverages are built on the premise that should a claim arise, the insurance company will respond to that claim to mitigate or eliminate any risk to an insured. The life cycle of the claim is the business of the insurance industry's casualty claim departments. Quality and expertise may vary from company to company, but generally the top insurance carriers take pride in providing detailed and proficient claim handling along with a commitment to excellence and attention to customer detail. Risk management must include not only an understanding of what an insurance policy covers in order to properly anticipate and place risk, but also an understanding of the claim process. A claim is an anticipated personal or business event, and the risk manager will need to work closely with its insurance adjuster in responding to the claim by promptly reporting actual and potential claims and working closely throughout the investigation and discovery process in order to properly evaluate exposure and strategic resolution. Keeping risk contained is of mutual benefit to the insurance carrier and the insured.

Returning to our shopkeeper with her injury-prone customer, once an accident has occurred in the shop and the customer is on his way to the doctor, the claim process begins which will hopefully resolve in the best possible outcome for the shop owner and customer. The shopkeeper, being astute and responsible, completes a timely incident report documenting what happened along with the time, date and conditions, making careful note of any witnesses including their contact information and snapping a few pictures to include in her email to her insurance broker or directly to her insurance carrier. The claim process begins with a claim representative inputting the information electronically and taking preliminary information from the insured. The claim is opened in a database system with confirmation of an active policy in force and routed for handling to the appropriate claim professional. Proper claim handling is another procedure that is unique to each carrier but is segmented by line of business, often geographically and usually by severity. The mention in the claim reporting of fractured bones as a result of the fall over the dog will likely route this claim to a mid-level claim examiner. Algorithms are often in place to predict exposure and assist in the claim being properly assigned.

Claim professionals are extraordinary at what they do and provide a model of effective and efficient risk management along with compliance with regulatory and ethical standards. Part detective, part lawyer, part analyst and ardent multitaskers, claim examiners handle multiple claims both new and pending, customers, emails and phone calls, a constant barrage of new information, and even often suspect or exaggerated claims, all the while responding professionally and with the utmost customer service. The very best are highly sought after and well paid, enjoying the "never a dull moment" interesting aspects of the job.

The claim process begins with confirming coverage. As one sage claim adjuster noted before her retirement, there is no point in working a claim for which there is no coverage. Confirmation of coverage consists of again confirming a policy is valid and in place for the policy period in which the occurrence or offense took place. Further, the facts are reviewed to determine whether the insuring agreement has been met. Does the claim qualify as bodily injury or property damage caused by an occurrence or personal injury or advertising injury caused by an offense? It should be noted the more involved claims with complex coverage issues are handled by adjusters experienced in recognizing coverage problems, analyzing policies and drafting written letters communicating coverage determination outcomes with insureds and often their counsel.

Once coverage is confirmed, an investigation into the claim begins. The insurance industry is heavily regulated with insurance commissioners at the state level standardizing insurance adjusting by way of fair claims practices acts mandating prompt investigations and response times to conclude on liability and respond to requests in order to protect consumers. A thorough and complete investigation is the foundation of claim handling. An in-depth investigation will determine the outcome of a claim or lawsuit and provide a proper analysis of liability and damages. The claim professional who is curious about the facts, pays attention to detail and does the work to follow up with witnesses, obtain scene investigations and snoop around for more information can turn the direction of the claim to a positive outcome for the insurance company. The claim adjuster will review the matter with the insured representative, carefully gathering information and reviewing the incident report and pictures. He or she will speak with the claimant asking how the accident occurred, how they are injured and what treatment has been received along with a prognosis for recovery. Medical records will be obtained for verification and, depending on need, perhaps reviewed by a nurse consultant. The adjuster should speak to witnesses as well. The adjuster should consider any potential for risk transfer. Is there a third party such as a landlord or contractor who may have contributed to or may be responsible for the injury based on work or contract or a lease? The investigation should be well documented in a claim file with a plan of action clearly outlined along with a timeline for completion.

Once the investigation is fully underway or completed, the evaluation of liability can be made. An insurer is responsible to pay damages the insured is legally obligated to pay; therefore, liability is very important in evaluating risk. In the majority of claims, liability is based on negligence. Was the insured negligent for the operation of a vehicle in running that red light? Was the insured property owner negligent for creating or failing to address a dangerous condition on its property? In making this determination, a claim adjuster applies the elements of negligence to the facts. Negligence is found when four principles are met: duty, breach, causation and damages. The first element of negligence, duty, is created by statute or case law. Is there a duty to a third party to prevent harm? A land owner has a duty per a long line of common law to a guest or invitee on its premises to make conditions safe or warn of dangerous conditions. If there is a failure of duty, there is a breach. Should the breach be the legal cause of the damages, then negligence is found, as all four elements of the concept are present.

In considering negligence, the adjuster will also consider possible defenses or mitigating factors. Building on the foundation and resting on a solid investigation, the adjuster will consider whether the person making the claim, the claimant, was the cause or partial cause of his or her own injury. Was a condition on the premises open and obvious? How many times had the claimant visited the premises prior to the accident? Did the insured regularly inspect the property and document those procedures? How long did the dangerous condition exist, and did the insured have adequate notice of the condition so as to prevent the accident? Is the condition up to code? Experts may even be brought in to inspect the condition or conduct tests, such as coefficient of friction, should a claim include an allegation the floor surface is excessively slippery. In addition, the analysis into liability should include possible third parties and risk transfer. The adjuster must carefully consult with the insured or its risk manager to discover who else may have control over a dangerous condition. Perhaps the dog in our shopkeeper's store belongs to someone else, or if there is a trip and fall on stairs, perhaps the steps in our shopkeeper's store had recently been installed by a general contractor, or perhaps the steps are excessively slippery due to a new type of wax applied by a janitorial company. In addition, the shopkeeper may be a tenant with a lease that includes language making a landlord or property manager responsible for whatever the dangerous condition may be. All of these factors are considered and if found relevant, the claim is noticed or even tendered to the responsible third party to hold harmless the insured for any damages. Once the adjuster considers the elements of negligence, defenses and possible risk transfer, an assessment of liability is made applying a percentage on the insured, claimant and any others.

In addition to investigating liability, an adjuster must evaluate the damages. This is done by obtaining documentation of what the claimant has lost, be it in the form of property that must be restored to present value or injury to a person in a physical sense. Property damage is much more objective, while a bodily injury is much more subjective. The process of evaluating bodily injury begins with the medical damages documentation. The claimant must provide his or her confidential medical records and bills for review. The adjuster will consider the diagnosis and treatment and even look for clues of a preexisting medical condition that may actually be at the root of the injury, making the important negligence element of causation less likely to be established. The adjuster at that point may request medical records going back several years to confirm causation. The amount of money and reasonableness of treatment is taken into account and then a subjective number is added for general damages, perhaps more commonly known as pain and suffering. Other elements considered as part of the damages evaluation are any future medical costs (special damages) and loss of earnings for time lost from work due to the injury and any future lost wages (referred to often in the claims world as loss of earnings, or LOE). Additional household expenses and even a spouse's loss of consortium claim for loss of help around the house and marital relationship may be included in the overall evaluation of damages. The emotional distress of a close family member who may have witnessed the accident can sometimes be a damages element in particularly tragic claims. The investigation into damages may include the assistance of a nurse or doctor to review the medical records and even conduct an independent medical exam (IME) of the claimant. Forensic accountants and complete employment or tax records are obtained to formulate an assessment of loss of earnings, as well as to confirm the injury and any claims for ongoing or future medical treatment.

An evaluation of liability and damages includes a consideration of fraud. Insurance companies employ special investigation units consisting of adjusters, former detectives and law enforcement to review claims for what may be a fake or staged accident, as well as fake or exaggerated injuries. Suspect claims are reported to the authorities and the Insurance Crime Bureau for input into their databases, which generate reports listing all past insurance claims a claimant has made. It is far from uncommon for personal injury attorneys to refer clients to chiropractors and doctors working with them to build up the medical specials. Certain "hell hole" jurisdictions will perform unnecessary surgeries, preying on the unaware or unprotected for profit. California has seen a surge of privately owned surgical centers where pain management and surgeries are performed outside the arena of health insurance or Medicare, generating massive bills on a lien basis. In claims where an injury is under investigation for fraud sub rosa or surveillance may be conducted to confirm whether the claimant is indeed as impaired or limited in activity as claimed. Often video surveillance will show a claimant working or living a normal life without the disabilities claimed.

The process of investigating a claim to evaluate liability and damages allows the adjuster to arrive at an estimated cost or risk the claim presents. That dollar amount is then set aside as a loss reserve on the file. A loss reserve is an estimate of the eventual claim payment and is set aside representing a balance sheet liability for the insurance company. The accuracy and continual monitoring of reserves for the claim and any associated expenses is an important business aspect of claim handling. Risk managers likewise have an interest in an accurate reserve practice by its carrier in order to keep down overall insurance premiums based in part on loss runs. A large account can demand some say in how a carrier sets its reserves.

Resolution

The claim adjuster has no doubt in a timely manner completed its gathering of the facts and analyzed liability and damages to come to a conclusion on the evaluation of the claim. Based on this outcome, the decision is then made whether to deny or accept the claim or negotiate a compromise resolution. If no liability exists, a letter will be sent to the claimant stating the reasons why their claim is denied and include language advising as to the applicable statute of limitations within which to file a lawsuit against the insured. Most states also require the carrier to include contact information for the local department of insurance, where a claimant can find consumer remedies. If the claim is accepted an offer will be made based on the evaluation of damages. Oftentimes the process will include some back-and-forth discussion and negotiations before a settlement number is agreed upon. State insurance regulations govern the evaluation and negotiation process prohibiting the lowballing of an offer. The adjuster must evaluate and negotiate in good faith.

If the evaluation reaches a dollar amount over the adjuster's personal authority, the adjuster will need to go through the steps required by that insurance company to obtain the necessary authority. Authority levels vary from company to company and by adjuster experience level, with some companies closely guarding authority at a regional or home office level, while others delegate to the field to allow for prompt local response to claims.

Inevitably, a certain percentage of claims that come in the door of the claims department will end up as litigated files. Either the lawsuit is the first notice of the claim, or the inability to reach a settlement agreement over value or disagreement over liability will result in the claimant, now plaintiff, filing a summons and complaint against the insured. Some claims involve such complex facts and damages that they are best sorted out through the discovery process of litigation.

Once suit is filed against an insured, the claim adjuster will again confirm the listed defendants qualify as insureds under the policy and refer the file to defense counsel to protect the interests of the insured. The insured or risk manager will be advised and contacted to discuss the anticipated process and make introductions to the assigned defense counsel. Unless other arrangements are made for a large account or high self-insured retention, most general liability and personal lines policies do not allow for the insured to have choice of counsel. An exception to this would be jurisdictions such as

California that give a right to independent counsel when coverage issues create a conflict between the insured and the carrier.

Insurance companies are increasingly relying on the use of "house counsel" as a way to minimize legal expenses while providing quality legal protection for insured clients. House counsel are attorneys employed by the insurance company to act as defense counsel. These attorneys have a unique, tripartite role with their employer, the carrier and the insured, their client. In all dealings, however, the attorney's primary duty is to protect and serve their client. A tripartite attorney-client relationship exists as the attorney, carrier and client work together for their mutual interest, keeping all communication privileged.

The more traditional, although increasingly less common, approach to handling of the insured's defense is the handling of the defense by an outside insurance defense law firm. The carriers maintain a list of preferred panel firms who agree to provide a defense at an agreed upon hourly rate that is typically discounted based on volume or work assigned to that particular firm. Often the relationship between counsel and carrier is a close and trusted one based on years of working together closely on various files.

Managing the litigation is an important role claims adjusters are tasked with providing their insureds. The adjuster will provide defense counsel with a copy of the claim file and investigation and continue an active role in discussing and approving work necessary to the defense of the insured. A claims best practice is to meet with the defense counsel within the first couple of weeks of receipt of the suit and agree upon an action plan for discovery with time frames for completion. The discovery plan typically would include interrogatory production, gathering of all present and past medical and employment records, setting the depositions of plaintiff and relevant witnesses and parties. The action plan should be documented in the claim notes and periodically revisited and updated as the case progresses. If the initial discovery gets the case to a place where questions about liability and damages are answered, it is incumbent on the adjuster to consider whether an offer can be made and the case settled. If not, the litigation phase typically moves to more in-depth and expensive discovery such as an IME by a defense-retained doctor and the retention of experts. The adjuster works closely with the defense counsel in authorizing the appropriate use of outside experts. Solid experts are vital in defending disputed claims of damages and liability.

As the litigation progresses the decision must ultimately be made whether the case should be resolved or tried. Factors that go into this decision include the evaluation of liability and damages, strength of available defense arguments, fraud or damage build-up, covered versus uncovered damages, sufficiency of policy limits to provide adequate protection from exposure, venue, judge and even the competency and reputation of the plaintiff attorney. It takes a certain stomach and fortitude to turn the outcome of a case over to 12 strangers, and it is a decision weighed carefully on facts, reason and experience. The majority of claims are ultimately settled by insurance companies, but a small percentage are unable to be resolved due to an inability to reach a consensus on value and liability or if gross evidence of fraud and overreaching is present and is tried.

The settlement of the claim, even those that are in litigation, is overseen and most often handled by the claim adjuster, and if the insured has a financial stake in the claim, then the insured risk manager will participate in the decision-making. After all, it is the adjuster and insured who in most instances control the money. The adjuster will often work with his or her defense attorney to review the strengths and weaknesses of a case and arrive at a value and strategy that then leads to discussion with the plaintiff attorney and ultimately a settlement.

More frequently, cases are negotiated with the help of a mediator in a private mediation setting, especially if they represent a higher worth. A highly skilled and experienced mediator is invaluable in facilitating the settlement of some of the trickier negotiations by educating plaintiffs on the trial process and jury risk and assuring plaintiff lawyers they have achieved the best result possible for their clients. Adjusters, with their defense attorneys, work toward a "getting to yes" position of compromise, where both sides typically give up something to reach a settlement and avoid trial. Early neutral evaluation is a second pair of eyes by a former judge or another lawyer offered candidly and with confidentiality, usually arranged through an alternative dispute resolution company to provide an objective assessment of a case or any part of a case at any stage of the litigation that would be useful. This is especially helpful at times when each side is in love with their position on a case but is concerned they may have blinders on when it comes to arguments of the other side. A neutral analysis can be a powerful and effective tool for decision-making and even settlement.

While it is an added cost, especially with high demand mediators, private mediation provides individual attention to a case facilitating resolution or at least giving the negotiation every effort possible for success before trial. In the past, trial judges would set aside time to hold settlement conferences in an effort to reduce trial court pendings, but in the age of ever tighter civil budgetary constraints, the effectiveness of this practice is minimal.

Another tool available as an alternative means to resolve a claim is arbitration, which if the parties agree may be binding on the outcome of the dispute. Arbitration looks like a mini-trial, with witnesses and briefs presented to an agreed upon arbitrator or panel of arbitrators who weigh the evidence and render an outcome. Benefits may be less expensive and time-consuming than a trial, with privacy and in some instances a better outcome as the arbitrators may understand the issues, especially if they are complex, more easily than jurors as at public trial.

At any time during the claim or case process the claimant or plaintiff can make a demand on the insurance company to settle. A demand should be based on confirmed evidence of liability and damages and reflect a proper settlement evaluation. A well-formulated demand is not only beneficial to the claimant or plaintiff but also is an asset to the insurance company conducting its own evaluation of risk. Too often, however, demands are made prematurely or for some disproportionate to reality so that they do not add value to the negotiation process. Claims adjusters do not need to wait for a demand to make an offer, but a well-reasoned demand can force the process into negotiations.

A current trend or tactic is for claimant or plaintiff attorneys to make a "policy limit" demand early and often in the claim process regardless of whether they have actual knowledge of the policy limits or existence of any excess policies in an attempt to put the insurance company on the defensive to protect itself from any potential, no matter how remote, of an ultimate jury verdict in excess of its policy limits that could then be used by an insured to claim bad faith against the carrier for failure to settle at or within the policy limit, thus opening up the policy limits. A policy limit demand must be acknowledged and, if premature, responded to setting forth why and what is needed in order to make an offer or accept the demand. An offer for something less than the policy limits is deemed a rejection of the demand and could carry weight in a subsequent bad faith litigation should there be some misstep or miscalculation of the claim's value. The offer must be based on a reasonable evaluation of liability and damages, not just a notion the claim's adjuster has. Policy limit demands should be shared with insureds and risk managers and discussions should be had as to how to respond with open communication as to any risks involved.

Trial is indeed a last resort and last phase of the claim process. The insurance company will have considered the decision carefully internally and will have communicated with the insured and defense counsel on any decision to try a case while fully vetting the potential risks. A trial hands over control of the outcome to juries who may view the facts much differently than the insurance company, leaving the outcome up in the air. Entering into a high/low agreement before trial is one way to mitigate risk, as is having a highly experienced trial attorney well matched to the plaintiff attorney's capabilities and charisma. Nonetheless, jury outcomes and apportionment of fault are increasingly difficult to predict. It is becoming more and more difficult and time-consuming to seat a jury, especially as prospective jurors have busy lives and are increasingly resistant to serve their civic duty in this capacity, and there is no question the trial process can be fraught with delay and wasted time.

Trends

Emerging trends in personal injury litigation, together with the current political climate, impacts claim handling, loss runs and trial strategy. We are seeing an increase in the value of settlements and verdicts, especially in parts of California such as Los Angeles and the Bay area, as well as Las Vegas, Nevada, and other parts of the country. We are seeing very creative liability theories parlayed into high verdicts. What would have been a soft tissue neck and back injury with chiropractic treatment is now steroid injections and the threat of surgery on simple claims to fusions and insertions of spinal pain pumps on the more serious end. Even embellished claims involving serious injury, say to a motorcyclist or a wrongful death case, are settling at or obtaining jury verdicts at a much higher price in recent years and in certain venues. The insurance industry is seeing an uptick in sophisticated fraud, such as the use of private surgical centers operating on a lien basis outside of health insurance constraints along with the prescription pain medicine and the opioid crisis driving claimants to seek medication.

In recent years personal injury plaintiff attorneys have joined forces to work together to maximize payouts by insurance companies. There are annual gatherings of plaintiff attorneys to share information and strategies. Plaintiff attorneys literally share a database of information on insurance companies and often refer or bring in big-name plaintiff attorneys to drive up case value. Plaintiffs recently shared the strategy of making an early and persistent "policy limit" demand, and so carriers are seeing this tactic on almost every file. Another strategy plaintiff attorneys are using is to "control the mediation" by setting parameters or disallowing the mediator to speak directly to their client, the plaintiff.

Trial tactics have included the use of the so-called reptilian theory based on the book *Reptile: The 2009 Manual of the Plaintiff's Revolution* by authors Don C. Keenan and David Ball. Through their books, videos and seminars, the authors advise plaintiff attorneys to appeal to the "reptilian" part of the human brain that would trigger survival instincts by alluding to the immediate danger posed by the actions of the defendants. The argument is then broadened into the danger posed by the defendant is an immediate threat to the community and only the jury, they are told, has the power to prevent future danger and protect the community by deterring the defendant from this dangerous action by hitting them with large sums of money to be paid to the plaintiff. The desired outcome is that a jury will make a decision based on instinct and emotion rather than logic and reasoning. A seasoned mediator recently advised an assembled group of defendants that the millennial juror no longer makes a decision on facts and reason but purely on emotion.

The reptilian theory is especially dangerous when defending wealthy stakeholders or corporations, as the plaintiff attorney theme becomes even more appealing that only money will correct an injustice and make an impact on the "evil" defendants who prey on the poor. An example of this theme is a recent case involving a landlord of a large apartment complex where unfortunately a child was struck by a motorist exiting the property. No matter the child was unattended by an adult and had darted in front of the car; the theory against the landlord was that it did not provide a safe play space, did not enforce rules about playing in the street and cared more about saving money than the safety of young children. A long list of low-income tenants was prepared to testify of complaints against the unresponsive property management setting up a have-not versus have theme for the jury. The sympathetic nature of the case would play to the so-called reptilian part of the human brain that this landowner posed a danger to the poor that only the jury could correct by way of a large verdict for the plaintiff. The response by the defense, risk manager and carrier is to be aware of this strategy, remind jurors they are rational decision makers, point out the clear facts that should not be oversimplified into a theme painted by the plaintiff attorney and educate judges by way of trial briefs.

The current political climate and progressive thought of income redistribution favors plaintiffs more than the defendants in litigation. Jurors are less willing or incapable of reasoning through evidentiary-based fact patterns and applying logic to arrive at an outcome based on law. As a result, insurance companies are more often looking to contain damages by way of settlement rather than risk an adverse verdict. The make-up of the judicial bench appointed or elected will also determine how evidence is admitted at trial and align with the current political trend to drive up settlements and verdicts. For example, in the case involving the child struck by a motorist at the apartment complex, the judge was able to add to the plaintiff's social justice theme by keeping out of the hands of the jury evidence of the mother's gross neglect and investigations by child protective services deciding that the evidence was more prejudicial than probative. The exclusion of this critical evidence negatively impacted the defense. An awareness of these trends is important to the business of risk management and protection of clients and insureds.

Conclusion

A look inside an insurance casualty claims department has provided an understanding of the types of exposures the liability policy is meant to protect against and the claim process once a claim is submitted. Discussed have been the types of claims typically covered by commercial general liability and personal lines liability policies. Reviewed was the claims handling process and how a claims professional reviews coverage, investigates a claim and evaluates exposure based on liability and damages to derive an appropriate financial reserve for the claim and for making decisions. A look at the decision process of choice of counsel and what the terms house counsel and panel counsel mean was included. Also addressed was how decisions are made to resolve a claim and at what price and how mediation is a useful tool. The chapter concluded with a discussion of some of the challenges faced by casualty claims and how the current political climate impacts trial strategy, torts and claim values with emotion versus evidentiary-based decisions. The risk manager will do well to understand the process of the claims department in order to work well with his or her insurance carrier and to hold down the cost of insurance that results from incurred claims and to protect clients against exposure.

8

CONTRACT RISK MANAGEMENT WITHIN AN OPERATIONAL CONTEXT

James N. Phillips Jr.

Contracting

Introduction

"Don't panic" was on the 1979 fictional book *The Hitchhiker's Guide to the Galaxy* by Douglas Adams; we too can benefit from that admonishment of *don't panic* as we dive into contract management and risk. Often contracting is seen as mysterious and messy, such as making sausage, or the process is messy but the results are good. Contracting is more than just a piece of paper or an agreement between two people or companies; it reflects an understanding what the requirement is, addresses the risks, and sets in place strategies to ensure the outcome is achieved.

Contracting is not just one office or directorate; it is a team of people from both buyer and seller that is dedicated to achieving the outcome that has been mutually agreed to. The challenge then becomes clearly articulating what is needed in developing tool understanding, a meeting of the minds between buyer and seller. Contracting therefore demands focus clarity, and follow-through.

This chapter is to help the reader better understand contracting and the different facets of contract management risk so that they may better practice the discipline The chapter is not intended to go deep into the weeds, however, it may do so where there is a learning point beneficial to the student's understanding. The chapter includes figures to aid the student in understanding key points of contract management and risk. Finally, there may be some information that is redundant or even presented differently within this book; in these instances the book is designed to explore thought, as contracting is not a science but an art. Where there are differences the student is challenged to explore the differences, as many differences are related to context. Contracting professionals work with words, and their ability to craft words to achieve the meeting of the minds is essential. So *don't panic*. Contracting professionals are thinking professionals; enjoy the ride!

Players in the Contracting Game

As said before, in contract management there are two principals: the buyer and seller. In many respects the buyer and seller both will have a team of people focusing on the contract (Table 8.1).

The list is diverse but is not exhaustive; however, there are three key members of each team that help drive the contracting relationship: the contracting manager, the legal team, and the program manager (the "key three").

DOI: 10.4324/9781351107242-11

Table 8.1 Contract Team

Buyer	*Seller*
• Contract managers	• Contract managers
• Legal team	• Legal team
• Program management	• Program management
• Financial	• Controller
• Cost or price analysis	• Technical expert
• Technical experts	• Marketing and sales
• End user/customer	• Logistics
• Logistics/supply chain	• Information technology
• Information technology	• Security
• Security	• Engineering/design
• Engineering/facilities management	• Proposal development team
• Unions	• Bid/no-bid team
• Training staff	• Unions
• Human resources	• Human resources

The contract managers focus on the process, that is ensuring that the contract is met. The legal team focuses on the practice, which ensures the contract is compliant with internal policy and guidance and external laws and regulations. The program managers focus on contract performance and outcomes. It is vital that these three work in concert for the contract's successful outcome.

Organizationally contracting has been placed under legal and finance, however, in recent years it has held its own spot with room at the C-level in an organization. Contract management is first and foremost a business discipline and not a legal or accounting discipline. While contract management does have accounting and legal flavors, it is still a business discipline and must advise decision makers of its professional opinion. As a business discipline the contract manager's opinion may consider legal opinion, not as the final word but in an advisory capacity. An opinion by a lawyer about a business decision is tantamount to asking the pope his opinion about hip-hop; the pope's opinion is not authoritative in matters not of faith and morals.

This position is a contentious position, as lawyers are often placed in the middle when a contract goes poorly, and yet a poorly performed contract demonstrates the need for sound contracts management and the value of the key three people to be on the same page.

Why Do Contracts Matter?

Contracts are the primary vehicle with which commerce is conducted. Every day people, companies, and governments (buyers) use contracts to secure goods and services necessary for their well-being. For instance, people may have a cell phone contract, companies may contract out information technology (IT) services, and governments may contract for housekeeping services. Contracting occurs when buyers require something that they cannot perform in-house as efficiently as it can be performed on the outside. Therefore, contracts are legally binding agreements in which a buyer agrees to pay a sum certain (consideration), and a seller agrees to provide a particular good or service to the buyer.

Useful Definitions

The Contract Management Body of Knowledge (CMBOK), Sixth Edition, defines a contract as "A mutually binding legal relationship obligating the seller to furnish supplies or services, and the buyer to provide consideration for them." In this definition, it presents the principal relationship of the buyer and a seller. The CMBOK defines the buyer as "the contracted party with the requirement for goods and/or services to be fulfilled by one or more sellers." Furthermore, the seller is defined as "the contracted party tasked with fulfilling the buyer's requirement for goods and/or services." The definition of a contract establishes a relationship between a buyer and a seller.

It is generally understood that a contract for goods or services required by a buyer are either not available internally or that the cost of fulfilling goods or services would be prohibitive for the buyer. For instance, where the ability to fulfill a requirement from internal resources is not possible, it would make sense to acquire that capability or capacity from an external source. Similarly, buyers may have the skills and ability to meet the requirement, but other internal demands may make the choice prohibitive. Such is the case with what is called a "make or buy" decision. A make or buy decision is made at an early stage of acquisition planning to determine what is the best approach to meet the requirement.

In many ways, we are all contract managers, we have purchased or rented cars or homes, we have secured insurance, and bought food, among many other goods or services. Contract management is not just for major corporations and multinational conglomerates; it is the voice of commerce. Whether it is bartering or a legal document, a contract has been made and has to be managed.

The basic elements for a contract are simple: a buyer, one who needs and is willing to pay for goods or services; a seller, who provides the goods or services; and consideration (this for that). Whether eggs are purchased at a grocery store or directly from a farmer, the farmer expects to be paid in exchange for providing the eggs; for example, in consideration for providing me the eggs (something of value to the buyer), I will pay you 2 euros (something of value to the seller). This is the basic equation of all transactions.

The profession of contract management is taking this equation to a higher level, and while the equation does not change, the complexity and risk does. In the case of the farmer and their chicken eggs, there is an implied warranty that the eggs offered are in fact unfertilized chicken eggs and not have broken shells. Also, there are other warnings that may come, such as consumption of uncooked eggs may expose the consumer to the risk of salmonella poisoning, therefore consumption of uncooked eggs is not recommended. As the exchange becomes more complex, the greater the need for oversight, the mitigation of potential risks.

The complexity/risk table below (Table 8.2) is a general representation that buyers and sellers experience related to complexity and risk. While it is not necessarily true for individual and unique instances, when taken as a whole it accurately depicts the relationship. In scenarios 1 and 2, it suggests a simple relationship between a buyer and a seller during the exchange of commerce on a daily basis; contract management is conducted by the buyer and seller.

In scenarios 3–5, the levels of complexity and risk increase. Complexity is compounded by consumer safety laws, patent rights, various terms and conditions, and many other requirements that need to be met or fulfilled. Coupled with complexity are the related risks to nonperformance,

Table 8.2 Complexity/Risk Table

Scenario (Buyer/Seller)	*Complexity*	*Risk*
1. Person to person	Low	Low
2. Person to business	Low to medium	Low to medium
3. Business to business	Medium to high	Medium to high
4. Government to business	High	High
5. Multinational corporation or government to multinational corporation	High	High

noncompliance, product liability, and so forth that must be mitigated. This is the environment where the professional contract manager is found.

Contract managers are actively used in scenarios 3–5. Their focus is to craft documents called contracts and manage contracts after they are signed by both parties, buyer and seller. A common misconception suggests contracts are only used by governments when they buy goods or services from industry. This is patently false. The reality is this: whenever and wherever goods or services are exchanged, a contract follows. Whether it is a cell phone agreement, software license purchase, purchasing real property, or selling helicopters to the government, a piece of paper (i.e., contract) is there memorializing the exchange and identifying what each party committed to.

The Contract Life Cycle

Pre-award Phase

To further understand what a contract is, it is beneficial to present the elements that go into planning for a contract. There are three phases to the contract life cycle: pre-award, award, and post-award, as identified in the CMBOK (Figure 8.1).

The pre-award phase addresses acquisition planning and solicitation development. Learning from what was discovered in the buyer need in market research and acquisition plan emerges, which leads to the development of the solicitation. According to the CMBOK, the acquisition plan includes:

- Description of need
- Required capabilities
- Delivery or performance requirements
- Cost targets
- Conditions or constraints
- Cost/technical/schedule trade-offs
- Cost/technical/schedule risks
- A plan of action.

Perhaps the most critical element in the pre-award phase's acquisition planning begins with the description of the need.

Make or Buy Decision

While the need is being discerned, the question of whether the need can be satisfied with in-house resources or external resources is answered. The Checklist for Defining the Need and the Make or Buy Decision Tree will help guide the buyer on creating a better understanding of the need as the buyer moves toward creating a solicitation.

Where the need is satisfied internally, there is no requirement for a contract; however, where the need cannot be satisfied with internal resources, external resources must be sought to meet the need.

It is the need that drives the whole contracting process. The need (or bona fide need) represents a desired end or solution which the buyer is looking for and which will satisfy the need. In defining the

Figure 8.1 Contract Life Cycle

need, the buyer uses market research to inform them about the capability and capacity of the market (i.e., seller to satisfy the need). The buyer in gathering its market research begins to better understand how the market is able to provide a solution to a future requirement response.

Award Phase

The award phase represents the nexus of the buyer's analysis of the seller's offers and making a source selection decision based on objective criteria stated in the buyer's solicitation. Based on the information provided, the buyer will determine, for instance, the method of solicitation, fixed price or cost reimbursable, financial incentives for delivery or performance, and terms and conditions. In public procurement, it is common to have transparency so that prospective sellers will know that the procurement system and resulting contract are fairly administered to all who participate.

Post-award Phase

The final phase is the post-award phase. In this phase, there are two domains, contract performance and contract closeout. Each domain is distinct and necessary for contract completion. There are four elements in the contract performance domain:

- Administer contract
- Ensure quality
- Subcontract management
- Manage changes.

According to the CMBOK, to administer a contract is the oversight of the contract performance pursuant to the fulfillment of the contract terms, conditions, and specifications. To ensure quality requires the seller to ensure that the products and services delivered to the buyer conform to the contract requirements. For the seller, this represents their quality control system, and for the buyer, it represents their quality assurance system as described in the quality assurance surveillance plan (QASP). Subcontract management is the process of contract management of subcontracts, with the prime contractor being responsible for the performance of the supply chain. Finally, managing changes occurs out of the necessity that things may change, and as they do such changes must be managed to ensure configuration control of the contract and subsequent contract performance.

Solicitation Methods

Table 8.3 provides a general framework for understanding solicitations; however, the disciplined practitioner will recognize that these two represent opposite ends of a continuum. For instance, in a

Table 8.3 Understanding Solicitations

Sealed Bid	*Negotiated Procurement*
• Requirements are clear and not complex • Solution is known • Communication with seller is to clarify but will not result in amending the bid • Low risk (low uncertainty and ability to perform) • Fixed price • Examples are construction projects, commodity items, and commercial items	• Requirements are unclear and complex • Solutions may evolve • Communication with seller is to clarify and may result in amending the proposal • High risk (high uncertainty and ability to perform) • Cost reimbursement • Examples include research and development, where alternatives may be considered, such as best value or trade-offs

negotiated procurement it may result in a fixed-price contract. Or in a negotiated procurement, there may be elements that are fixed price and cost reimbursement.

Contract Types

The choice of the contract type is a risk mitigation strategy. For instance, choosing a firm fixed price (FFP) contract is less risky for the buyer than a cost-reimbursable (CR) contract. Yet in choosing an FFP the trade-off is in allowing competition to drive price, as the solution is often not in question. However, for a CR the risk to the buyer is increased as the buyer accepts a portion of the performance risk once held by the seller. The most common reason for this risk transfer is unknowability. As once shared by former US Secretary of Defense Donald Rumsfeld:

> There are known knowns. These are things we know that we know.
> There are known unknowns. That is to say, there are things that we know we don't know.
> But there are also unknown unknowns. There are things we don't know we don't know.

It is in the risk categorized in the known unknowns that CR contracts dwell, and sellers are hesitant to invest 100% of their effort when the return may be negligible or a loss. In this case the buyer would share the burden of the risk with the seller by paying for all incurred costs that are allowable, allocable, and reasonable. Often the CR is incentivized by the buyer so as to create an incentive for finding a solution or finding economy; such incentives are stated as incentive fee (CPIF), award fee (CPAF), and fixed fee (CPFF).

Another understanding of contract risk is related to contract pricing. For instance, when a buyer chooses a fixed-price contract, it is generally understood that risk has been transferred to the seller. Similarly, when a buyer chooses a CR contract, risk is now shared between buyer and seller. Sellers who are working on a requirement that is unclear or complex will find having their costs covered through a cost reimbursable contract beneficial. It is important to note that in the partnership between buyer and seller, the seller may insist on having its risks mitigated through this risk sharing agreement.

Contract Risk

A common misconception that is made is equating risk management and contract risk management as the same, so it is treated the same; however, such treatment is misleading. Risk management, from a macro view, is defined by Marquette University as a continuing process to identify, analyze, evaluate, and treat loss exposures and monitor risk control and financial resources to mitigate the adverse effects of loss. A better definition which is closer is the following:

> Enterprise risk management (ERM) *provided by the Risk Management Association*, is defined as an organization's *enterprise risk* competence—the ability to understand, control, and articulate the nature and level of *risks* taken in pursuit of business strategies—coupled with accountability for *risks* taken and activities engaged in.

Accordingly, contract risk management is not to be confused with risk management or even enterprise risk management (see Figure 8.2).

Similar to enterprise risk management's focus on the enterprise (i.e., the organization), contract risk management focuses on the contract life cycle, particularly the contract document. So what is contract risk management?

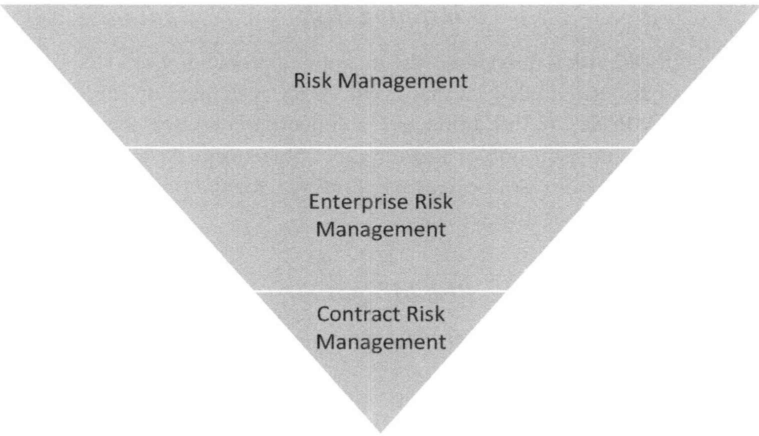

Figure 8.2 Contract risk management.

> Contract risk management is an essential component of managing the legal risk of an organization. The crux of legal risk management is the process of analyzing an organization's exposure to risk and determining how to best handle such exposure through identification, assessment, and prioritization. Legal risk management is vital to an organization's success. Therefore, an organization cannot be successful without effective contract risk management.

The risk management hierarchy is helpful to understand where contract risk management is compared to risk management. Yet it doesn't explain how to do contract risk management. This is a good model to follow, adapted from the International Organization for Standardization (ISO) 31000 on Risk Management:

- Establishing the context
- Identifying the risks
- Analyzing those risks
- Evaluating the risks
- Treating those risks.

This flow provides a good method to assess contract risk vulnerability. Consider applying this model to people, processes, performance, and price (see Table 8.4).

Table 8.4 Risk Vulnerability

	People	*Processes*	*Performance*	*Price*
Establishing the context				
Identifying the risks				
Analyzing those risks				
Evaluating the risks				
Treating those risks				

This table allows for contemplating risk and risk mitigation strategies that will be employed.

Defining Risk

According to the CMBOK, risk is defined as "the measure of probability of a risk event (an unwanted change) occurring and associated effect of that event." Risk as defined by the Project Management Body of Knowledge (PMBOK), Fifth Edition, as " an uncertain event or condition that, if it occurs, has a positive or negative effect on one or more project objectives." As in the PMBOK definition, risk in and of itself is neither positive nor negative; however, for the purpose of discussion, risk will be generally referred to in the negative sense.

Risk Mitigation

Risk mitigation is commonly aligned with four strategies: acceptance, avoidance, limitation, and transference.

- *Acceptance*: Risk acceptance does not reduce any effects; however, it is still considered a strategy. This strategy is a common option when the cost of other risk management options, such as avoidance or limitation, may outweigh the cost of the risk itself. A company that doesn't want to spend a lot of money on avoiding risks that do not have a high possibility of occurring will use the risk acceptance strategy.
- *Avoidance*: Risk avoidance is the opposite of risk acceptance. It is the action that avoids any exposure to the risk whatsoever. Risk avoidance is usually the most expensive of all risk mitigation options.
- *Limitation*: Risk limitation is the most common risk management strategy used by businesses. This strategy limits a company's exposure by taking some action. It is a strategy employing a bit of risk acceptance along with a bit of risk avoidance or an average of both. An example of risk limitation would be a company accepting that a disk drive may fail and avoiding a long period of failure by having backups.
- *Transference*: Risk transference is the involvement of handing risk off to a willing third party. For example, numerous companies outsource certain operations, such as customer service or payroll services. This can be beneficial for a company if a transferred risk is not a core competency of that company. It can also be used so a company can focus more on their core competencies.

Contracting combines a variety of the risk mitigation strategies to minimize the impact on contract outcome; for instance, risk transference is the most common method used in contracting. In this strategy, one or more of the risk categories below are transferred from a buyer to a seller to satisfy a particular need identified in the contract. It is important to note, however, that risk resides with the buyer even though they may never transfer 100% of the risk.

Contracts as a Key Risk Management Tool

Contracting is not the only risk management tool, however it plays an important role in an organization's risk management strategy. In the book *Today and Tomorrow*, Henry Ford explained he was able to manage his risk by owning all aspects of automobile production. As the Ford Motor Company owned forests, farmland, mining, and transportation systems, thus there was no need for Henry Ford to contract other services or to buy goods. In this case he accepted all risk as he had control of all aspects of production. Such is not the case these days for the Ford Motor Company or for any corporation, business, or government. The integration of other businesses into the overall supply now satisfies requirements for goods and services needed on their core business objective. As such, contracts have become a risk management necessity, this has driven a greater need for intelligent contracting.

Risk and Market Research

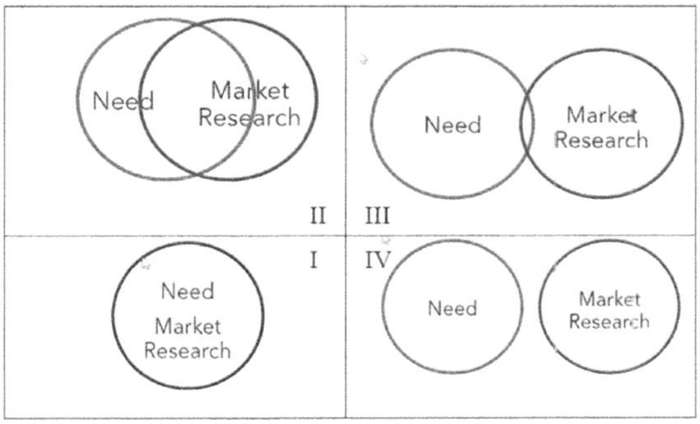

Figure 8.3 Risk and Market Research.

There are in general four relationships of varying degrees between the buyer's need and market research. In Figure 8.3, each block represents the risk potential that is presented. For instance, in Block I the circles for both need and market research overlap, which suggests that need can be met by the market and as such will have a lower risk. Comparatively speaking, Block IV presents that there is absolutely no overlap, which suggests a higher risk for the buyer in seller performance. Both Blocks II and III are degrees of overlap and suggest greater risk than Block I but lesser risk than Block IV.

Bidding Versus Negotiated Procurement

Throughout this process the buyer will be assessing risk. Each action taken or strategy employed is designed to mitigate the buyer's risk; for example, in looking at solicitation there are two commonly used methods which will be used to compare and contrast.

The first is bidding, and the second is negotiated procurement. In bidding the requirement and its outcome are well known to the buyer. Communication with the seller is unnecessary and in some instances prohibited, as the point of a bid is to achieve the lowest price bid from a seller offering a good or service meeting the minimum performance requirements. Having said that, communication related to minor informality or irregularities may be necessary, but only for achieving clarity, such as an arithmetic error.

Lowest Price Technically Acceptable

Negotiated procurement, on the other hand, offers the buyer a wider latitude in achieving clarity and understanding. Also, using negotiated procurement techniques there are gradations of alternatives, which include lowest price technically acceptable (LPTA) contrasted against best value or trade-offs. According to the CMBOK, the LPTA

> source selection process is appropriate when best value is expected to result from the selection of the technically acceptable proposal with the lowest evaluated price.

Best Value

At the other end of the negotiated procurement continuum is best value. Best value, like LPTA, is also a source selection process; unlike LPTA, best value employs various strategies to achieve its end. A best value source selection strategy is riskier as it requires the buyer to better understand its requirement and the market's potential response to that requirement and imputing value as to degrees of importance. This strategy is also referred to as trade-off, where the buyer assesses the seller's proposal and rates the proposal as being a best value or not.

Risk Analysis Tools

The Failure Modes and Effects Analysis (FMEA) tool is used in conjunction with other risk identification and assessment tools such as brainstorming and cause and effect diagramming, to name but a few. Brainstorming, when used in managing contract risks, is a risk identification tool. Brainstorming is best used in small groups and where contribution by the participants as welcomed. Here the small group is given a specific contract outcome for which they then identify the likely risks. The second tool is a fishbone-type diagram, also known as the cause and effect diagram. This diagram starts with the effect (outcome) and then works backwards to determine potential causes. Each cause represents a single bone in the entire fishbone.

The potential causes to a specific effect are represented by people, processes, performance, or price. The fishbone diagram does not stop at people, processes, performance, or price; rather it digs deeper into the potential risk; for instance, if people are the cause, what are more specific causes that relate to people, such as work hours, compensation, training, certification, and so forth? So, once the fishbone diagram is filled out, the results can be transferred to an Adapted FMEA worksheet next (see Figure 8.4).

Adapted Failure Modes and Effects Analysis

The FMEA tool provides a discipline approach to documenting contractual, and there are several blocks to attend to. Using the example earlier:

1. *Process description* will be one of the bones of the fishbone, in this case *people.*
2. *Potential failure mode, noncompetitive compensation* will be used.
3. *Potential effects of failure* represents what happens to the people when there is a poor compensation system, *high turnover rate.*

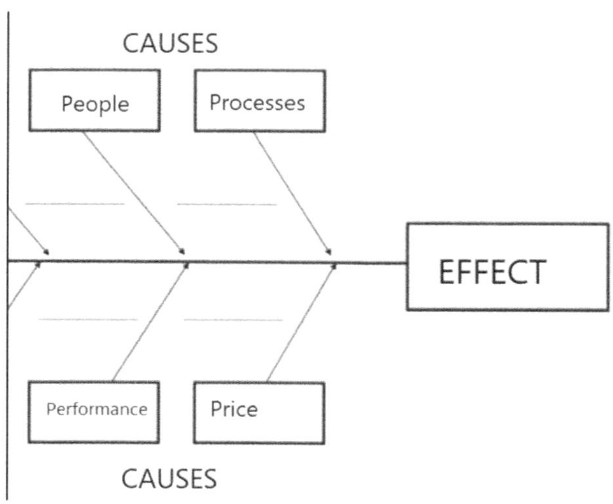

Figure 8.4 Sample fishbone-type diagram/cause and effect diagram.

4. *Potential causes* are where further analysis is warranted, such as what are the potential causes for a high turnover rate? For example, where a location has a dearth of a particular discipline, such as IT professionals in Silicon Valley.

Also on the form there are two columns which represent severity and probability of occurrence. Severity assesses the impact on the effect should that cause occur. For instance, if the prospective contract is with a company which is about to renew its labor agreement with the union, what is the impact if a contract is awarded to a company whose labor force might walk out on strike? High! Probability on the other hand suggests that the likelihood of a strike is less when companies and unions are at peace and are working off a labor agreement. So what is the probability of a strike? Low!

The Adapted FMEA forces the buyer to address the potential risks of a particular procurement with the intention of creating visibility of the risk and a mitigation strategy for the risk. In the PMBOK, the documentation for listing each risk is a risk register, which is a document in which the results of risk analysis and risk response planning are recorded.

Contract Risk Analysis Tool

The contract risk analysis tool (CRAT) focuses on a simple analysis of the contribution of buyer, seller, and the requirement, as contrasted by the Adapted FMEA, which addresses the totality of risks within a contract event. The results from the CRAT present to the buyer the performance risk in the contract. It is generally understood that an experienced contract manager knowledgeable of the requirement and working with an ethical incumbent seller will pose less performance risk than a seller who isn't. The CRAT represents a quick yet meaningful analysis of performance risk.

Contract Risk Rubric and Scoring Matrix

Risk is contextual, and the contract risk rubric and scoring matrix (see Table 8.5) provides this context. The rubric defines what the scores mean and should be expanded when appropriate. The scoring matrix provides a means of quantifying the risk. For example, the scoring rubric and matrix reflects the additive total from the CRAT. If the CRAT when scored is 3–5, this suggests less performance risk when taken to the scoring matrix. Conversely, scores of 11–15 on the CRAT suggest a higher performance. While no tool can assure *zero* performance risk, the CRAT, scoring matrix, and rubric, used as a predictive tool, indicate degrees of performance risk. The scores are not the answer but serve as a starting point for a deeper dive into the performance risk.

Table 8.5 Contract Risk Rubric and Scoring Matrix

1	• Low performance risk • Risk of a performance problem is minimal • No need to change
3	• Moderate performance risk • Risk of a performance problem is moderate • Assess deficiencies and apply resources or training when appropriate
5	• High performance risk • Risk of a performance problem is high • Assess the significant deficiencies/weaknesses • Apply resources or training when appropriate

3	**5**	7
5	9	*11*
7	*11*	*15*

Bold: low performance risk
Italics: high performance risk

Contract Types as Risk Mitigation Strategy

There are generally categories of contract types which are fixed price and cost. In choosing a fixed price contract vehicle, the buyer is saying the performance risk is low, there is a clear understanding of the requirement, there is adequate competition, the goods or services are reasonably available in the marketplace, and competition should drive the price. Fixed-price contracts are generally considered a lower risk, because the performance risk is transferred to the seller.

On the opposite end of the continuum are cost contracts. In a cost contract, there is a sharing of the risk. Often sellers will not accept a fixed-price contract and the risk is too high, rather a cost contract is used to help them better manage the risk. In a cost contract, as compared to a fixed-price contract, there are incentives that may be built in to help encourage the seller to find economies and savings in the process. These economies are often captured in performance or cost savings or other economies they may achieve, including value engineering. It is important to know that the incentives relate to what the buyer desires and not what the seller desires. For instance, the buyer states that they want something delivered in six months and the seller states they can deliver in three months; in this case faster is not better, as there are other considerations to be addressed. Other risk mitigation strategies include the use of terms and conditions in the contract which address what the buyer desires, such as delivery or pricing/invoicing terms. A mitigation strategy that is not commonly used but does have importance is liquidated damages.

Liquidated Damages

A risk mitigation strategy used often in manufacturing and construction is liquidated damages. According to the CMBOK, liquidated damages are "a contract clause providing for the assessment of damages on the seller for its failure to comply with the certain performance or delivery requirements of the contract." Further liquidated damages are "used when the time of delivery or performance is of such importance that the buyer may reasonably expect to suffer damages if the delivery or performance is delinquent." An example in manufacturing where liquidated damages would apply is the failure of a particular part used in the assembly of an automobile to be available, thus shutting down the assembly line. Such a shutdown would be expensive and affect automobile production, payroll, and the whole supply chain. Another example is in construction, where the general contractor fails to deliver a usable space when it is required, thus injuring the buyer by having them extend a current lease or procure storage, which would not have been required if the space was built out on time. A liquidated damages clause is powerful, however it should not be punitive, in that liquidated damages represent making the buyer whole.

Managing Contract Risks

There are two elements that must be addressed when managing contract risk. The first is to thoroughly understand risks that the requirement and potential solutions present. Second, what is the willingness to accept an adverse outcome resulting from that risk (i.e., risk tolerance). A comprehensive and disciplined approach toward understanding risks and risk tolerance is through the use of the FMEA tool. This tool is used in engineering, but contracting personnel, both buyer and seller, can benefit from a practicing a disciplined approach to risk that a FMEA brings.

Note on best practices: As a mental exercise, when looking at the best practice, think about what cause was there that prompted the need for this particular best practice.

Contract Management (Post-award Contract Management)

Post-award Contract Management Today

This section uses the available literature which presents performance risk in the light of contract management and performance risk. The literature used includes insights provided by the US government and the national government of the United Kingdom (UK), as well as the CMBOK maintained by the National Contract Management Association (NCMA) and insights from the International Association for Contract and Commercial Management, now known as World Commerce and Contracting Association.

Contract management, as presented in this chapter, refers to the period which occurs immediately after contract award and concludes with contract closeout. A review of literature also presents another term, contract administration, which is also used. Arguably contract management is the most important function in the contract life cycle, as it is the very function that ensures contract compliance, mitigates performance risk, and satisfies the desired outcome. And yet, within procurement those assigned to contract management duties are the least capable of meeting the desired outcome. This chapter focuses on the concerns and best practices identified in the literature that will educate and inform the contract manager.

Introduction to Contract Management

An often lamented aspect of the entire contracting process is contract management. Why is this, and what can be done about it? The remainder of the chapter will focus on the aspects of contract management where contract managers can make a difference. Consider the following statement made in 2014 report by the National Audit Office (NAO) in the United Kingdom:

> Traditionally, the procurement profession has had a low status in the civil service, while contract management has been seen as low status within the procurement profession.

This quote suggests two things: first, that procurement in general is a prestige problem; and second, contract management is seen as less prestigious. This chapter is not to address procurement as a whole but rather to focus its attention on contract management and its improvement.

Words Mean Something

The contracting profession is a profession of words. In this chapter, we will be using terms that may have different meetings in different countries, so there will be attempts to reduce the ambiguity and provide clarity to the reader.

The audience for this chapter is both commercial and government; accordingly, we will use terms found in common sources where appropriate, however there may be a need to define the term where no common definition is available. The use of common terms is not often in question, however there will be key words and phrases that are used which will need to be defined. Accordingly, the following definitions will be used to aid the reader in understanding what is meant.

Buyer—the contracted party with the requirement for goods and/or services to be fulfilled by one or more sellers. (CMBOK, Sixth Edition)

Commercial—reflects a general categorization of all nongovernmental entities such as non-governmental organizations (NGOs), universities, corporations, large and small business concerns.

Contract—a mutually binding legal relationship obliging the seller to furnish supplies or services and the buyer to provide consideration for them. (CMBOK, Sixth Edition)

Contract management—the act which occurs immediately after a contract has been awarded/commissioned and extends to the contract's completion (referred to as post-award contract administration, contract administration, and contract oversight). Not to be confused with *procurement*, see below.

Contract management life cycle phases—contracts have a distinct beginning and end, and the contract life cycle defines these parameters. The contract life cycle generally consists of three contract phases: pre-award, award, and post-award. (CMBOK, Sixth Edition)

Contract management practices—practices which have the purpose to reduce or eliminate risk of an adverse performance outcome; such practices include inspections, audits, and surveys.

Government—a political-socioeconomic entity whose duty is to provide for its constituents, often referred to as the public or its citizens.

Procurement—all stages of the process of acquiring property or services, beginning with the termination of need for the property or services and ending with contract completion and closeout. (The government contracts reference book)

Seller—the contracted party tasked with fulfilling the buyer's requirements for goods and/or services. (CMBOK, Sixth Edition)

Different Titles, Same Duties

Post-award contract oversight may be an unfamiliar title for many. Other alternative titles which may be more familiar to the reader may include:

- Contract administrator
- Contract manager
- Contracting officers representative (COR) or contracting officer's technical representative (COTR)
- Buyer's or owner's representative.

The actual title used may be different, but the duties of contract oversight are fundamentally the same (i.e., looking out for the buyer or seller's interest).

Conventions

Whenever possible, we will use phrases such as *buyer* and *seller* regardless of who the buyer or seller is, government or commercial. We will refer as *contract management* for all post-award contract administration work. We will refer as *award* for contract commissioning or signing. These conventions are set aside to provide clarity to the text below.

The Literature

The term contract management is more frequently used in commercial contracting and less in government contracting; however, what is required by a contract manager is still the same. The US government through its subordinate offices—such as the Office of Federal Procurement Policy (OFPP), Merit Systems Protection Board (MSPB), and Government Accountability Office (GAO)—produces a wealth of information as to education, training, delegations, skills, and abilities necessary to perform contract management. Further guidance is provided by the executive agencies of the US government. The national government of the United Kingdom, particularly the national audit office, has also provided insight into contract management. Finally, additional guidance is provided through the National Contract Management Association's *Contract Management Body of Knowledge (CMBOK Guide)* Project Management Institute's *A Guide to the Project Management Body of Knowledge* (PMBOK Guide); and the World Commerce and Contracting Association.

No Industry Standards

The procurement profession has been behind in producing a comprehensive body of knowledge. The National Contract Management Association is working to produce such a standard in its CMBOK, in a similar way to that of the Project Management Institute's PMBOK. It is not the intention of this chapter to create such a standard.

What Is the Need for Contract Management?

Contract management is arguably the most important function in the procurement process, as contract management is the only link to a successful outcome. Thus, the more complex the buyer's requirements are, the more complex the contract management processes and practices are.

This requires the contract manager to exercise due diligence in not only understanding the contract document but also understanding its relationship to the intended outcome. So what is the intended outcome, and just as important, how do we know we have achieved the intended outcome?

Intended Outcome (Cullen)

The phrase psychological contract (PsyCon), coined by Dr. Sara Cullen, refers to the contract we thought we had (the desired outcome) rather than the contract that was actually written (the contract outcome). Here Cullen opines that the contract that is written is not used; rather it is the psychological contract which is being exercised, and will not be used unless a problem occurs. Cullen's position is supported by professional experience and the literature. So what is at play? To achieve parity, the PsyCon need to be identified and addressed earlier in the procurement cycle. In the above illustration, the PsyCon needs to be reflected in the buyer's requirements, and where those are deficient, it will shift to the contract manager to fill in the gaps.

Cullen suggests that there are two points: the one we think the contract should be (PsyCon) and the other (what the contract actually says). Here she suggests our default position is what she thinks the contract should do (PsyCon), which holds the lead position until a problem occurs, at which time it is the actual black-letter words of the contract that dictate performance. To the degree that the these two positions are separated will result in performance risk.

As you can imagine, where there is a gap between the buyer's requirements and the contract manager's processes and practices, there will be a dissonance. This dissonance must be resolved as it reflects the performance risk. If the contract manager's processes and practices do not match up to the buyer's requirements, something will need to occur; either an experienced and trained contract manager would know what to do, or most likely there will be an inexperienced or poorly trained contract manager, who will substitute their desires for that which is in the contract.

Who Serves as Contract Manager?

Contract management is seldom performed by the person who wrote the contract, rather it is frequently a delegated task. It is often assigned to the office that will benefit from the contract and delegated to a person within that office. Assignments of a contract manager may be carefully made or handed out to the least busy person. Ownership of the assignment by the person is linked to the value they place on the actual contract and its outcome. An inexperienced and poorly trained contract manager may have a tendency to deviate from the contract, taking the easy way out or pursuing what the contract should have had!

Principle Contract Management Functions

There are three fundamental functions to be performed by the contract manager:

- Verifying performance
- Reporting deficiencies
- Approving payment requests.

Regardless of the quality of the individual or the buyer's requirements, contract management is an action performed by a trusted individual who is delegated by the buyer to ensure that the seller's performance fulfills "the contract terms, conditions, and specifications" of the contract.

Verify Performance

Verify performance is not just contract completion but has to do with meeting contract terms and conditions, the requirements of the contract, and achieving goals or incentives and quality standards. Yet the popular reason for contract management is to verify seller performance in the contract. So verifying performance is the foremost important aspect of contract management. A key concern with all contracts, particularly for service contracts, is whether the contract is being performed within scope and on schedule. The role of the contract manager is to ensure decision makers have the correct performance information related to the degree that a contract is on target for completion. In verifying performance, it's not just pass or fail; it is also degrees of completion and data that confirms it.

Start

- Perform pre-award surveys.
- Conduct post-award orientation conferences.
- Report to the contracting office any inadequacies noted in specifications.

Performance

- Assign and perform supporting contract administration.
- Issue work requests under maintenance, overhaul, and modification contracts.
- Contract compliance with contractual quality assurance requirements.
- Perform production support, surveillance, and status reporting, including timely reporting of potential and actual slippages in contract delivery schedules.
- Submit required reports.
- Perform engineering surveillance to assess compliance with contractual terms for schedule, cost, and technical.
- Cause release of shipments from contractor's plants according to the shipping instructions.
- Accomplish administrative closeout procedures.

Report Deficiencies

The second function which is necessary in contract oversight is reporting deficiencies. Reporting deficiencies in contract management requires the contract manager to identify potential performance problems which affect the contract's quality, cost, or schedule. Experience and the literature have shown that this function is where problems frequently occur and why it is given the color red.

Contract management fails when it is silent as to reporting deficiencies to decision makers. Failing to report is a tacit approval and an invitation to unauthorized changes in the contract's scope and schedule, which often will affect the contract's cost or price.

Approve Pay Requests

The third function is reviewing request for payment by the seller tendering an invoice. This function is not just to sign and approve an invoice; more importantly it is to verify work that is complete for which invoicing is appropriate and to ensure the proper penalties and incentives have been applied. Additional related tasks include:

- Review and approve or disapprove the seller's requests for payments.
- Make payments on assigned contracts.
- Ensure timely notification by the contractor of any anticipated overrun or underrun of the estimated cost under cost-reimbursement contracts.
- Analyze quarterly limitation on payments statements.
- De-obligate excess funds after final price determination.

These three fundamental functions provide a high-level understanding of what is required by contract manager; however, there are other areas that require consideration when performing contract management, one of which is higher-level contract management systems.

Higher-Level Contract Management Systems

Large companies and national governments create contract management systems to save time and resources. These systems when initiated allow the seller to demonstrate to the buyer their processes, which the buyer may or may not approve. In these instances, both buyer and seller have multiple contracts financially worth millions or billions, so such systems create an economy. Once a system is put into place, the system is audited and not the multiple contracts. These systems are often validated by a third party or by the buyer in advance. Systems may include:

- *Accounting system*—a system that identifies and categorizes business costs in a consistent manner, thus allowing for proper reporting of costs and determining a likability and allowability of cost elements.
- *Estimating system*—the contractor's policies, procedures, and practices for generating cost estimates and other data including in proposals submitted to customers in the expectation of receiving a contract award.

Other Higher-Level Contract Management Systems

Like the aforementioned systems, the following are similar in process but of a unique character:

- *Purchasing system*—the contractor's policies, procedures, and practices for approved purchasing on items used in a contract.
- *Quality system*—the contractor's policies, procedures, and practices for approving and shipping conforming material to a buyer without individual or unit inspections, such as the ISO standards.

- *Property system*—manages buyer property used by the seller during the creation of product for the buyer; this includes equipment, jigs, and raw material.
- *Traffic-shipping system*—manages the traffic or shipping of goods from the seller to the buyer.
- *Packaging/preservation system*—manages the packaging and preservation of goods required by the buyer with specific requirements for long-term storage or packaging for inclement weather.

Approved Systems

In the seven systems listed, what is missing is the word *approved*. With an approved system, the buyer may use the system to supplement their contract management. An approved system allows the buyer to forgo any inspections or audits that they might have performed on a routine basis. an approved system provides the buyer a degree of cost savings related to time and transfers the burden of performance to the seller. Incidentally, sellers value approved systems, as they allow them to be more efficient and ultimately enable them to be paid faster.

Contract Management Metrics

Effective contract management requires the use of meaningful metrics. Identifying the discriminating a few metrics requires that the contract manager first understand the contract and then the service or work to be performed.

General Types of Performance Metrics

The performance metrics selected must offer clear and demonstrable evidence of the success of each of the following aspects, even in areas where a metric is hard to quantify:

- *Quality*—conformance to contract requirements and standards of good workmanship.
- *Timeliness of performance*—adherence to contract schedules, including the administrative aspects of performance.
- *Client-supplier relationship*—being reasonable and cooperative, having a commitment to customer satisfaction, having integrity and ethics.
- *Cost control*—forecasting and containing costs on changes and cost-reimbursement contracts.

Each of these types represents a characteristic of contract management metrics which would aid in performance assessments. With these four categories in mind, what sources would you consider to further identify your performance metric? Sources for metrics would include:

- The contract requirement;
- Industry benchmarks;
- Value chain map and analysis (performance metrics should support a focus on value-added activities away from non-value-added activities);
- Similar past relevant contracts;
- Customer strategies;
- Expert opinion.

S.M.A.R.T. Metrics

Creating a metric is not sufficient. A metric should be S.M.A.R.T.:

- *Specific*—clear and focused to avoid misinterpretation. Should include metric assumptions and definitions and be easily interpreted.

- *Measurable*—can be quantified and compared with other data. It should allow for meaningful statistical analysis. Avoid "yes/no" measures except in limited cases, such as start-up or systems-in-place situations.
- *Attainable*—achievable, reasonable, and credible under conditions expected.
- *Realistic*—fits into the organization's constraints and is cost-effective.
- *Time-bound*—states the time period in which each metric will be accomplished.

A word about assumptions: as noted above, it is always important to identify any assumptions made related to the performance being measured. Assumptions can be as simple as an empty office (housekeeping) or good weather (groundskeeping), or more complex, such as no changes to routing important supply shipments (every Tuesday).

Measurable Performance Words

Measuring performance requires the creation and use of performance metrics that allow the quality of a service to be measured. Consider the following words in creating metrics:

• Completeness	• Auditability/clear documentation
• Cost	• Responsiveness
• Availability	• Security
• Capacity	• Standards
• Reliability	• Usability
• Flexibility	• Accuracy
• Satisfaction	• Risk
• Timeliness	• Safety

Performance measures are rooted in the proper metrics used and linked to successful contract outcomes. The contract manager must focus their attention on the desired outcome, which means their performance measures must measure the proper things. It is necessary then for the contract manager to understand the contract to know the requirement and then create the appropriate metrics to achieve that outcome.

Risk Management

Managing risk is an important aspect of managing service delivery and must be reflected in the design of performance metrics. The fulfillment of the contract may be endangered by several kinds of risk, some within the supplier's control and some beyond it. Identifying and controlling (by avoiding or minimizing) risks is a vital part of managing a contract. Business continuity plans and contingency plans provide backup strategies and actions to recreate/restore/relocate a business or project and are used to help prepare the client for possible situations where the supplier is unable to deliver contractual requirements. Performance metrics should reflect risk management objectives.

Best Practices of Contract Oversight (Adapted From an OFPP Memo 9/6/2011)

- *Continuity of understanding*—If an individual is performing pre-award tasks, such as requirements determination and proposal evaluation, it is recommended that they be delegated contract oversight via an appointment memorandum at that time that addresses both pre-award and post-award responsibilities.

- *Clear understanding of duties*—At the time of appointment, the buyer should meet with the person performing contract oversight in person, if practical, to ensure they understand their duties, roles and responsibilities in regard to the contract and in regard to organization-specific processes and requirements. Persons performing contract oversight should be informed that their duties, responsibilities, and obligations are limited to those articulated in their appointment letter and must be exercised in accordance with the organization's policies.
- *Read and understand the contract*—Persons performing contract oversight are critical in ensuring successful contract outcomes. As such, they must read and understand the contract and work closely with their buyers.
- *Proximity to performance*—People performing contract oversight who are physically located where the contract is being performed can help facilitate effective communication with the seller.
- *Affirmative acknowledgement as key role*—It is highly encouraged that the person performing contract oversight and their supervisor sign the appointment letter *acknowledging acceptance* contract oversight responsibilities. It is recommended that these responsibilities be added as a critical element in their individual performance plans. The contract oversight performance management process should allow for buyer input in their performance appraisal.
- *Supervisor/manager acknowledgement*—It is also a best practice for their supervisor/manager to have a performance standard related to oversight of its employees' contract oversight responsibilities.
- *Organizational learning*—Contract oversight mentors are very helpful in acquainting new persons performing contract oversight with specific organizational requirements and enhancing the expertise of persons performing contract oversight at all levels. It is also helpful to build the community of persons performing contract oversight within the organization to facilitate collaboration and sharing of best practices.

So, are these best practices enough? No, however this is a good start.

What's Next?

In 2012 I co-authored the book *The COR Member of the Acquisition Team: The Contracting Officer's Representative (COR) Guide to Performance and Quality*, where we focused on ways to improve post-award contract oversight. The book was written to bring to light the challenges of contract oversight as a unique discipline that is not unique to the US government but is common to the buying community. A major point of the book relates to ownership of the need. In most instances, buyers are identified as those who write contracts and are seen as owners and the persons who have contract oversight responsibilities work for them, so to speak. The reality is that the person who performs contract oversight has two masters: the buyer and their manager/supervisor. The buyer is worried about the contracting process, while the supervisor manager is worried about the satisfaction of the need or performance outcome. The person who performs contract oversight reports worries about both.

In my 16 years' worth of empirical study of contract oversight, I have noticed the following that I would also offer as additional *best practices* for both US government and industry:

- Evaluate each requirement from the *bottom up* to assess the complexity and define what is to be measured. Contracts, specifically service contracts, must be performance based and as such need to be measurable. To be measurable means that there are one or more elements in the requirement that can be defined and from which a measurement can be made in terms of quality/scope, schedule, and cost. A *bottom-up* approach will look at the requirement and properly assess what is to be measured and apply the proper means of measurement; conversely, a *top-down* approach will attempt to apply a universal measurement technique to a requirement which may not be the best fit.

- Create a performance-based requirement which prominently features aspects of the requirement to be measured.
- Identify the appropriate measurement practices and tools. There is no universal application of how to measure all things; each one is tailored. For instance, time can be measured as speed (miles per hour), duration (number of days), or response. Each instance of time is represented in different charts or graphs.
- Engage with industry, which means ask questions and seek to understand. This engagement is not only face-to-face but through professional reading of the subject matter so as to become schooled on the subject.
- Create a library of similar measures for analogical use. Organizational learning is vital to continuous improvement and achieving successful outcomes; therefore, mining the past information is a time saver and may reduce engaging in duplicative errors when performing contract oversight (see Table 8.6).
- Use a quality assurance surveillance plan (QASP). This is used when performing contract oversight and provides the person who is performing contract oversight a great tool to ensure performance. A QASP is a necessary part of performance-based contracting.

A QASP has five parts: performance objective, performance standard, acceptable quality level, monitoring methods, and incentive. Most specifically for this chapter, the focus is on the monitoring methods used in contract management, which are:

- *Random sampling*—a statistically based method that assumes receipt of acceptable performance if a given percentage or number of scheduled assessments are found to be acceptable.
- *Periodic sampling*—similar to random sampling, but it is planned at specific intervals or dates.
- *Trend analysis*—should be used regularly and continually assess the contractor's ongoing performance over time.
- *Customer feedback*—firsthand information from the actual users of the service.
- *Third-party audit*—contractor evaluation by a third-party organization that is independent of government and the contractor.

Table 8.6 Organizational learning example

Question	*Techniques to Measure*
What additional skills, knowledge, or abilities are required to successfully perform the post-award functions of the contract oversight?	Ability to use the techniques below
Identify the deliverables (both priced and unpriced)	Analysis of contract/word search
What are the performance measurement techniques which will be used?	Brainstorming, cause and effect, FMEA
What are the most appropriate ways to document/present performance measurement?	Flow chart, milestones, value stream mapping, Program/Project Evaluation and Review Technique (PERT) chart, spreadsheet, earned value management, charts and graphs
Identify if the contract has interim milestones or actions that may be measured	Flow chart, milestones, value stream mapping, PERT chart, spreadsheet, earned value management, charts and graphs
What contract close out elements can be planned to facilitate that close out?	Flow chart, milestones, and PERT chart

Overcoming Obstacles

Post-award contract management is not unique. The way a contract is measured through its performance, the key is to find that which is to be measured. While there may be aspects of the contract that can be measured, not everything needs to be measured, so it is necessary to uncover the important few that represent the best indicators of contract performance. Therein lies the challenge of contract management.

Up and Coming

Over the past 30 years there have been initiatives undertaken to automate portions of the contract management process. While contract management does focus on the process, it also engages intellectual rigor, using business acumen to achieve the outcome being sought by an organization. At present, there are two positions related to this. One position seeks to fully automate the contract management processes, while the other position doesn't. The fully automated position suggests that in using artificial intelligence in blockchain methodology, one could create a usable contract; the other side would contend that each contract is unique and as such would be managed separately. Perhaps somewhere in the middle is the ideal.

Summary and Conclusion

Industry requires contract management, as does government. There is a similarity between contract management practices used in the US government and industry. The US government has produced volumes of standards related to contract oversight, while industry has virtually none. This dearth of contract management standards in industry causes confusion. Both the CMBOK and the PMBOK offer some industry standards, but still more needs to be done. The focus of this chapter was on the foundational functions of contract management, which are to verify performance, report deficiencies, and approve pay requests.

These three foundational functions serve as the platform for building and understanding the contract oversight practice. By using the *best practices* from the OFPP, as well as through professional experience, industry is provided a baseline from which to build contract management programs. The additional information related to the QASP and measurement methods provides an operational understanding of contract management and performance.

The scope of the chapter was on an operational understanding to be used by industry buyers and government buyers; however, the scope did not include areas such as subcontract management, creating a contract management program, or delineating responsibilities of key personnel.

The fundamentals of contract management are universal and necessary for successful contract performance. The good news is that there are usable standards, and the better news is that the standards can be applied right now.

Bibliography

Benchmark of Contract Management (2018). *International association for contract and commercial management.* Retrieved from: https://www.worldcc.com/Resources/Content-Hub/View/ArticleId/9180/2018-BENCHMARK-REPORT-interim-report.

Clark, B. (2015). What is Contract Performance Management? *LinkedIn* [Blog post]. www.linkedin.com/pulse/what-contract-performance-management-brian-clark/.

Contract Management Body of Knowledge (CMBOK). (2019). Sixth Edition. National Contract Management Association, McLean, VA.

Contract Management, Professional Standards Version 1.0 (2017). *Government commercial function (United Kingdom).* www.gov.uk/government/uploads/system/uploads/attachment_data/file/683151/6.4006__CO_Commercial_Capability_Programme_Framework_Interactive.pdf.

Cullen, S. (April 28, 2017). Contract management is an investment not cost. *LinkedIn Blog*. www.linkedin.com/pulse/contract-management-investment-cost-dr-sara-cullen/source.

Cullen, S. (September 26, 2017). Contract success—it is in your mind. *LinkedIn* [Blog post]. www.linkedin.com/pulse/contract-success-your-mind-dr-sara-cullen/?trk=v-feed.

Define Contract Management Metrics, United States Postal Service. http://about.usps.com/manuals/spp123108/html/pp_ps2_023.html.

Elsey, R. D. (October 2007). *The contract management guide.* The Chartered Institute of Purchasing and Supply. www.cips.org/documents/CIPS_KI_Contract%20Management%20Guidev2.pdf.

Federal Acquisition Regulation. www.acquisition.gov.

Garrett, G. A., and Rendon, R. G. (2005). *Contract Management Organizational Assessment Tools.* McLean, VA: National Contract Management Association.

Good Practice Contract Management Framework (C) (2016). National Audit Office, United Kingdom. www.nao.org.uk/wp-content/uploads/2016/12/Good_practice_contract_management_framework.pdf.

Government Commercial and Contracting: An overview of the NAO's Work (Spring 2016). National Audit Office. www.nao.org.uk/wp-content/uploads/2016/05/Government-Commercial-and-Contracting-overview-NAOs-work.pdf.

International Association for Contract and Commercial Management. (2015). Commercial Excellence; Ten Pitfalls to Avoid in Contracting. www.IACCM.com.

Jones, B. (November 2017). 4 important performance metrics for contract management, contract insight—contract management software blog. *Cobblestone Systems.* http://blog.cobblestonesystems.com/contract-management-software/leaders-with-contract-software/4-important-performance-metrics-for-contract-management/.

Mackie, Ian, and Langley, J. (2015). Commercial skills and competency framework for developing and practitioner levels. *Government Commercial Function.* www.gov.uk/government/uploads/system/uploads/attachment_data/file/501136/Commercial_Skills_Framework_v_October_2015__1_.pdf.

Phillips, J. N., Jr., Jennings, M. P., and Paramore, S. L. (2012). *The COR member of the acquisition team: The contracting officers representative (COR) guide to performance and quality.* National Contract Management Association, Vienna, VA.

Reddaway, J. (November 2016). Commercial and contract management: Insights and emerging best practice. National Audit Office United Kingdom. www.nao.org.uk/wp-content/uploads/2016/12/Commercial-and-contract-management-insights-and-emerging-best-practice.pdf.

Transforming Contract Management. (September 2014). Report by the comptroller and auditor general, Home Office and Ministry of Justice. National Audit Office. www.nao.org.uk/wp-content/uploads/2014/09/Home-office-ministry-of-justice-transforming-contract-management.pdf.

9

CONTRACT RISK AND UNCERTAINTY MANAGEMENT

Don Shannon

Using contracts to direct work to another entity is often seen as a risk reduction tool through the mechanism of risk transference. But by doing so, one trades one set of uncertainties for another. The Contract Management Body of Knowledge (CMBOK) details several areas in which the contract manager should be prepared to identify and control uncertainties. In the following sections I will elaborate on several of the uncertainties inherent in contracts and provide some insight as to what can or should be done to mitigate their effects.

The Uncertain Nature of Contracting

The principal set of business (or management) risks encountered when contracting or subcontracting work is the buyer's reduced control over the outcome. The cost, schedule and quality components of fulfilling a need are no longer within the buyer's direct control. Consequently, the buying company must rely on a contracting professional to properly structure the contract instrument and enforce its terms so as to achieve a satisfactory outcome. Although this contract management effort may be divided between a contract manager and a project manager, this arrangement is not always the case. However, in the end the same functions are performed, be it by one person or a dedicated team. The tools they use to do this are described below.

Selection of Contract Type

When forming a contract, the contracting party has an extensive array of contract types at their disposal including fixed price, time and material, and cost reimbursement. Each of those contract types then has a number of sub-types such as cost plus fixed fee, cost, cost plus incentive fee and so forth.

The type of contract selected apportions the cost risk between the contracting parties. Fixed price contracts favor the buyer, while cost reimbursement contracts favor the seller. The numerous contract types and variations available offer a well-graduated scale to apportion contract cost and performance risk between the parties.

Contract type selection goes hand in hand with the specificity of the contract requirements such that loosely defined requirements—often jokingly called "bring me a rock"—entail the greatest risk, and therefore the buyer must indemnify the seller to some extent by offering a cost reimbursement contract. Under such an arrangement the seller has a responsibility to make their "best efforts" at fulfilling the contract objectives but may stop work when the funding is fully expended. The buyer

 DOI: 10.4324/9781351107242-12

then has the option to either end the project or provide added funding. This type of contract is often seen in the basic research phase of projects. The seller may be paid a fee for their work over and above their costs to incentivize them to accept the work. In the case of academia or nonprofits, the fee is often not paid.

If the requirements are more fully developed, then the buyer may tend toward some sort of fixed-price contract. Here the seller is obligated to complete the work for the agreed amount and in doing so assumes the majority of both the cost and the performance risk.

Selection of Provider

Performance risk is often controlled in contracts through the selection of the providing firm. In some cases—as with purely commercial items or in cases where the principal distinguishing feature among offers is cost—the selection of seller may simply hinge on the offered price. This is always the case in sealed bids and low-price technically acceptable solicitations. The assumption is the products or services offered are essentially the same, so price is the deciding factor.

However, there are a number of other possible criteria considered when selecting a seller, and it is here that the government has a definite edge. The government maintains and references several databases of vendor information as a part of their pre-award vendor qualification process. Many of these databases are also available to and require references for government prime contractors in their selection of subcontractors as well. Sources like the System for Award Management (https://sam.gov) and the linked databases for excluded or debarred entities are required searches in the pre-award process.

Both industry and government buyers alike investigate the prospective offeror through various record searches including the government Federal Awardee Performance and Integrity Information System (FAPIIS) which consolidates access to the Contractor Performance Assessment Reporting System (CPAS), the Past Performance Information Retrieval System (PPIRS) and the Excluded Parties List System (EPLS) or commercial sources such as Dun & Bradstreet.

The Downside of Cost Transparency

While commercial entities are usually constrained as to the insight they have into the offeror's cost data, the government and (to some extent) government contractors have much more detailed insights through the requirement for certified cost or pricing data or the lesser requirement of other than certified cost or pricing data. Although the threshold requirements for certified data is now $2 million, other than certified data may be requested under a much broader range of circumstances.

Cost or pricing data are subject to audit prior to the contract award. Requiring such data in conjunction with the remedies available for defective cost or pricing information can provide the government with a reasonable assurance that the price offered is appropriate. Market pricing and competitive offers will add to the government's confidence, typically leading to a determination of "fair and reasonable" pricing. In some circumstances the government is free to do a cost realism analysis to ascertain if the offered cost or price is properly aligned with the contract requirements so as to rule out offerors who either fail to understand the work requirements or are attempting to "buy in" to the contract.

Contingencies, Changes, Claims and Disputes

The methods and options for dealing with cost risk are a significant concern in any type of contract for both the buyer and the seller. One strategy commonly used on commercial projects is to calculate the amount of a *contingency* to cover unexpected (risk-related) costs. While this is perfectly acceptable in commercial contracts, it is not permitted in government contracts since the government offers various relief granting clauses in their contracts to provide for recovery. (One aside here: the government, in FAR 31.205-7, distinguishes between what are called *allowances* for such things as scrap products and spoiled goods that are predictable, and *contingencies* which are not.)

Several clauses including "changes", and "changed site conditions" provide relief and therefore mitigate the seller's risk for changes occurring in the project scope during contract performance. Of course, there is always the risk that some ambiguity in the work description or acceptance criteria will result in the contractor being required to perform more or different work than was originally contemplated. Such controversies may result in alleged changes being made to the scope without the benefit of a written change order (e.g., a "constructive" change) and lead to a claim being filed by either party.

Generally, the risk of a contractor being compelled to perform (additional or changed) work without compensation is relatively low. What is at risk, however, is the adequacy of the compensation provided. Although the contractor is free to file for an "equitable adjustment" for unilateral changes made by the government and to submit claims for constructive changes or disputes, the entitlement and quantum of such adjustments to the contract value are subject to the contracting officer's approval. The contractor is protected from unfair determinations by the disputes clause and various venues for relief including negotiation, mediation and several boards or courts.

Ensuring Adequate Contractor Performance

Both government and commercial contracts share certain protections to ensure the contractor completes the work in a timely manner and according to the terms of the contract. Both types of contracts have quality assurance provisions and acceptance criteria protecting the buyer from substandard performance. Both have the ability to assess liquidated damages should the contractor fail to complete their work in a timely manner.

Where they differ is in the means of enforcing those terms. Commercial contracts generally rely on civil law and enforcement by the courts for breach and the associated damages. Government contracts have similar protections, albeit assessed and enforced with different tools.

The government's trump card is the ability to terminate for default, which carries with it an administrative sanction limiting the contractor's ability to compete for future work for five years with any federal agency. While punitive damages are not available, the government enjoys the ability to make claims for actual damages and/or assess the contractor for the "additional (or excess) costs of reprocurement" from the defaulting contractor, thus indemnifying them from increased costs for a replacement contractor.

Finally, both government and commercial contracts commonly use bonds to protect the interests of the buyer. Although the cost of the bond is generally included in the seller's price, the bonding process effectively transfers significant risk to a third party. Bonds are often required for performance on both services and construction contracts (Miller Act), and payment bonds are required by the government on construction projects over $150,000. Finally, bid bonds are required on construction projects to ensure the offeror will actually be bound by a contract should their bid be accepted.

The Effects of Uncertainty on Contract Performance

Cost estimates are notoriously uncertain and consistently inaccurate. Despite our best efforts to accurately estimate contract costs, we typically miss the mark more than 75% of the time. Here are the results of two published studies showing the extent of uncertainty on program costs witnessed in many of our projects—and by extension, our contracts.

The first study[1] by Bent Flyvbjerg and Alexander Budzier dealt with software projects. The results from this study appear to contradict the second study by John Holloman (dealing with oil and gas infrastructure projects)—until one realizes the horizonal axes on the summary charts are flipped. This means that estimates examined by Flyvbjerg range from +20% of the actual cost to −70% of the actual cost.

These are almost the exact percentages observed by Holloman—the difference being that Holloman's data is drawn from a different "industry" and his presentation of the data more accurately reflects the characteristics of the underlying log-normal distribution. By that I mean it has a mound shape and a very long tail extending to the right. These are characteristic of the log-normal distribution and hint at the possibility for significant outliers out to 300% of the estimated cost or beyond. These are the "runaway" programs that seem to make headlines from time to time.

Also note that the mean of Holloman's "as estimated" is actually 107% of the estimate, as it includes a 7% contingency. Therefore, roughly 9% come in under the original estimate (less contingency) and only 17% come in at or under the "adjusted" estimate with contingency. That means roughly 83% of programs overrun by more than the 7% contingency. These percentages seemingly align with Flyvbjerg's chart, although Holloman's is somewhat more pessimistic.

In summary, the approximate range of ranges for accuracy or uncertainty around the reference amounts are as follows:

- P10: −32% to +8% (average about −9%)
- P50, or mean: 0% to +88% (average about 21%)
- P90: +34% to 190% (average about 70%)

The Uncertain Nature of Contract Requirements and Costs

The buyer and the seller must come to a meeting of the minds concerning what the requirements for a given contract require of each. These requirements are embodied in the contract terms and conditions, as well as the contract technical requirements, such as the statement of work.

The risks when forming a contract are many, but one of the top three is the degree of specificity and/or completeness in the work specifications (design or drawings), or the statement of work. When soliciting a contract, the buyer must ensure specifications are accurate and complete. Those who write the specifications bear the risk for any ambiguity in those specifications being interpreted against them through the doctrine of *contra proferentem*.[2] Similarly, the seller in responding to the solicitation must guard against making exaggerated promises or offering defective pricing. Thus, the stage is set for a difficult and often litigious phase of contract management. Here are some of the more common uncertainties.

Imprecise Work Statement and Specifications

Inaccurate or incomplete work or design specifications can be classified as an epistemic risk and should be considered during risk management activities.[3]

1. Bent Flyvbjerg and Alexander Budzier, Why Your IT Project May Be Riskier Than You Think, *Harvard Business Review* (September 2011).
2. Literally, "against the drafter"; see https://definitions.uslegal.com/c/contra-proferentem-doctrine/.
3. AACE International Recommended Practice No. 17R-97 Cost Estimate Classification System TCM Framework: 7.3—Cost Estimating and Budgeting Rev. November 29, 2011.

> Epistemic uncertainty on the other hand represents a more general and resolvable lack of knowledge. We lack in knowledge, but are aware of our lack, so that the opportunity presents itself for us to reduce this uncertainty.[4]

In practice we find that although there is inherent uncertainty in the designs or specifications, the effects of that uncertainty can be mitigated through improved knowledge. This is certainly the case when estimating a project such as a new building or weapon system.

The American Association of Cost Engineers (AACE) in their Recommended Practice 17R-97 provides the following continuum of estimates and their perceived accuracy at various points in the project definition.

AACE identifies five specific estimate classes ranging from Class 1 (very inaccurate) to Class 5 (very accurate).[5] As shown there, an improvement in the accuracy of the estimate—*and a concurrent reduction in epistemic uncertainty*—can be achieved by spending the money to improve the quality or robustness of the design. This is also true in other applications where similar benefits may be obtained by improving the quality of the project requirements or specifications. In other words, we are becoming more definite concerning what we are asking the contractor to do and as a result reducing uncertainty.

As noted above, as the specificity and accuracy of the work requirements or design improve, the plus-minus error in the cost estimate decreases accordingly. Ultimately, we develop a detailed estimate at about the 65%+ design maturity that supports a deterministic estimate with ±10% to 15% accuracy. Further design (to the 90%–100% complete point) improves the accuracy to ±5%, which is about as accurate as estimates ever get. However, even with these highly refined designs, we often miss the mark.[6]

Uncertainty and Single-Point Estimates

Estimates of project cost or schedule tend to be expressed as deterministic, single-point estimates comprising the summation of several lower-level (again single-point) estimates. For example, if one were to start at the lowest level of detail and sum the individual cost estimates for a project work breakdown schedule (WBS), they would arrive at an overall estimate for the total project cost.

What is missing from this approach is the understanding that any single-point estimate for cost, effort, performance time and so on is by its very nature uncertain and is, therefore, stochastic rather than deterministic. Stated another way:

> High-quality cost estimates usually fall within a range of possible costs, the point estimate being between the most likely costs and the least likely costs. . . . there is always a chance that the actual cost will differ from the estimate. Moreover, lack of knowledge about the future is only one possible reason for the difference.[7]

Consequently, the technique of using a single-point estimate to represent an uncertain value is flawed.

4. Epistemic, ontological and aleatory risk, Matthew Squair, blog post (November 10, 2009); see https://criticaluncertainties.com/2009/10/11/epistemic-and-aleatory-risk/.
5. AACE International Recommended Practice No. 17R-97 (November 29, 2011).
6. Estimate Accuracy: Dealing with Reality John K. Holloman, PE CCE CEP, 2012 AACE International Transactions.
7. Covert, Raymond P., 2013. Analytic Method for Probabilistic Cost and Schedule Risk Analysis. [Report] NASA.gov, April 5, www.nasa.gov/.pdf/741989main_Analytic%20Method%20for%20Risk%20 Analysis%20-%20Final%20Report.pdf (March 6, 2014).

> Estimates of cost and schedule duration of a task or project are uncertain values, so we do not know the exact, discrete values until it (the work) is complete. Given the inherent uncertainty of estimates, the only way to portray them is with probability distributions of possible costs and schedule durations (or dates).[8]

Optimistic Cost Estimates

One of the prime factors in this uncertainty is that the estimator often lacks detailed historical data that provides a basis for estimating the new project. In effect, if we are doing something that we have not done before, what do we base the estimated cost or schedule duration on for accomplishing that work? It is at this point that we encounter "expert opinion" or "engineering judgment" as the basis for our cost and schedule estimates, and it is here that we encounter a major source of optimism in the estimates.

> People remember past task durations as being shorter than they actually were, and therefore, when they consult them to predict the next task, they underestimate how long that task will take. . . . Experience with a task seems to negatively affect predictive ability. The person who would seem to have the best ability to predict—an expert—is also the person who is most likely to be biased.[9]

The Cost of Uncertainty

When one looks at how much a contract "costs", three values should be identified. To the buyer the contractor's price is the principle concern, as it goes to answer the question, "Can we afford this?" Knowledgeable contract and project managers also consider (or should consider) what will it actually cost them when all is said and done, considering that the awarded price seldom is the final price as changes are made to the contract, overruns can happen, and uncertainties (both risks and possible rewards)—like finding asbestos insulation on all the pipes in a renovation project—can happen.

Discrete Uncertainties

When most people think of risk management, they zero in on the discrete uncertainties to the detriment of other less obvious uncertainties. The "usual suspects" of such analysis tend to range from the cost impact of material price increases to things like late delivery by subcontractors to uncertain building site conditions. Many companies have gone so far as to build checklists of these "known unknowns" complete with ranges of probabilities and consequential impacts.

Systemic Uncertainty: The "Elephant in the Room"

As John Holloman points out in *Project Risk Quantification*,[10] the effects of systemic uncertainty generally exceed those of the project-specific (aka discrete) uncertainties. Hollmann notes that systemic uncertainty is often the largest component of total uncertainty yet the least well understood.

8. *Ibid.*
9. Michael Roy and Nicholas Christenfeld, Bias in Memory Predicts Bias in Estimation of Future Task Duration, *Memory and Cognition*, 2007.
10. John K. Holloman, *Project Risk Quantification, A Practitioner's Guide to Realistic Cost and Schedule Risk Management* (Probabilistic Publishing, 2016).

Characteristics of Systemic Uncertainty

Systemic uncertainty is a conglomeration of various environmental and organizational flaws responsible for the suboptimal performance of a particular entity. These factors exist in all organizations but are seldom quantified or even acknowledged as a part of formal risk management. Generally, these factors are quantified by analysis of historical project costs. Systemic risk is approximately equal across a range of similar projects. Systemic risk comprises two types of uncertainty, as discussed below.

THE EPISTEMIC COMPONENT

Systemic uncertainty has the following characteristics:

1. It is generally similar between or among companies within an industry.
2. It encompasses environmental factors, such as business or economic conditions, the political environment, interest rates, exchange rates and so on.
3. It is reflective of business practices, management efficiency and corporate culture.
4. It can be subdivided into two general classes of uncertainty: aleatory and epistemic.

THE ALEATORY COMPONENT

The aleatory component of systemic uncertainty is akin to variability. If one does a task several times, the difference between performance on one trial and the next is attributable to the aleatory (probabilistic) nature of the task. Tasks are considered independent trials of an event whose outcome is a random variable defined by some probability or frequency distribution. How long one takes driving to work is a good example—some days are faster than the others, but we can generalize the time within a range of values.

Mitigating Systemic Uncertainty

The epistemic component of systemic uncertainty is driven by a fundamental *lack of knowledge* or (in my opinion) a systemic inefficiency. The epistemic nature of these risks means they can be mitigated through "buying down", that is, obtaining more knowledge or better knowledge. For example, if epistemic risk results in subpar performance, then improving business systems or better understanding how business systems contribute to organizational performance can mitigate that risk.

Government contracting officers are well aware of the effects of systemic uncertainty and have a number of tools available to mitigate that risk. These include the authority to invoke requirements for contractors to "improve" their knowledge or abilities with certain business-wide infrastructure requirements such as

- An acceptable accounting system
- An acceptable cost estimating system
- An approved purchasing system
- A compliant earned-value management system
- An approved material management system
- An approved property management system.

Quantifying the Effects of Uncertainty

Notwithstanding the fact that one can identify the various dimensions of uncertainty with relative ease, how does one translate these dimensions into an overall uncertainty score suitable for our estimate? Many are the times I encountered the sage old veteran manager who would add x% to the budget "just to be on the safe side" (Hence the 7% contingency in the above illustration.) Often they were proven right, so perhaps they intuitively knew a thing or two about uncertainty.

The ultimate questions are:

1. How much should be added to the estimate for uncertainty?
2. How do you factor that additional cost into the contract price?

Quantifying Discrete Uncertainties

Discrete uncertainties are quantified during the qualitative risk analysis process.

Dollarizing discrete risks can be controversial. The classical approach is to calculate the "expected value" by multiplying the probability of occurrence times the likely outcome. This approach is now discouraged because it may overstate the potential liability. The *US Air Force Cost Risk and Uncertainty Analysis Handbook*[11] provides the following recommended approach:

1. If there are only a few discrete uncertainties, their cost impact on the TBE (a cost estimate that is the arithmetic sum of the program's elements) should be included in the form of supplemental "what-if" cases regardless of their probability of occurrence. Funding at the "expected value" (probability of occurrence times the cost impact) is not recommended.
2. If there are many discrete uncertainties, then they should be listed and uncertainty assigned via a discrete distribution (e.g., triangular) and totaled using a simulative process (Monte Carlo) or an analytical technique such as method of moments.

Quantifying Systemic Uncertainties

Several studies have been conducted seeking to address the "how much" issue.[12] These studies have produced a number of parametric models which consider various inputs—such as design maturity, project complexity and technology risks—to estimate the plus-minus percentages for systemic contingency.[13]

To use the model, one enters the traditional single-point estimate for each WBS element. This estimate is then modified based on the user selections of criteria for three historically significant uncertainty drivers—in this case, design maturity (factor 1) selects which of three historical data tables (class 3, 4 or 5) is selected; project complexity (factor 2); and technological maturity (factor 3). Each factor is described by the user of the model adjectivally using words such as "conceptual, budgetary or detailed" for the design and then "low, medium or high" for factors 2 and 3. Based on these inputs the model selects appropriate factors from the historical data and then applies a correction factor to the single-point estimate to derive a three-point estimate for that WBS element. Finally, the model uses either a simulative or an analytical solution to sum the individual elements to obtain the risk-adjusted estimate highlighted in yellow at the lower left.[14]

Parametric models such as this are commonly used for top-level project estimates, especially in the oil and gas industry. Such models tend to be very proprietary and closely guarded, however (generic) models developed by Rand and others are available in open literature.

11. *US Air Force Cost Risk and Uncertainty Analysis Handbook*, April 2007.
12. *Ibid.*, Project Risk Quantification.
13. *Ibid.*, Uncertain Estimating.
14. The exact process used and the mechanics of the process are beyond the scope of this article but are readily available in articles on Monte Carlo simulation and the FRISK technique using the Method of Moments.

Interpreting the Model's Results

Using this modeling technique, the deterministic original single-point estimate of $407,717 is now expressed as a random variable using a triangular frequency distribution with a minimum value of $338,511, a mode of $510,365, and a maximum of $676,018. The arithmetic mean of the distribution—expressing a 50/50 chance of finishing at or below that value—is $508,298.

Depending on the risk tolerance of the owning organization, the project should be budgeted at the $P_{(80)}$ to $P_{(90)}$ range (or roughly $570,000).

Aggregating the Uncertainty

Pricing Uncertainty

Much of the project uncertainty can be "bought down" either through well-defined specifications (as above) or proper application of business practices, as discussed in the following section. But savvy managers know that nothing is ever certain until its done, so only the most naïve manager would quote a project without some "slack" in both the schedule and the costs. This slack is a factor (x) added to the estimate such that:

$$tc = pe + y \pm x$$[15]

where
tc = the cost at completion
pe = the point estimate of cost
y = estimating error (including optimism)
x = the uncertainty in the estimate.

If the estimate is being performed to identify funding requirements for an infrastructure project or a major system acquisition, the risk-adjusted (i.e., "uncertain") estimate is very valuable in defining the capital budget.

If the estimate is being done by a contractor in response to a solicitation, then the value of x, while good to know, may or may not be of immediate use. The risk-adjusted estimate, while a "best practice," may not comport to FAR Part 31 estimating procedures. Its use for pricing contracts varies by contract type.[16]

Overlooked Risks—Contract Management and Third-Party Risks

With the abundance of tools at their disposal, why is it then that we have epic contracting failures and enormous cost or schedule overruns on government megaprojects such as the Healthcare.gov website or weapons systems such as the Navy's A-12 Avenger program? Although vastly different in many respects, these two programs offer insights into uncertainties not typically evaluated as a part of the overall risk analysis.

Case Study #1: The A-12 Avenger 1984–1991

In acquisition circles the case of the Navy's A-12 Avenger aircraft and its resulting cancellation by then Defense Secretary Dick Cheney in 1991 is a well-known instance of how things go wrong. As

15. Uncertain Estimating—Methods and Techniques for Controlling The Uncertainty In Your Estimates, Don Shannon, Contract Management Magazine (October 2018), pp. 23–35.
16. That is, fixed-price or cost-reimbursement type contracts, as per FAR Part 31.

with most situations where things go terribly wrong, what happened with the A-12 was not simply the case of one thing veering off track; it was a combination of factors that have been discussed above plus a management environment that tried to suppress the facts. So what really went wrong?

Contract Type: Setting the Stage

The A-12 Full Scale Development Contract (N00019-88-C-0050) was (at inception) a $4.8 billion fixed-price incentive contract for eight flight-test aircraft and five full-scale ground-test articles. The contract established a target price of $4.379 billion, a ceiling price of $4.777 billion and a 60%/40% share line between target and ceiling with economic price adjustment.[17]

In the late 1980s, both General Dynamic and Boeing were in a financial bind. As noted in the Beech report on the A-12:

> Moreover, the aerospace contractors, who had sustained financial setbacks because of government defense cuts, were under pressure from upper management to maximize cash flow. They relied heavily on progress payments given at various points in the development process, . . . Such pressure would create an incentive to be optimistic, since progress payments would be reduced if the contractor or the government estimated an overrun.

Boeing and General Dynamics accepted a fixed-price incentive contract for developing the prototype aircraft—a high-risk decision borne out of financial desperation.

> Somewhere along the line, the contractors began to see that they had made a gigantic mistake in taking on the program under a fixed-price contract, which the Navy had imposed in an effort to get a grip on weapons costs. It was too inflexible to allow for unforeseen costs, say industry and Pentagon officials, even though such costs are inevitable when contractors are working on the frontiers of technology.

The Navy had insisted on a fixed price in order to control program costs. However, the contract type (FP incentive fee) selected was inappropriate for a developmental effort because the requirements were likely to change and many technical uncertainties had to be addressed. Such a contract type would be more appropriate for an aircraft that had been through initial testing and acceptance and was just entering full-scale production.

Fixed price contracts are generally not used for contracts where there are significant uncertainties or where reliable estimates of cost cannot be established. FAR 16.202-2 states fixed price contracts shall not be used unless "Performance uncertainties can be identified and reasonable estimates of their cost impact can be made, and the contractor is willing to accept a firm fixed price representing assumption of the risks involved."

The Navy was criticized for taking advantage of the (desperate) contractors in this situation, and ultimately the use of fixed price contracts for developmental purposes was disallowed. In 1988 Congress passed Section 8118 of the Defense Appropriations Act which prohibited DoD from awarding a fixed-price contract in excess of $10 million for development of a major system or subsystem

> unless the Undersecretary of Defense for Acquisition determines, in writing, that program risk has been reduced to the extent that realistic pricing can occur, and that the contract type permits an equitable adjustment and sensible allocation of program risk between the contracting parties.

17. US Department of Defense Audit Report 91-059, titled *Review of the A-12 Aircraft Program* (February 28, 1991).

Changing the Program Assumptions[18]

Initial estimates of the A-12 program cost had been based on requirements for a projected fleet of 858 aircraft. This estimate was subsequently reduced to 620 aircraft in December 1989. Further reductions in the number of aircraft were possible due to uncertain participation by the Marine Corps, the Navy electing to reduce the total number of carriers and the Navy potentially reassigning various mission roles such as refueling to other platforms.

Second, cost estimates for the program were based on promises of funding to the contractors, which the Navy was finding hard to live up to. According to the contract terms, such delays would enable the contractors to "renegotiate costs and specifications in a noncompetitive environment" and would likely result in additional cost overruns.

Adding fuel to the fire, the Navy and Air Force had agreed to share non-recurring engineering costs based on the assumption the Air Force would join the program in 1993 with an estimated procurement of some 400 aircraft. However, the Air Force reevaluated the service life of existing aircraft, which the A-12 would ultimately replace, and decided not to buy the A-12 until 1998, thus adding an estimated $2.4 billion to the Navy's share of nonrecurring engineering and tooling costs. Finally, revised inflation rates between 1988 and 1989 resulted in an $11.5 million increase in A-12 program costs.

Over-Optimistic Contractors

The A-12 contractors, General Dynamics and McDonnell Douglas, clearly underestimated the technical difficulties of constructing a carrier-based ground attack aircraft incorporating stealth technologies.

> "Overly optimistic A-12 contractors, who miscalculated the extent of the technical difficulties in producing such a plane and shielded the problems from the government. An inquiry by Navy Deputy General Counsel Chester Paul Beach found that General Dynamics and McDonnell Douglas discovered "increasing cost and schedule variances" but did not alert the Navy in a timely fashion.[19]

The technology issues were exacerbated by mutual distrust between the two partnering contractors.

> "There were technologies that could have helped in the overall [A-12] effort, but they weren't willing to share those," said the analyst. "If you have a technological advantage, how willing are you to share that if . . . it could help you in some other program?"[20]

Consequently, when a review team looked at the program in 1989 with the expectation of a first flight in 1990, there were clear signs the program was in deep trouble with missing tooling and much engineering of the airframe yet to be done.[21] It was clear that the first flight milestone would not be met.

18. Navy A-12 Cost and Requirements, Report to the Chairman, Committee on Armed Services, House of Representatives, Government Accounting Office, December 1990.
19. Dr. David D. Christensen, Cost Overrun Optimism: Fact or Fiction?, *Defense ARJ* (July 2015), Vol. 22, No. 3: 254–271.
20. David Montgomery, How the A-12 Went Down, *Air Force Magazine* (April 1991).
21. Beach, Chester Paul, A-12 Administrative Inquiry Washington Dep't of the Navy November 28, 1990).

Cancellation

On January 5, 1991, Defense Secretary Cheney cancelled the A-12 program. At the time of cancellation, the program was at least $1 billion over budget, the aircraft was 8,000 pounds overweight, and the program was 18 months behind schedule. Secretary Cheney stated:

> The A-12 I did terminate. It was not an easy decision to make because it's an important requirement that we're trying to fulfill. But no one could tell me how much the program was going to cost, even just through the full scale development phase, or when it would be available. And data that had been presented at one point a few months ago turned out to be invalid and inaccurate.[22]

Contracts to General Dynamics and McDonnell Douglas were terminated for default. What followed was lengthy litigation over the propriety of the cancellation and the damages to be assessed.

Advocacy and Poor Business Judgement

The above program management issues were compounded by advocacy issues, as the Navy passionately wanted the aircraft to replace an aging and increasingly vulnerable A-6 Intruder with more capable and survivable stealth aircraft. Consequently, both Navy and contractor management were unwilling to be the bearer of bad news to the Secretary of Defense and the prospect that such news would cause the program to be cancelled. As one leading critic of the A-12 program noted:

> Program managers are advocates by necessity. When taken to the extreme, program advocacy can result in the suppression of adverse information about the status of a program. Such was the case in the Navy's A-12 program. In "A-12 Administrative Inquiry," Beach (1990) speculates that such "abiding cultural problems" were not unique to the Navy.[23]

Air Force Magazine[24] summarized the issues of why the A-12 was cancelled:

> Overly protective Navy officials, who didn't want to endanger the plane by pointing out problems. A Pentagon analyst first detected a possible cost overrun two years ago, but the Navy program manager continued to describe the A-12 as being on track until after a major Pentagon review last year.

Therefore, not only did Navy management fail to consider potential program risks and account for their effects when budgeting for and funding the program, but they actively concealed facts from upper management on the optimistic belief that "things would get better" and thus compounded the problem. This in the face of "research (that) has shown that, once a program is more than 15 percent to 20 percent complete, it is highly unlikely that the final cost overrun will be less than the present cost overrun."[25] Despite these facts, contractor and government program managers often claim optimistically that dramatic recoveries from cost overruns are possible.

22. Stevenson, James P. *The $5 Billion Misunderstanding: The Collapse of the Navy's A-12 Stealth Bomber Program.* Naval Institute Press (2001).
23. *Ibid.*, Cost Overrun Optimism.
24. *Ibid.*, How the A-12 Went Down.
25. *Ibid.*, Cost Overrun Optimism.

Lessons Learned

The Navy should have been acutely aware of the risks they faced, and one would note that:

1. Requirements (and assumptions based upon them) were not stable. Both technical and programmatic requirements were in a constant state of flux.
2. Technology being used was immature. In 1990 stealth technology consisted of the F117 Nighthawk (Lockheed Martin) and the B-2 (Northrop). Neither McDonnell Douglas nor General Dynamics had produced a stealth aircraft, hence there were considerable technical unknowns.
3. Project complexity called for two contractors to work together to solve various technical challenges, even though these same two contractors were competing on an Air Force program: the Advanced Tactical Fighter.

Inserting the $4.8 billion and the various risk factors into the proposed parametric model referenced above provides the following results. The Navy should have expected the cost to be more in the area of $6.5 billion and should have sought program funding in the range of $8 billion to $8.5 billion. In retrospect, this is precisely where things were heading in 1991 when the program was cancelled. At that time the program had expended on the order of $5 billion.

It is pretty clear when looking at the above plot—which admittedly uses generalized factors not specifically tailored for aircraft development—where costs were likely heading. This is especially true if one considers that when the program was terminated, not one of the eight flight test aircraft had been built. We start with the $4.8 billion contract value and then adjust for the stated risk factors. If we add in the estimated $1 billion the program was seen to be over budget as of March 1989,[26] we start to see that the cost was growing in a predictable manner, and by contract termination, the Navy's A-12 cost estimate at contract completion had risen from an original estimate of roughly $5 billion to the $7.5 billion cited in the GAO report.[27]

The Navy's biggest error however, was their irrational belief that "things would get better." Christensen has shown that once project is approximately 20% complete, the Cost Performance Index (CPI) seldom gets better.[28]

Case Study #2: Healthcare.gov Website

There is no better example of the issues posed by overlooked risks or their potential to turn a program into a disaster than the US government healthcare website. Just about everything that could go wrong with an acquisition eventually did go wrong on this program.

The Patient Protection and Affordable Care Act was a signature piece of legislation and a key achievement of the Obama administration. A central provision of the law required the establishment of state health insurance exchanges, now commonly referred to as marketplaces, by January 1, 2014. Marketplaces permit individuals to compare and select private health insurance plans. For states that

26. Lt. Col. Louise A. Eckhardt, Bureaucratic Politics: Explaining Cancellation of the Navy A-12 Aircraft, Lt. Col. Louise A. Eckhardt, National War College, 300 5th Avenue, Fort Lesley J. McNair, Washington, DC 20319-6000.
27. Government Accountability Office Report Status of Navy A-12 Contract and Material at Termination NSIAD-91-261 (July 24, 1991).
28. Christensen, David S., and Carl Templin (2001). "EAC Evaluation Methods, Do They Still Work?" Working paper. Cedar City: Southern Utah University.

elected not to establish a marketplace, PPACA required the federal government to establish and operate a federal marketplace.[29]

To meet the tight deadlines, the Centers for Medicare and Medicaid Services (CMS) used existing indefinite quantity, indefinite delivery (IDIQ) contracts and issued task orders to incumbents to get a contract in place. While this was expedient, it limited competition and short-circuited the normal solicitation process where more refined requirements would have been demanded and offerors would have provided more detailed technical proposals. As the GAO noted, the task orders were awarded without full appreciation of the true requirements for the system, which consequently led to numerous requirement changes. This is a significant risk factor and is aligned with the CMS failing to adequately document an acquisition strategy.

Systemic risk includes all of the corporate and environmental factors that affect every contract effort attempted by an organization and are the sleeping "elephant in the room",[30] generally going unnoticed yet constituting a major portion of the contract risks faced by an organization. CMS was well aware of the time constraints and lack of formal planning with Healthcare.gov but carried on anyway. However, CMS compounded their risk by failing to effectively deal with two areas: introducing a new management technique (Agile development) and ineffective program oversight.

First Use of Agile Development

The Agile development methodology has rapidly become a standard development technique for complex software projects. However, the Healthcare.gov website was the first significant program by the Department of Health and Human Services (HHS) to use this methodology, and the inherent risks of implementing a new management approach on what was a very high-visibility and politically important project were ill-advised. As the GAO noted:[31]

> To help manage compressed time frames for FFM and data hub development, CMS program officials adopted an iterative IT development approach called Agile that was new to CMS. Agile development is a modular and iterative approach that calls for producing usable software in small increments, sometimes referred to as sprints, rather than producing a complete product in longer sequential phases. The Office of Management and Budget issued guidance in 2010 that advocated the use of shorter delivery time frames for federal IT projects, an approach consistent with Agile. However, CMS program officials acknowledged that when FFM and data hub development began in September 2011, they had limited experience applying an Agile approach to CMS IT projects.

One of the hallmarks of Agile software development is the ability to trade off requirements freely. "Agile development allows for prioritization and assignment of requirements (features) to successive software releases (sprints) determined by the development team and stakeholders".[32] This trade-off is accomplished by the product owner (in this case a government technical manager but not the traditional contracting officer's representative) working directly with the software development team to shuffle requirements and schedules so as to create product functionality in short bursts of work (sprints) leading to the creation of various software releases incorporating those functions or features.

29. GAO-14-694 "Ineffective Planning and Oversight Practices Underscore the Need for Improved Contract Management."
30. *Ibid.*, Project Risk Quantification.
31. *Ibid.*, Ineffective Planning and Oversight.
32. Ray W. Stratton, PMP, EVP, Making EVM work in Agile Development Projects, Measurable News, *The College of Performance Management* (2016) Issue 2.

Because CMS was new to Agile, many of these trade-offs or added requirements resulted in additional costs—costs the contracting officer was totally unaware of.

Ineffective Management Oversight

The GAO Report on this project cited numerous lapses in management ranging from a failure to enforce the creation of a written acquisition plan to allowing technical managers to direct contractors to perform work that was outside the contract scope.

> We (the GAO) identified approximately 40 instances during the Federally Facilitated Marketplace (FFM) (system) development in which Centers for Medicare & Medicaid Services (CMS) program staff inappropriately authorized contractors to expend funds totaling over $30 million because those staff did not adhere to established contract oversight roles and responsibilities.[33]

Further, the GAO noted that CMS documents showed that the cost growth was the result of at least 40 instances in which work was authorized by various CMS program officials, including the government task leader (GTL)—who is responsible for day-to-day technical interaction with the contractor—and other staff with project oversight responsibilities, who did not have the authority to approve the work. This was done without the knowledge of the contracting officer or the contracting officer's representative. This inappropriately authorized work included adding features to the FFM and data hub, changing designs in the eligibility and enrollment module, and approving the purchase of a software license. CMS later determined that the work was both necessary and within the general scope of the task order, but the cost of the activities went beyond the estimated cost ceiling established in the order and thus required a modification.[34]

Other oversight issues were also noted. For example, despite the HHS requirement for a written acquisition strategy, the GAO found:

> CMS program and contracting staff did not complete the required acquisition strategy for FFM and data hub development. . . . the documents do not include the rationale for all decisions and did not address a number of planning elements required in HHS acquisition strategy, such as organizational factors, technological factors, and logistics. . . . In the absence of an acquisition strategy, key risks and plans to manage them were not captured and considered as required.[35]

The lack of planning and oversight combined with the unfamiliar Agile software and the unrelenting schedule all combined to elevate the risk for the Healthcare.gov project off the charts. It became a "Black Swan" with costs spiraling out of control, the schedule slipping, and ultimately failing to make its debut with anywhere close to the expected (and promised) features set in place.

Third-Party Contract Risks

The preceding discussion dealt exclusively with the risks encountered by the contracting parties, that is, those with contractual privity. However, not all stakeholders in contractual transactions are in privity. We have to also consider the third-party and even fourth-party risks as well.

33. *Ibid.*, Ineffective Planning and Oversight.
34. *Ibid.*
35. *Ibid.*

Third parties are often the sponsors or benefactors of a contract action. Such is the case when government procurement offices contract for the acquisition of goods or services that ultimately will be used by various departments or agencies. The position filled by the contract manager was once called the "procurement agent", in that they filled two roles: procuring needed goods or services and acting as a trusted agent or go-between for the benefiting department.

Consequently, many of the risks described above can (and properly should) be thought of as third-party issues as well. For example, the issues of underperformance, late delivery, nonconforming, delivery, cost overruns and so forth are all issues that ultimately affect the sponsoring organization. It is their budget that is decremented by overruns. It is their performance that is impaired by lack of a key deliverable or a schedule extension. While the procuring agency may suffer a loss of reputation and additional administrative workload, it is the sponsoring third party that bears the brunt of the consequences.

Avoiding these potential risks requires strong cooperation and communication between the sponsor (be that a government organization, a surety remediating a covered loss or any other third-party beneficiary), the contracting (i.e., procurement) team, and the performing contractor. Sitting in the hot seat in this scenario is the contract management team. As a fiduciary to the sponsor, they ultimately must exercise their authority to discharge their responsibility to identify, quantify, classify and address each risk. Therefore, the principal risk from the sponsor's point of view is how effective the contract management team will be in doing so.

Adding layers to the procurement action aggravates the existing uncertainty associated with communicating requirements. It can become very much like the game of "telephone", where each successive link in the communication chain adds distortion or miscommunication to the message. This problem was something I had to deal with on a daily basis when managing construction contracts, as the owner would be on the construction site and I, the contracts manager, was some distance away. Many changes or deviations originated from the owner and were directly communicated to the contractor. Obviously, such direct communication from the owner (a third-party beneficiary) and the performing contractor were potential constructive changes to the contract and a significant risk.

Other third-party risks included performance or compliance issues from the sub-contractor. Again, these uncertainties have been presented above with respect to the prime contractor, and the uncertainty is how well will the prime contractor manage their subcontractors. There is one area of uncertainty is unique to the prime contractor/subcontractor management issue, and that is the issue of claims.

Generally, claims between the subcontractor and prime contractor do not affect the buyer as the buyer is shielded by privity. In other words, there is little basis for the third party to file a claim with the buyer since they do not have a contractual relationship with them. However, there are exceptions.

Lacking privity of contract with the government, the subcontractor's options are limited to the following:

1. A sponsored claim. Sponsored claims are permitted by the Federal Acquisition Regulation under the Contract Disputes Act by a ruling known as the *Severin* doctrine. *Severin* holds that claims can be sponsored by the prime contractor as "pass-through" claims on the behalf of the subcontractor to the extent that the prime contractor itself is liable to the subcontractor.[36]
2. A claim against a surety under a payment bond required by the Miller Act.
3. The Tucker Act. If the subcontractor can show that an actual or implied contract existed between itself and the government, a claim can be made directly by the subcontractor under the Tucker Act. However, there is strong precedent showing "the Tucker Act does not give a right of action against the United States in those cases where, if the transaction were between private parties, recovery could be had upon a contract implied in law".[37]

36. *Severin v. United States Court of Claims*, 99 Ct. Cl. 435 (1943).
37. *Merritt v. United States*, 267 U.S. 338 (1925).

Conclusion

There is a difference between knowing the tools and techniques described in this article and applying those principles in a challenging environment. Contracts personnel have a virtual arsenal of tools at their disposal to manage the risk associated with contracts. Using those tools to make effective business decisions is a core competency of the contract management profession. The above cases clearly illustrate that there is much room for improvement in our efforts to identify, quantify and effectively manage risks. These cases also make a strong argument for professional integrity and the need for subordinates to press for adherence to established processes and regulatory compliance in the face of demanding time limits or bureaucratic pressures.

10

FINDING OPPORTUNITIES IN RISK FOR SMALL BUSINESSES AND SUBCONTRACTORS

Linda Harris

Introduction

In a world that fosters hopes, dreams, and innovation, we find in that world one that fosters entrepreneurship. The American Dream romanticizes the picture of the small business entrepreneur and their journey, often offering a misleading portrait of the path to success. The French meaning of entrepreneur is "one who undertakes." Every year in the United States there are many individuals that start their journey to open a small business—and sadly, and almost equally, is the number of businesses that close. According to the Small Business Administration (SBA), there are over 32 million small businesses in the US, with small businesses representing 99% of all businesses in the country. Small businesses are the most significant contributor to GDP and assist in creating a balanced economy; however, starting a business is a risk.[1]

Risk is at times the fence that keeps an individual focused on safety, from leaping into the unknown, and it can also be the reason some individuals risk everything and jump gladly off the cliff into the unknown, but when one jumps, they should do so knowing they will meet the face of risk over and over again. Entrepreneurs tend to evaluate risk based on topics and trends that highlight internal and external risks, ignoring the impact of systemic risks. The most significant systemic risk is the ability of the entrepreneur not just to mitigate risk but to embrace it. The mindset of an entrepreneur is the differentiator between the successful entrepreneur and one who quits, for it is not always how well they plan for risk or how they manage it, but if they can embrace the chaos it causes as part of their journey.[2]

The entrepreneurs who start these businesses are often admired, whether they fail or succeed, and that is because of the considerable risk it takes to begin the journey of owning a business. Risk is the undeniable part of the journey, and small business owners will expect it, plan for it, attempt to mitigate it, and at some stage within the business's life, they will dance with it, and at that time, they should embrace it. It could be the last dance or the first steps in a life journey where the fluidity of the movement, accompanied by grace and composure, leads the way to innovations and greater productivity.

1. Small Business Administration (2021). Small Business Office of Advocacy. www.sba.gov/sites/default/files/advocacy/SB-FAQ-2016_WEB.pdf.
2. Conner, D. R. (1998). *Leading at the Edge of Chaos*. New York: John Wiley.

DOI: 10.4324/9781351107242-13

Many books and classes address risk and attempt to increase the ability of an entrepreneur to prepare for it. The Federal Deposit Insurance Incorporation (FDIC) and US Small Business Administration (SBA) provide training materials on risk management for small businesses. The mission of this literature is to assist entrepreneurs in taking the first step toward building a better business.[3] A pretest includes questions directed to the entrepreneur:

1. What type of risks can be controlled?
2. Is it possible to create a business plan that prepares for every type of risk?
3. What should you do with the identifiable risks that could halt, slow, or affect your business's profitability?
4. If you need help managing risk, what should you do?
5. What are the common ways to avoid risk?

Out of the list of questions, number 5 stands out. Why would the SBA suggest to "avoid" risk and provide the following as choices as answers to the questions above:

a. Communicate risks you have identified to employees.
b. Make your expectations clear to employees.
c. Develop support systems to care for your family's needs.
d. Train staff on the business continuity plan.
e. Purchase insurance.
f. Plan emergency contingencies.

Because entrepreneurs cannot avoid risk, they must embrace it and meet it head-on. These questions for the business plan are standard fare in understanding how one must plan for risk, but no literature, class, or life experience can thoroughly prepare an entrepreneur for risk. The argument is that the entrepreneur's attitude, spirit, and true grit will assist them in embracing the risk, because the unknown impact of unplanned business interruptions is the very risk the entrepreneurs either faced or ignored when they started their business.

The SBA is the leading organization providing support to small businesses, and they should challenge themselves to assist in changing the view of risk from something that should be avoided or mitigated to something an entrepreneur must marry to survive. Once married, the small business owner should learn to love or at least appreciate their relationship with risk.

Chaos and Risk

There are several definitions of chaos according to Webster's Dictionary; the first words are obsolete (chasm, abyss, a state of disarrangement where chance is supreme) and a list of synonyms including confusion, disarray, dishevelment, disorder, disorderedness, disorderliness, disorganization, free-for-all, havoc, hell, jumble, mare's nest, mess, shambles, snake-pit, tumble, and welter.[4] Many of these words inspire panic and fear, but Conner, in the book *Leading at the Edge of Chaos*, places them as steps in a dance. The arrangement of steps in a dance is often the order of a beautiful ritual, but improvisation of steps can turn an ordinarily beautiful dance into an extraordinary experience that even bystanders will feel they have lived. Hearts will race faster as the audience becomes part of the

3. Small Business Administration (n.d.). Risk Management Guide. www.sba.gov/sites/default/files/files/PARTICIPANT_GUIDE_RISK_MANAGEMENT.pdf.
4. Merriam-Webster (n.d.). Chaos. www.merriam-webster.com/dictionary/chaos;Merriam-Webster (n.d.). Failure. www.merriam-webster.com/dictionary/failure.

journey of the dance. This is chaos at its best, a journey of the unexpected where each bystander waits hopelessly for the next step, embracing the unknown with anticipation.

The Beauty of Chaos

The first thing an entrepreneur should learn is to embrace risk and the chaos it brings, and *Leading at the Edge of Chaos* is should be a must-read on this subject. Conner prepares the reader for the journey of developing the mindset that embraces risk and chaos, leading to the development of a nimble organization. The premise in discussing chaos is through organizational change. Entrepreneurs must be prepared to lead change by understanding what risk is the chaos that ensues, how to predict it, manage it, and, most importantly, prepare their team for change. One learns that the turbulence in an organization is seen through the viewer's perception as chaos or construct. In the current business climate, the state of rest is short-lived; risk is the ever-present factor that energizes the company, creating either fear or innovation—and when it is embraced, both. Business life spans, along with "new technology," have declined. Business lifespans only last as long as an organization can remain ahead of the pack or, at best, can remain current. New technology is only new until you or your competitor brings the next product to market.[5]

Business successes used to be measured on the reputation of a company to stand on the results of its last product or innovation, but now they are also judged by how far they have surpassed the competition; today's leaders must be prepared to function in a constant state of change; any change is a risk, but change is the reality of businesses today, and change is constant. Tom Panaggio, the author of *The Risk Advantage*, states that risk is the unwavering self-motivating willingness to step outside your comfort zone, and that separates leaders from the rank and file.[6] There are often two ways change is managed: one is the mindset of the entrepreneur who has the innate understanding that continued change is necessary for success or survival; the second is when change becomes a necessary response to survive or to avoid failure. The first relies on the mindset of the entrepreneur, because playing it safe rarely leads to innovation. Solomon Timothy, the founder of Clickx, wrote an op-ed for *Inc. Magazine*[7] and said that avoiding risk was suffocating his business:

> In my early days of starting my own business, I let the fear of those risks control my decisions. I was scared of failing, of making the wrong decisions, and of losing everything. . . . I quickly learned that playing it safe meant I was suffocating my own business growth. I was making small gains, but they weren't enough to bring my agency to the next level. So, I made it my goal to stop running from risk and to embrace it instead.
>
> As an entrepreneur, risk is inevitable. If you're too scared to handle that risk, your entrepreneurial goals will never come true. Embracing risk is easier said than done, but you'll see how natural it can feel once you get started.

Below is a list of his recommendations:

1. Identify open opportunities.
2. Understand you won't always succeed.

5. Conner, D. R. (1998). *Leading at the Edge of Chaos*. New York: John Wiley.
6. Panaggio, T. (2013). *The Risk Advantage: Embracing the Entrepreneur's Unexpected Edge*. Austin: River Grove Books.
7. Timothy, S. (2019, April 12). How to embrace risk as an entrepreneur. *Inc.* www.inc.com/young-entrepreneur-council/how-to-embrace-risk-as-an-entrepreneur.html; Thomas, G. S. (2012, July 24). Recession claimed 170,000 small businesses in two years. *Business Journal on Numbers*. www.bizjournals.com/bizjournals/on-numbers/scott-thomas/2012/07/recession-claimed-170000-small.html.

3. Stay nimble.
4. Find the right team.

Timothy concludes that entrepreneurs must identify the "right risk," otherwise known as the calculated risk. At times identifying the right risk is a challenge; the most consistent risk is change, both predictable and not.

The second way change is managed is often a result of a business disruption. Panera Bread and other retailers became creative when the COVID-19 pandemic hit. To remain relevant to their customers, they quickly offered purchases of groceries like milk, bagels, bread, cream cheese, and additional items such as fresh produce. "Our mission has always been to make good food accessible," says CEO Niren Chaudhary in an interview with *Fast Company*. "We want to strengthen our off-premise channels to better serve the consumer and keep as many people employed as we can."[8] CNBC reports other large companies pivoting during the pandemic. "While thousands of smaller eateries have been forced to temporarily shutter during the coronavirus pandemic, many of the country's biggest restaurant chains have been forced to make major changes, too."[9] As we learned in the recession of 2008, no company is too big to fail. Pivoting to avoid failure is not uncommon, and what most businesses need to accept is there will be failure and there will be loss; this is part of the risk one takes in opening a business.

Risk and Failure

Changing the view of "risk" within the organization's culture creates an environment of continual response and renewal. To change the culture of the organization to one that thrives on risk and views risk as an asset, and embraces the ensuing chaos, the owner must model transformational leadership during a state of panic so much so that employees willingly embrace the new concept and they create a culture that is nimble and responsive in a crisis. The renewal begins when the team that becomes capable of change embraces the volatility and chaos resulting from the unexpected risks. The team's adaptability to volatility drives the nimbleness of the business and the ability to determine what the value of change is and initiating the change that provides value. Mastering change is not defined by success alone, as change is mastered only by including the failures a leader will make on their journey; knowledge and humility create a wise leader.[10]

Loss is referred to as a moment in time, associated with everything from socks to loved ones. For an entrepreneur, the loss of an employee or client can be devastating, but is it a failure? Failure is associated with an action or inaction. Webster's Dictionary defines failure as[11]

1a: omission of occurrence or performance, specifically failing to perform a duty or expected action // failure to pay the rent on time
b(1): a state of inability to perform a normal function // kidney failure
(2): an abrupt cessation of normal functioning // a power failure
c: a fracturing or giving way under stress // a structural failure.

8. Gagne, Yasmin (2020, April 8). Out of avocado? Panera Bread's new grocery delivery service can help. *Fast Company*. www.fastcompany.com/90486835/out-of-avocado-panera-breads-new-grocery-delivery-service-can-help.
9. Lucas, Amelia (2020, April 8). Panera Bread is selling groceries as restaurant sales plummet. CNBC. www.cnbc.com/2020/04/08/panera-bread-is-selling-groceries-as-restaurant-sales-plummet.html.
10. Conner, D. R. (1993). *Managing at the Speed of Change*. New York: Random House.
11. Merriam-Webster (n.d.). Chaos. www.merriam-webster.com/dictionary/chaos; Merriam-Webster (n.d.). Failure. www.merriam-webster.com/dictionary/failure.

Then the definition of failure is given to us in two quotes by Michael Jordan. The first is "A loss is not a failure until you make an excuse." The second is "I've missed more than 9000 shots in my career. I've lost almost 300 games. 26 times, I've been trusted to take the game-winning shot and missed. I've failed over and over and over again in my life. And that is why I succeed."[12]

Failure is the definition that an entrepreneur gives to it; again, the view of risk and failure is all a mindset: by embracing risk and failure and displaying this for employees allows the individuals within the organization to purge previous perceptions and embrace what was a crisis as a commitment to renew. What an entrepreneur needs to understand is that failure is also a moment in time, and failure is something that happened—not who the person is. During times of disruptive change, all sorts of feelings are heightened: loss of control, the interruption of power, fear of failure. In response, leaders often unconsciously respond with behaviors that reveal their struggle to adapt to the very change they are championing.[13]

How does a small business owner plan for a business interruption, either a small or a catastrophic event? In reality, a business owner cannot anticipate every risk. Missing from previous traditional risk-mitigating business plans is the impact of the community surrounding a business. Waking up in the middle of the night to find out that not only has the incident changed an individual life, but that of an entire community. This reality challenges traditional business plans; small business owners must consider the forces of nature and the chaos that ensues. A risk assessment includes viewing everything as a potential threat and opportunity, and the FDIC and SBA plan, although basic, if followed, creates a platform that provides some preparation in the areas of planning and recovery an entrepreneur can control, but it does not fully identify those they cannot. We only must look at our recent business interruptions, such as hurricanes, floods, fires, and the COVID-19 pandemic, to understand how the mindset drove entrepreneurial response, ingenuity, or innovation.

In 2018 and 2019, various government agencies were funding emergency preparedness seminars for small and diverse businesses. The training included how to pack a go-bag for the house and car, duck and cover for earthquakes, have an emergency preparedness plan tucked in your child's lunch box, and encourage people to locate alternate routes securing the safety of their families. Business owners were encouraged to "Write It Down," have a plan, and provide a plan for their family if they were separated from them, understanding that to focus on stabilizing their business, they had to stabilize their home first. A business interruption can be as simple as a power outage or as catastrophic as a fire or flood, but in all events, business owners must have a strategic plan on who to notify and how they would continue to operate; this includes ensuring their employees' safety, especially if they have to shelter in place, their obligations to the customer and their supply chain, and an endless list of additional critical tasks. Most of the continuity plans provided to small businesses suggested a plan for two weeks or up to 30 days; however, as we have now learned, the length of recovery is as predictable as the next disaster.[14]

In some industries, chaos and the changes resulting from a disaster increase the number of business opportunities available to small businesses. Although the next disaster may not be as predictable as we would like, the need for small businesses to assist in the recovery efforts is a predictable event. The various emergency preparedness sessions delivered to small businesses suggest one part of their business continuity plan should include taking advantage of the contract opportunities that the Federal Emergency Management Association (FEMA) and the Army Corps of Engineers facilitate during

12. Jordan, M. (2016, January 14). 75 motivational Michael Jordan quotes. *Addicted 2 Success*. https://addicted2success.com/quotes/75-motivational-michael-jordan-quotes/.
13. Carucci, Ron (2016, October 24). Organizations can't change if leaders can't change with them. *Harvard Business Review*. https://hbr.org/2016/10/organizations-cant-change-if-leaders-cant-change-with-them.
14. Small Business Administration (n.d.). Risk Management Guide. www.sba.gov/sites/default/files/files/PARTICIPANT_GUIDE_RISK_MANAGEMENT.pdf.

the recovery efforts. One reason to create an operational contingency plan is that those small businesses prepared for a disaster or business interruption are best prepared to win government contracts that assist in disaster relief.

In the United States, the first agency to respond to a disaster is FEMA; they are the "boots on the ground," managing the aftermath of disasters. At a small business emergency preparedness training event in California, the Army Corps discussed their response to the 2018 flood in Montecito, California. In addition, a representative from the California governor's office provided context on the support and contracting that took place after the Camp Fire in Paradise and the Woolsey Fire in Malibu. The Camp Fire killed 85 people and burned 95% of the town; the Woolsey Fire destroyed 1,600 structures and burned nearly 97,000 acres.

All these disasters devastated the surrounding communities, and it is often difficult to imagine a silver lining; however, the remediation contracts after the Montecito flood were awarded to small 8(a)-certified small businesses. The US government has small business contracting goals set each year. The goals in 2019 were that overall, 23% of federal dollars should benefit small businesses, and 5% should contract with small diverse business enterprises. By utilizing the set-aside programs enacted by Congress in 1984, the government can expeditiously award contracts to contractors that have past performance doing business with the federal government. These contract awards provided the ability of small businesses to assist in the remediation and repair of the incident, but nothing was business as usual, and accepting the contract posed a significant risk to small businesses. The awarded contracts were to construction firms for the remediation of the mudslides in Montecito. Construction firms had to use drones and helicopters to survey the damage and provide pricing for the cleanup. Logistics were essential in coordinating where the debris would be placed until it could be hauled away. A contractor who received a contract discussed the issues they faced once their contract began. They were hired to remove the mud and debris. Usually, a contractor uses a backhoe and digs out the excess mud; however, when the mud removal consists of significant landslides, it is often difficult to determine the support for the machinery that is essential for the cleanup. The backhoe was brought in, but unfortunately, it started to sink; the ground below the mud was insufficient to support the machinery.

The contractor resolved the issue and proceeded with the cleanup, but additional fees were negotiated. The emergency preparedness sessions had two goals: one to stress preparation and the other to stress the ability to take part in the contracting efforts for remediation, repairs, and disaster response. Although a disaster may present new opportunities, winning the award is often associated with many new risks. An entrepreneur must move from the traditional mindset of playing it safe and challenge themselves: did they embrace risk enough to develop an organization nimble enough to respond to a disaster or prepare enough to take advantage of opportunities that arrive due to disaster?

No matter the risks, many contractors are willing to do business with the federal government. According to the Government Accountability Office (GAO),[15] as of December 31, 2017, 19 federal agencies had entered into contracts and obligated over $5.6 billion on those contracts to support efforts related to Hurricanes Harvey, Irma, and Maria. The Department of Homeland Security, FEMA, and Department of Defense components, including the Army Corps of Engineers, accounted for approximately 97% of those obligations.[16]

Federal agencies have obligated more than $2 billion for products, such as food, water, and shelter, and about $3.6 billion for services, such as power restoration.

The rate of competition for federal contracts was higher in the immediate aftermath of the three recent hurricanes the GAO examined than for Hurricane Katrina during the same time period.

15. Government Accountability Office (2019, August 1). Contracting for Disaster Response and Recovery. www.gao.gov/.
16. Contract obligations by top 10 contracting agencies, in support of Hurricanes Harvey, Irma, and Maria, through December 31, 2017.

Federal agencies are generally required to award contracts based on full and open competition. However, an agency may award a contract non-competitively when the need for goods and/or services is urgent—as in the case of a natural disaster. GAO found, for the three hurricanes: the percentage of total obligations reported under competitive contracts was 73% as of December 31, 2017; and the percentage of contracts awarded competitively within the first 90 days after each hurricane's landfall was approximately 74%—an improvement compared to landfall was approximately 74%—an improvement compared to the first 90 days after Hurricane Katrina's landfall when the competition rate for contracts was about 53%.[17]

FEMA's current mission is "Helping people before, during and after disasters." To advance that mission, the US Army Corps of Engineers provides support with procurement and contracting. Both agencies utilize small businesses to fulfill their missions post-disaster. FEMA has a preapproved contractor list on its website in addition to a list of the commodities they purchase during disasters. There are 89 advanced contracts listed on the FEMA website. Small businesses can contact FEMA directly and market their solutions or initiate a conversation with the current contract holders.[18]

It appears some industries flourish during a crisis, and these are those that take part in the recovery efforts during and post-disaster. Recovery is as imminent as the disaster, and the opportunities are at times as unpredictable; however, a business able to take part in disaster recovery and participate in contracting is an example of the mindset when companies embrace the risk, expect it, and use it to their advantage.

A small business owner must possess the hard skills and the soft skills to overcome the risks they face; they must be aware of industry changes, not only in their industry but any that could negatively impact their business. When construction, medical supplies, and organizations providing basic living supplies flourished, many other industries did not. In October 2020, *Small Business Trends* reported that 45% of small businesses have earned half or less of their income and with the SBA reporting that small businesses have closed.[19] In 2008 a global economic depression occurred, and small businesses suffered; there were substantial losses.[20] According to an article published in the *Business Journal*, based on federal data more than 170,000 small businesses in the United States closed between 2008 and 2010, according to an analysis of US Census Bureau data.[21]

Entrepreneurship plunged during the recession. The number of self-employed Americans fell 4% to 9.8 million between November 2007 and June 2009, according to Census Bureau data cited by the Federal Reserve Bank of Cleveland.[22] Twelve percent more businesses shut down in 2009 than in 2007. Many started small businesses because they had no other choice, but many small businesses are not thriving. Nearly four in five businesses have no employees at all, and they make an average of $45,000 per year.[23] According to the Census Bureau, small business applications continued to wane from 2007 through 2017, and new startups that employ workers continue to fall, according to the Kauffman Index of Entrepreneurial Activity. The recovery from the recession was slow due to

17. Government Accountability Office (2019, August 1). Contracting for Disaster Response and Recovery. www.gao.gov/.
18. FEMA Small Business Program, Government Accountability Office (2019, August 1). Contracting for Disaster Response and Recovery. www.gao.gov/.
19. Rathone, Sandeep (2020, October 13). 45% of small businesses have earned half or less of their pre-COVID revenue during pandemic. *Small Business Trends*. https://smallbiztrends.com/2020/10/alignable-road-to-recovery-report.html.
20. Small Business Administration (2021). Small Business Office of Advocacy. https://advocacy.sba.gov.
21. Scott, Thomas G. (2012, July 24). *Business Journal*; Small Business Administration (2021). Small Business Office of Advocacy. https://advocacy.sba.gov.
22. Economic Commentary, Federal Reserve Bank of Cleveland (March 24, 2011). https://www.clevelandfed.org/newsroom-and-events/publications/economic-commentary/economic-commentary-archives/2011-economic-commentaries.aspx.
23. US Census (2012). https://www.census.gov/library/publications/2011/compendia/statab/131ed.html.

changes in lending practices; banks became risk-averse. In 2019, there were 774,725 businesses less than a year old—an increase of 41,000 from 2018. So in essence, just as we were experiencing our most robust small business revival, another economic tsunami took place.[24]

Although hundreds of thousands of businesses closed when the pandemic hit, they also opened in record numbers, with more filings for corporate employer identification numbers (EINs) than in 2019, according to the Census Bureau. Why? Typically, these businesses fill the gaps that existing businesses either do not see, cannot respond to fast enough, or are too afraid to take the risk of pivoting during a crisis. Some of the surges in small businesses were due to increased services, such as delivery drivers, personal shoppers, and other types of independent contractors that created their "own job" when faced with the scarcity of employment options.

The *Wall Street Journal* published an article in September of 2020 based on some of the census data, aptly titled "Is It Insane to Start a Business During the Coronavirus? Millions of Americans Don't Think So."[25]

The article reviews the highs and lows of small business data gathered by John Haltwanger's research:

> "This pandemic is inducing a surge in employer business at a pace that takes us back to the days before the decline in the Great Recession," said John Haltwanger, an economist at the University of Maryland who studies the data . . . and what could lead to this increase. . . . The jump may be one sign that the pandemic is speeding up "creative destruction," the concept popularized by economist Joseph Schumpeter in the 1940s to describe how new, innovative businesses often displace older, less-efficient ones, buoying long-term prosperity.

Innovation during a crisis makes us once again revisit the ability of the entrepreneur to embrace risk. The US Chamber of Commerce published an article "Why You Should Consider Starting a Business Now,"[26] which mentions three reasons why entrepreneurs should launch their business: bootstrapping know-how, business model changes, and time of innovation. Although these are good reasons to take the risk to start a business, they are also the essential steps existing businesses need to take to continue to operate.

Bootstrapping is what an entrepreneur does to navigate a change, not letting the change navigate them, or in other words: "When life hands you lemons, make lemonade." During the pandemic, most businesses changed some form of their model, and for some, it included putting a remote working policy in place. For those businesses that continued to operate, there were six-foot social distancing efforts, masks, temperature monitoring, split shifts, adaption to new client guidelines for safety, and unfortunately, salary reductions and furloughs for those companies hardest hit. Yet some were able to pivot.

As Mauro Guillén outlines in an article for the *Harvard Business Review*,[27] three conditions are necessary for a business to pivot successfully:

- Align the firm with at least one trend that the pandemic created or intensified (e.g., remote work);
- Laterally extend the company's existing capabilities in a way that cements its original strategic intent;
- Offer a sustainable path to profitability that preserves/enhances brand value in the minds of consumers.

24. Kauffman Indicators of Entrepreneurships (March 2021). https://indicators.kauffman.org/reports.
25. Guilford, G. and Scott, C.L. (2020, September 26). Is it insane to start a business during the coronavirus? Millions of Americans don't think so. *Wall Street Journal*.
26. US Chamber of Commerce. Why you should consider starting a business now. https://www.uschamber.com/co/start/startup/starting-a-business-in-difficult-times.
27. Guillén, Mauro (2020, July 7). How businesses have successfully pivoted during the pandemic. *Harvard Business Review*. https://hbr.org/2020/07/how-businesses-have-successfully-pivoted-during-the-pandemic.

Competitively achieving these points requires business leaders to be exceptionally aware of current short-term conditions and resources. But it also requires considering broader opportunities that can have a long-term influence on the brand's perception and operation.[28]

Why do some entrepreneurs and businesses flounder in crisis and others generate success? The foundation of entrepreneurial resiliency is ages old; although the challenges change, the foundations of embracing risk and navigating the change are as essential as the business plans each business should have. For some entrepreneurs, risk resiliency and innovation are part of their nature, and they are the ones that will risk everything during a pandemic. For other entrepreneurs, they have an entrepreneurial mindset, yet they need to establish the management skills to lead their team during change. In 1993, Daryl R. Conner wrote another book titled *Managing at the Speed of Change*. The book's summary[29] indicated the key wisdom entrepreneurs learn from change.

Essential wisdom in a nutshell:

- To prosper, remain competitive, or survive, leaders need to respond to a growing number of profound changes in how they govern countries, structure companies, conduct business, treat employees, and deal with customers.
- The main ingredient of success is the ability of resilient people that must understand and use to their advantage the principles underlying basic human patterns that operate during change.
- People who demonstrate resilient characteristics most often prosper during disruption and disorder. They regain equilibrium faster, maintain a higher level of productivity and efficiency, preserve their emotional and physical health, and achieve more of their objectives than people who experience future shock.

To achieve the above, entrepreneurs need to understand their assimilation capacity. Assimilation is the process we use to adjust to the positive or negative implications of a significant shift in our expectations. People need to adjust to changes they were unprepared to face. Future shock is that point when humans can no longer assimilate change without displaying dysfunctional behavior.

As of 2022, the big push for agencies is to assist small businesses with their resiliency plans, but one thing remains constant, according to *Harvard Business Review*, when it comes to organizational change: failure continues to be more common than success. A McKinsey survey included assessment on the success of transformation efforts by entrepreneurs. Nearly 3,000 participated and discovered the failure rate to be higher than 60%, while *Harvard Business Review* conducted a study that suggested more than 70% of transformation efforts fail. The pattern is clear, and diligent leaders often devote countless resources to planning out the perfect change management initiative. To raise the odds of success, however, experience suggests the place that leaders need to begin their transformation efforts is not their organizations: it's themselves.[30]

Conclusion

Embracing risk is the driving force to creating nimbleness within an organization, and it defines the paradigm shift that moves from the "known zone" to the "unknown zone," where leaders move their teams from paradigm shift to paradigm renewal. Again, the mindset of an entrepreneur is the

28. Merchant, Priya (2021, January 12). Pivoting during the pandemic. *Entrepreneur*. www.entrepreneur.com/article/362003.
29. Conner, D. R. (1993). *Managing at the Speed of Change*. New York: Random House. pp. 1–6.
30. Carucci, Ron, (2016, October 24). Organizations can't change if leaders can't change with them. *Harvard Business Review*. https://hbr.org/2016/10/organizations-cant-change-if-leaders-cant-change-with-them.

differentiator between the successful entrepreneur and one who quits, for it is not always how well they plan for risk or how they manage it but if they can embrace the chaos it causes as part of their journey (Conner D. R., 1998). Constant change is managed by responding to the change instead of trying to prevent the change; this mindset is where the team understands that volatility is the norm and can now succeed and thrive in an unpredictable environment. To some, grit is the determining factor—the determination to keep going when all efforts appear futile—and that stems from the entrepreneur's attitude and spirit; these will assist the entrepreneur in embracing the risk. Conner and Panaggio both describe the people that succeed as the "winners"; this chapter has emphasized it is the mindset of the entrepreneur, but nothing summarizes it more than a quote from *Managing at the Speed of Change*: "We can either learn to manage change at a speed that will accommodate future transformations that face us or pay dearly for not doing so. The opportunity to choose is ours. The responsibility to act is yours.[31]

References

Carucci, R. (October 24, 2016). Organizations Can't Change If Leaders Can't Change With Them. *Harvard Business Review*. https://hbr.org/2016/10/organizations-cant-change-if-leaders-cant-change-with-them.

Conner, D. R. (1993). *Managing at the Speed of Change*. New York: Random House.

Conner, D. R. (1998). *Leading at the Edge of Chaos*. New York: John Wiley.

Federal Emergency Management Agency. (n.d.). FEMA Small Business Program. www.fema.gov/business-industry/doing-business/small-business.

Gagne, Y. (April 8, 2020). Out of Avocado? Panera Bread's New Grocery Delivery Service Can Help. *Fast Company*. www.fastcompany.com/90486835/out-of-avocado-panera-breads-new-grocery-delivery-service-can-help.

Government Accountability Office. (August 1, 2019). Contracting for Disaster Response and Recovery. www.gao.gov/.

Jordan, M. (January 14, 2016). 75 Motivational Michael Jordan Quotes. https://addicted2success.com/quotes/75-motivational-michael-jordan-quotes/.

Kauffman Indicators of Entrepreneurship. (March 2021). https://indicators.kauffman.org/reports.

Lucas, A. (April 8, 2020). 2020, April 8). Panera Bread Is Selling Groceries as Restaurant Sales Plummet. *CNBC*. www.cnbc.com/2020/04/08/panera-bread-is-selling-groceries-as-restaurant-sales-plummet.html.

Merchant, P. (January 12, 2021). Pivoting During the Pandemic: How These Businesses Succeeded. *Entrepreneur*. www.entrepreneur.com/article/362003.

Merriam-Webster (n.d.). Chaos. www.merriam-webster.com/dictionary/chaos.

Merriam-Webster (n.d.). Failure. www.merriam-webster.com/dictionary/failure.

Panaggio, T. (2013). *The Risk Advantage: Embracing the Entrepreneur's Unexpected Edge*. Austin: River Grove Books.

Rathorne, S. (October 13, 2020). Trending. *Small Business Trends*. https://smallbiztrends.com/2020/10/alignable-road-to-recovery-report.html.

Scott, Sloane. (March 24, 2011). Economic Commentary. *Federal Reserve Bank of Cleveland*. https://www.clevelandfed.org/newsroom-and-events/publications/economic-commentary/economic-commentary-archives/2011-economic-commentaries.aspx.

Small Business Administration. (2021). Small Business Office of Advocacy. www.sba.gov/sites/default/files/advocacy/SB-FAQ-2016_WEB.pdf.

Small Business Administration. (n.d.). Risk Management Guide. www.sba.gov/sites/default/files/files/PARTICIPANT_GUIDE_RISK_MANAGEMENT.pdf.

Thomas, G. S. (July 24, 2012). The Business Journals on Numbers. *Business Journals*. www.bizjournals.com/bizjournals/on-numbers/scott-thomas/2012/07/recession-claimed-170000-small.html.

Timothy, S. (April 12, 2019). How to Embrace Risk as an Entrepreneur. *Inc*. www.inc.com/young-entrepreneur-council/how-to-embrace-risk-as-an-entrepreneur.html.

31. Conner, D. R. (1993). *Managing at the Speed of Change*. New York: Random House.

11

SUPPLY CHAIN RISK MANAGEMENT CONSIDERATIONS IN AN EVER-CHANGING WORLD

Jessie Castro

Introduction

Following a global pandemic, how do businesses thrive today when yesterday's rules no longer apply, when once-thriving markets, pre-pandemic, have all but shifted their business priorities to play catch up to the promises made to their shareholders, stakeholders and investors. Today, economies are no longer bound by established borders or geographical location. Multinational corporations, consortiums and private entities are growing at a scale that dwarfs the GDP of many countries. With people so interconnected, the perception of a business can skyrocket to the top of their industries overnight with a tweet or a blog from a social media influencer, or can even cause the market to standstill. Conversely, one fact check off base or a debunked assertion can equally cause any social, political or financial capital to dissipate. Businesses that have stood the test of time and have consistently been able to weather the ebbs and flows of society do so by maintaining consistency in their core values and compliance to the ethics set by expectations of their leaders.

These days, information is power, but the speed of relevance is equally key. The world's currency is data, and those that can access, interpret and deploy tailored experiences for their consumers are the ones that stand to gain the advantage in today's economy. Successful application of knowledge-based solutions is dependent on how an entity collects, analyzes, utilizes and retains key information on how their consumers, competitors and economies in their respective countries operate. Think of the reach companies such as Amazon, Facebook, Google or even consumer data obtained by service provides like Netflix and YouTube have in the lives of their customers.

> Now, imagine if allies and adversaries deployed misinformation campaigns via tweets, memes and posts on a multitude of social media platforms to cause disarray without leaving a trace of where it came from. Just the act of introducing doubt, can cause markets to tumble and elections results to shift in a split second.

Sound familiar? The notion that knowledge is power still holds true in today's competitive marketplace, but what about accountability? How the knowledge of contractual requirements, obligations and buyer/seller exposure to risk (and how the tiered supply base for a prime contractor is affected) will be covered in this chapter. Additionally, proactive compliance strategies to set the stage for an entity's success will be introduced.

DOI: 10.4324/9781351107242-14

Even today, countries still struggle to maintain antiquated processes and procedures to retain their supply base in order to procure and keep up with emerging technologies, platforms and equipment to stay afloat. The key phrase is "keep up," as opposed to "looking ahead," to leverage, consolidate or negotiate favorable strategies that mitigate risk and maximize profit.

This is the world today. Data is currency, and the sophistication of those who know how to yield and deploy the application of data to obtain their desired outcomes can pivot strategies and thrive. Those that do not keep up get pushed out of the front page of topics trending that day.

Unfortunately, this scenario is also the state of the traditional acquisition processes at the federal, state and local levels.

From the perspective of federal contracting as it relates to the speed of relevance, far too often requirements in a solicitation are a reactive approach to quickly plug gaps in key capabilities, which often are out of reach for end users (due to timing of access to earmarked funding or fiscal year). When businesses are not incentivized or are intimidated by the sheer volume of special requirements blanketed by liabilities not covered by the customer; it's the public that will not reap the benefits of a well-thought-out solicitation. Many times, requests for proposals fall behind or do not come to fruition because the technology available outpaces the process and funding requirement budgetary support. Industry, today, prefers to respond to less onerous commercially available equipment that may be good enough to meet the needs in a cost-efficient way. Gone are the days where a key critical technology is wholly initiated and funded by the government. Today's acquisition process requires potential suitors of coveted government contracts to have skin in the game. This means that suppliers will need to provide their own internal investments to be considered viable contenders. The issue with that "pay-to-play" approach is that businesses will also spread out their financial risk exposure but also sell their products internationally. This puts the government in a tough position, because we no longer have a technological edge when it comes to our adversaries. Shareholder value in many cases takes precedence over the needs of national security. That is why having a core ethics and compliance infrastructure along with a world-class contracts and supplier management organization can properly navigate a company's trajectory in dealing with the government.

Though information and technology processes have moved ahead, the process for contracting and subcontracting has not been kept up with industry best practices. Perhaps successful knowledge transfer and access to tribal knowledge of a particular topic may also be due to the need to train more individuals, departments and leaders or contracting best practices. The guidelines and policies written for the government industrial sectors have struggled and move at the speed of traditional contracting in order to maintain compliance. However, competitors in other countries and sectors have not had to abide by the same rules of the free market economy, which too can be a double-edged sword due to ethics concerns or preferential treatment for companies with inside knowledge. Overall, applying industry best practices and utilizing contracts and compliance professionals are best suited to create the environment for businesses and organizations to compete on a global scale and execute with velocity.

The speed of relevance has brokered new challenges to how consumer information is collected, how data is distributed and by whom it is consumed, all of which sets the stage for how the data is protected. When a business environment is in lockstep with its contracting organization (and departments are training on compliance best practice), there is no limit to opportunities that organizations can achieve because they move with purpose and understand the requirements, factors, risks and relevance. Additionally, the feedback loop for continuing improvement is established since contract parameters established can push to enforce guidelines. There are checks and balances built in to be challenged by evolving thresholds where a "healthy tension exists" among departments that want to push ahead and maximize profits, while compliance organizations watch over their respective organizations to properly temper their colleagues to ensure compliance within the polices and guidelines set up for the entity.

In an article by Virginia A. Suveiu titled "Contract Risk Management to Survive and Thrive in the 21st Century," she points out that "What is changing, however, is the perspective on the importance, and inevitably, the intrinsic value of contract risk management to an organization."

From the perspective of a contracting professional, it is essential to have a solid grasp of risk management principles in order to be able to navigate the complicated US government procurement process and provide meaningful feedback to our customers. As professionals, we provide guidance on business decisions before we commit the company to a binding agreement. In a "more-for-less" business landscape with a short turnaround time, proactive compliance education is key to winning and maintaining a competitive edge. However, even if a contracts organization is entrusted with the responsibility to commit a company to execute a particular work scope, all the other functions have to provide their own oversight to justify the business decision and provide the resources to be successful. That is where educating our peers will need to take place. Operational approval must be confirmed. So there really are checks and balances in the company I work for. The best environment is one that provides a good collaboration with all parties involved at the very start of a new business pursuit. A risk mitigation mindset balanced with forward-thinking talent makes for a strong business strategy.

This chapter also aims to explore the intricacies of compliance, while working in an environment that is shifting away from traditional roles of a contract or sub-contract professional; to building a presence in market shaping initiatives that aligns with an organization's need to grow the core business and create new sources of revenue.

In today's more-for-less environment, cost control and budget optimization seem to be the recurring theme that organizations, companies and the government tend to use as the tagline for reasons why extra scrutiny is applied to requirements, solicitations and subsequent contract awards. In the contexts of government procurement, "Spend your budget or risk losing it in the next year" tends to be the driver in why there is a rush to spend funds toward the end of the fiscal year, the expectation between customer/suppliers to do their due diligence in offering a fair and reasonable price on behalf of customers and taxpayers. However, the extra layers of oversight can become redundant and leave many to feel that the cost of scrutiny actually costs everyone more in the end and can discourage future business, decreasing a diverse pool of suppliers because it is no longer profitable. Here is where there is an opportunity to look at this dynamic differently.

Depending on the size and sophistication of the company, oftentimes before an organization chooses to expend resources in contemplating a new business capture (i.e., a broad agency announcement [BAA], request for information [RFI] or straight request for proposal [RFP]), these "opportunities" usually have a metric associated with the ability to win that particular project or program. Whether or not companies realize it, the conversation of risk analysis is happening before they actually document it. It comes down to the thoughts, "Do companies really want to pursue this solicitation? Is it worth it? How much time, energy and resources are needed to execute it?"

There are a lot of tools, techniques and metrics out there. These models are great to utilize when working to articulate the idea behind the support needed to quantify the cost realization in applying a risk mitigation strategy. The problem is, are organizations using these tools effectively? Are the results being shared throughout the organization? For example, the use of a compliance checklist is great, but only if the proper methodology is applied within the functions these tools were designed to support.

Working for a global company in a fluid business environment, success is often defined in the news that does not make the headlines. In a corporate environment, power may be perceived by an individual, organization or business unit to make and enforce decisions. Perception of power can be interpreted by how many layers it takes to get to decision makers.

It's a Business Decision

As a contracting professional who has been through the full spectrum of procurement, from early development through product life cycle sustainment, much of what I have experienced is a microcosm of what is to come. The challenge I face is that the work I do deals a lot with the unknown. There aren't any benchmarks or a special formula to compare past performance to work that has never been done before. Risk can be high, and the return on investment will not be realized until later down the line.

Additionally, in a previous profession I managed major suppliers, both domestic and international. My experiences exposed me to a wide range of the supply base in the aerospace and defense industries (commercial, military, research and space). I was able to identify and shape new capabilities while also working to sustain existing product lines. The common theme in many of the suppliers I worked with was the massive cost of compliance to provide redundant reporting to our customers (whether they are commercial or government).

The most successful entities are the organizations that are empowered by their leadership to make and own the results of a business decision. Teams that are rewarded for focusing on improving the effectiveness and efficiency across the life cycle of products and services are the ones that build a culture of openness, accountability and continual improvement. This means, in your department, business or organization, can you observe and explore creative solutions to reach your goals? Do you feel you are empowered to do so? That applies on both the technology side and business side of things. Creativity doesn't have to just be applied to a new widget; it can extend to the type of contract or agreement set. That is where having the right contracts team, armed with the proper rules of compliance, comes into the strategy. That well-thought-out strategy can properly position the company to reap the benefits of a new full production line and perhaps product sustainment services for years to come.

Another example is the widespread methodology for technology deployment of such additive manufacturing techniques. For example, one can apply a rapid prototyping capability (i.e., create a model quickly and see if the asset can be quickly deployed, then scale the model and focus on continuing improvement). This approach is also used to quickly deploy incremental software releases (e.g., software "sprints" in the gaming industry). Why not apply these methods and creative rapid procurement arrangements in procurement and compliance? This Agile acquisition platform is a driver to quickly deploy assets and personnel to where they are needed most.

An example of how this was used successfully in the past can be best illustrated by examples from the type of customers we interface with. My exposure to the industry base ranged from commercial entities such as small business innovative research (SBIR) to large corporations, universities and government customers. This portfolio entailed working with and managing a diverse set of personalities, conflicting agendas, goals and budgets. The result translates into a whole slew of agreements, contracts and transactions which define the type of relationship we will have during that specific period of performance. More specifically, my team led proposal efforts, provided guidance and interpretation of key terms and conditions, including working with internal customers on complex intellectual property and liability requirements, consulting on intellectual property protection strategies, subcontract sourcing support and so on.

Over the last decade, the convergence of federal and commercial practices is finally being realized. Thought competition remains tough; companies like Amazon, Google, Lockheed Martin and SpaceX are making waves in growing their portfolio of technology and are quickly gaining market share in areas traditionally left to traditional aerospace companies.

For a business to grow and stay ahead of competition, organizations should align their compliance organizations at the forefront of market capture. Companies should really look within and see if there is a contracts organization to leverage. Contracts/compliances and even sub-contracts/

procurement need to be a part of a company's strategic initiative. My hope is for the reader of this chapter to understand the importance of engaging their contracts department early in the decision-making process to:

- Identify and manage risk effectively.
- Build a collaborative environment.
- Articulate requirements to other business functions.
- Apply compliance best practice principles.
- Face challenges of business-to-business (B2B) compliance.
- Talk about emerging issues.

Identify and Manage Risk Effectively

From the perspective of risks in federal contracting, in Gregory A. Garrett's book *Contract Administration: Tools, Techniques and Best Practices*, he defines risk in US federal acquisition management as "a measure of future uncertainties in achieving program performance goals and objectives with defined cost, schedule, and performance constraints." In other words, risk is a measure of probability relative to an event occurring and the effects that are associated with it.

Managing risk means understanding relationships on an individual basis and extending your range out to the organizations (both internal and external) to effectively manage the outcome. For example, as contracts professionals, their role is expected to balance the application of Federal Acquisition Regulations (FAR) clauses versus commercial requirements entails identifying clauses that may benefit the business bottom line, and may cause a business risk to the company. Once clauses are identified, contract professionals are then tasked with the appropriate interpretation, as it applies to the specific business arrangement—at that time! At least with FAR, DFAR and other US flowdowns, there is a set way to interpret the language. With commercial entities, the words and clauses are wide open. Competition is the driver.

Build a Collaborative Environment

In the competitive business environment we are in today, companies cannot afford to sit by and wait for change to happen. That change cannot happen unless you get the buy-in of the stakeholders. If it were only about metrics, numbers can always be tweaked to back up whatever agenda leadership has in mind. The issue is when people are involved; that is more difficult because it deals with habits and a culture. We all know that habits are hard to break; culture shift is difficult to implement.

Oftentimes in a corporate environment you will hear a push for "first time quality, being lean, implementing customer-focused strategy, or being agile"; these are all ways companies signal to their employees and their customers that change is coming. These slogans are a great step in the right direction. The problem is sustainability (if there is no real employee buy-in)! If a cultural shift is not ingrained in the company's DNA, the charge for change will lose steam and the initiatives will just be ideas that were great at the time and get shelved. What is often the cause for a company to shift their business approach is usually due to a cost-cutting initiative. More often than not, if a change is going to happen, and the government customer is involved, that is usually because of a punitive measure directed at a contractor. When companies lose a big competitive proposal, when funding gets cut for a program, when a company gets bought out, all of a sudden, people start watching out for all the little things that they could do to cut costs. Unfortunately, that is a common story in today's environment.

To start this push for change much earlier, organizations can get their ear to the ground and listen to ideas of their best asset: their employees. Employees who are seasoned and experienced in understanding the nature of the challenges can apply creative approaches to effect long-term change. To do this, companies will have to go beyond a silo mentality.

Breaking down the barriers and engaging all the teams early on, building a collaborative environment to educate all parties—these will help instill trust and empower others to mitigate risk.

This task has to start with leadership in the organization. Companies must recognize that their workers closest to the work will be able to share knowledge in real time. Leadership must provide the strategic framework in which the concerns can be identified and interpreted and a risk mitigation plan executed. For this to happen, the organizational boundaries must be eliminated. Where I've seen an effective implementation of the type of candid dialogue take place is where companies hold kick-off meetings to discuss future business pursuits. My company will often defer to contracts to help set the tempo on any unique risks associated with the business pursuit. From there, the team will decide as a committee whether or not to move forward. This forum empowers each function to have a vote in the task. This forum also puts the functions on notice and holds everyone accountable.

Leaders, though not involved in the day-to-day work, really play a big role in advocating their confidence in the team to get the job done. This political capital resonates internally and empowers the group to make the right business decisions.

Articulate Requirements to Other Business Functions

As the role of contracting and compliance professionals continues to evolve, their presence in shaping future business in the organization and their impact on key decisions are becoming more prominent. Dedicated corporate risk and customer requirements make their presence known in the purchased orders issued to major suppliers and sub-tier vendors, since companies now realize they have liabilities that extend beyond the company product deliverables.

Examples in the context of traditional federal contracting can give the perception that contracts can only effect change and exert their influence as contracts professionals toward their customer counterparts. At times, they may even limit interaction to a very transactional relationship relative to organizations maintaining a qualified government property system, compliance to keep a current estimating ticket for proposals, a quality management system in line with the latest ISO standards and so forth. When it comes to contract implementation, or if by chance an audit is required post-award, these examples will most definitely come up with the Defense Contract Management Agency (DCMA). One reason contracts may choose to play a bigger role is because DCMA may levy a corrective action request (CAR) if the organization does not properly document and show progress in meeting key required standards. A CAR is sent to a supplier where an item or process is in nonconformity and a remedy is required. CARs are normally determined during quality assurance activities.

The government has many tools at its disposal to effect change for products that are not up to par or are less than what are needed. The reality is, companies look at it primarily through the lens of cost implications. Companies often overlook the impression they leave their customers and the impact of confidence in their product. Companies need to take notice and adapt to leveraging real-time data available to them, so they can change trajectory mid-stream before it is too late. That is where the value of a contracts professional comes into play, because they have a pulse with their customer (if they are actively engaged with their contract). I've seen the organizations I've worked with in the past be on the reactive side, and even today the current culture does not understand the implications of a government-imposed corrective action—until now! For example, the reason resources being deployed to discuss compliance is because companies do not want a fee withholding on future contracts for being noncompliant.

Knowledge share in this sense is quantifiable because "What division wants their fee withheld?" The impact would hurt our ability to put earnings into future technology investments.

In contracts, we often act as the primary contact between the new business capture team, strategic development, engineering business unit and office of general counsel, ensuring that all legal and contractual matters are addressed efficiently and promptly and are also profitable for the business. That profit loss (P&L) responsibility has traditionally been with the program manager. With the challenging business environment of today, that P&L and risk responsibility is being impressed upon contracts. The only issue is, our organization usually does not get compensated for the risk mitigation or the crisis averted. Again, our victories come from the news or issues that never come to fruition. "Crisis averted!"

Functionally, the contracts department provides guidance on all issues related to pre- and post-award contract administration. We are tasked with the interpretation and application of FAR, DFAR and other regulations governing the administration of all contracts and subcontract agreements.

The ability to articulate requirements in a professional manner can be a challenge if you do not have the correct medium in which to convey your message.

A robust contract compliance program with active training is a great way for other functions to visualize the methodology. It is a great way to articulate the thought process and a step-by-step check to measure against. This also helps break out tasks in a way that promotes collaboration with affected departments.

Much of the US government lays out their criteria in the expectations when it comes to solicitation. I've been hearing more and more terms like "performance-based metrics," and although that is not a new term, it comes down to the same theme of "more for less." That also gives a tone of extra scrutiny (i.e., audit) when it comes to new awards.

Apply Compliance Best Practice Principles

In the past, many organizations would use their best judgment or intuition reasoning (i.e., educated guess) for their decision-making process. Nowadays there is so much accountability that everything is traceable. The rationales need to be backed up with substance. For example, in proposals a basis of estimate has to be adequately justified. The math has to make sense, complexity has to be accurate and the rationale has to be relevant. "Judgment" as a justification for why a method is applied just doesn't work anymore. That type of thinking for companies that offer competitive proposals will find that business is not that way anymore.

In Garrett (2009), many companies refer to a consolidation of project-related information and risk on one document as a "Project Doability Analysis." The form is tailored and used by any organization to briefly summarize the opportunities and risk before a company moves forward. My company has a similar type of form, and that reference is known as our executive review. I've also seen a four-panel chart on one PowerPoint slide. The premise is the same: get all the key items together and have contracts brief the leadership team on the opportunity, the cost benefit, the risks and, if need be, the risk mitigation plan.

That compliance meeting allows for the key decision makers to properly discuss, debate and decide the path forward. The decision also serves as a great historical document for future reference. Oftentimes companies forget the history of similar projects in the past.

That also serves as a great tool in discussing decisions. When looking at corporate competency, the government will take that into account when conducting analysis prior to award. Companies can lower their risk exposure if they take lessons learned and past performance into account.

Face Challenges of Business-to-Business (B2B) Compliance

The challenge of being responsive to complex inquiries in fact-finding from another company (prime) is that they are often your competitor. Companies that frequently changes roles from being prime one day and supplier the other are usually in the middle of trying to satisfy customer requests, yet at the same time being the guardian of the company's proprietary information. There is a balance; unfortunately, the organizations that are successful in finding that balance usually don't share the success stories among their peers. That is why the use of a case study share site or a database that houses special agreements would be an effective tool in maintaining relevant documents. Further, the use of memoranda of agreements (MOUs), master agreements, and nondisclosure agreements (NDAs) are key in opening up the channels of communication between two businesses. In a B2B environment, everything is negotiable. Regarding contractual obligations and revisions, companies will need to identify and mitigate risks through consultation with their respective legal and risk management counterparts to determine their risk exposure and also understand their capacity to negotiate. When you engage legal and risk, it will set the negotiations team up for success because they are made aware of the pitfalls and not get caught signing up for a bad contract. This will also ensure they are compliant and protect the company's interest.

"In the Trenches"—Talk About Emerging Issues!

Most recently, I concluded negotiations with a company that took over a year. My company was a supplier to a competitor that owned an indefinite delivery, indefinite quantity (IDIQ) contract. The government customer wanted us to perform a study, and we had almost 100% of the effort in this particular task order (in other words, the work was a pass-through). Everything from the RFP to the proposal submission went smoothly. We knew that this work was going to be relatively easy to execute if we could get on contract before the funding ran out. The anticipated issues would lie in our ability to negotiate terms and conditions with this prime.

The core of our inability to find resolution dealt with one main theme: liability and precedence. My company pushed hard for an exclusion of liability clause in our contract, because we did not want to accept any risk that the prime was not able to flow down to suppliers. Further, since the prime owned the IDIQ contract, we had no visibility into other efforts relative to what the government customer intended to do with the results from our task order research. What I found most intriguing in is this particular contract was that the statement of work (SOW) was low-risk, based on all the internal analysis that we performed, very similar to the opportunity and risk model (ORM) this course covered. The type of techniques I talked through with the team included utilizing our compliance matrix, running a cost/benefit analysis, and really just using past experience to properly confirm that the SOW was not going to yield any proprietary information or give our prime any competitive information later down the line. In fact, this work involved a study with the only deliverable being a report. Once I reassured the business team that no data or intellectual property would be delivered, they began to back off of further approvals.

The heart of the issue was setting a precedent with our prime in future dealings. We wanted to send a clear message that our efforts would not indemnify the prime. The concern was trying to find out which company would budge first and give up their ability to accept liability. When that failed, I pushed for a mutual liability which extended to "We cover our liability and you cover yours." Even that was unacceptable.

In the end, it took me calling my technical and legal team together and explaining to our leadership that the information was not going to represent an adverse risk to the company. There were too many pockets only looking at their particular areas (i.e., a silo mentality) and not seeing the broad picture and what we were really going to deliver (i.e., a notional research paper). The research deliverables were internally quantifiable, and that satisfied our risk and insurance department's concerns. Once our team was all on the same page, I was able to present a way out for our prime. I told them if they flow down the limitation of liability FAR clauses, we would back off on the exclusion of liability requirement.

Ultimately, we were able to tailor language that capped the liability down to just the specific study, and my company was able to make an exception, so long as the prime was able to flow down FAR 52.246-23 Limitation of Liability (FEB 1997) and 52.246-25 Limitation of Liability–Services (FEB 1997).

This strategy allowed our prime to feel as if we were backing off that requirement, due to pressure—when really we did our own analysis and concluded that this research would benefit us later down the line. In fact, we wanted the government to get the research and perhaps fund another solicitation down the line.

In this example, we were able to engage all parties and turn the tools of risk mitigation and compliance into a negotiation technique and a strategic advantage. We were able to quantify our concerns to the customer and get them to accept our position, based on our ability to articulate the perceived risk we were obtaining. This due diligence helped position us for future opportunities and lay the groundwork in creating a template for articulating risk to our internal customers.

Industry Lessons Learned

- Communicate often and early.
  - Connect with the industrial base and leverage purchasing power.
  - Understand who the power brokers are and who the real decision makers are in your organization, local and federal government.
  - Use language that resonates with this current administration to align their agenda with your mission statement. If you need to reorganize and rename your department or division, use that as a strategy that decisions makers can point to use push their vision forward.
  - The tone in industry during this unique time in history will be a heavy emphasis in regulation and compliance to help steer industry to manageable economic norms and revitalize the workforce. However, the caveat is that there will also be a push for more regulation and adherence to ethics, diversity and inclusion, and conflicts of interest which will in turn drive overhead costs that will flow down to consumers. There needs to be an open dialogue on how to meet in the middle and find a balance.
  - There will be a stronger emphasis in supporting small business that represent the local community. This strategy is needed in order to engage the community and push federal funding toward job creation.
- Identify potential vendor risks.
  - In the current state of the economy, during a global pandemic with climate factors affecting access to commerce, the supply base is at great risk. Access to logistical channels via, land, ocean and air are at a premium. Additionally, growing external threats such as identify theft, cyber intrusion and a contentious political environment are major factors to doing business. Corporation that can afford teams to lobby local, state and federal governments have a front row seat to the way the environment will be shaped, so these entities can prepare or hire consultants to allow them to adapt.
- Develop effective strategies for addressing higher-risk vendors.
  - Once the pandemic hit, the business models for companies were pushed to their limits. The traditional brick-and-mortar establishments that relied on analog approaches were the first to be hit. Many states issued stay-at-home orders which caused businesses and consumers to make tough choices on what were really necessities and forced them to adapt or risk losing their base.
  - Business that thrived in this new dynamic were quick to adopt new methods of payment; many took their businesses fully online and leveraged e-commerce. Other companies simply took the opportunity to retool their infrastructure and reduce their employee footprint.

What has changed in the last year has been our newfound reliance on social media, telepresence (e.g., video telecoms, podcasts, live streams). What that approach did was increase the virtual footprint of these businesses and expand their customer base internationally. Now a small business could project a larger presence virtually and level set their professional identity.

A key test of these success stories is, can these businesses scale up, once the economy fully opens up?

Companies that can best leverage technology and quickly adapt to innovation, such as leveraging talented individuals, can utilize a more nimble infrastructure to offset the costs associated with carry large overhead. Businesses that are early adopters of 5G technology, those that understand how keep their supply chain in check and can quickly adapt their logistics architecture will have the advantage. Additionally, those that can transition to a cloud network or even use blockchain to ensure security for their transaction will have the advantage when they need to scale up.

- Align vendor control environments with your internal framework.
- Implement ongoing oversight using metrics and external alerts.

Conclusion

Much of what has been discussed comes down to a common theme: communicate, follow through and collect lessons learned! Communicate and don't stand by on the sidelines. Deploying proactive strategies to educate and engage teams opens up opportunities to establish a rapport that is unique to the skill set as contract professionals. Further, establishing a platform that contracts can use to shape the conversation within the organization leaves the door open for ongoing dialogue with a focus on continuous improvement to calibrate strategies for evolving issues. Having other functions understand how contracts can set the stage for success to affect the bottom line and maintain compliance ethically.

Contracts and procurement is a profession that is evolving, and companies will need to adapt to these roles to be competitive. Businesses cannot afford to be complacent and outdated in their approaches. Those contracting organizations that can successfully communicate the intricacies of compliance while working in an environment that builds a presence in market shaping initiatives will align the company for growth business and sustainability.

A contracts department has to communicate and assert its presence among its business peers. Once it is able to establish trust, identify and articulate issues up front; this approach positions the business to make good, sound business decisions organically. This proactive approach would lessen the exposure for future issues and save a lot of money. Further, being able to effectively communicate concerns and present solutions for the team to consider up front will ensure the stakeholders look to contracts as an effective bridge and partner in the success of the company.

Another aspect to consider is to position your organization to be relevant and open to the latest information possible. Information flows so quickly, and there are so many lessons learned that contracting professionals share. Organizations that are opening themselves up to knowledge share and building information centers of excellence are creating foundations for other business partners to speak candidly about issues and concerns.

Collectively, contract professionals' value to an organization will grow exponentially when they are in tune with industry best practices. Professionals who work to share that information throughout the business also evolve their functional support. Standards from organizations such as the International Organization for Standardization's (ISO) 31000 or ISO 9000, or even utilizing knowledge from NCMA or applying lean principles helps further the reach and helps translate an organization's maturity.

In conclusion, acquisition professionals are constantly striving for improvement. More for less should really resonate as evolving and growing by reading what the data is trending toward. Proficient contracts/sub-contracts and compliance professionals are the barometer of a fluid, changing business climate.

Bibliography

Contract Management Body of Knowledge(CMBOK). Sixth Edition. McLean, VA: National Contract Management Association, 2019.

Garrett, Gregory A. (ed) (2009). *Contract Administration—Tools, Techniques and Best Practices*. Wolters Kluwer.

Suveiu, Virginia. (May 2015). Contract risk management to survive and thrive in the 21st century. *Contract Management—Voice of the Professional Contract Management Community*, pp. 31–37.

PART III

Corporate Compliance and Ethics Challenges

12

OPERATIONALIZING COMPLIANCE

Best Practices

Tom Fox

Perhaps the most consistent process in the compliance field is its evolution. Compliance programs began in response to the US Sentencing Guidelines for Corporations back in 1992. Since that time, everyone involved, from the Department of Justice (DOJ) and Securities and Exchange Commission (SEC) to corporations and compliance practitioners, have evolved in their thinking over what constitutes a best practices compliance program.

There are several reasons for this evolution. Perhaps the most forceful drivers have been the regulatory/prosecution side and the corporate response. When I began in the compliance arena in 2007, having a paper program in place run by lawyers was about as good as it got. The company where I worked focused on compliance in the supply chain, which was so far beyond cutting edge that we might as well have been on Mars. Now having a paper program has been discarded as worse than useless, and compliance for your supply chain is table stakes to get into a minimum compliance program.

Looked at from another perspective, as companies have come before the DOJ and SEC and presented information on their remediation efforts, the DOJ and SEC have come to appreciate what can be done to prevent, detect, and remediate efforts by a company. As the DOJ and SEC perspectives evolved, they communicated that information in enforcement actions. Two of the clearest examples were the General Cable Corporation Non-Prosecution Agreement[1] (NPA), which was the first time the DOJ laid out a requirement for *tailored* training, and in the SEC civil action[2] involving Key Energy Services Inc., which discussed *transaction* monitoring for the first time in a Foreign Corrupt Practices Act (FCPA) enforcement action. The Evaluation of Corporate Compliance Programs–Guidance Document[3] (2019 Guidance) is the thinking of the DOJ's on what constitutes a best practices compliance program. It is a preeminent roadmap to a best practices compliance program.

1. www.justice.gov/criminal-fraud/file/921801/download.
2. www.sec.gov/litigation/admin/2016/34-78558.pdf.
3. As of this printing, the most recent Guidance is found here from 2020: https://www.justice.gov/criminal-fraud/page/file/937501/download. Although the updated guidance does not include major changes, it does provide additional details to further explain how the Criminal Division will evaluate programs. In March of 2022, the Assistant Attorney General of the Criminal Division, Kenneth Polite, reiterated the importance of the 2020 Guidance, based on the 2019 Guidance, see: https://www.justice.gov/opa/speech/assistant-attorney-general-kenneth-polite-jr-delivers-justice-department-keynote-aba.

DOI: 10.4324/9781351107242-16

Hallmark I: Commitment From All Leadership

This requirement moved beyond the ubiquitous "tone-at-the-top" as it focuses on the conduct of senior management. The DOJ wants to see a company's senior leadership actually *doing* compliance. The DOJ asks if company leadership has through their words and *concrete actions* brought the right message of doing business ethically and in compliance to a company. How does senior management *model* its behavior on a company's values and, finally, how is such conduct monitored in an organization? The 2019 Guidance drives this home with the following questions: "What concrete actions have they taken to demonstrate leadership in the company's compliance and remediation efforts? How have they modelled proper behavior to subordinates?"

However, this commitment has been extended far beyond simply senior management. It has been extended down into middle management. This is certainly appropriate as it is usually middle management which has the most day-to-day contact with employees. There is also the understanding to fully operationalize your compliance program, corporate departments other than compliance, and legal must be involved. This means human resources (HR), IT, security, treasury, finance, supply chain/procurement, and most importantly, business and operational managers, must all be a part of your company's compliance solution. The 2019 Guidance makes this clear with the following question: "What actions have senior leaders and middle-management stakeholders (e.g., business and operational managers, finance, procurement, legal, human resources) taken to demonstrate their commitment to compliance or compliance personnel, including their remediation efforts?"

Finally, the evolution in the role of the Board of Directors. A Board of Directors should have a true compliance expert sitting on it, coupled with a Compliance Committee, separate and apart from the Audit Committee. The Compliance Committee should be chaired by the Board's compliance expert. In addition to this great compliance expertise focus, a Board should now exercise real oversight of the corporate compliance function. This exercise comes from holding "executive or private sessions with the compliance and control functions" and by providing the answers to such questions as "What types of information have the board of directors and senior management examined in their exercise of oversight in the area in which the misconduct occurred?"

Hallmark II: Written Standards

Written standards consist of a Code of Conduct, Policies and Procedures and Internal Controls. The Ten Hallmarks moved us past the state where written standards were lawyer written and lawyer driven to wave in a regulator's face during an enforcement action by using it to claim we are an ethical company. Now companies need to show how the written standards were developed and, equally important, who was involved in their development. The business/operations part of your organization should be consulted and be a part of this process going forward.

There should be business unit input into the written standards. You should not only train your employees on them but they must be tested to determine effectiveness. When was the last time you tested the *effectiveness* of your written standards? Testing for effectiveness is mandated under the COSO 2013 Internal Controls Framework,[4] so that model can be one to use to test the effectiveness of your compliance internal controls.

Finally, accessibility. Can your employees even access the information contained in your written standards and understand it? The original formulation of the Ten Hallmarks required that your Code of Conduct, together with policies and procedures, be translated into local languages so employees outside the United States could understand them. Accessibility also means training, so your training must also be in local languages where appropriate.

4. www.coso.org/Pages/ic.aspx.

Hallmark III: Compliance Authority and Resources

The role of a Chief Compliance Officer (CCO) and compliance function has grown in prestige and in the eyes of regulators. The original Ten Hallmarks made clear that a CCO should have the ability to report up to the Board and have sufficient authority and standing within an organization. A corporate compliance function is also required to have sufficient resources to affect its obligations.

The 2016 FCPA Pilot Program[5] was the first time the DOJ laid out specific information about the expertise it expects from a corporate compliance function. A compliance practitioner must now have both quality and experience. Most importantly, this expertise and experience is not limited to simply reciting the FCPA or even understanding compliance. Now every compliance practitioner must have sufficient understanding of the business, the transactions the companies engage in, and the data and information which flows therefrom. In short, to help fully operationalize compliance in your organization, you must be able to read a spreadsheet. Finally, there must be adequate compensation paid to and opportunity for promotion for those in the compliance department within an organization.

The 2019 Guidance added components on stature of both the compliance function and the compliance professional within a company. In addition to the obvious comparisons of a corporate compliance function with other strategic functions in the company in terms of stature, compensation levels and rank/title, there were new areas of inquiry. They included a reporting line up to the Board and chief executives, resources, and even access to key decision makers. You need to consider what has been the turnover rate for compliance and relevant control function personnel. Finally—and this is the area that may, at the end of the day, prove the most decisive—what role has compliance played in the company's strategic and operational decisions? If compliance has not played a role in strategic and organizational decisions, it cannot adequately begin the risk management process, which still serves as the basis for your compliance regime.

Hallmark IV: Risk Management

Under the original formulation of the Ten Hallmarks of an Effective Compliance Programs from the 2012 release, *A Resource Guide to the US Foreign Corrupt Practices Act*[6] (2012 FCPA Resource Guide), the risk assessment was articulated as the cornerstone of all compliance programs. However, now a full risk management program is the standard for any best practices compliance program. This consists of three components. First is forecasting, which allows you to consider your business strategy and weed the risks you can foresee. By starting with forecasting, a compliance function utilizes risk assessment to consider issues which forecasting did not predict for or issues which the forecasting model raised as a potential outcome which warranted a deeper dive. The second is that risk assessments allow you to evaluate and measure known risks. If you are moving into a new product or sales area and are required to use third-party sales agents, a risk assessment would provide information that a company could use to ameliorate the risks. Third is risk-based monitoring which allows you to monitor both the compliance risks you know about and detect those you do not know, on an ongoing basis. The basis of your compliance program in many ways turns on the robustness of your risk management process.

The DOJ formulation takes a more tactical approach that you must be able to articulate and justify your risk assessment process. From there the next question is, how you used the information going forward. As compliance evolves, and corporate compliance programs become more sophisticated, compliance is seen not as simply a legal prophylactic, but as a business process. Seen in this light, it is clear the risk management process should begin with forecasting as it attempts to estimate future aspects of your business. Compliance professionals should be able to say with some degree of

5. www.justice.gov/archives/opa/blog-entry/file/838386/download.
6. www.justice.gov/sites/default/files/criminal-fraud/legacy/2015/01/16/guide.pdf.

authority, what will happen in the next 3, 6, 12 to 24 months. This can facilitate resource deployment where deemed appropriate in order to meet these future demands. This ties back into process management and process improvement. There is a balance between what is actually important for your business or for proper execution versus the practical aspects of the whole process.

Hallmark V: Communication and Training

One of the key goals of any compliance program is to train employees in awareness and understanding of the FCPA, your specific company compliance program, and to create and foster a culture of compliance. Beginning in the fall of 2016 through the announcement of the FCPA Pilot Program, the DOJ began to talk about whether you have determined the effectiveness of your training. This continued with the 2019 Guidance where they asked, "How has the company measured the effectiveness of the training?" This point has bedeviled many compliance professionals yet it is now a key metric for the government in evaluating compliance training.

Most companies have not considered this issue, the effectiveness of their compliance program. I would suggest that you start at the beginning of an evaluation and move outward. This means starting with attendance, which many companies tend to overlook. You should determine that all senior management and Board members have attended compliance training. You should review the documentation of attendance and confirm this attendance. Make your department or group leaders accountable for the attendance of their direct reports and so on down the chain. Evidence of training is important to create an audit trail for any internal or external assessment or audit of your training program.

Also raised in the 2019 Guidance was the focus of your training programs, where the DOJ inquired into whether your training was *tailored* for the audience. This added new requirements. One is that you must assess your employees for risk to determine the type of training you might need to deliver. This means that you should risk rank your employees. Obviously, the sales force would be the highest risk but there may be others which are deserving of high-risk training as well. From your risk ranking, you need to then develop training tailored for the risks those employees will face.

The key going forward is that you have thoughtfully created your compliance training program, not only in the design but who receives it, all coupled with back-end determination of effectiveness. Finally, all of this must be documented.

Hallmark VI: Incentives and Discipline

Incentives

The 2012 FCPA Resource Guide stated the

> DOJ and SEC recognize that positive incentives can also drive compliant behavior. These incentives can take many forms such as personnel evaluations and promotions, rewards for improving and developing a company's compliance program, and rewards for ethics and compliance leadership.

This same concept was expanded in the 2019 Guidance with questions about both the carrot and the stick. The DOJ wants to know how companies "incentivized compliance and ethical behavior." Equally importantly, they want to know about incentives awarded "as a result of compliance and ethics considerations."

As your compliance program matures and your strategy is more fully operationalized, your sales force should embrace this operationalization to help achieve compliance. The prescription for you, as the compliance practitioner, is to revise the incentive system to focus your employees on the goals of your compliance program. This may mean that you need to change the incentives as the compliance programs matures, from installing the building blocks of compliance to integrating anticorruption compliance with the DNA of your company. There are three key questions you should ask yourself in modifying your compensation structure. First, is the change *simple*? Second, is the changed *aligned* with your company values? Third, is the effect on behavior *immediate* due to the change?

Discipline

The original formulation of the Ten Hallmarks stated, "DOJ and SEC will thus consider whether, when enforcing a compliance program, a company has appropriate and clear disciplinary procedures, whether those procedures are applied reliably and promptly, and whether they are commensurate with the violation." In the 2019 Guidance, the requirements around discipline expanded to "Have the disciplinary actions and incentives been fairly and consistently applied across the organization?" Similarly, the FCPA Corporate Enforcement Policy,[7] released in November 2017 stated: "Appropriate discipline of employees, including those identified by the company as responsible for the misconduct, either through direct participation or failure in oversight, as well as those with supervisory authority over the area in which the criminal conduct occurred."

One of the areas which can work to more fully operationalize your compliance program is to ensure that discipline is handed out fairly across an organization and to reward those employees who integrate such ethical and compliant behavior into their individual work practices going forward. In addition to providing a financial incentive for ethical behavior, it also provides a sense of institutional objectivity. Institutional objectivity comes from procedural fairness and is one of the areas that will bring credibility to your compliance program.

Today, this is called institutional justice, which recognizes that there are fair procedures, not arbitrary ones, in processes involving rights. Considerable research has shown that people are more willing to accept negative, unfavorable, and non-preferred outcomes when they are arrived at by processes and procedures that are perceived as fair. As you incorporate the institutional justice in your compliance program, consider these three key areas: (1) administration of discipline; (2) employee promotions; and (3) internal investigations.

Hallmark VII: Third Parties

Third parties are still recognized as the highest risk for corruption. Management of third parties is therefore a critical component for any best practices compliance program. The 2012 FCPA Resource Guide discussed three prongs on inquiry. The first focused on *risk-based due diligence*, mandating companies to understand the qualifications and associations of its third-party partners, including its business reputation and relationship, if any, with foreign officials. Second is a *business justification*, requiring companies to understand the business reason for including the third party in the transaction. Third is *compliance terms and conditions* in the commercial contract.

This original formulation has expanded into five distinct steps: business justification, questionnaire, due diligence, compliance terms and conditions, and management after the contract is signed. Understanding and properly using each step is critical to fully manage the life cycle of third-party relationships. It begins with the following:

> How has the company's third-party management process corresponded to the nature and level of the enterprise risk identified by the company? How has this process been integrated into the relevant procurement and vendor management processes?

7. www.justice.gov/criminal-fraud/file/838416/download.

> What was the business rationale for the use of the third-parties in question? If third parties were involved in the underlying misconduct, what was the business rationale for using those third parties? What mechanisms have existed to ensure that the contract terms specifically described the services to be performed, that the payment terms are appropriate, that the described contractual work is performed, and that compensation is commensurate with the services rendered?

This first set of queries clearly specifies that the DOJ expects an integrated approach that is operationalized throughout the company. This means your compliance process must have a process for the full life cycle of third-party risk management. Moreover, the management of the third-party relationship after the contract has been signed is becoming much more important. This integrated approach is further confirmed by another series of questions in the 2019 Guidance.

> Management of Relationships—How has the company considered and analyzed the compensation and incentive structure for the third parties against compliance risks? How does the company monitor its third parties? Does the company have audit rights to analyze the books and accounts of third parties, and has the company exercised those rights in the past? How does the company train its third-party relationship managers about compliance risks and how to manage them? How does the company incentivize compliance and ethical behavior by third parties?

Managing your third parties is where the rubber meets the road in your overall third-party risk management program. You must execute on this task. Even if you successfully navigate the first four steps in your third-party risk management program, those four are, in reality, the easy steps. Managing the relationship is where the real work begins. Here the DOJ inquires the following.

Hallmark VIII: Reporting and Investigations

This was one of the shortest of the Ten Hallmarks. It had three parts: (1) internal reporting, (2) investigations, and (3) remediation. The 2019 Guidance gave extended discussions on what the DOJ expects in this area, beyond the basic formulation found in Hallmark VII.

Reporting

The 2012 FCPA Resource Guide had as clear and concise a statement about hotlines as any other requirement found in Ten Hallmarks of an Effective Compliance Program. It stated: "An effective compliance program should include a mechanism for an organization's employees and others to report suspected or actual misconduct or violations of the company's policies on a confidential basis and without fear of retaliation."

The 2019 Guidance reinforced this language with the following Confidential Reporting and Investigation: "How has the company collected, analyzed, and used information from its reporting mechanisms? How has the company assessed the seriousness of the allegations it received? Has the compliance function had full access to reporting and investigative information?"

This is more than simply maintaining hotlines. Companies have to make real efforts to listen to employees. You need to have managers who are trained on how to handle employee concerns; they must be incentivized to take on this compliance responsibility, and you must devote communication resources to reinforcing the company's culture and values to create an environment and expectation that managers will raise employee concerns.

The Investigation Protocol

The 2012 FCPA Resource Guide had only a short statement about investigations, which stated: "once an allegation is made, companies should have in place an efficient, reliable, and properly funded process for investigating the allegation and documenting the company's response, including any disciplinary or remediation measures taken."

This was expanded in the 2019 Guidance to both how a company performs its investigation and what it does with the information collected in the investigative process. Regarding the former, the 2019 Guidance states: "How has the company ensured that the investigations have been properly scoped, and were independent, objective, appropriately conducted, and properly documented?" Regarding the latter, it states,

> Have the company's investigations been used to identify root causes, system vulnerabilities, and accountability lapses, including among supervisory manager and senior executives? What has been the process for responding to investigative findings? How high up in the company do investigative findings go?

Moreover, with the advent of the SEC Whistleblower Program,[8] companies must quickly and efficiently investigate all hotline reports. This means you need an investigation protocol in place so that the entire compliance function is on the same page and knows what to do.

Your company should have a detailed written procedure for handling any complaint or allegation of bribery or corruption, regardless of the means through which it is communicated. The mechanism could include the internal company hotline, anonymous tips, or a report directly from the business unit involved. You can make the decision on whether or not to investigate with consultation with other groups, such as the Audit Committee of the Board of Directors or the Legal Department. The head of the business unit in which the claim arose may also be notified that an allegation has been made and that the compliance department will be handling the matter on a go-forward basis. Through the use of such a detailed written procedure, you can work to ensure there is complete transparency on the rights and obligations of all parties, once an allegation is made. This allows the compliance department to have not only flexibility but also the responsibility to deal with such matters, from which it can best assess and then decide on how to manage the matter.

Remediation

The 2012 FCPA Resource Guide stated: "Companies will want to consider taking "lessons learned" from any reported violations and the outcome of any resulting investigation to update their internal controls and compliance program and focus future training on such issues, as appropriate." Clearly lessons learned are near and dear to the heart of any "nuts and bolts" compliance practitioner, as it clearly means you need to input your investigative findings into the solution of the issue which led to the compliance failure.

This was expanded in the 2019 Guidance with the following requirements around root causes analysis: "What is the company's root cause analysis of the misconduct at issue? Were any systemic issues identified? Who in the company was involved in making the analysis?"

8. www.sec.gov/whistleblower.

Finally, in the FCPA Corporate Enforcement Policy, the DOJ had several pronouncements on the remedial aspect of any investigation. Initially, it noted there should be a "remediation to the root causes" and then went on to add the following points:

- Appropriate discipline of employees, including those identified by the company as responsible for the misconduct, either through direct participation or failure in oversight, as well as those with supervisory authority over the area in which the criminal conduct occurred; and
- Any additional steps that demonstrate recognition of the seriousness of the company's misconduct, acceptance of responsibility for it, and the implementation of measures to reduce the risk of repetition of such misconduct, including measures to identify future risks.

There is nothing like an internal whistleblower report about a FCPA violation, the finding of such an issue, or (even worse) a subpoena from the DOJ to trigger attention from the Board of Directors and senior management to the compliance function and the company's compliance program. You may find yourself in the position that you will have to have some very frank discussions about what to expect in terms of costs and time outlays. While much of these discussions will focus on the investigative process and those costs, these discussions will allow you to initiate the talk about remediation going forward and begin to explain why money must be budgeted for the remediation process.

One of the things rarely considered is how the investigation triggers the remediation process and what the relationship is between the two. When issues arise warranting an investigation that would rise to the Board of Directors level and potentially require disclosure to the government, there is usually a flurry of attention and activity. Everyone wants to know what is going on. You will have everyone's attention on remediation, and you must use that attention to provide for the required steps to not only fix the issue but, as the FCPA Corporate Enforcement Policy says, implement measures to reduce the risk that the same or similar conduct will occur again.

Hallmark IX: Continuous Improvement

Hallmark IX of Ten Hallmarks of an Effective Compliance Program, as articulated in the 2012 FCPA Resource Guide, stated:

> Finally, a good compliance program should constantly evolve. A company's business changes over time, as do the environments in which it operates, the nature of its customers, the laws that govern its actions, and the standards of its industry. In addition, compliance programs that do not just exist on paper but are followed in practice will inevitably uncover compliance weaknesses and require enhancements. Consequently, DOJ and SEC evaluate whether companies regularly review and improve their compliance programs and not allow them to become stale.

The 2012 FCPA Resource Guide made clear that each company should assess and manage its risks. It specifically noted that small and medium-sized enterprises likely will have different risk profiles and therefore different attendant compliance programs than large multinational corporations. Moreover, this is something that the DOJ and SEC consider when evaluating a company's compliance program in any FCPA investigation. This is why a "check the box" approach is not only disfavored by the DOJ, but, at the end of the day, is also ineffectual. It is because each compliance program should be tailored to the enterprise's own specific needs, risks, and challenges.

This insight was expanded upon in the DOJ's 2019 Guidance which listed four areas of continuous improvement, each further refined with multiple attendant questions. They were:

A. Internal Audit

What is the process for determining where and how frequently internal audit will undertake an audit, and what is the rationale behind that process? How are audits carried out? What types of audits would have identified issues relevant to the misconduct? Did those audits occur and what were the findings? What types of relevant audit findings and remediation progress have been reported to management and the board on a regular basis? How have management and the board followed up? How often does internal audit conduct assessments in high-risk areas?

B. Control Testing

Has the company reviewed and audited its compliance program in the area relating to the misconduct? More generally what testing of relevant controls, collection and analysis of compliance data, and interviews of employees and third parties does the company undertake? How are the results reported and action items tracked?

C. Evolving Updates

How often has the company updated its risk assessments and reviewed its compliance policies, procedures, and practices? Has the company undertaken a gap analysis to determine if particular areas or risk are not sufficiently addressed in its policies, controls or training? What steps has the company taken to determine whether policies/procedures/practices make sense for particular business segments/subsidiaries?

D. Culture of Compliance

How often and how does the company measure its culture of compliance? Does the company seek input from all levels of employees to determine whether they perceive senior and middle management's commitment to compliance? What steps has the company taken in response to its measurement of the compliance culture?

Keeping track of external and internal events which may cause change to business process, policies, and procedures is a key step to meeting this requirement. Some examples of these potential events are new laws applicable to your business organization and internal activities that drive changes within a company (i.e., a company reorganization or major acquisition).

Continuous improvement requires that you not only audit but also monitor whether employees are staying with the compliance program. In addition to the language set out in the 2012 FCPA Guidance, two of the seven compliance elements in the US Sentencing Guidelines call for companies to monitor, audit, and respond quickly to allegations of misconduct. These three activities are key components enforcement officials look for when determining whether companies maintain adequate oversight of their compliance programs.

Finally, the 2019 Guidance was the first time the DOJ so prominently recognized corporate culture as a key metric of a company's overall commitment to compliance and as a measure of its compliance program. You need to begin to assess, improve, and remediate your culture going forward. Always document, document, document everything you do, so if the DOJ or SEC come knocking there will be evidence of your efforts.

Hallmark X: Merger and Acquisitions

Pre-acquisition

The 2012 FCPA Resource Guide stated

> mergers and acquisitions present both risks and opportunities. A company that does not perform adequate FCPA due diligence prior to a merger or acquisition may face both legal and business risks. Perhaps most commonly, inadequate due diligence can allow a course of bribery to continue—with all the attendant harms to a business's profitability and reputation, as well as potential civil and criminal liability.

While most compliance practitioners have been long aware of the requirement in the post-acquisition context, the 2012 FCPA Resource Guide focused many compliance practitioners on the need to engage in robust pre-acquisition due diligence.

The 2012 FCPA Resource Guide emphasized the pre-acquisition phase, and the 2019 Guidance took a deeper dive into the need for the compliance component of your merger and acquisition (M&A) regime to begin with a preliminary pre-acquisition assessment of risk. Such an early assessment will inform the transaction research and evaluation phases. This could include an objective view of the risks faced and the level of risk exposure, such as best/worst case scenarios. A pre-acquisition risk assessment could also be used as a "lens through which to view the feasibility of the business strategy" and help to value the potential target. Most interestingly, the DOJ made the question "How has the compliance function been integrated into the merger, acquisition, and integration process?" a basic inquiry in the 2019 Guidance.

This focus on pre-acquisition due diligence has become much more central to a best practices compliance program. The DOJ mandates that a thorough due diligence be performed at this stage in the M&A process. The DOJ asks: "Was the misconduct or the risk of misconduct identified during due diligence? Who conducted the risk review for the acquired/merged entities and how was it done? What has been the M&A due diligence process generally?"

Post-acquisition

The 2012 FCPA Resource Guide language stated

> pre-acquisition due diligence, however, is normally only a portion of the compliance process for mergers and acquisitions. DOJ and SEC evaluate whether the acquiring company promptly incorporated the acquired company into all of its internal controls, including its compliance program. Companies should consider training new employees, reevaluating third parties under company standards, and, where appropriate, conducting audits on new business units.

The pre-acquisition process sets up a company's post-acquisition integration. Obviously any ongoing misconduct identified in the pre-acquisition phase must be stopped and then remediated. From there a company must also work to integrate the acquired entity into its overall compliance framework.

There was no new information in the 2019 Guidance or FCPA Corporate Enforcement Policy changing any of the deadlines for completion of the post-acquisition integration as was originally formulated in the 2012 FCPA Resource Guide and the enforcement actions involving Johnson & Johnson[9]

9. www.justice.gov/sites/default/files/criminal-fraud/legacy/2011/04/27/04-08-11depuy-dpa.pdf.

and Data Systems & Solutions LLC[10] or Opinion Release 08-02.[11] The general guidelines presented in these FCPA enforcement actions were that the post-acquisition integration, investigations, and remediations had to be completed in 18 months or "as soon as is practicable."

Root Cause Analysis

One item in the 2019 Guidance supplemented the Ten Hallmarks of an Effective Compliance Program from the 2012 FCPA Resource Guide. This was the performance of a root cause analysis for any compliance violation which may lead to a self-disclosure or enforcement action. This require was previously articulated in the FCPA Corporate Enforcement Policy brought forward this requirement for a root cause analysis as a "Demonstration of thorough analysis of causes of underlying conduct (i.e., a root cause analysis) and, where appropriate, remediation to address the root causes."

The 2019 further expanded on this language by mandating that a company not only perform a root cause analysis but asking if any systemic issues were identified in the process. From there the DOJ wants to know what steps in your remediation process were tied to these findings. Initially, you need to understand the difference between a root cause analysis and a risk assessment. Obviously, you would perform a root cause analysis after an incident occurs so to that extent it is reactive rather than proactive. The site Thwink.org has defined root cause analysis as follows:

> The purpose of root cause analysis is to strike at the root of a problem by finding and resolving its root causes. Root cause analysis is a class of problem solving methods aimed at identifying the root causes of problems or events. . . . The practice of root cause analysis is predicated on the belief that problems are best solved by attempting to correct or eliminate root causes, as opposed to merely addressing the immediately obvious symptoms.[12]

Well-known fraud investigator Jonathan Marks has defined a root cause analysis as "a research-based approach to identifying the bottom line reason of a problem or an issue; with the root cause, not the proximate cause the root cause representing the source of the problem."[13] He contrasted this definition with that of a risk assessment, which he said "is something performed on a proactive basis based on various facts. A root cause analysis analyzes a problem that was previously identified through a risk assessment."

Marks also contrasted a root cause analysis with an investigation. He noted, "in an investigation we are try to either prove or disprove an allegation." This means that in a compliance investigation you may be trying to prove or disprove certain transactions could form the basis of a corrupt payment or bribe by garnering evidence to either support or refute specific allegation or allegations. You do not assess blame, and that is the point where a root cause should follow to determine how the compliance failure occurred or was allowed to occur.

This requirement for a root cause analysis is a basic investigative tool that the DOJ now requires companies to incorporate into their best practices compliance program. Not only must you engage in a root cause analysis but you must document your protocol and then show how you fed the information you obtained back into your remediation.

10. www.scribd.com/document/97479341/Filed-dss-Dpa.
11. www.justice.gov/sites/default/files/criminal-fraud/legacy/2010/04/11/0802.pdf.
12. http://thwink.org/.
13. https://boardandfraud.com/2018/01/17/root-cause-analysis/.

Conclusion

Compliance best practices will continue to evolve. The same process which has occurred since 2012 when the original FCPA Resource Guide was released is still in place. Moreover, both the DOJ Antitrust Division[14] and the Department of Treasury, Office of Foreign Asset Control[15] (OFAC) have fully embraced corporate compliance programs as key elements in the enforcement of antitrust laws and trade sanctions.

All of these pronouncements are publicly available at no charge to the compliance professional. There is simply no excuse not to have at hand the latest and most up-to-date formulation by the DOJ on any best practices compliance program. Moreover, each one of the DOJ releases allows every compliance professional and every company to benchmark their compliance program against the current best practices.

The original formulation of the Ten Hallmarks of an Effective Compliance Program from the 2012 FCPA Resource Guide still provides the basic framework for any anticorruption compliance program. The information provided in the 2017 FCPA Corporate Enforcement Policy and the 2019 Guidance further refined and amplified additional information which allows a corporate compliance program to meet the ever-changing business risks around bribery and corruption.

14. www.justice.gov/atr/page/file/1182001/download.
15. www.treasury.gov/resource-center/sanctions/Documents/framework_ofac_cc.pdf.

13
INTERNAL INVESTIGATIONS

Michael Volkov, Matt Stankiewicz and Noah Smith

The Importance of Internal Investigations

The internal investigation is the central fact-finding component of any functioning corporate compliance program. An early mentor in the field used to harp on its importance, often explaining that internal investigations are where the "rubber meets the road" for the compliance program. This proves true in practice, as internal controls must be supported by effective enforcement mechanisms. Moreover, proper enforcement cannot occur unless the company first uncovers exactly what occurred by conducting a thorough review to understand any reported allegations.

This is the crux of the internal investigation. A proper, well-scoped investigation is the most reliable tool for key decision makers to quickly and efficiently obtain the information they need to protect their company from misconduct. The access to information provided by a strong internal investigations function allows those decision makers—who could be the board, senior management, or otherwise—to properly resolve violations of company policy or law. Without knowing the details of what occurred, these decision makers could not properly mete out discipline and create effective remedial controls for continued success. A strong internal investigation program can also have a profound impact on the organization's culture by encouraging employees who witness misconduct to speak up.

Federal Guidance Pertaining to Internal Investigations

The most successful companies will apply sufficient resources toward ensuring adherence to the internal investigation standards outlined in federal guidance. The Department of Justice (DOJ) certainly understands the importance of sound internal investigations procedures, as it has continually reiterated the need for effective investigations in evolving iterations of its compliance guidance through the years. For example, in its Foreign Corrupt Practices Act (FCPA) Resource Guide developed jointly with the Securities and Exchange Commission (SEC), the government instructed that the businesses should devote resources toward ensuring that companies' processes for investigating allegations should be "efficient, reliable, and properly funded."[1] As an overarching guidepost principle, companies should maintain detailed records of any disciplinary or remedial measures that result, and they should use any "lessons learned" from the inquiry to identify gaps and improve the overall program.

1. www.justice.gov/sites/default/files/criminal-fraud/legacy/2015/01/16/guide.pdf.

DOI: 10.4324/9781351107242-17

The 2015 Yates Memo changed the landscape and revealed the critical need for effective investigations.[2] The Yates Memo made clear that, in order to receive *any* cooperation credit during government prosecutions, the company must provide all relevant facts and information regarding the alleged misconduct. This includes disclosing names and providing extensive evidence about culpable individuals. These principles apply to both criminal and civil cases across a variety of legal risk areas, including antitrust, FCPA, fraud, cybercrime, sanctions and export controls, and money laundering—to name just a few.

In mid-2019, the DOJ's Criminal Division released its *Evaluation of Corporate Compliance Programs* guidance, which further highlighted how sharp internal investigations practices tend to promote ethical and successful workplaces.[3] Best-in-class compliance programs should ensure that employee complaints are encouraged, routed swiftly to proper personnel, assessed as to their seriousness, resolved in a timely and professional manner, and followed up on with the appropriate remedial or disciplinary procedures. The guidance further explains that investigations should be properly scoped, independently conducted, objectively scrutinized, thoroughly documented, and conducted by qualified and independent investigators. Regardless of any given investigation's specific outcome, company leaders should be internalizing and implementing takeaway lessons by identifying recurring patterns of misconduct, curing any systemic deficiencies, updating internal controls, and improving overall compliance efforts, including future employee training initiatives. To allow company leaders to conduct these remedial analyses, complaints and investigations must always be centrally tracked.

The Anatomy of an Internal Investigation

The general internal investigation process typically proceeds as shown in Figure 13.1.

Intake of Employee Complaints

The investigation begins with the initial source of the complaint, as this is the first place to potentially uncover useful information. Proper complaint intake procedures are therefore critical. Different companies could utilize a range of different complaint intake sources, including human resources departments, internal audit departments, compliance departments, reporting hotlines,

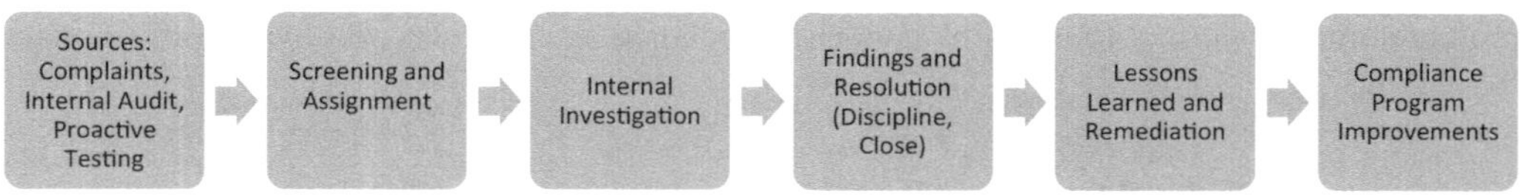

Figure 13.1 General internal investigation process.

2. www.justice.gov/archives/dag/file/769036/download. In March 2022, Attorney General Merrick Garland reiterated and built upon Deputy Attorney General Lisa Monaco's October 2021 speech where she announced the DOJ's reinstatement of the 2015 Yates Memo, see: https://www.justice.gov/opa/speech/attorney-general-merrick-b-garland-delivers-remarks-aba-institute-white-collar-crime.
3. www.justice.gov/criminal-fraud/page/file/937501/download. As of this printing, the most recent Guidance is found here from 2020: https://www.justice.gov/criminal-fraud/page/file/937501/download. Although the updated guidance does not include major changes, it does provide additional details to further explain how the Criminal Division will evaluate programs. In March of 2022, the Assistant Attorney General of the Criminal Division, Kenneth Polite, reiterated the importance of the 2020 Guidance, based on the 2019 Guidance, see: https://www.justice.gov/opa/speech/assistant-attorney-general-kenneth-polite-jr-delivers-justice-department-keynote-aba.

or third-party intake providers. The most common intake source, however, remains complaining employees' direct managers or immediate supervisors. This underscores the importance of managerial training, which familiarizes managers with how best to handle reports of unethical or unlawful internal conduct. Again, this is the first, and at times only, opportunity to gain valuable information into the allegations.

Triage of Employee Complaints

Once a complaint is received, it must be appropriately triaged. One common and effective way to categorize complaints is by subject matter. It may make sense to assign more serious issues to in-house legal teams or external legal counsel, while relegating more routine personnel complaints to human resources managers. Undoubtedly, issues involving significant legal, financial, or reputational risks—particularly the types of issues that could land the company in a news headline—should be managed by subject matter experts with the proper experience to isolate and resolve potential misconduct. When the need to investigate serious issues like these does arise, management should be kept aware throughout each step of the process to institute appropriate crisis response measures as necessary. However, regardless of how "routine" certain issues may appear at first glance, there is cause to exercise caution when triaging and categorizing employee complaints, as even seemingly run-of-the-mill issues can—and certainly at times, do—ultimately expand into larger issues.

Principles of Sound Investigatory Practice to Bear in Mind

As you begin the investigation, be aware of several key principles that should always guide your actions. First, above all, is confidentiality. Limit access to investigative information to only those with a need to know. Second, ensure the security of witnesses and other participants in the investigation. Reporters and witnesses must not be subject to any form of retaliation for assisting investigators in their efforts. Third, ensure competency by enlisting the support of staff who have been properly trained within their particular areas of expertise. Fourth, maintain professionalism throughout the entire process by analyzing and discussing the matters under investigation through a lens of objectivity, impartiality, integrity, fairness, and diligence. Be sure to address conflicts of interest and focus on the search for truth. This is not ultimately about punishment or retribution. Rather, this is about unearthing facts and determining whether the allegations are substantiated. Finally, stay timely by aiming to address concerns as promptly as possible. In general, 60 to 90 days is a suitable target time frame for most routine investigations; but of course, never sacrifice the investigation's overall quality in the name of expediency.

Planning and Preparation

The investigations program should maintain a level of uniformity throughout the entire process. To aid in this endeavor, companies should develop standard operating procedures for each phase, from complaint intake to final resolution and follow-up steps. There may be multiple procedures for different types of investigations. For most investigations, the first step is to develop an investigation plan. Review the allegations, lay out the basic facts, and identify the potential violations. Then, gather the written text of the policies or law that may be implicated by the alleged misconduct. The basic elements of the alleged violation should be spelled out so that subsequent document review and witness interviews can be targeted toward that objective. Think about which facts would need to be proven for each element of the offense to be substantiated. Once this has been defined, the document collection plan, procedures for contacting witnesses, witness interview procedures, final investigation reports, and ultimate resolution will each flow more easily. Always tailor your information collection procedures to the ultimate objective of the investigation, compiling evidence that is both relevant and material to the underlying allegations at issue.

At this point, open the case file and begin to document every investigative step taken. This will aid you throughout the investigation, to maintain a repository of all relevant information, but can also be hugely beneficial in the future to definitively demonstrate to any regulators or auditors who may inquire that the investigation was conducted properly and according to established procedures. "Documentation" should be construed very broadly in this context to include thorough records of all evidence collected. This includes recording information such as interview subjects, date and time of the interview, and listing any additional observers or participants. Create summary documents, such as time lines, to organize information or develop the facts uncovered into a narrative. Rigorous documentation must begin at an early stage to ensure nothing becomes overlooked as the narrative develops. Even when investigations appear simple or routine, they often indicate broader systemic issues. As one mentor used to say, in the beginning you don't know what you don't know.

Document Collection and Review

Begin to identify the documents necessary for the investigation, brainstorming which documents you would need to prove or disprove the allegations, where those documents may be located, and who has access to or control over those documents. Those individuals—the "custodians"—must be issued preservation notices as soon as possible. The concept of "document review" should be interpreted expansively as well. Depending on the nature of the allegation, the review of documents may require computer file collections or cell phone data backups to preserve electronically stored information such as emails, text messages, and other digital records. Gather pertinent individuals' calendars, expense reports, time records, personnel files, and anything else that could shed light on their activities during the events in question. Review any prior relevant investigation reports to better understand the historical context of related company misconduct.

As you think critically about the information needed and where that information may be located, think further about what type of internal or external support will be needed to perform a thorough investigation. For example, the information technology department is often critical in pulling relevant emails. Also think about what subject matter experts will be needed; if the allegations relate to highly technical areas, then the support of these experts may be necessary. If, for example, an employee was accused of fraudulent accounting practices, then forensic accountants become helpful investigative allies. In most interviews, human resources personnel can serve as key partners through their specialized knowledge of the employee population or specific individuals. Human resources may also provide deeper insights into bad actors' potential motives or background information.

Conducting the Interviews

Throughout the document review process, you must identify the witnesses who may have information related to the allegations. Then, plan an interview schedule around these individuals. Typically, it makes sense to interview the alleged perpetrator last—after the available information becomes more developed, the narrative feels more complete, and the events are more fully understood. You should initially make contact with the complainant and, subsequently, the other alleged perpetrators, if possible, and gather any relevant intelligence and records that may be in their possession. Unfortunately, always anticipate that individuals may have engaged in some level of collusion or conspiracy.

To preserve the investigation's independence and integrity, subjects of the investigation should be walled off from outside information sources to the extent possible, including any senior management that may be involved. At least initially, the operative standard is fairly straightforward. That is, if an individual has some interest in the outcome of the investigation, then that individual should be excluded from accessing information about the investigation. These individuals should generally continue to be walled off until the conclusion of the investigation. Too often, a senior leader will consider themselves to be "cleared" and then gain access to the investigation, only for new information to arise later on that implicates that leader once more. Suddenly, the entire investigation is tainted due to his or her involvement.

As you begin conducting interviews, always remember why the investigation is occurring. You are on the search for truth. You are not the police, nor are the interviewees your friends. You should constantly be operating in the mindset of an objective fact-finder who is seeking to understand what occurred. You are not a prosecutor, and your objective is not necessarily to prove the allegation, and an equally plausible outcome is a finding that the allegation is unsubstantiated.

Additionally, investigators should determine whether to conduct the interview under the protections of attorney-client privilege. Not all investigations will require it, but companies should err on the side of protecting themselves by utilizing privilege if the circumstances suggest some conceivable anticipation of litigation in the future. Again, a reasonably tailored approach is preferred. It may not be plausible to ensure that attorneys conduct every single interview, but sensitive or risky issues should be handled by legal counsel to preserve the privilege. Even in circumstances where attorneys are not involved, many companies use a process where the General Counsel or Chief Legal Officer creates a standard form to authorize the internal investigation. This helps to imbue the process with legal review and authorization, as all subsequent steps will be understood as having been taken for the purposes of analyzing legal issues and providing legal advice to the company. Non-attorneys may then conduct interviews and report the results to internal legal personnel. With this approach, basic privilege protections may remain intact because the interviews are conducted under the authority of the legal department.[4]

An Upjohn warning may be necessary before questioning begins. The Upjohn warning is necessary for a company to maintains the right to control attorney-client privilege, which becomes imperative to take advantage of the cooperation credit discussed in the Yates Memo. The Upjohn warning effectively provides witnesses with the knowledge that counsel conducting the interviews are counsel for the corporation, not for the witness, and that the attorney-client privilege over the information disclosed during the interview is held by the company. The Upjohn warning should not be taken lightly, so be sure to provide it at the outset of every interview where needed. Develop a formal Upjohn script to ensure that all key points are addressed in a uniform manner. To elevate these procedures further toward best practice, provide a written description of the Upjohn warning and other salient points about the interview. Have the witness read and sign this statement, and include it in the interview file. Be prepared to answer certain questions, such as "Do I need a lawyer?" or "Will I lose my job?" Your responses should be consistent.

Use an interview outline of the key topics to discuss to guide your discussion with the witness. Don't read from a script, but interviews of this nature will inevitably wind along various tangent pathways, so it is helpful to have a basic reference guide on hand to bring your lines of questioning back on track if needed. Start with basic questions about the witness's relevant roles and responsibilities. While useful for background context, these easier questions may also alleviate any nervous energy from the witness.[5] Try to develop a rapport with the witness while establishing the universe of the witness's relevant activities. As you question the witness, your inquiries should become progressively more specific to drill down on your targeted elements of the alleged offense. This type

4. Courts do not like to see broad assertions of privilege across all investigations. Determine which investigations should require privilege and focus efforts on those. Ensure that all precautions are taken to maintain the privilege, including official letters from the internal legal department to authorize the investigation.
5. It is important to note that any interview in this manner can be stressful for an interviewee. Nervousness is common, and it's certainly not indicative of guilt.

of progression can also help investigators in assessing witness credibility. It could be revealing when interviewees attempt to backtrack and rework previous answers to shoehorn excuses for problematic behavior. Work in more open-ended questions as well, to allow the witness to explain all relevant information. Focus on the witness's impressions and stories.

Documents are another powerful interview tool when used correctly, and relevant documentary evidence should be weaved into critical junctures throughout the interview. Be sure to prepare these documents ahead of time by ordering and organizing them well in advance of the interview, so that they are easily accessible when needed. For more difficult or evasive witnesses, it can help to lead with the documents on difficult questions. Asking the witness to walk you through the documents and explain specific terms and phrases helps jog witnesses' memories and can elicit more truthful information. If a document is written by someone else, consider asking questions like "What does this mean?" or "How did you interpret this?" If a document is written by the witness, consider asking questions like "What did you mean here?" or "Why did you say it like this?"

Finally, while remembering to always be respectful and professional, do not accept unbelievable explanations. It is perfectly understandable to press for better understandings of critical issues, so be assertive without being aggressive. Be persistent and test every witness. Make sure to get their full explanations on the record.

Preparing the Final Report

After the document review and witness interview phases are complete, the investigators must distill all of that information into a comprehensive and objective report. Bear in mind that the investigator is not the "change agent," meaning that the investigators themselves are not the appropriate individuals to recommend disciplinary measures to or explain how internal processes and procedures should be reformed. The goal of the report is to lay out all of the factual information uncovered throughout the interview so that the ultimate decision makers have everything they need to assess the allegations and make the final determinations—including discipline and other remedies.

The report itself should include an introduction that outlines the allegations and the elements of the offense at issue. Following the introduction should be a section detailing the procedural steps taken during the investigation. The main body of the report should involve a detailed outline of all the facts and evidence uncovered, along with an analysis of whether the available evidence satisfies the elements of the alleged offense. The body of the report should methodically and chronologically walk through the facts by utilizing both documentary evidence and witness statements. Weave in credibility determinations, assessing the weight of each testimonial statement. Acknowledge any contradictions in the facts and provide possible explanations for those inconsistencies. Apply the facts to the elements of the offense and provide an ultimate analysis. Your conclusion should reach a determination as to whether the allegations were substantiated. Finally, remember that sloppy reports lead to sloppy results, which often leads to unwanted litigation.

Disciplinary Authority

After completing the report, it should be handed off to the ultimate decision maker to determine what will happen next. Companies that want to stay ahead of the game may consider convening an investigations committee. Investigations committees can serve as useful cornerstones of high-functioning investigations programs by acting as an impartial final authority to monitor open cases, close out cases, administer discipline as appropriate, and oversee the development of the broader investigations program. Committees like these will go a long way with government regulators in demonstrating compliance. Ideally, the committee should convene at the conclusion of each investigation to review the report, the underlying facts, and the investigatory analysis. The committee's ultimate disciplinary or remedial decisions should be prompt, fair, and consistent with applicable policies and comparable incidents. Consistency is incredibly important here. Uneven discipline threatens to undermine the investigation program's integrity and legitimacy—along with the overarching company culture—if employees begin losing faith in the process.

14

HUMAN RESOURCES CONSIDERATIONS

Silvia Van Dusen

The human resources (HR) function in an organization can at times be thought of as completely an administrative function. In reality, the HR function is critical to creating, continuously improving, and maintaining a culture that supports corporate excellence. One of the cornerstones of corporate excellence is compliance. Compliance is the first step to "doing the right thing" or exemplifying the corporate value of integrity often found in many corporate guiding principles or values.

Compliance is often complex for an organization to achieve. The more multifaceted and diverse an organization becomes, the more likely it is to find challenges with meeting requirements. Labor laws not only vary globally but also within regions. The labor law landscape is quite different even from state to state in the United States. This complexity is one of the reasons why HR or labor law compliance can be challenging and difficult for companies to achieve; the other and sometimes more powerful challenge to compliance is the perception that compliance takes away from flexibility and creativity. In modern businesses and in many industries the desire for agility and creativity is directly correlated with competitiveness and overall business success. The drive to be first to market allows for agility and creativity but may appear to be hindered by the requirement to be in compliance. As example, there are many labor laws related to how people should be paid, when they are to take rest and meal periods, and how overtime is calculated. When a company is working on a "hot" project, these laws without good processes and understanding may be perceived as obstacles to getting the work done. This is probably one of the reasons the US Ninth Circuit Court of Appeals has seen an increased in wage and hour lawsuits, in the last several years, especially in class actions. According to Seyfarth Shaw's 2021 class action litigation report, 2021 showed the highest settlement numbers in their report's history.[1]

The challenge of compliance is not only when an organization has grown, but this challenge is likely to happen to newly established companies without the means and processes to have the internal or external resources to clearly understand and manage all the regulatory requirements.

Human Resources Role in Compliance

It is not unusual to have HR be one of the last departments created when a company is in its infancy. This is unfortunate, since HR can help build the foundation for compliance to be in the fiber of the company culture by creating an HR-compliant organization starting with the founders.

1. Seyfarth Shaw, LLP, *Workplace Class Action Litigation*, 2022, 18th ed., https://www.seyfarth.com/news-insights/seyfarths-18th-annual-workplace-class-action-report-2021-spikes-highest-settlement-numbers-in-reports-history.html

DOI: 10.4324/9781351107242-18

Since HR is seldom part of the start-up process, it is important for HR to build a compliance review system as soon as it becomes a functional area of the organization and make sure to create the strategies to build a learning culture and corporate respect for subject matter experts. In the HR arena, compliance review systems provide an opportunity for HR leadership to truly develop knowledge within the organization, partnering with every aspect of the business to ensure HR compliance is incorporated in business decisions. When HR is involved as a partner in the way business is done, then it is no longer looked upon as an obstacle to getting things done, but an actual asset. HR becomes the subject matter expert to help the business achieve goals, live values, and create the desired culture. HR experts must be willing to engage in the business and understand the business strategy to help the business achieve compliance without sacrificing culture or goals. The balance between, culture, compliance, and strategy is one of the key contributions HR leaders can provide to an organization.

In order for HR leaders to contribute at this higher level, the HR structure has to be designed to provide an agile, compliance-knowledgeable, strategic, and culture-centered HR business unit. The HR business unit has to be developed with the competencies required to be successful in the overall business. With the understanding that each business is different, the structure and competencies required are not the same from industry to industry as well as the size or type of company. The creation of the HR structure and competency model should start with the alignment to the company mission, vision, and values. As the structure is created the individuals in the HR roles must have the required competencies to build credibility in the organization. This credibility is built differently in each organization. In organizations where creativity is highly valued, the HR unit must have creativity as part of their competencies. Although, an HR person may have the HR functional competencies, they may not have the business competency to be successful in a certain business. We often call this "fit", but a more objective, easier-to-align approach to fit is to understand the competencies necessary to align with the business, including making sure the person has the right attributes to conform to the organization's compliance requirements. This is extremely important when organizations "parachute in" top executives instead of growing internal talent. When leaders are brought in from other organizations, the vetting process on behaviors is extremely important. High-level vetting should include a complete background and reference checks by an expert company, and in some cases pre-employment personality profiles and/or testing may be appropriate. There are quite a few validated instruments that may help select the right fit. Some of these instruments and tests provide insight into honesty, empathy, emotional intelligence, and compliant behavior.

This is another way HR can support the organization, by providing more objective ways to hire for fit. This is beyond the job description or hard skills; this is about aligning the true person and their behaviors to the organization. Situations such as the Uber founder incidents of harassment and Harvey Weinstein incidents would be completely preventable with a strong alignment in the organization and some level of autonomy for HR. When Uber received the recommendations from their internal culture assessment/investigations, the recommendations by former US Attorney General Eric H. Holder included[2]

> "Employment Actions. The Human Resources organization should take employment actions delegated to the Human Resources organization by the Board and Special Committee." And "Use Compensation to Hold Senior Leaders Accountable. The Board should consider incorporating ethical business practices, diversity and inclusion, and other values from Uber's Business Code of Conduct into its executive compensation program. Experience shows that compensation provides a powerful tool for creating incentives for behavior,

2. *Washington Post* (2017), Holder Report Recommendations for Uber, https://apps.washingtonpost.com/g/documents/business/read-holder-report-recommendations-for-uber/2470/

> and reinforcing a company's values. Many leading companies have incorporated similar metrics into the compensation packages for senior executives as a way of ensuring that their compensation practices reward conduct that is consistent with the cultural environment that they hope to create."

Due to some of these situations/incidents, we may see in the future a higher possibility of HR reporting in to the board with some protection and independence from executive leadership.

Knowing HR or having HR subject matter expertise is not sufficient to create culture or understand strategy, and most of all it does not build credibility in the organization.

HR must go beyond compliance knowledge. HR must have the ability and competencies to mesh their compliance knowledge and build the desires culture with the understanding of how the compliance elements can be incorporated into an organization without negatively affecting the desired or already created culture. A culture of compliance is generated by the vision, values, and belief systems of the organizational leadership, and it has to be a nonnegotiable standard in the organization. Without this level of commitment from the ownership or leadership, compliance will eventually drift and become secondary to other elements in the organization. Doing the right thing and doing things right must be first among other equally important business requirements. Leaders within the organization must also believe that the organization is better because it has high ethical standard. It is the responsibility of the senior leaders and/or the board in organizations to clearly send the message via their actions that achieving compliance is not an obstacle to achieving business goals and creating a successful organization.

Entrepreneurs and New Companies

Often new companies are established based on a vision or a dream of the founder. Entrepreneurs are often driven by the excitement of creating a new company and making the vision or dream a reality. Often new companies are started with limited resources and ingenuity. This creates a culture from inception of "getting things done" and valuing those team members who are committed and engaged in the vision. Often individuals who are driven to start-ups are searching for a flexible and less structured work environment. Some of these individuals are fleeing the traditional organizations with their thick handbooks, written rules, and other policies and procedures that are perceived as limiting flexibility and the fun, creative work culture. However, some of these traditional rules are in place in established companies to meet compliance requirements, and as stifling as they may seem, some may be necessary to create that compliance. Uber has had its share of bad publicity and lawsuits due to their culture of "everything goes" and lack of HR compliance structure. In a recent lawsuit, one of their female engineers claimed that when she brought up concerns about harassment, her complaints were ignored and she was later terminated.[3]

Can We Have It All?

One must ask, can you achieve the fun, agile, creative culture and still maintain compliance? Or are these polar opposites and cannot truly be achieved concurrently?

The answers to these questions may be answered by starting at the core of company culture. All companies have values, even if they have not been formally developed or established. Values are how the management or ownership of the company behaves, what they value, and how they do business.

3. Wakavayashi, D., 2018, Former Uber Engineer's Lawsuit Claims Sexual Harassment, *New York Times*, www.nytimes.com/2018/05/21/technology/uber-sexual-harassment-lawsuit.html.

Many companies that formally establish their values include in their mantra a value related to honesty or integrity in their value. The integrity value is often described or defined by "doing the right thing". For example, companies Apple has in their core values "We don't settle for anything less than excellence in every group in the company, and we have the self-honesty to admit when we're wrong and the courage to change".[4] Their self-honesty implies that they will do the right thing. Other companies such as Google say it right out in their values: "Honesty and Integrity in all we do". These values can be used as cornerstone to companies building compliance. When company management/ownership forgoes compliance to be agile, they exemplify the violation of the integrity value. When company management/ownership makes the decision to be noncompliant or fails to evaluate compliance as part of their process, they are basically saying that they will do what they want, not necessarily the right thing. Part of having integrity built into the culture and values of an organization is placing the adherence and understand of compliance as a top priority, not because you have to but because you want to. Often integrity is defined as doing the right thing, even when no one is looking or even if you can get away with not doing the right thing.

Achieving Compliance

Achieving compliance is not a result that comes from simple desire or a policy statement. A structure and a process to ensure compliance needs to be created in organizations. The achievement of compliance starts with clarity and understanding. The processes to achieve compliance need to encompass a review system/framework of questioning decisions, processes, and policies. There are internationally accepted standards, such as the International Organization for Standardization under the ISO 19600:2014 Compliance Management System,[5] with a complete framework to achieve compliance. The ISO 19600 standard is based on the principles of good governance and provides guidance for establishing, maintaining, and improving an effective and responsive compliance management system. The ISO 19600 standard was designed to be sufficiently agile to be implemented in organizations of any size or industry.

Many companies may not be able to invest or do not have the resources to implement a full ISO standard. This resource constraint should not be an obstacle for creating a review system/framework to achieve compliance. A simple internal process such as the compliance review framework outlined below may be sufficient if well designed and implemented to build a culture of compliance. The key to any compliance framework is leadership's willing to challenge their decisions, conduct objective research on decisions before they are implemented, and have the ability and willingness to restructure or change the decision in order to be in compliance. These added steps to decision-making may appear at times to be unnecessary, but due to the dynamic nature of compliance and the constant change in the regulatory environment, a lack of process can end up becoming compliance errors by ignorance that could be at certain times considered leadership negligence.

A compliance review system does not have to be difficult, it can be quite agile and simple.

A review system/framework to achieve HR compliance can be as simple as:

1. At the decision/action step, evaluate all elements that contribute to the decision. This includes any decision in the organization of substance. Decisions that may need to be reviewed for compliance and ethics can include, but are not limited to, rewards systems, business decisions on contracts, decisions on sales strategy, and product performance decisions.

4. Sabutey F., 2017, The 7 Core Values Which Made Apple the Most Valuable Brand in the World, *Expand*, www.expandgh.com/7-core-values-which-made-apple-most-valuable-brand-in-the-world/.
5. ISO 19600:2014, Edition 1, www.iso.org/standard/62342.html, revised to ISO 37301:2021, https://www.iso.org/standard/75080.html.

2. Review the decision/action with subject matter expert for compliance. This can include outside subject matter experts such as attorneys, board of directors, or other third parties. Internal subject matter experts can also be used as long as the culture allows for candid feedback and authority to question the decisions/actions.
3. Have the subject matter expert conduct research to confirm changes in regulations or requirements do not affect action or decision. This may include looking at risks and conducting risk analysis. The subject matter expert may at this moment recommend further evaluation, such as an investigation, or review any other processes in the organization preventing ethical behavior or compliance.
4. Either move forward or adjust decision/action in order to be in 100% compliance.
5. Incorporate and communicate the compliance or new knowledge within the company.
6. Educate leadership on the changes and how they may or may not affect the business.

Step number three is critical to an effective review system. The subject matter expert must be a person who confirms the compliance via research and current information, not do "what has always been done" or what they think they know. This is particularly true in labor law compliance. The ever-changing landscape and constant significant changes, even from month to month, can affect compliance if the loop is not properly followed.

Steps five and six create sustainability. Without the incorporation and communication with leadership, the compliance is not sustainable. These steps in the review system/framework also create the process of accountability and a learning organization. They force the people within the organization to maintain their knowledge and skills in the areas of compliance. As most companies have learned, ignorance in HR compliance is not bliss and can be very costly.

The Technology Challenge

As much as technology improves our lives and continues to provide incredible opportunities for efficiencies, learning, and growth, it also creates challenges in many areas.

Technology has changed the way we interact and how we work. The question is, how do companies stay ahead of the compliance issues that may be created by technology. For example, before email, texting, and other digital communication platforms, individuals would take vacation and truly leave the work behind. Now with technology it is not unusual for people to stay connected to work while on vacation. Some of the compliance questions related to this example are whether they are really on vacation? and whether they should be paid for this time. The same question applies to daily work: people are connected on the weekends and after normal work hours. Some countries, such as France, have actually created legislation to address the vacation and after hours infringement on personal life versus work life created by technology.[6]

Another example of how technology has a potential impact on compliance can be seen by how social media has blurred the line between business and personal lives. Behaviors either in business or personal life can become public in social media very quickly, making individuals and companies accountable to the public and/or their customers. An illustration of how technology has created compliance accountability is in allegations of sexual harassment or hostile work places becoming public via social media, almost putting the companies on notice to take action to become compliant or suffer the consequences to their reputation. The ride-sharing service company Uber has had many scandals initiated by social media that have resulted in the departure of top executives, including one

6. Morris, D., 2017, New French Law Bars Work Email After Hours., *Fortune*, https://fortune.com/2017/01/01/french-right-to-disconnect-law/.

of the founders. This sends the message to companies on how powerful technology has become in holding accountability for compliance.

Organizational Culture: The Real Path to Compliance

While achieving compliance is a basic requirement for a business, the business culture is really what ultimately decides if compliance is achieved. The root of the word culture comes from the Latin *cultus*, which means "to care." The Society for Human Resources Management (SHRM) defines organizational culture as what defines the proper way to behave within the organization. Organizational culture sets the context for everything an enterprise does.[7]

What does that really mean? An organization's culture is its values (what the organization cares about), behaviors, assumptions, beliefs, and habits—basically what the organization stands for and how it makes decisions. It has been said that individuals and business stand for what they tolerate. Therefore, if you tolerate behaviors that lead to noncompliance, the business culture becomes a culture that accepts noncompliance or does not care about noncompliance.

Culture in a business is present from the very start with or without deliberate design. Culture normally starts with the founder: when people start a business, they begin with a rudimentary vision of what the business is going to become, how they are going to work to achieve their goals, and their values. Values at the early stages of a business are based on the basic personal values of the founder. Since normally the business is based on the behaviors of the first employees, this is normally the founder. When a founder first chooses to hire people, they have a tendency to hire people who are like them. This starts to create the first steps toward culture. Most businesses are started by friends and/or family members, so the first people are not only hired or join the organization for their technical expertise but also because they share a common vision and have similar backgrounds, and potentially the same values. However, this is when vision starts becoming dynamic and changing, as people with different experiences, knowledge, and backgrounds come into the organization. When organizational leaders choose to not spend time on culture during the early stages, culture can be heavily influenced by different people in the organization, and smaller subcultures within the organization may develop.

This culture development and subculture development can happen in both new and in mature organizations. In larger, more mature organizations, subcultures can develop in different departments, divisions, business units, and/or subsidiaries. New leadership in departments of business units can affect culture and create organizational subcultures. These cultural misalignments in organizations can be detrimental to any leader or to Human Resources compliance efforts.

Cultural misalignment may be a root cause when pockets or areas of an organization behave less ethical or are less compliant than other areas of the organization. Ethical breaches that may end up in compliance breach may start with misalignment. Some examples of cultural misalignment and how it can affect an organization can be seen in the Wells Fargo case. In April 2018 the *National Law Journal* reported that Wells Fargo was assessed $1 billion in penalties due to violations of consumer protection laws. Additionally, it was reported in August 2018 that Wells Fargo Bank would pay a $2 billion civil penalty to settle claims that its home mortgages contained misstated information, in violation of the Financial Institutions Reform, Recovery, and Enforcement Act of 1989.[8]

7. SHRM, 2018, Understanding and Developing Organizational Culture. www.shrm.org/resourcesandtools/tools-and-samples/toolkits/pages/understandinganddevelopingorganizationalculture.aspx.
8. Scarcella, M., 2018, Documents: Feds Hit Wells Fargo for $1B Penalty for Consumer Abuses., *National Law Journal*, www.law.com/nationallawjournal/2018/04/20/documents-feds-hit-wells-fargo-for-1b-penalty-for-consumer-abuses/.

Originally, Wells Fargo claimed these unethical and noncompliant actions were not mandated by Wells Fargo Bank and were not present at every branch, business unit, or division. They claimed that the behaviors that became norms in certain areas of the business with certain individuals, units, or branches. However, in a press release dated April 10, 2017, Tim Sloan, president and CEO of Wells Fargo, commented on the findings regarding the board's investigation into the company's retail banking sales practices. Sloan stated:

> "Nothing is more important to Wells Fargo's future than ensuring we have a culture and operating model that works for all our stakeholders—our customers, team members, investors, and communities," Sloan said. "With that principle in mind, we will ensure this report becomes a powerful complement to the ongoing self-examination of our culture and practices that we have been conducting as a leadership team and a company.
>
> "We've changed leadership; held executives accountable; changed how we compensate and lead our retail bankers; centralized key control functions, such as risk management and human resources; and taken steps to promote a workplace where team members are encouraged to raise concerns. We have also retained independent third parties to provide their advice and feedback to help us identify possibilities for additional improvements across the company."[9]

Wells Fargo suffered greatly as an organization due to this misalignment. They had to answer to their customers, their reputation was blemished, and their financial consequences have been significant. As stated above, the compliance failures were cultural and based on the acceptable behaviors within the organization and its reward system. We can find similar situations of subculture where unethical behaviors resulted in noncompliance, such as when the now-infamous Arthur Andersen shredded documents associated with the Enron case. The issue with Arthur Andersen is deeper than the Enron situation. Arthur Andersen created this unethical behavior, as it started to reward people not for being good auditors and following all the audit principles; instead they rewarded their auditors for securing consulting assignments from the audits, creating an immediate conflict of interest and the foundation for noncompliance.[10] These unethical decisions were created by subcultures within the organizations, where leadership failed to look at what subcultures were developing within their organizations and put in place sufficient processes/systems to ensure the way of doing business or treating their customers were ethical.

One of the key contributions made by a strong Human Resources presence in an organization is to be accountable for the identification of the true organizational culture and ensure the culture is ethical. A culture without ethics cannot be a culture that embraces compliance. A compliant culture cannot exist without a strong ethical foundation/framework. Human Resources can create the process to support/create the culture of compliance with some of the following processes.

On-Boarding Programs

A strong on-boarding program provides new people joining the organization with the proper expectations. All people joining the organization are provided with the same set of standards, behavioral expectations, a review of policies/procedures, and clear direction of what to do if the expected

9. Business Wire, 2017, Wells Fargo Statement Regarding Board Investigation into Community Banks, Retail Sales Practices, https://newsroom.wf.com/press-release/community-banking-and-small-business/wells-fargo-statement-regarding-board
10. McRoberts, F., 2002, The Fall of Andersen, *Chicago Tribune*, www.chicagotribune.com/news/chi-0209010315sep01-story.html.

behaviors in the organization are not as defined. The organization requires a personal commitment from the individual that they agree with the culture, ethical standards, and procedures of the organization.

Awareness Training

In order for anything to become second nature or part of the way things are truly done, constant communication of expectations and how to handle situations must be present. Creating an ethical culture is not done by a "tell it and leave it" approach. It is done by repetition, constant communication, and exemplification of what is expected.

Thoughtful and meaningful annual awareness training programs reinforcing the culture requirements provide for a safe place to discuss and address potential issues. These meaningful discussions help redirect and prevent noncompliant behaviors. These type of awareness programs only work if they have the full support or leadership. They need to be part of the way the organization communicates, valued by leadership, well developed, and engaging. This requires constant redesign and introspection by the company leadership. A thoughtful and meaningful annual awareness program would incorporate a review of compliance policies, new compliance requirements, samples of industry noncompliance issues, awareness and recognition of compliant behaviors by individuals in the organization, and feedback from participants to continuously improve the awareness training.

Policies and Procedures for Safely Reporting Noncompliance

It is imperative that Human Resources leads the development and implementation of well-developed policies and procedures for reporting any misalignment with compliance expectations. These policies must incorporate any regulations regarding the process for addressing noncompliance, expectations, consequences, and protection to those who report issues. There are many regulations currently in effect that protect individuals against retaliation for reporting noncompliant behaviors. Such regulations include the Whistleblower Protection Act of 1989 and the Whistleblower Enhancement Protection Act of 2012, as well as many other federal and state regulations, such as sexual harassment laws, discrimination laws, and environmental laws providing protection to individuals who report regulatory violations or noncompliance. In order for these policies to be really absorbed and incorporated in the day-to-day way of doing business, the policies need to be drafted to reach the organization at almost an emotional level. The policies cannot be perceived as just rules that collect dust. They need to truly connect the company culture. They need to be written in a way that they reach the population of the organization. For example, if the organizational culture is highly creative and fun, writing a policy that would be only handed via paper distribution without video and other modern communication platforms like social media, it would be unlikely the policy would reach the intended audience or that it would be even incorporated in day-to-day business. Not only is it not effective to have policies that are not incorporated into the organization, but it actually hurts the business to have policies that are not followed. Organizations need to take a pragmatic approach when writing an implementing policies and procedures. It is the role of Human Resources to build these procedures so they speak to the workforce, making sure they are relevant to the organization and at the same time compliant. This is a balance between a legal/compliant policies and engaging employee communications.

Accountability Processes

Having all the onboarding, training, and policies in place is worthless unless the company actually holds itself and everyone accountable. Accountability can be separated into audits and actions.

Audits

An organization can build accountability for compliance by auditing. Auditing can be done internally by building self-auditing processes based on industry acceptable standards or by hiring third parties. Human Resources leadership can be the champion to ensure third-party auditors focus on the correct areas of compliance and lead the organization to taking the proper actions when failures are identified. These audits are about living the values of the organization (self-governance). Self-governance is about being purpose-inspired in leading with moral authority/values.[11]

Actions

To create accountability in an organization, leadership must be willing to take action on audit findings and behaviors. Accountability has to be at every level in the organization. Accountability does not need to be punitive, unless the behaviors are such that there are no other alternatives. Accountability is really about the way people are rewarded what they are rewarded for, as referenced above in the situation with Arthur Andersen: how training and development programs are evaluated and decided upon. The actions to achieve accountability include the due diligence to understand the problems, find the process failures, and be willing to give people the direction to fix them. Address the failures that are behavioral in a consistent and immediate manner.

Creating an Ethical Organization From a Human Resources Viewpoint

Ethical behaviors in organizations are directly aligned with a culture that embraces compliance. If organizational leaders use a consistent approach to ensure their behaviors are ethical, the question of compliance only becomes a question of ensuring knowledge of the compliance requirements. The model previously described can ensure compliance, but without true ethical leadership, the value of ethics, and integrity, the model of compliance loop will not be truly effective.

Ethical behaviors in an organization must start from the executive level. The expectations on how people behave what is tolerated is defined at the executive level and also confirmed. In order for this to happen, all executives within an organization must have the same behavioral standards, and the guiding principles and values must be exemplified the same way by each executive in the team. When there is ethical misalignment at the executive level, the organization will not be able to create a culture of compliance. The Human Resources leadership role, among others, is to be the censurer of the ethical alignment. Human Resources has the needed visibility across the organization to the way decisions are made; it is the role of HR to support each vertical of the organization to align to the corporate guiding principles. Human Resources, regardless of the industry or size of the company, is the department that interacts with every other part of the organization. HR can influence many of the most important decisions and can therefore have maximum impact on building and maintaining a culture of compliance.

It is not unusual to hear people in organizations express the point of view that the rules do not evenly apply to everyone in the organization, that some departments or executives make their own rules. If not carefully managed or evaluated, this can eventually turn into unethical decision-making, cultural misalignment, and eventual noncompliance. This is particularly true if senior leadership or ownership has a blind spot for a certain department or people. Often when the "rain makers," such as sales executives, technology, developers, or senior technology experts, may break the rules, the organization rationalizes the toleration of the ethical breach because the business is dependent on their

11. LRN, 2016, Ethics and Compliance, Program Effectiveness Report, https://content.lrn.com/research-insights/2016-e-c-program-effectiveness-report.

technical knowledge or outputs. Once an individual or individuals in an organization are given a free pass not to follow the foundational rules that ensure compliance, ethics, and value alignment, then the erosion of a culture of compliance starts. Human Resources has failed the organization if these breaches are accepted without consequences, rationalized, or tolerated. For example, if one executive of the organization decides he/she will allow their employees to work remotely, although the organization does not allow or have systems in place for remote work to be applied equitably within the organization, the executive is starting to create a subculture within the organization. Tolerating the subculture or not following the company structure and system can eventually deteriorate to unethical behaviors, not necessarily from the executives but from other parts of the organization where the view of not following the rules does not have consequences. Therefore, coming to the conclusion that not following the rules, even when it may be an ethical or compliance breach is accepted within the organization. One way to avoid this type of issues is for Human Resources to help align the business and department needs with the processes and systems within the organization. Human Resources can lead the management to clarity and ensuring inconsistencies are addressed appropriately, so alignment in organizational behaviors is part of the management process. In order for this behavioral alignment to be effective, the leadership of the organization must believe the company culture or the team is more important than personal beliefs or ensure that their personal belief system is properly aligned to the company's values. Value alignment can be considered the "fit" of people in the organization. Companies need to first understand if their stated values are actually the way they do business. Stated values versus actual actions could be the reason Google recently eliminated the "Do no harm" value out of their stated values. This happened after Google was criticized for their involvement with artificial intelligence government contracts.

Human Resources Compliance and the Company Board

The main role of the board of directors of an organization is to protect the shareholders' value, and it is considered the highest governing authority within the management structure in an established organization or publicly traded company. Many non-public companies also have boards of directors, and many smaller companies have advisory boards.

Long-established boards of directors for public companies have structured processes to ensure the business is maximizing shareholder value. Eva Sage-Gavin, in her article published in *Human Resources Executive*, proposes that the top Human Resources professional should have independence and a direct line of communication with the board of directors to address risks related to talent management.[12] According to Equilar, HR's board involvement has made some significant increases in the last few years. From 2005 to 2017, the number of HR executives on US public boards almost tripled, from 84 to a record high of 243. Although this increase is impressive, there's still more work to be done, considering that only 3.7% of US HR professionals who are named corporate officers have a seat on their company's board.[13] It appears that boards are starting to see the value of including HR experts on their boards to grapple with compliance issues related to the #MeToo movement, diversity, and rising employee activism, according to *Workforce* magazine. One example of this change is the naming of Kathleen Wilson-Thompson to Tesla's board of directors.[14] Tesla, has had its share of HR compliance challenges, including lawsuits from African American current and former employees

12. Sage-Gavin, E., 2018, Taking Talent Management to the Board, *Human Resources Executive*, http://hrexecutive.com/chros-take-talent-management-on-board/.
13. Equilar, 2018, The Rise of the CHRO: From the Corner Office to the Boardroom, www.equilar.com/blogs/356-rise-of-the-chro-in-the-boardroom.html.
14. Rafterm, M., 2019, Tesla's CHRO Director Pick Points to a New Era, Workforce, www.equilar.com/blogs/356-rise-of-the-chro-in-the-boardroom.html.

and contractors accusing Tesla of rampant racism and race-based harassment, according to the *New York Times*.[15]

As the future of compliance continues to be shaped, the necessity for HR professionals to prepare themselves to become board members is imperative, and the transformation of boards toward having HR on their boards may provide the perfect solution to prevent and manage compliance in organizations.

Compliance and the New Gig Economy

The gig economy is a fairly new term to refer to the independent contractors or short-term workers. The gig economy has become more popular in the last few years due to remote workers and new nature of work, with companies like Uber and Lyft that have built their business model around a mobile applications and work being done by freelancers or independent contractors. For example, Intuit estimated that in 2018, about 34% of the American workforce engaged in some type of gig economy type of work, and it estimated that it would increase to 40% in by 2020.[16] The trends of a mobile, less controlled workforce brings about a whole new set of compliance challenges to companies and individuals. In traditional standard company-employee relationship, the responsibility and liability to ensure compliance rest almost completely on the company. Gig work assignments challenge the traditional model and starts creating a potential shared responsibility between the contractor and gig worker. This shared responsibility may require a whole new thinking on how to structure work, changing all the assumptions on how systems, processes, behavior management, and culture are established.

Since the gig economy is new, there's not much history or knowledge on how to actually establish organizational compliance with gig workers. There have been some court challenges to the definition of independent contractors as to when someone preforming work for a company is truly independent or a gig worker, versus when the individual may actually be an employee of the organization. In 2018 the California Supreme Court made some additional clarification to the definition of an independent contractor in *Dynamex Corp. Inc. v. California*. The California Supreme Court clarification created the ABC test in order to classify as an independent contractor. This test requires for all three requirements to be met by the individual, the requirements are (Kim, 2018):[17]

- A: The worker is free from the control and direction of the hiring entity in connection with the performance of the work, both under the contract for the performance of the work and in fact.
- B: The worker performs work that is outside the usual course of the hiring entity's business.
- C: The worker is customarily engaged in an independently established trade, occupation, or business of the same nature as the work performed.

The second requirement has the potential for analysis. For example, are Lyft and Uber affected by this decision? Probably not, since the usual course of business for both Lyft and Uber is technology, they provide a software application for ride-sharing, and they are not in the driving business. Based on this decision, Lyft and Uber would have a difficult time having a software developer as an independent

15. Hepler, L., 2018, Menial Tasks, Slurs and Swastikas: Many Black Workers at Tesla Say They Faced Racism, *New York Times*, www.nytimes.com/2018/11/30/business/tesla-factory-racism.html.
16. Gillespie, P., 2017, Intuit: Gig Economy Is 34% of US Workforce, *CNN Money*, https://money.cnn.com/2017/05/24/news/economy/gig-economy-intuit/index.html.
17. Kim, T., 2018, The Dynamex Decision: the California Supreme Court Restricts Use of Independent Contractors, *Sheppard Muling, Labor & Employment Law Blog*, www.laboremploymentlawblog.com/2018/05/articles/class-actions/dynamex-decision-independent-contractors/. In September 2019, California Governor Gavin Newsom signed Assembly Bill (AB) 5 into law, which, as discussed in this section, addresses the employment status of workers when the hiring entity claims the worker is an independent contractor, not an employee, see: https://www.dir.ca.gov/dlse/faq_independentcontractor.htm.

contractor. Regardless of where the court battles regarding the definition of an independent contractor fall in the future, the growth in gig workers is likely to continue. As our society continues to value independence, flexibility, and time off, the shift toward less structured work will continue. This means that organizations will need to shift their policies, systems, procedures, and culture to accommodate the changes in the way work will be performed.

When work is being performed by an independent contractor or gig worker, the ways of working take on the values of the individual doing the work, similar to the values of the founder or entrepreneur of a company, therefore behaviors with the people doing the work will vary significantly without shared systems, processes, and values. This could potentially mean that the company providing the product will have very limited influence on how the work is being performed and the behaviors of those preforming it. For example, an e-commerce company hires independent drivers to deliver its products to residents although a contract may be in place on expectations on the results, such as timely delivery in a legally compliant professional manner. These expectations not being met may result in cancellation of the contract, but unfortunately with an unsupervised self-guiding workforce, the company not be aware of the ethical or compliance breach for a while. There's a possibility that technology advances will provide some of the foundation to help organizations manage and confirm compliance for gig workers. Consumer feedback may be sufficient to create some compliance, but this takes time to gather. Potentially, analytics and predictive analysis models will become the answer to managing gig workers. Sites such as Yelp can score the way people work, not just the companies. Some of these analytics are in place and working quite well in the area of service feedback for some companies such as Lyft, DoorDash, Uber, and other consumer-facing gig workers. The service feedback is probably not sufficient feedback to confirm or create a culture of compliance.

Without a feedback system, companies addressing the relationship with the gig worker who fails to follow the expectations of the company has to be almost immediate. The danger with these feedback processes is that they have to be validated and carefully navigated, since the relationship based on how is managed can shift from an independent contractor or gig worker to an employee-employer relationship, creating different compliance challenges.

The shift of the way work is done from the traditional 9-to-5 model to a more fluid, flexible model with each individual contributor has more impact on how the work is perform and will only increase the complexity of compliance, not decrease it. Company leaders, especially HR leaders, will have to reinvent the way culture is built to positively impact organizations employing gig workers to ensure compliance. Some companies are even considering offering benefits to gig workers to stay competitive and attract talent, but these companies may face obstacles related to the current legal definition of who is an employee and how the employee-employer relationship is defined.

Key Ending Points

- A culture of compliance must come from top leadership and the board.
- Human Resources is the business area in the company that defines and develops the internal culture to ensure compliance.
- Compliance in Human Resources is dynamic, and organizations must stay current in order to achieve compliance.
- Building a consistent system to ensure compliance in the Human Resources/labor area is critical to building the culture. Compliance happens with consistency and systems.
- Human Resources must have a certain level of autonomy to ensure compliance.
- Compliance does not have to be an enemy for an entrepreneur.
- Company boards or advisory boards would benefit from having Human Resources professionals as a key board member.
- Independent contractors and the new gig economy are reshaping the way companies can control compliance.

15

SELF-REGULATORY ORGANIZATION'S ROLE IN PROMOTING ETHICAL BEHAVIOR IN INDUSTRY

Laura McNamire

Alternative dispute resolution (ADR) offers an important alternative to litigation, which can be a cost-prohibitive and extremely protracted method of resolving conflict, sometimes spanning years before reaching its conclusion. Arbitration and mediation can provide an economical and efficient way to obtain a much more timely resolution of disputes. However, some have raised concerns with the fairness of consumer arbitration, and Congress has in recent years sought to address those concerns by introducing bills to limit or ban consumer arbitration altogether.

The Financial Industry Regulatory Authority (FINRA) is the self-regulatory organization (SRO) for the securities industry and operates the largest securities dispute resolution forum in the United States. This chapter will give a high-level overview of FINRA and its ADR forum and highlight some of the issues raised in the current debate about the fairness of consumer arbitration. This chapter will also delve into a comparison between FINRA arbitration and litigation, and discuss the differences between FINRA's arbitration program and other arbitration programs.

Overview of FINRA and Its ADR Forum

What Is a Self-Regulatory Organization (SRO)?

An SRO is an organization that exercises regulatory authority over an industry or profession. It plays a vital role in promoting ethical behavior in the industry that it regulates. It has enormous power to create and enforce rules promoting ethics, integrity, and honesty. In order to continue doing business in their industry, members of an SRO must comply with these rules.

FINRA is a primary example of an SRO. It is a not-for-profit organization authorized by Congress to protect America's investors by making sure the broker-dealer industry operates fairly and honestly. It plays a critical role in ensuring the integrity of America's financial system—all at no cost to taxpayers. Working under the supervision of the Securities and Exchange Commission (SEC), FINRA writes and enforces rules, examines securities firms for compliance with those rules, fosters market transparency, and educates investors.

DOI: 10.4324/9781351107242-19

FINRA oversees approximately 630,000 brokers and more than 3,600 broker-dealers across the country, and analyzes billions of daily market events.[1] In 2018, FINRA brought more than 900 disciplinary actions against registered brokers and firms, levied $61 million in fines, ordered $25.5 million in restitution to harmed investors, and referred more than 900 fraud and insider trading cases to the SEC and other agencies for litigation and/or prosecution.[2]

As an SRO, FINRA is dedicated to protecting investors and safeguarding market integrity in a manner that facilitates vibrant capital markets. FINRA fulfills its mission of investor protection and market integrity by creating and enforcing rules designed to ensure the following:

- Every investor receives the basic protections they deserve.
- Anyone who sells a securities product has been tested, qualified, and licensed.
- Every securities product advertisement used is truthful and is not misleading.
- Any securities product sold to an investor is suitable for that investor's needs.
- Investors receive complete disclosure about the investment product before purchase.

FINRA touches virtually every aspect of the securities business, from registering and educating all industry participants to examining securities firms, writing rules, enforcing those rules and the federal securities laws, informing and educating the investing public, providing trade reporting and other industry utilities, and administering the largest dispute resolution forum for investors and firms.

FINRA Dispute Resolution Services

FINRA's dispute resolution forum—FINRA Dispute Resolution Services—oversees the resolution of securities disputes through two non-judicial proceedings: arbitration and mediation. Arbitration and mediation are two distinct ways of resolving securities and business disputes between and among investors, brokerage firms, and individual brokers, and offer a prompt and inexpensive means of resolving issues. FINRA administers between 4,000 and 8,500 arbitrations and numerous mediations annually. FINRA maintains a diverse roster of over 7,800 arbitrators and numerous mediators to resolve disputes.[3]

Arbitration

Arbitration is similar to going to court but is usually faster, cheaper, and less complex than litigation. It is a formal alternative to litigation in which two or more parties select a neutral third party, called an arbitrator, to resolve a dispute. By arbitrating a claim, you cannot have the same matter decided by a court of law. In resolving disputes through arbitration, an arbitrator or panel (consisting of three arbitrators) will listen to the arguments set forth by the parties, study the testimonial and/or documentary evidence, and then render a decision. When an arbitration case goes to hearing in a FINRA arbitration, it takes approximately 17 months on average for the case to be decided.[4] The arbitrator's decision, called an award, is final and binding. There is no appeal process through FINRA arbitration, and only very limited grounds upon which a judge can grant a motion to vacate the award.

1. www.finra.org/about.
2. www.finra.org/about/what-we-do.
3. www.finra.org/arbitration-mediation/dispute-resolution-statistics.
4. www.finra.org/arbitration-mediation/dispute-resolution-statistics.

Mediation

Mediation offers a flexible alternative to arbitration and can be initiated at any time before arbitration commences and even during an arbitration case before it concludes. It is an informal process in which a trained, impartial mediator facilitates negotiations between disputing parties, helping them find a mutually acceptable solution. Both parties in a dispute must agree to mediation.

Mediation is a voluntary process, so either party can decide to stop at any time. The mediation process is, in most cases, significantly faster than arbitration, and unlike arbitration, mediation does not impose a solution. It is not binding until the parties reach and sign a settlement agreement.

Current Debate About the Fairness of Consumer Arbitration

Congress and the SEC have the ultimate authority to restrict mandatory pre-dispute arbitration agreements in securities-related disputes. FINRA does not mandate that investor disputes must be resolved in arbitration unless the investor wants it, nor does it require its members to include pre-dispute arbitration clauses in their account opening agreements.

Over the years, there have been numerous bills introduced into Congress, and several in the states, which are aimed at limiting or eliminating mandatory arbitration. One such bill is the Forced Arbitration Injustice Repeal (FAIR) Act of 2022 (H.R. 963), which was approved by the House of Representatives on March 17, 2022, and, as of the date of this writing, awaits Senate action. If enacted, the FAIR Act would eliminate mandatory pre-dispute arbitration agreements for consumer disputes and bar class action waivers, among many other things. Another recent example is a bill signed into law by California Governor Gavin Newsom on October 13, 2019 (SB-707). It focuses on the need for arbitrator diversity in order to fairly adjudicate claims, and it requires arbitration providers to report on the demographic data of their arbitrators.

These bills, and others like them, seek to address the major criticisms of consumer arbitration. This section will highlight some of those criticisms, such as the unfairness of arbitration rules, lack of transparency, prohibition of class actions, and arbitrator diversity, and discuss how FINRA's process addresses those concerns.

Criticism 1: Arbitration Rules Are Unfair to Consumers

Rule Making Process

FINRA's rule making process is transparent and multifaceted. FINRA is regulated by the SEC, which must approve all rule changes after a period of public comment.

FINRA is in constant communication with its constituents in order to get feedback on the dispute resolution process. When they suggest a rule change to improve the process, FINRA first presents it to the National Arbitration and Mediation Committee (NAMC) for review and discussion. The NAMC provides policy guidance to FINRA's dispute resolution staff and comprises 13 investor, industry, and neutral (arbitrator and mediator) representatives. A majority of the NAMC members and its chair are public, which means that they are not affiliated with the securities industry.

The next step is to send the rule change to the FINRA board for approval. Once approved, it is then filed with the SEC. The SEC staff will review the proposal and may request changes. It is then published for public comment in the Federal Register. There is a period during which anyone can submit written comments on the proposal, which may include supporting the change or raising potential issues with it. FINRA reviews and analyzes every comment letter, and provides the SEC with written responses. Once all the issues have been analyzed, the SEC either announces its approval of the proposed rule in the Federal Register or sends it back to FINRA for consideration of changes.

In deciding whether to approve the rule change, the SEC will determine whether it is in the public interest. After receiving SEC approval, FINRA announces the new rule language and effective date in a Regulatory Notice to the public.

Hearing Location and Service of the Claim

FINRA has at least one hearing location in every state and Puerto Rico (70 in total), and the hearing is held in the location closest to where the investor lived at the time of the events giving rise to the dispute. When the investor files an arbitration claim, FINRA will serve that claim on the brokers or firm named as parties, thereby relieving the investor of the burden of having to find proper service addresses.

Senior or Seriously Ill Investors

If the investor is a senior or has a serious health issue, they can request an expedited arbitration proceeding, which reduces the amount of time it takes to complete the arbitration. Under this process, FINRA staff will complete administrative tasks, such as sending arbitrator selection lists and scheduling the initial conference call, in an expedited fashion. FINRA also asks the arbitrators to be sensitive to the needs of senior or seriously ill parties when scheduling hearing dates, resolving discovery disputes, or considering hearing postponement requests.

Arbitrator Selection Process

FINRA's arbitrator selection process allows each separately represented party an equal opportunity to choose arbitrators. The process uses a computer algorithm to randomly generate potential arbitrators from the roster. The number of arbitrators that parties select depends on the type of case. In investor cases requesting damages of more than $100,000, the parties choose from a list of ten chair-qualified public arbitrators, 15 public arbitrators, and ten non-public arbitrators. In general, public arbitrators are not affiliated with the securities industry, while non-public arbitrators have some background or experience in securities.

In 2011, FINRA changed its rules to allow parties to select all public arbitrators to hear their case. This change was in response to feedback from investors, who perceived non-public arbitrators as having a potential bias toward the securities industry. The rule change now allows any party in an investor case to strike all the non-public arbitrators on their list and select only public arbitrators for their case. Making this change helped to boost investor confidence in the fairness of the FINRA dispute resolution forum and in the arbitrators deciding the merits of their cases.

Arbitrator Removal

Once an arbitrator is appointed to a case, the FINRA director of arbitration will only remove an arbitrator from the case in very limited circumstances. Before the first hearing session begins, the director will only remove an arbitrator if it is reasonable to infer that she/he is biased, lacks impartiality, or has an interest in the outcome of the arbitration. However, in an effort to ensure the fairness of the forum for investors, close questions regarding challenges to an arbitrator by a customer will be resolved in favor of the investor.

Fees and Costs of Arbitration

FINRA's fee structure favors the investor. The industry parties contribute approximately 85% of the forum costs through the payment of member fees. Investors pay only a sliding-scale filing fee to commence an arbitration, based on the amount they are claiming in damages. The filing fee starts at $50 for claims under $1,000 and is capped at $2,250 for claims over $5 million. The investor can request a deferral of the filing fee if they are able to show that they are experiencing financial hardship.

FINRA does not require the investor to submit any further fees until their case has concluded, and the arbitrators will decide how to assess any additional fees at that time. In fact, the arbitrators may determine to assess all of the fees (including the filing fee) to the industry parties. If the arbitrators do assess fees to an investor, the investor can request that FINRA waive those fees at the end of the case due to financial hardship.

Suspension of Firms and Brokers for Nonpayment of Awards

If the arbitrators issue an award finding that a member firm or broker is liable to an investor for damages, they must pay that award within 30 days of receipt, unless they have a defense to nonpayment, such as bankruptcy. If they do not pay within that time, FINRA will begin an expedited suspension process. If the firm or broker is suspended, they can no longer do business until they pay the damages.

Criticism 2: Lack of Transparency

Arbitration Awards

FINRA, unlike most other arbitration forums, makes all of its arbitration awards available to the public at no cost. Awards can be viewed online through the Arbitration Awards Online database on the FINRA website, printed, or downloaded as text-searchable PDF files. When FINRA receives notice that an award is later vacated or confirmed by a court, it will also post a copy of the order (once received) to the Arbitration Awards Online database. This is important so that the investing public can research the award history of a securities firm or broker before doing business with them.

Statistics

FINRA provides detailed, up-to-date case statistics on its website in order to provide the public with as much data about the substance of cases as possible (while still preserving the confidentiality of individual cases). The information available includes the number of cases filed and closed each year, the most common causes of action and securities at issue, and a summary of how cases close (whether by award or settlement).

The statistics also include detailed data about the results of customer cases, highlighting the percentage of cases where the customer was awarded damages. There are also statistics regarding the damages awarded to customers when they choose a panel of three public arbitrators, as compared to having a non-public arbitrator on the panel.

FINRA also provides detailed data about its roster of over 7,800 arbitrators, including a breakdown of the number and type of arbitrators in each hearing location. There is a map that indicates the current number of cases in each city, along with the number of non-public and public arbitrators that are available to serve on those cases.

Finally, FINRA provides information about the number of cases in its mediation program, what percentage have settled (between 78% and 86%),[5] and the average turnaround time.

Arbitrator Disclosure Reports

When selecting arbitrators, parties want as much information as possible about who will be deciding their case. Accordingly, FINRA provides parties with a detailed arbitrator disclosure report for each arbitrator to use when they select their panel. Each report contains information about the potential

5. www.finra.org/arbitration-mediation/dispute-resolution-statistics.

arbitrator's employment history, education, relevant training, disclosure/conflict information, and a narrative section providing any additional information. The report also lists all of the awards that the arbitrator has issued so that parties may review the details of those cases and how the arbitrator ruled. Finally, the report lists all open FINRA cases that the arbitrator is assigned to, including the name of counsel in those cases. This is important so that parties can contact those counsel, if they choose, to get evaluations of the arbitrator's service.

Criticism 3: Class Action Waivers

Another common complaint is that arbitration agreements preclude consumers from creating or joining class actions to resolve disputes. Although investors cannot bring a class action claim in arbitration, FINRA rules specifically allow for investors to participate in class actions in court. FINRA rules state that member firms may not enforce an arbitration agreement against a member of a class action with respect to any claim that is the subject of the class action. The only exceptions to this are if the class certification is denied, the class is decertified, the investor is excluded from the class by the court, or the investor elects not to participate in the class action. FINRA rules also prohibit firms from attempting to prevent investors from participating in judicial class actions by adding waiver language to customer account agreements.

In 2014, the FINRA Board of Governors issued a decision finding that a firm had violated FINRA rules when the firm attempted to keep investors from participating in judicial class actions by adding waiver language to customer account agreements. The Board noted that FINRA rules (as approved by the SEC) provide for customer class actions to be litigated in court, while FINRA arbitration is available for customers to make individual claims against firms. The Board also noted FINRA's complementary rules to separate class actions from individual claims—one to prohibit any class actions in FINRA arbitration and a second to prevent FINRA firms from using an arbitration agreement to defeat a putative class action in court.[6] The firm entered into a settlement with FINRA, agreeing to pay a fine of $500,000 and to notify all of its customers that the class action waiver requirement had been withdrawn from its customer account agreements and was no longer in effect.

Criticism 4: Arbitrator Diversity

FINRA is committed to achieving arbitrator and mediator diversity and believes that it is vitally important that its pool of neutrals reflects the varied backgrounds of the parties who use the FINRA arbitration forum. Accordingly, FINRA has bolstered its recruitment efforts in recent years to add more diverse arbitrators—in age, gender, race, and occupation—and continues to work toward this goal.

Ongoing recruitment initiatives thus far have included more than 100 women and minority organizations nationwide to source and recruit all types of people through on-site events, targeted recruiting advertisement, and direct marketing campaigns.

To track its progress, FINRA employs a third-party consultant to survey—on an anonymous and voluntary basis—the demographics of the neutrals on its roster each year. FINRA makes that data publicly available on its website in order to provide transparency about the current makeup of its arbitrator roster. The demographics are broken down by gender, race, LGBTQ status, and age, and also include data about FINRA mediators.

6. *Department of Enforcement v. Charles Schwab & Company, Inc.*, Complaint No. 2011029760201 (April 24, 2014), https://www.finra.org/sites/default/files/NACDecision/p496824.pdf.

In 2019, 39% of new arbitrators were women (up from 26% in 2015) and 19% were African-American (up from 4% in 2015).[7] FINRA has stated that although it is encouraged by the short-term results and incremental progress, it recognizes that this is a long-term effort and will continue its efforts in this area.

FINRA Arbitration Versus Litigation

Arbitration is an important alternative to litigation as a method of resolving a dispute. Both are adversarial processes, where the opposing parties provide evidence and testimony to an impartial fact-finder, who will decide the outcome. There are many differences, however.

Arbitration is generally confidential in that the documents submitted in arbitration are not publicly available, unlike court-related filings. However, the parties themselves are not bound by confidentiality; they may share information related to their case (unless it violates any settlement terms). Only FINRA staff and arbitrators are bound by confidentiality. If an award is issued at the conclusion of the case, FINRA posts it in its Arbitration Awards Online database, which is publicly available.

Time

The time to conclude a case in litigation or arbitration varies and can be affected by many factors, including the number of parties and witnesses involved, the complexity of the issues, the volume of discovery, and the schedules of the parties and arbitrators. However, as arbitration is a less formal process than litigation, it typically results in notably faster turnaround times than court cases. In 2019, the average processing time for a FINRA case from service of the claim to close of the case was 14.2 months (increasing to 16.9 months for cases that went to hearing).[8]

In addition, because FINRA awards are final and binding, there is no lengthy appeals process like there is in litigation. Although federal and state laws provide that a party may challenge an arbitration award in court, the grounds upon which a court will vacate an award are extremely limited. Specifically, the law permits a district court to vacate or overturn an arbitration award if it finds that:

- The award was procured by corruption, fraud, or undue means.
- There was evident partiality or corruption in the arbitrators.
- The arbitrators were guilty of misconduct in refusing to postpone the hearing, even in light of sufficient cause shown, or in refusing to hear evidence pertinent and material to the controversy, or of any other misbehavior by which the rights of any party have been prejudiced.
- The arbitrators exceeded their powers or so imperfectly executed them that a mutual, final, and definite award upon the subject matter submitted was not made.
- The arbitrators disregarded a clearly defined law or legal principle applicable to the case before them (manifest disregard of the law).
- There is no factual or reasonable basis for the award (complete irrationality).[9]

Discovery

In both arbitration and litigation, the discovery process allows the parties to obtain facts and information from other parties in order to support their own case and prepare for the hearing. However, in

7. www.finra.org/arbitration-mediation/our-commitment-achieving-arbitrator-and-mediator-diversity-finra.
8. www.finra.org/arbitration-mediation/dispute-resolution-statistics.
9. For more information, view the Federal Arbitration Act, 9 U.S.C. § 10.

general, discovery is much more limited in arbitration than in court. For example, FINRA's rules provide that depositions are strongly discouraged and are only permitted under very limited circumstances, such as an ill or dying witness, an essential witness who is unable to travel, or to expedite large or complex cases.

Also unlike litigation, FINRA provides a discovery guide for investor disputes, which contains guidelines to help parties and arbitrators during the discovery process. The discovery guide provides lists of presumptively discoverable documents, which the parties should exchange on their own. However, parties still retain the flexibility to file objections to those documents or request others that they feel are relevant. The arbitrators will decide any discovery disputes raised by the parties.

The production of documents in FINRA arbitration does not create a presumption that the documents are admissible at the hearing. A party may object to the introduction of any documents as evidence at the hearing, and the arbitrators will decide what evidence to admit. In FINRA arbitration, unlike court, arbitrators are not required to follow state or federal rules of evidence in deciding what to admit at the hearing. The rules of evidence are not usually used in arbitration because it is less formal and allows for more a liberal introduction of evidence than would be permitted in court.

Motions to Dismiss

Unlike in court, motions to dismiss a claim prior to the conclusion of the investor's case in chief are discouraged in arbitration. This helps to ensure that the investor gets the opportunity to present his or her case to the arbitrators, except under very limited circumstances.

FINRA rules provide that arbitrators cannot act upon motions to dismiss before the investor's case in chief, unless the case is ineligible for arbitration due to time limitations, the claims were released by a signed settlement agreement, the claims were previously adjudicated on the merits, or the moving party was not associated with the accounts, securities, or conduct at issue. If a panel grants a motion to dismiss, the decision must be unanimous and accompanied by a written explanation. If the panel denies a motion to dismiss, the moving party may not refile the denied motion, and the panel must assess the related forum fees to the moving party. Finally, if the panel deems a motion to dismiss frivolous, it must also award reasonable costs and attorneys' fees to compensate for the motion.

Cost

The cost of an arbitration case is determined by the amount of the claim, the number of hearing sessions, the number of discovery motions, and any postponements. However, due to the shorter duration, truncated discovery and motion practice, and lack of appeals process, arbitration is generally much less expensive than court.

FINRA Dispute Resolution Services Versus Other Arbitration Providers

FINRA Dispute Resolution Services is distinct in that it is overseen by the SEC, as discussed above. In addition to approving all arbitration and mediation rules, the SEC conducts regular examinations of the program. The US Government Accountability Office also has the ability to conduct special inquiries into the program.

FINRA's rule making process is also distinct as it requires a transparent process whereby the public may provide comments and feedback prior to any substantive change.

Further, FINRA's program is distinct in that it will suspend its members from doing business if they do not pay an arbitration award to an investor.

Future of Arbitration

The future of arbitration will undoubtedly involve the use of technology. In the last five years, FINRA has gone paperless and now requires parties (except pro se investors) to use an online portal to file and receive case documents, select arbitrators, and schedule hearing dates. Parties are currently able to utilize videoconferencing during hearings to accommodate witnesses, and many attorneys employ some form of technology in the presentation of their case.

In many current cases, however, arbitrators still review paper copies of exhibits during evidentiary hearings. In the future, it is entirely possible that parties will utilize technology to allow arbitrators to review exhibits electronically, perhaps through the use of iPads or laptop computers.

Parties may also want to more fully utilize videoconferencing technology to eventually have evidentiary hearings where all the participants are entirely remote. This will require technical proficiency by the parties and arbitrators, but as we all get more comfortable with our smartphones and the use of technology, there is no end to the innovation that may be useful in arbitrations.[10]

10. Due to the pandemic, FINRA Dispute Resolution Services allowed hearings to proceed virtually, see: https://www.finra.org/media-center/finra-unscripted/zoom-arbitration.

16

RISK AND COMPLIANCE CONSIDERATIONS IN THE STARTUP WORLD

Cynthia Fascenelli Kirkeby

What Is Compliance?

If you mention compliance to most startup founders, their eyes glaze over. Ask them to give you a definition and they'll be hard-pressed to come up with one even though it will affect the health and success of their company.

According to Encyclopedia.com:

> The word compliance can be defined as the act of adhering to or conforming with a law, rule, demand, or request. In a business environment, conforming to the laws, regulations, rules and policies is the part of business operations often referred to as "corporate compliance."

They continue to put business compliance into context by specifying that

> Corporate compliance involves keeping a watchful eye on an ever-changing legal and regulatory climate and making the changes necessary for the business to continue operating in good standing within its industry, community, and customer base. In a broader sense, corporate compliance extends beyond mere legal and regulatory conformity into the realm of promoting organizational ethics and corporate integrity.[1]

And although it seems compliance is merely one giant headache, there are good reasons to implement business compliance systems, and there are unfortunate pitfalls when they are overlooked. The ever-changing regulatory climate is both an opportunity that many startups exploit and a potential bomb waiting to take them out. An example of this duality is Uber, which has become a force to be reckoned with in the transportation industry by ignoring the regulations that were established for taxi companies. At the same time, Uber has accumulated enormous fines in a host of areas for noncompliance that would have put most companies out of business. Only massive investments from the venture capital sector has kept Uber in business; however, the question remains whether their taste for the bleeding edge of business disruption pays off in the end.

1. "Corporate Compliance." Encyclopedia of Bioethics. www.encyclopedia.com.

DOI: 10.4324/9781351107242-20

Corporate Culture as the Base of Compliance

Corporate culture is a continuously discussed topic at startup events. Founders and speakers discuss how to develop it, how to shape it, how to expand it, and how to benefit from it. The earlier definition of *corporate compliance* points to the idea that a startup's corporate compliance essentially begins in the core values of the company. If a company's corporate culture is focused on ethical choices and values, then compliance becomes a natural offshoot of that focus. Harvard Business Review published *Six Components of a Great Corporate Culture* (Coleman, 2013) which outlined the areas of a company's culture that they felt identified some of the best startups. The second and third components identified by Coleman were values and practices. *Values* establish the mindset of the organization and put an emphasis on how the company will deal with important issues as it moves forward, and *practices* put those values into tangible form as a set of guidelines. In this way Coleman's values and practices equal the corporate compliance strategy of a startup. A startup team should discuss these essential ideas and write them into the company handbook. What are the core values of the company? Which ethical considerations drive the choices that have to be made on a day-to-day basis? Do you always strive do the right thing, or do you use every incident that brings you an advantage regardless of the collateral damage? Define your culture. Define your compliance strategy.

Sometimes, the lack of these guidelines also becomes part of the corporate culture, as we've seen with Uber. So many fines were accumulated by the company under the direction of Travis Kalanick, the company's founder, that the Board of Directors finally replaced him with a new CEO in 2017 (della Cava, 2017). Dara Khosrowshahi, the new CEO, has his work cut out for him as he tries to establish a new corporate culture with ethics at its core—a difficult task considering the current pattern of behavior.

Google, on the other hand, began their company with ethics at its core with "Don't be evil" in its Code of Conduct as its unofficial motto. Despite articles written in 2018, including one by Kate Conger of Gizmodo titled "Google Removes 'Don't Be Evil' Clause from Its Code of Conduct," Google's stated ethos has not changed. The parent company of Alphabet instigated the rewording of their Code of Conduct from a statement in the negative ("Don't be evil") to a positive version ("Do the right thing"). This change in wording has subtle differences that still bother many people. Doing the "right thing" could be something evil if the ethical core of the company has been compromised. Google, however, only recently adopted the Alphabet version of the Code of Conduct, and keeping true to their original ethical base, they insisted on keeping the original motto as the final line in their Code of Conduct. It reads, "And remember . . . don't be evil, and if you see something that you think isn't right—speak up!"

Death and Taxes

You can't escape either death or taxes, and startups should not mess around with this one. Founders should find a good accountant and have them take care of the company's finances. Web versions of QuickBooks, Xero, FreshBooks, and other accounting systems have made this much simpler, allowing the accountant to set up the appropriate accounting categories and reconcile the company's books remotely. Just remember that corporate tax filings are done in March, a month before personal taxes are due in April.

Human Resources—One of the Most Complicated Compliance Issues That All Startups Face

Employment and human resources (HR) compliance has become an almost terrifying compliance issue for startups of all types. There are questions you are not allowed to ask when you interview someone for a job, including questions about their race, religion, gender or sexual orientation, pregnancy status, disability, marital status, number of children, citizenship, arrest record, and former salary. And this is just a partial list. Asking any of these questions is a violation of the law and can trigger EEOC (US Equal Employment Opportunity Commission) fines or a potential lawsuit if the issues cannot be swiftly resolved.

In California, when there is a dispute involving employees, the state weighs heavily in favor of the employee, and most of the fines they impose accrue daily against the employer until the dispute is resolved. HR is not for the faint of heart. Although it used to be possible to handle the required postings and paperwork needed to remain in compliance as a small company 20 years ago, today the requirements are so complicated and onerous that smart firms contract out their HR needs as soon as they hire their first employee.

Even with only one employee, there are numerous compliance issues around something as simple as employment posters. Every poster represents specific rules that are related to a particular compliance issues that require particular protocols or responses. Some of the employment posters represent federal laws, while others represent employment laws that are specific to your state.

According to JJ Keller, which specializes in HR compliance training, the failure to post required state and federal employment posters can result in fines as high as $23,486. Failure to post OSHA (Occupational Safety and Health Administration) notices alone can result in fines of $14.502 (as of 2022). It doesn't take much in the area of business compliance to put you out of business, if you're not paying close attention.

The Basics You Need as Soon as You Add Your First Employee

According to a *Nolo* article by Bethany K. Lawrence, titled "Hiring Your First Employee," there is a minimum of 13 basic compliance issues that must be put in place as soon as you have your first hire:

1. Your EIN (Employer Identification Number), which is required by the federal government;
2. State unemployment taxes;
3. Workers' compensation insurance, in case someone is injured on the job;
4. A payroll system so that you can withhold taxes;
5. W-4 forms for each employee (federal tax form);
6. I-9 forms for each employee to verify the employee is legally eligible to work in the United States;
7. A form filed with the New Hire Reporting Agency for your state, which allows the state to track down parents who haven't paid required child support;
8. Employment posters for state and federal agencies, which must be posted in your business;
9. Form 940, which reports your federal unemployment taxes;
10. OSHA safety measures;
11. Your employee handbook;
12. A formal employee personnel file;
13. Any employee benefits program forms and filings.

And this is just the beginning. If you have more than one employee, there may be other requirements, and if you live in California there are even more policies that are either required or highly recommended.

Five Critical Policies That Must Be in Place if You Are a California Employer

The California Employment Law Report posted a list of five essential policies that you must add if you are a California employer. This list, compiled by Anthony Zaller, points out the fact that California has an especially heavy compliance burden for employers:

1. *At-will employment policy*—Under California Labor Code section 2922, "An employment, having no specified term, may be terminated at the will of either party on notice to the other."

2. *Anti-harassment, discrimination, and retaliation policy*—The California Fair Employment and Housing Council has specific criteria for compliance in this area.[2]
3. Timekeeping policy—Hourly, nonexempt employees must have their start and stop times tracked, and your policy must specify *how* you are tracking this data.
4. Break policy—You must also track hourly, nonexempt employees' two 15-minute breaks and their 30-minute lunch time.
5. Paid sick leave—In some cases sick leave has compliance requirements at the city level. You should check your local business department for policy and tracking requirements.

Exemptions to the Minimum Wage Law: Exempt Employee Status

Under the Fair Labor Standard Act (FLSA), there are only a handful of ways that an employee does not qualify for minimum wage and overtime pay requirements, and an enormous number of companies get this wrong. Section 13(a)(1) of the FLSA allows the following employees to receive an exemption from both pay requirements: executive, administrative, professional and outside sales employees, as well as certain computer employees. It is critical to understand which employees qualify and which ones don't. According to startup attorneys in Silicon Valley, employee classification is one of the top compliance mistakes in new companies.

The following descriptions from the Department of Labor are important criteria for all businesses, regardless of their size. Please keep in mind that job titles do not determine whether or not an employee is exempt. Each employee's status should be evaluated separately. To be exempt, please remember that *all criteria* in their classification must be met to qualify.[3]

W-2 or 1099: That is the BBQ (the Big Basic Question): Determining whether someone working with your company is an outside contractor or an employee has become an ever-increasing nightmare for companies. Startups in particular have enormous challenges in this area when people decide to work together to create a company. They are usually working for equity (a piece of the company) in order to get things off the ground. Cash-strapped founders often cut corners that put them in violation of the letter of the law. However, ignoring the rules is usually done at their peril. Even for the founders who try to pay attention to the regulations in their state, it may be nearly impossible to keep on top of the compliance requirements.

When trying to determine whether a person is an employee (W-2) or an outside contractor (1099), the two primary determining factors are time and control. If your company tells the person when they are supposed to be in a particular place and how they are supposed to accomplish the tasks at hand, then they are an employee. If the worker determines their own hours, uses their own equipment, and decides how they are going to accomplish the needed tasks, then they are usually an outside contractor.

Obviously, there are extremely broad gray areas related to this issue, which is why startups often get in trouble. Outside contractor agreements can help to clarify this issue and should be used whenever possible; however, putting an outside contractor agreement in place will not protect an employer if they are treating the person in question like an employee.

2. www.dfeh.ca.gov/wp-content/uploads/sites/32/2017/06/DFEH-Workplace-Harassment-Guide.pdf.
3. Executive exemption, www.dol.gov/whd/overtime/fs17b_executive.pdf; administrative exemption, www.dol.gov/whd/overtime/fs17c_administrative.pdf; professional exemption, www.dol.gov/whd/overtime/fs17d_professional.pdf; computer employee exemption, www.dol.gov/whd/overtime/fs17e_computer.pdf; outside sales exemption, www.dol.gov/whd/overtime/fs17f_outsidesales.pdf; highly compensated employees, www.dol.gov/whd/overtime/fs17h_highly_comp.pdf.

The incidents to the right are mere samples of the fines Uber has received for failure to comply:

- 2016, California fine for $7.6 million for failing to report data on their drivers[4]
- 2018, settlement of nationwide case requiring a fine of $148 million for hiding a massive data breach, affecting almost 60 million customers[5]

The California A, B, C Test[6]

To clarify these relationships, the California Supreme Court created the A, B, C Test. To qualify as an independent contractor, all three parts of this test must be met:

1. The worker is free from the control and direction of the hirer in relation to the performance of the work, both under the contract and in fact.
2. The worker performs work that is outside the usual course of the hirer's business.
3. The worker is customarily engaged in an independently established trade, occupation, or business of the same nature as the work performed for the hirer.

As a little extra insurance of the status of the working relationship, it would be beneficial to see a copy of their business license. This solidifies the third criterion and generally establishes that they are an independent business and not an individual seeking employment.

The Gig Economy

The gig economy has compounded this issue. Uber drivers and TaskRabbit gig workers are in one of those gray areas. These are people who have control of their time. They can choose whether or not they take a particular ride request or odd job. They are in control of their supplies and materials since they have to have their own car or tools (although Uber has run into additional trouble by involving themselves in car leasing operations). In Uber's case, the drivers are told where to go, how to get there, where and how to get to the next destination, and they are not in control of the setting of their fee for their service. Likewise, TaskRabbit sets the price for the contractor within their system and the person can merely accept or reject the gig.

One of the other factors that points to both of these services being employers instead of merely connecting services is the fact that most of the people involved are individuals without companies of their own. It's even seen in the way the workers refer to their work with the company. A person drives *for* Uber or works *for* TaskRabbit, unlike those who work for companies that are part of platforms such as Home Advisor or Angie's List, who would never say either of those things. These workers are all part of separate companies who say that they get their leads *through* Angie's List or Home Advisor. It is interesting that a simple preposition can often be a primary indicator of this important company relationship.

Employee versus independent contractor status continues to be one of the most complicated and frustrating compliance issues related to business today, and we have further information on this issue in other chapters of this book by experts in this area.

4. Digital Trends, https://www.digitaltrends.com/mobile/uber-in-more-regulator-bother-as-california-fines-it-7-6m/.
5. www.tnw.com.
6. See www.dir.ca.gov/dlse/faq_independentcontractor.htm. In September 2019, California Governor Gavin Newsom signed Assembly Bill (AB) 5 into law, which, as discussed in this section, addresses the employment status of workers when the hiring entity claims the worker is an independent contractor, not an employee, see: https://www.dir.ca.gov/dlse/faq_independentcontractor.htm.

Specialized Agency Compliance Issues

Different industries may have specialized agency regulations with which they are required to comply. Agriculture, biotech, and pharma industries have the FDA. Aerospace has the Federal Aviation Administration (FAA). Banks and FinTech companies have the Consumer Financial Protection Bureau (CFPB), the Federal Deposit Insurance Corporation (FDIC), and the Financial Crimes Enforcement Network (FinCEN).

Sample case:[7] *Financial Crimes Enforcement Network (FinCEN) and Ripple Labs*	• XRP is cryptocurrency of Ripple Labs • In 2015, US Department of Justice initiated a civil action against Ripple Labs • Ripple failed to be in compliance, in particular failing to register as a money-services business and failing to maintain an anti–money laundering (AML) program

Be sure to check with your specialists in your industry to see if there are special compliance protocols that you need to meet. It's not fun to have a surprise from an inspector that you didn't even know existed.

Virtual Currency: Part of the Wild, Wild West of Compliance

Bitcoin, Litecoin, Ethereum, Ripple, and other cryptocurrencies are treading on the dangerous edge of compliance. In addition to all of the normal financial service compliance issues, which are substantial, the cryptocurrency startup world also has to deal with uncertain Securities and Exchange Commission (SEC) rulings, regulations surrounding the prohibition of creating private currency systems, and specialized regulations and compliance related to financial crimes through the Financial Crimes Enforcement Network (FinCEN) and the Bank Secrecy Act, such as money laundering, bribery and corruption, human trafficking, and the funding of terrorism.

A simple oversight in this very complicated area can easily cause the demise of a startup in this sector. One of the more confusing areas for founders of cryptocurrency companies is related to confusing and evolving SEC rulings. The industry doesn't seem to be able to decide if cryptocurrency is an actual currency or a traded security, like a stock. Because of the interest in trading cryptocurrency and its volatility, most government agencies are trying to classify them as securities. This creates a litany of specialized problems. If Bitcoin is a security, then every time you convert it into something like Litecoin, it becomes a taxable event. Can you imagine being taxed every time you convert your US dollars for euros when you travel? This could eventually destroy the viability of cryptocurrency. For the brave individuals who are trying to start a company in this sector, compliance is going to be their primary focus.

Unintended Consequences and Apathetic Agencies

In 1987, my partners and I started a furniture manufacturing company in Southern California. Although most furniture companies were located in North Carolina, at the time there were more than 40 furniture manufacturers creating furniture in this area of the country. In recent years there have been articles that have blamed Chinese and Mexican furniture imports for the demise of what was, at that point, a thriving Southern California industry.

7. www.jdsupra.com/legalnews/sec-action-could-have-rippling-effects-2276292/; see also https://procoinnews.com/ripple-sec-settlement-talk-confirmed/.

Thirty years later, virtually all of the large-scale furniture manufacturers have closed down operations, but if you asked the manufacturers what killed their businesses, it wasn't the imports (although they were a factor); it was the Air Quality Management District (AQMD). This agency put policies in place that had no solutions. That left each of the manufacturers one of three choices: move their manufacturing facility to a state that didn't have the same restrictions, move their manufacturing to Mexico and possibly assemble in the United States, or shutter their company. None of the options was very appealing, since it could cost hundreds of thousands, if not millions, of dollars to move, and closing the company was obviously the undesirable nuclear option.

I had the opportunity to ask one of the AQMD policy attorneys about the issue around 2010. How could they make policies that had no solutions? His answer was shocking, but not surprising. He told me that his job was only to make the policies. If the industry needed to create solutions to deal with the restrictions that resulted from his policies, that was of no concern to him. I pressed the issue and asked him how he could in good conscience implement a policy that had no solution and would result in the forced closing of an existing company. His response, once again, was beyond frustrating. He said that the resulting consequences to the manufacturers were not something that he was required to take into account. That answer still makes my head hurt when I think about it.

In Southern California, the AQMD created compliance requirements that had no solutions. The only choices the manufacturers had were to move out of the state, out of the country, or to shutter their doors. All three eventually happened, and a thriving California industry has essentially disappeared.

> *A note to policy makers*: It's important to take into account whether or not the policy that you're creating actually has a solution that can be implemented. You hold people's lives and livelihoods in your hand, and you can destroy them with the stroke of a pen.

Cybersecurity Compliance in the United States and Worldwide

Europe leads the way in cyber protection for the consumer with the implementation of the General Data Protection Regulation (GDPR), which went into effect on May 25, 2018. The GDPR is designed to give the consumer more control over their personal data with regard to collection and consent. As a business, you must comply with GDPR regulations if you reside in the European Union (EU) or if you make services or products available to people from the EU.

In January 2020, the California Consumer Privacy Act (CCPA) went into effect. This set of laws puts restrictions on how a company can collect and use data, as well as what sort of control consumers can exercise over their own information. The CCPA brings California to the forefront of privacy restrictive policies in the United States and heralds the beginning of the shift toward EU-like standards.

Insurance as Compliance Protection

Insurance may not something that comes immediately to mind related to compliance when a company is starting out. However, there are two essentials that must be in place to start: (1) workers' compensation insurance and (2) liability insurance. You cannot hire an employee or lease a space without these policies in place.

There are also other policies that should be considered, such as directors and officers liability (D&O) insurance, which indemnifies officers and directors, as well as the company itself, from alleged wrongful acts in their official capacity as officers and directors. This policy is sometimes confused with errors and omissions (E&O) insurance, which protects a company from a liability complaint by a client caused by an error or omission in the service or product policies used by the company. Finally, because online advertising and social media have become such essential parts of internet marketing, advertising liability insurance is a relatively inexpensive coverage that can protect the company from claims of slander, defamation of character, libel, copyright infringement, and various other advertising-related risks. Please keep in mind that depending on your business sector, there may be additional policies that should be in place.

Pricing Compliance

Throughout the years, corporations have gotten into trouble for discussing their pricing with their competitors and agreeing on their pricing models. This is an illegal practice under Federal Trade Commission (FTC) guidelines. Any written or verbal agreement between competitors that raises, lowers, or stabilizes prices within their industry (or just between their companies) is called *price-fixing*. You would be amazed to find that it is not just the giant corporations that have run afoul of this statute. Mitsubishi Corporation was found guilty of price-fixing graphite electrodes on a global basis and fined over $130 million. Vitamin maker F. Hoffman-LaRoche Ltd. was convicted of the largest price-fixing and antitrust cases in history with more than $750 million in fines. There was also an ongoing battle over price-fixing and restraint of trade against US dentists in the who are attempting to block non-dental providers from performing teeth whitening services. The FTC took the side of the non-dental providers, while some states have enacted local laws to protect the licensed dental groups. In February 2015, the US Supreme Court overturned the tight protections the lower courts had put in place to protect dentists and ruled that the FTC can charge dental groups with anticompetitive and unfair actions. The Court's opinion, authored by Justice Anthony Kennedy, stated that "Active market participants cannot be allowed to regulate their own markets free from antitrust accountability."

Price-fixing continues to be one of the most egregiously and intentionally violated compliance issues in business. Consortiums and cartels continue to be formed for this nefarious purpose, and massive violations continue to occur.

Benchmarking programs are a way for companies to legally have an idea of the range that businesses in a particular sector are charging without running afoul of these regulations. Each company is still free to choose to stay within the benchmarked range on the high or low end, or to completely disregard the range all together when setting their prices, but it does let the company know where they stand in relation to other businesses performing a similar service or selling a similar product.

The Value of Intellectual Property (IP) Compliance

This is the fun and valuable side of compliance.

One of the things that can dramatically increase the value of a startup is intellectual property. There are four primary types of IP:

1. Patents (including utility patents, design patents, and plant patents)
2. Trademarks (including service marks and certification marks)
3. Copyrights
4. Trade secrets.

Each type of intellectual property has its unique compliance requirements, length of protection, benefits, and challenges.

Patents

Patents must be filed within very specific time constraints in order to be valid. Out of the patents filed in the United States, the percentage approved has varied between 60% and 89% depending on the year. The average patent takes about two years to be approved, with another year added if there was a provisional patent application filed first. Technology patents can take four years or longer to reach the grant phase. Utility (and plant) patents have a patent term of 20 years from first filing (if filed on or after June 8, 1995), and 17 years from the date of issue or 20 years from first filing, whichever is longer (if filed before June 8, 1995). Design patents filed on or after May 13, 2015, have a term of 15 years from the date of grant, and those filed prior to that date have a term that is one year shorter.

Patents are very valuable. Although most people think a patent gives you the right to make something, they actually give you the right to prevent others from making something that you've patented. It may seem like a subtle distinction, but having the ability to keep an infringing product from entering the market is a substantial advantage. Patents typically cost thousands or tens of thousands of dollars to file and process; however, considering the cost of having a competitor knock off a product you have developed, the cost is relatively inexpensive. Patents have enabled my companies to keep foreign companies from replacing my product with cheap knockoffs and have added enormous value to my ventures through the years. One of the first things an investor will ask is "Do you have any IP and is it defendable?"

A quick note on deepfakes:

> The term "deepfakes" refers to the broad scope of synthetic images, video, and audio generated through recent breakthroughs in the field of machine learning, specifically in deep learning.[8]

Trademarks, Service Marks, and Certification Marks

This category of intellectual property is essentially a protection of the good will of a company by protecting its designation of origin. According to the US Patent and Trademark Office (USPTO), a trademark "distinguishes the source of the goods of one party from those of others," while a service mark distinguishes the source of a service instead of goods.

The value of a trademark attaches with use. Trademarks do not expire as long as the mark is in use, and they do not have to be officially registered, although there are definite reasons to do so. The mark can be a name, phrase, design, sound, color, or other identifying element.

Although you can obtain common law protection on a trademark, registration with the USPTO brings with it a presumption of nationwide ownership and the exclusive use of the mark related to the goods and services listed in the filing. What this means is that if someone marks a product with your trademark and you didn't produce it, you can have it removed from sale and destroyed. The items are considered counterfeit and the manufacturer is an infringing party that can be fined and/or imprisoned.

Trademarks typically cost between $275 and $400 if you file them yourself and $1,500 to 2,000 if you have an attorney help you.

Copyrights

Copyrights are a rather remarkable type of intellectual property protection. Copyrights attach with creation. They are good for the life of the author plus 70 years. This was established because many times the value of an author's or artist's work is not realized until after their death. This provision of copyright law allows the creator's estate to benefit from their life's work, even if they were not able to do so.

8. https://cset.georgetown.edu/wp-content/uploads/CSET-Deepfakes-Report.pdf.

Even though it is not mandatory to file a copyright with the Library of Congress, there are a number of reasons to do so. A copyright gives you a public record of your ownership of your creation. This also gives you an official document if you decide to sell the rights to your creation. You also cannot sue someone until you have a filed copy of your copyright. *and* if you file before it has been infringed or within five years of first publication, then the presumption in court is that you are the creator and you are allowed to seek statutory damages and attorney fees.

Because the cost of filing a copyright is minimal ($50 at the time of this publication), artists, writers, musicians, and other creators should avail themselves of the protections afforded by prompt compliance.

Trade Secrets

The value of a trade secret is firmly rooted in proper compliance. A trade secret is a type of intellectual property that protects things like formulas, manufacturing processes, sales lists, and other information that a company does not want generally known. However, to qualify as a trade secret, compliance steps must be put into effect and enforced.

At a minimum, trade secrets usually have the following criteria according to the World Intellectual Property Organization (WIPO):

- The information must be secret (i.e., it is not generally known among, or readily accessible to, circles that normally deal with the kind of information in question).
- It must have commercial value because it is a secret.
- It must have been subject to reasonable steps by the rightful holder of the information to keep it secret (e.g., through confidentiality agreements).

When discussions center around the IP of a company that is potentially being acquired, there is a tiered ranking that is often discussed. The value of the company increases with the protection.

1. Are there any patents?
    - Provisional patent applications;
    - Non-provisional patent application (not yet granted);
    - Granted non-provisional patent application;
    - Patent Cooperation Treaty (PCT) filing (international);
    - Filed and granted international patent;
    - Is there one patent?
    - Are there multiple patents that cover the essential business? (This is sometimes called a patent wall.)
2. Are there any trademarks or related certifications? (Have they been filed?)
3. Are there any filed copyrights on logos, website designs, and so on?
4. If there are any claimed trade secrets, have they been properly categorized, and have compliance measures been put in place and followed?

As you can see, the value of intellectual property is dependent on compliance with necessary filings and documentation. Compliance in this area can have a huge impact in determining your company's value.

In summary, although compliance issues can be the bane of employers, there are also upsides to certain types of compliance. By building a culture which has values and practices that support a healthy compliance structure within your company, you will avoid many pitfalls that have destroyed companies in the past. You might want to consider taking a line out of Google's Code of Conduct: "Don't be evil, and if you see something that you think isn't right—speak up!"

Bibliography

Coleman, J. (2013). Six components of a great corporate culture. *Harvard Business Review*. https://hbr.org/2013/05/six-components-of-culture.

della Cava, M. (2017). Uber selects Dara Khosrowshahi as new CEO to replace Travis Kalanick. *USA Today*. www.usatoday.com/story/tech/2017/08/27/uber-selects-expedia-ceo-take-over-kalanick-reports/606816001/.

Department of Justice (1999). F. Hoffmann-La Roche and BASF agree to pay record criminal fines for participating in international vitamin cartel. F. Hoffmann–La Roche agrees to pay $500 million, highest criminal fine ever. www.justice.gov/archive/atr/public/press_releases/1999/2450.htm.

Department of Justice (2001). Mitsubishi corporation fined $134 million for its role in international price-fixing cartel. www.justice.gov/archive/atr/public/press_releases/2001/8186.htm.

Encyclopedia.com. (2019). Corporate compliance. www.encyclopedia.com/science/encyclopedias-almanacs-transcripts-and-maps/corporate-compliance.

Green, Geoffrey, and Westman-Cherry, Melissa (2015). Supreme Court: Self-interested boards must be actively supervised. *FTC, Bureau of Competition*. www.ftc.gov/news-events/blogs/competition-matters/2015/02/supreme-court-self-interested-boards-must-be-actively.

Lim, S. (2019). How to tell if your corporate culture is healthy. *Investopedia*. www.investopedia.com/terms/c/corporate-culture.asp.

Vinton, Kate (2015). Virtual currency startup fined $700,000 for violating Bank Secrecy Act. *Forbes*. www.forbes.com/sites/katevinton/2015/05/05/virtual-currency-startup-fined-700000-for-violating-banksecrecy-act/#8182cfb7b6f2.

17

CORPORATE COMPLIANCE AND ETHICS CHALLENGES

An European Perspective

Claudiu Jipescu-Munteanu

The European Roots of Corporate Compliance and Ethics

The European Legal Theory on the Connection Between Law and Ethic

The European legal theory concerning the connection between Law and Ethic generally evolved into two main opposed directions: (1) the Law is based on Ethic and (2) the Law and Ethic are disconnected concepts.[1]

1. Under the *first approach*, the Law and Ethic are the two faces of the same coin: one objective (the Law) and the other one subjective (the Ethic). A well-known French scholar, Georges Ripert, believes that there is actually no significant difference between the legal rules and the ethic (moral) rules, as the Ethic penetrates the Law easily via the legislator or the judge ethical conceptions. Ethic rules are located at the edge of legal rules and they are applied whenever the later are lacunar or even in conflict with the moral laws.[2] The French scholar gives as examples some Civil Law institutions such as the enrichment without cause or the good faith exercise of contractual rights. In his view, whenever the Law goes against Ethic, the Law will end up by becoming irrelevant.
2. Under the *second approach*, the Law is disconnected from any other reality and represents the State's expression. The State is the only ground of the Law, there is no Law in absence of the State.[3] Thus, according to Carre de Malberg and Hans Kelsen, even ethically wrong (unjust) legal rules represent the Law as they as long as they are enacted by the State. One cannot say that the Law has to be ethical as there is no such a thing like an absolute Ethic. A legal rule can be in line with a certain legal system and can, at the same time, conflict with another legal system; for example, the monogamist family rules in the European and North American legal systems against the polygamist family rules largely accepted in the legal systems of Muslim countries.

1. Nicolae Popa, *General Theory of Law*, 3rd ed., CH Beck, Bucharest 2008, p. 112.
2. G. Ripert, *La regle morale dans les obligations civiles*, 3rd ed., LGDJ, Paris, 1935, quoted by Popa, *supra* note 2, p. 112.
3. Popa, *supra* note 2, p. 113; Simona Cristea, *General Theory of Law*, 3rd ed., CH Beck, Bucharest, 2014, p. 4.

DOI: 10.4324/9781351107242-21

So everyone seems to agree on the fact that the legal rule is different from the ethical rule especially by the fact that such a legal rule triggers a legal responsibility and a sanction/punishment applied by a public authority in case of breach,[4] while in case of breaching an ethical rule, the sanction is represented by the public disapproval, as opposite to the specific sanctions occurring in case of breaching a legal rule.

While the lack of a specific sanction/punishment might induce the impression of superiority and completeness of the legal rules against the ethical rules, one can say that the legal rules cannot fully achieve their social regulatory purpose in absence of the ethical rules.

As opposite to totalitarian regimes, the European Union's member states legislators do not aim to regulate in detail all and any kind of social relationships as this is seen as a bureaucratic and destructive approach. The legal rules are critical for organizing the society, but the day-to-day existence of communities is largely governed by soft rules having a different nature than the legal rules, such as the ethical, cultural or economical rules.[5] The absence of legal rules in some sectors of our society does not mean the absence of any rules, but quite the opposite sometimes; that is, a large variety of rules, many of them ethical rules that are, in many occasions, filling the gap and supplementing the legal rules.

The legal profession in several EU countries is, actually, a good example as the specific lawyers' legislation is supported by local deontological guidelines (lawyers' code of conduct), and while at the EU level it exists an EU Legal Profession Code of Conduct.[6] The breach of deontological rules can have legal consequences as the professional liability of a lawyer in case of damage caused to a client will not be judged on the basis of breach of lawyers' legislation only, but also in case of breach of the lawyers' codes of conduct.

Historical Concepts in Europe That Anticipated Corporate Compliance and Ethics

There are two concepts that are generally considered as historical precursors of the modern concepts of Corporate Compliance and Corporate Responsibility: the *honorable businessman* and the *lex mercatoria*.[7]

The Honorable Businessman

This concept has roots reaching back to antiquity, but it was confirmed in the late middle ages as businessmen organized themselves into influential guilds and developed their own codes of honor. The golden age of this concept was during Italian Renaissance, when Italian business handbooks primarily addressed the economic fundamentals of business and recognized importance of trustworthiness and good reputation in business.[8] Honorability assumes a generally accepted social code of conduct as an ethical reference point.

The honorable businessman concept is one, but not the only, root of Corporate Responsibility and Compliance as the individualistic responsibility model and honorable merchant has little in

4. Popa, *supra* note 2, p. 114.
5. Catalin Constantinescu, "*Quelques points concernant la relation entre les normes juridiques et les normes éthiques dans la vie universitaire roumaine*", AUB Drept, Forum Juridic no. 1/2021.
6. Adopted by the General Assembly of CCBE on October 28, 1988, and subsequently amended. See here for the English version: www.ccbe.eu/NTCdocument/EN_CCBE_CoCpdf1_1382973057.pdf.
7. Brigit Spiesshofer, *Responsible Enterprise. The Emergence of a Global Economic Order*, 2018, CH Beck Hart Nomos, p. 17.
8. *Ibid.*, p. 17.

common with 21st-century entrepreneurs. This concept needs to be in line with 21st-century global competition economy whose disruptive forms of economic activity cannot be cured through an appeal to honesty alone.[9]

Lex Mercatoria

The roots of lex mercatoria, a medieval concept, go back to the Roman law. This concept is experiencing a renaissance as the "new customary global law".

In essence, this was the unregulated commercial practice (medieval universal trade law) of the European medieval merchants with their private ad hoc arbitration that aimed to become the blueprint for the development of an universal legal order outside the law created by the States. According to critics however, *lex mercatoria* was a Eurocentric set of commercial rules based on western commercial practices and developed by European judges and jurists.[10]

At the same time, such *lex mercatoria* emphasizes the fact that a global set of rules that are independent and detached of the national legal systems (having a transnational nature) is probably one of the best examples of customary rules, accepted by the persons taking part in commercial transactions and not bound or limited by national laws, but rather freely overlapping such laws, a "growing" and "grown" law.[11]

This situation of a supranational legal practice is often present in our days across the EU jurisdictions when it comes about the Mergers and Acquisitions (M&A) transactions that are drafted in line with what is called the "international market practice" of M&A transactions, largely inspired from the Anglo-Saxon legal system. Thus, the shares sale purchase agreements or the business transfer agreements include massive sections of clauses of Representations and Warranties given by the sellers and buyers, while these concepts are unknown to the EU civil law systems, not being provided by the European Civil Codes. It is true that such agreements are submitted by the parties to the outside EU laws, such as the English law, but they are concluded between EU resident companies and are (especially now, after Brexit) to European arbitral or national courts. The legal consequences triggered by the applicability of Anglo-Saxon law concepts into the Civil Code jurisdictions, are insufficiently analyzed for the time being.

The main difference between the concept of corporate ethic (corporate responsibility) and the lex mercatoria is that, while the latter is a set of rules governing private agreements related to trade of goods and based on the pacta sunt servanda principle (the binding nature of contracts), the corporate responsibility liaise rather with the public order (mandatory) rules, such as labor and environmental protection, anticorruption and anti–money laundering, fair taxation and third-party rights.

Corporate Ethics and Corporate (Social) Responsibility as a European Union Policy

European Union General Policy

The concept of Corporate Ethic and Responsibility is directly or indirectly addressed in several enactments at the EU level, starting with EU Treaties, the EU Charter of Fundamental Rights, but also by the secondary EU legislation concerning companies, labor, environmental and integrity related regulations that limit the enterprises' freedom and call for responsibility. This is supplemented

9. *Ibid.*, p. 19.
10. Maniruzzman, American University International Law Review, 14/1999, pp. 656, 691, cited by Spiesshofer, *supra* note 8, p. 21.
11. Spiesshofer, *supra* note 8, p. 221.

by the European Convention on Human Rights (ECHR) and through the recommendations of the Council of Europe on human rights and business, particularly on the implementation of the UN Guiding Principles.[12]

The essential aspect of these EU regulations concern the human rights guarantees of the EU Charter of Fundamental Rights and their direct applicability between private parties.[13]

The European Charter of Fundamental Rights and the ECHR contain basic human rights corporate social responsibility requirements such as the prohibition of slavery, servitude, forced or compulsory labor, and human trafficking (Art. 5); the right to freedom of assembly and of association (Art. 12 (1)); the prohibition of discrimination (Arts. 21 (1), 23); the right to fair and just working conditions (Art. 31); the prohibition of child labor (Art. 32 (1)); and environmental protection (Art. 37)) that imply a duty to protect for European and national bodies, and a corresponding right to protection for the parties concerned.

In this context, the European Court of Human Rights (ECtHR), whose jurisprudence is authoritative under Art. 52(3) of the EU Charter as far as the fundamental rights correspond to those of the ECHR, postulated that the EU Charter contains, in principle, a "state duty to protect", an obligation to protect individuals from human rights violations by enterprises. At the same time, the EU fundamental rights cannot bind private persons and individuals directly as under Art. 51(1) of the EU Charter; only the Union and its institutions and member states are the addressees of the provisions of the EU Charter.[14] Thus, direct third-party applicability between enterprises and private parties is questionable at best.

The EU Commission introduced a new conception of corporate social responsibility. In its Communication from October 25, 2011, "A Renewed EU Strategy (2011–14) for Corporate Social Responsibility", the Commission defined the corporate responsibility as the "responsibility of enterprises for their impacts on the society". The compliance with the applicable law should be the minimum responsibility of enterprises. In order to fully meet their responsibilities, enterprises should also introduce processes that integrate social, environmental, ethical, human rights and consumer concerns into their strategies and activities in close cooperation with their stakeholders. Thus, enterprise responsibility has a positive objective, that is, to maximize "shared value" for their shareholders, their stakeholders and the general public; and a negative objective, that is, to identify, avoid and minimize their possible negative effects

We can therefore note that the (new) corporate social responsibility's definition covers compliance with applicable law as a minimum standard, corporate governance and, additionally, social, environmental and ethical expectations.[15] The EU practically integrates the corporate social responsibility, especially human rights and climate change, as cross-sectional issues in their policies and elaborates them in a mix of hard law, soft law and soft instruments.[16]

National Strategies at the Level of EU Member States

While the enterprise responsibility is an integral part of the social market economy and regarded as such at the EU level, the member States maintained rather a soft law kind of approach as to the rules governing the enterprise responsibility on their own territory. This situation lead to the

12. United Nations Guiding Principles on Business and Human Rights: www.unglobalcompact.org/library/2.
13. Pursuant to Brigit Spiesshofer, other essential aspects concern also EU's strategies in the corporate social responsibility field and the application of Article 5 (1) of the Treaty of the European Union (TEU), cited book, p. 210.
14. *Ibid.*, p. 211.
15. *Ibid.*, p. 213.
16. Spiesshofer, *supra* note 8, p. 217.

development of a-national norms, following ideas of lex mercatoria and human rights as global standards (although, for the reasons shown above, the corporate social responsibility issues such as environment protection and fight against corruption) materially belong to the *ordre public* (public order) and not to private law rules.

The vectors have been the large enterprises that elaborated detailed codes of conduct combining soft law and national hard law sanctions. The basic problem of any soft law is represented by its limited enforcement mechanism, therefore in order to have penetrative power, it has to be transferred into hard law opening up the legal or contractual enforcement sanctions systems. Corporate social responsibility norms can, for example, be transferred into liability laws, contractual general terms and conditions, or be included in an internal regulation of an enterprise as a code of conduct, and thus become legally binding.

One example in this respect is the EU Corporate Social Responsibility Reporting Directive that introduces the reporting obligation and the linked sanctions through (hard) law, while pointing to soft law with regard to the standards for non-financial reporting. This is in line with the financial reporting standards, which complement the legal accountability obligations, such as International Financial Reporting Standards and US Generally Accepted Accounting Principles that are seen by law as they are considered and followed in the transactions' practice like states' legal provisions.[17]

Same is the case of internal guidelines (code of conducts) of enterprises: they bind the enterprise leadership and employees, while their violation can be sanctioned through company and employment law and lead to liability or dismissal. Also, the publication of inaccurate corporate responsibility policies can create liability on the basis of unfair competition or serve as the basis for a complaint by an affected party.[18]

In conclusion, in the EU, the enterprise responsibility remains a smart mix of hard and soft law and informal steering instruments, which amalgamate with international (human rights), European and industry-specific requirements, showing a high degree of heterogeneity, as opposite to the US responsible business conduct (RBC) approach that takes into account the positive and negative aspects of responsibility and introduces an integrated comprehensive responsibility conception that covers not only aspects concerning the human rights but all corporate responsibility issues.

Private Corporate Responsibility and Compliance Principles by European Enterprises

Role of Enterprises: Business and Ethics

Since the 1990s, in a multilayered way, European and Anglo-American business ethics have dealt with the societal functions and tasks of companies under the conditions of globalization, with the "should-expectations" on the enterprise leadership and employees (morality, integrity at micro-level), on enterprises (economic/political responsibility at meso level) and on the framework conditions of a social and ecological market economy (at macro level).[19]

By way of example, in the early 1990s, when multinational companies started to invest in the Central and Eastern European countries, the main problem they faced was the choice of one of the following alternatives: either the strict compliance with the ethical code of the firm from the country of origin or adapting the company's policy to the local traditions and business style of the target country. Thus, such corporations faced conflicts, more or less flagrantly, between the laws of their country of origin and the set of moral values that the respective corporations affirmed in their code

17. *Ibid.*, p. 228, fn. 78.
18. *Choc v. Hudbay Minerals Inc.*, 2013 ONSC 1414.
19. Spiesshofer, *supra* note 8, p. 416.

of conduct.[20] It is interesting to note that the collapse of communist regimes in Central and Eastern Europe at the end of 1989/beginning of 1990 and the increased attention of multinational companies toward investments in this region coincided with the commencement of the globalization process.

The business ethics approaches raise several fundamental questions, out of which the following seem relevant for our analysis:

1. One of them is the relation between the moral values and the legal framework (the "ordoliberal approach").[21] Thus, if the regulatory framework implements society's moral values, then the role of the enterprise is limited to its observance of this legal framework during its business activities (what is called the "compliance"). If however the regulatory framework does not reflect the moral "ought" and present governance gaps, then enterprises should have the duty to fulfill the claims of the moral responsibility that is normally implemented in the regulatory framework. It is of course to be discussed which kind of moral should be taken into consideration (see earlier discussion) and fact is that the enterprise investing is the one that assess the guiding moral values that should be, in its view, reflected by the legal framework of the country where such enterprise is investing. In other words, the question is what is "legitimate", particularly in the intercultural context, and how should this be determined, operationalized and enforced. Additionally, the question is raised as to whether compliance with the regulatory framework is still sufficient, and to what extent enterprises, considering their increase in power through globalization, should assume political responsibility alongside their economic responsibility.[22]
2. A second one concerns the integrative business ethics in the sense that large enterprises become quasi-official institutions that fulfill a political function and integrate economics and ethics. Conflicting values could be brought into balance through communication processes between enterprises, states and civil society, within the framework of public-private partnerships. As opposite to the classic liberal economic model, this approach would integrate enterprises into a political decision-making and consensus building process.[23]
3. A third one concerns the governance ethics approach; that is, where the nation state, with its territorially linked political and legal system, shows itself to be inadequate, there is a need for adaptive mechanisms of global and local, economic and political governance, and enterprises are highly adaptive global governance structures. This raises the unresolved problem of the nature of the moral system: which one from different cultural traditions should apply? Enterprises find themselves between Scylla and Charybdis: their approach could lead to friction with the legal system of the host state, to "value imperialism", and to the imposition of standards that are not appropriate regarding the economic and political situation in the host state. If they follow the standards of the host state, they risk opening themselves up to criticism and the loss of reputation and acceptance in their home state.[24]

Multinational Companies Applying Ethics in International Business

Ethics in international business refers to the ethical dimension of any business relationship between two or more countries or between private partners in different states. Ethics in international business addresses a morally acceptable code of conduct for decision makers and executives on different

20. Irina Eugenia Iamandi, Academy of Economic Studies, Bucharest, Faculty of International Economic Relations, *Master International Business Course*.
21. As called by Brigit Spiesshofer, *supra* note 8, p. 416.
22. *Ibid.*, p. 416.
23. *Ibid.*, p. 417.
24. *Ibid.*, p. 417.

hierarchical levels of a company operating not only domestically but also in other countries.[25] It is known that moral values and principles vary fundamentally from one culture to another, and what is ethical in a certain geographical space can be considered completely immoral in another part of the world.

Multinational companies are the main actors in the international business environment, being considered, according to some authors, the main economic powerhouse of the world, with not only interests but also worldwide responsibilities. Corporate obligations or responsibilities relate to the promotion of general economic growth and social progress and aim at maintaining and promoting standards and ethical behavior norms.

There have been a number of cases where these companies, particularly strong internationally, have been accused of exploiting the world's least developed countries (e.g., the US multinationals that use cheap labor from underdeveloped countries) that do not meet the high standards protecting the environment in developed countries, and implementing them in poorer and less advanced parts of the world, which accept high levels of pollution in return for jobs for their populations.

Another famous case is Nestlé, which produces a wide variety of food products. The company was accused of "ethical and moral" behavior for using advertisements that encouraged mothers in less developed countries to give up breastfeeding and use the powdered milk that was prepared and marketed by the company. So mothers adopted for their children their diet with milk powder; however, because of excessive poverty, they diluted the product with water until it lost its nutritional qualities. The result was an increase in infant mortality and the company attracted public opinion disapproval. Although Nestlé won the lawsuits, demonstrating that it complied with the World Health Organization's rules, the company continued to be in the attention of the above-mentioned institutions and organizations and the general public for such unethical conduct.

As mentioned above, the ethical principles of large EU-based multinational companies are reflected in their codes of conduct that, once implemented based on internal regulations, by the effect of labor legislations they usually bind the enterprise leadership and employees, while their violation can be sanctioned through company and employment law and lead to liability or dismissal.

Thus, the typical code of conduct[26] addresses the following business ethic topics:

1. Companies declare themselves as strictly committed to high standards of legal compliance and business ethics. This shows that the code of conduct (addressing business ethics) is supplemental to the observance of laws and regulations (the compliance point of view).
2. However, not many codes are addressing also the situation of silence/lack of provisions and conflicts between the code's provisions and local laws. In case the code is silent and provides no direct guidance, the recommendation is to obey "high ethical standards" in every aspect of the work; in other words, to be guided by the "common sense". The employees are encouraged to make assessments based on their own experience (how the respective decision would affect the image of the company; what family and friends could say about it). Still, if the solution is unclear, the managers and employees are encouraged to speak up and seek advice from advisors.
3. The code of conduct binds usually the members of the management of the respective company (i.e., board members or executive directors, ordinary managers) but also employees and is applicable in all companies' subsidiaries. The company is usually investing in in-house trainings aiming to keep the management and employees fully informed and seek expert advice when in doubt. A chief compliance officer is appointed at the company level in order to keep the code up to date and revise it whenever necessary. Changes to the code are approved by the board.

25. Iamandi, *supra* note 21, p. 10.
26. Such example is the Code of Conduct of the Germany-based company BASF available here: www.basf.com/global/en/who-we-are/organization/management/code-of-conduct.html.

4. The first topic of codes of conduct that is addressed is the corruption fight and the recommendation not to get involved in corruption, whatever form it takes. Any lobbying and political communications should be made on transparent basis, and any financial support for political parties or organizations close to such political parties is forbidden.
5. The second topic concerns the trade laws governing the import/export of products and/or services. All regulations should be observed, especially control of exports into suspicious or embargoed areas/countries.
6. The third topic concerns the anti–money laundering aspects. The identities and credentials of all customers and business partners should be carefully controlled and checked. Constant vigilance should be kept in relation to activities of business partners so to be aware of the payment irregularities or suspicious behavior.
7. Observance of antitrust laws is the fourth important topic; that is, the fact that the enterprise is committed to observe the free and fair competition rules and strictly obey to applicable laws and regulations so to avoid agreements between competitors, to have transparent interactions with customers and suppliers and avoid abuse of dominant market position.
8. Gifts and entertainment to customers or business partners are prohibited, except for small gifts or modest invitations.
9. Conflict of interests are to be avoided so to prevent a conflict between private and professional life.

And, finally, usual corporate social responsibility topics included in the codes of conduct are as follows:

1. Observance of human rights, labor and social standards, in accordance with the United Nations Universal Declaration of Human Rights, UN Guiding Principles of Business and Human Rights, OECD Guidelines for Multinational Enterprises, and the Tripartite Declaration of Principles Concerning Multinational Enterprises and Social Policy (MNE Declaration) of the International Labour Organization (ILO).
2. Environmental protection: companies are committed to energy efficiency and climate protection, as well as sustainable solutions.
3. Health and safety rules: besides the obvious purpose of avoiding labor accidents, their observance will maintain at a high level the trust of employees, customers, business partners and other stakeholders.
4. Protection of information and intellectual property, as they are among the most valuable assets of the enterprise. Such information cannot be shared on social media or in public places.
5. Take care of the protection of the personal data (General Data Protection Regulation [GDPR]). All personal data collected by the company will be processed fairly, transparently and in full compliance with the applicable legal requirements.
6. Keeping accurate books and records in view of proper accounting and financial reporting.

18
FINANCIAL CONSIDERATIONS
A Global Perspective

Philip Wood

What This Chapter Is About

This chapter explains how you understand the legal jurisdictions of the world quickly and make sense of the noise.

In substance, if you know the basics of the law in four jurisdictions in terms of their underlying approach, then you will have a feel for the fundamentals in 85% of the legal jurisdictions of the world. Altogether, there are 321 jurisdictions.

Three of the four founding jurisdictions you need to understand are England, France and Germany. Between them, they were the main founders of three distinct legal ideologies: the Anglo-American common law group, the Napoleonic group and the Roman-Germanic group. Roughly the proportions are 40%, 30% and 20%, with the rest of the world taking up the remaining 10%.

I call this threefold division the Triple Polarization. The ideologies crystallized in the 19th century and the foundations were more or less settled by 1870. That development also coincided with what the economists call the Great Divide, when the economies of Europe and America pulled away from the rest. This in turn influenced the spread of European laws via their empires and via copying by other countries.

I split the common law group into two: the English common law group and the American common law group, represented here by New York. I do so because of the special contribution which the American group has made to the international development of law.

Understand these four—England, France, Germany and New York—and you can solve the puzzle.

Legal Fields Covered by This Chapter

The domains of law dealt with here are largely wholesale financial, commercial and corporate law—the law relevant, for example, to international banking and bond issues, to bankruptcy, to large corporations and to the sale of everything which is sold, whether goods or foreign exchange or securities. I do not deal with consumer law, small litigation, family law, the law of succession, constitutional law, ordinary criminal law or the like.

I do not deal with regulatory law, such as banking or securities regulation. Regulatory law is different from ordinary private law because of three characteristics:

- A regulator has legislative powers to make rules, executive powers to administer them and judicial powers to enforce them, subject to various checks on this concentration of legal power. Effectively regulatory agencies are a delegation of governmental power.

 DOI: 10.4324/9781351107242-22

- Offences of the regulatory codes are typically subject to administrative penalties. These are criminal in nature because they are not purely compensatory. Regulators can, for example, impose fines and disqualify people from the industry. However normal criminal protections in favor of the accused are generally diluted (e.g., the right to silence).
- The regulatory rules are extremely detailed codifications, massive in extent, exceeded only by taxation laws.

Because of these differences people often refer to law and regulation as different things.

However the division of the world's jurisdictions into families of law for our fields of law is often also valid in other areas of law, since each of the families of law often have different approaches across the whole spectrum of law—but not always.

What Is a Jurisdiction?

The 321 jurisdictions of the world are encased in just under 200 sovereign states. Thus the United States has 51 jurisdictions—the states and the District of Columbia. The British Isles have seven, mainly England, Scotland, Northern Ireland and a few small islands in the English Channel off the coast of France, dating back to the Norman invasion of 1066. On the other hand, France and Russia are unitary jurisdictions.

The tests of a separate legal jurisdiction are:

- *Territory*: It must have territory, however small. The smallest jurisdiction is the Vatican, at 0.17 km^2. It is also the smallest sovereign state. Pitcairn Island in the Pacific has 4.6 km^2. Russia is by far the largest jurisdiction, with about 17 million km^2, and Canada is next with about 10 million km^2. China follows with about 9.5 million km^2, about the same size as the United States. Both New York (122,000 km^2) and England (130,000 km^2) punch well above their relatively small size.
- *Population*: It must have people who live there more or less permanently—not just visitors. Thus Pitcairn Island, with a population of around 57, just makes it—these are mainly descendants of the mutineers of the ship HMS Bounty in 1767. The Johnston Atoll, belonging to the United States, does not qualify, nor does Bouvet Island (Norway) in the South Atlantic, the most remote island in the world: it does not have a resident population.
- *Government*: It must have a government, in the minimum sense of a de facto government which is in charge. Thus the Turkish Republic of North Cyprus would qualify, even though it is not recognized by any sovereign states except Turkey.
- *Distinct system of law*: It must have a system of law which is different from that of the sovereign state it is part of. One practical test is whether a practitioner would regard the law as sufficiently different to warrant legal advice from a locally qualified practitioner. In our field, the states or provinces of the United States, Canada and Australia would normally qualify, but not the cantons of Switzerland or the provinces of Mexico, Brazil or South Africa.

This is not a legal definition but a convenience definition. The first three tests are commonly used to define a sovereign state. It is the fourth test—a different system of law—which distinguishes jurisdictions from sovereign states. Many jurisdictions are also sovereign states where they are not divided into separate provinces or the like.

Legal systems were historically transmitted by imperialism or settlers or by emulation or copying. Copying still continues since it is easier to borrow than to duplicate the thinking. There is nothing wrong with that. The first step is to know the main families of jurisdictions.

American Common Law Group

The first group here is the American common law group, comprising about 61 jurisdictions. These are mainly the US states plus about ten others scattered round the world, such as Liberia, Puerto Rico, the US Virgin Islands and a number of Pacific Islands, such as Guam, the Marshall Islands and Palau.

Although this group is based on English common law, history has led to distinctions (e.g., in the approach to litigation). The amount of case law on every subject is vast, an astonishingly rich and fertile assembly of legal thinking, reflected, for example, in the famous Restatements and the Uniform Commercial Code.

The influence elsewhere of US legal thought is also very great, especially in relation to bankruptcy law, the law of security interests and in some regulatory fields, such as financial regulation, the resolution of banks, and antitrust (competition law). All the latter fields were substantially invented in the United States. In addition, US lawyers have shown marvelous ingenuity and creativity in the transactions they have developed.

Unlike some of the legal empires of the past, this is not a territorial empire. It is an empire of the mind. It is the empires of the mind which matter.

English Common Law Group

The ideology of the English common law jurisdictions was developed initially by England and expanded elsewhere in profusion. At the relevant time, England's law was largely not codified so other countries had nothing to copy out from. Not so with the civil code group—the French codes date from the first decade of the 1800s, and the German codes were in the works in the last quarter of the 1800s. The main German civil code was enacted in 1900, but the influential Bankruptcy Act stems from 1879, replaced as late as 1999.

There are 84 members of this group—or 65 if you treat each of Australia and Canada as substantially a unified bloc.

The members are almost wholly the former British Empire, including

- In Europe: England, Northern Ireland, the Republic of Ireland and the Isle of Man, Gibraltar and both Cypruses, but not Scotland (which is a mixed jurisdiction). Malta is also in the mixed group.
- In the Americas: the Canadian provinces (except Quebec, which is in the mixed group), Belize, Guyana and 16 Caribbean islands, such as Bermuda, the Bahamas and Cayman, plus various islands in the Atlantic.
- In the Middle East, only Israel.
- In Africa: Ghana, Nigeria, the two Sudans, Uganda, Kenya, Tanzania, Zambia, Malawi, other African territories and some Indian Ocean islands such as the Seychelles and Mauritius (which were formerly French but are now virtually wholly anglicized in our areas of law), but not the southern African cone countries, most of which are in the mixed group.
- In Asia and Oceania: Pakistan, India, Bangladesh, Sri Lanka, Myanmar, Malaysia, Singapore, Hong Kong, Brunei, Australian states and territories, New Zealand and a few others.

The 61 jurisdictions in the American group are treated a separate group although their origins are in the English common law. The 18 members of the mixed civil/common law group discussed below (including China and Japan) have elements of the English group (see later). So the overall influence of this ideology is large globally, about 40%.

The original tenets of the approach were based on 19th-century philosophies of developing countries—Adam Smith's laissez-faire (the "invisible hand of the market") and the mottos "capital is king" and "the railways must be built." All this was tempered by Victorian moral values.

By an extraordinary and unexpected twist of history, one can see these influences of a rapidly developing country in China's commercial laws; for example, insolvency set-off and the adoption of the trust for all assets. Singapore and Hong Kong may have provided reassurance that it was safe to adopt this bold experiment.

A challenge for this precocious ideology is to retain its original simplicity, versatility and freedom.

Napoleonic Group

The Napoleonic group, originating in France, comprises a huge 86 jurisdictions in all parts of the globe, phenomenally successful as a legal ideology. You could divide it up into smaller groups:

- The European group: France (including about ten French island dependencies elsewhere), Belgium, Luxembourg, Spain, Italy, Portugal, Greece, Bulgaria, Romania, Greece, Monaco and Andorra.
- The traditional group, which have not changed as much as in, say, France and Belgium. The traditional group include nearly all of Central and South America, the whole of North Africa (including Egypt and also Lebanon, the United Arab Emirates (UAE) and Jordan in the Middle East), some Caribbean islands, four Indian Ocean islands (including Madagascar), the Philippines, and islands in the Pacific.
- The Ohada group: 17 sub-Saharan countries more recently adopting a harmonized version of French business law, including the Ivory Coast and the Democratic Republic of the Congo. Other African members include Mozambique, Angola and Ethiopia.
- The Sharia group, such as Syria, Iraq and Iran—about seven of them.

The Napoleonic codes of the first decade of the 1800s were the first truly great universal codification since Justinian's codes of Roman law around AD 530. The first version was composed in six weeks on the orders of Revolutionary leaders in the 1790s, but later progress was more measured. Napoleon himself attended many drafting meetings. The codes are charismatic. Stendhal is said to have read sections of the *Code civil* every day to refine his feeling for the language.

Other version of the codes were drafted in, for example, Italy, Spain, Latin America and Egypt.

Napoleon observed from lonely St Helena, "It is not in winning 40 battles that my real glory lies . . . my *Code civil* will not be forgotten, it will live forever."

Roman-Germanic Jurisdictions

There are about 34 jurisdictions in this group. These include:

- Germany, the Scandinavian and Baltic countries, Czech, Poland, Slovakia, Hungary and countries in the former Yugoslavia in the Balkans, plus Austria, Switzerland and Turkey—a sizeable chunk of Europe.
- The Dutch group, comprising the Netherlands, Indonesia, Suriname and the former Netherland Antilles territories in the Caribbean.

If you added the affiliated members of the mixed civil/common law group—which includes China, Japan, Taiwan, Korea and the Southern African cone jurisdictions (see next)—the global influence of this ideology is enormous, a gigantic contribution to civilization.

Thailand is marginally in this group.

In the main the ideology was a late 19th-century project of Germany, with major contributions from the Netherlands, Switzerland, Austria, Scandinavia and others.

Kemal Ataturk in modernizing Turkey in the 1920s borrowed the new Swiss Code of 1907 pretty much word for word. Note that Russia's first civil code in the 1990s was influenced by the new Netherlands code, then in draft—I keep Russia in the New group, see below. This in turn influenced other countries in the former USSR. Countries borrowing a set of laws frequently look to the latest model, as with cars.

The overall approach in commercial and financial law of this group is often midway between the Napoleonic and the English common law—a balance.

The systematic working out of this ideology was an extraordinary intellectual feat which was, and still is, transmitted to most countries in the group entirely by the quality of the product.

Mixed Civil/Common Law Group

The Mixed civil/common law jurisdictions have a special fascination. The group is a small group of 18 out of the total 321.

An astonishing group at first sight. The fact that China and Japan should find themselves in the same group as Swaziland, Jersey and Liechtenstein is part of the wit of history. But it is perfectly explicable.

The members have origins in one of the two main civil code groups (the Napoleonic or the Roman-Germanic) and have at least two of the three uniquely common law superpriority claims on insolvency. These are insolvency set-off, a universal corporate security interest and a universal trust, as discussed later.

The Channel Islands, which are British possession in the English Channel just off the coast of France, came with the Norman invasion of England in 1066 and have anglicized pre-Napoleonic Norman law. The southern African cone countries—just on the edge of this group—inherited a commercialized Roman law from Holland. These are South Africa, Botswana, Lesotho, Namibia and Eswatini.

China, Japan and Taiwan imported common law features, especially the trust. Scotland, like South Africa, has a direct view back to Rome. The influences in Panama included the canal and its large ship register. The Principality of Liechtenstein has every institution known to the human mind.

Is this group just a product of history? Or will this one day be the winning group?

Islamic Group

The Islamic group has about 11 jurisdictions. They include Afghanistan, Bahrain, Kuwait, Libya, Maldives, Oman, Saudi Arabia, Somalia and Yemen.

Strict Sharia law applies in the commercial sphere, including the objection to interest, insurance and the assignment of claims. One result is that bankruptcy laws tend to be quite thin (e.g., Kuwait 1980) or virtually nonexistent (e.g., Yemen). As in Europe at the time when usury was unlawful, Islamic financiers use title finance transactions, such as conditional sales, leases and repos as substitutes. But Afghanistan has a Secured Transactions Law 2008 and an Insolvency Law 2018.

Djibouti, Iran, Iraq and Syria are treated a part of the Napoleonic group but could equally well be here. Their codes are French-inspired, though with a Sharia override, as in Iran (1932, override 1982).

Jordan and the UAE are considered Napoleonic now. Many other jurisdictions belonging to other groups (to come) have a de facto Sharia coloring, but mainly applicable to individuals.

The financial center enclaves in Abu Dhabi, Dubai and Qatar are based on English law.

The codes of Syria, Libya, Iraq and Somalia are all based on the Napoleonic Egyptian codes (1949) of Sanhuri, "the legendary arch-codifier."

Saudi's Bankruptcy Law is 2018.

Ancient legal history in the region is astonishing. Our oldest law codes come from Mesopotamia (present day Iraq), for example, Hammurabi's code (1732 BC). The oldest we have heard of is the Code of Urukagina, about 2380 BC, long before the religious codes. Moses with his ten bullet points on the mountain was much later—perhaps 1750 BC. The Arabs had a renaissance of law in the ninth century AD. History does not stop now.

New or Transition Groups

The New group of 20 jurisdictions are a romantic and ancient group, linking Europe to China, plus a few others. The main countries in this group are Albania, Armenia, Azerbaijan, Belarus, Bhutan, Cambodia, Georgia, Kazakhstan, Kyrgyzstan, Laos, Moldova, Mongolia, Nepal, North Macedonia, Russia, Tajikistan, Turkmenistan, Ukraine, Uzbekistan, and Vietnam.

They all switched to market economy laws. Some are not so interested at present (e.g., Turkmenistan and Tajikistan).

Nearly 30 years have passed since the fall of the USSR. Maybe you need half a century to think about your codification of morality, including in the commercial sphere.

China is in the Mixed group.

Nepal and Bhutan are underlying English.

At least five have insolvency set-off, which is a good litmus test: Albania, Azerbaijan, Cambodia and North Macedonia.

Five have a secured transactions law based on Article 9 of the US Uniform Commercial Code (e.g., Armenia).

Unallocated Group

The Unallocated group of about seven includes the Vatican, Cuba and North Korea.

In addition, the high seas and space are each governed by their own bodies of law.

Legal Indicators

It is not feasible to go through a whole legal system to understand it. Instead it is sensible to use legal indicators which you drop into a legal system like litmus paper.

Legal indicators must be (1) measurable, (2) symbolic and representative, (3) economically important and central to transactions, and (4) indicative of intense conflicts about what is just and fair. Taxonomy in other areas—plants or the elements or stars—also proceeds on the basis of indicators. You must be able to distinguish one thing from another in a way which matters. The indicators you use must be the right ones.

Codification does not seem relevant because most important law is codified anyway. Some common law jurisdictions are highly codified (e.g., India and California). What matters is what the law says, not how it is written down. As to the doctrine whereby courts follow the judgments of higher courts, civil lawyers cite case law almost as enthusiastically as common lawyers do. These indicators have low explanatory power. Vague statements about culture or governance are often difficult to prove.

Insolvency as the test: The crucial test is insolvency. Set-off and a great many other things do not matter fundamentally if people stay solvent and can always pay. You only need set-off involving vast amounts if the counterparty is insolvent. You also only need security interests if debtors become insolvent. Trusts must work on the trustee's insolvency. These institutions are systemic.

One can best test the approach of a legal system on its insolvency rules—in financial, commercial, corporate and many other realms of law—because this is when people suffer losses, sometimes enormous losses, sometimes losses which not only destroy the lives of individuals but can destroy whole economies. This is when the law has to make up its mind as to who gets paid, whether by set-off or security interest or trust or other priority.

On bankruptcy creditors are paid everywhere according to a ladder of priorities with a rather large number of steps or rungs, at least six of them, divided into sub-classes. It is the bankruptcy ladder of priorities which determines who the winner is and who the loser, who is the victor and who is the victim, who survives and who gets drowned. The ladder defies all notions of equality of treatment in an emergency and is one of the most complicated moralities of all in this arena of law. The law is forced to decide at last.

At the top of this ladder in some jurisdictions, but cut off in others, are the claimants with a set-off or security interest or a claim of a beneficiary under a trust. The rest are pulled down in the swirling water—gasping for that last bubble of oxygen. Bankruptcy is a spoliator and destroyer.

Bankruptcy is a stimulant to the enactment of laws. For example, the Great Depression in the United States led to a huge expansion of regulatory law, increased even more by the global financial crisis from 2007, as was also the case in the rest of the world. The collapse of large corporations, such as Enron in the early 2000s, spurred laws on corporate governance and financial statements. When large bankruptcies cause losses, the legislator reaches for the legal wand.

Key bankruptcy indicators: Three key indicators drawn from the impact of bankruptcy are:

- The availability of insolvency set-off;
- The scope of corporate security interests;
- The availability of the trust over all assets.

These three main indicators are each of major importance in modern economies and essential to financial stability. They are revelatory of many other aspects of a legal system so they are efficient. They are discussed later.

There are other indicators, some of which are quite technical. For example, the ability to trace embezzled or other wrongfully taken property and its proceeds through commingled bank accounts on the insolvency of the holder, called restitutionary tracing or real subrogation in civil jurisdictions, appears to be exclusively a common law remedy, not found in the other groups. This is not of great economic importance but it is a powerful final nuancer which can tip the scales.

In the realm of financial regulation, the key indicators are somewhat different. They include criminalization, the aggressiveness of enforcement, national protectionism, heaviness of investor protection and consumerism.

The key indicators of corporate law would include other factors, such as financial assistance by a corporation to buy its own shares (as where a target corporation guarantees a bank loan to the bidder for the target's shares). This doctrine is hardly ever a problem in the United States but is highly relevant in many other jurisdictions. The rule stems mainly from the notion that share capital should be subordinated to creditors on insolvency. Another corporate indicator is the liability of the directors for deepening an insolvency. Both these indicators are insolvency indicators.

Financial law indicators are on a straight line from pro-creditor to prodebtor, but corporate law involves a triangle of creditors, shareholders and management at the apexes. Hence the analysis of the tugs of three magnets, not two, is more complex in the endeavor to measure corporate law.

Why Did the Triple Polarization Happen?

The question of why the Triple Polarization happened is intriguing. There were many influences. The timing of the Industrial Revolution in the three key western European countries in relation to the crystallization of their commercial legal systems played a significant role. The English pro-creditor, pro-business ideology was developed during the Industrial Revolution when development and enterprise were uppermost. The Napoleonic view was based on earlier views before the impact of the Industrial Revolution could influence the codes on which the ultimate codes were based. They were therefore more orientated toward an agricultural economy as opposed to business. The German view was adopted in the middle of the Industrial Revolution in Germany but might have been more conservative about backing business because it was professors' law rather than practitioners' law.

One must not forget the imprint of the footsteps of ancient Rome, whose legal system survived the collapse of Rome's territorial empire for centuries until rediscovered in Europe in the 11th century, a homecoming.

In any event it seems clear that, as will be seen, by 1870, the Triple Polarization and the basic indicators had crystallized and that, notwithstanding many erosions and splinterings, they remain in force to this day—giant shadows of the past. Since then, this or that jurisdiction has shifted on the three main indicators and others like them. But there has been no grand reconciliation.

Governing Law Generally

The object of following sections is to bring out some of the differences between jurisdictions by comparing various factors which a transactor would consider in deciding the governing law of an international contract—a very common situation.

All Contracts Must Have a Governing Law

Every contract must be determined the law of a legal jurisdiction. A contract cannot exist in a legal vacuum. If you do not choose the law expressly, the court will choose for you—which may not be the result you want. Most jurisdictions will honor a clear express choice by the parties in their contract. So how do you choose? A great deal can depend on your choice.

We are concerned here mainly with large international banking contracts between parties of comparable bargaining power, such as bank loan syndications, international bond issues, derivatives contracts and the like—not with contracts with consumers or small businesses.

Jurisdictions to Choose From

The main possibilities are to choose a member of the family group whose core legal ideology matches your expectations.

This section compares the laws of England, New York, France and Germany as a proxy for the others in the same group. You do not get exactly the same result from, say, England, Hong Kong, Ontario, Singapore and New South Wales, but the similarities are striking. This would also be broadly true of, say, Switzerland, the Netherlands and Germany, or France, Belgium and Luxembourg.

As discussed, the four principal ideologies of English law (to which we add New York law as representative of the US group), French law and German law have been phenomenally successful and made a huge contribution to world civilization. Yet, for historical reasons, French and German law, say, are very different from English law, as is New York law.

English and New York law enjoy a dominant position as the governing law of major international financial contracts (and certain other large contracts too). Those governing laws are now international public utilities—ideologies which no longer just belong to the jurisdictions which are their custodians. It is difficult to come by reliable figures, but the aggregate share of these two jurisdictions as the governing law of the classes of wholesale international contracts we are discussing could be as high as 80%. In any event, they serve the international business community, not just their own populations.

Nevertheless in today's world, the competition between legal systems is sharper and different choices are more widely debated.

The differences between the ideologies do not mean that one is good and the others bad. They each present a spectrum of solutions which typically are well within the range of what is legitimate and defensible. The question is, what ideology is most suitable for the particular transaction; what is most protective of the interests the parties wish to protect and the risks they want to avoid?

Legal systems have to make choices, such as between whether to protect debtors or creditors or between predictability and what the courts on the day, not the parties, think is fair. Those choices are almost always hard to make and each has strengths and weaknesses. Whichever policy you choose, you will generally have some losers, some victims of an injustice. The balance is often difficult and controversial.

When parties choose a governing law, they also typically choose the courts of the country of the governing law as well, either exclusively or non-exclusively. That means that that the court is interpreting its own law and also applies its own conflict of laws doctrines: hence you know where you are. Similar principles apply to choice of courts as to choice of law; for example, commercial orientation, protection of the transaction, predictability, certainty, fairness, familiarity and the like.

The following points are a few of the main comparative points—in fact there are dozens of them. The importance which market participants give to one factor or another will vary. It is important that there is a choice, and clients are entitled to know what they are choosing.

Predictability

The predictability and certainty of contract terms is generally important to commercial parties. They will generally have specifically negotiated their terms.

Commercial parties normally cooperate in good faith and do not call "Snap!" on the slightest pretext. But if all the efforts to solve a break-down in relationships are in vain, the parties need to know where they stand strictly.

A key characteristic of English contract law is that the courts will normally uphold what the parties agreed, subject to some basic principles of contract. Banks and corporations control their own deals. Business parties are entitled to decide for themselves what they think is just and fair.

In the symbolic Monday/Friday case of *The Laconia* (1977), the ship charter hire fell due on a Sunday. So the charterer paid on Monday. The shipowner sent the money back and repossessed the ship at once on the Monday. The hire was payable in advance so it should have been paid on the Friday. This was an express event of default and the charter said that time was of the essence. *Held* by the House of Lords: the shipowner was entitled to repossess. The charterer could have negotiated a grace period but didn't. So what was the court to do—three days, three weeks, three months, who knows? The court said it was up to the parties to agree their risks (e.g., a grace period after notice, as is commonly done). If there was any doubt about whether the shipowner could repossess and the shipowner was wrong, then the shipowner could be liable for very substantial damages for wrongfully taking over the ship and interfering in the charterparty. Effectively the shipowner would be liable for exercising a right which it had agreed. Both the parties had comparable bargaining power.

This was an extreme case. One test of a legal system is whether it can cope with the occasional commercial abuse in favor of the higher ideal of predictability. The case is essentially a litmus test, the question being whether the other desired jurisdiction would reach the same decision on exactly the same facts.

The same result has been upheld in England in a long line of decisions on the acceleration of loans by a bank or a bank syndicate and the appointment of a receiver. Typically, in these cases responsible banks would have been in discussions with the borrower for many weeks and longer, until there was really no point, until the position was hopeless. Clauses providing for immediate acceleration of loans on an event of default have consistently been upheld.

The underlying policy is discipline of payments according to what was agreed when it is other people's money. Creditors often need payment on time to pay others (e.g., deposits out of loans). Timing can be crucial and therefore systemic in the case of central counterparties and the provision of collateral. Small businesses also suffer if, say, a supermarket does not pay them on time.

There are times when banks or corporations need to act swiftly; for example, in fast-moving markets where minutes or even seconds can count in relation to a close-out or sale or there is a threatened attachment or a set-off must be exercised as against a deposit on an aircraft or ship in fleeing its creditors.

It is suggested that the same result seems not to be consistently available in the case of, say, France, Germany or New York. They all have statutory overrides for vague "good faith". This in practice can on occasion be used to delay creditors, sometimes for months or more. In France the courts are specifically authorized to defer payments for up to two years and reduce the interest rate.

Good faith is enshrined by France CC art 1134, Germany BGB (Civil Code) s 242, US Uniform Commercial Code s 1–203 and Restatement (Second) of Contracts s 205. Members of the relevant groups tend to take a similar approach. The general doctrine of good faith was explicitly reaffirmed in the French contract reforms in 2016.

If parties prefer that good faith should apply in their contract to override its terms, then they could also still apply English law and insert a good faith clause and other provisions for mediation, cooling off, grace periods, notices of action and the like. The English courts respect good faith clauses; for example, *Horn v Commercial Acceptance Ltd* [2011] EWHC 1757 (Ch). The difference is that in the case of English law, it is the parties themselves who are trusted to decide the ideology.

To ensure predictability, the English courts have a doctrine that lower courts will follow higher courts (precedent), so that you know where you are. This is specifically not the case in France or Germany (or most members, of the relative groups), nor in practice is it the case in New York—largely because of jury trials and for other reasons. It may well be that in practice courts everywhere tend to follow a cluster of decision of higher courts, but this seems less clear in the case of the other groups.

The French courts are particularly prone to rewriting contracts in favor of debtors and to imposing reorganization plans on insolvency over the heads of creditors. The Civil Code expressly instructs the courts to back debtors in case of ambiguity.

In this matter, the issue is whether the parties want to have the court honor the terms they have agreed, even if they turn out to be unfair to one party, or whether they wish the court to override the agreed terms and substitute its own view.

Liability

One of the most important legal aspects of the law of contract is whether one of the parties can exclude liability in relation to the performance of the contract, such as contracts for the sale of goods which turn out to be defective.

Significant applications of this contest arise in relation to financial contracts, such as prospectuses for the sale of securities, offering memoranda for bank loan syndications, and contracts for derivatives. In most commercial jurisdictions, a prospectus for the offer of securities to the *public* and derivative contracts with consumers are regulated, and the ability for an arranger to exclude liability is restricted. We are dealing here with private contracts between parties of comparable bargaining power, which are outside the grasp of regulation.

If the contract states that the arranger has no liability to a business buyer of a derivative or for statements of an issuer in an offering circular (outside public issues) or in a bank syndicate offering memorandum, that will be normally be upheld by the English courts, except for fraud or the like.

There are numerous English cases which uphold disclaimer clauses in business situations which clearly state that the counterparties are not to rely on the arranger and that the arranger or underwriter has no duty to check the information of the borrower or issuer. For example, in the *IFE Fund* case (2006), Goldman Sachs was held not liable to bank syndicate members for an information memorandum which was allegedly wrong but had an explicit standard disclaimer. In the *Springwell* case (2010) JPMorgan Chase was not liable to a Greek family-owned shipping company for selling notes based on Russian GKOs. Springwell claimed $700 million. The court upheld the exclusion of liability clause.

There are a number of US cases to the same effect.

The rationale of the English courts is that in the offering circular cases, the parties should be able to apportion the risks themselves, including who does due diligence. Also, the claimant may sometimes just be looking for a big pocket to pay when the borrower or issuer is insolvent. The prospectus is that of the issuer, not the arranger.

In the derivative mis-selling cases outside the consumer arena, typically the counterparty has just lost the bet. If the counterparty did not understand the risk, the underlying rationale of the court is that the counterparty should have got its own advice and paid for it, instead of attempting to negate the deal after the event.

The effect is that the parties are in charge of and control the documents which they negotiated. English law does not rewrite legitimate contracts.

French contract reforms in 2016 require parties to disclose any information which is "essential" for the other contracting part, a duty which presumably extends to a guarantee or information memorandum. In the United States, juries impose their own idea of fairness.

Heads of terms and mandates to arrange financings: Because of the duty of good faith, it is much harder under French and German law to terminate negotiations on a contract before it has been agreed. English law generally honors "subject to contract" clauses so that parties are not bound unless they intended to be—important for credit contracts, as indeed any other major contract.

Insulation

A fundamental reason for a choice of law which is external to the country of the borrower of counterparty is to insulate the obligation against changes in the law of the debtor country. If, say, a loan is governed by the law of the debtor's country, then normally any moratorium or the like in the debtor's country is recognized under the governing law because the parties took the risk of that law, but not if the governing law is a foreign law. See for example the English case of *Re Helbert Wagg* [1956] where a German law of the 1930s in effect cancelling a foreign sterling loan from an English bank was recognized in a loan agreement governed by German law. Contrast *National Bank of Greece and Athens v. Metliss* [1958] where a Greek decree reducing the interest rate on a loan was not allowed to change an English law contract. So you can insulate by choice of law. US case law is to the same effect although the test is not what the governing law is, but rather where the loan is located—a less clear test, although you often get the same result.

This point was comprehensively debated and researched in in the early 1970s at the time of the inception of the Euromarkets. A number of Latin American countries argued that their syndicated bank credits from foreign banks should be governed by their own law and contain an arbitration clause. With very few exceptions the foreign banks refused to lend on that basis, and in the end English or New York law and courts were agreed in most cases.

However, some countries will defeat this insulation even in the case of the choice of a foreign governing law in the case of exchange controls. A provision in the International Monetary Fund (IMF) Agreement (article VIII 2b) requires the courts of member states (more or less the whole world) to recognize complying exchange controls of a member state in the case of "exchange contracts". In other words, the government of the country of the borrower or issuer can unilaterally change the deal by an exchange control—which they often do on insolvency if the sovereign itself is the debtor or if the borrower is locally important. Both New York and English law insulate even against these foreign intrusions by exchange controls and do not apply article VIII 2b to loans and bond issues—they are not "exchange contracts." But the insulation can be overridden in France, Germany and Luxembourg because of case law on the article. In those countries the borrower can in effect unilaterally change the deal even if governed by a foreign law.

In practice, exchange controls are the most frequent way in which countries postpone or discount their foreign debt obligations. Exchange controls can block the country's whole corporate sector and its banks. They are particularly common in emerging countries, thereby striking at project finance and local corporate and bank finance. India, China and South Africa have exchange controls. In the European region, exchange controls were introduced in the 2010s in Greece, Iceland, Cyprus and the Ukraine to cope with a sovereign insolvency or bank collapse. If a debt-ridden country or one of its dominant companies has financial problems, this is a way out for them, instead of negotiating an agreed restructuring.

Creditor Orientation

Legal systems tend to adopt positions on whether they are pro-creditor or pro-debtor, a choice which can profoundly affect outcomes.

English law is generally respectful of the position of creditors in comparative terms. As a generalization, it does not subordinate the interests of creditors to those of the insolvent debtor.

This is dramatically shown by the superpriority granted to the triple privileged claims—insolvency set-off (and netting), a universal corporate security interest which is easily enforceable, and the universal trust (e.g., for custodianship, central depositaries, client assets, syndicate agents holding collateral and bondholder trustees).

Each of this trio of common law protections reduces risks massively and protects, for example, banks that are at the center of risk and stability. On one view, banks and corporations are crucial to prosperity. The argument here is that, if one strips aside all the veils of incorporation, it is not the bank which is the lender. It is the citizen who places his or her salary in the bank who is the ultimate creditor, the creditor who is being protected in substance. It is the citizen who switches on the light.

Insolvency set-off: Insolvency set-off is the set-off of mutual claims by a party where its counterparty is insolvent (i.e., where each owes the other one or more debts). If set-off is allowed, the solvent creditor is in effect paid in priority to the other creditors. If set-off is not allowed, then the effect is that the debtor is paid (because the creditor still has to pay the debtor), but the creditor is not paid (because the debtor is hopelessly insolvent and the dividend is nil or trivial).

The flows in foreign exchange, derivative and securities markets go through world GDP every few days, so very large amounts are at stake. Set-off can sometimes reduce exposures by as much as 90%. In England set-off is compulsory and automatic on insolvency in all material cases. That is not so in France (and most members of the Napoleonic group). Both the US and German bankruptcy laws allow insolvency set-off, so the majority international opinion favors set-off.

Note that netting is a more intricate subject. If parties have a series of contracts between them, then on the insolvency on one party, the other party has to be able to cancel all those contracts, calculate the losses and gains on each contract and then set them off. Cancel, calculate, set-off. Many jurisdictions neuter contract termination clauses on insolvency, as is the case in the United States, Germany and France, thereby preventing netting unless exempted.

If we did not have the colossal risk reductions through set-off and netting in financial markets and through central counterparties, there would be nothing on the plate for breakfast. Nearly all advanced countries have installed special protections for set-off and netting in financial markets, so it is in the regions where these impenetrable and often narrow statutes do not apply that set-off becomes an issue.

Security interests: These are mortgages and charges creating security for a debt. In England it is possible for a corporation to create a fixed and floating charge over all its present and future assets to secure all present and future debt owing by the corporation and on a default to enforce this immediately by a private sale. This is also broadly the position in the United States, at least in relation to movables under Article 9 of the Uniform Commercial Code. The contrary is the case in most Napoleonic jurisdictions: normally universal charges are not available or for all debt, and enforcement may be led by the courts. The position in France and Belgium has been improved. Most Roman-Germanic jurisdictions are in between.

Trusts: The question of whether a trust exists matters only on the insolvency of the trustee. The test of a trust is whether the real owners of the asset whose title is held by the trustee gets its asset back if the trustee becomes insolvent. It does not matter whether you call this a trust or a fiducia or bailment or deposit or the man in the moon. That is the test and the main risk. The biggest trusts nowadays are enormous; for example, settlement systems for securities, such as the Depository Trust Company in the United States (half the GDP of the world) and Euroclear in Brussels (one and half times the GDP of the EU), that is together about $55 trillion.

In the United States (including Louisiana) and England, anybody can declare a trust of any transferable property present and future. This covers custodianship of securities at a depository (essential for collective investment schemes, central securities depositories and many others), a bondholder trustee or an agent bank holding security for the syndicate. In the other two groups, trusts are often limited. France has a Trust Law 2007, but the trust must be registered. Germany and Switzerland have trust laws for investments, but not generally for all property.

In many cases, not just under the Hague Trusts Convention 1985, one can choose the governing law which validates the trust. So parties requiring this protection can in these cases choose a system of law which has a full trust.

If the trust is not recognized, the assets of the trustee go to its private creditors, not the beneficiaries—a mournful prospect if the assets are a few hundred million. The real owner is effectively expropriated.

The German-based systems have a strong policy against trusts, outside special statutes, a policy stemming from 19th-century academic theory. Trusts are everywhere in financial transactions. Even a turnover subordination trust can be suspect in a non-trust country if the junior creditor is insolvent, thereby destroying the subordination in that case.

Hence as regards the trio of the three superpriority claimants, the Anglo-American groups have all three, the Roman-Germanic one and a half, and the traditional Napoleonic none—in each case subject to various exceptions. A neat triptych: one panel all blue, the second panel half blue and half red, and the third panel all red.

Director liability for deepening an insolvency: The more pro-debtor bias of France and Germany on insolvency is illustrated, for example, by the compulsion of directors to apply for an insolvency proceeding when the company is insolvent, thereby in many cases prejudicing the chances of a work-out or a negotiated pre-packaging (i.e., a private agreement with a court stamp on it). England has the concept of wrongful trading, which codifies director duties of care to creditors when a corporation is insolvent. Case law shows that directors are personally liable only in case of extreme irresponsibility. In the United States, this liability is almost unheard of—at least in Delaware.

Avoidance of preferences: These are an additional measure of pro-debtor or pro-creditor attitudes. English law has potent protections against the claw-back of preferences (e.g., in rescues or leveraged deals). These protections are generally weak in Roman-Germanic jurisdictions and even weaker in the Napoleonic jurisdictions and the United States. Claw-backs can threaten a work-out rescue by increasing the liability risks of the creditors and management.

Collective action clauses: A further example is collective action clauses in bonds. The US Trust Indenture Act of 1939 does not permit the majority bondholders of a corporation to bind the holdouts to changes of principal and most changes of interest. The debtor has to go into Chapter 11 to achieve creditor voting on a plan. English law has substantial case law on bondholder voting and no-action clauses which respect the benefits of a financial democracy in getting a deal through. Many countries in the other Napoleonic and Roman-Germanic groups have installed bondholder community statutes which provide for bondholder voting (e.g., Germany, Switzerland and Japan).

One could cite many other situations. Bankruptcy is a destroyer and a spoliator. One tests the views of a legal system on bankruptcy one way or the other. It is on bankruptcy that jurisdictions have to decide which way to jump.

Commerciality: Preventing the Nullity of Transactions

Does the law have a strong policy in favor of upholding transactions and ensuring that they are not nullified by some formality?

There are numerous illustrations. One example of this is that English law recognizes title finance transactions, such as repos and finance leasing, without recharacterizing them as a security interest—in which case they might be void for lack of registration or filing. Predictability is fundamental to English law. The United States generally does recharacterize, as do Australia, Canada and others but not Hong Kong or Singapore. France varies on this issue. Title finance is everywhere, from the humble retention of title clause for sold goods to grand title transfers under the ISDA master agreement.

There is of course much more to the issue of recharacterization than predictability.

Freedom of Contract

What is the degree of freedom of contract? There are an enormous number of situations.

English law and its counterparts generally favor freedom of contract in financial and commercial dealings. This original approach was that any fettering or manacling of the parties is justified only if it liberates us, improves our chances. Standing back, one may say that generally the purpose of a legal restriction is to free us, just as we have rules about our societies so that we can survive.

An example of freedom of contract is that (apart from a minor exception) English law does not override non-assignment clauses in commercial and financial contracts. France, Germany, the United States and many other countries, including Australia and most of Canada, do in significant cases. They do not allow the parties to decide for themselves. Clauses restricting assignments are part of the English ideology of freedom of contract. They are also the first line of defense for netting which might otherwise be lost in the case of an assignment. They prevent the contract landing in the hands of an unfriendly counterparty or a competitor or another intervener who upsets the transaction.

Hence the choice of law may decide whether the parties espouse the mandatory marketability of contracts or their own freedom to choose. Both routes have a substantial body of adherents.

There are many other examples, including predictability, maintaining the commercial validity of transactions, and a general orientation toward markets and commerce.

Language

English is the lingua franca of international business. It is hard to conduct litigation or to know one's rights and protect oneself when statutes and case law are in a foreign language, as well as court proceedings.

Market Acceptability

Both English and New York law have a proven track record of market acceptability over two centuries of use. They are acceptable in all markets, which helps the deal. Commercial parties know what is on offer, the law is familiar from constant use by international parties, there is a large body of consistent case law, and no extra investigation is required. This not generally true of either Germany or France or indeed most other jurisdictions.

Stability and the Rule of Law

All four jurisdictions have stable legal systems and a strong adherence to the rule of the law. The legal infrastructure is sound and efficient.

The United States has certain legal policies which are tougher than the other jurisdictions. For example, cases involving foreign banks have led to administrative fines which are a multiple of the fines in the UK, France or Germany. The litigation system has a strong plaintiff orientation—class actions, jury trials, unlimited discovery of documents, punitive damages, no costs even if the plaintiff loses, and a relative freedom to make accusations of criminality and racketeering. These litigation principles appear to be uncommon elsewhere, although individual aspects may be found in the rest of the world (e.g., class actions).

Conclusion on Governing Law

One should underline the point that legal systems have to make choices in their policies. These choices are typically not right or wrong, but they do not suit everybody. The positioning of a legal system is something which societies have to work out for themselves. What the situation requires is clarity on what the choices are so that people can make an informed choice between the competing ideologies on offer.

Why It Is Necessary to Understand Jurisdictions

The reason that the law has become a behemoth difficult to comprehend stems from a number of factors.

The most obvious fact is the huge upsurge in the amount of money around—the financialization of the world. Around 1830, the population of the world reached 1 billion for the first time. A century later, in 1930, it was 2 billion. Then rapidly it bounded up in increasingly short leaps to top more than 7.5 billion now.

A lot more people produce a lot more. In 1980, the GDP of the world in adjusted dollars was roughly $20 trillion ($700 billion in 1830). Now it is over $80 trillion—four times as much as 1980. All this money does not go under the mattress. Much of it ends up in banks, pension funds and investments. This leads to more prosperity. But it also leads to more mayhem, which in turn leads to more law as legislators wave the legal wand to banish crises.

To be more specific, one can identify a number of factors which since 1980 have resulted in an increase in the volume of law and the complications of practicing the law.

The first is new financial inventions. The obvious examples are derivatives and securitizations. Both were of respectable antiquity (grain for derivatives, forfaiting of bills of exchange for securitizations) but what was new was the volume and sophistication. Derivatives flowed originally from the advent of floating currencies after the Vietnam War so that currency values and interest rates were volatile—so people need to hedge the risks. The impulse behind securitizations in the 1980s was the need to finance home loans for the increasing population by in effect refinancing bank loans in the capital markets.

The second factor is the increase in the number of jurisdictions adopting market economies, especially after the collapse of the Soviet Empire, the last of the 20th century round of collapsing empires.

In 1980, financial lawyers dealt with only a few jurisdictions. Socialist countries were largely excluded. Now there are 321 jurisdictions with separate laws—only a few remain withdrawn from the business of business on the planet. Aside from the multiplier effect on law and transactions, other progeny was the greater interplay of conflict of laws.

The third factor is the tiering and layering of legal regimes domestically. At one time legal regimes had two tiers—the individual and the merchant. But now, for example, there are at least eight tiers of law for security interests in England, ranging from the law applicable to clearing systems at the freest down to the law applying to charges created by non-business individuals—the most restrictive. Multiply 8 by 321 and you get over 2,500.

England also has at least 25 different types of bankruptcy regime. Multiply 321 by 25 and you get over 8,000.

Other Factors

The closeness of the embrace between jurisdictions forced into each other's arms by trade links and population growth led to extraterritorial laws to cope with cross-border contagions. The result is that lawyers must deal not only with their own laws but also those of others. Examples are antitrust (competition), sanctions, insider dealing, market manipulation and bribery. The close squeeze also invited more shoving and hustling in terms of foreign litigation and the imposition of foreign laws, sometimes aggressive in their scope.

Another consequence of the increase in jurisdictions has been the need to take account of political risks and rule of law risks, as well as the inefficiency of the local legal infrastructure. The black-letter law might be acceptable, but these other risks can be deal stoppers.

Then finally, there is the dilation in financial regulation as a result of the global financial crisis, an increase which needs no further elaboration. Financial regulation hardly existed in 1980, except in the United States as a result of the Great Depression.

Impact on the Number of Lawyers

The above has led to an increase in the number of lawyers in the world. Just by way of order of magnitude without being precise, there appear to be somewhere between 6 and 7 million lawyers in the world, depending on who you count—maybe more. The United States, which is the world's largest legal market, has about 1,350,000 lawyers. The main 45 countries which have GDPs per capita in excess of $20,000 (there are quite a lot more than 45) have about 1,370,000 lawyers. Brazil, Russia, India and China are said to have about 2,600,000 lawyers between them. Then there are the other 150 or so other countries to be added.

As world population is rather more than 7 billion, the average seems to be very roughly one lawyer per just over 1,000 people. Recently it was recorded that New York has one lawyer per 115 people, Californian one per 246, the UK one per 324—these figures are constantly changing. In 1980 socialist and very poor countries had a tiny number of lawyers compared to what they have now.

One can therefore say that, notwithstanding predictions to the contrary, cold winds do not blow through the empty halls of the faculties of law, nor have the cloud-capped towers of the law firms or in-house lawyers vanished into airy nothingness. The law has not become a desolate ruin in the desert amidst the lone and level sands stretching far away.

Are There Any Solutions?

So how do we solve this problem of the law's increase?

The chances of legislatures reducing the amount of law seem remote. This pruning has hardly ever happened in history, notwithstanding the boasts of politicians to do something about the situation. The law doesn't often go on a diet.

The second way out is for the law to be pared down by greater codification (i.e., distillation). This was the solution of Justinian with the Roman law codification in 535 and that of the great codifiers of the 19th century.

This is not likely to be a solution either because the codifiers were distilling the principles of case law, whereas the problem we have now is a mountain of statutes and regulations which, as mentioned, seem immune to distillation in practice.

Third, jurisdictions could harmonize. The United States achieved substantial harmonization in, for example, the Uniform Commercial Code, and the experience is similar in countries such as Canada and Australia.

But in these cases there was substantial agreement on basic policies—derived from the English-based common law systems. Contrast Europe. But when it comes to the difficult points, agreement seems very difficult. After 15 centuries there is still no agreement on the trust in Europe—a simple issue if ever there was one. At the international level, financial law is like a stone hitting a windscreen—shattered and fissured.

Finally, we may be saved by artificial intelligence. We surely need legal tech to enable lawyers to practice at all. The quicker it arrives, the better—in my estimation we are still in the foothills of the potential. But if we humans cannot devise the answers, it seems unlikely that we can instruct our robots on devise them instead.

There is another answer. This is that there is a way of grouping systems of law, as I have described. Often there are only three answers to a legal problem. The art is to know what the problem is and to know the three answers. This chapter aimed to suggest a framework for that endeavor.

Conclusion

The laws of the 321 jurisdictions reflect the intense beauty and aspirations of human philosophies over centuries of thinking. Our laws are not perfect, but then nor are we.

On July 2, 1816, at 3:00 p.m. the French frigate *Medusa* struck a sandbank 60 miles off the coast of west Africa. The terrified crew and passengers built a raft out of planks of the ship and 147 people got on the raft. The captain and the crew climbed into the six ship's boats to row to the shore "to get help." Only 15 got off the raft when it was rescued by another French ship. Nearly all the rest were killed in the fighting for the brandy and the biscuits. The raft is portrayed in a stupendous and justly famous canvas by Gericault which hangs in the Louvre in Paris.

On August 5, 2010, at around lunchtime, 33 miners in a mine in Chile heard a thunderous crack and rumbling of rock above them. They were trapped more than 2,000 feet down. Yet they all escaped after 69 days. So what was the difference compared to the raft?

One difference was that the Chilean miners elected a leader who then made rules rationing food and water and sharing what they had, They had a constitutional law and a rudimentary legal system. But on the raft the captain left the ship and they had no rules about food and drink. They had no laws, just anarchy. The Chileans survived, but those on the raft did not. We have laws to survive.

I believe that our laws are our most important codifications of our moral systems—the rules which we need for our survival. We have a duty to survive. These rules do not only cover murder and other serious crimes, or our constitutional laws, or our family laws—they also cover taxation and the laws of money, banks and corporations. They cover us in a terrible emergency too, as best they can. They are our scriptures. We should look after our scriptures. To do that, we must first understand them.

Bibliography

Supporting citation for the propositions in this chapter may be found in the revised version of the author's Law and Practice of International Finance series published by Sweet & Maxwell, London, in nine books in 2019.

There is a full treatment of governing law and jurisdiction agreements on a comparative basis in *Conflict of Laws and International Finance* (which is volume 8 in the series, 3rd edition), including the case law on exchange controls and article VIII 2b of the IMF Agreement. Factors relating to the choice of governing law are in chapter 3.

The main classification of the world's jurisdictions into their families of law and a comparative treatment of debtor/creditor orientation in many different contexts is in *Principles of International Insolvency* (volume 1 in the series, 3rd edition). There is a short summary in chapter 2.

Volume 2 *Principles of International Insolvency: Jurisdictions of the World I* contains summaries of insolvency law in all 321 jurisdictions of the world which facilitates a comparative study.

Volume 3 *Comparative Law of Security Interests and Title Finance* (3rd edition) deals with world comparative security interests, relevant to the discussion in this chapter about security interests. See especially the summary in chapter 2. Its companion, volume 4, has summaries of security interests in all the world's jurisdictions.

Volume 6 on *Set-off and Netting, Derivatives, Clearing Systems* (3rd edition) contains citation and commentary supporting the assertions in this chapter about set-off, including a study of the main netting carve-out statutes in chapter 8 and a world survey of set-off and netting in chapter 9.

International Loans, Bonds, Guarantees, Legal Opinions (volume 5, 3rd edition) contains discussions of such matters as exclusion clauses in information memoranda (chapter 2), of cases on loan accelerations (chapter 16), bond trustees (chapter 32) and collective action clauses in bonds with the relevant case law and country studies.

Volume 1 mentioned above has details on the recognition of the trust internationally (chapters 13 to 15) and see also volume 4 for a country by country survey of trustees of security.

On liability for bond prospectuses, see also *Regulation of International Finance* (volume 9, 2nd edition), chapter 35.

For the treatment of turnover subordinations on the insolvency of the junior creditor, see *Project Finance, Securitisations, Subordinated Debt* (volume 7, 3rd edition) chapter 11, and volume 4 containing jurisdiction summaries, often including this point.

PART IV

Cyber, Data Risks, and Technological Considerations

19

CONSIDERATIONS FOR A SUCCESSFUL CYBERSECURITY PROGRAM

Kristine A. Hayes Munson

If you remember nothing from this chapter, remember that your organization is at risk for a cybersecurity attack. Robert Mueller, when serving as FBI director, sounded a somber warning regarding the evolution and prevalence of cybercrime to 2012 RSA Cyber Security Conference attendees. He stated, "I am convinced that there are only two types of companies: those that have been hacked and those that will be. And even they are converging into one category: companies that have been hacked and will be hacked again" (Mueller, 2012). Former executive chairman and CEO of Cisco Systems John Chambers took this warning one step further by stating, "There are two types of companies: those that have been hacked, and those who don't know they have been hacked" (Kerravala, 2015).

Every organization including global Fortune 500 firms, local small businesses, and educational institutions face the risk of cyberattack. How successful will your organization be at thwarting the attack? Will your organization's defenses halt the attack? Will the intruder breach your organization's network? How long would it take your organization to detect, investigate, contain and recover from a cybersecurity breach? Recall these highly publicized cybersecurity breaches. These firms may be more like yours than you want to admit.

- RSA: 40 million employee records compromised in the March 2011 RSA breach
- Yahoo: Information taken from 3 billion Yahoo user accounts in 2013–2014;
- Target: Credit/debit card information from 110 million Target customers exposed in 2013;
- Equifax: Personal information stolen from 143 million Equifax customers in 2017;
- Atlanta: Ransomware crippled the City of Atlanta in March 2018, prohibiting it from accepting payment for taxes and fees.

These cybersecurity breaches are only a handful of examples of which you've probably heard and by which you may have even been impacted. It is more a matter of "when" rather than "if" an organization will experience a cybersecurity attack. An organization makes the headlines when it discloses a cybersecurity breach publicly. At this point it is too late. The damage is done. Each breach costs the victim firm millions of dollars in reputation damage, recovery costs and monetary damages. According to IBM's 2017 Cost of Data Breach Study, the average cost of a lost or stolen record is $141. CEOs and other senior management team members are forced to resign. The organization's reputation is damaged in the eyes of its current and future customers. Experts anticipate cybercrime will "cost approximately $6 trillion per year on average through 2021" (Eubanks, 2017).

DOI: 10.4324/9781351107242-24

The media rarely reports about an organization building a strong cybersecurity program. Savvy customers expect organizations with whom they do business to put in place a robust cybersecurity program. Request for proposals (RFPs) routinely include cybersecurity questions because prospective customers want to make sure their data provide to the firm will be secured appropriately. Once a customer decides to do business with an organization, clients frequently request an update on an organization's cybersecurity program to ensure ongoing due diligence in protecting the customer's data. Regulators and other external auditors include cybersecurity topics in examinations of an organization's internal controls.

A successful cybersecurity program aligns with the business's strategy and protects the organization's data assets. Accountability for an organization's overall cybersecurity rests with the board of directors. The senior management team sets the tone from the top for cybersecurity, building a strong cybersecurity culture and adequately funding a cybersecurity program. Cybersecurity professionals, who report in to the C-suite, secure organizations by combining their technical expertise with strong general, risk and project management skills. Business owners and management play a pivotal role in ensuring data security and make risk-based decisions using their understanding of the data's value and the impact of unexpected data loss or unauthorized data disclosure. Other key cybersecurity program stakeholders include, but are not limited to, information technology (IT), business continuity, finance, legal, human resources, internal audit and enterprise risk management. Each individual employee serves as the first line of defense in the war against breaches.

This chapter provides a high-level overview of considerations for building a world-class cybersecurity, risk-based program to secure your organization's data, regardless of your organization's size. Each topic covered could be a stand-alone chapter or book. There are other cybersecurity topics which were omitted due to space constraints. No discussion is included regarding specific cybersecurity technical tools, as technical tools used to combat attacks change as rapidly as the threat environment. Hopefully, this chapter will "whet your appetite" and give you place to start in your own journey to better understand how to protect your organization's data using best cybersecurity risk-based practices.

What Is the Difference Between Information Security and Cybersecurity?

Data is your organization's most valuable asset and must be protected. Each organization's data is as unique as the organization itself. Data comes from many sources. Your organization possesses proprietary information or the "secret recipe" that makes its products and services unique from other firms. Ongoing operations generate data, such as personal information in the form of employment records for current, past and potential employees. Data can be physical, on pieces of paper housed in filing cabinets or on an employee's desk. Each time you print a document, it becomes physical data to be protected. Data also exists electronically, housed in an organization's databases or file system. You create data each time you make a presentation deck or input information into an application. Incoming and outgoing emails are also data requiring protection.

Individuals frequently use the terms information security and cybersecurity interchangeably. However, the phrases have clearly differentiated meanings to security professionals. *Information security* protects the confidentiality, integrity and availability of your data regardless of its source or how it is stored. Security professions use the acronym CIA to refer to confidentiality, integrity and availability of data. Confidentiality implies that only those individuals who are authorized to do so access your organization's information—electronic and physical data. Confidentiality is especially important when securing private personal information or proprietary information and ensuring that information is not disclosed to any unauthorized party. Integrity connotes that the organization's information is complete and intact. The information security program protects information from inappropriate modification or deletion. Availability means that the information user can access the data reliably in a timely manner.

Cybersecurity is a subset of information security. It narrows the security focus down to protecting data stored electronically. Cybersecurity programs protect electronic data in the cyber realm, taking into account confidentiality, integrity and availability. This chapter focuses on securing electronic data.

What Types of Electronic Data Exist?

Estimates claim that at least 85% of an organization's business assets are now electronic (Eubanks, 2017). Before you can protect your organization's electronic data, you need to understand what kind of data exists within your organization and where it can be found. In other words, you need to complete a data asset inventory. Generally speaking, there are two types of data to be captured in the inventory: structured data and unstructured data. *Structured data* is housed within application databases used by internally developed or third-party applications. Completing a structured data inventory involves inventorying the organization's application suite and documenting what data each application contains, because end users read, write and modify structured data through an application with direct database access being prohibited. The application makes the decisions as to where in the database to place the data rather than the user. Application databases rarely, if ever, store structured data on a user's physical PC or laptop. Rather they store data so that it can be accessed across the enterprise by those users who have been granted the required application and data access entitlements.

Unstructured data is housed in the file system and created via word processing, presentation, spreadsheets, email or related applications. If data is extracted from an application in the form of a report and saved outside of the application, that report becomes unstructured data. Unstructured data can be saved locally to a physical PC or to an organization's network drives. It may be accessible to only the individual who created the data, or it could be placed in a shared directory so others can read and update it. IDC's research asserts that 90% of an organization's data is unstructured data (Schubmehl, 2014). Inventorying unstructured data is fraught with multiple difficulties because of the difficulty of seeing the data as a whole. Data ownership must be assigned to all inventoried structured and unstructured data.

Who Owns the Data Requiring Protection?

Your first instinct in answering this question is to say the organization owns the data requiring protection. Technically, this is a correct response. A cybersecurity program requires that a more defined, named person or position plays the role of data owner.

Data ownership must be assigned to the data produced as part of business operations. The *data owner* is the person who is responsible for the business process which creates and uses the data. Neither IT nor the cybersecurity team is the data owner. Rather those teams take actions to safeguard and protect the data based on the business manager data owner's directions and requirements. The data owner is a member of the organization's business management team and understands the data's tangible and intangible value to the organization. A senior human resources (HR) manager owns data which originates in HR such as personnel records, whereas the chief operations officer owns data related to your organization's intellectual property.

The data owner classifies the data based on its use and the impact to the organization associated with data loss. The data owner identifies personally identifiable information (PII), personal health information (PHI) or business proprietary data. The data owner is one of the key subject matter experts who participates in the cybersecurity risk management program. She works with the organization's legal team to determine which laws and regulations apply to the data that she owns and makes decisions regarding how the data is used and who can access the data. We will discuss these responsibilities in greater detail throughout the chapter.

Where Is the Electronic Data Requiring Protection?

Structured data and unstructured data stored on the organization's network can be housed on servers found on your organization's premises (*on-prem*) in a data center owned by your organization or in a co-located (*colo*) data center where a specific space or cage is managed by the organization. In an on-prem or colo operation, the organization supports its own infrastructure comprising networking, storage and physical or virtual servers. Internally developed or licensed, third-party applications run on the infrastructure. In this model the organization assumes all responsibility for mitigating cybersecurity risks via its own cybersecurity program.

The organization may elect to house data in the cloud where the firm contracts with a third-party vendor to house the data across the service provider's geographically dispersed data centers, where new capacity can be added on demand. A shared responsibility for cybersecurity exists in the cloud. The organization's management, including its chief information security officer, must understand the shared security model and know who is responsible for which security function. Cloud service can be broken into three categories (Table 19.1).

Organizations may also house data in a combination of locations based on business requirements. For example, a firm may maintain some data on-prem for legacy, internally developed applications while using a SaaS model for other data.

From What and Whom Are We Protecting the Data?

This chapter started by mentioning some infamous cybersecurity breaches where data was exfiltrated from the organization's systems or modified so the systems no longer function. Look at the news today. There is a high probability of another cybersecurity breach being reported.

These successful attacks provide organizations with intelligence regarding known threats in the environment. A *threat* is an intention or potential event which will cause harm to an organization by

Table 19.1 Three Categories of Cloud Service

Infrastructure as a Service (IaaS)	The third party provides a basic level of cloud service which includes networking, storage and virtual servers allowing the organization to quickly scale as demand grows. It can be described as a virtual data center. The organization is responsible for securing the applications, data and operating system using the cloud-based infrastructure. The service provider protects the network, storage and servers. The other cloud service models discussed below use IaaS as their foundation. IaaS examples include Microsoft Azure (Azure), Amazon Web Services (AWS) and Google Cloud Platform (GCP).
Platform as a Service (PaaS)	The third party provides infrastructure, as well as databases and programming languages, to the organization so the organization can develop and run applications developed by the organization itself to support its products and services. The organization reduces its cybersecurity responsibilities in this model as it is responsible for securing only the applications and data. The service provider protects the other systems. PaaS examples include Azure, AWS and GCP.
Software as a Service (SaaS)	The third party provides software and houses the data contained within that software. The organization pays a subscription fee to use the software. It saves money by minimizing the staff required to develop and support the software. The service provider develops the application and supports the infrastructure used to run the application. The organization transfers the cybersecurity protection risk to the service provided in this model for the application, data and infrastructure. Examples of such software include SalesForce and Google Docs.

breaching the organization's data. Threats can come from external sources or from within the organization. Cybersecurity professionals develop threat scenarios to analyze different types of threats. The scenarios examine the tactics, techniques and procedures (TTPs) an attacker may use in each scenario. One scenario type is that the attack is a one-time attack where the damage is done immediately. Compare this to a bank robbery in the brick-and-mortar world. Another scenario type focuses on *advanced persistent threat* (APT), where attackers possess the financial resources which allow them to persistently or continually attack the organization over an extended period. An APT attacker adjusts their strategy as the organization changes its defensive tactics to prohibit attack.

Scenarios examine who the possible attacker, referred to as a *threat actor*, may be and their motivations for the attack. Threat actors can be internal or external to the organization. Verizon's 2018 annual *Data Breach Investigations Report* (*DBIR*) asserts that 73% of attacks were perpetrated by outsiders in 2017 while only 23% involved insiders (Verizon, 2018, p. 5). Organizations routinely test their cybersecurity defenses as compared to the threat scenarios using penetration tests conducted by "white hat" hackers external to the organization.

Internal Threat Actor

The CERT Insider Threat Center confirms the Verizon DBIR assertion mentioned above that insiders perpetrate fewer data breaches than external parties (CERT Insider Threat Center, 2016, p. 4). *Internal threat actors* are individuals such as employees, contractors and vendors who are (or were) authorized to access the organization's network and data. Insiders know the organization and know where its crown jewels or most valuable data can be found. An insider may inadvertently disclose information by sending data to the incorrect party accidently or be the unwilling victim of a phishing attack. We'll discuss phishing in more detail when we discuss external threat actors. Worse case, an insider may maliciously sabotage the organization's technology systems and data, steal and disclose intellectual property, or commit fraud using the data. Malicious insiders exploit technical vulnerabilities and business process weaknesses.

Multiple motivations exist for insider threat attacks. Moore's research shows that 70% of insider theft of intellectual property occurs within the last 60 days of the person's employment with the organization (Moore, 2013, pp. 12–13). The CERT Insider Threat Center provides additional reasons why insiders perpetrate malicious cybercrimes, including:

- The individual is disgruntled due to perceived injustices with the organization
- The employee failed to receive an anticipated raise or promotion
- A contract is coming to the end and there is uncertainty regarding its renewal
- Anytime workforce reduction occurs through layoffs

(CERT Insider Threat Center, 2016, p. 43)

Discouraging the internal threat actor requires organizations to adopt a robust internal security policy and build a cybersecurity-aware culture. The policy documents the standards for appropriate use and access of the organization's data. It should be coupled with ongoing employee cybersecurity education and awareness training which empowers employees to become an organization's first line of defense. Cybersecurity training starts the day an individual joins the organization and continues throughout their tenure. Mechanism exist for employees to report potential cybersecurity incidents to a response team. If a third party including contractors can access the data, appropriate cybersecurity language must be included in the contract.

Data owners play an indispensable role in safeguarding data by limiting data access. Remember, we previously discussed that data owners approve who can access the data for which they are responsible. Access should be granted using the least privileged access model. In other words, only those individuals with a need to know or use the data to successfully execute their job responsibilities should be granted access to data. A cybersecurity best practice is for data owners to review or recertify users who can access the data on at least an annual basis.

External Threat Actor

External threat actors execute most cyber breaches and include cybercriminals, nation states and hacktivists. Cybercriminals are looking for a way they can monetize the attack and receive a return on their investment. Verizon (2018) reports that financial gain is the primary motivation for threat actors (p. 6). Attackers can *exfiltrate* your data and sell it, or they may opt to encrypt the organization's data via ransomware because they see income potential in the ransom payment. The second most common motivation for attacking a system is espionage perpetrated by a nation state or state-sponsored attackers (ibid). Other attack motivations such as hacktivism follow distantly behind (ibid).

How Long Does It Take an External Threat Actor to Compromise Your Network?

Repeatedly for many years, Verizon's DBIR warns readers that attackers breached the victim in a matter of minutes, if not seconds. Threat actors use *vulnerabilities* or weaknesses in an organization's cybersecurity defenses to attack the organization. Vulnerabilities can exist in the operating system, database management system or application software. The good news is that these vulnerabilities can be addressed through a rigorous, regular patching and upgrade program.

Yet Verizon (2016) reported that most attacks exploit known vulnerabilities where a patch was previously distributed, and the victimized organization failed to deploy the patch in a timely manner to all systems with the vulnerability. In 2017, the worldwide WannaCry ransomware attacks exploited a known Microsoft Windows vulnerability where the previously distributed operating system patch was not deployed. Patched systems were safe. *Ransomware* encrypts your organization's data and demands a ransom payment. Upon payment of the ransom using bitcoin, the attacker promises to decrypt your data. The WannaCry attack attributed by the United States to North Korea succeeded in over 100 countries and famously paralyzed British hospitals. Victim organizations struggled with the decision to pay or not to pay the ransom. Many organizations globally followed the FBI's recommendation not to pay the requested ransom. Others paid and were still unable to recover their data fully. The WannaCry attack and its impact are estimated to have cost $4 billion globally.

People can be the organization's biggest vulnerability. Employees can fall victim to *social engineering attacks* and *phishing attacks*, which are also known as business email compromise (BEC) attacks. Attackers use social engineering to learn about an organization and its employees. Attackers study the targeted employee's social media accounts to gain valuable information regarding this individual. Company information is gleaned from exploring the company's online presence. The threat actor crafts a phishing email where the recipient clicks on a link or attachment containing malware using the gleaned information. A famous example of a successful phishing attack occurred during the 2016 US presidential election. Clinton campaign chairman John Podesta responded to a phishing email, providing hackers with his password and access to his emails. Armed with his password, attackers downloaded his emails and published them on WikiLeaks.

What Are the Characteristics of a Cybersecurity Breach?

A cybersecurity breach is different than an incident. Verizon (2016) defines an *incident* as "a security event that compromises the integrity, confidentiality or availability of an information asset" (5). An incident can be something as simple as a virus detected and removed by antivirus software.

Verizon (2016) defines a *breach* as "an incident that results in the confirmed disclosure (not just potential exposure) of data to an unauthorized party" (p. 5). In other words, a cybersecurity breach occurs when an unauthorized party accesses, steals or discloses confidential, proprietary data such as PII, PHI or proprietary data. Data integrity may also be threatened as part of a cybersecurity breach. Every organization is a potential target. Breaches must follow public disclosure laws and regulations. Incidents not rising to the level of a breach need not be reported publicly.

A breach can be broken down into five components:

1. Compromise
2. Exfiltration/data manipulation
3. Discovery/investigation
4. Containment
5. Return to normal operations.

The *compromise* is the entry into your organization's systems. It takes minutes or seconds for an attacker to breach an organization's network and weeks or months to *discover* a breach and that the data has been *exfiltrated*. Customers and law enforcement agencies are frequently the ones who discover the breach first rather than the organization itself (Verizon, 2015). The faster a data breach is discovered, the quicker it is contained. The quicker a data breach is contained, the lower the cost of the breach. Think of *containment* as stopping the bleeding on a physical wound.

Consider, for example, the now infamous Russian hack on the Democratic National Committee (DNC) during the 2016 US presidential election campaign. The DNC failed to detect the breach independently and learned of the matter from the FBI, who first contacted the DNC in September 2015 and again in November 2015. Yet the DNC seemingly ignored those warnings and took no significant action to contain the breach until after April 2016. The DNC subsequently reported that breached their network as early as July 2015. In other words, the Russian attacker known as Cozy Bear was in the DNC's network for approximately eight months before they took any action—near the average time of 257 days that a typical breach causes a firm to lose data, according to IBM's 2017 Cost of Data Breach Study. Russians gained and later leaked information from the DNC's email, backups, VOIP calls, and chats. The DNC spent over a million dollars to contain the breach and return to normal operations (Barrett, 2018).

Incident Response Plan

When a breach is discovered, organizations invoke their predefined cybersecurity incident response and, if required, business continuity plans during a breach's containment phase. Incident response plans provide information regarding the technical, management and legal responses to an detected event. These plans document who to involve in halting the breach, ensuring the business can continue to function, and listing who to notify when based on the severity of the breach. Notifications may include law enforcement agencies such as the FBI, regulators and individuals whose data was compromised. For example, if an organization believes the breach is criminal activity, law enforcement should be notified immediately. If the breach is inadvertently exposing data to a third party, no law enforcement involvement is required.

A key element used to create an incident response plan is a business impact analysis (BIA), where the organization determines what the impact to its daily operations would be if a system ceased normal operations. The organization's business continuity team prepares the BIA in conjunction with the organization's various business units, and the cybersecurity team leverages it. The BIA assesses the criticality of organizational systems and prioritizes recovery efforts based on the impact of a system being down on the individual business unit as well as the entire organization. The BIA documents downtime estimates such as:

- Maximum tolerable downtime (MTD) or maximum tolerable outage (MTO): The longest amount of time an outage can continue and the business remain viable.
- Recover time objective (RTO): The targeted amount of time to restore the business to an operational level. In other words, the business requires that critical systems be functional four hours after the incident, or financial losses would will exceed a tolerable level set by management.
- Recovery point objective (RPO): The targeted time prior to restore data to its last known good point prior to the incident. For example, the maximum amount of data loss is 30 minutes.

Once the breach is contained, then the hard work of returning to normal operations begins. Recall the November 2014 malware attack on Sony Pictures. The malware allegedly unleashed by North Korea exfiltrated data including salary information, Social Security numbers and management emails, which was later released online. Plus the malware "erased everything stored on 3,262 of the company's 6,797 personal computers and 837 of its 1,555 servers" (Elkind, 2015). The studio rebuilt its technology infrastructure from the ground up while using manual, paper-based and cash-based processes to continue daily operations.

Is My Organization's Cybersecurity Program Adequate?

There are no easy answers to the question regarding the adequacy of an organization's cybersecurity program. An organization's cybersecurity program protects it from attack daily. Attackers have the luxury of specializing in one type of attack. If they are unsuccessful in breaching one firm, they move on to the next until they are successful. They enjoy the luxury of time. Think advanced persistent threat, where the key word is "persistent." An organization's cybersecurity program requires expertise and success for every type of attack every time an attacker launches an attack. Chances are high that your organization has employed the basic elements of a cybersecurity program, such as deploying firewalls, requiring access controls for people logging on to the network, implementing virus/malware detection software and patching on a regular cadence. Cybersecurity programs require continuous improvements and enhancements to keep up with the ever-changing threat environment.

What should my organization do to enhance its data security? Implement employee training? Require the use of two-factor authentication? Launch a data leakage program? Patch more frequently? The answer is, it depends. Organizations make hard, economic choices on what investments to make to secure their data in an environment where technology constantly changes. Adopting a *risk management program* to assess cybersecurity risks, monitor cybersecurity risks and respond to cybersecurity risks will assist firms in answering these hard investment questions. A cybersecurity risk management program is similar to risk management programs used in other areas of the organization's business. In the best-case scenario, the cybersecurity risk management program is a component of the organization's larger enterprise risk management process.

An ongoing risk assessment process forms the backbone of an organization's risk management program. A *risk assessment* looks at risk, likelihood and impact. Subject matter experts from throughout the organization participate in the cybersecurity risk assessment, rather than limiting the analysis participants to only cybersecurity professionals. The business data owner is indispensable in the risk assessment process as they possess the greatest insight into the risk's potential impact.

- *Risk*: Risk events are identified by looking at known threats in the environment and vulnerabilities. Vulnerabilities can be technical in nature. Business policies and operational procedures can also be a vulnerability. The subject matter experts must take the time required to identify all relevant risks and to adequately define those risks. Tools such as brainstorming can be used to jump-start the risk identification process.

- *Likelihood*: This analysis determines what the likelihood, possibility or probability is that the risk would occur. Factors to consider include a potential attacker's ability and intentions along with the organization's overall cybersecurity practices. Likelihood also considers time. What is the likelihood of the risk occurring in three months versus one year or five years from now? The participating subject matter experts assign a numeric probability to each potential risk event, usually using a predefined definitional scale.
- *Impact*: The risk assessment final component is to determine what would be the impact to the organization if the risk occurred. What adverse impact would the organization experience? Potential impacts include, but are not limited to, reputational, legal liability, loss of business, event cost and inability to do business. The participating subject matter experts assign a dollar amount to the impact.

Results of the completed risk assessment are communicated throughout the organization. Members of the board of directors, C-suite executives and other business management team members, as well as IT team members need to understand the cybersecurity risks faced by the company. Together they decide what actions an organization will take for identified risks. Based on the organization's risk tolerance, risk can be:

- *Accepted*, and no further action will be taken by the organization regarding the risk. Accepting a risk is an appropriate action if the risk is determined to be low or below the established risk tolerance. For example, an organization may choose to accept the risk of a third-party representative logging onto the network because that individual only authenticates on-site and passed a required background check prior to being granted network access.
- *Mitigated* by funding and executing projects to change processes, procedures, controls or systems to reduce the risk. A cost benefit analysis must be undertaken for each project to ensure the project's resulting benefits and cost do not exceed the costs associated with the risk's impact. Most organizations choose to mitigate the risk of a phishing attack by investing in technology to minimize the number of phishing emails reaching the end user's mailbox and by training end users on how to spot and report a suspicious email.
- *Transferred* by working with another organization to assume all or part of the risk. One strategy to transfer cybersecurity risk is moving infrastructure and applications to the cloud using the IaaS, PaaS or SaaS models. The cloud provider now becomes the primary risk owner. Cybersecurity insurance can also be purchased, making the insurance company the primary risk owner.
- *Avoided* by taking such actions removing high-risk systems or applications from the organization's IT platform. An organization may avoid the risk of infecting the network with malware from unauthorized devices by systemically prohibiting the use of USB storage devices on company PCs and by no longer allowing guest laptops to connect to the network.

Residual risk is any risk remaining after the organization takes the required actions to mitigate, transfer or avoid the risk. The risk assessment should be updated to reflect the residual risk. The entire risk assessment itself must be reviewed and updated on a regular basis, usually annually. Additionally, a third-party risk management (TPRM) program will need to be added to the overall risk management plan to assess risks associated with transferring risks to a vendor.

Risk monitoring is the second leg of an organization's risk management program. Monitoring involves continual tracking of the organization's efforts to mitigate, transfer or avoid risks. It also involves monitoring the environment at large to determine if there are any significant changes. The third leg of a risk management program involves determining if one of the risk events occurs and activating pre-defended incident response programs and business continuity programs.

Which Regulations Should be Used as an Input Into the Cybersecurity Risk Assessment?

Before examining which regulations impact your organization's cybersecurity, you must first understand the organization's business, the type of data used by that business and the geographic locations in which the organization does business. Cybersecurity, at its heart, is a business concern. Business operations produce unique (and some not so unique) data. Who is the best person to understand the business and know the data? The data owner.

The organization's legal team continuously scans the environment identifying new or changed laws and regulations that apply to the organization as a whole. They then communicate broadly the changes to the business management team, which includes the data owner. The data owner must identify the potential applicability of the law or regulation and work with legal to determine the actions to be taken for compliance.

Table 19.2 shows a representative sample of laws and regulations to be considered for inclusion in the cybersecurity risk analysis, which focus on protecting data about the individual or PII. This is not a comprehensive list. It shows that laws can be international in scope, US-based, or US state–based. No unified data privacy standard exists, although the European Union's General Data Protection Regulation (GDPR) mandate does so for countries within the EU.

US public companies must also comply with the Security Exchange Commission's (SEC) guidance on disclosing cyber risks and incidents in its publicly available financial reporting in the annual report on Form 10-K and quarterly reports on Form 10-Q. The SEC issued its more recent guidance in February 2018. This guidance expands on its original 2011 guidance. According to the guidance, the SEC "believes that it is critical that public companies take all required actions to inform investors

Table 19.2 Sample Laws and Regulations

General Data Protection Regulation (GDPR)	The European Union regulation impacts organizations globally, not just firms based in the EU. It unifies EU privacy regulations and is quickly becoming the gold standard on how to protect an individual's (data subject's) information. A data subject is defined as anyone who is an EU resident. Organizations who control or process the data subject's data must take appropriate actions to adequately secure the data subject's data and obtain the data subject's informed consent to collect the data. The data subject can request to be forgotten, requiring organizations to delete their data. Cybersecurity breaches must be reported to the regulator within 72 hours. Fines for failure to comply can range as high as 4% of global revenue. This law became effective on May 25, 2018.
Health Insurance Portability and Accountability Act of 1996 (HIPAA)	This US regulation protects the confidentiality of an individual's health care records. Individuals have the right to be able to see their health care records and obtain a copy of those records. HIPAA prohibits health care providers from sharing a patient's records unless permission is obtained. Patients must be provided with records of who has accessed or seen their health care data.
Massachusetts 201 CMR 17.00: Standards for the Protection of Personal Information of Residents of the Commonwealth	This is one example of a privacy law passed by a US state. Most states have similar statutes and regulations. These regulations apply to the personal information of citizens of Massachusetts. One of its provisions states that personal information must be encrypted if it is transmitted or stored on a portable device, like a laptop. Other provisions discuss access control to personal information and maintaining firewalls, patching and up-to-date software for systems attached to the internet. Personal information is defined as a person's first and last name in combination with their Social Security number, driver's license number and/or financial account information.

about material cybersecurity risks and incidents in a timely fashion, including those companies that are subject to material cybersecurity risks but may not yet have been the target of a cyber-attack" (SEC, 2018, p. 4). Items to be considered for inclusion in the disclosure include:

- Cybersecurity event occurrences;
- The probably and impact of future cybersecurity events;
- Cybersecurity protection costs;
- Costs to comply with cybersecurity-related laws and regulations;
- Any pending litigation or remediation costs from cybersecurity incidents.

Do Other Groups Exist Which Can Provide Information To Be Used as an Input Into the Risk Analysis?

Industry groups can establish standards to which an organization must comply, recommended cybersecurity benchmarks and opportunities for information sharing regarding the threat environment. Table 19.3 shows some examples of such groups.

Table 19.3 Industry Groups

Payment Card Industry (PCI) Security Standards Council	This global organization defines standards to be used by organizations who accept payment cards (credit cards). Members include firms such as American Express, Discover Financial Services, JCB International, MasterCard and Visa Inc. Standards include such items as protecting payment information through use of a secure network, encryption for the transmission of cardholder data, a vulnerability management plan and access control.
Center for Internet Security, Inc. (CIS)	CIS is a nonprofit global organization which provides recommended configuration benchmarks for networks, operating systems and applications used in public or private firms. These best practice recommendations are developed with input from a global community of IT professionals. CIS continuously monitors cybersecurity threats, provides alerts to subscribers and recommends mitigation strategies.
National Cyber-Forensics and Training Alliance (NCFTA)	The nonprofit NCFTA fosters partnership between industry, government and academia. Law enforcement agencies such as the FBI participate in this organization. It uses a collaborative approach to identify, mitigate and disrupt cybercrime. Near-real-time information is provided to member partners, enabling them to secure their organizations against active, current threats.

What Frameworks Exist to Help My Organization Determine the Adequacy of Its Cybersecurity Program?

A *framework* can help your organization evaluate its current cybersecurity posture, determine your organization's ideal cybersecurity position and guide your organization in its decision-making processes. They assist organizations to develop and implement policies, standards and operating procedures using tools of the organization's choice to protect its data. By definition, a framework is applicable across multiple industries and technologies and applies to small, medium and large firms. Framework use is voluntary by an organization, whereas compliance with laws and regulations is required. Organizations may ask third-party reviewers to assess their compliance with the framework and, if the assessment is favorable, use the results as a marketing tool.

Three well-known cybersecurity frameworks are shown in Table 19.4.

Table 19.4 Typical Cybersecurity Frameworks

Information technology—Security techniques—information security management systems—Requirements	This standard, published by the International Organization for Standardization (ISO), discusses the implementation, maintenance and continuous improvement of an information security management system.
COBIT	COBIT is developed and maintained by ISACA, a global professional association focused on information systems. The framework focuses primarily on enterprise IT governance and management (GEIT). It is based on five principles and seven enablers. Information security is included as part of the overall governance model. COBIT focuses on meeting identified stakeholder needs as criteria for success.
CIS Controls	In addition to identifying configuration benchmarks, CIS identifies 20 cybersecurity controls based on best practices from its members. Controls are divided into three prioritized action groups—basic (controls 1–6), foundational (controls 7–16) and organizational controls (controls 17–20)—which are used to define what all organizations should be doing to build an in-depth cyber defense.

These frameworks are updated frequently, so be sure to check each framework's website to determine the most current version before selecting one to use.

How Does My Organization Select a Cybersecurity Framework?

Selecting a framework is a decision an organization needs to make based on its business requirements. Each framework referenced above has its own unique strength and weaknesses. A fourth framework, the *US National Institute of Standards and Technology (NIST) Cyber Security Framework (CSF)*, encompasses the frameworks listed above and contains elements of the cybersecurity risk management program previously discussed. NIST CSF is a voluntary framework created as a direct result of US Executive Order (EO) 13636, Improving Critical Infrastructure Cybersecurity, issued by President Barack Obama in February 2013. The framework is industry nonspecific, technology neutral, and free to use. Industry representatives provided input into the NIST CSF design. ISACA, the COBIT 5 author, participated in the NST CSF's development and advocates its use in conjunction with COBIT 5. The NIST CSF also aligns to the ISO/IEC 27001:2013 and the CIS controls. Because of this alignment with other frameworks, its adoption is growing throughout the United States and abroad.

The CSF framework is broken into three sections: (1) Framework Core; (2) Framework Implementation Tiers and (3) Framework Profiles. A spreadsheet can be downloaded from the NIST website to help organizations walk through the specifics of each section. The spreadsheet also clearly identifies the framework's mapping to other frameworks.

Five high-level functions or activities used to obtain cybersecurity-desired outcomes make up the Framework Core:

1. *Identify*: Understand the organization. Outcome categories addressed are asset management, business environment, governance, risk assessment and risk management strategy.
2. *Protect*: Safeguard critical service delivery. Outcome categories addressed are identity management and access control, awareness and training, data security, information protection processes and procedures, security continuous monitoring, and detection processes.
3. *Detect*: Identify a cybersecurity incident when it occurs. Outcome categories addressed are anomalies and events, security continuous monitoring and detection processes.
4. *Respond*: Contain a cybersecurity incident. Outcome categories addressed are response planning, communications, analysis, mitigation and improvements.

5. *Recover*: Maintain resilience and restore the business to normal operations after a cybersecurity incident. Outcome categories addressed are recovery planning, improvements and communications.

Four Framework Implementation Tiers ("Tiers") identify the sophistication of the organization's cybersecurity program: Tier 1 Partial, Tier 2 Risk Informed, Tier 3 Repeatable, and Tier 4 Adaptive. Firms assess their risk management process, integrated risk management program, and external participation to place themselves within a specific tier. The tiers are not maturity levels, although firms are encouraged to move to the higher-level tiers as part of their continuous cybersecurity improvement processes. Firms then continue by creating a current state and desired future state Framework Profile ("Profile"). The profile aligns the Framework Core and Tiers to firm's business requirements, the risk appetite and available resources.

NIST identifies seven steps for organizations to use to implement the CSF and to repeat over time for ongoing assessments for use continuous improvement processes. Notice how these steps encompass and refine the cybersecurity risk management program previously discussed.

- *Step 1, Prioritize and scope:* The organization makes strategic decisions regarding the firm's overall cybersecurity program.
- *Step 2, Orient:* The organization identifies systems, assets, regulatory requirements and risk approach.
- *Step 3, Create a current profile:* The organization identifies the current state of its cybersecurity program.
- *Step 4, Conduct a risk assessment:* The organization uses its risk management program to determine the likelihood and impact of a cybersecurity incident.
- *Step 5, Create a target profile:* The organization determines the ideal future state of its cybersecurity program.
- *Step 6, Determine, analyze, and prioritize gaps:* The organization compares the current profile to the desired future profile to determine gaps. It creates a prioritized action plan for addressing the gaps, keeping in mind the cost and benefits of each proposed project.
- *Step 7, Implement action plan.* The organization completes the projects required to close the gap between the current state profile and the desired future state profile.

How Does My Organization Manage Cybersecurity Projects?

Both the cybersecurity risk management program risk assessment and the NIST CSF assessment identify potential projects to address gaps and continuously improve the firm's cybersecurity program. Cybersecurity projects are similar to any other project undertaken by the organization. They are temporary efforts scoped to deliver a unique produce, service or process which moves the firm toward its overall strategic objectives. Typical projects undertaken include, but are not limited to, implementing process changes to strengthen controls, which are frequently supported by a technical tool, automating manual processes, replacing or upgrading end of life and end of support hardware and software, creating a cybersecurity training program, and addressing penetration test findings. Each project results in organizational change. Project managers incorporate tactics to help the organization adopt the changes into each project.

A successful cybersecurity program oversees multiple projects simultaneously. Some of the projects should be targeted, quick wins that can be completed in 90 days or fewer. Other projects in the program will be larger, long-term projects with multiple phases that may run for several years. A cybersecurity program/project management office (PMO) is a team that oversees the projects being executed and helps maintain the balance between shorter versus longer duration projects.

The Project Management Institute (PMI) captures traditional and emerging project management best practices in its *Guide to the Project Management Body of Knowledge* (*PMBOK Guide*), which includes the American National Standards Institute (ANSI) standard *The Standard for Project Management*. The *PMBOK Guide* breaks project management into five repeatable project management process:

- *Initiating*: The firm selects, charters and funds a project based on its ability to meet business requirements defined in a business case. A project manager is assigned who leads an analysis to identify stakeholders who may be positively or negatively impacted by the project.
- *Planning*: The project manager and project team document how the project will be managed in the project management plan, refine the project scope and requirements, identify the tasks required to deliver the project, develop the project's schedule and create a budget forecast.
- *Executing*: The project team completes the identified tasks to create the project's deliverables and thus fulfill the work defined in the project's scope.
- *Monitoring and controlling*: The project manager compares the project's scope, schedule and budget performance to the baselines established during the planning processes. Change requests are reviewed and approved to address baseline variances by a change control board. Completed deliverables are validated by the quality control processes and accepted by the project's internal sponsor or external client.
- *Closing*: Work associated with the project is completed and lessons learned are collected. The project manager and project team members are assigned to other projects within the organization. The project's deliverables are transferred to business-as-usual operations teams.

Project managers use different methodologies to manage projects through the various phases. A traditional or waterfall methodology defines requirements up front and uses a "big-bang" approach to complete each deliverable in its entirety prior to going live. An agile methodology breaks projects into small user stories and focuses on delivering minimally viable product during each short-term iterative deliverable release. Software development teams generally prefer an agile environment.

Conclusion

Together we've covered the high-level elements that make a world-class cybersecurity program. Organizations use a cybersecurity risk management program to assess, monitor and respond to threats and vulnerabilities. Inputs to the risk assessment process include known threats, laws, regulations, standards/benchmarks from industry groups and framework assessment models. Stakeholders judge an organization's cybersecurity program to be a success if no significant breach occurs. A firm's cybersecurity program will also be judged successful if it takes minutes or days to identify and contain a breach before any significant data loss occurs, rather than months. Cybersecurity professionals cannot achieve success in a vacuum. The organizations must establish a cybersecurity-aware culture where the tone is set from the top, where management provides adequate funding and each employee vigilantly strives to protect the organization's most important asset: its data.

Bibliography

A Guide to the Project Management Body of Knowledge (PMBOK Guide). Sixth Edition. Newtown Square, PA: Project Management Institute, 2017.

Armerding, Taylor. (January 26, 2018). The 17 biggest data breaches of the 21st century. *CSO*. www.csoonline.com/article/2130877/data-breach/the-biggest-data-breaches-of-the-21st-century.html.

Barrett, Brian. (April 20, 2018). DNC lawsuit reveals key details about devastating 2016 hack. *Wired*. www.wired.com/story/dnc-lawsuit-reveals-key-details-2016-hack/.

Beer, Jonathan. (May 16, 2017). WannaCry ransomware attack losses could reach $4 billion. *CBS News*. www.cbsnews.com/news/wannacry-ransomware-attacks-wannacry-virus-losses/

Bonazzo, John. (March 28, 2018). Atlanta ransomware attack shows cities not prepared for long-term security breaches. *Observer*. http://observer.com/2018/03/atlanta-cyberattack-ransomware/.

CERT Insider Threat Center. (December 2016). *Common sense guide to mitigating insider threats*. Fifth Edition. Software Engineering Institute. Carnegie Mellon University. https://resources.sei.cmu.edu/asset_files/TechnicalReport/2016_005_001_484758.pdf.

CIS Controls. Center for Internet Security, Inc. (March 19, 2018). www.cissecurity.org/controls/.

CISM Review Manual. 15th Edition. Schaumburg, IL: ISACA. 2015.

COBIT 5: A Business Framework for the Governance and Management of Enterprise IT. Rolling Meadows, IL: ISACA, 2012.

Coman, Eamonn. (August 27, 2013). When to use SaaS, PaaS, and IaaS. *ComputeNext*. www.computenext.com/blog/when-to-use-saas-paas-and-iaas/.

Cybersecurity Nexus: Implementing the NIST Cybersecurity Framework. Rolling Meadows, IL: ISACA, 2014.

Elkind, Peter. (June 25, 2015). Sony Pictures: Inside the hack of the century. Part 1: Who was manning the ramparts at Sony Pictures. *Fortune*. http://fortune.com/sony-hack-part-1/.

Eubanks, Nick. (July 13, 2017). The true cost of cybercrime for business *Forbes*. www.forbes.com/sites/theyec/2017/07/13/the-true-cost-of-cybercrime-for-businesses/#41b678aa4947.

Gregory, Peter H. *All-in-One: CISM Certified Information Security Manager Exam Guide*. New York: McGraw-Hill Education, 2018.

ISO/IEC 27001:2013, *2017 Cost of Data Breach Study: Global Overview. Ponemon Institute*. (June 2017). www.iso.org/obp/ui/#iso:std:iso-iec:27001:ed-2:v1:en.

Kerravala, Zeus. (July 24, 2015). John Chamber's 10 most memorable quotes as Cisco CEO. *NetworkWorld*. www.networkworld.com/article/2952184/cisco-subnet/john-chambers-10-most-memorable-quotes-as-cisco-ceo.html.

Meeuwisse, Raef. (2017). *Cybersecurity for Beginners*. Second Edition. London: Cyber Simplicity Ltd.

Moore, Andrew P., Collins, Matthew L., Mundie, David A., Ruefle, Robin M., and McIntire, David M. (December 2014). *Pattern-based design of insider threat programs*. Carnegie Mellon University. https://resources.sei.cmu.edu/asset_files/TechnicalNote/2014_004_001_427430.pdf.

Moore, Andrew P., McIntire, David, Mundie, David, and Zubrow, David (March 2013). *Justification of a pattern for detecting intellectual property theft by departing insiders*. Carnegie Mellon University. https://figshare.com/articles/Justification_of_a_Pattern_for_Detecting_Intellectual_Property_Theft_by_Departing_Insiders/6575015.

Mueller, III, Robert S. (March 1, 2012). Prepared remarks for RSA cyber security conference. *FBI*. https://archives.fbi.gov/archives/news/speeches/combating-threats-in-the-cyber-world-outsmarting-terrorists-hackers-and-spies.

National Institute of Standards and Technology. (February 2014). *Framework for Improving Critical Infrastructure Cybersecurity. Version 1.0*. Gaithersburg, MD: Information Technology Laboratory National Institute of Standards and Technology.

National Institute of Standards and Technology. (September 2012). *NIST Special Publication 800-30 Revision 1, Guide for Conducting Risk Assessments*. Gaithersburg, MD: Information Technology Laboratory National Institute of Standards and Technology.

Office of Consumer Affairs and Business Regulation. (November 13, 2009). 201 CMR 17: Standards for the protection of personal information of residents of the Commonwealth. *Commonwealth of Massachusetts*. www.mass.gov/regulations/201-CMR-17-standards-for-the-protection-of-personal-information-of-residents-of-the.

Puffer, K. (September 16, 2015). Security incident vs. security breach. *NY InfoSec, Inc.* https://nyinfosec.com/2015/09/security-incident-vs-security-breach/.

Schubmehl, David. (July 15, 2014). *Unlocking the hidden value of information* IDC Community. https://idc-community.com/groups/it_agenda/bigdataanalytics/unlocking_the_hidden_value_of_information.

SEC. "Commission Statement and Guidance on Public Company Cybersecurity Disclosures." Securities and Exchange Commission. (February 26, 2018). www.sec.gov/rules/interp/2018/33-10459.pdf.

2016 Data Breach Investigations Report. *Verizon Enterprise*, 2016. www.verizonenterprise.com/resources/reports/rp_dbir-2016-executive-summary_xg_en.pdf.

2016 Presidential Campaign Hacking Fast Facts. (February 21, 2018). *CNN*. www.cnn.com/2016/12/26/us/2016-presidential-campaign-hacking-fast-facts/index.html.

2018 Data Breach Investigations Report. *Verizon Enterprise*, 2018. www.verizonenterprise.com/resources/reports/rp_DBIR_2018_Report_en_xg.pdf.

US Blames North Korea for "WannaCry" Cyber Attack. *Reuters* (December 18, 2017). www.reuters.com/article/us-usa-cyber-northkorea/u-s-blames-north-korea-for-wannacry-cyber-attack-idUSKBN1ED00Q.

20

VALUE AND RISK IN THE FOURTH INFORMATIONAL REVOLUTION

Peter Coffee

The plural of the Latin *datum*, "data," has an origin that may surprise those who assume its original meaning to be something like "fact" or "measurement." The word actually comes from a root meaning "an item given." One might therefore say that until it has been transmitted from one person (or process, or device, or place, or event) to another, a piece of "data" does not truly exist: like the "sound" of a tree that falls where no one hears it, *data has no impact—and in a sense, no existence—until it conveys knowledge*, in some form, across some sort of channel.

This is not just a matter of wordplay: it implies a mandate, to everyone involved, to understand that data is what the receiver *understands* it to mean, not what the sender *intended* to impart. Until it has been received, it has not been truly given—and in that important sense, it is not data.

When it first appeared in English-language works in the 1640s, *data* was only used in the context of mathematics; it became more generally used to mean "numerical facts collected for future reference" around 1900 and took on the modern meaning of "transmittable and storable information by which computer operations are performed" a little before 1950.[1] Respecting that long history, this chapter will shine a harsh and revealing light on some things that we have learned—or in too many cases, apparently failed to learn—over a period that starts many decades before we were exchanging or analyzing data in any context resembling modern information systems.

Where this chapter is trying to make a key point, the reader won't have to dig it out: prominent, numbered "takeaways" will make those statements (one may hope) both apparent and unforgettable, because "data" is about what's *received*.

Data: The Defining and Durable Asset

Remember "data processing"? Essentially unseen before 1950, the phrase enjoyed a spectacular rise in mind share (as measured by the Ngram Viewer of Google Books) through the mid-1980s; then it rather quickly declined to less than a third of its peak share of in-print interest.

Those who were braving the perils of the IT arena during that period can tell their juniors what was going on as the 20th century ended: that was the time in which desktop "personal" computing was in its ascendance, while data processing was dismissed as an old-fashioned set of ideas and practices.

1. www.etymonline.com/word/data.

DOI: 10.4324/9781351107242-25

Data processing, as then perceived, managed information as a colorless noun; personal computing, and the 1990s emergence of the internet, celebrated information as the innovator's what-if analysis and the web designer's animated on-line infotainment. Data processing was an overhead activity, a cost center, a necessary evil of recording and reporting; computing was creation. Data was a boring side effect of activity. Code was an exciting opportunity.

Today, finding data boring is *so* last century. Approaching this still-new century's third decade, it's clear that data is back. Big data, data science—and with them, the apprehensions and complexities of the European Union's General Data Protection Regulation (GDPR) along with other (some would say overdue) laws and regulations.

Any old machine-learning algorithm, it appears, can now tell us things that we used to pay an expensive programmer to figure out—but having unique (and hard to acquire) data, well, that's actually valuable, and becoming rapidly more so.

It's required a bit of a journey, through a series of labels, to obtain for data the honor of defining this era. In 2011, David Kirkpatrick in *Forbes* asserted[2] that "Every company is a software company." We could have argued, then, that this was merely a repackaging of long-standing truth—because all companies are in a sense the compilation of their procedures, and the sum of their experience-based efficiencies. That's the difference between a company and a bunch of random people working together in a factory or office or store.

It might have seemed at the time that being a "software company" was sexy, while doing mere data processing was legacy dullness. This was a tempting, but ultimately short-lived misunderstanding. It's now clear that data has never been in a greater turmoil of new ways for it to arise, new needs to understand its meaning, new consequences for its mismanagement, and new value in its creative and insightful use. It has never been more in need of our best thinking on proactive measures for its protection and control.

Hence, this chapter.

Code Is What We Try to Do the Same; Technology Is What We Try to Do Differently

Expressing things that we routinely do in the form of computer code, rather than filling three-ring binders with company policies, pours old wine of habit and practice into an updated bottle—with complications, though, that can be painfully and expensively surprising. This chapter will explore some of these considerations, notably in the discussion below of the risks created by careless use and inadequate governance of spreadsheets.

A double distillation of the spirit of the software company idea, though, yielded Peter Sondergaard's Gartner Symposium assertion[3] in 2013 that "Every company is a technology company." Every company being a technology company must not be misunderstood to mean that all companies are defined by the gadgets that they build, for clearly there are still companies whose essential activity is something more real world, like extracting natural resources from the earth or flipping hamburgers or filling seats in theaters. *Technology is not the device that is built, but is rather the organization and the sharing of knowledge to enable new ways of getting things done.*

Let this be emphasized: the roots of the word "technology" are Greek words meaning the *description* of a *means of gain*.[4] Any resulting gadgets are (perhaps) a useful outcome, but they are not the essence.

2. www.forbes.com/sites/techonomy/2011/11/30/now-every-company-is-a-software-company/.
3. https://blogs.gartner.com/mark_raskino/2013/11/28/every-company-is-a-technology-company-more-and-more-evidence/.
4. http://web.engr.oregonstate.edu/~funkk/Technology/technology.html.

Data Is What We Know—and Technology Changes Our Relationship With Knowledge

As noted earlier, words have meanings that it is not mere entertainment to dissect and examine. It is more than just wordplay to insist that technology is a behavior, not a thing, because becoming a technology company requires that organizations become at least as invested in their processes of head-up anticipation and transformation, as they are head-down focused on their skill in doing what they have always done.

If that does not seem like a novel idea, then it may be useful to look back and realize what a radical change of thinking this has represented over just the past several decades. Between roughly 1950 and 1980, it was that era's thought leadership to tell an organization that it must create and sustain a culture of primarily incremental refinements: a process that "aims to create improvements that can be put into place on the same day."[5] It was therefore startling, at the time, when Tom Peters recanted his own best-selling early-1980s business bible, *In Search of Excellence*, in which he had admonished business leaders to "Stick to the knitting—stay with the business that you know."[6] His 1987 epiphany, *Thriving on Chaos*, instead asserted that "There are no excellent companies" and added, "If it ain't broke, you just haven't looked hard enough. . . . Fix it anyway."[7]

When Peters and other thought leaders newly demanded that organizations adopt a culture of self-disrupting improvement, they paved the way toward a change in the relationship between organizations and knowledge. Power had previously derived from ownership of long-lived secrets: Coca-Cola's formula[8] for flavoring syrup, for example, or the closely guarded metallurgical process—modern-day alchemy—that makes the distinctive sound of Zildjian cymbals[9] the preference of rock stars.

As success came to depend more on a relentless pursuit of transformation through intentional and accelerating processes, companies had to confront and accept new vocabularies and practices of "open source" and "crowdsourcing." In a notable counterexample against the old idea that "secrets are power," the data from a mineral company's prospecting expeditions was once considered a crown jewel secret: all conversations about that data would have been about cost of acquiring it, uncertainties in evaluating it, and confidentiality in using and protecting it. Turning this set of concerns inside out, Goldcorp achieved literally billions of dollars in returns[10] by offering, in March 2000, a half-million-dollar prize for successful suggestions, enabled by its startling grant of public access to the company's prospecting data.

What's glimmering through the dust of our traditional data archives is, therefore, this challenging idea: that a traditional focus on preserving secrets, in today's new world of collaboration, risks following a familiar path in a way that is just as counterproductive as keeping one's money under the mattress. To hide one's data from all others may protect those assets from some kinds of risk, but today it also means accepting a certainty of lost opportunities to generate new value. Remember: data is something *given*.

The notion of such an "open data" approach may be much more palatable to a startup, which can hope to gain a flying start from the wisdom of the crowd while taking little risk; it may seem much more heretical to an industry incumbent that has much more history and might seem to have much more to lose. It requires conviction to accept that in a world of accelerating change, making only incremental progress from even the most elevated starting point of the best-established industry leader will not outpace a challenger's exponential progress—even when it begins from a much lower origin.

5. www.bidsketch.com/blog/business/kaizen-benefit/.
6. https://en.wikipedia.org/wiki/In_Search_of_Excellence#Themes.
7. http://articles.latimes.com/1987-10-11/books/bk-13230_1_peters-and-waterman-tom-peters-bantam-books.
8. https://en.wikipedia.org/wiki/Coca-Cola_formula.
9. https://zildjian.com/information/history-zildjian.
10. www.ideaconnection.com/open-innovation-success/Open-Innovation-Goldcorp-Challenge-00031.html.

A key realization, for organizations of any age or size, is that an open approach can yield far more value from data today than was possible to unleash in a connection-poor, computationally limited, collaboration-averse past era—but it requires the acceptance of prudent risks. Data discipline that once pursued zero leakage of proprietary facts must pivot toward a discipline of risk optimization: a much less simple goal to define, and a much less simple accomplishment to measure.

> *Takeaway #1*: The habit of data hoarding must become a commitment to value-creating collaboration.

Data Is a Medium of Exchange—Not Just a Store of Value

The mental model of data as something to keep in a vault, and to guard against all but a handful of obvious and predictable uses by a limited group of insiders, must therefore be replaced by something that looks much more like the marketplace behaviors surrounding other productive assets. There must be investment, there must be exchange, and there must be considered analysis and conscientious mitigation of risk.

Again remembering that data is "something given," it may require vigorous leadership from the top of an organization to change a mindset that data is "something kept." One may need to redraw the organization chart, literally—creating innovative roles like "chief customer experience officer," rather than having C-suite titles defined by an activity and perpetuating activity-based silos of storage.

It is unrealistic to expect a person whose door is labeled, "VP of Activity X" to invest great effort in sharing data with the VPs of W, Y, and Z: there will be a temptation to say, "cross-function connection is the job of the chief information officer." If line-of-business systems are designed as silos, though, their later interconnections will be both costly and fragile; the movement of useful data among them will be complex and error-prone.

Senior leadership must drive into organizations the recognition that huge opportunity costs are incurred from failure to make data a non-siloed resource. Survey results (of 500 US and UK companies, each with at least 500 employees) published in August 2018 found:[11]

- Around three-quarters of survey respondents believed their organization "has more data than ever, but is struggling to use it to help generate useful business insights."
- The greatest stumbling block hindering attempts at better utilizing data was said to be data silos: only 2% of respondents considered their business to be effectively silo-free.
- Lack of a "coordinated data strategy" was named by 37% of respondents as a barrier to effective sharing.

In addition to assisting line-of-business leaders in coordinating their data strategies, a crucial role that *will* belong largely to the chief information officer, will be leadership in addressing new demands for a social consensus on data management practices—that is to say, the back-office operations that once were strictly technical or commercial concerns. Going forward, it will no longer be enough to invest in greater efficiencies of data collection and use, even though many organizations would regard that as a major strategic effort just now beginning to gain momentum. It increasingly appears there also must be regulation that contemplates and limits unacceptable behaviors involving the stewardship and exploitation of data.

11. http://blogs.lse.ac.uk/businessreview/2018/07/25/data-silos-are-the-greatest-stumbling-block-to-an-effective-use-of-firms-data/.

Unfortunately, regulators are inclined to write rules that amputate risks with a machete rather than trimming them with a scalpel: industry leaders will have to demand entry to the halls of government if they want to make their case for minimizing the future cost and difficulty of bringing innovative applications to market.

Regulation is widely recognized as needed, though, because the long-term self-interest of data-intensive companies has not (as things turned out) prevented careless and even knowingly abusive behaviors. Revelations like the role of Cambridge Analytica[12] in the US presidential election of 2016 have done long-lasting harm to people's trust in any institution that has data collection and monetization as prominent components of its operation—whether in the profit sector,[13] or in the professions,[14] or in government.[15]

Note, moreover, that even in a case as paradigm-shifting as the Goldcorp example described above, the process absolutely had to begin with a *kind* of data that would have been utterly recognizable over a hundred years ago. As observed by crowdsourcing analyst Keith Rozario,[16]

> This doesn't mean the $10 million Rob McEwen spent on the geologist was wasted: it could be argued that without that $10 million dollar data mining, they wouldn't have had much to share with the crowdsourcing participants. *However, had the geologist viewed it as a data collection exercise, the results might have even been better.*" [italics added]

Thinking about one's organization as a data collector, curator, custodian, and creative but prudent investor, is perhaps the new defining competence of the strategic business leader. Especially in historically risk-averse domains such as finance, health care, and government, optimization rather than minimization of risk may be quite a challenging change of the definition of "right thing"—but that which is hoarded, rather than exchanged for mutual benefit, is not really "data" at all.

Collaboration is at least a two-sided thing, though, and data received from others requires the same scrutiny as any other "thing given." The folk phrase "gift horse"[17] is not as inimical as "Trojan horse," but both include the idea that things may not be what they seem—and data may come in the gift-wrapped package of a peer-reviewed scientific paper or other authoritative dress while failing basic tests of confident belief.

Researchers Nick Brown and James Heathers, notably, rejoice in their nickname as the "data thugs" who estimate[18] that their tools and practices of data scrutiny "have led to corrections to dozens of papers and the full retraction of roughly 10 more." Some of their methods are sophisticated, but in one case they observe that a nutritional study's published results implied that "at least one child in the sample would have had to have eaten roughly 60 carrots in a single sitting." Sometimes, it's that easy to recognize a gift of data that should be declined.

Greater Value—and Greater Risk

We may therefore say that people finally found the right phrase with the statement in 2014 by Marius Moscovici at TheNextWeb[19] that "Every company is now a data company." Software merely represents

12. https://en.wikipedia.org/wiki/Cambridge_Analytica.
13. https://variety.com/2018/digital/features/facebook-privacy-crisis-big-data-mark-zuckerberg-1202741394/.
14. www.sciencedirect.com/science/article/pii/S1877050917317015.
15. https://academic.oup.com/idpl/article/4/2/96/734798.
16. www.keithrozario.com/2012/07/opensource-gold-the-greatest-crowdsourcing-story-ever-told.html.
17. https://en.wiktionary.org/wiki/gift_horse.
18. www.sciencemag.org/news/2018/02/meet-data-thugs-out-expose-shoddy-and-questionable-research.
19. https://thenextweb.com/dd/2014/04/07/spotify-effect-every-company-now-data-company/.

what an organization does, letting it do those things reproducibly and efficiently but not self-disruptively. Technology (as a behavior) is a search for new value, and it is a leadership challenge that should not be taken lightly—but without sources and processes for acquiring and using differentiating data, being a technology company is being an enterprising explorer who's bereft of reliable maps.

Being a data company means embracing a truth that is in some ways the oldest definer of humanity, seeming to be suddenly new—for ultimately, what has every human culture or organization ever been, if not the sum of the things that it knows? Every other advantage that an organization might have is increasingly vulnerable, whether to duplication or to obsolescence: behaviors can be copied, inventions can be reverse-engineered, technologies can be overtaken by new discoveries. Durable value, however, resides in the data that an organization accumulates through experience, and in the insights that only the perspective of experience can fully apply to what is known by anyone who cares to look—but what may be apparent only to those who are looking for it.

At the same time, though, there has never been so much risk attached to our knowledge: the obligations that it creates, the damage that it can do, and the opportunities that arise for unintended bias and distortion—in systems that are faster than we can manage but for the foreseeable future will continue to be stupider than we imagine.

Scale, Ubiquity, Information and Intelligence

If "we are what we know" is an ancient truth, and "every company is now a data company" is just a modern phrasing of that idea, then what is actually new and transformative? The answer requires going below the surface of another modern phrase, "the fourth industrial revolution," to appreciate the *patterns* of past and present revolutions—even if an organization does not think of itself as being in the space of "industry"—and to recognize the appearance of the same patterns in our relationship with what we know, and not just with what we make and what we do.

Early in 2016, discussions led by Klaus Schwab of the World Economic Forum at Davos[20] drove the phrase "fourth industrial revolution" to a rapid peak of global mind share. Too quickly, though, the phrase came to be used as a headline for lists of new technologies such as quantum computing, 3D printing, and robotic drones.

All of those were interesting means of economic sector disruption, but all of them were utterly dependent on new sources and new uses—and potentially, new associated risks and duties—of data. To understand both the generality of impact and the challenge of creating new value, we need to rise above the inventory of technologies to recognize more powerful general patterns; we need to understand the importance, and the challenges, associated with similar developments in what might seem the entirely abstract domain of data management.

Scale: The First Revolution

It's been common to label the industrial revolutions in terms of what many would consider their defining technologies, often enumerated as steam, electricity, computers/automation, and (most recently) artificial intelligence and robotics.[21] There's a genuine hazard, though, in thinking of the revolutions to date as either rip-and-replace successions, or as bells-and-whistles enhancements, of the tools that people have used. It is far more useful to examine the manner in which companies, and communities, have organized their activities to use new tools well. We will be more specific about

20. www.weforum.org/agenda/2016/01/the-fourth-industrial-revolution-what-it-means-and-how-to-respond/.
21. https://en.wikipedia.org/wiki/Fourth_Industrial_Revolution#Stages_of_Industrial_revolutions.

this farther on, when we have shown that it is more powerful to define the revolutions by their *effects*, not by their enablers.

In the first revolution, what matters is not that people harnessed the power of steam, but that they made power *scalable*. The transformative change was from horsepower packaged in units of one horse to horsepower in quantities of dozens or hundreds with the capacity to operate for hours at a time.

The most disruptive upside of scalable power was a far greater availability of what had previously been the luxuries of the few, but what have since come to be seen as basic necessities. Unconsidered miracles of our daily lives, like textiles, paper, and glass, were both manufactured and consumed by something that had never existed before: a middle class,[22] not owners of the productive resource but also not mere field-tilling serfs. Their labor was worth more because it was amplified by machines' power.

What changed society most, in the process, was the massive migration (and political evolution) of populations from the entrepreneurial farm to the wage-earning city—a consequence doubtless unimagined by engineers but one that was inherent in the mechanics and thermodynamics of steam-driven machinery, whose economies of scale led to concentration of production.

There are entire books that could be written about this, but this is not that book or even that chapter: for our present purposes, let's see what this pattern brings to the domain of data.

In a striking parallel, the first revolution of data was likewise one of scale: specifically, the introduction of enablers like punched cards and tabulating machines,[23] often attributed to the 1890 US census and the use of that technology by the company that eventually evolved into IBM.

Notably, a major finding[24] of that 1890 census was that the "frontier" of US westward development had essentially disappeared, that the further development of the US economy would be one of enrichment in activity rather than expansion of territory. The same might be said of data today, as the mere achievement of collection at scale is now being overshadowed by the challenge of discovery of patterns and delivery of understandable insights.

Further, *even in this first pre–electronic revolution of data scale we find the first examples of data risk.* Early 20th-century record storage mishaps, and gaps in data governance, resulted in the *loss* of most of that 1890 census data. The resulting furor led to the creation of the US National Archives and Records Administration in 1934.[25] One wonders how many corporations are having the foresight, even today, to institute such responsibilities and disciplines, so as to avoid a costly reactive response to what may be a crippling data loss—because many organizations today find themselves in a shockingly similar situation of what has been called a "Digital Dark Age."[26]

During the late 20th and early 21st centuries, rapid succession of radically different mechanisms of data storage—and obsolescence of proprietary data formats associated with bygone business software products—have deprived many organizations of reliable access to information ranging from the mundane to the priceless. In 2018, for example, engineers at NASA were forced to go through an almost archeological process[27] to make 20-year-old data from a Jupiter exploration mission accessible to more modern analytical techniques. Going forward, merely the safe archival of records is grossly inadequate if it is not accompanied by equal vigor in assuring that the meaning of the raw bits can be also fully preserved.

22. www.ukessays.com/essays/history/the-three-main-classes-that-emerged-during-industrial-revolution.php.
23. https://en.wikipedia.org/wiki/Punched_card.
24. https://en.wikipedia.org/wiki/1890_United_States_Census.
25. https://en.wikipedia.org/wiki/National_Archives_and_Records_Administration.
26. https://en.wikipedia.org/wiki/Digital_dark_age.
27. www.theregister.co.uk/2018/05/01/fortran_data_galileo_ganymede_moon/.

> *Takeaway #2*: Modern data is a combination of the bits that represent it, the hardware that can read it, and the software that can render it so people can understand it. Absent any of these, the others are not enough.

Distribution and Decentralization—Revolution Two

Consider next the example of the second industrial revolution, in which the scalable power of the first revolution became easily distributed and activity thereby decentralized. Rather than the massive, steam-driven factories of the first revolution (which required activity to be organized around them), the second revolution was that of the electrical grid that allowed power to go almost anywhere.

Electricity's relative ease of distribution was compounded by the development of electrical motors of many sizes, allowing that power to be used in even small hand tools as well as in massive factory installations. To look at this from the other direction, any mere replacement of steam with electrical power—in an otherwise unchanged factory arrangement—left much of the value on the table. "Electricity triumphed only when factories themselves were reconfigured," wrote economist Tim Harford in 2017.

Consequently, the second revolution's effects were as much organizational and cultural as technical: "Workers had responsibility for their own machines; they needed better training and better pay," Harford continued. "The electric motor was a wonderful invention, once we changed all the everyday details that surrounded it." Like the social consequences of steam, the personal empowerments of electricity were not an engineering phenomenon but were perhaps the most significant impacts of that technical change on organizations and societies.

It must therefore be strongly emphasized, and clearly understood, that revolutions must be pursued to their logical conclusion, with all of the disruptions that this may entail, rather than being half-heartedly followed only as far as their obvious and superficial benefits can be easily seen. It was true for the volts and amps of electricity; it is true for the bits and the bandwidth of a data-driven world.

> *Takeaway #3*: Incremental replacement of technology is inadequate without re-examination of processes for organizations—and of roles and skills for people.

Networks: The Data Grid

Asking again if data pursued a parallel journey, we quickly see that the corresponding second data revolution began with the emergence in the 1960s of the first meaningful data networks—created for tasks ranging from airline reservations to national defense.[28] Going even beyond the reach of the electrical power grids, data networks could quickly evolve from wired to wireless connectivity, and quickly went global with the launch of pioneering communication satellites like Telstar.[29]

Data networks also began to achieve fault tolerance, of the kind that we expect from our power grids, when their original "circuit-switched" model—seen in concrete form in an old-fashioned office switchboard, with its tangle of cables and plugs—was overtaken by packet-switched networks.[30] These allowed data to find an adaptive path, despite potential network damage; such networks were also convenient to join and leave, when one could simply plug in to data as easily as plugging in to

28. https://en.wikipedia.org/wiki/Computer_network#History.
29. https://en.wikipedia.org/wiki/Telstar.
30. https://en.wikipedia.org/wiki/Packet_switching.

a power outlet using multiple-access networks like Ethernet.[31] It is difficult for those who were not present at the time to appreciate what an enormous change this was in the simplicity of participating in an emerging data-centric world.

Crucially, though, the flexibility of the data packet model was also a vulnerability: a packet could deceptively claim to originate from a trusted source, while actually coming from a malicious actor. With what today seems ludicrous naïveté, the internet's original protocols were entirely unprotected (and largely remain so today) against this kind of deliberate sabotage or misrepresentation.

As was acknowledged in the *Washington Post* in 2015,[32]

> "We didn't focus on how you could wreck this system intentionally," said Vinton G. Cerf, a dapper, ebullient Google vice president who in the 1970s and '80s designed key building blocks of the internet. "You could argue with hindsight that we should have, but getting this thing to work at all was non-trivial."

If there is one overarching lesson in all of this, it is perhaps to design for the success (and scale) that a system may someday have, from the beginning—instead of deferring critical considerations until *after* a primitive version has grown too quickly to be easily improved.

As now seems a chronic pattern, though, *we find in even the earliest stages of the second data revolution some warning signs of need for governance and risk management.* In 1987, networks serving avant-garde organizations like IBM became the means of their own self-destruction with the appearance of what's usually considered the first "network worm": the "Christmas Tree" attack,[33] in which an apparently innocuous greeting re-sent itself to every entry in a recipient's email contact list. The lessons of experience proved dismayingly ineffective: 13 years later, the so-called Love Bug worm[34] would use the same techniques to achieve similarly anti-productive results.

Power grids began with simple circuit breakers, to detect a problem and limit the impact of local damage—preventing the propagation of harm. One might have thought that even the earliest data networks would have learned from this example, but it appears that such lessons must be learned all over again and again.

> *Takeaway #4*: For every data channel, ask not merely "Can we make it work?"; ask also, "How can we tell that it is 'working' in ways that we don't actually want?"

Microprocessors—The Data Motors

The 21st-century replays of 1980s network attacks were dismaying for their failure to learn from experience, and to institute more nuanced management and control—and they were also a far greater nuisance, to many more people, than their forebears. That growth in the affected population was the result of the other half of the second data revolution: the emergence of microprocessors,[35] echoing the second industrial revolution's emergence of tiny electrical motors.

The electrical revolution's miniature motors made many things "power assisted," ranging from hand tools to automotive windows and rear-view mirrors. They were convenient when they worked,

31. https://en.wikipedia.org/wiki/Ethernet#History.
32. www.washingtonpost.com/sf/business/2015/05/30/net-of-insecurity-part-1.
33. https://en.wikipedia.org/wiki/Christmas_Tree_EXEC.
34. www.zdnet.com/article/love-bug-could-it-have-been-prevented.
35. https://en.wikipedia.org/wiki/History_of_personal_computers#Market_size.

but their complexity created new failure modes with greater costs of repair than the simpler mechanisms that they replaced. Similarly, the second data revolution's microprocessors made many things "smart"—but arguably to a fault, because they introduced obscure complex behaviors and opaque data flows that compounded rapidly over the following decades.

In July 2018, Bernardo Rodriguez, chief digital officer at the iconic quality measurement firm J.D. Power, wrote:

> In the automobile industry, the single factor that continues to pull down our annual Vehicle Dependability ratings is persistent customer dissatisfaction with the "center stack," which is the area in the center of a car's dashboard that houses things like built-in voice recognition systems, navigation, and Bluetooth connectivity.[36]

He continued,

> While the quality and reliability of the core elements of a car—the engine, the transmission, the braking systems—are the best they've ever been in history, automakers are struggling when it comes to the newer, fast-changing technologies that connect people to their cars.

This is a vivid, everyday, costly, and frustrating example of turning our engines of power into engines of data, more quickly than we are learning to make those data engines reliable and maintainable.

As the computational heart of the personal computer, the microprocessor was initially embraced as an affordable environment in which to learn the arts of computer programming. This was technology delivered to technophiles, and it hugely expanded the population of people who could create the software of "every company a software company" in the phrase of this chapter's opening paragraphs. So far, so good.

What quickly followed, though, were consumer-oriented software products that attempted to abstract away the complexities of writing code, as well as devices (for both consumers and industrial applications) that contained some surprising and deeply embedded assumptions.

The computer spreadsheet, for example, superficially seemed to be a mere automation of the large-format, grid-ruled sheets of paper that had long been used by accountants and engineers to perform a wide variety of numeric tasks. The computer spreadsheet was, indisputably, successful in hiding the realities of the computer under the façade of that familiar way of working: in many cases, it was said, a new computer buyer walked into a retail store demanding "VisiCalc and something to run it."[37]

Like any power tool, though, the spreadsheet accelerated the damage created by the clumsy and inexperienced as effectively as it amplified the skills of the expert. Not merely simple human error, but psychological effects of overconfidence in results,[38] and misapplication of spreadsheets to tasks far better suited to more robust database technologies, are among the consequences continually being documented by organizations such as the European Spreadsheet Risks Interest Group.[39]

Spreadsheets—Power Tools With No Safety Guards

It might seem odd, in this discussion that's centered on data, to spend the next few paragraphs talking about the "spreadsheet" genre of personal productivity software. These software products are

36. https://sloanreview.mit.edu/article/putting-customer-experience-at-the-center-of-digital-transformation/.
37. https://en.wikipedia.org/wiki/VisiCalc.
38. www.sciencedirect.com/science/article/pii/S0749597884710028.
39. www.eusprig.org/basic-research.htm.

> Directors of companies, charities, departments of government and other organisations have numerous statutory, fiduciary, reporting and compliance obligations. Penalties for failing to meet them include fines, jail sentences, undesired share price movements and unplanned career changes. The ability to meet these obligations is undermined if the information upon which decisions are based turns out to be flawed. In most businesses, a majority of that information is derived from spreadsheet models.
>
> Research has repeatedly shown that an alarming proportion of corporate spreadsheet models are not tested or controlled to the extent necessary to meet these obligations. Uncontrolled and untested spreadsheet models pose significant business risks, including:
>
> • Lost revenue, profits, cash, assets and tax
> • Mispricing and poor decision-making due to prevalent but undetected errors
> • Fraud due to malicious tampering
> • Systemic financial failure due to overdependence
>
> Furthermore, an inability to show that spreadsheet-based business information has been subject to procedures designed to ensure it is reliable is in itself a failure of fiduciary and regulatory compliance.
>
> www.eusprig.org/about.htm

Figure 20.1 Hazards of end-user access to data containers with computational powers.

positioned, and their use is taught, as if they were primarily for making calculations: as if they were the successor to paper and pencil and adding machine, not to the file cabinet. It's natural to think about spreadsheets as calculation tools rather than data storage facilities, since terms like "formulas" and "logic" are more often the subjects of a spreadsheet conversation than are data-oriented terms like "tagging" or "range check."[40]

Even so, the soberly business-focused publication *Forbes* has called Microsoft Excel "the most dangerous software on the planet. Yes, more dangerous than rogue code running a nuclear power plant, than the Stuxnet that was deliberately sent off to sabotage Iran's nuclear program."[41] As everyman's accumulator of inaccurate, inconsistent, and compromised data, the spreadsheet is a recurring character in huge numbers of undesirable situations.

One need only skim the archives of the aforementioned EuSpRIG[42] to realize that, even though they were never intended to be used as robust data containers, computer spreadsheets represent today's "long tail" of data: in aggregate, representing uncountable examples of small but crucial data stores that suffer from inadequate rigor of collection, governance, or understanding.

"Why Are We Here?", asks the EuSpRIG website. Their explanation of origin and purpose is worth quoting in its entirety (Figure 20.1), as it might justify writing an entire book rather than merely a single element of a single chapter.

In his satirical lexicon, "The Computer Contradictionary," Stan Kelly-Bootle lambasted the spreadsheet as "the Uzi of creative corporate accounting," further dubbing it "the chief culprit in the 1980s savings & loan scandal": its failure, he said, was the perhaps unconscious shift in use from

40. www.zdnet.com/article/excel-errors-microsofts-spreadsheet-may-be-hazardous-to-your-health/.
41. www.forbes.com/sites/timworstall/2013/02/13/microsofts-excel-might-be-the-most-dangerous-software-on-the-planet.
42. www.eusprig.org/index.htm.

"What if?" to "Why not?"[43] It is one thing to ask probing questions of data to see what it knows, but quite another thing to beat it until it says what you want to believe—but if anyone was wondering what the business books were talking about instead of the declining meme of data processing, just look at the complementary rise of what-if analysis.

Of even greater concern, perhaps, because it can so easily be accidental, is the blending of data with (the equivalent of) code that a spreadsheet invites—but which it then fails to make apparent. A paper spreadsheet requires some external agent to perform the operations on its values: either a documented set of instructions, or an engaged and presumably knowledgeable person, will be "in the loop." A software spreadsheet is different, in that once it has been created, that engagement is over unless there is some (rarely seen in practice) process of initial and (preferably) ongoing audit of how it works—beginning with where the data originates, and following the data and operations path all the way through the spreadsheet grid (and possibly through other linked spreadsheet files) to every result that it reports.

How can a blending of data nouns and operation verbs so easily occur? A spreadsheet might include, for example, a cell containing an estimated future rate of inflation to be used in a financial analysis. An adjacent cell might even contain a helpful label of, in this case, "inflation rate"—and most spreadsheet programs, such as Microsoft Excel, include a formula convention that lets other cells refer to the thus-labeled "global variable" cell, either by name or by an "absolute" reference location such as B32 (look in column B, row 32, no matter how many columns and rows that may be distant from the cell where that reference is being used).

The problem is that the label next to the cell is merely descriptive, not enforced by any higher-level logic. Someone might carelessly include an estimated inflation rate in a formula as a constant value, making no reference at all to what is believed by a reader of printed output to be the value used throughout. Alternatively, if someone accidentally enters (in a cell that could be anywhere in the grid) a reference to "B$32" (*without* the initial $ sign), then any copies of the resulting formula might look at C32 or D32 or E32 as that formula is copied rightward (e.g., to future years). If those unintended references point to empty cells, the inflation rate being used in those cells will be silently and invisibly assumed to be zero. Complications could ensue.

In the words of Business2Community contributor Greg Poirier,

> Spreadsheets are nasty little things that are isolated by nature, and seldom shared. When they are shared, they are not done so with an eye on collaboration. Worst still, updates don't propagate across the organization, but errors in formulas do.[44]

If the "official" databases in an organization (the ones used for vital tasks like financial management and regulatory compliance) are what the organization knows, then the spreadsheets are in a sense the organization's subconscious beliefs: they can affect its behavior without awareness or reflection.

> *Takeaway #5*: Data accumulates where people find it convenient to use it—and people use it as they find convenient, whether or not they understand the consequences.

43. https://books.google.com/books?id=tZKCZje8178C&pg=PA199&lpg=PA199.
44. www.business2community.com/sales-management/%e2%80%8band-the-worst-crm-in-the-world-ishint-it-is-not-salesforce-01268557.

Smart Devices—Power Tools With No "Off" Switch

For all the issues that they may engender, at least our spreadsheets are visible as software, with human beings consciously and intentionally involved in everything they do. The logic is open to inspection and testing. Results can be checked. They *can* be turned off. We know when we are putting data into them, and we are engaged in the process of taking data out and deciding what to do with it.

A far more subtle and difficult problem, though, has been (and is quickly becoming, at massive scale) the addition of microprocessors and connections to global networks in formerly straightforward products such as home appliances. In 2016, a six-figure number of internet-connected devices were found to have been enlisted in a network attack[45] against an important element of the internet itself. The so-called Mirai malware, it was reported at the time,

> scours the Web for "Internet of Things" devices protected by little more than factory-default usernames and passwords, and then enlists the devices in attacks that hurl junk traffic at an online target until it can no longer accommodate legitimate visitors or users.

Even an unusually conscientious owner of one of these devices, it appeared, would have found it inconvenient or even quite infeasible to alter default security credentials that were deeply embedded into the device. Communication capabilities that were entirely invisible in normal use, perhaps only present as unintended leftovers from device development and testing, had their passwords hard-coded into so-called firmware in the devices.

As with the automotive systems earlier described, this issue is another example of the widespread phenomenon of devices being made complex more quickly than they were made manageable—or even maintainable. In 2018, for example, hot-tub manufacturer Zodiac had to advise the owners of some of its products that management aids for operating their devices were going to be offline for several hours due to software maintenance in a central facility; this was followed, however, by a period of about four days during which many features were entirely inoperable due to "intermittent connectivity issues" associated with some unspecified complications during that process.[46]

The Zodiac episode was "a first-world inconvenience, at best," acknowledged writer Jason Perlow on the web site ZDNet,

> But it could have very well been worse if this was a critical infrastructure control device, such as for IoT-enabled environmental controls in a multi-dwelling building in a city experiencing frigid cold weather. Or in a place like Florida, during the summertime, when air conditioning is absolutely essential. People could die, especially elderly people.

Perlow was not proposing that hardware be made fail-proof—for that is never going to happen. He was militating for conscientious process design. The company, he accurately and straightforwardly observed, had

> failed to do proper A/B testing, and clearly, it lacked proper internal processes to roll out changes in a manner that minimized the possibility of downtime or even rolling back the mistake quickly from an untarnished backup when it was recognized. Period. Full stop.

It was, he said, "a process fail."

45. https://krebsonsecurity.com/2016/10/hacked-cameras-dvrs-powered-todays-massive-internet-outage/.
46. www.zdnet.com/article/swim-at-your-own-risk-how-botched-iot-can-sink-your-precious-first-world-life/.

In August 2018, this crossed the line from anecdotal stories of "stupid technology tricks" to become a subject of formal warning[47] from the FBI, which warned:

> Cyber actors actively search for and compromise vulnerable Internet of Things (IoT) devices for use as proxies or intermediaries for Internet requests to route malicious traffic for cyber-attacks and computer network exploitation.

That August 2018 warning included a pointer to an earlier alert from October 2017,[48] which urged buyers of devices to

- Look for products from manufacturers with a track record of providing security to their internet-connected products. Look for companies that offer firmware and software updates, and identify how and when these updates are provided.
- Identify what data is collected and stored by the devices, including whether you can opt out of this collection, how long the data is stored, whether it is encrypted in storage, and if the data is shared with a third party. Also identify what protections and policies are in place in case there is a data breach.

These are absolutely the kind of recommendations that the present author has also made since (at least) June of 2014:[49] "When we think about the stories that data can tell, we quickly realize the need to rise above Stupid Technology Tricks: to meet high expectations for reliability of data flow, accuracy of data values, and control of data visibility." Such advice, one must concede, carries much more weight when it comes from the FBI.

Even the FBI, though, can probably do little to accelerate the process of figuring out how to handle the increasing data content of what used to be a purely mechanical possession such as an automobile. When a modern car is designed to give its owner information and even control via smartphone application, who has what responsibilities for a clean handover of the machine to its next owner without lingering residues of connection? "The response from the car industry," wrote industry observer John Leyden[50] in August of 2018, "has been to put the onus on the previous owner to delete data while minimising the role of auto manufacturers to come up with a well thought through process and for dealers to enforce it." Law, practice, and customer expectation are all clearly moving targets.

For those who find it difficult to be sympathetic owners of hot tubs or luxury cars, who can always make the effort to flip a switch or tap a reset button on a screen we can go one level deeper to the kind of problem that has no switch to flip and no button to press: the kind of problem that arises when a dependency is not fully considered, and when an engineered behavior is unconsciously treated as being as certain and reliable as the rising of the sun or the falling of Newton's apple.

A startling example of this invisible uncontrollability was in early 2018, when there was a dispute concerning the shared responsibility for managing electrical power delivery across 25 European countries.[51] Network glitches disturbed the sine-wave frequency of the alternating-current power mains supply, causing conventional "synchronous motor" clocks to drift by many minutes during the period of conflict.

47. www.ic3.gov/media/2018/180802.aspx.
48. www.ic3.gov/media/2017/171017-1.aspx.
49. https://diginomica.com/2014/06/12/assuring-trust-wears/.
50. www.theregister.co.uk/2018/08/21/connected_car_data_handover_mess/.
51. www.bbc.com/news/world-europe-43321113.

Customers had no way to see, and in many cases lacked the knowledge to comprehend, the mechanism or the occurrence of this problem except in its symptom of their clocks becoming inaccurate. The assumption of a known, unvarying frequency of the alternating current from power outlets was literally hard-wired into the system—and into the devices that relied upon it.

> *Takeaway #6*: Every interface between two systems implies a data-transfer contract—and every such exchange should be subject to audit and correction.

Revolution Three—Everything Informed

The presence of invisible, uncontrollable, even unmaintainable "smartness"—which might be better termed "idiot-savantness"—in network-connected devices brings us now to a third revolution, in which the pathways of the physical industrial world and the abstract digital world have permanently converged.

The third industrial revolution is typically considered to be marked by the emergence of electronics: that is, the use of analog and (later on) digital signals, amplified and detected by (initially) crude vacuum tubes and subsequently by increasingly sub-microscopic transistors. The distinction between electronics and electricity is that the former involves the precise manipulation of electron behaviors and effects, rather than electricity's gross flow control of the bulk goods of volts and amperes.

To speak of the third *industrial* revolution as having converged with a third *data* revolution invites the question, "Can data also be manipulated as a physical thing, like (as it turned out) an electron? Or is data a pure abstraction?" Most people in the workforce today were not even alive when the notion of information as a thing, rather than a state of mind, was first proposed to (what may surprise the modern reader) considerable initial skepticism.

It was only in the late 1940s that Norbert Wiener[52] introduced two transformative ideas about data, under the general heading of the word he coined at the time: "cybernetics."[53] Now a part of the language, embedded in words like "cyborg," cybernetics represented a fusion of (1) control and communication as processes and (2) information as a quantifiable thing.

When Wiener and other theorists first broached the latter notion of information as something we could measure, many reacted as if they were trying to put a dimension on pure thought. Information had long been thought to be a state of mind; "to inform" was a verb, meaning to alter that state. Wiener made information physical by asking a few simple questions that led, as a matter of mathematical proof, to something that almost everyone today knows is true, even though they probably don't know why.

It's a conventional wisdom that "computers only understand things as ones and zeros," and many people recognize the word "binary" (having only two possible states) as describing that system. Wiener showed the way to this world, in which we all now live, with a few simple questions.

Suppose, said Wiener, that we want to represent a number with some desired accuracy. We can understand Wiener's approach in terms of a children's guessing game. Imagine one player choosing a number, and the other being challenged to guess the chosen value. If the players agree to use the range from 1 to 100, the guesser can begin by asking if the number is less than 50. This immediately rules out half of the possible values. If the number *is* less than 50, the guesser can then ask if the number is less than 25, and so on, until the exact value is known.

52. https://en.wikipedia.org/wiki/Norbert_Wiener.
53. https://en.wikipedia.org/wiki/Cybernetics:_Or_Control_and_Communication_in_the_Animal_and_the_Machine.

At any point, if an exact result isn't needed, the guesser could stop. "It's between 18 and 21? That's close enough." Intuitively, that person would be applying the notion of "enough bits of accuracy." A binary "base two" notation can represent 32 different values, ranging from 00000 to 11111 (00000, 00001, 00010, 00011, 00100 . . .) with only five of the "binary digits" which we for short call "bits."[54] One could break up the range from zero to 100 into 32 rough sub-ranges, each needing only five bits to identify the sub-range that one had in mind. And that might be enough.

Wiener demonstrated that for any given cost in hardware of representing a value, and for any given task of representing a range of values, a system based in this manner on powers of two—a binary system—would always be the least expensive approach. It is, therefore, not the proper relation of cause and effect to say that computers work with ones and zeros because that's what their hardware can do. Rather, it's that computer hardware is built that way (rather than using continuously variable voltages and currents, like the very earliest "analog computers")[55] because doing it binary-digitally is less costly.

As almost always, though, you get what you pay for. From the moment that one decides to measure, record, and store any finite number of bits—whether as holes in a punched card, or as quantum states in an electron well, or in any other form—one has made an irrevocable decision about how much understanding is "enough." A sundial, tracking the passage of time as our planet turns, could in principle be read to any desired fraction or sub-fraction of a second if one looked closely enough at the moving shadow—but a quartz wristwatch that only jumps its second hand once per second is unable to disclose any more precision than that, no matter how carefully it's examined. "Digital" is discrete, not continuous.

Our a priori decisions about data capture are important because we can be wrong, as it turns out, about what's worth knowing. People often use the DNA blueprints of living things as the ultimate standard of precision in an enormous space of options. It's often remarked that there are more possible variations on a human DNA molecule than there are atoms in the universe. Really, though, that's not the most illuminating comparison.

For any given human being, the number of *different* genomes that would produce an apparently *identical* person (because much of our DNA is so-called junk) may possibly outnumber the known universe's atoms by a factor of $10^{6,141,012}$—yes, 10 followed by about 6 million zeros. Or should we look more carefully at the dismissive "junk" label? That term "does need to be totally expunged from the lexicon," said Ewan Birney of the European Bioinformatics Institute in Cambridge,[56] because perhaps as much as 80% of our genes may actually play functional roles (compared to the 1970s assessment that 97% of our DNA was "noncoding").

"It was always clear that there was regulation. What we didn't know was just quite how extensive this was," said Birney, and in a connected world it's becoming clear that this is more than a biological comment. In every situation, we're increasingly awash in opportunities to capture information that might matter someday—that might turn out to play, as the biologists put it, a "regulatory" even if not a directly "coding" role—and that, once discarded, can never be re-created.

It is not merely a question of "capture or not?" When we consider costs of sensing, recording and storing on the input end, and when we consider questions of personalization and privacy on the back end, we need to ask what we can let pass. What should we record *only* in anonymous aggregates and averages? What do we record in all available detail? And what do we capture, not only in its own right, but with an accompanying envelope of "metadata" that represents when, where, how, in association with what, and under what potentially relevant circumstances?

How far might this go? With people wearing network-connected devices that capture time- and geo-tagged "digital breadcrumbs" of their every activity, we can choose to capture the time and the

54. https://en.wikipedia.org/wiki/Bit.
55. https://en.wikipedia.org/wiki/Analog_computer.
56. www.scientificamerican.com/article/hidden-treasures-in-junk-dna/.

location in which a question was asked; the times and the sequences in which the questioner got what answers, from whom; the actions subsequently taken, when and where and in the company of whom. And this is just the beginning: what about the music that was playing in the location where a choice was made, and the colors that were present, and perhaps even the smells that might have played a part?

What we capture, and analyze, and can control on future occasions, we can engineer instead of leaving to luck or happenstance. Choosing not to do this will soon seem as half-hearted as using default fonts in monochrome layouts in advertising. Engineering the scent of an environment, for example, was at the end of 2014 considered to be "where music was 15 years ago," in the words of one player in this space at that time.[57]

Since this is clearly about choice, we should consider examples both of choosing *not* to capture and of discovering that new data manipulation skills can reveal information from our data that we did not *intend* to capture.

In the first case, when Apple executives came on stage back in March of 2015,[58] before the first public reveal of the Apple Watch, they talked about their introduction of their ResearchKit software framework[59]—which devoted considerable, proactive attention to the security and confidentiality of the personal data that would soon be recognized as among the most compelling opportunities of wearable technology, in personal fitness, and even in advanced medical care. Apple set a high standard, in this case, for rigorous control of data transmission and access privileges as initial requirements, not afterthoughts.

We may call this a "trust-first" approach, in which we establish permissions, then construct secure containers, and only then collect and seek value from data.

Even Apple's somewhat older HomeKit[60]—we're talking about your lights and your air conditioning, not your body and your brain—imposes security requirements that initially saw device vendors complaining that Apple was making it too difficult to build cheap hardware. "Apple is requiring device makers using both WiFi and Bluetooth LE to use complicated encryption with 3072-bit keys, as well as the super secure Curve25519, which is an elliptic curve used for digital signatures and exchanging encrypted keys," reported *Forbes*[61] in 2015, adding an anonymous developer's comment: "This is one of those things that Apple does. . . . They force an issue. It's like that here. Regular Bluetooth has an issue—it's not secure."

With these actions, at some cost to themselves, Apple has made a statement that responsibility for data protection is part of the price of admission to the market that they create.

But what about the second case, in which *data* turns out to contain *information* that was not meant to be captured? In 2015, researchers at MIT reported[62] that "just four fairly vague pieces of information—the dates and locations of four purchases—are enough to identify 90 percent of the people in a data set recording three months of credit-card transactions by 1.1 million users."

If it has long been true that "we are what we know," is today's newer truth "we are what others can know about us"?

> *Takeaway #7*: Every decision about the capture, representation, and storage of data is a possibly irrevocable decision about what is *not* worth knowing—but might also let people someday know things that were never *meant* to be captured.

57. http://adage.com/article/cmo-strategy/smell-money-marketers-sell-scent/296084/.
58. www.apple.com/live/2015-mar-event/.
59. http://researchkit.org/.
60. https://developer.apple.com/homekit/.
61. www.forbes.com/sites/aarontilley/2015/07/21/whats-the-hold-up-for-apples-homekit.
62. http://news.mit.edu/2015/identify-from-credit-card-metadata-0129.

Revolution Four—Intelligence

With the worlds of the physical and the abstract—the atoms and the bits, in the memorable coinage of Nicholas Negroponte in *Being Digital*[63] in 1995—now clearly converged, *we can consider the fourth revolution of intelligence—whatever that word really means, for like "information" it seems to be a moving target. As soon as we understand what we previously thought it entailed, we move the goalposts.*

Chess-playing software, as it turned out, did not have intelligence. It only had chess-playing skills. What used to be "machine vision" is now just a supermarket's bar-code reader. What used to be "passing the Turing test" by successfully imitating a human in conversation is now just the use of stress-harmonic detection and word choice analysis to know when a service call should be escalated to a supervisor, and so on.

The casual application, though, of increasingly capable machine learning algorithms to cornucopias of data brings with it truly dangerous ease of finding and relying upon utterly *un*informative coincidences in the form of spurious correlations. To note one example from a web site devoted to this subject,[64] it is not completely impossible that the number of letters in the winning word of the Scripps National Spelling Bee can predict the number of people that will be killed in the same year by venomous spiders—but there would be a skeptical examination of any conceivable causal link before anyone made any important decisions based on the surprising historical strength of that relationship.

> *Takeaway #8*: We can argue about whether AI is "really intelligent," but even its most optimistic champions don't call it "artificial good judgment."

The New Rules: Making Them, Following Them, Enforcing Them

We have seen the risks of undisciplined scale in the loss of data from as long ago as 1890. We have seen the dangers of undisciplined distribution, as data networks without circuit breakers have invited data to destroy its own distributed environment, as long ago as 1987. We have seen the potential for costly errors in the ungoverned use of spreadsheet software, and the potential for privacy-threatening insights from voracious capture of transactional metadata, in the cascading and turbulent stream of a growing volume of incidents and research discoveries even before we began this century.

Each of the four revolutions has increased the value of data while also creating new risks. The obvious risks are those that can be mitigated by obvious methods, such as minimum strength of passwords and minimum frequency of password change. The more complex risks simply end-run around such protections, like a thief who does not even try to pick a lock but simply smashes it with a hammer—or cuts through the wall, or tunnels in from the building next door.

For an example of such a "side-channel attack," consider the researchers who found that computers' processing chips make distinctive noises as they perform specific operations. According to a report from December 2013,

> The researchers successfully extracted decryption keys over a distance of four meters (13 feet) with a high-quality parabolic microphone. Perhaps more intriguingly, though, they also managed to pull of this attack with a smartphone placed 30 centimeters (12 inches) away from the target laptop.[65]

63. https://en.wikipedia.org/wiki/Being_Digital.
64. http://tylervigen.com/spurious-correlations.
65. www.extremetech.com/extreme/173108-researchers-crack-the-worlds-toughest-encryption-by-listening-to-the-tiny-sounds-made-by-your-computers-cpu.

If you saw someone crack a password by analyzing CPU sound signatures in a *Mission: Impossible* or Bourne franchise movie, you might very well roll your eyes, but this is real—and this is not the only such cross-mode connection between simple observation and successful compromise. Even something as easy as recording the sounds of a keyboard can narrow the search space enormously[66]—and that's all that's needed.

Rather than ever believing that all attacks can be foreseen, and effectively blocked by rigorous design and enforcement of security rules and practices, it is far more likely that the pattern-recognition capabilities discussed in other applications above can also be applied to recognize and take prompt action against novel and unexpected attacks, simply by recognizing the unusual—at a scale we can't afford with living brains.

What may also be happening, finally, in response to growing public awareness of these risks is that people are becoming more accepting of the need for some reduction of convenience as the price of getting these risks under control. To borrow the example of "Pretty Good Privacy" security guru Philip Zimmermann, we tolerate the cost and inconvenience of envelopes rather than conducting business with postcards: it's about time we added that common-sense level of protection to an ever more fully connected world.[67]

There are abundant precedents for the idea that personal accountability becomes a necessary companion to personal power, as a technology ceases to be the privilege of the expert or especially wealthy few, but instead becomes an everyday convenience to the point of being perceived as a near necessity for all. We put number plates on our automobiles, for example, to make them identifiable, and to trace them to responsible individuals who are accountable for their actions in shared spaces.

The European Commission observes, in what seems a natural parallel notion, that

> A potential obstacle for the achievement of a single market for the [Internet of Things] has to do with issues linked to the capacity to handle a large diversity and very large volumes of connected devices, and the need to securely identify them and be able to discover them so that they can be plugged into IoT systems.[68]

It's certainly not too soon to get serious about making that happen.

What takes us forward from recognition to action? What makes this explosion of scale, ubiquity, information richness and sensitivity, and unintended-consequences intelligence all behave?

Protection Through Reorganization

One of the most deeply rooted problems is a habit of hierarchical privilege, where the owner of a physical machine can do anything with that machine—including anything that views or manages the data that it stores. A user name of "root," deriving from the origin point of a tree of data folders, has traditionally represented that total power. Subsets of that power can be granted to sub-managers and to end users, but the notion that someone has to be trusted by everyone else has been the starting point for the vast majority of data-leakage and data-corruption incidents.

The resulting, simple hierarchy of privilege is well recognized as a source of significant risk. According to results reported in May 2007 by Newton, Massachusetts-based Cyber-Ark Software, a survey of more than 200 IT professionals found one-third of them actually admitted to abuse of their administrative access privileges to examine sensitive data unrelated to their job functions. About one-fourth reported knowledge of former employees who retained access to "sensitive networks"

66. www.inf.ed.ac.uk/publications/thesis/online/IM100855.pdf.
67. www.philzimmermann.com/EN/essays/WhyIWrotePGP.html.
68. https://ec.europa.eu/digital-single-market/en/internet-things.

long after their termination, and one-third stated a belief that they could do likewise with little risk of detection.[69]

The notion of a privilege hierarchy appears to be so inherent, in the architecture of data storage and management, that many are genuinely unaware that alternatives even exist. Among the most important developments now in progress are therefore the emerging models of the metadata-based cloud platform, and the shared-truth distributed ledger (often called by the name of a particular approach called a "blockchain").

Multi-tenant Clouds

As to the cloud, exemplified by a service provider such as Salesforce, the change is from a model in which possession implies control to a model in which various privileges are explicitly and separately defined and granted.

In the Salesforce model, there is no single table in any physical database instance that represents data assets specific to any individual customer organization. Rather, there are massive sets of data elements, whose individual structure includes a representation of which customer organizations may have access to any given element—with further control of which individual subscribers within those organizations can exercise which specific privileges.

By matching privilege sets to individuals, rather than issuing application-specific login IDs and passwords that are all too often shared among several users, the multi-tenant model exemplified by Salesforce can improve the effectiveness of many data governance measures. Not only the data elements, but the endpoint locations and even the times of day when access is allowed, can be managed with relative ease.

Consider the further governance improvements that can result from this granularity. There might be tasks, for example, involving data update—such as revising the credit rating of a customer—that do not require the person making the update to know what the previous value of a datum may have been. In a multi-tenant model of the kind described here, the privilege of editing can be decoupled from the privilege of reading: an employee could have a task-specific user interface that enables entry of new values without providing visibility of the values being replaced, and without giving inappropriate access to data that the employee's role creates no legitimate need to see.

A long-sought goal of IT governance, the granting of "least privilege"[70] as needed by business process, rather than as dictated by technology's clumsy controls, is thus brought much closer to achievement.

Global Shared-Truth Ledgers

The other, rapidly accelerating approach to increased confidence in data integrity is shared-truth distributed ledgers, concisely described by one observer as repositories in which "unrelated transactions are bundled into blocks, which are chained together using [cryptographic] hashes and (in most cases) broadcast to all participating entities for batch processing."[71] Entire chapters, indeed entire books, are being rapidly written and intently read as companies and industries grasp the implications.

69. www.thefreelibrary.com/Cyber-Ark+Software+Survey+Reveals+Scandal+of+Snooping+IT+Staff.-a0164217574.
70. https://csrc.nist.gov/Glossary/?term=5232.
71. https://bitsonblocks.net/2017/02/20/whats-the-difference-between-a-distributed-ledger-and-a-blockchain/.

Bankers look to this transformation for acceleration of transactions, shrinking days to seconds.[72] Manufacturers and shippers look to it for improved consistency and reduced costs in supply chain management.[73] Researchers look to it for reduction of data falsification, saying that the general model's four main properties—"Identity, Timestamping, Content and Immutability"—could play a valuable role in addressing "diminishing trust in science and scientists" due to high-profile cases of questionable (or even fraudulent) data manipulation.[74]

Many of what have been regarded as inherent risks, with high costs of mitigation, in the realm of all data operations to date are consequently coming to be recognized as artifacts of design choices. They may have been competent and pragmatic optimizations at the time, but they were made in an era when connectivity around the entire planet was costly, intermittent, and slow—instead of being nearly free, almost always-on, and continually growing faster.

All future discussions of data will incorporate growing attention to the connectivity-intensive, shared-truth trend. In the short run, there will be as many vague and self-serving definitions of terms surrounding these ideas as there have been around past phrases du jour, like "artificial intelligence" and "cloud computing": it is therefore useful to have specific criteria on hand, like those offered, for example, in August 2018 by researchers at the Judge Business School at the University of Cambridge, who proposed[75] that a distributed ledger technology should minimally be expected to:

1. enable a network of independent participants to establish a consensus around . . .
2. the authoritative ordering of cryptographically validated ("signed") transactions. These records are made . . .
3. persistent by replicating the data across multiple nodes, and . . .
4. tamper-evident by linking them by cryptographic hashes. Finally, that
5. The shared result of the reconciliation/consensus process—the "ledger"—serves as the authoritative version for these records.

If it doesn't satisfy all five of these elements, it may have the superficial form of a buzz-phrased "blockchain model" while missing some of the most important advantages or even creating new vulnerabilities.

Protection Through Regulation—Before GDPR, and After

Concurrently with new data architectures in the technical realm come new norms and requirements in the legislative and regulatory realm. Prior to the introduction of the European Union's GDPR[76] in May of 2018, even a diligent effort to understand data-related regulation across multiple jurisdictions encountered wildly varied approaches and enormously uneven enforcement.

Specific domains such as health care were earliest to the party, so to speak, due to the inherent sensitivity of their subject matter. A regulation like the US Health Insurance Portability and Accountability Act (HIPAA) is notable for what it says about the enormous scope of responsibility for data, extending well beyond the boundaries of IT systems.

72. www.ft.com/content/541414c0-3834-11e6-a780-b48ed7b6126f.
73. https://medium.com/@philippsandner/application-of-blockchain-technology-in-the-manufacturing-industry-d03a8ed3ba5e.
74. www.bio-itworld.com/2018/02/07/scientific-data-doctoring-could-blockchain-technology-help-stamp-it-out.aspx.
75. www.theregister.co.uk/2018/08/14/distributed_ledger_technology_system_cambridge_university_report/.
76. www.eugdpr.org/.

In the course of the first publicly discussed HIPAA audit, taking place in March 2007,[77] a list of 42 points of inquiry—to which the auditors apparently asked for response within ten days—made it clear that organizations were thenceforth going to be living in a world of rigorous scrutiny affecting every interaction that acquired or used others' information. Every organization should wonder if it could demonstrate documented and enforced policies for items of auditor inquiry that included "regularly reviewing records of information system activity, such as audit logs, access reports and security incident tracking reports," or "creating, documenting and reviewing exception reports or logs. Please provide a list of examples of security violation logging and monitoring."

How quickly, if at all, could an organization unravel its own tangles of database/spreadsheet/document interactions in response to an audit demand to "provide a list of all information systems that house ePHI [electronic protected health information][78] data, as well as network diagrams, including all hardware and software that are used to collect, store, process or transmit ePHI"? How readily could most organizations even respond, accurately, to the much simpler question, "Please provide a list of all users with access to ePHI data. Please identify each user's access rights and privileges"?

Note also that the scope of a HIPAA audit is not limited to electronic information, but may even address such issues as a paper form filled out by a patient being left on a desk, where it is visible to other patients.[79] Data governance is about data, not about technology—and even though HIPAA's audit regime is specific to health care, one must expect that other sectors will soon adopt similarly stringent guidelines.

> *Takeaway #9*: Responsibility for data does not begin when something is typed in or piped in. It does not end when something is printed out or wired out. It begins when a question is asked, or an input is invited; it ends only when any and every record is provably destroyed

Even as corporations and other institutions confront the burdens of regulation, individuals should be taking care not to assume that those regulations are being effectively implemented and enforced. For example, the most recent available audit of US federal agencies by the Government Accountability Office (GAO) reported that

> federal agencies continued to experience weaknesses in protecting their information and information systems due to ineffective implementation of information security policies and practices. Most of the 24 Chief Financial Officers Act (CFO) agencies had weaknesses in five control areas—access controls, configuration management controls, segregation of duties, contingency planning, and agencywide security management.[80]

In another high-profile discovery, revealing alarming noncompliance with widely discussed restrictions on data sharing, it became known[81] in June 2018 that the US National Security Agency (NSA) had been receiving telephone records "that NSA was not authorized to receive" since (it appeared from their announcement) perhaps as early as 2015.

77. www.computerworld.com/article/2541971/security0/hipaa-audit—the-42-questions-hhs-might-ask.html.
78. www.virtru.com/blog/what-is-ephi/.
79. http://blog.securitymetrics.com/2015/08/reception-desks-hipaa-compromise.html.
80. www.gao.gov/products/GAO-17-549.
81. www.nsa.gov/news-features/press-room/statements/jun-28-2018-ufa-cdr-decision.shtml.

We may therefore be, at most, merely hopeful that the recent emergence of GDPR—given the growing importance of the EU marketplace—will lead many companies to adopt and observe its strictures globally, as Microsoft announced its intention immediately upon GDPR taking effect.[82]

It is still much too early, though, for anyone to be able to claim a complete understanding of the practical effect and extent of GDPR's requirements. "The regulation is intentionally ambiguous, representing a series of compromises," wrote anthropology and information science professor Allison Cool[83] in the weeks before GDPR went live. She continued,

> It skirts over possible differences between current and future technologies by using broad principles. . . . I interviewed scientists, data managers, legal scholars, lawyers, ethicists and activists in Sweden. I learned that many scientists and data managers who will be subject to the law find it incomprehensible. They doubted that absolute compliance was even possible.

One must also consider the quite real prospect of unintended consequences that could result from GDPR protections being applied to everyone, the just and the unjust alike: when a malware campaign is launched in a GDPR-compliant world, suggests IBM Security Vice President Caleb Barlow,

> The difference this time is they're able for the first time to do it with complete anonymity. . . . Now when they strike, normally a campaign might only last a few hours to a few days, as they're sending out millions of spam messages. In the future, two or three months from now, those same campaigns may last 30 days or more before the security committee is able to rally to close them down because of this increasing attack surface due to the privacy that the bad guys now enjoy.[84]

With any new regulation as complex as GDPR, it is commonly anticipated that only the case law resulting from adjudication of actual complaints and disputes will provide trustworthy guidance on what will be considered lawful conduct. Until then, one can only make good faith, prudent man, competent practitioner efforts, and hope to set the precedent rather than being bludgeoned by it.

Further, it is not enough to have the text of a country's laws at hand without also knowing something about law enforcement practices, judiciary efficiency and ethics, and customer expectations based on varying cultures and histories. The need for legal expertise is not reduced merely by the emergence of GDPR as something of a global reference model.

Faced by both the growing complexity of many compliance requirements, and the rising level of potential damage (both financial and reputational) in the event of even accidental errors, many organizations may be moved to consider increased reliance on external resources for what they may have always previously considered internal control and compliance roles and duties. This should be done with care: in 2015, the US Securities and Exchange Commission (SEC) issued a warning[85] that

> certain outsourced Chief Compliance Officers could not articulate the business or compliance risks . . . or, to the extent the risks were identified, whether the registrant had adopted written policies and procedures to mitigate or address those risks. . . . The staff identified several areas where the registrant did not appear to have policies, procedures, and/or disclosures in place necessary to address certain risks.

82. https://internetofbusiness.com/microsoft-adopts-gdpr-globally-supports-privacy-for-all/.
83. www.nytimes.com/2018/05/15/opinion/gdpr-europe-data-protection.html.
84. www.techrepublic.com/article/heres-whats-next-for-the-gdpr/.
85. www.sec.gov/ocie/announcement/ocie-2015-risk-alert-cco-outsourcing.pdf.

The short form of the SEC warning was that "Some standardized risk checklists utilized by outsourced CCOs were generic and did not appear to fully capture the business models, practices, strategies, and compliance risks that were applicable"; that an organization, not an outsourced compliance expert, "is ultimately responsible for adopting and implementing an effective compliance program and is accountable for its own deficiencies." Outsourcing the workload does not outsource the accountability.

> *Takeaway #10*: If your data situation looks to be well in hand, look harder.

In Conclusion: This Is Just the Beginning

The present and future of data stewardship cannot be understood or predicted by a simple evolution—"bigger, better, faster and cheaper"—from the first half century or so of what we now consider traditional databases and data-based services. Long-standing models of data's origin, collection, ownership, protection, monetization, regulation, and litigation are not merely at the foundation of established business and technical practices: they are also embedded, often only by implication, in many aspects of law and precedent.

One can see the slow-motion train wreck of old ideas about data in the renewed controversy[86] in August of 2018 over data files that can be used by a 3D printer to produce an untraceable gun. Are data files a form of speech, protected in the United States by constitutional guarantees? Or is a data file, in a world where bits can direct the manipulation of atoms, a "munition" subject to regulation? This is not even the first time that such a question has arisen: in 1994, export of the book *Applied Cryptography* by Bruce Schneier was ruled to exclude the export of floppy disks[87] containing the sample code in the book. Packaging the code in a form that was directly machine readable was considered to cross a boundary separating "information" from "function."[88] More than 25 years later, this remains an area of important unanswered questions.

If anyone has difficulty getting business leaders to take this all seriously, and to see the present and future of data as a strategically vital and financially impactful domain, there are compelling arguments to appeal to either fear or greed, depending on the audience.

To persuade the fearful, share studies like the *2018 Cost of a Data Breach Study: Global Overview*, conducted by Ponemon Institute LLC with the sponsorship of IBM.[89] Released in July 2018, this study's key findings included increased estimated average cost of a data breach, projected at $3.9 million per incident; and increased likelihood of a "material breach" for an organization, projected at almost 28% over the coming two years. Dan Torpey, the US leader of Investigation and Compliance services at Ernst & Young, was stark in his assessment[90] that "there are companies that have been breached and companies that don't know they've been breached"; further, that the uncertainties and possible excesses of regulatory response are in their way just as much a source of risk as are cyberthreat and fraud.

Note well that it's not just the vendors of defensive expertise and tools who assert that the risks are real. In June 2018, *The State of Industrial Security 2018* report produced by Germany's Pierre Audoin Consultants stated that

86. www.theregister.co.uk/2018/08/27/3d_gun_injunction/.
87. www.ka9q.net/export/history.html.
88. www.ka9q.net/export/mcnamara-response.html.
89. www.ibm.com/security/data-breach.
90. http://fcpacompliancereport.com/2018/04/iic5-dan-torpey/.

> over three quarters of the companies surveyed state that it is very likely or at least quite likely to become a target of a cybersecurity attack. . . . Despite this, only 23% are compliant with minimal mandatory industry or government guidance and regulations around cybersecurity . . . [and] 48% don't have specific incident response programs.

To inspire the greedy, share studies like the *2018 Data Value Report* from Vanson Bourne, sponsored by SnapLogic,[91] which included findings that "on average, respondents estimate that their organization only uses around half (51%) of the data that it collects or generates," and also that "respondents estimate an annual revenue increase of $5,156,891, on average, as a result of using data more effectively."

To thrive in an environment of massive, technology-driven disruptions of many markets and huge reshaping of social norms and personal expectations, we must confront both the possibility *and* the necessity that traditional models must in many cases be turned inside out, rather than being merely accelerated and enlarged. Differences in degree become differences in kind when data arises, not only from intentional transactions with known partners, but also as a side effect of everyday actions that are measured and analyzed by unknown and unaccountable corporations and government entities.

When rapidly evolving laws and regulations may be infeasible or even logically impossible to satisfy in full, a reasoned and responsibly considered posture of good-faith effort is (one may argue) the best that can be achieved: it has been the goal of this chapter to support that process of informed consideration and prudent choice.

91. www.snaplogic.com/resources/research/2018-data-value-report.

21

THE CONVERGENCE OF SOCIAL MEDIA, TECHNOLOGY, AND DATA

Jeff Koller

Without question, the world and evolution of social media and cybersecurity-related issues is in a daily state of change with no retraction in site. In fact, one could confidently wager that this topic evolves so quickly that weekly updates on new aspects of cybersecurity, technology, and social media are not fast enough and far between. On a daily basis, our world is inundated with the immediate impact of viral videos showing dire and unfathomable events directly impacting the very lives of individuals. We are seeing massive, ongoing, and organized protests calling for social change coordinated through social media. And during this time, our world has been enveloped in a global pandemic called COVID-19, which literally resulted in a near-pervasive shutdown of society as we sheltered in place. More so than any other time, we have been tethered to our devices for news, socialization, and even as a means to order our next meal, groceries, and other needed items.

As such, we no longer have the option to turn a blind eye toward the inextricable integration of social media in society, technology, the importance of data security and insuring ourselves against inevitable cyber-related events. The reality that the concept of managing ones' own risk or that of one's employees has always been an intricate dance between productivity, safety, privacy, and technology evolution. It's apparent that a meteoric-type jet pack was strapped on to the practice of managing risk as social media, cybersecurity, and data management tightly intertwines its presence in everyday life, both personal and professional.

The pervasiveness of data breaches and incidences of ransomware have resulted in the complete loss or denied access to pivotal data held by the largest and most sophisticated of corporations, governmental entities, and professional entities such as law firms, healthcare providers, and publicly traded companies. We've seen social media sway elections, impact the stock market, drive the overthrow of governments, lead to the demise of prominent public figures and overnight ascending of unknown individuals into either quickly fleeting or sustaining stardom, decisive and immediate terminating employment decisions, the movement of societal endeavors, and the increase of communication between friends and family. In short, we've seen the best and worst of individuals in their public domain posts, and we've come to the realization that even the most well-resourced of entities are subject to human frailty, error, and the brilliance of hackers providing, perhaps unknowingly, access to the most private of our information.

As our reliance on each of these technologically based platforms increases, so does the profound societal impact it has on us as individuals, a collective society and global perception. The monetary and psychological impact is unparalleled with the promise of it not going away but increasing. There's no doubt that our advancements have resulted in significant benefits to many, but at what cost? This

DOI: 10.4324/9781351107242-26

chapter will explore the intersection of social media, technology, and big data as it relates to us as individuals, as well as in a broad cross-section of society and business. After all, society and business are inextricably intertwined with the other. We'll look at this from the perspective of risk management, legal, and responsive planning when something goes awry. Unfortunately, the latter is the inevitable; however, anticipating and planning is something we can control, discuss, implement, and act upon. After all, there's no need to conjure up hypothetical scenarios from which to learn as there are a multitude of daily published human miscues from which to stare at, digest, discuss, and then ponder: What were they thinking? How could that have occurred? How could we have prepared better? How could we respond better? Are there readily available resources to educate and try to keep informed? Do we have insurance coverage for such an incident?

When Did It Begin For You?

We all have a memory of when we first connected with social media by downloading and signing into a platform. The reason could have been for your use, the desire (but, more like need) to know what your children were doing on social media, professional, or a combination of any of the above. This could have been Facebook, Twitter, LinkedIn, MySpace, Instagram, Snapchat, or the like. Nowadays, the list can go on and on with the varied applications and online social media portals growing daily. At present, there are tens of thousands of available smartphone applications covering the gambit of tools, games, social media, graphic editing tools, emoji builders, dating, social platforms, and information portals. There's no doubt many must think how did one function just a few years in the past and then wonder are you any more efficient, more aware, or far too connected, wishing to retreat back to a time of greater anonymity.

Here are but a few perspectives of what has driven social media to its unquestionable position of dominance and presence in our everyday lives as it is:

- Unfiltered
- Spontaneous
- Free
- Readily available
- Ubiquitous
- Contemporaneous
- Permanent
- Promotional
- Informative
- Persuasive
- Beneficial
- Detrimental.

We've learned that demographically certain applications appeal greater to one age spectrum over another. For example, Millennials may be drawn to Instagram and Snapchat, while Gen Xers may favor Facebook along with their time line neighbor Baby Boomers, perhaps embracing Tinder and leaving behind MySpace.[1] Regardless of the platform used, the general consensus is that social media has changed the way we communicate with friends, family, and those across the country and globally, as well as every service provider and commerce portal we may currently utilize or consider. With

1. See generally, Brooke Auxier and Monica Anderson, Social Media Use in 2021, *Pew Research Center*, www.pewresearch.org/internet/2021/04/07/social-media-use-in-2021/.

many, there's a constant desire to let as many know as possible what you're doing, eating, experiencing, and thinking (or in some cases not thinking) as this portal sometimes gives license for some outlandish publications of one sort or another. What we do know is the communication is instantaneous, can be impactful, and should be considered permanent. That's right: that rant, photo, video, and image can be quickly engraved into the social media environment, a virtual permanently indelible chalkboard not subject to the passage of time or erosion. At times these posts unite individuals, causes, and communities around a common focus, platform or message while prove devastating to others in their professional or employment capacity. We would also be remiss not to acknowledge the dreadful cyberbullying from which no one is immune; however, it predominantly targets our youth.[2]

The following will review and discuss from a practical, user-friendly perspective a multitude of issues brought about by the pervasive world of social media from a risk management, legal, individual, and corporate impact perspective. As we've seen, entire social movements have been born, nurtured, and grown in immense proportions such as #NeverAgain, #MeToo, #BlackLivesMatter, #GeorgeFloyd, governmental uprisings and overthrows, to political campaigns and societal influences on the same.[3] When we look at all that has been published and shared on social media, we must quickly acknowledge and embrace that there is little in the way of filtering. Today's technology, availability, and ease of use provides us the stage to instantaneously share images from photos, streaming video, and text that can range from raw, highly disturbing, horrific, and dire but also inspiring, positive, instructive, and beneficial.

From a business perspective, we are frequently plunged into unchartered waters in how we respond to social media activities that can be detrimental both individually and commercially. It ranges from bullying, defamatory statements, and impactful dissemination of images and content that has derailed and shattered once untouchable professional careers, commercial and personal brands, legal settlement agreements, and others all in the span of minutes utilizing a small yet powerful handheld device sending (posting) an image, a video, a meme, or a statement, at times embodied in 140 characters or fewer. These communications are freely initiated and spread through free platforms that are viewed across the globe and ubiquitously available by using a simple hashtag symbol which makes social media posts universally searchable regardless of whether the viewer is a "contact," "friend," or "follower" across multiple social media platforms.

In looking at this all-encompassing topic, the logical place to start when we talk about social media is what exactly are we talking about. The basic premise is that social media is user-created content added to application platforms residing on our phone, tablet, and computer utilized by an individual. By platform, we mean applications like Twitter, Instagram, Facebook, LinkedIn, Snapchat, and the like. Yes, even email is a social media platform, as that content can be easily copied, forwarded, and embedded in a separate platform for broad distribution well beyond what the writer intended at the time of it being composed and posted.

The evolution of platforms is not going to be stagnant but boundless, and only capped by the creativity and imagination of those who launch them. This need to communicate is married with society's ongoing norm and its need to be aware of "what's next," "what's favored," "what's trending," and "what's happening" versus "what's fallen out of favor." No doubt we've moved to a digital platform for communication, advertisement, promotion, and tracking, and with daily sophistication

2. One resource that offers multiple channels of education on social media platforms and their interaction with one another is Social Media Marketing Examiner (www.socialmediaexaminer.com/) The group's newsletters, conferences and podcasts offer an inclusive and informative window into the various available social media channels.
3. Diana Daly, *Humans R Social Media*, Open Textbook Edition 1, University of Arizona, 2021, https://opentextbooks.library.arizona.edu/hrsm/.

improvements by both developers and users, a far majority of society has no idea of what is occurring around them or *to* them in the cyber world.

Social Media Puts Us In An Ongoing Risk Management Role

The news has always provided a portal of information, a funnel if you will, into what is going on in our community, the country, and globally. It wasn't that long ago where learning of an event was dependent on us reading the paper, watching the news, or surfing the internet. No doubt, all of this could be filtered and edited subject to publication constraints and network guidelines. However, now, with push notification applications a part of every current handheld device, we are easily inundated multiple times each day with breaking news, updates, and happenings. This is the antithesis of information receipt which may have previously been restricted, censored, or tethered in its content.[4]

The endless possibilities of doing a hashtag search of a particular topic, event, name, phrase, or anything of interest can quickly yield current, hot-off-the-fingertip informational updates. Companies across the globe are hiring and training teams of social media first responders to canvass various platforms at the ready to respond and interact with a now global audience. In many respects, the speed and fulfillment of an interaction, inclusive of a request, with a company through a social media platform is far more expeditious, productive, and impactful than a customer service email or much less a potentially interminable maze of caller options to ultimately be directed to a bot or, if you're fortunate, a living, breathing customer-centric service representative.

Frequently, banner snippet ads populate your home screen unless you are adept enough to put those to sleep through your device's settings feature. All too often, information goes "viral" and can literally be at the fingertips of millions of readers within minutes. Oftentimes these morsels of information contain a troubling, perhaps shocking image in the form of a video or photograph, or a socially repugnant, even perplexing statement by a noted societal figure whether meant for a small audience or the entire audience of their followers.

Impulsiveness Can Be Irreversible

When we look at the volume and frequency of online activity from the perspective of "every minute of every day," it is both daunting and jaw-dropping as to the prevalence. Just a few morsels of such activity are provided by a 2019 statistical study published by DOMO setting forth *every minute* frequency occurrences such as over 231,000 Skype originated calls, over 55,000 photos posted to Instagram, in excess of 694,000 hours of video streamed through Netflix, over 18 million text messages sent (many emanating from certain political figures), Americans utilizing over 4.4 million gigabytes of data, and almost 4.5 million Google searches initiated. These are just a few to pique your attention should you need to further your appetite of curiosity as to this "every minute, of every day activity."[5]

Of course, with such a volume of postings and activity, there are those activities which one would surmise are regrettable, posted at a moment of conscious weakness, perhaps caught in a festive moment with friends, or simply a way to visually verbalize a desire to rebel against something or

4. See, e.g., Natalie Jomini Stroud, Cynthia Peacock and Alexander L. Curry (2019), The effects of mobile push notifications on news consumption and learning, *Digital Journalism*, Volume 8, Issue 1, pp. 32–48, www.tandfonline.com/doi/abs/10.1080/21670811.2019.1655462.
5. Data Never Sleeps 8.0 [Infographic], DOMO, www.domo.com/learn/infographic/data-never-sleeps-8. See also generally, Yogesh K. Dwivedi et al. (2021), Setting the future of digital and social media marketing research: Perspectives and research propositions, *International Journal of Information Management*, Volume 59, 102168, www.sciencedirect.com/science/article/pii/S0268401220308082.

someone. Such judgment calls, or lack thereof, could be couched in a young man posting a photo of himself flipping the bird as he syphons gasoline from a police car, the individual captured in his restaurant uniform licking a stack of hard-shell tacos, another utilizing a food chain's sink for a post-shift bath, or one simply using the presence of the presidential motorcade to express their political preference with a raised single-finger solute as it passes by. Of course, we've often heard that a picture is worth a thousand words, and such postings often far exceed this measure. Without question, we also can't evade the power of video to capture an escalating event often from start to some pivotal moment and then the aftermath. (YouTube has over 4.5 million videos watched every minute of every day, according to Domo.com.) In fact, many of us have unlimited data plans that allow us the platform to stream live events as they're unfolding before our eyes, even creating our own online channel for such purposes. The sophistication of these ubiquitous devices can provide quality capturing and production at the touch of a thumb or other trained digit.

Now, that's not to say that one can't have a similar negative impact with 140 characters or fewer, perhaps in conjunction with a hashtagged word or phrase or a robust list of followers to equally draw ire, disdain, and an immediate and decisive detrimental response. We've seen this in the late-night missives of well-known celebrities, prominent professional and political figures, and others removed from such public positions of notoriety only to be thrust into the spotlight due to the viral outgrowth of their posting(s). Such conjurings are a daily occurrence, and gone are the days of simply being able to paint over something on a wall, scratch out something written by another, or shred an unwanted photo. Those days have passed, and many of us are grateful we did not grow up in such a vividly public time. We have also learned all too well that even deleting a post, deactivating a social media platform, or moving something to private is not a cure. With the ongoing and pervasive canvassing of the internet wild, posts can be quickly unearthed and permanently captured by an independent service entity such as a news agency searching for topically relevant posts, perhaps simply married to a hashtagged term, phrase, or name. From there, one's ability to virtually reach through the internet and forever claw back that post are forever obliterated, and if this isn't believed, it doesn't take long on any given day or week to view such notable misadventures on the internet.

Online resources like Timemachine.com allow someone to search for a specific individual's last 3,200 tweets, inclusive of accessing a link that was cross-posted with the tweet. There is no prerequisite of following them on Twitter to review this tweet history. If you're interested in reviewing a website's content from years ago, you can utilize Archive.org, which over the years has archived billions of web pages preserving content which may otherwise no longer be available. If you're looking to capture the entirety of web pages, there are other options available in lieu of taking a screenshot, which only captures what's actually visible on the screen/monitor. One such service is PageVault.com, which provides a subscription plan that allows you to log into a separate server, and by searching the web for a particular site using your preferred browser you can then capture the entirety of the desired page which may extend well beyond what you can see (e.g., someone's Facebook timeline, LinkedIn listing, YouTube channel).[6] The image is continuous, like a paper towel roll, as compared to the print screen version which is like quilting together individual sheets. The image is captured with supporting metadata such as date, time, browser engine, operating system, length of document, internet service provider used, and captured URL, among other document foundation morsels pivotal for legal evidentiary purposes. If you're looking to cross-search multiple social media platforms simultaneously for a particular individual or activity within a specified geo-location, then you may wish to review the capabilities of services such as X1 Discovery.

6. See, e.g., Jeremy Harris Lipschultz, *Social Media Communication: Concepts, Practices, Data, Law and Ethics* (Routledge, 2020), www.routledge.com/Social-Media-Communication-Concepts-Practices-Data-Law-and-Ethics/Lipschultz/p/book/9780367195007.

How can resources like this be used in conjunction with one another? Imagine you wish to retrieve from the internet someone's LinkedIn page and any other publicly available social media platform that may exist that you've yet to discover. You could start your search process by accessing Page Vault, through which you could then login to X1 Discovery for a cross-platform search. After locating what you're looking for, you could use Page Vault's website capture service to retrieve the entirety of their page (which is typically quite a bit longer than a single page) in a medium that is authenticated via the metadata information provided by Page Vault's platform. Of course, there are other services available, inclusive of utilizing retained professionals to conduct, harvest, and preserve desired web-housed information, if available.

New Language Frontier: Emojis and More

Our embraced use of advancing technology has also brought about a different way for us to communicate with one another using emojis in our messaging. Emojis are tiny pictures of facial expressions or objects used in text messages, emails, and on social media. The use of emojis has grown exponentially as a way to communicate beyond text-driven content. They provides the writer a means to more precisely express themselves utilizing one or multiple emojis in conjunction with one another whether facial expressions or images. When combined, they can stand for what would have normally been a text written communication; however, with emojis the message is not always clear or obvious. As such, the growing presence of emoji messages are increasingly becoming present in lawsuits. At issue is what do these emoji messages mean and how are they to be interpreted?

The enthusiastic embrace of emojis and emoticons has been breathtaking. Emoji is the fastest growing form of language in history based on its incredible adoption rate and speed of evolution. This development also has major implications for how humans communicate with each other. We're not just watching the birth of a new type of language; we are creating a new way of communicating with each other.[7]

One initial study reported that 92% of the online population uses emojis, and another report indicated that 2.3 trillion mobile messages incorporated emojis in a single year. The "face with tears of joy" emoji has appeared in over 1.6 billion tweets, and domain names that incorporate emojis are being developed.[8] With this increased use, there will be ever-growing challenges of interpretation in lawsuits, as attorneys seek out the meaning behind such messages and their relevancy to the factual issues in the case. At the moment, "emoticons and emojis have fixed emotional resonance, clear dictionary definition, or established grammatical rules for interpreting them in the various contexts in which they appear." Also, it is widely understood that the use of emojis "creates situations where the sender and recipient make reasonable—but different—interpretations of the same message."

Lawyers are now seeking insight through multiple resources to interpret the subjective meaning the sender/author meant to attach to the emoji and/or emoticons presence in a message. Resources such as Emojipedia.org, seminars, articles, academic publications, studies, commonality of use, and case precedent are but a few of the channels available to further discern and interpret what was meant by the emojis presence in a message. "There are no limits to the emoji possibilities. The reality is people are just going to keep using their technology to communicate."[9]

7. See, Eric Goldman, Surveying the Law of Emojis, Santa Clara Univ. Legal Studies Research Paper, 8–17, May 1, 2017, last revised May 2, 2018, Santa Clara University School of Law, https://papers.ssrn.com/sol3/papers.cfm?abstract_id=2961060.
8. 2015 Emoji Report, Emoji Research Team; see also Qiyu Bai, et al. (2019), "A Systematic Review of Emoji: Current Research and Future Perspectives," *Frontiers in Psychology*, Volume 10: 2221, www.ncbi.nlm.nih.gov/pmc/articles/PMC6803511/.
9. Mike Cherney, "Lawyers faced with emojis and emoticons are all," *Wall Street Journal* (January 29, 2018), www.wsj.com/articles/lawyers-faced-with-emojis-and-emoticons-are-all-1517243950.

Preparing: It's Not a Matter of If, But When

So, what can one do? The first place to start is with yourself. Simply, one must become their own risk manager both in their personal and professional lives. Realizing this is a simple tenet to write; however, to place into practice is a far deeper challenge, as seen by everyday occurrences from all individuals regardless of their station in life, wealth, training, and intellect. It seems for many the urge and desire to share is unbridled. It makes sense, after all, as this is a central platform of our educational and personal development, right? Early on, our writings and drawings are posted for all to see in our class, examples of exemplary work are displayed to others and there's an interwoven societal need to be seen, liked, differentiate oneself, and be accepted by others. This isn't a scientific hypothesis premised on field research and studies, but simply borne from our own reality proven by the fact you're most likely nodding your head in the affirmative as you read this very statement.

As co-workers, managers, owners, and trainers, we can speak to the downsides of errant practices on social media, as well as cybersecurity. As to the latter, this is a whole other realm ripe with danger as nefarious fraudulent emails looking like the real deal from a known individual or company comes with it an attached malware payload (i.e., virus) attachment urging you to open it. Or, perhaps, an embedded link encouraging you to "click me" so as to access some important information, or provide access to an upload portal for certain requested information (e.g., upload relevant employee payroll data to this site at the fraudulent request of your company's chief financial officer). We're quickly becoming accustomed to phrases like phishing, spear phishing, smishing, vishing, ghosting, spoofing, packet sniffing, and whaling.[10] Although these phrases in and of themselves are intriguing, the very import which is attached to them is quite ominous, negative, and likely harmful.

So, again, we ask ourselves, what are we to do? Of course, abstaining from the internet, inclusive of the online general use for email, information, and shopping purposes, may be an available individual option; however, such doesn't appear to be the case in our respective professional worlds. Routinely, if you were to take inventory of some of those around you in your daily lives, inclusive of yourself, you most likely encounter those who are retracting themselves from an online presence for one of several reasons probably already touched on above. No doubt, there could be many more not mentioned, nor even discovered as of yet. This leaves us with again pondering, what are we to do?

Training ourselves and being trained by our employers through developed processes and programs is definitely one channel to manage and be a preventative to this risk. And, with all training, regardless of how good, repetitious, and improved upon it is, we must accept that there will still be those individuals that succumb to an inherent weakness, lack of judgment, or even fatigue to the actions of "write, click, attach, or send" and possibly repeat over and over again. For those occurrences, we must develop an immediate evaluative and action-focused response plan knowing that inaction (doing nothing) is a form of taking action. However, as a society, it's pretty well evidenced that we don't respond well, but in fact negatively, to silence or inaction following a notable event, whether in the form of a published statement, unearthed negative action or conduct, or possibly a posted video streaming a tragic event. This doesn't even touch on the internal chaos that can ensue within the impacted entity. So having a response plan and process created, embraced, communicated, and practiced in advance is beyond recommended; it should be required. Keep in mind, in some professional sectors such inaction or inappropriate action could be subject to civil liability, as well as criminal culpability. After all, training for an eventuality so that a response is second nature is interwoven in our military, law enforcement, first responders, medical professionals, and many other private and public sector entities, not to mention us as individuals. Isn't it true that individually many of us have gone

10. See, e.g., Karen Freberg, *Social Media for Strategic Communication: Creative Strategies and Research-Based Applications* (Sage, 2018), https://us.sagepub.com/en-us/nam/social-media-for-strategic-communication/book258081.

through earthquake, fire and evacuation drills, driver's training, and possibly CPR and first aid training to name a few? Three central tenets can sum the above: anticipate, communicate, and educate.

By adding social media and cyber incident plans and responses is only a natural outgrowth of those societal happenings that are an evolution of society's progression into new areas of daily happenings. If you're wondering what incidences could be used, or, better yet, how could one replicate such situations from which to initiate your training and response plan protocol, you need look no further than your daily news or the internet for prior notable events. Better yet, this is by no means a costly endeavor to replicate a scenario, and to have available what response was mounted and communicated from which you can judge the strengths and weaknesses of that response. How would you have done it better? What would you have done differently? How could you prepare? What could you have in place? What do you currently have in place? These are but a few self-reflective inquiries to pose to yourself and others.[11]

From natural disasters, overnight corporate implosions, product recalls, ransomware attacks, data breaches, physical property destruction (e.g., computer servers destroyed by fire, flood), the loss of central pivotal company figures through disciplinary action, termination or a life altering event, and individually undertaken events such as intentional shootings. Unfortunately, this list is not exhaustive, and our ability to train/prepare for all eventualities isn't tenable; however, can we do better than what we've been doing? Can we insure against such possibilities with those insurers that provide such coverage? Keep in mind that meaningful monetary insurance coverage for cyber liability is relatively new in the realm of insurance. In some cases, law firms have greater cyber coverage than they do covering claims of professional malpractice.[12]

Are we able to determine what is the likelihood of one occurrence over another based on the nature of our business? The answer, of course, is yes we can, and the information available to us is predominantly and freely available on the internet.

For example, with regard to social media, cybersecurity, and data breaches, do you have an employee policy discussing and outlining appropriate and inappropriate conduct, as well as behavior? Do you have provisions in your client retention agreements discussing such topics as social media use during representation, appropriate means of communication (e.g., use of email with possible confidential attachments), and preservation of then-existing social media posts/information? Of course, we must also realize that in some instances, certain desired and implemented policies may run afoul of labor rules, privacy rights, may cause potential clients deciding not to retain your services, and may violate constitutional safeguards, all of which are topics beyond the content overview intent of this chapter. But, these are topics easily located with current information by way of a focused Google search.

That said, it is advantageous to turn your attention to such concerns and seek the requisite professional input/consultation from a legal professional versed in the topic. These are not nebulous archaic topics, but quite the contrary they are poignantly before us as an integral part of our world. Ignorance or ignoring will not suffice, particularly when professional practice mandates, inclusive of ethical licensure requirements, speak directly to requirements of competency and having a knowledge base of such areas.

11. James M. Davis and Bradley H. Dlatt, "How to prepare yourself and your clients to respond to data breaches," *American Bar Association Journal* (September 19, 2019), www.abajournal.com/voice/article/how-you-and-your-clients-can-be-ready-for-and-respond-to-a-data-breach. See also National Conference of State Legislatures, Security Breach Notification Laws Study (April 15, 2021), www.ncsl.org/research/telecommunications-and-information-technology/security-breach-notification-laws.aspx.
12. National Law Review (March 7, 2019), "Cybersecurity: Understanding Cyber Insurance for Law Firms," Volume 11, Number 310, www.natlawreview.com/article/cybersecurity-understanding-cyber-insurance-law-firms.

What Do You Mean I'm Ethically Required To Learn About This Stuff?

It seems redundant at this point to discuss one's ethical mandates in the legal sector not only for legal practitioners but for those they supervise. The reality is the American Bar Association (ABA), as well as individual state ethical rules for legal professionals, intersect social media and cyber incidents in more areas than one would care to acknowledge. As a legal practitioner, employee in a law firm setting, or an individual/entity retaining the services of a law firm, the following only highlight those areas where ethical mandates intersect our social media and cyber frontiers.

- Handling of confidential information;
- Advertising/promotion;
- Communicating with represented parties;
- Communicating with those in possible need of representation;
- Acting competently;
- Violation of laws;
- Preservation of information (i.e., unlawful destruction of information);
- Suppression of information—discovery obligations/requirements;
- Communicating with jurists;
- Communicating with jurors;
- Communicating with witnesses;
- Supervising staff;
- Duties to prior clients;
- Trial publicity.

Ethical mandates are not confined to just legal practitioners. One doesn't have to think too far afield to realize those in healthcare, public accounting, the clergy, and a number of professional trades are all beholden to a set of professional rules or guidelines.[13]

The above represent viable areas of awareness and concern for both the practitioner and the client. Again, we must embrace and be reminded that we are all individuals who act in a specified capacity, but are inherently still subject to the weaknesses social media can extort, technology can trigger, and the calculated deception undertaken by others that can ensnare us in a virtual ambush of sorts. What is a growing realization is that practitioner ignorance is no longer a shield but is more appropriately to be viewed as a sword from which we must defend. Our shield is education, awareness, preparation, and a good dose of reality mixed in with the realization that technology is only advancing. This advancement is at a pace that far exceeds both the evolution of the law and our general reasonable person standard of not only absorbing but comprehending its functionality and impact. We also must embrace the reality that there are incidences and occurrences that will befall our society that we've yet to fathom, nor experience as there are those out there that are constantly conjuring up incidences and events yet to be launched, implemented, or triggered. Unfortunately, our minds are drawn to a certain level of paranoia as these yet to be known conjurings are more often damaging and traumatic rather than beneficial, nurturing, and for the greater good.

Currently, it's not a matter of finding the means from which to educate oneself about legal ethical requirements; it's more a matter of filtering out and determining what are the best resources. For example, legal publications on a near weekly basis have articles relevant to these topics, specific publications have emerged from nonexistence or relative obscurity just a few years ago to national

13. See generally, Association of International Certified Professional Accountants, Professional Responsibilities: https://us.aicpa.org/interestareas/personalfinancialplanning/resources/practicecenter/professionalresponsi bilities.

and global resources, podcasts are readily and freely available, blogs and share sites bringing industry practitioners together to share best practices and incident response plans, conferences, state bars and the ABA provide real-world ethical opinions on the topic, and there is a myriad of entities and consultants at the ready to provide you their services.[14]

The challenge before you now is to not only educate yourself and others but to execute and follow the tenets garnered from those educational efforts. This challenge is real and not easy, as the complexity and sophistication of the implements used to breach our security in the cyber world are only growing in numerosity and impact, while at the same time our reliance on social media for engaging the world is deepening in our daily lives. The choice is squarely before you to either shield and hibernate, or to adapt, learn, and employ safe practices.

14. American Bar Association, Standing Committee on Ethics and Professional Responsibility, Formal Opinion 483, "Lawyers' Obligations After an Electronic Data Breach or Cyberattack," (October 17, 2018), www.americanbar.org/content/dam/aba/administrative/professional_responsibility/aba_formal_op_483.pdf.

22

RECORDS MANAGEMENT/ RECORDS RETENTION RISK CONSIDERATIONS

Patricia Lee-Gulley and John Drudi

Records Management

Proper records management is a function which has become of vital importance in ensuring an organization's efficiency, vitality, and even survival. In today's electronic age, the volume and categories of records which pass through an organization have been increasing rapidly, with liabilities and compliance duties in relation to them increasing exponentially. Records management programs can protect an organization from significant risks such as compliance issues, litigation demands, disaster recovery, confidentiality breaches, and security threats. Consequently, a vigorous records management system should be part of every organization's sound risk management strategy. Of course, included within sound records management methods are records retention policies and procedures which encompass how long documents are saved and when they are erased or destroyed, as well as preserving documents which are potentially relevant to litigation.

But what is records management? The International Organization for Standardization (ISO) defines "record management" as the "field of management responsible for the efficient and systematic control of the creation, receipt, maintenance, use, and disposition of records, including the processes for capturing and maintaining evidence of and information about business activities and transactions in the form of records." ISO further defines a record as "information created, received, and maintained as evidence and information by an organization or person, in pursuance of legal obligations or in the transaction of business."[1] The Association of Records Managers and Administrators (ARMA) defines a record as "evidence of what an organization does. They capture its business activities and transactions, such as contract negotiations, business correspondence, personnel files, and financial statements." ISO 15489-1:2016 further provides that managing records encompasses the following:

1. Creating and capturing records to meet requirements for evidence of business activity;
2. Taking appropriate action to protect their authenticity, reliability, integrity and usability as their business context and requirements for their management change over time.

1. International Organization for Standardization, "Information and Documentation—Records Management. Part 1: General," ISO 15489-1:2001 section 3.15, revised by ISO 15489-1:2016, https://www.iso.org/standard/62542.html.

DOI: 10.4324/9781351107242-27

While definitions may vary, it is clear that records management encompasses a systematic application of management principles to an organization's records and recorded information. These records necessarily include paper documents and electronic documents. An "electronic document" is "information recorded in a manner that requires a computer or other electronic device to display, interpret, and process it."[2] More simply put, it is a document that is stored electronically within a computer file. Such information includes spreadsheets, emails, invoices, sales orders, photographs, recorded telephonic communications, videos, photographs, and so on.

Records retention, or data retention, is the continued storage of an organization's data for compliance or other business reasons. It is a significant element of records management. Records retention is the subject of various regulations which dictate how long each record must be retained and when (and the manner) said record may be destroyed. A strong, compliant records retention policy is an important aspect of sound records management.

Records management is, therefore, a system of methodologies used to provide a comprehensive program for managing the creation, capture, indexing, storage, retrieval, retention, and disposition of the records used by the organization. Records retention is a subset of records management and focuses on the storage and disposal of records and data. When accomplished properly, a competently designed records management system—including a sound record retention policy—provides significant benefits to the organization which is able to successfully implement it.

The Benefits Related to Establishing a Dynamic Record Management Program

To be effective, record maintenance programs must be legally defensible; that is, they must be constructed so that any documents disposed and retained thereunder are done so appropriately, so that the responsible organization does not face liability for improper destruction or failure to retrieve the record when necessary. Such a program should also allow for legal holds, in which documents relevant to a litigation are not destroyed.

There are substantial benefits to establishing a legally defensible record maintenance program. These include substantial benefits relating to compliance with legal and regulatory requirements, litigation response, business continuity, cost savings, and avoiding the dangers associated with saving too many records (discussed below). ISO lists many of these benefits:

1. Improved transparency and accountability;
2. Effective policy formation;
3. Informed decision-making;
4. Management of business risks;
5. Continuity in the event of disaster;
6. The protection of rights and obligations of organizations and individuals;
7. Protection and support in litigation;
8. Compliance with legislation and regulations;
9. Improved ability to demonstrate corporate responsibility, including meeting sustainability goals;
10. Reduction of costs through greater business efficiency;
11. Protection of intellectual property;
12. Evidence-based research and development activities;
13. The formation of business, personal and cultural identity;
14. The protection of corporate, personal, and collective memory.[3]

2. www.businessdictionary.com/definition/electronic-document.html.
3. ISO 15489-1:2016 (Introduction).

Business realities often mandate that a *risk-based* approach to records management be utilized. Under a risk-based approach, records managers establish a well-defined execution model that meets legal and regulatory requirements and at the same time is not cost prohibitive and resource intensive.[4] Under such an approach, the highest risks to an organization related to its records are determined. This involves an analysis of the risk's probability, likelihood, and severity. The appropriate risk control method is then determined and implemented, and continual monitoring and updating occurs. A risk-based approach is therefore tends to be more proactive rather than reactive—ISO 31000 standards envision a proactive approach to risk management. A risk-based approach therefore enhances an organization's performance and improves its strategic information use.

While many of the benefits associated with an appropriate records management process system are self-evident, several require further in-depth analysis.

Cost Savings

A systematic records management program can result in cost savings which exceed the costs of the program. Efficiencies added by such programs can reduce the costs of doing business in several ways. There are substantial costs associated with the retention of older and irrelevant documents which include enhanced retrieval, storage, and other costs. Therefore, an effective records management program can reduce labor costs associated with retrieval of needed documents. It can also reduce the risk and cost of vital records being adversely impacted or destroyed. Perhaps most importantly, by appropriate records management, an organization can reduce records volume, storage requirements, and associated costs.

There are other dangers associated with saving too many records unnecessarily. For example, when a party is sued, excessive and/or improperly managed records can impair an organization's ability to timely and appropriately respond or defend against the lawsuit, resulting in adverse results. The costs associated with searching and locating old and voluminous records can be time-consuming and costly.

Additionally, when involved in a litigation, an organization will likely receive a demand for production of documents in its possession which are responsive to the matter—even those documents in its possession which could have been legally disposed of due to passage of time. Said documents will need to be produced and may be harmful to the organization's position. Additionally, as discussed below, once the litigation has begun, the organization may not dispose of relevant documents. Therefore, a records management system which includes a written policy to dispose of documents when appropriate can avoid liability relating to improper or unsupportable destruction of documents which may have been potentially relevant to the legal matter (the standard pertinent to such liability is dependent upon the laws of the jurisdiction in which the dispute is determined).

Identifying and Preserving Vital Records: Business Continuity

Vital records are those records which are necessary for the organization to resume operations in the event of a disaster. As part of its record management program, an organization should identify and protect such records in the event of emergency. Such records are necessary for the survival of the organization. The elements of a vital records plan should include:

- Identification of your vital records;
- Identification of disaster types and other events which you need to protect them from;

4. "Calming the Data Storm: A Risk Management Model for Mitigating Risks", ARMA, Information Management (July–August 2008).

- Deciding on a strategy for protecting your vital records;
- Planning the procedures for accessing vital records in the event of a disaster.[5]

Records management processes should identify and afford protection for the vital records which are needed to resume operations after a disaster. The accessibility of such documents is a clear benefit of a proper records management program. A successful records program will provide for preservation of vital records. In the event of a catastrophe, the costs pertaining to obtaining vital records are substantially reduced.

Records Management Is Essential for Compliance Activity

Federal and state laws have imposed an abundance of mandatory retention requirements dependent upon either the nature of the business or other activity, or the specific type of record at issue. These requirements must be carefully researched by any organization before conducting business in the locale which is subject to said requirements. Additionally, if the organization has any operations or relationships outside the United States, then there are retention requirements imposed by foreign jurisdictions which may need to be considered.

The compliance aspect of records management and document retention can involve the laws of multiple jurisdictions and localities, which oftentimes may overlap. As such, an organization which is subject to the laws of different jurisdictions may opt to adopt the most stringent requirement imposed on it. Alternatively, if possible the organization may be able to segregate or organize its files in a manner which allows for compliance with laws applicable only to the transaction or subject at issue. For example, if the organization has multiple international activities and clients, it may be able to segregate the matters pertaining to a foreign jurisdiction (e.g., the European Union) to comply with the differing laws of that jurisdiction—and allow the solely US-related matters to be handled consistent with the laws of the United States.

Records management is also complicated by the fact that very few of the laws applicable to retention schedules appear in isolation. They are usually contained among statutes and regulations which are designed to address other subject matters, such as data privacy, cybersecurity, and other legal obligations.

FEDERAL LAW

The federal government has imposed numerous record management and retention requirements upon organizations subject to its purview. These requirements range from the industry specific to those which encompass nearly all organizations, depending on the nature of the record. Some of these requirements are contingent upon the size of the organization at issue—usually the number of employees.

There is no single comprehensive federal law regulating records management, data privacy, cybersecurity, or records retention. Instead, there is a patchwork of industry-specific federal requirements. We shall briefly examine four of them: the Sarbanes-Oxley Act, SEC Rule 17(a), Gramm-Leach-Bliley, and the Federal Acquisition Regulation (FAR).

Sarbanes-Oxley

The Sarbanes-Oxley Act, passed in 2002, established new record requirements for all US public company boards, management, and public accounting firms. The Act takes a broad view of records,

5. ANSI/ARMA 5-2003: Vital Records Programs.

defining them to include any material which contains information about a company's plans, results, policies, or performance. The act provides that emails are considered a business record and must be maintained.

Sections 103(a) and 801(a) of the Act require public companies and registered public accounting firms to maintain audit work papers, documents which form the basis of an audit or review, and all information supporting any conclusions for at least seven years. Section 802 pertains to the retention and destruction of records. It makes it a crime to intentionally destroy, alter, mutilate, conceal, cover up, or falsify any records, documents, or tangible objects which are involved in or could be involved in a US government investigation or prosecution of any matter, or in a Chapter 11 bankruptcy proceeding. Private companies are also expected to comply with section 802, with fines and up to 20 years' imprisonment for failing to comply.

SEC Rule 17(a)

SEC Section 17(a) of the Securities and Exchange Act of 1934, and its corresponding regulations under Rule 17(a), contain various record creation and retention requirements applicable to financial institutions, brokerage firms, and anyone else dealing in securities under the oversight of the SEC. These rules contain various requirements, including:

- Rule 17(a)-3, requiring companies to create *accurate* records of all records required under the Act;
- The originals of all communications regarding customer accounts and trading records must be kept for at least six years, and during the first two years they must be kept in an "easily accessible place";
- The organization must retain other records such as compliance manuals, associated person records, powers of attorney, working papers, and written agreements entered into for at least three years;
- All reports produced to review for unusual account activity must be retained at least 18 months;
- Electronic records must be stored in a secure, non-erasable location;
- Broker dealers must notify their examining authority at least 90 days prior to their use of an electronic storage media of their intent to do so.

The Act is extremely complex, and compliance with all the requirements of this Act are beyond the scope of this chapter. There are various software packages offered to assist in the technical compliance with this Act, and several third-party providers who provide outside support services which assist in ensuring compliance.

Gramm-Leach-Bliley

The Gramm-Leach-Bliley Act (GLBA), or the Financial Modernization Act of 1999, applies to organizations which provide financial products or services to consumers. The Act requires such organizations to explain their information-sharing practices to their customers and to safeguard sensitive data. The organizations are required to prepare a written information security plan and to implement measures and safeguards based on the company's size and complexity, the nature of its activities, and the sensitivity of information it handles. The organization must have appropriate document storage and destruction protocols in place. The organization must comply with the Federal Trade Commission (FTC) disposal rule, which applies to disposal of consumer information. The FTC disposal rule is discussed in further detail below.

Federal Acquisition Regulation (FAR)

The FAR contains numerous records management and retention requirements. Most notably, FAR subpart 4.7, "Contractor Records Retention," contains express requirements imposed on contractors relating to records retention. The specific requirements, record types, and pertinent retention periods are set forth in that subpart.

Though perhaps technically dealing more with cybersecurity, the new rules promulgated under the FAR, set forth in FAR 52.204-21,[6] touch upon mandatory records management practices for organizations which contract with the federal government. Passed in 2016, this new regulation applies to all contractors who use information systems which may contain "Federal contract information," which means "information, not intended for public release, that is provided by or generated for the Government under a contract to develop or deliver a product or service to the Government." The regulation applies to any "covered contractor information system" which processes, stores, or transmits "federal contract information." The terms are interpreted broadly to cover any information provided by or transmitted to the federal government in connection with contract performance. FAR 52.204-21 will be included in all contracts with the federal government.

The regulation is but the first of even more regulations to come. It imposes 15 specific security requirements on contractors:

1. Limit information system access to authorized users, processes acting on behalf of authorized users, or devices (including other information systems).
2. Limit information system access to the types of transactions and functions that authorized users are permitted to execute.
3. Verify and control/limit connections to and use of external information systems.
4. Control information posted or processed on publicly accessible information systems.
5. Identify information system users, processes acting on behalf of users, or devices.
6. Authenticate (or verify) the identities of those users, processes, or devices as a prerequisite to allowing access to organizational information systems.
7. Sanitize or destroy information system media containing federal contract information before disposal or release for reuse.
8. Limit physical access to organizational information systems, equipment, and the respective operating environments to authorized individuals.
9. Escort visitors and monitor visitor activity; maintain audit logs of physical access; and control and manage physical access devices.
10. Monitor, control, and protect organizational communications (i.e., information transmitted or received by organizational information systems) at the external boundaries and key internal boundaries of the information system.
11. Implement subnetworks for publicly accessible system components that are physically or logically separated from internal networks.
12. Identify, report, and correct information and information system flaws in a timely manner.
13. Provide protection from malicious code at appropriate locations within organizational information systems.
14. Update malicious code protection mechanisms when new releases are available.
15. Perform periodic scans of the information system and real-time scans of files from external sources as files are downloaded, opened, or executed.

6. 52.204-21 "Basic Safeguarding of Covered Contractor Information Systems."

The contractor is further obligated under Regulation 52.204-21 to include the above provisions in the any subcontract in which federal contract information may be involved.

SPECIFIC FEDERAL DOCUMENT RETENTION REQUIREMENTS

The federal government also has implemented various records management and retention requirements which are applicable to all organizations—dependent upon the organization's activities and/or number of employees. These requirements are set forth in numerous statutes and regulations, and specify how long records pertaining to a specific activity or subject must be kept. Therefore, organizations must keep abreast of legal developments in order to comply. Assistance of counsel or other specialists may be desirable. The collaboration of these specialists (e.g., attorneys, accountants, human resources, compliance, risk management, etc.) and the overlap in their recommendations strengthen the entire program, giving greater assurance that compliance goals are achieved. Some of the more significant of these federal laws are shown in Table 22.1.

Table 22.1 Federal Record Retention Requirements

Record Source		*Law*	*Requirement*
Polygraphs	Employee Polygraph Protection Act	2 USC § 1314 3 USC § 414 29 USC § 2002	Three years from polygraph
Benefit plan records	ERISA	29 USC § 1027	Six years
Payroll records	Federal Insurance Contribution Act (FICA)	FICA Reg 3166001-1	Four years
Payroll records	Fair Labor Standards Act (FLSA)	29 CFR § 516.5	Four years
Employment and personnel records made by a covered contractor	Office of Federal Compliance Programs	41 CFR § 60-741.80	Two years from date of action or personnel decision involved
Employment contracts	Fair Labor Standards Act (FLSA)	29 CFR § 516.5(b)(4)	Three years
Employee evaluations	Fair Labor Standards Act (FLSA)	29 CFR § 516	Three years
Family and medical leave records	Family and Medical Leave Act (FMLA)	29 CFR § 825.500(b)	Three years after end of leave
Unemployment tax records	Federal Unemployment Tax Act (FUTA)	26 CFR § 31.6001	Four years from greater of tax payment or tax due
I-9 Forms (Employers with more than ten employees)	Immigration Reform and Control Act	8 USC § 1324(b)	Five years
OSHA forms pertaining to injuries and illness (ten or more employees)	Occupational Health and Safety Act (OSHA)	29 CFR § 1904.33	Five years following end of year
Records related to employee exposure to toxic substances or otherwise harmful physical agents	Occupational Health and Safety Act (OSHA)	29 CFR § 1910.1020	30 years after termination of employment
Records regarding employee exposure to noise	Occupational Health and Safety Act (OSHA)	29 CFR § 1910.95	Two years

(Continued)

Table 22.1 (Continued)

Record Source		*Law*	*Requirement*
Payroll records	Age Discrimination in Employment Act (ADEA)	29 CFR § 1627.3	Four years
Drug test results, physical exams, screening tests, job posting and ads, job applications, solicited resumes	Age Discrimination in Employment Act (ADEA)	29 CFR § 1627	One year
Hiring, promotion, transfer, layoff, recall	Age Discrimination in Employment Act (ADEA)	29 CFR § 1627.3	One year from action taken
Records or charges of discrimination and related personnel records	Age Discrimination in Employment Act (ADEA)	29 CFR § 1627.3	Final disposition
Benefit plans	Age Discrimination in Employment Act (ADEA)	29 CFR § 1627.4	One year after plan termination
Drug tests in transportation industry	DOT	49 CFR § 382.401	One to five years after test
Requests for reasonable accommodation	Equal Employment Opportunity Commission (EEOC)	29 CFR § 1602.14	Greater of one year after action made or record made
Hiring, promotion, demotion, transfer, layoff, discharge, etc. of employee	Equal Employment Opportunity Commission (EEOC)	29 CFR § 1602.14	Greater of one year after action made or record made

Additionally, there is authority which suggests that, in the absence of a specific federal legal requirement mandating retention, an organization should retain its records for three years. The Federal Paperwork Reduction Act of 1980, which became effective May 2, 1983, provides that the Office of Management and Budget will "not approve" requirements for retention of records "unless the submitting agency demonstrates that a longer period is necessary or unless the records relate to health, medical, or tax records." This three-year period should therefore be looked at as a minimum threshold date upon which records may be safely disposed.

STATE RECORD MANAGEMENT AND RETENTION REQUIREMENTS

All 50 US states have enacted data protection and cybersecurity laws, including requirements that a business notify consumers when their personal information is compromised. In fact, many states are in the process of updating their laws in the direction of the European Union General Data Protection Regulation (GDPR; see discussion below on the terms of the regulation). The state of the law is therefore very dynamic and quickly evolving, and the content and scope of these various laws is beyond the scope of this chapter. Organizations are again advised to seek the assistance of competent counsel (and other professionals) to determine the laws pertinent to their operations.

California law regarding privacy is worth discussion. California law impacting privacy and therefore record management includes the California Consumer Privacy Act of 2018 (CCPA) and the California Privacy Rights Act (adopted with the passage of Proposition 24 in the November 3, 2020, election).

The CCPA, effective January 1, 2020, contains various provisions pertaining to data privacy, cybersecurity, and record retention, including the following: (1) consumers have the right to know what personal information a business has collected about them, how it was obtained, and what it is used for; (2) consumers may opt out of allowing a business to sell such information; and (3) consumers have the right to demand the business delete their personal information. The Act applies to for-profit businesses which collect and control the personal information of California residents. Therefore, any organization which collects such information will need to consider compliance issues presented by the Act.

The California Privacy Rights Act (CPRA) operates to amend and expand the CCPA, and in fact replaces it. The CPRA took effect in 2023, but will contain a "lookback" period (which is the date companies dealing with consumers must be prepared to provide records upon the CPRA's effective date) of January 1, 2022. Regulations promulgated pursuant to the CPRA were scheduled for completion by July 2022. While the breadth of the CCPA is beyond the scope of this discussion, organizations which do business in California will need to consider its application to their activities. The scope of the Act includes:

- The Act allows consumers to opt out of the sale *and the sharing* of their personal information;
- Provides consumers with new rights (similar to the EU's GDPR) to access and opt out of automated decision-making, correct data, delete personal information, and discover an organization's period of data retention;
- Contains stronger protection for sensitive information;[7]
- The CPRA creates the Consumer Privacy Protection Agency (CPPA) to enforce privacy laws.

Regarding records retention and destruction, many states also have enacted their own records management and retention requirements which often mirror or impose more restrictive requirements than the federal government. An organization should research the law of the states in which it does business in order to ensure compliance with these additional state requirements. In the event that the state or federal law has different retention periods, the organization should follow the most restrictive requirement.

It is noteworthy that many states have adopted the Uniform Preservation of Private Business Records Act (UPPBRA), which is the state counterpart to the Federal Paperwork Reduction Act of 1980. The UPPBRA provides that, unless a specific period of time is stated for the preservation of a record, then the maximum an organization is required to preserve such records is three years from

7. Pursuant to Section 14 (definitions) of the Act, "sensitive personal information" includes:

(1) Personal information that reveals:

(A) A consumer's social security, driver's license, state identification card, or passport number.
(B) A consumer's account log-in, financial account, debit card, or credit card number in combination with any required security or access code, password, or credentials allowing access to an account.
(C) A consumer's precise geolocation.
(D) A consumer's racial or ethnic origin, religious or philosophical beliefs, or union membership.
(E) The contents of a consumer's mail, email, and text messages unless the business is the intended recipient of the communication.
(F) A consumer's genetic data.

(2)

(A) The processing of biometric information for the purpose of uniquely identifying a consumer.
(B) Personal information collected and analyzed concerning a consumer's health.
(C) Personal information collected and analyzed concerning a consumer's sex life or sexual orientation.

the making of the record. It is noted that several categories fall outside the UPPBRA, including corporate minutes and the sale of dangerous weapons or substances. Also, failure to preserve the records for the required three years may result in potential legal exposure,

In states which have *not* adopted the UPPBRA, the organization may be obligated to preserve the records for "a reasonable time"—a somewhat vague and open-ended standard. Determination of a "reasonable time" may depend on the law of the applicable jurisdiction. The assistance of competent counsel is recommended.

INTERNATIONAL RECORD RETENTION REQUIREMENTS

An organization which conducts any type of business overseas will need to keep apprised of pertinent international and foreign regulations regarding data privacy and record retention. These regulations often impose requirements which are distinct from those imposed in the United States. At this writing, the provisions of the European GDPR are having a substantial impact on companies which target customers located in Europe. This chapter will briefly discuss some of the key issues raised in the European Union, United Kingdom, India, and mainland China.

Any organization which conducts business overseas must ensure they are compliant with the foreign regulations. This includes conducting a comprehensive audit to map the organization's data owners. The organization must know where its data owners are located, where the sensitive and other data pertinent to these users resides, and the regulations applicable to the data.

The European Union General Data Protection Regulation (GDPR)

The European Union's GDPR applies to all European Union members. It went into effect on May 25, 2018. It is designed to "harmonize" European data privacy laws and to give greater protection and rights to individuals. Article 3 of the GDPR provides that the regulation applies to organizations which collect personal information from anyone in a European Union country. The Act applies to those who process and those who control such information. This Act therefore presents far-reaching application to non-European organizations which collect personal information from those residing in the EU—including use of websites and the internet to target individuals located in the EU.

The GDPR applies to "personal data". Personal data is given a broad meaning, and is defined as "any information relating to an identified or identifiable natural person ('data subject')." An "identifiable person" is one "who can be identified, directly or indirectly, in particular by reference to an identifier such as a name, an identification number, location data, an online identifier or to one or more factors specific to the physical, physiological, genetic, mental, economic, cultural or social identity of that natural person." The GDPR also prohibits the processing of additional "special categories" of personal data under some circumstances.[8]

The GDPR bestows eight rights on data subjects (which of course are subject to various exceptions):

1. Right to be informed. Individuals have a right to be informed about the collection and use of their personal data.
2. Right of access. Individuals must be given access their personal data.

8. GDPR Art. 9 provides: "Processing of personal data revealing racial or ethnic origin, political opinions, religious or philosophical beliefs, or trade union membership, and the processing of genetic data, biometric data for the purpose of uniquely identifying a natural person, data concerning health or data concerning a natural person's sex life or sexual orientation shall be prohibited."

3. Right to rectification. Allow rectification of inaccurate or incomplete personal data.
4. Right to "erasure" (i.e., right to be forgotten). Individuals have right to have personal data erased. There is a 30-day time limit to respond to erasure requests.
5. Right to restrict processing. Under some circumstances, an individual can restrict the processing of their personal data.
6. Right to data portability. Individuals can obtain and reuse their personal data.
7. Right to object. The individual can object to processing their personal data under some circumstances.
8. Rights regarding automated decision-making. Limits the use of automated decision-making including profiling.

The GDPR also obligates a company to report a data breach within 72 hours of discovery of the breach.

Violations of the GDPR rules can result in significant fines and penalties, including up to 4% of global revenues or €20 million—whichever is higher. The GDPR also allows any person who has suffered damage as a result of a violation to obtain damages, including those for emotional distress.

United Kingdom

The United Kingdom enacted the Data Protection Act of 2018. The Act is similar to the GDPR and governs how personal information is used by organizations, businesses, or the government. Since the UK is no longer part of the EU, it adopted its own Data Protection Act.

India

For years, India's primary data privacy law was contained in the Information Technology Act of 2000. The Act provided standards for data collection and use but did not address data storage methods or user consent and had no express provision for data security. The Act was revised in 2008 to add remedies for persons who incur loss due to inadequate private data protection.

India currently has pending a Data Privacy and Protection bill which would control data usage, surveillance, transfer, storage, security, and other concerns and would apply to private companies and governmental entities.

China

China's first national law which addressed cybersecurity and data privacy became effective June 1, 2017. The law requires critical data infrastructure operators (CIIOs) to store personal information and important data collected and generated within China. The law imposes data privacy obligations on network operators. It defines personal data to mean information which identifies a natural person either by itself or in combination with other information, and includes a person's name, address, telephone number, date of birth, identity card number and biometric identifiers. The cybersecurity law requires network operators to keep users' personal data in strict confidence, and must encrypt important information such as that related to national security, economic development, and social and public interest.

China also passed the Personal Information Security Specification (PI Security Specification), effective May 1, 2018. This is a comprehensive guideline which contains no penalties for breach. This act contains various new rights, including the rights of erasure, data portability, and the right to an appeal in the event an automated decision impacts the rights of a data subject.

Records Management Enables Appropriate Responses to Litigation

A competent legally defensible record retention system is of immeasurable value when an organization is faced with litigation (including arbitration). First, a proper retention system will make it easier for the organization to identify and locate records and documents which are necessary to assess the litigation and to defend and/or prosecute the matters therein. Second, it will be far easier for the organization to comply with its discovery requirements in the case, as it will be able to locate and produce records which are requested by the opposing party. Additionally, a proper retention system will have adequate safeguards against destruction of potentially relevant documents and will therefore avoid the penalties which attachment under a spoliation of evidence theory.

Arbitration, which is generally more informal than litigation, also benefits from a competent record retention system. Though more informal in nature, arbitration proceedings benefit equally from the ability to quickly locate and retrieve relevant documents. Also, arbitrations still involve substantial discovery proceedings and oftentimes require a quicker turnaround.

SPOLIATION OF EVIDENCE

"Spoliation of evidence" occurs when evidence relevant to a case is intentionally or negligently destroyed, hidden, or altered by a party connected to the case. It can occur during or prior to the institution of formal proceedings. The duty to preserve relevant evidence may arise prior to commencement of a lawsuit where it is "reasonably foreseeable" that a lawsuit will be filed. Certainly, when a party has notice of future proceedings, or when a complaint is filed, it will have a duty to preserve documents in its possession, custody, or control which are potentially relevant to the proceeding. Failure to do so will likely constitute spoliation.

There may also under some circumstances be a duty to preserve evidence which is in the possession of third parties, such as an organization's agents, attorneys, insurers, or experts. The test may be whether the organization has a right to obtain or "control" the information in the possession of those third parties.

The remedies against spoliation vary by jurisdiction, but can be severe depending on the circumstances. In some states, spoliation can give rise to an independent tort claim for spoliation, thereby entitling the party against whom evidence was despoiled to money damages. In other jurisdictions, criminal sanctions may result, including fines and jail time. In others, the penalty may be a jury instruction in the case in chief to the effect that the jury consider the spoliation when rendering a decision, and may include an instruction to the effect that the jury may conclude that the destroyed evidence would have damaged the spoiler's case.

In federal courts, there is no independent claim for spoliation of evidence. However, federal courts sitting in diversity[9] may apply the spoliation law of the state from where the case originates. However, most federal courts will sanction intentional spoliation, and many will punish negligent spoliation. Additionally, the failure to appropriately preserve the records mandated by the specific federal law requirements will be met with an adverse inference instruction.

Federal Rule of Civil Procedure 37(e), adopted in 2015, specifically imposes a duty on parties to preserve electronically preserved information (ESI) under certain circumstances. Where the ESI has been lost, and was lost after the duty to preserve the ESI arose, and this loss was due to a party's failure to take "reasonable steps" to preserve it, then the court will impose sanctions on the responsible party

9. Diversity is where a federal court has jurisdiction due to a difference in state citizenship of the parties and not because of another basis of federal subject matter jurisdiction. Federal courts in diversity will apply pertinent state law rather than federal law to the dispute.

if the ESI cannot be "replaced or restored" and the party seeking the ESI is prejudiced thereby. FRCP 37(e)(2) provides for the following sanction in that instance:

1. Presume that the lost information was unfavorable to the party;
2. Instruct the jury that it may or must presume the information was unfavorable to the party; or
3. Dismiss the action or enter a default judgment.

Based on the above potentially harsh consequences which may result in spoliation fact patterns, an organization must institute a record management program which locates the required documents and at the same time will operate to preclude any spoliation claims.

LEGAL HOLD NOTICES

To comply with an organization's preservation requirements, the organization will use a "legal hold" notice. This notice is sent to various custodians throughout the organization who may have potentially relevant documents and advise them to identify and preserve relevant records which need to be preserved. Care should be taken in the drafting of the legal hold notice to ensure that it encompasses the breadth of required documents, as the scope of discovery in legal proceedings can be quite broad. It should be sent by someone with authority in the organization, be plainly written, and should apprise of the universe of records to be preserved (e.g., emails, voice messages, text messages). Additionally, there should be follow-up to ensure that the notice will be complied with. Counsel (and management) should monitor the compliance activity related to the legal hold, as well as the retention and production of relevant documents, to ensure that it is not violated.

The Sedona Group is a prominent trade association[10] in the field of records management and e-discovery. Guideline 8 of the Sedona Group's commentary on legal holds provides the following factors which increase the effectiveness of legal hold notices:

- Communicates in a manner that assists persons in taking actions that are, in good faith, intended to be effective;
- Is in an appropriate form, which may be written;
- Provides information on how preservation is to be undertaken;
- Is periodically reviewed and, when necessary, reissued in either its original or an amended form; and
- Addresses features of relevant information systems that may prevent retention of potentially discoverable information.

The Dangers Associated With Saving Too Many Records

A properly designed, legally defensible document management and retention program will assist in avoiding the pitfalls associated with retaining too many records. Generally, the more records are retained, the more difficult it can be to quickly file and retrieve pertinent records. Appropriate destruction of records as allowed by law will reduce the quantity of irrelevant records and therefore

10. Records management trade associations play an important role in the field of records management, including but not limited to providing guidance to organizations, recommending best practices, setting guidelines, and educating organizations regarding records management and records retention issues. Some illustrative trade organizations include the Sedona Group, the Association of Records Managers and Administrators (ARMA), Institute of Certified Records Managers (ICRM), and Master of Archives and Records Administration (MARA).

result in less required storage space and associate supplies, leading to reduced costs. It will also enhance the speed of record filing and retrieval.

The program will also reduce litigation risk and costs, as fewer documents and proper organization of retained documents will result in reduced efforts and costs for document collection, review, and production in the event of a legal action against the organization. Also, risks associated with liability for lost documents can be reduced.

Document Retention Policy

Creation of a Formal Retention Policy

Based on the clear advantages inuring to an organization which has implemented a legally defensible records management/retention policy, the organization should strive to implement a suitable, effective document retention policy plan. The document retention policy will provide for the systematic review, retention, and destruction of documents generated in the course of the organization's business. The document retention policy will identify how the organization's documents are maintained, stored, and ultimately disposed of.

The policy must be a formal written policy, which must be actually enforced and audited. It must be tailored to the specific business to which it pertains and serve as a realistic policy of what the organization will undertake to manage its records in accordance with the law. It must be adhered to so that it can avoid claims for spoliation in the event of litigation. It should also provide flexibility so that it can be re-examined on a regular basis, to account for any deficiencies.

The creation and implementation of a record management and retention program is a substantial undertaking which utilizes personnel throughout the organization in order to be effective. However, there are several steps to the creation and implementation of a successful retention policy, which can be summarized as follows:

- The organization's business records must be examined and inventoried;
- The various laws applicable to the retention program must be surveyed and kept current;
- The organization's needs relating to record retention must be determined, along with needed support and an appraisal of necessary costs;
- The formal retention policy must be created, including the categories which will be used to store the records;
- The policy must be implemented;
- Compliance with the policy must be audited;
- The policy must be periodically evaluated and updated.

The various steps are discussed in detail below. Among these steps, there is no set formal order in which they may be accomplished. The foundation of the program, and the part which may be most labor-intensive, is performing the inventory of the organization's records and then surveying the laws which apply to those records. However, all the steps, in whatever order, are necessary to some extent in order to create a successful retention policy. We will examine each step in turn.

A Detailed Inventory Must Be Conducted Which Captures the Organization's Records

The first step in preparing a formal record retention policy is to conduct an inventory of the organization's records. This necessarily includes defining the parameters of the inventory, use of an inventory form which contains the information desired, and determining how the inventory will be conducted. After the inventory is conducted, the results should be analyzed and verified. It is important at the design stage that the buy-in of senior management be obtained and utilized, to ensure that the necessary input from employees is obtained. For best results, directives from senior management should be part of the inventory process. This will help ensure that the importance of the process is appreciated by all participants.

The scope of the inventory should be the first major consensus for those conducting it. The inventory should identify and capture all documents, both physical and electronic, that a business produces. Categories of documents should include all employment documents (including employee records, taxes, training manuals), workplace records (all safety documents, maintenance, products and services, shipping, insurance), sales records, audio, correspondence, accounting and tax records, legal records (contracts, real estate, corporate, lawsuits, intellectual property, insurance), advertisements and promotional materials, government records, and so on. The electronic records examined should include all emails, computer disks, spreadsheets, hard drives, web pages, and so on.

The scope of the information collected regarding each record type may vary by organization, but it is clear that basic information should be included regarding each record type in order to prepare the formal retention schedule. The minimum of information collected should include:

- The name and type of record;
- Whether the record is paper or electronic;
- Location of the record (department, computer system) including where it is stored;
- What application created the record (paper, email, Word, Adobe Acrobat, Excel);
- Date created and revised;
- Whether the record is vital;
- Whether there are other forms or versions of the record.

A specific inventory form should be tailored and developed for the organization's inventory, which includes information which is relevant to the retention schedule. The form should include the basic information about the organization's records. For ease of use, it may include an area where the retention period applicable to each record type may added later (or concurrently, if the legal survey has been completed). Table 22.2 shows a sample form.

Table 22.2 Sample Specific Inventory Form

Record Type	*Record Description*	*Media (Paper/ Electronic)*	*Location*	*Vital*	*Retention Period*
Legal records	Contracts	Paper	Legal department filing cabinets	Some	Continual
Intellectual property	Patents and trademarks	Paper	Legal department filing cabinets	Yes	Continual
Medical	Employee medical	Paper	HR	No	TBD
Sales	Invoices, bills of lading	Paper and electronic	Accounting, shipping	No	TBD
Tax	Tax returns	Paper	Legal	Yes	Continual
Accounting	Profit and loss statements	Paper	Accounting	Yes	Continual

After the survey form contents are determined, the information necessary to complete it should be obtained from the various departments of the organization. This is accomplished by use of one or a combination of three methods:

Direct review: The records are specifically surveyed by the team conducting the inventory. This involves physically inspecting the locations the records are located and completing the form. This method can use the other two methods to ensure a good result.

Distributing surveys: Surveys can be distributed to the organization's managers and department heads which request the information in the survey form.

Interviews: Interviews of key personnel with knowledge of the organization's records can be undertaken in order to determine the scope of the organization's records. Interviewees should include a cross-section of staff, department managers, and key employees.

A combination of the above three methods would likely have the best result. Records will need to be reviewed prior to this process to determine which of the organization's people would have the necessary knowledge of the organization's records.

When the inventory is complete, the results will need to be reviewed and verified. Also, the evolving nature of the technology and record-keeping must be taken into account: many of the results of a prior inventory may not be controlling in an inventory taken years later.

Determine the Laws Pertaining to the Organization's Records

Determining the retention schedule applicable to an organization's records requires research. As demonstrated in the discussion of laws applicable to records retention, there are different requirements dependent upon the type of organization or the type of record at issue. This step involves potential research at the federal and at the state and local levels of government. Some of the organization's records may need to be retained indefinitely, either due to legal or practical considerations.

An organization can use attorneys, accountants, or other professionals to conduct this research. There are other professional organizations which specialize in records management which may be consulted or retained. It should be emphasized that the laws are constantly evolving, and an organization will need to have a system by which its retention policy can be updated and revised depending on changes in the law.

Determine Organization's Needs for Document Retention, Needed Support, and Cost

After a proper inventory is conducted, and the legal requirements are appropriately researched, then the organization should be in a position to assess its needs for document retention. This assessment should take into account the nature of the business, including the business' need to access its records on a daily basis.

The organization should be able to determine how it wishes to manage its records. This should include whether some documents will be stored offsite, whether a third party will assist in the process, and the manner in which documents will be destroyed. The expense of storage will need to be determined. It may be more economical to create electronic copies of some documents rather than pay for storage. More recent documents should be stored onsite rather than offsite.

It may be desirable for some of the paper documents to be imaged. This will prevent accidental/inadvertent alteration. Investigation should be done to determine if this will be done in-house or whether an imaging service be retained. Estimates should be retained for all tasks.

No matter where stored, the records may be subject to discovery in the event of a lawsuit. Consequently, the organization must be mindful that they may need to be retrieved in the future. Additionally, the location where the records are stored will need to be sufficiently secure.

> ### Practice Pointer
>
> The record maintenance and retention policy should appropriately provide for the preservation of all insurance policies, which are often occurrence-based policies which can be triggered many years into the future. Oftentimes, old insurance policies cannot be located so that the appropriate carrier be put on notice.
>
> This is illustrated by a matter handled by the authors several years ago. The insured was a homeowners' association sued for a landslide which originated on association property and damaged homes located below. Most of the association's insurers during the relevant period of slope maintenance had denied coverage due to earth movement and subsidence exclusions contained in their policies. However, regarding the first-in-time insurer, the insured knew its identity but did not have a copy of the policy the insurer had issued. The insurer then contended that it had, pursuant to its own document retention guidelines, destroyed its own copy of the policy—but also contended that this destroyed policy had the same earth movement and subsidence exclusions contained in subsequent policies it had issued.
>
> Fortunately for the homeowners' association, upon conducting an exhaustive search of its business records, it was able to locate a declaration page to the lost policy, which conclusively showed that the first-in-time policy did not have such an exclusion. The carrier promptly paid the claim.

Create the Retention Policy

After the organization's needs have been determined and a cost structure and budget figured out, the formal policy should be drafted. The policy must be as clear and simple as possible, as this will enhance its chances for success. The policy must take into account the vantage point of the employee and must reflect realistic probabilities and capabilities.

The policy needs to be disseminated throughout the organization and employees given a chance to provide input and obtain training if necessary.

Characteristics of a successful policy include the following:

- It should state the overall objectives of the policy;
- It should spell out the roles and responsibilities of those in the organization regarding the retention policy;
- It should account for legal holds;
- It should have dates certain when records will be destroyed (e.g., once a year);
- It should have the partnership and input of the IT department, which can adopt technical safeguards to ensure that the policy is not frustrated;
- It should address and/or account for possible future platform migration;
- It may set forth various categories indicating the classification structures of the records management policy.

The classification formats for the records is extremely important. The policy should set forth the various categories in which the records will be placed. Regarding paper documents, this should already exist to some extent. As to electronic documents, the system categories should be spelled out in the policy so that everyone in the organization knows where to store and locate pertinent records.

For example, an organization may have several dozen broad classifications (such as finance, accounting, human resources, legal) and then have sub-directories for them including contracts, correspondence, medical, and spreadsheets, which can result in a system where everyone knows where the documents are stored and located, so they can save them in the appropriate areas. This makes it easier for the organization to store, locate, retrieve, utilize, preserve, and ultimately dispose of said records when appropriate.

There are pre-made classification schemes available from third parties, such as ECM, ERM/EDRMS, KM, trade associations, and enterprise search vendors. A benefit of these systems is that they may reflect industry best practices. Even these systems can be tailored by the organization to reflect its own needs and circumstances.

Practice Pointer

The record maintenance and retention policy should specifically address employee use of organization email addresses. Said policy should require emails containing personal information is to be used only sparingly or not at all, not to include sensitive matters, shall have a subject line which indicates it is purely personal, and be deleted by the user shortly after sending or receipt. Said policy should make clear that the organization owns all such emails and the employee has no rights of privacy in said emails. The organization should have a document retention policy which provides for the regular destruction of purely personal emails.

The organization policy should emphasize that under no circumstances is personal information to be included in business emails which also discusses business. The authors have seen many instances where employee emails which discuss relevant business also contain discussions of apparent extramarital affairs, crimes, obscenity, and so on. When personal information is commingled with information which is relevant to the lawsuit, it becomes more difficult to withhold.

Implement (Key Stakeholder Support, Realistic Goals, and Methodologies)

Perhaps the most important element in successful implementation of the retention policy is the support of key stakeholders, such as the chief executive officer. Other key stakeholders in the organization whose support may be significant include but are not limited to management, legal, regulatory/compliance, and financial. Without such support, any retention policy will likely fail. Therefore, key stakeholder approval should be obtained throughout the life of the retention policy creation. This includes approval of the goals, time frame, resources, scope, and budget of the policy. Presentations should be made to management and to department heads.

Communication of the policy's creation and requirements is essential, and it is critical that an organization's staff know that their participation in the program is mandated from the top of the organization. Executive sponsorship and support for the policy is critical to policy success.

Implementation should include appropriate training of the employees and staff who will be performing the necessary components of the policy. The organization will need to ensure familiarity with the policy and the specific employee's duties regarding records in their control which are subject to the policy. Employees should be trained to ensure they understand the records and information policies of the organization.

Implementation necessarily entails enforcement of the retention policy. The policy must be enforced consistently. Failure to do so may result in a claim that the organization improperly partially enforced its retention policy, thereby exposing the organization to liability, fines, or even criminal sanctions. Additionally, the records which are destroyed should be tracked to support the policy in case of challenge.

It is important to note that the retention policy must account for legal hold notices and ensure that records which are subject to preservation under a legal hold are not destroyed.

Audit Compliance

The retention policy will need to be audited in order to ensure that the organization is complying with its requirements. The organization must make sure that the employees are complying with the policy. The audits need to ensure that records are being appropriately classified, retained, and destroyed as the policy requires. The focus of the audit should be the most significant aspects of the policy, the areas with the highest degree of risk to the organization should they fail. It should also ensure that concerns due to employee turnover and new training are addressed by the program.

Audits should be conducted with the frequency required by laws applicable to the business, at a minimum. Certainly, the need for additional audit frequency may arise due to the particular circumstances of the organization. Audits of the record maintenance program should be undertaken at least once a year, even under optimal circumstances.

The audit can be conducted by internal auditors or risk managers. Sometimes, an organization will use outside auditors to assist.

A sufficient audit trail should be accomplished and retained so that the organization can document its efforts to ensure a proper record maintenance program.

Evaluate and Update

The policy must be continually evaluated and updated. Many of the items on which the policy is based are not static, and as they evolve and change the policy must be updated. The policy must be updated to reflect changing laws, storage and other costs, changes in technology, and the types of records the organization produces. The success of the program must be evaluated: Is the organization still retaining too many records? Have employees grown complacent?

Destruction/Irrelevant Records

The destruction of records which are slated for disposal is a critical issue. For one, the document retention policy must ensure that records are not destroyed prematurely. This includes the preservation of records which would be properly destroyed, except they are subject to a litigation hold. Additionally, the destruction must be complete, either by deletion, shredding, or other means. The records cannot be simply disposed of in a manner which could allow future discovery or retrieval by unauthorized third parties, as this would expose the organization to potential liability. This is especially the case when the documents contain sensitive or confidential information about a client, patient, or other entity. Therefore, the record retention policy must have clear guidelines on how records should be destroyed. In the case of paper documents, the organization may want to impose a "shred all" policy, which removes employee uncertainty regarding how to dispose of the records when indicated.

Additionally, there are some documents which should never be destroyed. This includes vital records, insurance policies, and records which the organization is legally required to hold in perpetuity. The policy should identify such records and ensure their non-destruction. Additionally, controls should be put in place to ensure that the applicable retention period has expired prior to the record's destruction. One such control could be required approval of all employees which are related to the record.

The destruction process should be properly documented. Many companies issue a certificate of destruction when a document has been destroyed, which state what record(s) are destroyed and the reason. Such certificates provide evidence that a record was destroyed in compliance with the organization's record retention policy.

Some electronic record management systems feature automated programs which will delete the record when it has reached the end of its life cycle. Such programs usually (and should) feature a safeguard which notifies a designated employee of such destruction before it is conducted.

Once established, the destruction schedule contained in the policy must be strictly adhered to, as failure to do so could result in an argument that the organization only selectively destroys its records. This exposes the organization to spoliation theories in litigation, adverse instructions, fines, and possibly criminal penalties. Strict observation of the destruction schedule will allow for a legally defensible program.

Specific US Rules Regarding Record Destruction and Disposal

The FTC "disposal rule" provides that any person who maintains or possesses consumer information for a business purpose must dispose of such information "by taking reasonable measures to protect against unauthorized access to or use of the information in connection with its disposal" (16 CFR § 682.3). "Consumer information" includes "any record about an individual, whether in paper, electronic, or other form, that is a consumer report or is derived from a consumer report." It also includes "a compilation of such records" (16 CFR § 682.1).

The FTC provides several illustrative, non-exhaustive "examples" of how the disposal rule applies:

1. Implementing and monitoring compliance with policies and procedures that require the burning, pulverizing, or shredding of papers containing consumer information so that the information cannot practicably be read or reconstructed.
2. Implementing and monitoring compliance with policies and procedures that require the destruction or erasure of electronic media containing consumer information so that the information cannot practicably be read or reconstructed.
3. After due diligence, entering into and monitoring compliance with a contract with another party engaged in the business of record destruction to dispose of material, specifically identified as consumer information, in a manner consistent with this rule. In this context, due diligence could include reviewing an independent audit of the disposal company's operations and/or its compliance with this rule, obtaining information about the disposal company from several references or other reliable sources, requiring that the disposal company be certified by a recognized trade association or similar third party, reviewing and evaluating the disposal company's information security policies or procedures, or taking other appropriate measures to determine the competency and integrity of the potential disposal company.
4. For persons or entities who maintain or otherwise possess consumer information through their provision of services directly to a person subject to this part, implementing and monitoring compliance with policies and procedures that protect against unauthorized or unintentional disposal of consumer information, and disposing of such information in accordance with examples (b)(1) and (2) of this section.
5. For persons subject to the Gramm-Leach-Bliley Act, 15 U.S.C. § 6081 et seq., and the Federal Trade Commission's Standards for Safeguarding Customer Information, 16 CFR Part 314 ("Safeguards Rule"), incorporating the proper disposal of consumer information as required by this rule into the information security program required by the Safeguards Rule.

The Act defines "disposal" to include (1) the discarding or abandonment of consumer information, or (2) the sale, donation, or transfer of any medium, including computer equipment, upon which such information is stored.

Additionally, at least 34 states and Puerto Rico have adopted laws which require either governmental and/or private entities to destroy, dispose of, or render personal information unreadable.[11]

International Rules Regarding Destruction

International laws regarding destruction of records, including private information, is beyond the scope of this chapter. However, there are several aspects of international law which are noteworthy. Under the GDPR, the "right to erasure" may obligate an entity to erase the personal data of an individual located in the EU under certain circumstances: upon request if appropriate, when the data is no longer needed, when the subject withdraws consent, the data is being used illegally, or if the data subject was a child at the time of collection. The same is true under the law of the United Kingdom. In China, China's Personal Information Security Specification (PI Security Specification) gives data subjects the right to request the pertinent data controller to erase personal data under some circumstances.

Records and Other Information Which Should Not Be Produced

There are some records or information which should not be produced in litigation, even though they may have some tangential relevance to the matter at issue. In some instances, such as patient information, the organization is precluded by law from providing the information. In other instances, the organization may be entitled to withhold the information entirely, or alternatively to produce the information pursuant to a strict protective order which precludes its dissemination to third parties.

Depending on the organization's business and the content of its records, any produced documents may need to be withheld for various reasons. This chapter will examine several of these bases: the attorney-client privilege, work product, trade secrets, and documents protected under HIPAA. The assistance of counsel should therefore be obtained to ensure that only appropriate matter is produced.

The Attorney-Client Privilege

In every jurisdiction, subject to few exceptions, a litigant may elect not to produce documents which are subject to the attorney-client privilege and are therefore protected from discovery. The attorney-client privilege protects communications between an attorney and the attorney's client.

11. The states and pertinent statutes are as follows:Alaska:

> Alaska Stat. § 45.48.500 et seq.; Arizona: Ariz. Rev. Stat. § 44–7601; Arkansas: Ark. Code §§ 4-110-103, 104; California: Cal. Civ. Code §§ 1798.81, 1798.81.5, 1798.84; Colorado: Colo. Rev. Stat. § 6-1-713; Connecticut: Conn. Gen. Stat. § 42–471; Delaware: Del. Code tit. 6, § 5001C to 5004C and Del. Code tit., 19 § 736; Florida: Fla. Stat. § 501.171(8); Georgia: Ga. Code § 10-15-2; Hawaii: Haw. Rev. Stat. §§ 487R-1, 487R-2, 487–3, Haw. Rev. Stat. § 261-17.7(d), and Haw. Rev. Stat. § 52D-14c; Illinois: 20 ILCS 450/20, 815 ILCS 530/30, and 815 ILCS 530/40; Indiana: Ind. Code §§ 24-4-14-8, 24-4.9-3-3.5(c); Kansas: Kan Stat. § 50-7a01, Kan Stat. § 50-7a03, and Kan Stat. § 50–6, 139b(2); Kentucky: Ky. Rev. Stat. § 365.725; Louisiana: La. R.S. 51:3074(B); Massachusetts: Mass. Gen. Laws ch. 931, § 2; Maryland: Md. State Gov't Code §§ 10–1303; Michigan: MCL § 445.72a; Montana Mont. Code Ann. § 30-14-1703; Nevada: Nev. Rev. Stat. § 603a.200; New Jersey: N.J. Stat. § 56:8-161, 162; New Mexico: N.M. Stat. § 57-12C-3; New York: N.Y. Gen. Bus. Law § 399-H; North Carolina: N.C. Gen. Stat. § 75–64; Oregon: Or. Rev. Stat. § 646A.622; Rhode Island: R.I. Gen. Laws § 6-52-2; South Carolina: S.C. Code § 37-20-190 and S.C. Code § 30-2-310; Tennessee: Tenn. Code § 39-14-150(g); Texas: Tex. Bus. & Com. Code § 72.004 and Tex. Bus. & Com. Code § 521.052; Utah: Utah Code § 13-44-201; Vermont: 9 Vt. Stat. § 2445; Virginia: Va. Code § 2.2-2009(F); Washington: Wash. Rev. Code § 19.215.020; Wisconsin: Wis. Stat. § 134.97; Puerto Rico: 2014 Law #234-2014.

The privilege encompasses correspondence, bills, ledgers, statements, time records, and other documents which "reveal the motive of the client in seeking representation, litigation strategy, or the specific nature of the services provided" (*Clarke v. American Commerce Nat'l Bank*, 974 F.2d 127, 129 [9th Cir. 1992]). The privilege must be timely asserted or it is waived. In some instances, the record at issue may only contain a brief reference to the legal advice, and therefore the privileged portion of the records should be redacted and the remainder produced. In most jurisdictions, if a document is withheld entirely on the grounds of privilege, then it must be logged. Assertions of privilege can be complicated, and legal assistance with its determination and assertion is recommended.

Privilege can be waived by failure to timely assert, disclosure to third persons, or tendering an issue regarding a privileged communication. Again, assistance of counsel is necessary in order to timely assert the privilege and to consider any waiver issues which exist.

Work Product

A party may be entitled to withhold production of documents which constitute an attorney's work product. "Work product" protection applies to the work of an attorney (and the attorney's agents) in preparation for litigation against the attorney's client. It includes documents prepared in anticipation of litigation or trial. The protection may extend to unrelated matters, so long as the records at issue were prepared in anticipation of trial. However, in most jurisdictions documents which are prepared in the ordinary course of business will not fall under this doctrine. Also, in many jurisdictions, the work-product doctrine may be overridden by a showing of need by the other adverse party. The protection afforded by the attorney work-product doctrine varies from jurisdiction to jurisdiction, so assistance of counsel is advised in order to determine its applicability.

Privacy and Trade Secrets

In many jurisdictions, privacy rights may protect certain documents from production. Usually, these claims may involve various items which may be considered private, such as sexual privacy, tax returns, bank statements, and news sources. The party affected must usually object to the discovery request or bring a formal motion for protective order, depending on the law of the pertinent jurisdiction. Many jurisdictions have notice requirements if the records requested implicate rights of a "consumer" held by a third party. A court may order the records withheld, only partially produced, or not disclosed to others and only used for purposes of the litigation. Privacy objections are complicated and vary depending on the jurisdiction, and assistance of counsel is recommended.

Trade secrets constitute another type of privacy objection. A "trade secret" is a formula, process, design, instrument, pattern, commercial method, or compilation of information which is not generally known or ascertainable by others and which a business can use to obtain an economic advantage over competitors or customers. The laws applicable to trade secrets vary from jurisdiction to jurisdiction. When an organization receives a demand for documents which may include trade secrets, advice of counsel should be obtained to ensure the trade secrets are adequately protected.

HIPAA

The Health Insurance Portability and Accountability Act of 1996 (HIPAA) applies to both the security and the privacy of health information. Organizations to which HIPAA applies includes health care plans and health care providers, and their business associates who perform certain activities on their behalf, such as legal, actuarial, accounting, consulting, data aggregation, management, administrative, accreditation, or financial services.

HIPAA's privacy rule protects "individually identifiable health information" held or transmitted by a covered entity or its business associate, in any form or media, whether electronic, paper, or oral.

Under HIPAA, "individually identifiable health information" is information, including demographic data, that relates to:

- The individual's past, present, or future physical or mental health condition;
- The provision of health care to the individual; or
- The past, present, or future payment for the provision of health care to the individual.

Additionally, the information must be that which identifies the individual or for which there is a reasonable basis to believe it can be used to identify the individual.[12] The "individually identifiable information" includes such items as name, address, birthdate, and Social Security number of the patient as well as the patient's relatives, household members, and employer.

Prior to producing records containing "individually identifiable information," such information must be removed. There are some disclosures to which HIPAA does not apply, such as disclosures to the patient, and the organization's own payment and health care operations, among others. However, application of HIPAA requirements can be complex and should be accomplished with competent legal advice.

Conclusion

To be successful, it is axiomatic that an organization must pay careful attention to its records management and records retention policies and practices. This is necessitated by compliance, cost, and operational issues. However, this is not an easy task, as the field of records management/records retention and the related subjects of data privacy and cybersecurity are dynamic and evolving quickly, both in America and abroad. For this reason, it is essential for an organization to obtain professional assistance to create a records management policy which complies with the applicable law, satisfies stakeholders, and efficiently reduces costs.

12. HHS.gov, Summary of the HIPAA Privacy Rule.

23

QUALITY MANAGEMENT CONSIDERATIONS

Shep Bentley

The Problem—How do we get what we want, assuming that what we want is a safe and effective medical product? Much of the problem with achieving quality for medical devices is that we are tightly constrained in the approach to the relationship between known good products and the abundance of innovation available to us in improving their manufacture. This is because we start out with a clinical need that is addressed by an existing standard of care supported by an existing technology, that is defended by regulations that are intended to protect the public health by disallowing changes that might introduce more harm than good. Generally, the principles of "Quality" promote the concept of continuous improvement; in the highly regulated medical device industry, improvement is made as the result of deliberate planning that starts with a risk/benefit analysis from which the decision to touch the device design and/or process to manufacture it complies with verification and validation regulations. That is to say, the quality of any medical device is inextricably linked to the process of risk management. In this industry, improvement is not continuous, nor is it continual. It is the result of assessments that drive a decision to undertake a new design or manufacturing process. As the world continues to offer access to new and improved materials and techniques, however, the problem becomes managing the balance between improvement for the sake of improvement, and improvement as the most reasonable course of action. Sometimes, there is no alternative to adapting to new materials and techniques, as the original ones disappear, are banned, or become nonviable.

The Solution—Fortunately, the relationship of quality to the highly regulated industry of medical devices has been the subject of intense study and interest by both the regulators and the regulated alike. With a shared goal of producing safe and effective medical devices within what has become one of the highest integrity industries in the world, professionals in quality have devoted themselves to forging a workable relationship between the safety and effectiveness of what is known and the possibility of access to products with better safety and/or more effectiveness. The counterintuitive goal of quality system requirements is *not* perfection of the outcomes of design or production efforts, but it is rather an acceptable level of safety and effectiveness. Why? Because regulators recognize that the costs associated with achieving perfection may result in a product that would remain outside of the reach of the general public, and thereby be a threat to the public health. Instead, the quality of the medical device must be "good enough". How good is "good enough"? Regulators stipulate acceptability rates explicitly for process outcomes, based upon a classification of risk level. It is left to medical device manufacturers to seek a level of performance that avoids a risk of hazard leading to harm of the patient and/or the user, as applicable.

DOI: 10.4324/9781351107242-28

Definition—Quality: the ability to achieve safety and effectiveness, as well as usability, and cybersecurity as applicable, of a medical device based upon its desired effect(s) of its intended use within its indication(s) for use.

Alternate Definitions—What else? In the European Union and markets that apply the same approach to medical devices for quality, the definition is the ability to achieve the desired performance of its intended use within its indication(s) for use.

Stakes—Why? The stakes for medical device quality represent the ability to achieve credible reliability of safety and effectiveness within the marketplace, to remove the doubts, fear, and uncertainty regarding the expectations of clinical outcomes from products, whether evaluated or else compliant without evaluation.

Past (History)—Why? The drive for medical device quality originated with federal reaction to the threat to the public health from the absence of acceptable safeguards in the design and manufacture of products that were intended to be used by clinicians and later by the public. Following the drive for food quality to overcome the "jungle" of unsafe meatpackers and others, drug quality with the formation of the Chemical Posse to put the purveyors of elixirs and liniments out of business, and cosmetic quality to prevent toxic compounds from being sold in the name of beauty, the Food and Drug Administration (FDA) was formed at the beginning of the last century 20 years before establishing the Food, Drug and Cosmetic Act (1938). Device quality would wait until the adoption of 21 CFR § 820, Quality System Requirements, on the basis of its preamble explaining the rationale for introducing the regulation of medical device quality on the basis of its risk classification. By doing so, the FDA required those designing the specifications, as well as creating the process for production to be considered as manufacturers, and to accept the full responsibility for design and process controls.

Threshold to Present—Where? From the Medical Device Amendments (1976) to the FDA Modernization Act (1997), the FDA codified the Good Manufacturing Practices (GMPs) and current Good Manufacturing Practices (cGMPs) for medical devices, and not just food, drugs and biologics, and cosmetics. It had become apparent that by 1976, the need for confirmation of the ability of a medical device to be used safely and effectively must be confirmed upon the basis of its perceived risk to its user and to the patient. The entire realm of devices was sorted into risk classifications: Class I for minimal risk, Class II for moderate risk, and Class III for significant risk. Certain devices remained either "unclassified" or else "not classified". The level of quality control required by each classification followed the perception of risk, with the lowest risk requiring only "general controls" (21 CFR § 820) and the higher risk levels requiring "general and special controls" (§ 820 plus the application of other unique quality standards or requirements).

Schools of Thought—math-centric; costly yet error prone (100%, 200%, 300% inspections) The concept of quality control that applied to device inspections started with the old school of linear testing and/or visual inspection of each article. The method of assuring a supposedly higher level of quality was to retest and/or reinspect. Therefore, the idea was that a batch of products that had been "100% tested and inspected" could be assured of a high level of quality, and that a batch that had been "200% tested and inspected" could be even more assured of a high level of quality. A batch with triple the quality control (i.e., "300%") could be quite assured of a very high level of quality, and so on. However, as the understanding of how to achieve quality and how to assure quality in terms overall process reliability evolved in the late 1970s and early 1980s, the FDA ensured that medical device manufacturers understood that the requirement for Statistical Process Control (SPC) applied to them at any risk classification. As the pioneers of SPC (W. Edwards Deming, Joseph M. Juran, etc.) (re)introduced their concepts to the United States after decades (in the case of Deming) of national deliberate neglect, medical device manufacturers recognized the need to adapt their quality control methods not only to comply with § 820, but to remain cost competitive in the medical device marketplace.

Reactive—inspection of quality into the product without world-class quality techniques—As quality control processes evolved to provide a level of assurance from statistical sampling measures, they faced the need to revalidate their processes in order to comply with the Process Controls within § 820. Without a firm understanding of SPC, many device manufacturers have remained reluctant to rely exclusively upon the accepted SPC tables published with ANSI/ASQ Z1.4-2003 (R2013) Sampling Procedures and Tables for Inspection by Attributes and ANSI/ASQ Z1.9-2003 (R2013) Sampling Procedures and Tables for Inspection by Variables for Percent Nonconforming, which standards (with numerous revisions) have become accepted by industry over the past few decades. Tables that originated during the height of the Second World War to secure the acceptability of scaled up production and rapid delivery of American warfighting materiel and logistical support items were neglected for decades. The revised standards for SPC in support of medical device production derive from these. Greater clarity of production problems is achievable by the proper use of SPC, as compared to full inspection.

Proactive—statistically savvy approaches—As trained statisticians have introduced both process engineering and quality engineering as instrumental sciences to device manufacturers, the savvy production facilities have incorporated their ability to perform process validation into process revalidation seamlessly in order to achieve highly competitive results, with optimal quality and significantly lower process (and process control) costs, much less rework and repair costs, product recalls, and costs of nonconformity. The American Society for Quality (ASQ) annually confirms candidates for the Certified Quality Engineer (CQE) by testing in the current body of knowledge for SPC and other aspects of Quality.

Regulatory minimum—regardless of statistical justifications, certain regulatory "musts" exist.—Nevertheless, the CQE and any medical device manufacturer per § 820 must perform various rigorous verification and validation steps for each design and process that supports the production of that design. These include Design Verification, Design Validation, Design Transfer, Process Verification and Process Validation. Essentially, there is some regulatory redundancy that theoretically catches the likelihood of an error in design safety and effectiveness, readiness for the safe and effective design to be produced, and the applicability and reliability of the process used to manufacture the device. Verification is the question: "Did I make the product right?" Validation is the question: "Did I make the right product?" This can be equated to passing design verification with a "square wheel", whereby each of the four angles are confirmed to be 90 degrees (versus 89–91–89–91). However, passing design *validation* would be exceedingly unlikely with a square wheel. Device quality requires the sequential passing of design and then process control measures.

History of the regulation—the preamble to the QSRs, etc. The Federal Register Act (1936) introduced the Federal Register to be the federal government's comprehensive source of all agency rules and regulations. It was amended in 1937 to provide a codification of all regulations every five years, and the next year (1938) produced the first publication of the Code of Federal Regulations (CFR). There are presently 50 volumes, and the 21 CFR is "Food and Drugs". For 60 years, the 21 CFR dealt primarily with food and drug quality. Achieving compliance to the regulation of medical device quality as required by the FDA for any manufacturer of medical devices intended for interstate commerce within the United States became a legal requirement with the introduction of § 820 (Quality System Requirements, or "QSRs") within 21 CFR. This all started in 1994, producing the "preamble" in 1996 and came about in 1997 as part of the FDA Modernization Act (FDAMA), as a means of codifying the GMPs that originally applied to the makers of drugs into the cGMPs for companies that developed specifications (designed), determined processes (manufactured) and labeled or relabeled, sold and handled complaints for medical devices. It is interesting to note that in 1994, the introduction of international standards for the quality of design (ISO 9001) and the quality of manufacturing (ISO 9002) were published in Europe and adopted across the "First World" as a means of demonstrating conformity to a system of achieving quality, regardless of the product designed or produced, and "certification" to the ISO standards became a requirement to achieve the Conformité Européenne (CE) mark, ascribing European Conformity upon the product from the certified company, and in theory a reliable level of quality in design and/or manufacture. The 21 CFR § 820 has never been a conformity scheme engaging with an assortment of private notified bodies for implicit results, but rather a compliance requirement to be explicitly followed with the force of law. A medical device that has been designed and/or produced outside of compliance to the QSRs may be considered to be misbranded and/or adulterated, and therefore in violation. A company that has outsourced the specification development of its device is nevertheless liable for the compliance with the § 820.30 (Subpart C—Design Controls) regulating the design of all classes of devices, just as a company that has (quite commonly) outsourced the manufacturing of its product to a contract manufacturer is likewise wholly liable for the compliance with the § 820.70 Production and process controls—§ 820.72 Inspection, measuring and test equipment—§ 820.75 Process validation (Subpart G—Production and Process Controls) regulating the methods of producing, controlling, and validating the processes involved in production of all classes of medical devices. The strength and clarity of contracts regarding compliant design controls and process controls by contractors may be reviewed by the FDA during an inspection, but these do not relieve the sponsor company of ultimate responsibility for compliance and of the liability for injury to the intended users. Where the § 820 is vague, there are today ample precedents to understand how the FDA perceives or could perceive compliance under the application of Food and Drug Law. The lengthy preamble to the § 820 offers the best insight to the application of the specific text of each subpart, for those seeking context and the rationales for the phrasing of the regulations. The rulemaking steps for federal regulations were applied, to include the comments period and review steps. Much of what is now enshrined within the preamble is taken directly from the original comments. While each April the Code is updated, the § 820 has remained stable. Its similarity to the ISO 13485:2016 is not apparent, but the FDA alters little of the MDSAP Companion Document (based upon the ISO 13485) when adding § 820 verbiage to it.

Standards—ISO 13485:2016, ISO 14971:2019—Outside of the United States, there evolved firstly within the British Standardisation Institution (BSi) and later the International Organization for Standardization (ISO) a set of requirements that revolutionized the approach to managing quality, regardless of industry. What appeared on the world scene as the famous ISO 9002 in 1994 dictated a common set of 20 quality management system steps for which any company, large or small, could gain a "certification". The arch goal was customer satisfaction. It was not well aligned with § 820, however. The ISO adapted to the medical device industry by introducing the ISO 13485 *Medical devices—Quality management systems—Requirements for regulatory purposes* that was quite similar to ISO 9002 (and companion 9001, later becoming simply 9001), but closer to what global regulators of devices required with regard to when and why to pursue design and process "improvements". For the ISO, the original goal was continuous improvement. This then was scaled back to the more realistic "continual" improvement, meaning improvement at intervals and not an unceasing enterprise. The FDA was not ready to embrace this approach until 2003, with the concern that "better is the enemy of good enough", and that a reasonably good medical device today might become a riskier device in its quest to become a "better" device tomorrow. What made the newer ISO 13485 standard acceptable was the inclusion of "national regulations" into the text as a driver of change, and not simply "customers". The FDA has subsequently moved closer over recent years to the ISO 13485 approach to GMPs, presently overtly accepting the 2016 version of the ISO standard in lieu of § 820. Although the ISO 13485 itself is not explicit with regard to how risk management is to be performed, the ISO 14969—*Quality Management Systems—Guidance on the Application Of ISO 13485:2003* was explicit that this must be achieved by means of using the ISO 14971 *Medical Devices—Application of Risk Management to Medical Devices*. Whereas the § 820 scarcely mentions risk management, the ISO scheme makes explicit a detailed approach to achieving conformity in the performance of risk management. For a period, it was possible to obtain an ISO 14971 "certification". As the application of explicit risk management approaches develop into a matter of compliance, however, this becomes a matter of great concern, as well.

Global Uptake—GHTF and the instantiations of the Precautionary Principle in the life sciences—The Global Harmonisation Task Force (GHTF) worked with stakeholders from around the world of regulated medical devices (the Tier One countries, such as the European Union, Australia, Brazil, Canada, Japan, and the United States) to promulgate and publish single harmonized documents addressing an approach common to each regulator, with the idea that each document would represent the globally acceptable method in the future. As the GHTF encountered resistance, however, it was replaced altogether by the International Medical Device Regulators Forum (IMDRF), which in recent years has been chaired by the FDA's Director for the CDRH, Dr. Jeffrey Shuren. The global uptake of IMDRF documents appears to be greater than from the GHTF outpouring, and the overall resistance to the IMDRF offering is less (certainly from the FDA).

United Kingdom—BSi, legacy—The United Kingdom since BREXIT has opted both into *and* out of the European Union's scheme for medical device regulations, with two BSi organizations (one based in Britain and one based in Amsterdam that is no longer British), and requiring that medical devices undergo an evaluation per the European Medical Device Regulation (EMDR) with a newly designated European Notified Body as well as a British Notified Body, at least during 2020. At the time of this writing (during the first months of the COVID-19 pandemic), the European Union based in Brussels has opted to extend the duration of the Medical Device Directive (MDD), set to expire May 26, 2020, by another year. The United Kingdom, however, drove the adoption of the EMDR within the European Union prior to BREXIT. Ironically, it may be that the United Kingdom adopts the full weight of the "European" Medical Device Regulation within its own jurisdiction prior to the European Union itself, in its effort to pursue a less abrupt effect of its departure on its neighbors. The effect of this may be to drive the American approach to medical device quality forward, as the world's device manufacturers shift to prioritize the acceptance of their device designs first by the FDA and only later by regulators in the European Union, and last by the United Kingdom at this time. The ultimate irony may be that the origin of the best regulatory schemes for medical device quality, namely BSi in particular, and the UK's Ministry of Health and Regulatory Affairs (MHRA) in general, may in the end not benefit the British public as much as the public of the United States having adopted the essence of the ISO 13485:2016 and the public of the European Union having adopted the EMDR. The United Kingdom is presently entering a period of regulatory confusion and ambiguity, as it strives for a new uniquely British approach to achieving medical device quality. Doubtless, however, it will emerge with a highly satisfactory system for regulating quality.

European—both Brussels-based and EFTA markets—The pursuit of medical device quality within the jurisdiction of the European Union and the European Free Trade Agreement member states has undergone a dramatic transition, drafted in 2012, signed into law in 2017 and replacing the previous conformity scheme between 2020 and 2021. The EMDR (EU) 2017/745 has altered compliance requirements as European Union Law replaces the MDD (1993) Council Directive 93/42/EEC and amendments 2007/47/EC, expanding the breadth and depth of medical device performance requirements, clinical proof demonstrations and risk management activities. The net effect of the regulation is to give the force of law to the norms that had been overseen by the several dozens of Notified Bodies based largely within the European Union member states, and presently the effort to designate a like number of Notified Bodies to provide the compliance assessments necessary to process existing and new CE certificates has lagged dramatically. There has been a substantial shift away from the decades-old view of the European Union as the starter market by medical device manufacturers, and a movement toward pursuit of the market of the United States as the initial regulatory hurdle, particularly by American companies.

Australian, Brazilian, Canadian—Tier One and influence on respective markets—As the influence of the ISO scheme for quality under 13485:2016 and the FDA 21 CFR § 820 have merged and spread to the rest of the world by means of the IMDRF until recently chaired by Dr. Jeff Shuren (FDA's CDRH Director), the markets of Australia (regulated by the Therapeutic Goods Administration, or "TGA"), Brazil (regulated by Agência Nacional de Vigilância Sanitária, or "Anvisa"), and Canada (regulated by Health Canada/Santé Canada) have agreed, along with Japan (Ministry of Health, Labour and Welfare, or "MHLW" or "Kōrō-shō" in Japanese), to adopt the Medical Device Single Audit Program (MDSAP) to assure medical device quality among these five members to their respective regulators. The fact of the existence of this program provides an aspiration for common cause in the quest for quality as it relates to the use of risk management to control design and processes developed in sponsor organizations that seek to make and sell products into these markets. Each regulator from Australia, Brazil, Canada, and the United States has introduced the unique verbiage into the first MDSAP Companion Document, as slight additions to the text of the original document. In awaiting the input from Japan, the MDSAP auditors began training to support four of the five markets that had agreed to allow (or in the case of Canada, to switch over altogether to) the MDSAP approach to device quality. Then came Japan.

Japanese—extreme? The world's most rigorous environment for medical device quality is Japan, whose Ministry of Labor, Health and Welfare (MLHW) has made it their business to set standards that depart from the rest of the world's harmonized requirements by a substantial margin. Within the MDSAP Companion Document, the regulators with by far the most particular requirements within the effort at "harmonization" are the Japanese.

Rest of World—India, South Africa, China, Singapore, Saudi Arabia, Russia, Mexico—The rest of the world has been rapidly developing medical device compliance requirements to the point that there is no nation in the world that has (or applies) zero regulation regarding medical devices. In India, the CDCSO has brought forward new regulation specific to medical devices within the past 15 years after regulating drugs only for most of its history. South Africa's South Africa Health Products Regulatory Authority (SAHPRA) does not have a medical device registration program in place, but leverages "country of origin" approvals and clearances. In the Peoples Republic of China, the National Medical Products Administration has recently replaced the China FDA (CFDA), that had replaced the State FDA (SFDA), introducing a large quantity of medical device regulations and the Guo Bai standards in recent years to replace their reliance upon foreign standards and regulatory concepts. Singapore, conversely, has moved steadily toward the IMDRF and the MDSAP approach to device regulation with open dialogue and consideration of mutually agreed upon regulatory theory. Saudi Arabia's Saudi FDA (SFDA) has borrowed the regulatory approach of the European Union to medical devices under the MDD, absent the EMDR. Russia's Minzdrav applies a likewise similar approach to that of the European Union. Mexico's COFEPRIS applies the "Registro" and "Permiso" for medical devices, to be obtained on behalf of sponsors by the prospective distributor(s).

Risk Management—the Precautionary Principle and its legacy in QMS standards and risk management standards. The conformity of medical devices to any meaningful quality standard or directive today is impossible without the application of risk management by its manufacturer. As conformity becomes a matter of compliance while the MDD is replaced by the EMDR, and as the MDSAP involving the regulators of Australia, Brazil, Canada, Japan and the United States has already adopted the provisions for the application of risk management as expressed within the ISO 14971:2019 standard. The standard specifies terminology, principles and a process for risk management of medical devices, including software as a medical device (SaMD) and in In Vitro Diagnostic (IVD) devices. The process described in the standard intends to assist manufacturers of medical devices to identify the hazards leading to harm associated with the medical device, to estimate and evaluate the associated risks, to control these risks, and to monitor the effectiveness of the controls. These risks of hazards leading to harms could stem from an absence of biocompatibility of materials used, lack of data or systems security, electrical shock, moving parts, radiation and inadequate usability. While the public welcomes the march of progress with regard to the further development on codifying risk management principles, it may be concerning to the sponsor organizations that are researching, developing and designing medical innovations that are likewise debating on the record the risks of the use of various materials. The application of the Precautionary Principle in the life sciences as a broad epistemological approach may be a boon to risk-averse regulators while being the bane to innovators, especially as compliance compels the availability of risk management activities that could (and do) introduce a level of liability to the managements of innovators and innovation sponsors. How is full disclosure of risk management activities during an FDA inspection to be handled? If full disclosure of hazard analyses is disallowed, then how is compliance to be confirmed? If full disclosure of hazard analyses is required, then how likely is it that these would be balanced and faithful records of the design risk discussions? The answers today are not yet obvious. The concern in the life sciences industry among those with the highest integrity and purest motives is that the introduction in Europe of the Precautionary Principle, originally developed within the environmental sciences, to the life sciences starting about 40 years ago generally in Germany as the "Vorsorgeprinzip", was not net beneficial to it. Nevertheless, there has been an inexorable movement toward the application of risk management along the lines of the precautionary approach. While the regulators of the world adopt and codify more risk management into revisions of industry standards, there is the old adage, "The greatest risk is the risk of avoiding all risks." It remains to be seen how far the precautionary principle can be taken as a matter of compliance, and if the reluctance of innovators to comply with its provisions within newer standards that have become the special controls for regulators will result in design stagnation, willful noncompliance or something else. The recent support of innovation as stipulated within the 21st Century Cures Act in the United States may nevertheless incentivize the imaginations of medical device designers, by offering breakthrough device designations and fast track review pathways for important new therapeutic product concepts.

Comparators—what is the same? (Quality of Life)—See Table 23.1.

Contrastors—what is different? (Approach to Market)—See Table 23.2.

Table 23.1 Comparisons

Comparisons 2020					
	Australia	*Brazil*	*Canada*	*European Union**	*United States*
Population	26M	211M	38M	514M	328M
GDP	$1.3T	$2.1T	$1.7T	$17.3T	$21.4T
ISO 13485:2016?	Yes	Yes	Yes	Yes	Yes**
ISO 14971:2007?	Yes	Yes	Yes	Yes	Yes

* Including the United Kingdom.
** With 21 CFR § 820 requirements.

Table 23.2 Contrasts

Contrasts 2020					
	Australia	*Brazil*	*Canada*	*European Union*	*United States*
Unique regulatory approach?	Yes, via TGA	Yes, via ANVISA	Yes, via Health Canada	Yes, via NBs	Yes, via FDA
Quality scheme	MDSAP/ISO	MDSAP/ISO	MDSAP only	ISO	MDSAP + QSRs
Fully harmonized pathway?	No	No	No	No	No
Acceptance of foreign mark?	No	No	No	No	No

Technology—what about innovations, such as digital health, SaMD, combination products, etc.? Traditionally, medical devices have represented a certain set of intuitive characteristics and attributes, hence the "Pre-amendment" list that serves as the origin of all predicate devices. That is, since 1979, if a moderate risk device could be compared to a device that was on the market on or before then as "substantially equivalent" and raised "no new questions of safety or effectiveness", it might "clear" an evaluation by the FDA using the 510(k) process. Historically, the vast majority of medical device types fit onto this regulatory pathway, and mostly without any requirement for clinical data. The FDA used to say, "A device rolls off the table and goes 'thunk!'" It has been a long time since this was true, but it may now be accurately claimed that the majority of prospective products that could be regulated as medical device types no longer fit neatly into the categories envisioned by the FDA in 1979. Not unlike how the US Patent Office contemplated closing in 1899 because everything that could be invented had been invented, 80 years later the FDA provided industry with the complete list of all medical devices. Any new moderate risk device would need to be compared to one of these. In the case of a significant risk device, the sponsor would need to undertake a clinical trial and demonstrate safety and effectiveness along with compliance to design controls and process controls in advance of a Premarket Approval (PMA). If a device could be considered a moderate risk device but was not comparable to a device that had been on the market in or prior to May 1979, then there could be an awkward effort to enter the market by submitting a flawed submission to be rerouted onto the regulatory pathway for a de novo 510(k). Although for a traditional 510(k) to clear a moderate risk product the sponsor could promise the FDA that it would undertake to fulfill the § 820 requirements, for a significant risk device the sponsor would be required to satisfy the § 820 requirements in advance of approval by PMA. Any device that did not have a predicate device would be viewed as a significant risk device, as it was new (de novo) and therefore unknown. With the passage of more than 40 years, however, the likelihood of forming a relevant comparison to pre-amendment device types has become less. Furthermore, the advent of technologies supporting products regulated as devices (such as software including "apps", novel accessories to old [and new] device types, digital health products, combination products that have drug and/or biologic components with a device primary method of action, and altogether new technology device types) that are inherently safe and essentially effective has created the need for new product codes and methods of evaluation. The FDA has released a record number of guidance documents and created various new meeting types for interacting with industry sponsors in order to facilitate clarity of understanding of their proposed devices, regardless of whether or not they go "thunk".

Classifications—how do we classify, and how does that influence medical device quality? Devices that are of minimal risk regarding the safety of their use by clinically trained professionals if for prescription use, or by the public if available by over-the-counter sale, are typically Class I; devices that are of moderate risk regarding the safety of their use by clinically trained professionals if for prescription use, or by the public if available by over-the-counter sale, or for which the effect may require specialized understanding, are typically Class II; devices that are of significant risk regarding the safety of their use by clinically trained professionals or for which the effect relates to a life threatening and/or debilitating disease or condition are typically Class III. There exist device types that are unclassified and not classified. Generally, Class I devices require no evaluation. Likewise, Class II devices generally require an evaluation and this is by means of a 510(k) submission that declares compliance activities in advance of confirmation by an onsite FDA inspection. Finally, all Class III devices require an evaluation and this is generally by means of the PMA submission. Compliance to § 820 for sponsors of Class III devices is confirmed before the approval by means of a Preapproval Inspection (PAI). A Class III device approval almost always requires original clinical data to support safety and effectiveness claims.

Alternative Classifications—why do classifications go up or down? Where? How often? With the current acceleration of innovation and development of artificial intelligence (AI), medical device data systems, medical image storage devices, medical image communications devices, and novel accessories that support technology platforms that previously may never have performed comparably, the FDA has revised numerous classifications. When a fundamental improvement in technology provides a rationale for revising the risk profile, the FDA may reduce the classification or "downregulate" the device. Conversely, when the history of use for a technology shows that there is a greater risk than previously perceived (such as with automatic external defibrillators (AEDs) which depend upon proper process controls to work well), the FDA may increase the classification (in this example, from Class II to Class III) or "upregulate" the device. This is observable on the FDA's Total Produce Lifecycle (TPLC) database, and although it happens, it is presently a rare occurrence. The TPLC database is posted and searchable within the FDA website.

Particular Quality Requirements—Special Controls beyond General Controls—In order to achieve full compliance of sponsors, the FDA relies upon a variety of other organizations to produce standards that it recognizes with a recognition number. These particular quality requirements and special controls originate from sources that represent the current knowledge of the state of the art for materials and techniques for testing and validating prospective products. These include the Association for the Advancement of Medical Instrumentation (AAMI), the American National Standards Institute (ANSI), the ISO which also includes the International Electrotechnical Commission (IEC), and others. The recognized standards are posted and searchable within the FDA website.

Down regulations versus Up regulations—what are the drivers, and how does this influence quality? (Infrared devices, AEDs, Tanning Beds) Changing perceptions of risk of use over time drive the regulation of infrared lamps down, removing the requirement for premarket evaluation by the FDA since 2017, while driving up the regulation of Automated External Defibrillators (AEDs) from Class II to Class III since 2015 due to poor quality of manufacturing resulting in numerous adverse events. Since 2015, tanning bed manufacturers must submit a 510(k), again, as a function of the current perception of risks of hazard leading to harm from the quality of the designs.

Safety—the first requirement—The most important requirement for satisfying compliance requirements for medical devices is safety. A device that is highly effective yet unsafe in terms of the severity of potential albeit infrequent harm or the frequency of mild harm faces regulatory challenges that are greater than those of a safe device that has some questions of effectiveness, generally speaking. The requirement imposed by the Hippocratic Oath "First do no harm" is interpreted to mean that a clinical benefit that is achieved at an unacceptable risk of hazard leading to harm of the patient and/or user is worse than a lesser risk product, almost regardless of the clinical benefit or absence thereof. The precautionary approach has made the question a matter of comparing *to do nothing* versus *to apply a potentially unsafe device*. However, if the clinical benefit could be shown to outweigh the risk of hazard leading to harm in most cases, or that the potential clinical benefit is great enough as with a rescue technology where the alternative is death or protracted excruciating pain, then the case for an otherwise risky device might be possible.

Effectiveness—where does it fit? The need for a device to achieve the desired effect of its intended use for its indication is almost as important as safety, generally. While there seems to be no point to design and develop a device that is ineffective regardless of safety, and while indeed this may be true, nevertheless the effectiveness of a prospective product only weighs into the scale after an acceptable level of safety could be established.

Usability—an afterthought? No longer does the dynamic contrast between safety and effectiveness suffice for the discussion of overall acceptability in the estimation of regulators. The attributes of usability, measured in terms of self-selectability (in other words, the subject device being the more obvious choice than other options for the indication(s) for use) and the ease of inference of proper use as compared to the risks of unintentional misuse/abuse of the device and its accessories, have become essential. Therefore, usability forms an odd co-factor to support arguments of safety by means of improved usability in certain cases, and conversely to support improved effectiveness in other cases. Although these tradeoffs between a diminished risk math for one factor in the support of an increased risk math for another factor have historically been binary in pursuit of a net improvement that could justify a conclusion of acceptability, with the introduction of this third factor (usability), the sponsor must apply a risk argument that satisfies a broader level of acceptability. As an example, if the use of a catheter is more intuitive for an interventional cardiologist (i.e., more usable), it may become a preferred device that improves effectiveness; however, its safety profile may become more challenging to confirm with prospective use in new anatomical locations. To address the competing yet ideally mutually reinforcing concerns with safety, effectiveness and usability, it is important to integrate these at the outset of the device design.

Cybersecurity—what is this? While it is certainly essential to confirm that an active medical device achieves satisfactory levels of safety, effectiveness and usability, those devices that require software to function may face an additional risk to the extent that there is any proposed connectivity to the internet or "hackability" of the device by means of any form of cyberattack. For this reason, an acceptable level of cybersecurity, which is a reasonable assurance that the device is designed to resist hacking, is essential. Risk management is to be applied to cybersecurity to facilitate an understanding of current vulnerabilities to hacking, whether as particularly targeting the specific device or as generally exposing the device to a vulnerable environment of use. Reconciling the demands of cybersecurity presents a tradeoff with privacy of data, in many cases, and regulators accept the understanding that there is no such state as complete cybersecurity. Nevertheless, the need for demonstrating mitigation of any likelihood of hacking as a hazard leading to harm of the patient and/or user is critical to the evaluation of affected devices. Therefore, the design of these devices ought to consider cybersecurity from the outset.

Efforts to accommodate innovation—21st Century Cures Act, Smart Regulations, Artificial Intelligence (AI) validations—all require a level of ability to demonstrate and confirm security of certain products that manage data as a potential tradeoff for the operational quality of each device, insofar as the protection measures (passwords, biometrics, data keys, cables, cards and encryption techniques) impede rather than enhance performance, as risk mitigation against the hazards of harm of compromise of data integrity and data security.

Disposability—what does this mean? How and when a device is to be disposed after its final use is yet another factor for the design of any medical device. Does the device become a biohazard after use, and need to be treated as hazardous waste? Does the device have batteries? Is the device intended for single use and become unusable after its onetime use? How easy or difficult is the disposal process, and what should be considered by the device user in advance or else immediately after the time arrives to consider the device to be waste? These considerations are best applied at the outset of the design process and risk management effort.

Target Population—How is this established and what happens when the product is used by the unintended users? The manufacturer has an obligation to know early and with reasonable certainty the profile of the user and/or patient for whom the device is intended, so as to support this target population with its design controls. As a "label" develops, the manufacturer confirms with testing and possibly original clinical data the satisfaction of the ability of the device to meet the needs of those individuals for whom it works best. May it be used on any gender? Children? People of all ages? Healthy as well as unhealthy? Do certain medical conditions make the product risky or else unusable altogether? The need to understand this label becomes the foundation of the regulator's ability to evaluate if the device is designed satisfactorily, and to contemplate what may occur if there is any prospective off-label use, by means of recommending precautions, warnings and contraindication statements within the labeling (instructions for use).

Benefit of Effect—how is this measured, and in the age of the Precautionary Principle, is this given adequate weight? Fortunately, as regulators are compelled to evaluate the risks of use in terms of safety and effectiveness as well as the previously discussed related factors, there is greater acceptance of a corresponding expression of benefits to each risk. For example, if the design of a device applies a material that enables the benefit of superb flexibility while at the same time introducing a level of toxicity, then there becomes a question as to whether or not the benefit of the effect outweighs the risk to patient safety. Regarding this question, an evaluator may perceive more than simply the hazard of harm without the context of the benefit of the effect, unless only the risk is conveyed for review. Without the associated expression of the clinical benefit, the risk represents a unilinear measure that provides no context and therefore denies the review staff with the means to understand more fully the argument for acceptance of the material's toxicity relative to the lives that its flexibility may save, if this be true.

Alternate Use (exemptions)—what happens when clinically trained professionals use the product in ways that are not intended, and what are the consequences of this sort of use, when it is the result of clinical decision-making? Only from clever alternate use of certain technologies may evidence of applicability be confirmed, and the practice of medicine is not impeded by those who decide on the acceptability of the original intended uses. Insofar as the different uses to which the device may be put are not a complicit effort by the manufacturer to broaden the label in advance of the appropriate communication with regulators, the alternate use for clinically relevant procedures (compassionate, emergency and humanitarian uses for which exemptions may be filed) may be allowable.

Off-Label Use (innovation during practice of medicine)—How do doctors get what they need in their hands, and how is the standard of care influenced by the practice of medicine? Although the promotion by manufacturers of any off-label use of the device by its market is strictly prohibited, a significant source of innovation and discovery comes from the use of devices outside of their intended uses by clinically trained professionals exercising the practice of medicine to advance clinical science. The considered estimation of a clinical situation by those trained to understand the decision-making process by considering the risks and benefits that apply to the use of a device in such a fashion that has not been envisioned by the manufacturer, or else may have been envisioned but not otherwise investigated or supported by design controls, is a source of research and development that provides enormously valuable design input to future devices.

Misuse (foreseeable)—predictable confusion—the application of usability studies and confirmation that foreseeable misuse is reduced to an acceptable level on the basis of risk, if not wholly eliminated, by means of detailed Usability Failure Mode Effects Criticality Analyses (UFMECAs) is part of both current design controls and risk management in all major markets for medical devices of the world. Reuse of single use devices is an example of misuse, and the manufacturer must undertake to contemplate the consequences and mitigate the worst effects.

Abuse (unforeseeable)—absence of self-selection—the application of usability studies may bring about the revelation of uses that do not suit the device whatsoever, to the extent that these identify the potential for the market to become confused and to adopt the device for uses that are incorrect. Abuse of the device may result from a name that is simply too close to that of an unrelated product, or it may stem from a perception of similarity to the shape of an unrelated product, or for any one of a number of reasons that design controls must attempt to comprehend.

Adverse Event Reporting—As a fundamental responsibility of any medical device manufacturer, the reporting to authorities of events from a serious malfunction or use that resulted in the potential (or actual) need for clinical intervention is central to the compliance requirements and the quality management system in place. Adverse Event Reporting must be controlled by a procedure, to which all affected staff are trained and internally audited routinely each year.

Data Trending (MAUDE + TPLC)—tables—Performance information is updated on the FDA website within the Manufacturers And Users Device Experience (MAUDE) and Total Product Life Cycle (TPLC) databases. As publicly available data, this information provides the market and manufacturers with ample detail from which to confirm clearly the current circumstances of devices by product code and manufacturer, going back at least 15 years, with downloadable spreadsheets (Excel) from which complete graphs and trend detail are easily produced

For example, see the new Guidance development trends, which show a significant increase in new Guidance documents for Medical Devices:

Table 23.3 Medical Device Guidance Documents Issued by FDA, 2002–2019

Medical Device Guidance Documents Issued by FDA: (1) Cross-Center Final; (2) Draft; (3) Total																		
	2002	*2003*	*2004*	*2005*	*2006*	*2007*	*2008*	*2009*	*2010*	*2011*	*2012*	*2013*	*2014*	*2015*	*2016*	*2017*	*2018*	*2019*
1	1	1	0	1	4	1	1	2	1	2	1	12	15	4	7	18	8	17
2	0	0	0	0	0	1	2	1	0	1	0	1	3	2	5	4	9	18
3	1	1	0	1	4	2	3	3	1	3	1	13	18	6	12	22	17	35

Source: www.fda.gov/Home/MedicalDevices/DeviceAdvice:ComprehensiveRegulatoryAssistance/Guidance Documents.

New Quality schemes—trends—Given the greater ease of understanding the FDA medical device premarket submission requirements with the increased number of Guidance documents issuing, and the greater frustration in preparing for the EMDR in May 2021 without visibility to designated Notified Body support in time for compliance to obtain the CE mark, members of the IMDRF are seeking to apply the Companion Document for the MDSAP based upon the ISO 13485:2016 versus certification to the ISO 13485:2016 by means of Notified Body audits. The total number of medical device manufacturers currently unprepared for the CE mark by means of the EMDR is approximately 80%.[1]

Effects of new quality schemes—current IMDRF versus ISO members, and current thinking—IMDRF is ascendant, as a reinvigorated resumption of the GHTF (now defunct); applying the ISO 13485:2016 plus various distinct regulations of its member markets, it has established a forward-thinking means of managing a newly harmonized approach to device quality and risk management.

Global trends in requirements—new harmonization? The IMDRF is expanding, and the newly independent United Kingdom is contemplating participation, as expressed in 2020 by the MHRA. The UK has historically been the source of the majority of original medical device quality concepts and regulations.

Time to market trends—data in the United States and European Union—The majority of the world's medical device manufacturers now pursue the United States as a first market, versus the European Union, likely due to the improved ease of understanding the FDA regulations as opposed to the decreased ease of achieving time and attention of a Notified Body much less the clarity of understanding of the new EMDR.

Summary—The foregoing figures demonstrate an unmistakable trend toward an acceleration the speed of device innovation and development, particularly in the area of digital health.

Future of Quality—offering methods for the future of medical devices including combination products with device primary methods of action, SaMD, and AI-driven devices. The movement toward rapid adoption of innovation and hybrid technologies that pair artificial intelligence with human expertise to create "synergistic" or "synthetic" intelligence (SI) is currently pointing the way to future regulations that comprehend novel effects of intended uses. The constraints of previous

1. Jon Speer, Regulatory Compliance and True Quality and Regulatory Affairs and Electronic Quality Management System (eQMS) and QMS Software and Medical Device Industry and EU MDR and MedTech Business and Design Reviews and Traceability and Medical Device Quality Management System (MDQMS) and Quality Assurance (March 29, 2020).

validation requirements, whether from guidance documents or final rules, are providing a foundation for departure from long-standing methods of assuring device performance. What constitutes adequate confirmation of reliability through testing and validation protocols is quickly and conscientiously adapting to proven innovation and technology, nearly concurrently. In the world today, the FDA is leading all efforts to support a balance in confirmation of safety, effectiveness, usability and cybersecurity of subject devices with a speedy and interactive review of information and data.

Conclusions

It is in this highly dynamic environment of daily (hourly?) innovation to develop abilities to diagnose diseases or other conditions, or cure, mitigate, treat or prevent diseases that the efforts to establish and maintain appropriate methods and measures to achieve quality based upon the understanding of risk of hazard leading to harm as well as the reasonable estimations of the likelihood of meaningful and enduring benefit provide the public with its best guarantee of safe, effective, usable and secure medical devices. Certainly, the dynamic relationship between successful performance of any product to achieve the desired effect of its intended use is generally in opposition to any unmitigated risks, and it remains counterintuitive that risk management could be complete for a medical device without consideration of the benefits attributable to its quality. To reach any conclusion on the basis of the expression of risk without a correlation to quality is an incomplete measure, and only by applying an understanding of what comprises device quality may a complete conclusion be reached. Therefore, the need in medical device regulatory affairs for a balance between the measure of risk and the measure of quality is essential.[2]

2. See generally A Standardized Expression of Benefit Is Missing from Our Risk/Benefit Analysis Paradigm (March 1, 2006), *Genetic Engineering and Biotechnology News*, Vol. 26, No. 5, www.genengnews.com/magazine/finding-a-balance-in-assessment-of-risk/.

24

DATA PRIVACY CONSIDERATIONS

An International Viewpoint

Marius Măgureanu

Brief Introduction to the Pivotal Year of 2018

In Brief

Although the General Data Protection Regulation (GDPR) was released as early as May 2016, in order for Member States in the European Union to have sufficient time to prepare and adapt the proper implementation of GDPR in their business models, it very often came to the fact that only beginning with 2018, when the date of May 25, 2018, approached, the date when the enforcement of GDPR began, that the entities concerned took steps to implement GDPR in a formal manner.

Therefore, in most business models, the changes that needed to be taken for GDPR to work properly were made in a hasty, formal fashion at first. Still, since the implementation is a work in progress and not definitive but needs to be overseen and constantly updated, this has become a norm and a point to consider in the case of business entities dealing with personal data. National authorities in the European Union have also provided sufficient information such that businesses are prepared to accommodate the requirements of GDPR and have provided clear and insightful information on the likely impact over a variety of business.

What Is Personal Data

Personal data represents any sort of information that relates to an *identified or identifiable living natural person*. Personal data need not directly and solely be able to lead to the identification of the said natural person; it is therefore enough that a piece of personal data that, collected together with other pieces of information, can lead to the identification of the respective natural person.

In that sense, the European Court of Justice has ruled in a Judgment of the European Court of Justice C-101/2001 of 06.11.2003 (Lindqvist) that

> referring, on an internet page, to various persons and identifying them by name or by other means, for instance by giving their telephone number or information regarding their working conditions and hobbies, constitutes the processing of personal data . . . within the meaning of . . . Directive 95/46/CE.

Personal data that has been de-identified, encrypted or *pseudonymized* but can be used to re-identify a natural person remains personal data and falls within the scope of the GDPR.

DOI: 10.4324/9781351107242-29

Personal data that has been rendered *anonymous* in such a way that the individual is not or no longer identifiable is no longer considered personal data. For data to be truly anonymized, the anonymization must be irreversible.

GDPR protects personal data regardless of the technology used for processing the personal data—both automated and manual processing and irrespective of the means used to collect and store such data, such as, but not limited to manual physical (paper form) records, IT system, video surveillance on videotape or else, geolocation and tracking devices.

Examples of personal data are name and surname; domicile; an email address that is composed of name and/or surname of the person; an identification card number (license plate number, identification card details, bank card details); location data (e.g., the location data function on a mobile phone); Social Security number, an internet protocol address; a cookie ID; phone number; voice of a natural person giving instructions in case of telephone banking service; faces of persons taped on video surveillance means; biometric data (e.g., fingerprints, retinal patterns, facial structure, voices, hand geometry, vein patterns or even some deeply ingrained skill or other behavioral characteristic); handwritten signature; keystrokes; or particular way to walk or to speak that may lead to identifying a natural person based on these traits.

European Legal Framework on Data Protection

Since there are only few, if any business models which do not involve the processing[1] of personal data in their daily business to some extent, data protection has become a legal and also business factor to consider when dealing with existing or new business models, which, apparently, prior to the enforcement of GDPR was not that relevant or less consistent.

This, albeit the fact that data protection legislation, in the form of the Data Protection Directive[2] was still applicable and largely departed from the same principles as the future to be GDPR when regulating the processing of personal data.

Prior to the adoption of GDPR, data protection legislation was available at the European level and took the form of:

- Article 8 of the European Convention of Human Rights, a person's right to protection with respect to the processing of personal data forms part of the right to respect for private and family life, home and correspondence.[3]
- Article 8 of the EU Charter of Fundamental Rights (the "Charter") states the right to personal data protection and enforces the following principles: processing of personal data must be fair, for specified purposes, based on either the consent of the person concerned or a legitimate basis laid down by law. Natural persons shall be afforded the right to access their personal data, have it rectified, and compliance with this right must be subject to control by an independent national authority.
- Lisbon Treaty is pivotal in European Data protection laws for mainly two things. It did raise the Charter to a status of binding legal document and has specifically mentioned the right to personal data protection[4] and the European competence to regulate data protection matters.

1. As defined under Art. 4 (2) of GDPR, "processing" shall mean "any operation such as collection, recording, organization, structuring, storage, adaptation or alteration, retrieval, consultation, use, disclosure by transmission, dissemination or otherwise making available, alignment or combination, restriction, erasure or destruction or personal data".
2. Directive 95/46/EC on the protection of individuals with regard to the processing of personal data.
3. Council of Europe, European Convention on Human Rights, CETS No. 005, 1950.
4. Article 16 of the TFEU.

- Council of Europe Convention 108[5] is the first legally binding instrument dealing with data protection. The Convention underwent a modernization process, completed with the adoption of amending Protocol CETS No. 223.
- Under European law, data protection has been acknowledged as a distinct fundamental right. It is affirmed in Article 16 of the Treaty of the Functioning of the European Union, as well as in Article 8 of the EU Charter of Fundamental Rights.
- Under European law, data protection was regulated at first by the Data Protection Directive as early as 1995 ("Data Protection Directive").

Still, since the Data Protection Directive required implementation in the national legislation of all Member States via national laws, the enforcement therefore was often inconsistent and led to setting different standards in the industry across the European Union. This had an impact especially on large enterprises, covering multiple jurisdictions in the European Union and which needed to adapt to various local legal requirements, which ultimately led to legal uncertainty and high legal consultancy/advisory fees.

Given the rise of information society services and the lack of jurisdictional barriers thereof, essential for building transnational business and the need to uniformly protect social challenges deriving from data protection and rise of information society services, a uniform regulation was required.

GDPR enforces a one-stop shop principle in the sense that, by being a Regulation, it is automatically implemented in the national legislation across European Member States, without the need for local national implementation measures. Still, Member States are required to adapt national legislation in order to comply to GDPR and in some instances, some margin of discretion is left to national legislative bodies to regulate further. Still, as GDPR is directly enforceable in the legislation of the Member States, differences of interpretation in terms of applying the provisions of GDPR should from now on be avoided.

Also, GDPR is supplemented, detailed and enforced via the guidelines issued by the European Data Protection Board (EDPB), which replaced and acts as successor of the former advisory board called Article 29 Working Party (Art. 29 WP), at its turn an advisory body made up of a representative from the data protection authority of each EU Member State, as an independent European body, which used to contribute to the consistent application of data protection rules throughout the European Union and promote cooperation between the EU's data protection authorities.

The EDPB, active since May 25, 2018, is composed of representatives of the European national data protection authorities and the European Data Protection Supervisor (EDPS). EDPB acts as the EU body in charge of the application of the GDPR as of May 25, 2018.[6]

Articles 64, 65 and 70 of GDPR deal with the main authorities that EDPB may exercise in the following directions:

1. Consistency: issue of legally binding decisions in cases where (a) a national supervisory authority of a Member State has raised a relevant and reasoned objection in cases of one-stop shops, (b) there are conflicting views on which of the supervisory authorities is the "lead authority", and (c) the competent national supervisory authority does not request or does not follow the EDPB's opinion.

5. Convention for the Protection of Individuals with regard to Automatic Processing of Personal Data (Council of Europe). The amending Protocol (CETS No. 223) to Convention 108 was adopted by the Committee of Ministers of the Council of Europe on May 18, 2018, on the occasion of its 128th session held in Elsinore, Denmark. References to the "Modernised Convention 108" refer to the Convention as amended by Protocol CETS No. 223.
6. Articles 63 to 76 and Recitals (135) to (140) of GDPR.

2. Advisory and consultation: EDPB may advise the European Commission in issues related to the protection of personal data within the EU, in cases that require amendments to the GDPR, or to European legislation involving personal data and the issue of adequacy decision by the European Commission in order to enable the transfer of personal data to a third country or other international organization.
3. Issue of recommendations and guidelines: the Board of the EDPB regularly issues guidelines, recommendations and best practice to ensure consistent application of GDPR.

Said guidelines aiming to confer a more in-depth knowledge on the meaning of the terms used throughout GDPR are:

1. Article 29 Working Party Guidelines on consent under Regulation 2016/679;
2. Guidelines on Data Protection Impact Assessment (DPIA) and determining whether processing is "likely to result in a high risk" for the purposes of Regulation 2016/679;
3. Guidelines on transparency under Regulation 2016/679;
4. Article 29 Working Party Opinion 4/2007 on the concept of personal data;
5. Article 29 Working Party Opinion 05/2014 on anonymization techniques;
6. Guidelines on Data Protection Officers (DPOs), as last revised and adopted on April 5, 2017.

The legal provisions in the GDPR are further supplemented by soft laws and binding court decisions.

As far as the enforcement from a territorial perspective is concerned, GDPR applies to controller[7] and processors[8] established in the European Union and to controllers and processors not established in the European Union, but which offer goods or services to data subjects in the European Union or monitor their behavior.

Immediate Consequences of GDPR Becoming Enforceable

The enforceability of the GDPR effective May 25, 2018, led to a number of immediate consequences.

Business entities have become aware of the necessity to review, or in most cases implement in their models the data protection framework. This mainly involved, at a minimum the following set of actions:

1. Self-auditing, data-mapping and self-testing of own activities related to the processing of personal data;
2. Drafting of appropriate data processing agreements and joint control agreements, where applicable;
3. Review and update of terms and conditions for the use of websites, cookies policy and privacy policies on their websites and/or web platforms;
4. Review and update of existing policies in business otherwise not mainly concerned with data protection as their primary scope of business, such as for example:

    - Real estate business, where landlords became aware of the necessity to implement data protection provisions in landlord's house rules, due to the existence of closed-circuit television

7. A controller is defined under GDPR Art. 4(7) as someone who "alone or jointly with others determines the purposes and means of the processing of personal data". A controller's decision establishes why and how personal data shall be processed.
8. A processor is defined under GDPR Art. 4(8) as someone who "processes personal data on behalf of a controller". The activities entrusted to a processor may be limited to a very specific task or context or may be quite general and comprehensive.

(CCTV), amending or updating parking regulation, as an effect of CCTV and license plate reader mechanisms being in place, updating terms regarding protection of identification data of visitors of office buildings who were required to provide a proof of identity prior to access being granted to them.

- Organizers of marketing campaigns: on occasion, consent of the recipients of marketing solicited email needed to be asked for again, as previous consent obtained under the former regime did not comply with the requisites of, for example, an informed positive consent of recipients. Marketing campaigns and regulations were adapted such as to implement also data protection regulations, which in many cases had failed to contain such, in the period prior to the enforcement of GDPR.
- General contractual framework, irrespective of business models or sector: since during the execution of any agreement, often personal data is exchanged, even when the agreement is concluded between business entities, either data protection clauses were taken over in the agreement or, depending on the case, data processing agreements between controllers and processors or joint control agreements between joint controllers, respectively, were put in place.

Principles Relating to Processing of Personal Data Introduced by the GDPR

In General

GDPR has introduced clearly spelled out principles applying to the storage, handling and processing of personal data, aiming to ensure the protection of personal data belonging to data subjects. To this end, personal data shall be:

1. Processed lawfully, fairly and in a transparent manner in relation to the data subject ("lawfulness, fairness and transparency");
2. Collected for specified, explicit and legitimate purposes and not further processed in a manner that is incompatible with those purposes (therefore adequately targeted and proportionate to the legitimate purpose), and further processing for archiving purposes in the public interest, scientific or historical research purposes or statistical purposes shall, in accordance with Article 89(1), not be considered to be incompatible with the initial purposes ("purpose limitation");
3. Processed in an adequate, relevant manner and limited to what is necessary in relation to the purposes for which they are processed ("data minimization");
4. Accurate and, where necessary, kept up to date; every reasonable step must be taken to ensure that personal data that are inaccurate, having regard to the purposes for which they are processed, are erased or rectified without delay ("accuracy");
5. Kept in a form which permits identification of data subjects for no longer than is necessary for the purposes for which the personal data are processed; personal data may be stored for longer periods insofar as the personal data will be processed solely for archiving purposes in the public interest, scientific or historical research purposes or statistical purposes in accordance with Article 89(1) subject to implementation of the appropriate technical and organizational measures required by this Regulation in order to safeguard the rights and freedoms of the data subject ("storage limitation");
6. Processed in a manner that ensures appropriate security of the personal data, including protection against unauthorized or unlawful processing and against accidental loss, destruction or damage, using appropriate technical or organizational measures ("integrity and confidentiality").

Rights of Data Subject and Enforcement

In order to give effect to the principles named in the previous section and to balance the powers of data subjects and controllers at the internal level of each controller, a self-testing of each controller shall be put in place and following rights shall be afforded and clearly communicated to data subjects, thus allowing them more control over how the personal data is processed by the controllers.

Right To Be Informed

This is a proactive obligation of the processor to inform data subject at the time when their personal data are being processed how and which personal data are collected, used or otherwise processed, as well as to be made aware of the risks, safeguards and their rights regarding processing.[9]

Under the GDPR, when personal data are collected from the data subject, the controller is obliged to provide the following information to the data subject at the time the personal data are collected:

- The controller's identity and contact details, including the details of the Data Protection Officer, if available;
- The purpose and legal basis for the processing (i.e., a contract or legal obligation);
- The data controller's legitimate interest, if this provides the basis for processing;
- The personal data's eventual recipients or categories of recipients;
- Whether the data will be transferred to a third country or international organization, and whether this is based on an adequacy decision or relies upon appropriate safeguards;
- The period for which the personal data will be stored, and if establishing that period is not possible, the criteria used to determine the data storage period;
- The data subjects' rights regarding processing, such as the rights of access, rectification, erasure, and to restrict or object to processing;
- Whether the provision of personal data is required by law or a contract, whether the data subject is obliged to provide his or her personal data, and the consequences in case of failure to provide the personal data;
- The existence of automated decision-making, including profiling;
- The right to lodge a complaint with a supervisory authority;
- The existence of the right to withdraw consent.

Article 12 of the GDPR sets forth that the above information shall be provided to data subjects in a concise, transparent, intelligible and easily accessible manner, using clear and plain language, in written form, including electronically where appropriate, and it may even be provided orally at the data subject's request and if his or her identity is proven beyond doubt. The information shall be provided without excessive delay or expense.[10]

Accountability Principle and Self-Testing

As mentioned above, under the accountability principle regime, the controller shall be responsible for, and shall be required to demonstrate compliance with the above-mentioned principles, related to the processing, handling and storage of personal data. To give effect to the accountability principle an internal analysis of each controller needs to be put in place, in order to formalize and evidence

9. Recital 39 GDPR.
10. GDPR Art. 12(5).

the fact that controllers have given effect to the accountability principle and that they have done so in consideration of their own business model.

This process commences by way of self-testing. Self-testing means that any controller should give thought and answer the questions below, prior to proceeding and implementing appropriate technical standards and formalizing documentation, and protocol these in a documented written instrument:

1. Which are the personal data which are processed by the controller? Here comes the balancing test into play, requiring that the controller only processes a respective amount of personal data collected from individuals required to meet the purpose of the processing. This represents a light touch risk assessment to check that any risks to individuals' interest and fundamental rights and freedoms of the data subject are proportionate for the controller's organization meeting the contractual obligations or the legitimate interest.
2. Is the personal data transferred to any third party, and if so, to whom? Does the processing of personal data comply with the principles and rules imposed by the GDPR?
3. Does the company implement a notification system of the persons affected, as well as to seek their consent to the processing of personal data by way of a contractual arrangement or on the basis of a clearly spelled out legitimate interest?
4. Are there procedures at the controller's level for the cases where the security of personal data is compromised?
5. Is the controller obliged to appoint a data protection officer?

Internal Analysis Part of the Accountability Principle

Unless it is obvious that an organization is not required to designate a DPO, it is recommended that controllers and processors document the internal analysis carried out to determine whether or not a DPO is to be appointed, in order to be able to demonstrate that the relevant factors have been taken into account properly. This analysis may be required by the supervisory authority and should be updated whenever necessary, if the controllers or processors undertake new activities or provide new services that might fall under the above-mentioned criteria for the mandatory appointment of a DPO.

Self-testing represents the backbone of the implementation of any data protection formal documents. This is because any internal procedures or agreements that are subject to data protection need to be revisited whenever the circumstances that were applicable on the date of their adoption have changed and second, as a formal implementation is to be avoided, and tailor-made internal procedures cannot be implemented unless self-auditing provide the answer to the substance beforehand.

Data Protection Officers

Data Protection Officers (DPOs) are persons who advise on compliance with data protection rules in organizations undertaking data processing. They are a part of the corporate governance of the business organization, act as a sort of compliance officers, acting as constant reviewers of legislation and data protection actions of the business organization that they are employed with.

They are also ensuring intermediary services between the supervisory authorities, data subjects and the organization which appointed them in this position and act as primary point of contact to the respective business organization, in matters related to data protection complaints of individuals.

Is the Appointment of a Data Protection Officer Mandatory?

Under GDPR, the appointment of a Data Protection Officer is mandatory in the following cases:

1. Where a public authority or body carries out the processing;
2. Where the controller's or processor's core activities[11] consist of processing operations which require the regular[12] and systematic monitoring[13] of data subjects on a large scale;[14] or
3. Where the core activities consist of large-scale processing[15] of special categories of data or personal data relating to criminal convictions and offenses.

All other business entities are not legally obliged to designate a Data Protection Officer. However, these entities may, if they wish to, voluntarily appoint a Data Protection Officer, in which case such person and its attributions shall be the same as the ones provided for in case of the Data Protection Officer appointed on a mandatory basis. GDPR also allows Member States to make such designation mandatory for more types of organizations than those foreseen under the regulation, wherefore Member States may extend the list of organizations that are mandatorily required to appoint a Data Protection Officer.

Who May Be Appointed as DPO

The DPO may be a staff member of the controller or processor (internal), or fulfill the tasks on the basis of a service contract (external).

11. According to the Guidelines on Data Protection Officers adopted by the Working Party on the Protection of Individuals with Regard to the Processing of Personal Data, "core activities" should not be interpreted as excluding activities where the processing of data forms an inextricable part of the controller's or processor's activity. For example, the core activity of a hospital is to provide health care. However, a hospital could not provide healthcare safely and effectively without processing health data, such as patients' health records; data should be considered to be one of any hospital's core activities and hospitals must therefore designate DPOs. On the other hand, processing personal data by an individual law office, as mentioned under para. 14 below, is not considered part of the core activities, although the lawyer requires the personal data in order to ensure legal assistance and representation of the interests of such client.
12. WP29 interprets "regular" as meaning one or more of the following: ongoing or occurring at particular intervals for a particular period; recurring or repeated at fixed times; constantly or periodically taking place.
13. WP29 interprets "systematic" as meaning one or more of the following: occurring according to a system; prearranged, organized or methodical; taking place as part of a general plan for data collection; carried out as part of a strategy.
14. According to the Guidelines on Data Protection Officers adopted by the Working Party on the Protection of Individuals with Regard to the Processing of Personal Data, examples of large-scale processing include: processing of patient data in the regular course of business by a hospital; processing of travel data of individuals using a city's public transport system (e.g., tracking via travel cards); processing of real-time geolocation data of customers of an international fast-food chain for statistical purposes by a processor specialized in providing these services; processing of customer data in the regular course of business by an insurance company or a bank; processing of personal data for behavioral advertising by a search engine; processing of data (content, traffic, location) by telephone or internet service providers. Examples that do not constitute large-scale processing include processing of patient data by an individual physician and processing of personal data relating to criminal convictions and offenses by an individual lawyer.
15. See, Guidelines on Data Protection Officers (DPOs), https://ec.europa.eu/newsroom/article29/items/612048.

The DPO shall be designated on the basis of professional qualities[16] and, in particular, expert knowledge of data protection law and practices[17] and the ability to fulfill the following tasks:[18]

1. To inform and advise the controller or the processor and the employees who carry out processing of their obligations pursuant to GDPR and to other Union or Member State data protection provisions;
2. To monitor compliance with the GDPR, with other Union or Member State data protection provisions and with the policies of the controller or processor in relation to the protection of personal data, including the assignment of responsibilities, awareness-raising and training of staff involved in processing operations, and the related audits;
3. To provide advice where requested as regards the data protection impact assessment and monitor its performance;
4. To cooperate with the supervisory authority;
5. To act as the contact point for the supervisory authority on issues relating to processing and to consult, where appropriate, with regard to any other matter.

Under Article 38(2) of the GDPR, it is set out that the Data Protection Officer acts as an independent authority within the company and may resort to a number of rights and guarantees to ensure that they may act in an independent manner.

Those basic traits of the functions of the Data Protection Officer are set out below:

- Data Protection Officers are not bound by instructions from the company, including from persons at a higher management level, as far as the delivery of their tasks is concerned;
- Data Protection Officers are immune from labor sanctions in connection to the way their advice was provided to the company, in the sense that, while their advice may be dismissed or not followed, they cannot be dismissed or penalized in any way for performing their tasks.

A group of undertakings may appoint a single DPO provided that he/she is easily accessible from each establishment. There is a preference that the place of establishment of the DPO is in the European Union.

16. It is a relevant element that DPOs should have expertise in national and European data protection laws and practices and an in-depth understanding of the GDPR. It is also helpful if the supervisory authorities promote adequate and regular training for DPOs. Knowledge of the business sector and of the organization of the controller is useful. The DPO should also have sufficient understanding of the processing operations carried out, as well as the information systems and the data security and data protection needs of the controller. In the case of a public authority or body, the DPO should also have a sound knowledge of the administrative rules and procedures of the organization.
17. The required level of expertise is not strictly defined but it must be commensurate with the sensitivity, complexity and amount of data an organization processes. For example, where a data processing activity is particularly complex, or where a large amount of sensitive data is involved, the DPO may need a higher level of expertise and support. There is also a difference depending on whether the organization systematically transfers personal data outside the European Union or whether such transfers are occasional. The DPO should thus be chosen carefully, with due regard to the data protection issues that arise within the organization.
18. Ability to fulfill the tasks incumbent on the DPO should be interpreted as both referring to their personal qualities and knowledge, but also to their position within the organization. Personal qualities should include for instance integrity and high professional ethics; the DPO's primary concern should be enabling compliance with the GDPR. The DPO plays a key role in fostering a data protection culture within the organization and helps to implement essential elements of the GDPR, such as the principles of data processing, data subjects' rights, data protection by design and by default, records of processing activities, security of processing and notification and communication of data breaches.

Relevancy of the DPO

Given the autonomy granted to the position of the DPO, in the sense that it *has autonomy* and related budget and decision-making powers to manage data protection noncompliance and related events, including reporting of such incidents to the relevant DPA, the functions that he/she must fulfill and the fact that nearly every company will deal at some point with data protection issues, the DPO should take a C-suite role in the corporate structure of such company, similar to CEOs, CFOs and COOs. Even if the GDPR does not position the DPO in the corporate structure of an entity, as it does not primarily deal with corporate structure issues, GDPR gives enough guidance to support the idea that the DPO should take over a C-suite position.

This would imply that the DPO would be in a better position, along with other C-suite roles, to take part in an executive-functional way to the management of the company, concerning data protection matters. As the CFO is responsible for the tax and financial matters and for conducting the financial records of a company, so should the DPO be clearly positioned to take over a similar role with respect to processing of personal data.

Simply having the DPO as an external advisor, albeit that it provides a certain autonomy specific to external advisors, does not sufficiently secure the fact that the advisor has day-to-day insight about the way personal data is being processed. Also, since the DPO is expected to implement and update data protection related policies, maintain close relationships with the chief information security officer (CISO), and advise and coordinate in-house training, ideally, as in the case of certain core functions of financial institutions, such role should be taken over only via labor agreement, therefore giving way to an employment law relationship, albeit stripped of the power to be directed by the superior management.

This would secure that the DPO is not simply a formal position that takes over such roles in many other companies as an external provider, but it is tied to the respective company.

Nevertheless, in Europe the role of the DPO has been taken seriously and many companies, despite not being mandatorily required to fulfill such a role, have decided to appoint a DPO.

Examples of Imposition of Administrative Fines—Jurisprudence

Administrative Powers

Each supervisory authority shall ensure that the imposition of administrative fines in respect of infringements of GDPR shall be effective, proportionate and dissuasive.

Noncompliance with an order by the supervisory authority, shall be subject to administrative fines up to 20 million euros, or in the case of an undertaking, up to 4% of the total worldwide annual turnover of the preceding financial year, whichever is higher.

Added investigative powers are granted to the authorities, as follows:

- To order the controller and the processor, and, where applicable, the controller's or the processor's representative to provide any information it requires for the performance of its tasks;
- To carry out investigations in the form of data protection audits;
- To notify the controller or the processor of an alleged infringement of the Regulation;
- To obtain, from the controller and the processor, access to all personal data and to all information necessary for the performance of its tasks;
- To obtain access to any premises of the controller and the processor, including to any data processing equipment and means, in accordance with Union or Member State procedural law;

- To lodge a complaint with a supervisory authority—without prejudice to any other administrative or judicial remedy, every data subject shall have the right to lodge a complaint with a supervisory authority, if the data subject considers that the processing of personal data relating to him or her infringes the Regulation.

Jurisprudence

Recent jurisprudence at the European level has shown that entities should be concerned with securing equipment under their control that grant access to personal data. Further, the recent jurisprudence described below shows that emphasis is put on the fact that those privacy policies and regulations should be tailor-made and drafted as accessible, clear and intelligible notions in mind, reproducing the exact way the company deals with the respective personal data. Abstract, protective and/or defensive wording that may be otherwise used in other circumstances should not be used in this case. Further, also the way that the information is structured is relevant when drafting privacy policies is relevant. Making wording difficult to grasp, or using any other language than plain, clear, accessible and concise language, leads to inappropriateness of those and thus to heavy fines.

Moreover, as you will notice in the Google case, even the ergonomics of the way that the information is structured may require scrutiny, as information which is largely disseminated, fragmented, and excessively spread out in various parts of a privacy policy may infringe the transparency and information obligations that the controller owes to data subjects.

CNIL Issues a 400K Euro Fine for GDPR Violations

Under the decision no. (original French nomination: "Délibération n°SAN-2019-005 du 28 mai 2019, Délibération de la formation restreinte n° SAN—2019-005 du 28 mai 2019 prononçant une sanction pécuniaire à l'encontre de la société SERGIC", an online real estate brokerage company has been fined by CNIL[19] with Euro 400,000 due to users of their online platform being granted unrestricted access to documents containing personal data (in the form of: identity cards, vital cards, tax notices, certificates issued by the family allowance fund, divorce decrees, account statements or bank related information) saved by other rental candidates by modifying the URL in their browser due to a faulty design of the website.

`The online platform missed a formal procedure of authentication of the users of the online real estate platform, but also the informational technical mechanisms to make authentication possible, thus allowing persons to access documents uploaded on the real estate online platform by other customers.

CNIL also underlines that this failure was aggravated by the nature of the personal data made accessible and by the lack of diligence of the controller in its correction, the vulnerability having been corrected only after 6 months and no emergency measure to mitigate the impact of this vulnerability has been taken during this period.

The documents sent by the applicants for the lease were finally kept for any length of time, therefore breaching the principle according to which personal data shall be processed for no longer than necessary for the purposes for which the personal data are processed, this to be assessed on a case by case basis by the controller.

The sanction was taken following an online check of CNIL, followed by an on-site check.

19. Commission Nationale de L'informatique et des Libertés (CNIL), standing as the French Data Protection Authority.

Deliberation of the Restricted Committee SAN-2019-001 of 21 January 2019 Pronouncing a Financial Sanction Against GOOGLE LLC

Deliberation of the Restricted Committee SAN-2019-001 of 21 January 2019 pronouncing a financial sanction against GOOGLE LLC gave insightful information on the above-mentioned requirements under the GDPR, as follows:

ON FAILURE TO COMPLY WITH TRANSPARENCY AND INFORMATION OBLIGATIONS, GOOGLE LLC HAS FAILED TO PROVIDE INFORMATION ON DATA PROTECTION THAT IS EASILY ACCESSIBLE FOR USERS

This is because:

(i) the general structure of the information chosen by Google LLC did not enable it to comply with GDPR, as the information provided to data subjects when seeking their consent was ergonomically unsuitable, by being largely disseminated, fragmented, and excessively spread out in various parts (Terms of Service, Privacy Policy) of the information provided.

"96. Firstly, the Restricted Committee recalls that, in accordance with the provisions of Article 12 of the Regulation, information must be provided in an "easily accessible" form. This accessibility requirement is clarified in the guidelines on transparency, in which the EDPB considers that "A central consideration of the principle of transparency outlined in these provisions is that the data subject should be able to determine in advance what the scope and consequences of the processing entails and that they should not be taken by surprise at a later point about the ways in which their personal data has been used. [. . .] In particular for complex, technical or unexpected data processing, the WP29 position is that controllers should [. . .] separately spell out in unambiguous language what the most important consequences of the processing will be: in other words what kind of effect will the specific processing described in a privacy statement/ notice actually have on a data subject?". The Restricted Committee also recalls that the accessibility requirement set out in Article 12 is based in part on the ergonomic choices made by the data controller.

97. In this case, the Restricted Committee finds that the general architecture of the information chosen by the company does not meet the requirements of the Regulation. Indeed, the information that should be communicated to individuals in accordance with Article 13 is excessively spread out across several documents: "Privacy Policy and Terms of Service", displayed during the creation of an account, and then the "Terms of Service" and "Privacy Policy" which are accessible subsequently through 14 clickable links on the first document. These different documents include buttons and links that must be activated to learn additional information. Such an ergonomic choice leads to a fragmentation of information, thus forcing the user to greatly increase the number of clicks necessary to access the different documents. They must then attentively read a large amount of information before they can identify the relevant paragraph or paragraphs. However, the user's work does not end there, since they will still have to cross-check and compare the collected information in order to understand which data is collected according to the various settings they may have chosen."

a) Language used when describing the scope/purpose of processing of personal data and its consequences was **too generic and abstract**, which impeded the users to **measure the extent of the processing and the degree of intrusion** in their private lives that they may experience. This was the case when the purpose of processing of personalized services in terms of **content and advertising** was said to be detailed as "*a necessity to ensure the safety of products and services, providing and developing services, etc.*" The same **vague** language was used also when stating that the "*information we collect is used to improve the services offered to all our users. [. . .] the information that we collect and how we use them depends on how you use our services and how you manage your privacy settings.*" The same approach has been used when describing the **legal basis** chosen to provide personalized services like ads. The Privacy Policy makes reference to the **consent of the user**, however Google LLC appears to make use of the **legitimate interest** as well, by stating that it conducts "*marketing to inform users about our services*" and above all to provide "*advertising to make many of our services freely available for users.*" It is not clear on what basis these processing are taking place.

Also, with respect to information on the **retention period of data retained for extended time periods for limited purposes** fails to precise the duration or criteria used to determine their duration, despite the fact that this information must be issued to users pursuant to Article 12, para 2 (a) of GDPR.

b) Information provided to users does not meet the objectives of accessibility, clarity and intelligibility laid down in Article 12 of GDPR and that certain information made mandatory by Article 13 of GDPR were not provided. This is because with regards to advertisement personalization "*99. . . . with regards to advertisement personalization processing, in order to find out the information collected for them for this purpose, a user must perform many actions and combine several document resources. As a first step, they must read the general "Privacy Policy and Terms of Service" document, before clicking on the "More options" button and then on the "Learn more" link to display the page "Personalized advertising". They will thus have access to a first description of the processing relating to personal advertising, which proves to be incomplete. To complete the information relating to the data processed for this purpose, the user will still have to consult, in its entirety, the section "Provider personalized services" contained in the "Privacy Policy" document, itself accessible from the general documents "Privacy policy and Terms of service"*"

c) Also, with regards to the **geolocation data processing**, the French authority claims that the same routed must be taken by any user wishing to track down information relating to the processing of geolocation data, which may be traced if accessing Privacy Policy and Terms of Service", "More options" and then "Learn more" until the page "Location History" is opened. Even this page does not contain all information as regards this topic, but the user needs to consult the Privacy Policy and consult the heading "Your location information". The information is neither available in full here, but the user needs to check every different source used to geolocate the user.

d) Also, if and when a user wished to have information on the **retention periods** for their personal data, they must review the Privacy Policy, then go to a heading called Exporting & deleting your information" and click on the hyperlink "Click here", contained in the paragraph on retention periods. The mere title chosen "Exporting & deleting your information is not easily comprehensible and is not correlated with the content of the information provider under this heading, wherefore it fails to be transparent and accessible.

ON FAILURE TO PROVIDE NECESSARY AND MANDATORY INFORMATION IN THE FORM OF INFORMATION TOOLS PRIOR TO THE USER REGISTERING ITSELF AS SUBSCRIBER OF THE GOOGLE SERVICES?

The multiple information tools that Google makes available to the users during their life as customer with Google, such as Privacy check-up tool and the Dashboard do provide indeed some degree of information on the processing of personal data and afford the right of the user to change preferences at any time. However, this information is relevant only if it is accessible to the user prior to registering as user of the Google service and not during his tenure. Such information must intervene at the time then personal data are obtained, therefore at the start of the data processing cycle, which is at the moment of registration as user and opening an account with Google, therefore accessing the Google ecosystem and not afterwards.

FAILURE TO SEEK AN INFORMED CONSENT OF THE USER

Given the fact that changing the configuration of the account prior to its creation requires for the user to click on an additional "More options" tab. Here, the displayed personalized advertising tab is pre-ticked with the consent of the user. WP29 Guidelines on consent specify that "*a controller must also beware that consent cannot be obtained through the same motion as agreeing to a contract or accepting general terms and conditions of services. [. . .] the GDPR does not allow controllers to offer pre-ticked boxes or opt-out constructions that require an intervention from the data subject to prevent agreement*".

Also, each purpose of processing must be consented upon individually and specifically by the user.

Case Involving Smaranda Bara and Others v. Casa Națională de Asigurări de Sănătate and Others

Case law of the CJEU[20] assessed that EU law impedes a national public administrative body to transfer personal data to another public administrative body, without the data subjects being informed of that transfer and of that further processing.

In the particular case involving Smaranda Bara and Others v. Casa Națională de Asigurări de Sănătate and Others,[21] the CJEU, the National Administration Agency had not informed the applicants that they had transferred their data to the National Health Insurance Fund prior to the transfer. The CJEU considered that the requirement under EU law to inform the data subject about the processing of their personal data is "all the more important since it affects the exercise by the data subjects of their right of access to, and the right to rectify, the data being processed [. . .] and their right to object to the processing of those data".

The principle of fair processing requires informing data subjects about the transfer of their data to another public body for further processing by the latter. According to Article 13 (1) of DIRECTIVE 95/46/EC of the European Parliament and of the Council of October 24, 1995, *on the protection of individuals with regard to the processing of personal data and on the free movement of such data*, Member States may restrict the right of the data subjects to be informed if it is deemed necessary to safeguard an **important economic interest of the state, including taxation matters**.

In broader terms, under Article 13 of the said Directive, the restriction of the scope of obligations and rights of data subject to be informed were restricted to cases of (a) national security; (b) defence; (c) public security; (d) the prevention, investigation, detection and prosecution of criminal offences, or of breaches of ethics for regulated professions; (e) an important economic or financial interest of a Member State or of the European Union, including monetary, budgetary and taxation matters; (f) a monitoring, inspection or regulatory function connected, even occasionally, with the exercise of official authority in cases referred to in (c), (d) and (e); (g) the protection of the data subject or of the rights and freedoms of others, **however formalized by way of legislative measures**.

As neither the definition of the data to be transferred nor the detailed arrangements for the transferring were laid down in a legislative measure, as imposed by the said Directive, but rather solely on the basis of a private arrangement between the two public authorities, the conditions for exemption under the said Directive were not met. The applicants should have been informed in advance of the transfer of their data to the National Health Insurance Fund and the body's subsequent processing of this data.

20. Court of Justice of the European Union.
21. CJEU, C-201/14, *Smaranda Bara and Others v. Casa Națională de Asigurări de Sănătate and Others* (October 1, 2015).

25

INTELLECTUAL PROPERTY CONSIDERATIONS AND BUSINESS RISK IN CHINA

Roger Philips

Intellectual Property (IP) Issues

It's no secret that China wants western technology. In the past Beijing insisted that in return for market access, western firms take on Chinese partners and share technology with them. Many US firms did just that, though sometimes withholding their very latest advances. Of course, there are other, less transparent ways of losing control of your intellectual property:

- Shadow factories manufacturing products identical to the ones being built legitimately for the foreign customer, using the same designs and expertise;
- Former employees competing with western firms using stolen IP;
- Fake look-alike Apple stores cropping up around the country, while the government restricts the number of legitimate stores Apple is permitted to open;
- Pirate copies of software, movies and books on offer for nearly nothing at street malls in every major city.

According to the OECD, 84% of fake goods seized by customs officials around the world originate in China (including Hong Kong), costing nearly US$500 *billion* annually, or 2.5% of global imports. Brands most often copied belong to US, French and Italian firms (www.oecd.org/industry/global-trade-in-fake-goods-worth-nearly-half-a-trillion-dollars-a-year.htm, 2016).

Chevy and Chery

In 1997 General Motors (GM) entered into a joint venture (JV) with Shanghai Automotive Industry Corp (SAIC) and Wuling Motor Corp., commonly known as SAIC-GM. The JV manufactures and sells Chevrolet, Buick and Cadillac brands in China. By 2003, China had become GM's second-largest market with a 13% share. Oddly by American sensibility, Buick is regarded in China as a high-prestige automobile and is in great demand.

The JV licensed the "Matiz" design from GM's Korean subsidiary Daewoo in 2002 and began producing it in China as the Chevrolet Spark. Shortly after its launch, though, GM had to contend with a copycat product, the Chery QQ. Chery Automobile Co. is a Chinese state-owned enterprise (SOE) based in Wuhu. (Note the similarity between "Chery" and "Chevy." One can hardly credit that this coincidence was accidental!) General Motors claimed the car was a copy of the Daewoo

DOI: 10.4324/9781351107242-30

Matiz. GM executives indicated that the two vehicles "shared remarkably identical body structure, exterior design, interior design and key components, and noting for example that the doors of the QQ and those of the Spark are interchangeable without modification." ("Chinese Chery QQ—a carbon copy of the Daewoo Matiz," MotorAuthority.com, July 6, 2006.)

The QQ far outsold the Spark, in part because of its price. At the time, it was perhaps the cheapest passenger car in the world; this was partly due, GM claimed, to the lack of need to recoup development costs. The Chinese government suggested mediation, but Chery was unresponsive, and even began exporting the QQ. In 2004, subsequent to an unsuccessful appeal to the State Intellectual Property Office, GM filed a lawsuit against Chery for piracy of the design. In response, Chery claimed it developed the QQ independently. The Chinese government, including the vice minister of commerce and the vice director of the State Intellectual Property Office, publicly supported Chery. These officials contended that GM didn't properly patent its technology. The suit was settled a year later for an undisclosed sum.

The *Detroit News* reported at the time had that "the dispute reflects the confusion, risks and ambitions in China's new auto industry, where global carmakers are battling pugnacious upstarts for a piece of what may become [and subsequently did become—ed.] the world's largest auto market."

According to the US China Business Council (USCBC), IP protection consistently ranks as one of the top concerns shaping the strategies and operations of foreign companies in China: "counterfeiters and infringers in China are increasingly sophisticated. They often exploit procedural loopholes, proactively seek to invalidate legitimate patents and trademarks, deploy advanced techniques such as reverse engineering, and find new ways to infiltrate legitimate distributions networks and build their own parallel networks" (2015).

So, what to do? Appropriate laws are in place. So first, be sure to register your patents, trademarks and copyrights properly with the relevant government entities. Do this early enough to prevent local businesses to appropriate your trade name and marks, for instance. Local legal assistance is required here. Then decide how aggressively to pursue discovered violations. It's an uneven playing field, and even if you win a case, the fines and damages may not be sufficiently significant to discourage rip-offs.

Don't be blindsided. Conduct periodic risk assessments of your vulnerabilities in country. Mystery shop, troll the Chinese internet and employ local consultants to see if your products, marks or technology are being illegally copied. Having a trusted Chinese partner to watch out for piracy can also be more effective than a foreign firm operating on its own. Join the USCBC, which regularly updates members on best IP protection practices. The US embassy in Beijing is a good source of local knowledge and advice, as is the US Department of Commerce website (http://export.gov/china is invaluable).

Here are some other ways to fight IP theft: separate manufacturing of critical parts in a country outside China with strong IP protection so that no Chinese factory can steal the entire design. Use the strongest available encryption and security technology to protect sensitive data. Be aware that Beijing controls the internet in China and that many key businesses are government-owned. Another approach is to make sure that local and provincial authorities are aware that if counterfeiting becomes a problem in their district, you will move your operation to another locality, costing the region jobs and revenue and costing the authorities possible bribes and kickbacks.

China has been taking steps to crack down on IP violations, but not until protecting domestic innovation becomes more important than appropriating foreign IP will Beijing really put teeth into enforcement. For more on this subject, consult *Best Practices: Intellectual Property Protection in China*, published by the USCBC in 2015.

Licensing, Joint Ventures and Acquisitions

It's often convenient, and sometimes necessary, for a western firm to hook up with a Chinese partner, or several. These may be charged with manufacturing, distribution, marketing or perhaps running government interference. While partners can be helpful to get started in China, many pitfalls await the unwary. Here are two significant historical cases where the western firm lost important markets and IP to a JV partner.

Danone and Wahaha

The story of the joint venture between French giant food purveyor Groupe Danone and the native Chinese Hangxhou Wahaha Group is a classic on how partners, playing by different rules, can get burned in China. To gain entry into the Chinese market, in 1996 Danone created a JV with Wahaha. Danone and its partner owned 51%. *Forbes* hailed it as a "showcase" joint venture. Danone naively believed that its majority stake would give it unchallenged control of the venture. The JV was assigned exclusive rights to the Wahaha trademark in China, though Wahaha later challenged the legality of this assignment.

The JV was exceptionally successful, with the Wahaha brand dominating the market in drinks in China. However, beginning around 2001, Zong Qinghou, Wahaha's founder and CEO, began secretly setting up parallel competing businesses outside the JV using the Wahaha trademark. Danone contended that by 2006 Zong had set up over 80 unauthorized companies selling copycat products under the Wahaha brand name.

Of course, Danone objected and began legal action, including filing for arbitration in Stockholm and bringing a lawsuit in Los Angeles which also named Zong's wife and daughter. What it didn't count on was Zong's ability to play on Chinese sensibility toward perceived foreign high-handedness. Zong and his executives publicly portrayed the French executives as evil and having taken advantage of an "unequal treaty," harking back to China's so-called Century of Humiliation by foreigners, incidentally including the French. With some justification, Zong objected to Danone's ownership of Wahaha's largest competitor, Guangdong Robust Group, as well as others. Danone retaliated by investigating Zong, his family and his executive team.

Danone's "reputation was badly damaged in China, where the feud erupted into a public brawl that became a case study in how a joint venture can collapse in China" (*New York Times*, September 30, 2009).

The French company sought several times to end the pain by buying out Zong, but these offers were rejected. Finally, in 2009 it was able to sell its 51% stake to Wahaha for an estimated US$500 million—undoubtedly a bargain price.

Lessons to be taken from this fiasco are several. First, the objectives of the partners were not clearly understood by either party up front. Danone was content to sit back and let Zong build the business, but Zong resented the degree of control exercised by the French, who in his eyes did little to grow the business. Danone probably jumped in with Zong, seeing a terrific business opportunity but failing to get to know the new partner personally well enough to be able to steer around his potential objections.

Other Lessons on Partnerships

Business in the United States is often impersonal, while in much of the rest of the world, especially Asia, the personal ingredient is paramount. Many trips to China by foreign executives, meetings over meals, reciprocal trips to the foreign headquarters by Chinese counterparts including local entertainment, sports events and so on, build a relationship that contributes to sufficient mutual understanding to align the interests and strategies of the partners.

In this author's view, every JV needs an exit strategy or prenuptial agreement, clearly agreed to up front. When the partners' interests diverge, as they often do over time, a clean divorce is far preferable to a public spat sullying the reputations of one or both parties.

Many foreign firms have made deals with new Chinese partners without adequately checking them out, only to be surprised later that the company isn't reliable. Or, you may believe you are dealing with a principal but find out after many trips and meetings that the representative you have met with has no power to bind the company and your time and travel have been wasted.

Also, beware of "ghost" companies. It's not uncommon to discover that the company you are dealing with isn't properly registered, or has taken the same name as a more well-known entity. It's imperative to engage local counsel to perform due diligence on any potential partner before negotiations get serious, and certainly before any deals are signed.

Chinese are famous for their hospitality during business negotiations. Beware of mao-taisoaked dinners preceding contract signings. But also note that the western view is that the contract is the final agreement between the partners, with mutually agreed changes and amendments being rare and arising only due to changed circumstances. To the Chinese, the contract is often just a starting point for future negotiations, not an end point. Be prepared for the Chinese side to reopen negotiations repeatedly during the relationship, even if circumstances haven't changed.

When agreement cannot be reached, the strength of the relationship can be tested. This is when the time and effort you have put into building the personal relationships within your counterparty become key.

> In China, the most typical process for resolving disputes centers achieving consensus between the parties involved. The *relationship* therefore is paramount, and the trust that underpins that relationship will be key to finding a common understanding. In the U.S., we tend to see disputes settled by lawyers in court or via the exchange of legal positions. In China, we expect to see disputes settled by partners getting together in a room and talking through the issues and differences.
>
> *(Lincoln Pan, June 23, 2016, https://blog.willis.com/2016/06/on-resolving-disputes-in-china/)*

This process is critically augmented by local advisers and supporters experienced in achieving consensus. The process might appear akin to western mediation, but it's more likely to succeed in less formal settings, such over drinks and dinner with the appropriate people in attendance. "Businesses need to be aware of local practices and expectations and they are likely to need some local expertise" (ibid.). If the dispute is serious, count on multiple attempts to resolve it. China values the concept of "face." Something of value must be on offer if a major concession is expected.

Changing and Conflicting Regulation

Carrefour

Carrefour, the French retail giant, got its foothold in China by ignoring national law prohibiting foreign ownership of retail stores all the while being supported by local governments happy to see its superstores built in their jurisdictions. To get a jump on potential competitors in the Chinese market, Carrefour opened its first store there in 1995. By 2007 it owned 100 hypermarkets to become the country's leading foreign retailer. Eventually Beijing came down on Carrefour, but the nominal punishment was well worth the early and substantial market penetration achieved (Fernandez and Liu, 2007).

The lesson here is to evaluate relative risks. Certainly, Carrefour took a chance, but weighing the benefit of being first to market with foreign hypermarkets versus an unknown future response from Beijing, Carrefour chose to deliberately ignore national law and move ahead. Carrefour is a smart company and undoubtedly modeled worst-case outcomes. Which was worse? Possibly being kicked out of China (low probability) or delaying and losing market advantage, perhaps never to catch up.

So we mustn't be too ironclad about obeying all laws and regulations, especially when regulations conflict and potential penalties are bearable.

After welcoming new foreign and high-tech enterprises for decades, Beijing has changed its tune. It seems the government is now more eager to protect established industries than to welcome more competition. There has been a number of recent instances of new regulations that have stifled planned expansion, resulting in lost investment. Two examples are in electric vehicles and foreign schools.

Electric Vehicles

In response to choking smog in the capital and elsewhere, Beijing has been offering substantial subsidies to electric vehicle (EV) purchasers—up to 60% of the vehicle's price. One result has been a flood of new entrants. "China's electric-vehicle industry, with 200-plus companies backed by a raft of billionaires, verges on a massive shakeout as the government imposes stricter technology standards on fledgling manufacturers and considers limiting their number to only 10" (Bloomberg, August 28, 2016).

As always, when governments attempt to jump-start infant industries, market economics get distorted. In this case, thanks to rich subsidies, many potentially weak entrants decided to try their luck. Money was raised and initial investments in plant and equipment made. Alibaba founder Jack Ma is among the many investors who have poured at least US$2 billion into building alternative-energy vehicles as China (ibid.).

"There are too many entrants in the sector, and some of them are just speculators," said Yin Chengliang, a professor at Shanghai Jiao Tong University's Institute of Automotive Engineering, who clearly holds no truck with Adam Smith's invisible hand. "The government has to raise the threshold. It's bad to see irrational investments in projects with low technology levels."

So Beijing is considering issuing only ten permits for electric vehicle start-ups. That won't limit established carmakers such as SAIC Motor Corp. and BYD Co. Those start-ups getting permits have more mandates to meet before switching on their assembly lines, as the government introduces stricter quality control measures. Even the lucky ten permit winners' products will have to meet 17 required technology standards.

One successful applicant is Beijing Electric Vehicle Co., which is controlled by BAIC Group, the state-owned manufacturer for Hyundai Motor Co. and Daimler AG's Mercedes-Benz. It will build a factory in the capital city that's capable of making 70,000 EVs a year.

Ban on New Foreign Schools

Investment in private schools across China has surged in recent decades. Education Ministry data from 2015 showed that China had 10,735 private schools offering grades 1 through 9, with more than 12 million students (grades 1 through 9 are the years of compulsory education in China). That is nearly 9% of all the students in these grades, up from 3% in 2004.

Driving the trend are wealthy families willing to pay for what they see as a higher-quality education. Some real estate developers promoted private schools as features to help sell apartments. Local government officials have accepted private schools as a way to provide more consumer choice and to stimulate the local economy, despite concerns that they exacerbate social inequality (*New York Times*, December 29, 2016).

In October 2016 the Shanghai Municipal Education Commission issued draft regulations that would sharply restrict international schools. Under the proposed regulations the authorities would no longer approve the establishment of any new private schools with "foreign influence" and would "bar foreign investment in private schools." However, these rules would not apply to international schools set up primarily to educate foreign students (ibid.).

Shanghai is the center of foreign culture in China, with the highest potential number of Chinese students whose families would like to see them obtain an international education. For those investors who were already far along in their planning to take advantage of the booming private school industry in Shanghai, this announcement came as a serious blow. Quickly changing regulations in China, arising from an opaque decision-making process, represent an ongoing risk for both new and established (foreign and domestic) enterprises in China. Firms need to do constant research into probable pending regulation changes, taking advantage of *guanxi*, government relations, trade associations and networking with other enterprises in their industries.

Acquisition Perils

As the era of foreign acquisition of Chinese national companies wanes, native Chinese companies have been ramping up their foreign buying. According to Bloomberg, a record US$246 billion of outbound takeovers was announced in China in 2016. "Last year's 137 percent surge in Chinese takeovers vaulted the country to No. 2 behind the U.S. on the ranking of global acquirers" (Bloomberg, 2017). Although Beijing is now attempting to slow this capital outflow, the lessons for the foreign acquisition target are to be cautious, know who you are dealing with, and have a break-fee in the agreement should the potential acquirer fail to consummate.

An example of how such a deal can go wrong for the target company is the abortive attempt in March 2017 by Chinese giant HNA Group's Pactera unit to acquire Jersey Holding, a subsidiary of US-based Ness Technologies, for US$325 million. Foreign acquirers of US companies must satisfy the US government that there is no security risk involved. The Committee on Foreign Investment in the United States (CFIUS) is charged with clearing such transactions.

Ness contended in its lawsuit against HNA that the company had

> provided . . . false, inconsistent, and misleading information to CFIUS and covertly worked to evade and frustrate CFIUS's ability to investigate and review the transaction, including by . . . implementing various schemes to disguise the true nature of their organisations, corporate structures, and ownership, . . . [including] that HNA founder Chen Feng and other executives held shares in several of its parent companies that they did not disclose.
>
> (Financial Times, *December 12, 2017, www.ft.com/content/ce65d6a8-def2-11e7-8f9f-de1c2175f5ce)*

Similarly, a Swiss takeover panel said in November 2017 that HNA had provided false information when it purchased the Swiss firm Gategroup for US$1.4 billion. Again, according the *Financial Times*, the panel held that shareholding disclosures were "untrue or incomplete" (ibid.).

The US FCPA

The US Foreign Corrupt Practices Act prohibits US firms and their employees from bribing foreign government officials. The penalties are potentially severe and include both fines and prison time for culpable executives. The United States is the only country in the world with such a stringent law on the books. So when bidding for business in a country rife with corruption, the US businessperson may be at a disadvantage.

In China, many of the largest firms, as well as smaller ones are wholly or partially government-owned. SOEs include the great majority of companies in energy, banking, transportation and telecommunications, for example. US firms must be aware that any bribery involving an SOE would fall under the FCPA. And apparently, many US firms are failing to recognize and control such activities. Regarding potential FCPA violations, "since 2008, the alleged misconduct occurred most often in China—33 times, more than all other countries combined" (Skadden Arps, June 2016, www.skadden.com/insights/publications/2016/06/china-and-the-foreign-corrupt-practices-act).

To avoid running afoul of the FCPA, it is recommended that companies doing business abroad establish robust internal compliance mechanisms and a corporate culture that eschews bribery and corruption. This rigor needs to extend to the ends of a firm's supply chains, as suppliers and subcontractors also can enmesh a firm in corruption-related difficulties.

Employment-Related Risks

Landmark Systems

There are several risks related to employment when doing business in China. The first category is risk to your expatriate employees on a temporary or short-term assignment. Case in point: while working for Landmark Systems Corp., based in Virginia, an employee was sent to China from the United States to troubleshoot Landmark's software installed at a local bank. The problem turned out to be worse than expected and was hampering bank operations, so the bank, using its government connections, prohibited the US employee from leaving the country until the software was fixed. As you can imagine, this "hostage-taking" caused some consternation back at headquarters. Happily, the software got fixed and the employee was allowed to return home. This kind of action is rare, but a company should be aware that a worker sent to China on assignment could run afoul of local customs, not to mention laws, as the following case illustrates.

Rio Tinto

A more famous example is the Rio Tinto case. The Australia-based mining company had sent its executive Stern Hu, an Australian citizen, to Shanghai to negotiate the price of iron ore to be sold to Chinese steelmakers. On July 5, 2009, Hu and three Chinese employees of Rio Tinto were arrested and charged with bribery and espionage. The case revolved around the Rio Tinto employees allegedly illegally receiving industry data crucial to the negotiations. Hu was sentenced to ten years in jail for espionage regarding state secrets. The arrests came soon after Rio Tinto had declined to sell an additional ownership stake to Chinese SOE Chinalco, which was considered by some to be retaliatory. The Australian government opposed this proposed transaction. To prevent further arrests, Rio Tinto, along with other foreign companies, immediately repatriated their remaining employees in China. As of July 2016, Hu was still imprisoned with an expected release date of 2018.

The main takeaway here is that many of the largest firms in China are completely or partially state-owned, and gathering trade secret market intelligence about or from these firms can be considered espionage—simply stealing secret government data. What might be considered market research could become espionage if SOEs are involved. Regarding this incident, Dr. Paul Monk of Austhink Consulting stated, "It's not unusual for the simple reason that the Chinese Government is one of the most secretive in the world. There is no free press over there. Anybody who tries to get this kind of information can be charged with stealing state secrets, just as Stern Hu has been" (July 2009). The Australian embassy maintained during the trial that the data found on Hu's computer was publicly available.

Had Hu and Rio Tinto been American rather than Australian, they might also have faced prosecution in the United States for violating the Foreign Corrupt Practices Act.

Reputational Issues

OSI

In July 2014 McDonalds, KFC, Pizza Hut (the latter two subsidiaries of Yum! Brands Inc.) and several other fast-food chains in China were discovered to be serving expired chicken and beef to customers. These products came from the Shanghai Husi Food Company, a Chinese subsidiary of US-based OSI Group, the world's largest food processor, which had printed fake expiration date labels for its products. Whether the fast-food chains were aware of this practice was not then determined, but this scandal was sadly typical of the state of the Chinese food chain (*Business in Contemporary China*, 2016). Shanghai police closed Husi's local plant and detained key employees. An insider revealed that the company's senior executives had encouraged the use of expired materials and the faking of quality supervision documentation.

Parent company OSI Group, which had established six other branches on the Chinese mainland in the company's 22 years of China operations, has found its practices under scrutiny, with shock waves resonating throughout the country's immense fast-food industry.

Ruling OSI guilty in January 2016 of violating sanitary regulations, a Shanghai court fined the company US$365,000 and issued prison sentences to ten of its employees. The court found that HUSI had reused returned meat to hold down costs. General manager Yang Liqun, an Australian citizen, was given a three-year sentence. OSI told the Xinhua news agency that the scandal had cost the firm nearly US$1 billion in lost revenue. In addition, the scandal "dragged down sales at McDonalds and Yum Brands in China" (Reuters, February 1, 2016).

One has to wonder, where was the parent company during the tainted meat period? Was there any independent oversight or auditing from the United States of Husi's operations?

Tainted Milk

A foreign firm need not own or control its investment in China to get dragged into a major reputation-sullying scandal. In 2008, it was discovered that many dairy suppliers in China had been adulterating milk and infant formula with melamine, a poison that boosts measured protein content. Eighteen babies died, 54,000 were hospitalized and some 300,000 others were affected. Subsequent prosecutions resulted in three death sentences, five jail terms and seven firings or forced resignations of culpable government regulators (*China Daily*, January 23, 2009).

The scandal began with revelations of contamination of China-based Sanlu's milk products. The New Zealand dairy cooperative Fonterra, which owned a 43% stake in Sanlu, said they were alerted to melamine contamination almost a month before the issue became public and pushed for a full public recall. There was an immediate trade recall, but local administrators refused an official recall (*South China Morning Post*, September 16, 2008).

Another type of reputational risk involves Chinese national employees of foreign-owned subsidiaries and suppliers.

Foxconn

Taiwanese firm Hon Hai Precision Industry Co., Ltd., doing business as Foxconn Technology Group, employs over 1.2 million workers, mostly in mainland China. The company makes most of Apple's products, as well as products for Acer, Amazon, Cisco, Dell, Microsoft, Sony, Toshiba and a host of other premier internationally recognized names. Its largest factory is in Shenzhen, China, where it employs several hundred thousand workers. This factory complex includes worker dormitories, cafeterias, a grocery store and a bank, all placed within a walled campus. As in many Chinese factories,

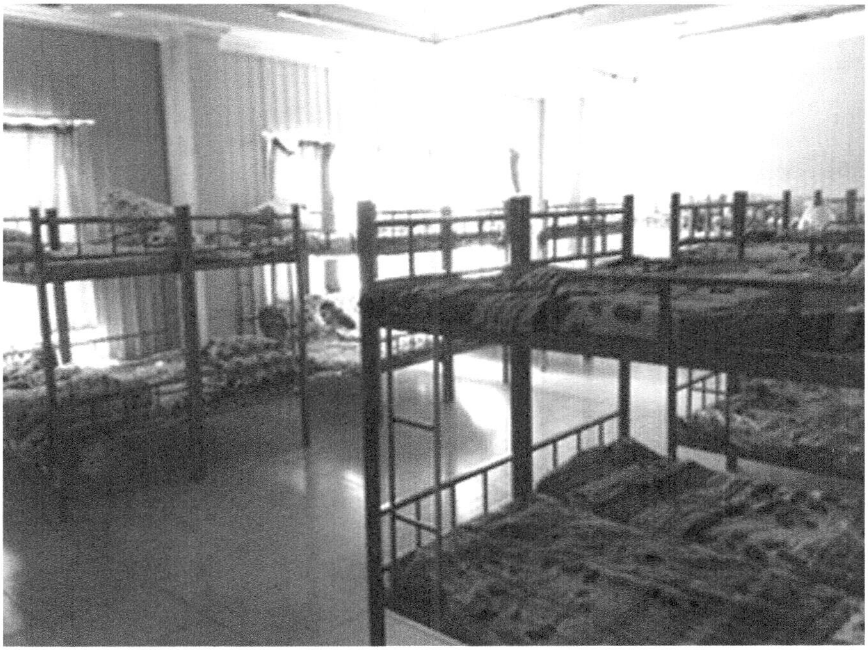

Figure 25.1 Typical Chinese factory workers' quarters.

Source: Photo by the author.

the workers live, eat and work in the same location. Living quarters are dormitory style. Many of the workers are migrants far from home, working six to seven days a week, 12 or more hours a day and seldom, if ever, being permitted to leave the factory compound.

A report from 20 Chinese universities described Foxconn factories as labor camps and detailed widespread worker abuse and illegal overtime ("Foxconn Factories Are Labour Camps: Report," Kenneth Tan, *South China Morning Post*, May 20, 2010); "Foxconn Security Guards Caught Beating Factory Workers," Shanghai: Shanghaiist, October 10, 2010).

These conditions can lead to serious mental depression. In 2010, Foxconn workers began committing suicide by jumping off factory buildings. A total of 14 employees died this way, making international news. When Foxconn is hit with accusations of labor abuse, its client companies can suffer reputational damage.

Nike

When supplier employment abuses are publicized, the foreign client firm must not attempt to hide behind a string of denials. A good model for dealing with this issue is Nike, which beginning in 1991 suffered from a withering string of exposes, protests and customer boycotts. In response, Nike issued a formal code of conduct for its suppliers and established a department tasked with improving factory labor conditions abroad. These steps, though salutary, proved insufficient. Criticism continued, sales were affected and the company was forced to lay off domestic workers.

In 1998 CEO Phil Knight announced that Nike would raise the minimum age for suppliers' workers, adapt OSHA clean air standards for their factories and increase monitoring. The following year, Nike created the Fair Labor Association (FLA), a nonprofit that includes other companies, human rights and labor interests ("How Nike Solved Its Sweatshop Problem," *Business Insider*, May 9, 2013). The FLA advocates for a minimum age and a 60-hour workweek. As of December 2017, there are FLA-affiliated companies in 20 countries, sourcing from factories and farms in 84 countries and employing 5.6 million workers (www.fairlabor.org/affiliates/participating-companies). Conditions at Nike's suppliers have improved, and the company now posts its commitments, standards and audit data for all to see.

IKEA

Chinese internet users went on Weibo (China's equivalent of the banned Twitter) to express anger at IKEA's recent TV commercial, calling it "sexist and twisted." The complainants were principally single women, an important part of IKEA's target demographic. The 30-second ad implied that without a potential marriage partner, a single woman in China would have no respect from her family.

"I just want to ask IKEA would they dare to show such an ad in their home country, Sweden?", a Weibo user wrote.

"We received some comments from social media, which reflect [the fact that] our television commercial has given people bad feelings," said a spokeswoman from IKEA China. IKEA responded by replacing the ad (Jane Li, *South China Morning Post*, October 24, 2017).

IKEA isn't the first foreign company to ignore the feelings of the Chinese consumer, continues Li. "In July 2017, an ad by German carmaker Audi that likened women to used cars also sparked outrage, with some people saying they would boycott the company."

"Don't ignore the feelings of the young and tech-savvy Chinese consumers, especially women," said Tang Xiaotang, of Chinese retail consultancy Nofashion. "Companies need to take a very careful approach when talking about topics related to nationalism and women's rights in China, as both are areas of high sensitivity."

Guarding Your Reputation

These events and others like them (though not always as deadly) have led foreign stakeholders to step up monitoring of their Chinese investments, suppliers and partners with on-the-ground monitors reporting to, and being paid only by, the head office. Monitors should be fluent in Chinese, authorized to conduct surprise inspections and snap audits (though being aware that a hidden set of books may exist), and to interview employees away from the workplace. Any delay or reluctance by the Chinese counterpart in honoring these inspection terms should be made grounds for terminating the relationship. If your firm sources from China or other Asian countries, establish standards for your suppliers, hire inspectors and join the Fair Labor Association. Set up an in-house watchdog to look closely for signs of trouble and be proactive. Preventing a hit on your reputation is much easier and less expensive than recovering it after it has been attacked.

Other Issues

Cybersecurity

China is acknowledged to possess powerful and sophisticated cyber hacking capability. Just as every firm must take all reasonable steps to protect its private data from unauthorized compromise from any direction, the vulnerability to China may be particularly high. Akamai Technologies, the US-based content delivery network and cloud services provider, found that by the end of 2014 around 50% of all cyberattacks worldwide originated in China.

To cite just one example, Dan Tehan, Australia federal minister for cybersecurity, revealed that in November 2016 a cyber hacker was able to steal "significant" data from an undisclosed Australian defense contractor (*The Australian*, October 10, 2017). *The Australian* went on to state that the hacker was based in China.

Beijing implemented a far-reaching new cybersecurity law effective June 1, 2017. This law, in addition to requiring built-in protection against hacking and malware, gives the government unprecedented rights to view internal company IP, including source code. All sensitive data must be stored domestically. Emphasis is on protecting personal data and individual privacy. Penalties for violation are severe, up to revocation of business licenses and fines of up to RMB 1 million. The law is so strict that in September 2017 the US government requested that China not enforce it so as not to disrupt international trade in services. Professional legal advice is highly recommended in this area (see https://assets.kpmg.com/content/dam/kpmg/cn/pdf/en/2017/02/overview-of-cybersecurity-law.pdf).

Insuring for Risk

It is usually desirable for firms to transfer some risk exposure to insurance companies. "China's insurance market is one of the most dynamic and changing in the world," according to Wise Xu, deputy CEO of Willis China. Xu goes on to advise that the market is very competitive. So shop around and negotiate for the best price. Note that insurance sales reps may not understand nuances of coverage they are selling. Also, be aware of China's changing insurance laws and regulations (*Navigating China's Growing Insurance Market*, Willis Towers Watson, May 28, 2015).

Chinese insurance regulatory oversight is becoming stronger, according to Claude Gallello, managing director of Willis International, New York. He further advises that there are special challenges in protecting company property, given that China is prone to natural as well as man-made catastrophes. China is well known for devastating earthquakes, train wrecks, and architectural failures due to rapid construction schedules and lax building codes. Furthermore, indications are that China is becoming a more litigious society and that liability claims are slowly rising (Willis Towers Watson, September 10, 2014).

Corporate Governance

One issue not addressed in this chapter regards corporate governance. Risks and protections afforded the passive or minority shareholder in Chinese corporations are different than in other jurisdictions. An excellent source of information on these topics is Feng Ma's chapter, "Managing Legal Risks in China" in the book *Legal Risk Management, Governance and Compliance* (Globe Business, 2013).

Conclusion

Despite the apparently daunting recitation of risks outlined above, many foreign firms have succeeded in China, with some now expecting the bulk of their future growth to come from that market. Certainly, China is different from any other country market in terms of business risks that may be encountered, but it is also unlike any other country market in possessing the largest population of potential customers. As outlined in this chapter, there are precautions that can be taken to keep business risk in China manageable. Forewarned is forearmed, as the saying goes, and in the above examples, most of the firms involved were taken by surprise, with a negative outcome. Being aware of risks likely to be encountered and taking reasonable and prudent steps to ameliorate the downsides can make doing business in China a more than acceptable proposition.

PART V

Best Practices Emerging From Lessons Learned

26
ENVIRONMENTAL COMPLIANCE RISK MANAGEMENT

Amber Baylor

Introduction

Environmental compliance relies on a multitude of self-monitoring reports and coordination with a variety of professionals (e.g., operations, legal, regulatory, engineering, nongovernmental organizations, and administration staff) to ensure achievement of environmental standards in a variety of matrices. Water, air, and solid matrices span the gamut of requirements for control, measurement, and reporting to local, state, and federal officials. The complexity of the matrices and the pollution control technologies utilized to minimize the risks to human health and the environment can be daunting for the nascent environmental regulatory professional. Compounding the complexities are fiscal repercussions for noncompliance through administrative civil liabilities and citizen lawsuits thus providing the impetus to ensure environmental compliance. Those potential fiscal repercussions are weighed in the analysis of environmental risk management and investment in pollution control technologies. This chapter provides an umbrella review of environmental regulations, systems to monitor the output of the pollution control equipment, communication between professionals charged with compliance, steps to take when environmental standards are exceeded, information management systems, enterprise risk management, and the basics of internal and external audits to ensure regulatory compliance.

What Are Environmental Regulations?

Before we start delving into how to manage environmental regulations, clear articulation of what environmental regulations are and how those regulations are updated is important. Environmental regulations are the set of enforceable rules resulting from either state or federal laws enacted by the governing body. The laws that enact the regulation start with bills that are carried by political representatives. Once the bill is passed by a legislative body, the law becomes a statute. The statute is then translated into a regulation. The regulation is then updated in the state or federal register, which is the official administrative record that an entity must abide in. An entity that must comply with that newly established regulation can be an individual, a nongovernmental organization, a corporation, or a governmental agency.

Environmental regulations can also be put into place outside of legal mandates by agencies that are provided statutory authority for protection of the environment. Legal mandates are politically driven processes that respond to acute or perceived management of human health or the environment that

DOI: 10.4324/9781351107242-32

are generally found in the mainstream public domain. However, state or local agencies may seek updating the code if there is due cause related to their perceived need if they have authority to create regulations. If a state agency that oversees a specific portion of the government code wishes to update that code, a notification procedure to the public begins and that proposed regulation will be released and then voted upon with the governing board that oversees management of the government code and associated agency in charge with enforcement of the rules within the code. This public notification process exists in both the legally driven and agency driven regulatory updates.

At the federal level, the Environmental Protection Agency (EPA)[1] is the lead agency which creates regulations on behalf of Congress and also enforces the environmental laws that have been established. The laws that the EPA regulate range from atomic energy, water, endangered species, toxic substances, air, energy, superfunds, noise, marine protection, and oil. More information about the range and depth of the laws EPA regulates can be found on their website.[2]

Environmental regulations are enforced through penalties that range from civil to criminal. The key difference between the type of penalties that can be levied are based on the concept of intent by the individuals that broke the law. In cases of civil violations, the burden of evidence must be just over 50% to prove that the entities knowingly broke the law. The civil cases are tried in non-judicial settings through administrative hearings conducted by the EPA.[3] This differs from criminal intent where there are focused actions by the defendant whereby the entity knowingly broke the law. In this instance, the entity is tried in a judicial setting, the case must be proved beyond a reasonable doubt, and the defendant can face monetary penalties and time in jail for their actions (or lack of actions) for compliance with the applicable law. The EPA's enforcement goals and framework for enforcement are articulated on their website.[4]

The types of laws and regulations by which an industry is regulated by, as well as the government body ultimately responsible for that regulation, should be the first key focus for anyone nascent to the industry. While the EPA is the federal agency, authorized by Congress to both regulate and develop regulations for the protection of the environment, that is not the case for all regulations. There are some laws that allow for the implementation of the regulations to be deferred to by states. For example, the Safe Drinking Water Act allows for states to claim primacy, which allows for direct regulatory oversight of public water systems. States may wish to develop regulations that are more stringent that the federal regulations, which is a key minimum requirement for the state to be granted primacy status by the EPA.[5] A reason why a state would want to have the authority to oversee regulation adherence relates to the policy interpretation of the underlying intent of the law. To review, the regulation is the interpretation of how the law should be carried out. In the practice of implementing regulation, this process is an iterative function, and the states may discover gaps in the intent of the law that the state would like to reconcile through the administration of their own program.

To run an effective environmental compliance program, the professional must first know the key legal and regulatory requirements by which the entity they represent will be held to. These laws and regulations are the basis for the permits that the environmental program will manage. In each of the permits or other rule-based documents, there is specific language as to the monitoring and reporting frequency to ensure that the entity is in compliance with the underlying law and is the focus of the next section in this chapter.

1. www.epa.gov/aboutepa.
2. www.epa.gov/laws-regulations.
3. www.epa.gov/compliance/how-we-monitor-compliance#investigation.
4. www.epa.gov/enforcement.
5. www.epa.gov/dwreginfo/primacy-enforcement-responsibility-public-water-systems.

How to Comply With Environmental Regulations?

As discussed previously, the EPA or other state entities provide administrative oversight of regulations. The most common administrative vehicle for oversight is called a permit. The permit is the document that articulates the underlying legal authority, provides the jurisdictional boundaries by which the permit oversees, articulates the sources of pollution that must be regulated, requires monitoring frequency on the pollution abatement control equipment/technology used to control the pollution, requires self-monitoring reports, notification procedures if a permit limit is exceeded, and the associated civil and criminal liabilities available when compliance with the permit is not adhered to.

While the permit or other rule-based document is the vehicle by which the overseeing agency communicates how to comply, the actual program creation and adherence to that program within the regulated entity is how compliance will be able to be achieved. One strategy for implementation of complex permits where there are multiple groups within an organization is a matrix system. This matrix system should be designed to connect the permit requirement to those responsible with implementation of the permit. A permit matrix may be focused on a piece of pollution abatement equipment or be focused on a larger permit which has many pieces of pollution abatement equipment. This permit matrix can be created in a software program that uses horizontal and vertical cells. A key design criteria difference in the choice of how to develop the permit matrix of the point of discharge. If the point of discharge from a treatment facility is the compliance point, then the permit matrix can be designed to incorporate all pieces of equipment used in treatment of water. On the other hand, if the permit is for one pollutant abatement technology, even if that technology is one of many at a single location, then it makes most sense to design the matrix to focus on the permit conditions associated with a single piece of technology.

In the case of a single technology permitted at a facility, the information about the permit should be included in the top of the permit matrix. Such identifying information includes the location of the equipment technology, the engineered specification of that equipment, the permit number, the expiration date of the permit, and any other relevant data related to the permit. Then for the design of a permit matrix, it should list horizontally the permit condition, the cited rule or regulatory requirement, pollutant limit, if there is a best management practice associated with the pollution abatement system, who is responsible for monitoring the equipment, how frequently the emission system should be monitored, where the data is being stored for future reference, what data approval path exists if applicable, and if there are any standard operating procedures related to the monitoring activities. Listed vertically are the related permit conditions that are contained within the permit. This type of matrix is a mapping exercise that is useful to organize the complexity of permit-related items and how an organization delegates the responsibility and who is ultimately responsible for the permit compliance activities.

Building on the permit matrix for a single piece of technology, the horizontally listed permit conditions start with the permit condition. The analyst or program manager will then begin to review the permit condition and to link the permit conditions to the conditions listed horizontally as articulated above. Beyond the listing out the information contained in the permit and coordinating with those entities internally, one of the most important management aspects is to then connect what is contained in the "rule/permit requirement" with external actions by the regulators. Rules can be updated in a more frequent manner than permit conditions, however tracking regulatory changes to the permits is an important aspect of management activities and will be discussed later in the chapter.

The pollutant limit is based on a numeric, but in some instances, a narrative requirement that the technology cannot emit. This "best available control technology" or the "best available technology" are common legal terms that denote that the regulated entity must evaluate in the design and installation of technology to limit pollutants from entering the environment. Environmental compliance professionals rely on monitoring to provide the evidence to regulators that the technology was designed properly, is functioning properly, and if not, then remedial action with additional monitoring should be employed to assist operations personnel in solving the problems associated with the pollutant exceedances. Monitoring requirements span all analytical criteria from volatiles, semi-volatiles, physical, chemical, radiological, biological, and microbiological limits as broad categories by which the permit will be required. Each one of these general categories contains specific methods that are used to prove that the monitoring is accurate. The EPA is the agency authorized to create and update methods that are then used in permits.[6] In general, a regulated entity cannot be regulated against a method that has not been released, through a public comment period by the EPA. Prior to release to the public, the EPA will validate the method through exercises with other laboratories to prove that the method can be successfully duplicated. This interlaboratory comparison is a requisite step in the approved method process which will be discussed in more detail later in this chapter. The EPA's Science Inventory publishes reports which evaluate these types of technical studies.[7]

The permit will refer to the list of approved methods that a regulated entity shall use to demonstrate compliance. The regulated entity may conduct those tests in their own laboratory or may have a commercial laboratory to perform those tests. In both instances, the permit matrix will serve as a guide to determine if the permit condition requires that the technology requires monitoring and if so, then who is responsible for those monitoring efforts? The matrix may also divide the responsibility into internal versus external laboratory if that level of specificity is required. However, a simple reference to the laboratory who will then make that determination would be sufficient.

Regarding monitoring, the laboratory or management should be the responsible entity directing staff the needed level of monitoring, or monitoring frequency required to demonstrate compliance. The monitoring frequency is the minimum level of analytical assessment of the permit compliance. However, although there is a minimal frequency by which the permit should be monitored, some entities choose the increase the minimum frequency to test how well the technology is functioning. This is a management level question as increasing the minimum frequency of monitoring also increases the cost for the permit compliance. With environmental regulations costs escalating with a diminishing return on the major reduction of pollutants, economic justification of the minimum frequency should be a key consideration in the management of permits and other related rules. However, due to this limitation, providing more sophisticated monitoring assists in the development of evidence-based policies to support regulatory updates.

In addition to monitoring by laboratories on the quality of the effluent leaving a facility, there are also field measurements that can be taken to demonstrate compliance in real time. There are many handheld devices and automated equipment that can also be or required to be installed for real-time monitoring. Sometimes, a regulator may require that a regulated entity report emissions data to the regulator in real time. An example of this type of equipment is called a continuous emissions monitoring system which is linked by an internet signal that will notify the regulator when the technology exceeds the permit conditions. This type of equipment is not normally deployed in environmental monitoring systems, as it is expensive to maintain and requires specialty trained personnel to keep the calibrated gases used to make sure there is an accurate reading maintained.

When monitoring of technology is completed, on either a daily, weekly, monthly, quarterly, semi-annual, or annual basis, reporting of those results is a requirement in most permits. However, there needs to be a technical review of the analytical data associated with the monitoring efforts. This step is considered a quality control (QC) check of the data. The QC of the data includes items such as the holding times associated with the method, the chain of custody, the raw data supporting the calculations used to summarize the data, and the historic tend of that data. Beyond the internal review of

6. 40 CFR Part 136.
7. https://cfpub.epa.gov/si/index.cfm.

how the data was produced in the QC process, the historic trends provide important information to determine if the pollution technology is failing or if there was some data quality check that was missing that could lead to an explanation of the deviation of the data. A large swing in data points could mean that the calculation was not accurate, for example. If the regulated entity does not produce the compliance data in-house, it would need to reach out to the external laboratory and ask the project manager for the raw data to back up the summarized data sheets. This will provide the evidence to the project manager that the data point was valid, and in cases where it was not valid, back-up to the regulators of the potentially honest mistake that was made to remedy a potential civil liability.

Once the data has been accurately QC'd, the report is then ready to be submitted to the regulator. The report is generally composed of the main components of the transmittal letter and the self-monitoring report. The transmittal letter includes any relevant or noteworthy items that you want or need to keep the regulated entity apprised of. This includes violations of permit conditions, missed monitoring events, or remedial actions taken by the regulated entity. An additional component of the transmittal letter is the attestation statement. This statement is the certifying statement that as the reporter of the monitoring information, you are stating that to the best of your ability, the information transmitted is accurate and complete. Included in the self-monitoring report are the analytical requirements of the monitoring period. Relevant information included in this report are the concentration of analytes in the waste stream, the amount of material discharge, and the expectant pollutant load. The permit governs how much of a load and/or concentration that the environment can bear without acute or chronic effects. Reporting of that information provides the regulator with key information related to the iterative function of the permit for potential future changes to the permit. The attestation statement also acknowledges that the submitter of the report is aware of the associated civil penalties for knowingly reporting false information.

This section covered the monitoring systems used to administratively oversee permit requirements, how to communicate the needs of the programs, develop standards, and manage the program are covered in more depth in the next part of this chapter.

Communication Protocols for Environmental Compliance

The compliance profession requires analytical skills related to the basic math used to demonstrate compliance. There are also important communication skills between departments in an organization, with regulators, and the public for management of a successful program. These communication skills should be clear, direct, and concise enough to capture the key components of the program.

One of the first areas of effective communication results from management oversight and setting forth the expectations of the program. This can range from formal, high-level policy direction from the board of directors on the minimum level of treatment for compliance, to more specific articulation of reporting date timing, exceedance thresholds and key performance indicators used to gauge the success of the program. The variety of standards that can be created to accomplish the oversight of the program should be listed and clear so that anyone in the organization can connect their job function to the required minimum standards. Employees should also have access to an anonymous system where they can report violations that may be occurring that management is not aware of.

In addition, management may set periodic goals within a permit cycle, annually, or as the political climate changes. Those management goals should be specific and achievable within the associated budget for the program. Without connecting the goals to the budget, program managers are doomed for failure. The management goals should also be included in a memo or other formal document that can be referenced and added to as needed.

Also related to budget are trainings that management should provide so that employees can adhere to the requirements as laid out in their job descriptions and in a more detailed manner, the specific permit requirements that they are responsible for. There are many ways that trainings can be attended to. For example, the EPA provides training through webinars that are free or low cost.[8] In addition, each regulated entity has industry-related advocacy and education groups whose mission it is to train personnel or to coordinate training opportunities with members. Changes in regulations, emerging contaminants, and new technologies are just some areas that should be the focus of new trainings to ensure that goals at the management or board level are achieved.

Training on how to implement new technology, maintain that technology, and comply with that technology should be accompanied by a set of standard operating procedures (SOPs) that relay the basic principles of how to achieve compliance. These SOPs are documents that should be updated on an annual basis or if there are new changes. The permit matrix described above can include an additional column as to the expected frequency of updating SOPs. By providing SOPs across the range of compliance activities, all staff understand how to perform their tasks in a clear and easy-to-understand manner.

Included in the communication requirements are periodic check-ins with regulators to determine if the goals of their program may predict changes in the permit conditions. While this communication is not to encourage regulators to change their approach to oversight of the permits they issue; the communication is to make sure that both entities move in step with the protection of public health and the environment. Communication related to resource changes, new technology opportunities, and changes in organizational structure are just some examples of how communication can be engaged with regulators.

The final piece of effective communication is the need for personnel to respond immediately to violations of the permit. Permits usually contain information as to when to notify regulated entities of events that can endanger human health or the environment. The notification procedure for events that are acute in nature can be required to be immediate or within two hours of the event. Therefore, clear communication requirements between staff and management is key for immediate response to permit exceedances and potential violations. In addition, biological response monitoring is an important measure to determine the effect of the spill on the environment. Ensuring that a biological assessment plan or other environment-related plan is in place provides the evidence that will be required to assess the effect and determine the type of violation that occurred (civil or criminal penalty). In addition, when potential violations do occur, there is usually a set number of days an interim report should be filed and then another set number of days that a final report is required to be submitted to regulators.

There are also violations that may occur based on review of self-monitoring reports by a regulated entity occurs. The regulators include the information related to the facts they discovered about a pollutant exceedance, anonymous citizen complaint, or any other permit-related administrative requirement that the regulated entity is charged with. In all of these instances, it is best to respond immediately to the email and letter accompanying the email indicating receipt of the letter with a proposed time frame for response. This lets the regulator know that you will look into the matter immediately, which can also affect the potential fees associated with permit exceedances. The more prompt the response, the better overall outcome from an effectiveness standpoint of management of the program.

The information in this section related to the communication of standards, goals, and communication protocols for the effective management of the compliance program. These communication strategies produce a result that can be linked back to the management and board oversight of the program. Management of all the communications and required reports in an efficient manner will be the focus of the next sections of this chapter.

8. www.epa.gov/advance/webinars-and-training.

Information Management Systems for Regulatory Compliance

Due to the breadth and depth of technical information and mandatory and non-required communication documents, systems for storing this information are required not only for present management of the program but for instances where reports need to be pulled for dissemination to the public and regulated entities tracking compliance. Storing information in a systematic manner will save the practitioner precious time and is also a key demonstration that the program is being ran successfully.

The definition of records can be quite broad depending on the type of system and the regulatory requirements with what the definition of records are. Permits, described earlier, usually contain a definition of what a record is and how long it is required to be stored. The required records should have a separate file system that the administrative office within a regulated agency keeps track of as the official version of that record. This makes for retrieval of the record much easier when there are requests based on the regulatory agencies or potential lawsuits. In addition, there are freedom of information act requirements that ensure that records are available to the public upon requests. Records related to permits would be a required record to produce.

Each regulated entity has their own strategy for record-keeping. These systems may rely on programmatic files that are then further organized by year. An additional system is storing records based on a library-based system of numbers associated with key file types which allows for searching and retrieving of files much easier and more efficient than sometimes random program names to files. This file system can also be referenced based on a master library outline that users of the system must utilize when storing files when more than one person has access to the files. This helps ensure that all files are accessible and easy to find. Another system of record-keeping that uses a number system is used when a report is needed to be created. Documents should be created in a chronological system so that there is an efficient collation of the report.

Beyond file storage is the storage of data in a database management system. There are many such commercial and noncommercial (free) systems that one can utilize to store analytical data that is then used to produce reports and then filed in the record-keeping system. One noncommercial database management system is called MySQL. This system is also the backbone of many commercial-type systems which couple the database with a graphical user interface (GUI) that provides the user with easier access to input data, especially if the user is not skilled in scripting language that is required to input and extract data from the database. A database of analytical records is one of the most efficient mechanisms to store and retrieve data and should be considered for oversight of a regulatory program. In addition, related the ethics of data production and reporting, most database management systems have the ability to pull a log of the inputs or deletions from the database which help reconstruct instances when there are discrepancies in reporting of data. With regulations becoming more stringent and sophisticated a database management system will not only help the environmental professional keep up with the pace of change, but it is also considered a key best practice for the management of data.

Outside of the internal management of records and data, there is information management which assists in the development of policies that occur by regulated entities. One of the easiest and lowest resource ways to be involved with conversations that are occurring related to developing regulations or technologies related to regulations are listservs. These are automated messages that are broadcast via email to individuals interested in certain topics. This is a great way to stay abreast of program changes at regulated entities.

Another mechanism by which to stay involved in the information needed to best manage an environmental compliance program are industry groups. These groups are financially supported by regulated entities as specialized interest groups to speak as the collective voice related to implementation challenges of regulations and to advocate on behalf of members why developing regulations may have key stumbling blocks that the regulator is not aware of. Many regulators do not come from industry so the practical application of the proposed regulation may not be understood. Direct dialogue by the industry groups with the regulators or the officials overseeing the staff at regulators is a good option to engage in when development of new policies is occurring. However, on the range of low- to high-resource needs, engagement with regulators through industry groups can be a very resource-intensive activity. This is due to the many number of regulated entities which may have slightly different needs or situations. These needs may not be met by all which can then stymie overall progress.

Included in the participation with industry groups and sometimes when common ground between members cannot be met, commenting on proposed regulations is another avenue for engagement with regulators. Public commenting is an art which requires the letter writer to clearly articulate what is good and what is bad in the proposed policy while also providing a clear ask to how the regulated party would like the regulation to be changed. This type of public commenting procedure can be very labor-intensive, as it involves direct engagement with the regulator, understanding the landscape of how the proposed regulation is anticipated to be implemented, and general coordination with other industry parties on how best to achieve goals. Public commenting also serves as the administrative record in case the regulation is to be challenged in a court case. Providing evidence to the court that the industry group exhausted all efforts to seek successful resolution is tool that can later be used by regulated entities.

This section reviewed strategies to keep the stream of information up to date and accessible for a variety of purposes. The next section will discuss how to balance time and risk associated with management of an environmental compliance program.

Environmental Risk Management

Environmental risk management at the very basic level is a balance between risks and opportunities. These risks present themselves in many ways, though not adopting a new technology, to not engaging in public commenting on the development of new regulations. When the benefits outweigh the risks, the choice on how to proceed is clear. However, when the risk of how to proceed are not clear, the practitioner and organization can spend valuable resources trying to chase a regulation.

For example, most environmental regulations contain legal mechanisms that require strict adherence to pollution reduction schemes. The governing body has legal authority to take civil and, in some instances, criminal actions against the entity who willfully breaks the law. The risk is quite high that the organization will face legal penalties, the management most likely relieved from their positions, and the tarnished public image of an entity that chose not to comply with the regulation.

However, especially in the case of new regulations or new policies, that risk of compliance may not be not fully understood, and so the associated interpretation by the entity may represent a risk when the entity may try to get ahead of others who may still be deciding how best to proceed. The risk here can also be considered high as a leadership position may not be the most cost-effective. Thus, the risks can be seen in the form of legal and economic factors that can produce unintentional results that the environmental compliance manager is charged with overseeing.

Each regulated entity must establish its own risk tolerance related to how it manages the unknown risks. To help inform risk tolerances, the entity should develop standards that structure as to how the compliance goals for the organization are to be met. This requires training from the bottom to the top with outlining of procedures to best accomplish the compliance standards. There also must be accountability related to meeting (or not meeting) those standards. The ability to report exceedances of the standard in an anonymous manner is also an important procedure as stated earlier in the chapter, to ensure that standards are being met, no matter the sometimes poor lapse in judgement.

Once the standards have been instituted by management, the associated risks should be articulated as low, medium, and high levels of risk so that risk tolerance thresholds can be established. These thresholds can then be used to create a more structured discussion with how regulatory risks can be managed. Without structure in the risk-based thresholds, an entity can never completely understand the true threats to their organization to weigh against the opportunities that can come from the regulatory process.

Standards based on the risk-based thresholds can be evaluated by performance reviews. These performance reviews take the form of audits of the program. There are internal and external audits. Most external audits are required due to the specific regulation that is being applied. The EPA provides guidelines related to their audit policy on their website.[9] An internal audit can be performed prior to an external audit to prepare for gaps in compliance that can be remedied in house. The regulatory profession does not have a single internal audit set of metrics that will work for each regulatory program. However, you can reach out to industry groups who will know which audit principles are integral for the program that the practitioner is managing. The most important audit principle is the role that ethics and integrity play in the oversight, management, and reporting of data in the environmental setting. Without these principles, an entity could fail all other standards due to improper behavior. The risks for an organization with poor ethics is quite high due to the connection to civil and criminal enforcement actions.

On the other side of the risk-reward equation lies opportunities. Opportunities in the regulatory or rule-making procedure can range in positive public awareness campaigns, reduced short- or long-term costs of the rule compliance, professional stature in government entities, educational opportunities, cleaner environment, setting of terms in direct negotiations, or a myriad of other reasons that may warrant a benefit to the organization. The opportunities also have costs in the need to hire technical staff to clearly communicate with regulatory staff, engage in the public comment period, and spend time with other professionals in drafting terms for the way regulations should be structured. While the ability to shape the direction that the regulation is going in can be important, that opportunity can also cost the organization monies that cannot be recouped. For example, for a small organization, the resources for this type of engagement are not normally available, thus many small organizations become members in larger coalition industry groups where their voice may be better heard with a smaller amount of resources spent.

In this section the risk management structures and thresholds were discussed to help professionals seek the best ways to manage their programs. Creating standards, evaluating risks, and allocating appropriate budgets to meet these challenges will ensure an efficient and effective environmental compliance program.

Final Remarks

Effective environmental compliance programs include knowledge of applicable environmental regulations, systems to monitor the output of the pollution control equipment, communication between professionals charged with compliance, standard creation and protocol development, use of information management systems, an understanding of enterprise risk management, and internal and external audits to ensure regulatory compliance. While this chapter provides the basis for a compliance program, the professional must be able to navigate the basic standards create working systems, and implement those systems daily. Direction from the board or other governing body related to how in depth the management of the system is required to understand how robust the system needs to be in order for the appropriate level of resources to be applied and what level of risk can be tolerated.

9. www.epa.gov/compliance/epas-audit-policy.

The environmental compliance professional must be able to work with staff members at all levels to support the systems created for success of the program. Practical implementation of policies is only as robust as the smallest unit,[10] therefore the professional must be able to link the sometimes vague environmental laws and regulations back to how those laws directly affect their management oversight to ensure that there are no missed details related to compliance with those mandates. The systems created require both a fundamental technical understanding of the requirements and a creative capability to read between the lines and communicate to those within the organization as to what is needed to stay in compliance. When those facets of met the environmental compliance professional will have an efficient and effective compliance program.

10. McLaughlin, S. Educational Evaluation and Policy Analysis Summer 1987, Vol. 9, No. 2, pp. 171–17.

27

COMPLIANCE LEADERSHIP

Don J. Polden

Introduction

The Importance of Leadership

The need for effective leadership is pervasive in our society. Leadership matters in many sectors of our society and in our communities, including political and governmental institutions, business organizations, many professions (such as law and medicine), and, significantly, for individual personal development. Leaders move our economic institutions, nonprofit and philanthropic organizations, and social and community groups, and they undertake the responsibility for articulating the goals and aspirations of varied groups and entities; they lead the groups' participants—whether they are shareholders or clients, advisory boards or employees—to achieve shared goals.

According to Stanford's Deborah Rhode, leadership training and education is itself a significant business enterprise which indicates its importance in our social and political communities and in our economic institutions. She notes that "leadership development is now a forty-five billion dollar industry, and an Amazon search reveals close to 88,000 leadership books in print."[1] However, she notes that that leadership education is virtually lacking in some critical areas of our society, such as law and medicine, while it is abundant in other areas such as business management and corporate operations.

Leadership education and personal leadership development in the United States occur in several ways. One important avenue through which leadership education occurs is by formal instruction at the college or university level, usually in courses that emphasize the prevalent theories of leadership, the biographies of acknowledged "great" leaders, and information about how leadership is developed in individuals.[2] Another route, which is common in many graduate business school programs, is to use empirical research to develop approaches to the development of sound, effective, or exemplary leadership abilities.[3] Personal and professional leadership development often attempts to enhance the leadership abilities of business executives, education administrators, professionals, and others so they can function at higher levels of competence in their positions. For key members of the organization,

1. Deborah L. Rhode, *Lawyers as Leaders* (Oxford University Press, 2013), p. 1.
2. See, e.g., Peter G. Northouse, *Leadership: Theory and Practice*, 7th ed. (Sage, 2015).
3. See, e.g., James M. Kouzes and Barry Z. Posner, *The Leadership Challenge*, 6th ed. (John Wiley & Sons, 2014).

DOI: 10.4324/9781351107242-33

there are useful leadership development and training programs that can be very helpful in advancing leadership and job performance abilities for these employees.[4] In addition, there are highly effective professional organizations and individuals that offer programs for personal or individual development of key leadership skills and abilities, such as by individual mentoring or coaching. Again, the goal of these high-level educational programs is to provide an employee or executive with a higher level of leadership ability to improve his or her ability to provide leadership to the organization.

Why do individuals and organizations spend billions of dollars, including the time key employees spend in leadership development programs and skills enhancement seminars, to build their key stakeholders' abilities to lead? The answer, I believe, is that well-led organizations are more successful—financially and otherwise—than organizations where leadership is lacking or, certainly where it is, failing. Moreover, many surveys have concluded that citizens have a greater sense of security and optimism if they perceive that their employer, organization, or government is led by capable, ethical leaders.[5] Importantly, countries, such as the United States, that are democratic republics, imbue their leaders with roles and responsibilities for maintenance of constitutionally based governance and protection of national institutions and governmental processes. These governmental initiatives and processes require great leadership.

Goals of This Chapter: Developing Leadership in the Risk Management Department

This section will introduce the important role of effective leadership abilities and the development of these abilities in the areas of risk management and compliance. It is intended to provide readers with insights into the importance of leaders and leadership in the context of compliance and risk management professionals in a variety of business organizations. Thus, the section provides an introduction to leadership theory and practice, including leadership approaches and styles that have been shown to be effective in advancing the interests of the organization. With this background in leadership fundamentals, the following section applies the leadership attributes in the context of the compliance function.

Leadership Overview: Learning Leadership for the Leader's Roles

What Do We Mean by Leadership? How Do We Define "Leader" and "Leadership"?

There are many theories of leadership and many perspectives on how leadership ability is developed in men and women. Moreover, there are many definitions of what defines an effective and capable leader and what constitutes the act of leadership. However, many of these theories and definitions share common aspects and similarities and can assist those who wish to promote leadership education. The following section provides an introduction to definitions of leadership and to prevalent theories of leadership—and, necessarily, permits a definition of who is a "leader" and what is viewed as leadership by society and our organizations.

At one time, the notion of who is a leader and how he or she leads a group was shaped by human observation and intuition, often influenced by the results or outcomes of the leader's activity. Leadership was defined by what the perceived leader did or didn't do and how he went about his work for the organization or group. Today, however, a great deal of the knowledge of effective leadership and

4. See, for example, the programs offered by the Center for Creative Leadership at www.ccl.org/Leadership/programs/index.aspx; and at the Harvard Business School at www.hbs.edu/leadership/.
5. James M. Kouzes and Barry Z. Posner, *The Truth About Leadership* (John Wiley & Sons, 2010), pp. 10–14.

effective styles of leadership is shaped by empirical analysis and a well-developed body of academic literature.

There are many definitions of leadership, but the simplest, and perhaps most inclusive, definition of leadership states it is a *process advanced through a personal relationship that influences individuals and groups toward established goals or desired outcomes.*[6] It is also very useful to think of leadership as a process by which an individual or group influences others to achieve positive, ethical change.[7] In this respect, leadership is really about a relationship of trust and confidence between the leader and his or her followers or constituents. More comprehensively yet, Joseph Nye defines the key functions of leaders in providing leadership: "The functions that leaders perform for human groups are to create meaning and goals, reinforce group identity and cohesion, provide order, and mobilize collective work."[8]

A few of the key concepts underlying the prevalent definitions of leadership (and the corresponding description of what leaders do) are:

- Leadership involves complex behaviors; it is a process of interactions with others.
- Leadership involves change; positive and ethical change; change is an outcome or goal of action by leaders; if an organization does not need change, then it doesn't need leadership.
- Effective leaders have many attributes that enable them to be successful in leading change, but one of the most fundamental is a having "vision"—an ability to conceive of a plan of action for how the change to the group or organization will benefit its members and the organization.
- Leaders inspire, motivate, and activate activity by their constituencies (followers, employees, team mates, etc.) toward a goal or goals; trust in the leader's vision for change moves the group toward achievement of the goals. In other words, leaders lead because those who choose to follow believe the leader to be credible and trustworthy and they share a vision for change.

These fundamental attributes of credible leaders and effective leadership are shared by most perspectives on and approaches to leadership, and together they form the core of most leadership development programs. The core attributes have been shaped by a history of leadership theories, some of which are discussed next.

Theories of Leadership

Mankind has had a long-standing love for its heroes and leaders. The Bible, the Koran, and the Talmud all feature stories of great and heroic figures who "lead their people" to safety, glory, or personal and religious growth. Gandhi rose from obscurity to spark an international movement marked by respect and compassion for the poor worker and his family. Early theories of who is a leader and how we know that he or she leads were built on these great historical leaders and the narrative accounts of their leadership. However, scholars and observers of less exalted, but still important, leaders began to construct more contemporary views of how we understand effectiveness in leadership and theories

6. Professor Deborah Rhode notes that "by some researchers' accounts, [there are] over 1,500 definitions and forty distinctive theories" of leadership." Rhode, *Lawyers as Leaders, supra* note 1, at p. 7 (citing Bernard Bass, *Bass and Stogdill's Handbook of Leadership: Theory, Research, and Managerial Applications*, 3rd ed. (Free Press, 1990), p. 11, and noting that "[t]here are almost as many definitions of leadership as there are persons who have attempted to define the topic"). Notwithstanding the plethora of definitions of leadership, the definition in text incorporates the key attributes of definitions across the spectrum.
7. Don Polden, Leadership Matters: Lawyers' Leadership Skills and Competencies, 52 Santa Clara Law Review, 899, 902–903 (2012).
8. Joseph S. Nye Jr., *The Powers to Lead* (Oxford University Press, 2008), in Deborah L. Rhode and Amanda K. Packel, *Leadership: Law, Policy, and Management* (Wolters Kluwer Law & Business, 2011), p. 17.

about how it was that particular leaders came to the forefront in their lives, jobs, or positions to become leaders and why and in what contexts people follow their leaders.

The most prevalent and historical theories of leadership[9] include:

- *The great man theory*. This perspective contends that leaders are born and not made and that great leaders arise when there is a social or communal need for leadership. This viewpoint is predicated on the idea that leadership ability is innate—you have it or you don't—and, therefore, that it is not an acquired ability. An important, but largely discredited, component of this theory is that leadership cannot be taught or developed in others.
- *Trait theory*. This perspective is similar to the "great man" theory and assumes that people inherit certain personal qualities that permit him to assume the role of, and be successful in the role of, leader. Again, this view has largely been discarded due to the lack of verifiable evidence that an ability to lead is a trait that one acquires through birth or position.
- *Behavioral theory*. This perspective asserts that leaders can be made and that leadership is really a set of behaviors that can be learned. This perspective is the antithesis of the "great man" perspective, and it argues that the capacity to lead is not inborn or inherent but rather the product of a deliberative process toward the understanding of and the development of the key characteristics and attributes of effective leadership.
- *Contingency theory*. This theory is similar to the behavioral perspective and argues that a person leads his followers due to the circumstances that he or she *is in* and to which the leader reacts. Some factors (or contingencies) that influence how the leader acts or reacts are the behaviors and needs of followers, the leader's preferred style of leadership, and various other situational factors.

Theories of leadership continue to be conceived as people attempt to explain why some men and women provide important leadership in a variety of social, political, and professional contexts and many constituents continue to follow them. The next section explains why people who provide or demonstrate leadership are able to influence others to follow and embrace the vision for change.

Types of Leadership

Related to the literature on theories of leadership are several perspectives on types of or approaches to leadership. The literature about types of leadership attempts to describe how the particular forms of leadership are practiced and conducted by leaders, including the circumstances they are in, the situations of their followers and their organizations, and the intended effects of the leadership practices.[10] Several of these types of leadership have been shaped by research in why people follow leaders and how those leaders embrace the need for change and motivate others to follow them.

Adaptive Leadership

This approach to leadership focuses on the activities of a person or persons to mobilize people around them to make progress on important goals, issues, and challenges facing them through diagnosis of a problem or challenge and then formulate action to address it.[11] But these actions occur within the

9. For more detailed descriptions of leadership theories, see Northouse, *supra* note 2, at pp. 19–257. See also http://changingminds.org/disciplines/leadership/theories/leadership_theories.htm.
10. See, for example, http://guides.wsj.com/management/developing-a-leadership-style/how-to-develop-a-leadership-style/; www.leadership-with-you.com/types-of-leadership.html.
11. Heifetz, R.A., Anchoring leadership in the work of adaptive progress, in F. Hesselbein and M. Goldsmith (eds.), *The Leader of the Future: Visions, Strategies, and the New Era* (San Francisco, Leader to Leader Institute, Jossey-Bass, 2006), pp. 78–80.

context of the problem, and therefore the leader must take action in the context of the challenge by adaption. These leaders mobilize through motivation and persuasion, organizing, orienting, and focusing attention on the issues and challenges and seek to bring the constituent group together for their common good.[12]

Transformational Leadership

This perspective, which is perhaps the leading theory of leadership used by business and political leaders, contends that people will follow someone who inspires them with a vision for achieving great things or improving the organization, for effectuating needed change in the organization or government. Such a leader inspires his or her followers by articulating a vision for how change (within the organization or in the political environment) can benefit everyone and then encourages and inspires them toward that change. It is important to note that the transformation often is mutual and reciprocal: the leader changes through his or her leadership conduct and relationship with his or her constituents, and the constituents or followers are changed by the leader's acts of his or her leadership.

The noted political scientist James MacGregor Burns was among the first to describe this form of leadership in the context of political leaders, and he examined why people will follow leaders who inspire them and who accomplish results by infusing their followers with enthusiasm and excitement about a shared goal or vision for their future.[13] According to Burns, the transformational leader brings the vision to life for her followers by her example and by her effective and inspiring communication to them.[14]

Transactional Leadership

Another type of leadership focuses on transactions or dealings between the leader and his or her followers or constituents.[15] The proponents of this perspective argue that effective leadership occurs within a framework of transactions in the workplace. The leader clearly articulates the structures within the workforce and how they are expected to perform. Reciprocally, employees or followers also know their roles and the expectations about their performance.

Situational Leadership

This type of leadership occurs when there is no one leadership style or approach, but rather leaders must choose the appropriate course of action based on each situation she faces with her constituents and according to the variables within that situation. This perspective recognizes that each situation calling for leadership is different, and the leader must determine what is necessary in each situation—what forces are pressing on the leader, what forces are pressing on his or her followers, what resources and competences are available in the workplace and the workers, and other similar considerations. A situational leader looks at the context of his workplace and adapts his approach or style to the developmental level of his employees or followers, including their level of commitment to the organization and their competence.

12. *Ibid.*
13. James MacGregor Burns, *Leadership* (New York: HarperCollins, 1978), pp. 4–5.
14. *Ibid.*
15. See Jim Allen McCleskey, *Situational, Transformational, and Transactional Leadership and Leadership Development,* 5 Journal of Business Studies Quarterly 117, 122 (2014).

Servant Leadership

Servant leaders focus on the growth and well-being of people and their communities, and not, as in other types of leadership, on power at the top of the organization. He or she shares the power of the organization (e.g., decision-making, planning, managing) with others by putting their needs first. The leader helps others to develop professionally, grow personally and perform as highly as possible.[16] Like adaptive leadership, servant leadership can be practiced or implemented by someone who does not have formal authority to lead.[17] The servant leader builds her leadership on a moral foundation through self-knowledge and the growth of personal conscience, and it is this foundation that permit her to inspire others to ethical, necessary action or activity.[18]

Interlude: Some Deeper Insights Into Leadership

Leadership and Management—Meaningful Distinctions

People often confuse, or conflate, leadership and management. They are different abilities. Some leaders are also effective managers; others are not. Some skilled managers have excellent leadership abilities; many do not. Warren Bennis, a great thinker on the subject of leadership explained the distinctions between managers and leaders as follows:

> The manager administers; the leader innovates . . .
> The manager has short-range view; the leader has a long-range perspective.
> The manager asks how and when; the leader asks what and why.
> The manager has his or her eye always on the bottom line; the leader's eye is on the horizon . . .
> The manager does things right; the leader does the right thing.[19]

Of course, there is no stigma in being a capable and conscious manager, and many organizations need effective management to permit them to achieve their mission. However, if an organization needs to change, adapt, achieve new goals, articulate, and pursue a vision of a new future, then it needs a leader.

Leaders' Attributes—How Followers Rate Leaders

How do followers—employees and others—rate the characteristics they most admire in effective leaders? Barry Posner and Jim Kouzes, authors of *The Leadership Challenge*,[20] have surveyed thousands of people across six continents and asked them to identify the top seven characteristics of exemplary leaders. Eighty-nine percent rated "honest" as a key characteristic, 71% identified "forward-looking," 69% identified "inspiring," and 68% identified "competent." The next most identified characteristic, "intelligent" was identified by 48%. So without question, the key characteristics most

16. R.K. Greenleaf, Essentials of servant leadership, in L.C. Spears and M. Lawrence (eds.), *Focus on Leadership: Servant-Leadership for the 21st Century*, 3rd ed. (John Wiley, 1977/2002), pp. 13–14.
17. Hamilton, *Ethical Leadership*, *supra* note 18, at 383, citing Heifetz, R.A., *Leadership Without Easy Answers*, p. 10, Belknap Press, 1994.
18. *Ibid*. at 383–84.
19. Warren Bennis, *On Becoming a Leader* (Cambridge, MA: Perseus, 2002), in Deborah L. Rhode and Amanda K. Packel, *Leadership: Law, Policy, and Management* (New York: Wolters Kluwer Law & Business 2011), p. 24.
20. James M. Kouzes and Barry Z. Posner, *The Leadership Challenge*, 6th ed. (John Wiley & Sons, 2017).

valued in admired leaders are their honesty, their ability to look toward the future, their ability to inspire others, and their competence and ability to get the job done.

Another thoughtful description of an effective leader's abilities and strengths identifies them as falling into five categories:

- values (such as integrity, honesty, trust, and an ethic of service);
- personal skills (such as self-awareness, self-control, and self-direction);
- interpersonal skills (such as social awareness, empathy, persuasion, and conflict management);
- vision (such as a forward-looking and inspirations); and
- technical competence (such as knowledge, preparation, and judgment).[21]

The highly valued characteristic of honesty is really about the leader's credibility and his or her followers' sense of trust with the leader. The interwoven characteristics of credibility and trust raise an issue of the ethical and moral foundations for a leader's actions. Leadership devoid of ethical compass is not true leadership, which is a useful way to distinguish political figures such as Hitler or Stalin, who are often described as "leaders" of their countries or sociopolitical movements but would not pass any ethics and values test or standard.

Leaders' Styles—What They Do to Inspire Others to Follow

As with the literature on types and theories of leadership, there are many topologies of leaders' styles. By "leaders' styles," we refer to how a leader gets things done; how he or she motivates and encourages his or her constituents to get the job done, or achieve institutional goals, or be successful. The literature on leaders' styles attempts to describe how leaders get results through their relationships with their employees or colleagues or teammates; how they move or motivate their followers to get results that advance their goals while also making the employees feel important to the mission of the organization or group. The following is a typology provided by Daniel Goleman, a Harvard University expert on leadership.[22] He describes six styles of leadership that are prevalent in our workplaces and other settings where there is a relationship between someone in charge and those who follow. Most of these styles are relatively observable in our lives, our work experiences, and in public life. Individuals interested in leading others should develop the capacity to employ them to get good results.

Importantly, these leadership styles, according to Goleman, come from the emotional intelligence of the leaders. Emotional intelligence refers to the capacity for recognizing our own feelings and those of others, for motivating ourselves, and for managing emotions in ourselves and in our relationships.[23] The four critical and fundamental capacities or abilities of effective leaders are self-awareness, self-management, social awareness, and social skill.[24] Our level of self-awareness permits us to understand our own emotions and understand their impact on our relationships and our work, permits us to perform accurate assessments of our strengths and weaknesses, and helps us develop and exhibit self-confidence. Self-management is important because it permits self-control, encourages our trustworthiness, permits us to take the initiative where it is needed, and focuses us on success and achievement of goals. The capacity for social awareness permits us to sense other people's emotions and needs and to demonstrate empathy for them. It also advances our abilities to organize effectively

21. Rhode, *Lawyers as Leaders*, *supra* note 1, at p. 4 (surveying dozens of references and points of authority).
22. Daniel Goleman, Leadership that gets results. *Harvard Business Review* (March–April 2000), p. 78. For more information about Professor Goleman's work, see www.danielgoleman.info/topics/leadership/.
23. Daniel Goleman, *Working With Emotional Intelligence* (New York: Bantam Books, 1998).
24. Goleman, *supra* note 22, at p. 80.

and to be cognizant of others' (e.g., customers or sports fans) needs and desires. Finally, the capacity for "social skill" permits us to provide leadership through conception and articulation of a vision for the group, the ability to build and maintain teams in the workplace, to effectively communicate with our constituents, and to be an honest and capable listener. This capacity also permits us to understand how to help others (e.g., our teammates or co-workers) develop their talents and to succeed.

Goleman's sweeping description of these key abilities has greatly advanced research and thinking on how effective leaders can lead groups in organizations. One of the most important findings that came from the research on these capabilities is that leaders with strengths in these abilities were far more effective in their work than peers who lacked such strengths and that they were able to create and sustain positive workplace "climates" that resulted in greater worker satisfaction and success of the organization. Of course, not every leader has a great abundance of every component of emotional intelligence, and many leaders are continually attempting to develop greater strengths in the components. As they become more proficient in many or all of these capabilities, their abilities to lead competently and successfully increase. In other words, these attributes can be learned and then refined and strengthened by the leader.

Building on his work on the components of emotional intelligence, Goleman identified six leadership styles that business executives use in the workplace. While Goleman's research focused on business workplaces, these styles are also observed in highly functioning leaders in other fields, such as law, medicine, and government.

Coercive Style

A leader using this style simply tells the follower (e.g., an employee) what he or she is going to do but doesn't solicit the employee's input, feelings, or suggestions. This leader believes in the adage "It's my way or the highway." This leadership style is generally not effective with highly educated or skilled employees, but it is often used in situations involving routine work, military combat settings, and other placements. Also, for example, athletics' coaches will often use a coercive, highly directive approach during critical periods of competition or preparation for competition or when more participative governance is not possible.

Authoritative Style

The authoritative leadership style involves motivating followers by making sure they know how their work fits in to the bigger vision for and mission of the organization. This leader inspires others by his or her knowledge, perceptiveness, expertise, and skills. This is one of the more effective methods of leadership with highly educated employees since it operates at a high cognitive level. The style is often used when challenges facing the organization or group have accelerated and it is necessary that a new, responsive vision or change in direction is necessary. A leader using this style demonstrates the ability to inspire her followers to keep in broader context the importance of their work and performances. This style is the most positive, and therefore most effective, of Goleman's typology of styles from the perspective of the enhancing the culture of the workplace and achieving commonly held enthusiasm for the organization's goals.

Affiliative Style

Leaders using an affiliative style value people highly and, while a coercive leader says "Do what I say," an affiliative leader says "Come with me; people come first and we go together." Such a leader builds cooperative relationships with strong emotional bonds; he or she builds loyalty and trust in the group or organization, especially if the group or organization has suffered through challenging and difficult times. It too has a very positive effect on the workplace or location of the relationship between the leader and his or her followers, and it can be especially effective when used by team leaders.

Democratic Style

A leader using this style builds trust and confidence in his or her followers and spends a lot of time getting "buy-in" from everyone. So all employees (or other followers) have a say in decisions that affect the team's goals. This approach works well when the leader is uncertain about what is the best outcome and what direction that organization should take, so he or she attempts to forge a consensus on how to proceed by bringing his constituents into the decision-making process. This style also works well in some workplaces where group orientation and shared commitment to the decision-making process moves the organization forward. However, this style is not as useful where the organization is facing an imminent and complex problem or where the followers lack the ability to make an effective decision regarding the particular problem or challenge.

Pacesetting Style

A leader using this style sets extremely high performance standards and then exemplifies them himself or herself. He or she challenges the followers to achieve his high standards and is critical of employees who fall short of his or her high performance. Often this style alienates employees who don't appreciate the leader's demonstrations of his or her competence and ability. However, it can be useful where the employees are highly skilled and self-motivated and are able to keep up with the leader's standards and high performance.

Coaching Style

A leader using this style spends a great deal of time helping employees identify their unique skills and weaknesses and encouraging their success. The leader makes agreements with individual employees about their personal growth and their success within the organization. Most leaders don't have time for this level of interaction with their employees but it is an effective approach when the organization has some key employees who are aware of their weaknesses and who are interested in self-improvement.

Goleman contends that these styles are all appropriate and useful depending on the leader's strengths and the circumstances or situation that calls for the leaders' action. In some (rare) circumstances, a coercive style is appropriate, such as when soldiers are in dangerous situations and democratic or highly participative approaches would not be safe for everyone on the mission. Moreover, he argues that effective leaders often use these styles in tandem or in conjunction with other styles. His research shows that the two most effective styles of leaders are the authoritative and affiliative, but also that leaders who have mastered four or more of the styles (especially the authoritative, democratic, affiliative, and coaching styles) have the very best workplace climate and business performance.

With these fundamental insights into leadership and the leaders "toolkit" of approaches and styles in mind, we turn to the application of key leadership abilities in the compliance and risk management department.

Demonstrating Leadership in the Compliance Department

This section discusses how effective leadership can be demonstrated in the compliance and risk management department, whether that is based in the organization's general counsel's office, in an office of compliance or in the organization's human resources office.[25] While the authority to implement the duties of the compliance function may differ between those departments or offices, the importance of leadership and how leadership should be practiced remain the same. Moreover, this discussion assumes, appropriately, that there is a "chief compliance officer" for the organization (irrespective of where that person is located within the organization leadership structure); someone with the authority and responsibility to fulfill and advance the compliance and risk management function across the organization.

As other chapters in the book describe, the compliance and risk management functions permeate the entire organization, and the success of the organization is highly dependent upon these functions being ethically and competently performed. The fundamental mission of the compliance function is to provide an essential line of defense or protection against activities that violate the existing internal or external norms of the organization.[26] But there are more roles that require leadership. According to a leading authority on the compliance and risk management function, "In addition to its role in preventing violations, the compliance function should play a strategic, advisory and consultative role in organizational decision-making."[27] The role of the department leader or leadership group becomes important for the entire organization because of the central role of the compliance function within the organization and because of the key goals of the compliance function to the organization.

To frame the reach of effective leadership in the organization, it helps to begin with the goals of the compliance function and their importance to the leader. The goals of that function include:

(a) providing input on the effective strategic management of the organization:
(b) deterring misconduct by employees, agents, or others whose actions can be attributed to the organization;
(c) enforcing the organization's code of ethics;
(d) investigating and identifying violations of the law;
(e) establishing and maintaining a culture of ethics and compliance within the organization; and
(f) lowering the organization's expenses by preventing legal violations in a cost-effective manner.[28]

Attaining these goals requires leadership within the department and across the organization, and this is especially important because of the ethical dimensions that inhere in the functions performed by the department. This is a very important issue for the chief compliance officer whether he or she is also the general counsel or head of human resources. The scope of the leader's duties include representing the compliance team across the entire organization as well as providing leadership within the compliance unit or department.

25. There are considerable differences between these organizational departments in how leadership can be demonstrated, but that topic is discussed elsewhere in the book. For purposes of these chapter, we can assume that the office must have effective leadership and that those leaders—general counsel, head of the compliance department or function, or director of human resources—must employ thoughtfully appropriate theories and styles of leadership.
26. American Law Institute, Principles of Law: Compliance, Risk Management and Enforcement, § 5.01 (Tentative Draft No. 1, April, 4, 2019) (hereinafter "ALI Principles of Compliance"). The Restatement further provides that "in many complex organizations, the compliance function is assigned to a specialized compliance department headed by an officer with a title such as 'chief compliance officer.'" *Ibid.*, cmt. a.
27. *Ibid.*, p. 162.
28. *Ibid.*, § 5.02.

So, how does a compliance department leader frame his or her leadership styles and approaches to the compliance team? What are the most effective practices that will ensure the success of the compliance functions in and across the organization?

The research in the field, as well as the best practices for organizational leadership, suggests that the following leadership approaches and practices will permit the department leader to excel in leading the compliance department in achieving its mission.

1. Establish yourself as a credible leader worthy of your team's commitment, respect, and effort.

   The single greatest attribute of an effective leader is his or her ability to be perceived as credible by followers and constituents. This requires that the leader earn the respect of his group "modeling the way" for them to follow.[29] This requires deliberate action that sets the tone, integrity, and purpose of the department; in other words, he or she creates a culture of compliance and leads others in building that culture.[30] How does a purposeful leader achieve this? She must have a clear understanding of her values as a person and as a leader. Leading leadership experts Jim Kouzes and Barry Posner refer to this a "clarifying your values," a process that involving candid assessment by the leader of his values and the reception of those values by his followers.[31] Similarly, Harvard's Daniel Goleman encourages leaders to develop an advanced capacity for self-knowledge, self-reflection, and self-management that will permit them to exercise the leadership styles necessary to create a culture of success in the organization.[32] Knowing your values permits you to lead by example and inspire the confidence of your group. If you don't know why others should follow you, they won't. Kouzes and Posner have assembled a substantial body of research as to why people follow a leader, and their findings are that it is all about trustworthiness, credibility, and honesty.[33] Successful leaders do what they say they will do.

2. Build your credibility by articulating a vision for the department around the ethical purposes of the compliance function. Make yourself a beacon of ethical wisdom and comportment for the department.

   Ethical leadership requires that those in leadership roles have three traits—they are themselves motivated by ethical beliefs and values, they expect others in the organization to be motivated by the same values, and they establish a "culture" of ethical commitment within the organization. It is difficult to sensibly preach ethical conduct without being highly ethical yourself. Ethical comportment and values are important for all lawyers and business leaders, but they are especially important for the leadership of the compliance and risk management unit. As the American Law Institute's (ALI's) Principles of Compliance state: "The compliance function is not exclusively concerned with legal norms. The organization may elect to impose other standards or norms of behavior on itself and its agents and employees."[34] The compliance function is inherently about setting and enforcing appropriate levels of ethical behavior, perhaps articulated formally in a "code of ethics" for the organization, across the organization. It is about compliance with

29. Kouzes and Posner, *supra* note 20.
30. The ALI explains that "the compliance function is a key element in establishing and maintaining an organizational culture of ethics and compliance within an organization . . . [and] . . . that the organization itself is committed to maintaining a culture of compliance." ALI Principles of Compliance, *supra* note 26, § 5.02, cmt. e, p. 163.
31. Kouzes and Posner, *supra* note 20, at 50–51 (describing research showing that "to be the most effective, every leader must learn to find the voice that represents who he or she is").
32. Goleman, *supra* note 22, at 80–81.
33. Kouzes and Posner, *supra* note 20, at 28–39.
34. ALI Principles of Compliance, *supra* note 26, at cmt. c, p. 163.

existent legal norms and requirements but also a statement about the organization's leadership's ethical values and expectations.

3. Communicate an inspiring vision for the success of the compliance mission and the team that is charged with achieving it.

In addition to strong ethical values, a core foundation to great leadership is the ability to communicate an inspiring and truthful message about the organization's needs and goals. An effective leader regularly engages in a significant amount of messaging and communications motivating others through various methods of inspired verbal and other communication. Leadership communications expert Deborah Barnett estimates that more than 80% of a leader's time is spent in communication with external and internal constituencies.[35] A chief compliance officer must be a master of timely, efficient and pertinent communications with her team and throughout the organization. This communication function of the chief compliance leader (and the compliance department) is crucial, as he or she must establish and maintain a culture of ethics and compliance across the entire organization, so persuasive communication is essential.

Leaders inspire others to action through honest communication encouraging them to join together to pursue the mission articulated by the leader and embraced by the group. Santa Clara's Bob Cullen, writing about lawyer-leaders, argues that of the many communication approaches, the most effective are those rooted in inspiration, personal appeal, and building teams or coalitions.[36]

4. Lead the team without fear of mistakes or failure; innovate and create a culture of experimentation and courage.

Leadership requires courage. It is most acutely necessary when there are challenges—external and internal—to the organization, and those situations require a fearless, but thoughtful, exercise of leadership. To grow the organization and the teams that drive positive change in the organization, it is necessary to create processes for innovation and change.[37] The process of innovation can be successful only where the team is comfortable with failure, when attempts at change do not succeed, and the team learns from the failure. Obviously, there is a point where too many failures accumulate and it becomes evident that change will not happen. But effective leaders inspire their teams to experiment and possibly even fail before success is achieved, important change is realized, and the team continues to push the mission forward.

This is daunting work in compliance and risk management departments because the essence of managing risk can be viewed as aversion to failure, to pursue change processes that are not likely to fail because that increases risk. It is therefore incumbent upon the leader of the department

35. Deborah J. Barrett, *Leadership Communication: A Communications Approach for Senior Level Managers* (Emerald Group, 2006), pp. 385, https://hodactuc.files.wordpress.com/2016/03/meeting_4_reading_leadershipcommunication-acommunicationapproachforsenior-levelmanagers-barrett.pdf.

36. Robert Cullen, *The Leading Lawyer*, 94–95 (West, 2010). Cullen cites research identifying the nice communication approaches available to leaders—rational persuasion, inspirational appeal, consultation, ingratiation, exchange, personal appeal, coalition building, legitimating, and pressure—and argues that lawyers are more successful by using collaborative and non-pressuring approaches.

37. See Donald J. Polden, *Lawyers, Leadership, and Innovation*, 58 Santa Clara Law Review 427, 436–442 (2018) (describing the importance of innovation processes in organization and the challenges to effective leadership of innovation in law firms). Polden points out that

> we know that innovation is a group process initiated by effective leaders and that it does not happen by itself, but rather, must be initiated and guided. We also know that innovation processes sometimes result in failure, often leading to further experimentation and adaptation, and hopefully, an approach that addresses the challenges facing the group. Finally, we know that innovation process results need critical assessment and monitoring to ensure that they result in what the organization needs.
>
> *Ibid.* at 439.

to lead the process by supporting and encouraging his team to pursue change needed to assure compliance with legal and ethical norms but also to brook acceptable risk that something will not work.

5. Encourage collaboration by the team.

   It should be obvious that the compliance mission will only be as successful as the compliance and risk management team, under thoughtful leadership, can accomplish through their commitment to the vision for the compliance mission. Once the vision for the success of the compliance function is articulated and embraced, it is then all about execution, and that is when a highly energized and committed team becomes essential. The instrumental importance of the leader does not end at getting shared commitment to an overarching vision for the success of the mission. Rather, it is critical that the compliance leader build and support a highly effective team to carry out the mission. There are few areas in large organizations where effective team work is as necessary as the compliance function, and that requires great leadership.

   What does an effective leader need to consider (and then act upon) in creating teams to implement the vision for the compliance function? Professor John P. Kotter of Harvard Business School has argued that for teams to effect significant change or respond to a critical challenge to the organization, they need to (1) have a sense of urgency; that the organization needs change and quickly; (2) a vision (often from the leader) for change; a purpose and direction; (3) communication about and agreement by team members (and, eventually, by key constituents in the organization) on the action necessary to address the challenge; and (4) an institutionalization of the changes and innovations into the organizations processes, culture, and habits.[38]

6. Support the team and value their successes.

   Organizational leadership is about motivation, direction, and inspiration of the group charged with fulfilling the mission. This requires great care and management by the leader throughout the group's effort, from the beginning to the end. As Kouzes and Posner have argued, credible leaders inspire loyalty and commitment by their followers,[39] from the creation of the new plan or strategic vision to the completion of the task or challenge or change. The leader must support the team through guidance, expectations for success, assessment (even criticism) for the team's efforts, and "thanks, for a job well done" at the conclusion.

   This view of the leader's role in the team-building process is critical to the role of creating and maintaining a "culture of compliance" that the ALI Principles of Compliance articulate as essential to the compliance and risk management function: "An active, vigorous and visible compliance function communicates to others in the organization not only that they risk sanctions if they commit violations, but also that the organization itself is committed to maintaining a culture of compliance."[40]

7. Expect, accept, and embrace accountability

   The ALI Principles of Compliance articulate the importance of compliance accountability: "organizations should undertake reasonable measures to ensure that employees conform to the requirements of law and the organization's compliance policies and procedures and code of ethics, as well as other applicable norms, when acting on behalf of the organization."[41] The compliance function is truly about accountability for ethical and legal activities and decisions

38. John P. Kotter, *Leading Change: Why Transformation Efforts Fail*, HARV.BUS.REV. 59 (March–April 1919), https://hbr.org/2007/01/leading-change-why-transformation-efforts-fail (January 2007).
39. James Kouzes and Barry Posner, *Credibility* (Jossey-Bass 2011), p. 27.
40. ALI Principles of Compliance, *supra* note 26, at cmt. e, p. 163.
41. *Ibid.* at § 5.03, cmt. a, p. 167.

across the organization. The role of the leader must be to articulate the need to such activities and decisions and to hold his or her team to those standards and to expect that all employees in the organization act with appropriate ethical and legal behavior.

Conclusion

The theme of this chapter is that leadership matters, and it especially matters in the compliance department or unit of nearly all organizations. To comply with the law and the internal and external ethical expectations of the firm's employees and customers is a core goal and mission of the compliance department. But this does not happen without inspired and energetic leadership. The chapter has described seven essential practices that the chief compliance officer (and his or her compliance unit or department) should implement to fulfill the compliance function. But, in many respects, thoughtful adherence to these practices is simply the beginning of the important process of developing a culture of compliance within the organization and inspiring the adherence and following of all members of the organization.

28

ETHICS AND LEADERSHIP

LaSharnda Beckwith

Introduction

Some would never attribute the lack of ethical behavior in organizations to a lack of a spiritual connectedness. However, one could argue that very point. Spirituality lies at the heart of the moral compass of individuals, and those individuals set the tone and establish the culture of the organizations they lead (Agbim et al., 2013). As scandals increase, public distrust also increases. Scandals range from discrimination, sexual harassment, unfair labor practices, cheating, fraud and the establishment of programs that profit the leaders while at the same time hurting the customers they serve.

Well before the scandals of the turn of the 21st century, including Enron, WorldCom and Tyco, corporations had struggled with their leaders behaving ethically. As other scandals have come to the forefront, there continues to be a repeat of unethical practices. In fact, because of leadership greed, laws were enacted to help protect the public. Although additional laws were established decades earlier due to unethical practices, they seem to have very little influence in changing behaviors. One such law was the Sarbanes-Oxley Act of 2002.

The Sarbanes-Oxley Act of 2002 is also known as the "Public Company Accounting Reform and Investor Protection Act" and "Corporate and Auditing Accountability, Responsibility, and Transparency Act." This is a US federal law that set new or expanded requirements for all US public company boards, management and public accounting firms with a number of provisions that apply to privately held firms also. Sarbanes-Oxley was enacted as a reaction to a number of major corporate and accounting scandals, including Enron and WorldCom.

Yet, after all the attention given to the biggest scandals of that era, we continue to see a rise in bad behavior. One of the largest corporate scandals of 2018 came from the sovereign wealth fund, 1Malaysia Development Berhad, which was created to attract foreign investment. Instead, criminal and regulatory investigations revealed embezzlement on an industrial scale. The scandal was shocking, but even more so when the perpetrators was to be the former Malaysian prime minister, Najib Razak, and his inner circle. This scandal was of epic proportions, with an estimated $4.2 billion in that fund embezzled. In addition, there were three senior Goldman Sachs bankers, one of which was the its Southeast Asia chairman and managing director. Not only were bankers involved, but an attorney trust account of two of the nation's largest law firms, Sullivan and Cromwell and Sherman and Sterling, were used to conceal the embezzlements (*The Hill*, December 31, 2018).

Uber Technologies former CEO, Travis Kalanick, did not help build the confidence of the public when he directed Uber drivers to continue working during a taxi worker stoppage, thus taking

DOI: 10.4324/9781351107242-34

advantage of the taxi protest. What further exasperated the public about the lack of moral leadership at Uber was when claims of widespread sexual harassment began to emerge. The public became so incensed with Uber that at least a half million users deleted their Uber accounts (*Wall Street Examiner*, 2017).

United Airlines was not that far behind on the list of corporate scandals over the last couple of years. The most notorious involved the forcible removal of a passenger on an overbooked flight. Although the CEO came forward and made a statement denouncing the treatment of this customer, the public was outraged that anything like this could happen in the first place. Protestors and disgusted customers had a huge influence on the call for better leadership oversight. Their voices and actions were so loud that the federal government got involved, and the CEO ended up being grilled by Washington lawmakers regarding United's policies and practices.

Finally, the Wells Fargo scam of 2017, which actually began in 2011, demonstrated how easy it is for leaders' goals in a corporation can create an atmosphere of greed, fraud and dishonesty. Wells Fargo employees had to meet steep sales goals and incentives under pressure, and they created over a million fraudulent accounts in customers' names. The schemes of Wells Fargo aren't new. In fact, the company has been caught in several scandals. Employees routinely created workarounds to meet the demands—mostly hitting targets—placed on them by senior management. The culture established by senior management provided the breeding ground for unethical behavior not only to evolve but to thrive. Senior leadership's sales goals were extreme, and the incentives for compensation and employment also added to the stress for employees in that environment.

These are only a few of the top scandals over the last decade that point to how leadership either actively engaged in unethical behavior or turned a blind eye to it when it was clear that it had become woven into their organizational culture.

Organizational Culture and Ethics

Organizational culture refers to the beliefs and values that have existed in the organization for a long time, and to the beliefs of the staff and the foreseen value of their work that will influence their attitudes and behavior (Tsai, 2011).

Leaders must adjust their leadership behavior to accomplish the mission of the organization, but not to the extent of using unethical means in doing so. Leaders must model ethical behavior, but the questions become "How?" and "What informs their moral core?"

Organizations are not unethical; leaders in scandal-ridden organizations are. Enciso et al. (2017) posited that business organizations should strive to create ethical cultures to win consumer loyalty. They should do so in order to safeguard long-term success.

To provide ethical leadership is one of the most important responsibilities of a leader, argues Johnson (2009). When leaders fail to carry out this task, it puts the organization, as well as careers, at risk (Johnson, 2009).

Ultimately, the leaders bear the responsibility of promoting ethical behavior. People imitate what they see the leaders do. Therefore, when leaders act badly, it is only a matter of time before others follow suit. When leaders learn to reward good ethical behavior and punish bad, this sends a strong message to others regarding the guiding principles of the company. Leaders must reinforce morally upright behavior and hold accountable those who do not follow the ethical code. In doing so, they create and cultivate a positive company culture.

Ethical Leadership

Effective leadership occurs when ethical leaders are in place. Ethical leaders understand how their behavior sets the stage for how employees and others will do business. If organizations want ethical employees, leaders must model ethical behavior. Leaders establish the organizational culture and thus, the need for ethical leadership and the ways in which it is manifested in organizations must be an intentional endeavor.

Kanungo and Mendonca (1998) proposed a three-component ethical leadership model: the ethics of the leader's motives, influence process strategies and the nature of the self-transformation needed for ethical leadership. They posit that before one can answer the question of how can we judge leadership in an organization to be ethical or unethical, one must define what is meant by "leadership" and "ethical" (p. 136). These researchers define leadership as having two dimensions, a set of role behaviors and an influence process. Ethical implies morality. What is considered morally right may conflict with what is legal. Thus, morals go beyond what is legal or procedurally right. To capture the essence of Kanungo's definition, he turned to Thomas Aquinas and found that in order for leadership to be ethical, they must be correct in three factors: the objective act, the motive, and the context.

Leaders are responsible for the actions of those in the organization; however, they are also responsible for the moral climate. If the leader is not developed morally, that leader may restrict the moral development of his or her followers. Leaders develop morally from character formation that is the direct result of practicing virtuous habits. Followers can be developed morally if the leader puts the right strategies and tactics in place and if a moral compass guides those strategies and tactics. Kanungo argues that ethical leadership is manifested on three dimensions: the leader's motives, influence strategies and character formation (Kanungo and Mendonca, 1998).

Bass and Steidlmeier (1999) postulated that underlying ethical leadership are three pillars: (1) the moral character of the leaders; (2) the ethical legitimacy of the values embedded in the leader's vision, articulation and program, which followers either embrace or reject; and (3) the morality of the processes of social ethical choice and action that leaders and followers engage in and collectively pursue.

Sekerka et al. (2014) argue that seeking positive subjective experiences, positive attributes of people, either individual or in groups, and positive practices can contribute to ethical and virtuous behaviors in organizations.

There are many ethical theoretical models for organizations to use if they find their leaders fall short in the area of ethical decision-making. However, research indicates that current ethical decision-making models may not be all that they are represented to be and may not yield comprehensive answers or lead to improved ethical decision-making. Barnett et al. (2007) posited that these models are not theoretically grounded. As such, one could argue that the missing component to these models rests with the spiritual foundation some attribute to the moral fiber of society.

Spiritual Connection

The moral compass many people have stems from a spiritual tradition, whether they practice that tradition or not. That tradition or its principles have been passed down from one generation to the next.

It is argued that spiritualty can support the workplace and can create a caring organization that will benefit from employees who are strong in personality traits, committed, productive and willing to engage in spirituality in the workplace (Subramaniam and Panchanatham, 2016).

Ashmos and Duchon (2000) posit that spirituality is not religion per se, therefore the idea of it should not tie to the notion of conversion or any other religious practice.

Giacalone and Jurkiewicz (2003) argue the need for a spiritual connection has become important to a wider audience, partly because of an ongoing upheaval in organizational structure, which often results in feelings of insecurity regarding one's place in the system. The character and ethical underpinnings of corporations are questioned, and organizations are asking themselves, "Are our leaders ethical?" because there continues to be issues with corporate finances, corporations ignoring generally accepted accounting procedures, and a disregard to do the right thing with regard to people, business and the environment.

Kumar and Kumar (2014) suggest that leaders who practice some form of spirituality, not institutionalized religion, and ethics in the workplace can transform the organization for better quality of life for its stakeholders.

The link between spirituality and work is not new. For centuries, people have tried to interpret their work through religious lenses (McGhee and Grant, 2016). Since the 1990s, workplace spirituality has gained momentum partly due to the enormous cost of disregarding human resource standards as they relate to business practices (Aburdene, 2007; Marschke et al., 2009).

Johnson (2009) posits that spirituality operates on two levels simultaneously: individual and collective. Individual spirituality evolves from the values, feelings and practices of each person in the organization (Johnson, 2009). This is the culture of the organization. Leaders who engage in spiritual behaviors commonly nurture their inner selves, and they strive to get in touch with their deep desires and feelings, seek purpose and establish deep connections with others and with a power greater than themselves (Johnson, 2009).

A leader who pulls from a spiritual connection generally cultivates a collective spirituality also. That collective spirituality should influence the workplace in a positive manner, thus affecting change in the organizational culture and fostering shared meaning and connection throughout the organization. Spirituality should impact values, and these values play an important role in our lives. Helping one to recognize, understand and articulate one's own set of values becomes critical in sound decision-making. When employees find meaningful alignment with their own personal values and those of their employer, a powerful connection is made. This connection creates opportunities for the person and the organization to produce and manifest growth in a variety of ways.

Johnson (2009) argues that spirituality motivates individuals to behave in a consistently ethical manner, maintain humility and treat others fairly (p. 78). In fact, the repeated practice of spirituality affects and fuels positive character traits of integrity, humility and justice.

According to Johnson (2009), spiritually motivated people seek to live by a set of universal principles. Leaders who follow the principles of love, truthfulness and respect for human rights and dignity are more likely to be people who act as moral persons. Johnson argues that these people do not fall to greed, ego or destructive motivations that undermine their careers, as was the case for former Enron CEO Jeffrey Skilling, former Tyco CEO Dennis Kozlowski, and former WorldCom CO Bernie Ebbers. Rather, they act honorable and honestly.

Integrity refers to how one lives up to their values and if they deal honestly with others. Integrity also informs ethical behavior and contributes to how others perceive the leader.

Jim Collins, the author of *Good to Great*, conducted initial research that identified certain traits of highly effective leaders; not only were they people of high morality, but they were also humble. Humility has been studied both as a separate entity and as seen within various forms of ethical leadership. Collins (2005) describes "Level 5 leadership" as an environment where the leader combines intense professional will with personal humility. Humble leaders place the needs of the followers above the organization, and this humbleness allows an organization to move forward

Caldwell also conducted a study of 12 ethical perspectives and found humility as an ethically relevant leadership construct that helped leaders build followers' trust and commitment (Caldwell et al., 2017). Caldwell et al. (2008) also posited that great leaders were known for "ethical stewardship" because they believed in creating committed relationships that maximized stakeholder value over the optimization of wealth.

Conclusion

Ethical standards are the principles and values of our society. In the western world, these principles can be based upon a particular religious tradition or believing in someone greater than oneself. It can also be based on valuing others and making sure the organization and its followers' needs are met before one's own. In large part, in western societies, ethical standards are based, in part, on Judeo-Christian principles. Generally, these ethical standards are what the majority of society views and accepts as good. It is also the way we behave without laws or regulations imposed to make sure we act appropriately.

Within society, sanctions are often imposed on those who fail to follow ethical standards, and laws dictate consequences for those found guilty of unethical behaviors (Chmielewski, 2004).

Ethics reaches far beyond the law. One wonders if ethics can be taught or whether they are innate. This is a question that remains. However, there are limitations as to what can be taught, as is seen through the years of ethics training, and we continue to see bad results. Do honesty and character come as a result of one's upbringing influenced by some sort of spiritual component? The answer remains unclear. Although most psychologists and researchers agree that ethics can be taught, why isn't it sticking? Is it perhaps the lack of spiritual foundation?

Bibliography

Aburdene, P. (2007). *Megatrends 2010—The Rise of Conscious Capitalism*. Charlottesville, VA: Hampton Roads Publishing, 144–145.

Agbim, K. C., Ayatse, F. A., and Oriarewo, G. O. (2013). Spirituality, ethical behavior and ethical business: The impact of relatedness. *Journal of Business Management & Social Sciences Research*, *2*(9), 76–86.

Arping, S., and Sautner, Z. (2012, August). The effect of corporate governance regulation on transparency: Evidence from the Sarbanes-Oxley Act of 2002.

Ashmos, D. P., and Duchon, D. (2000). Spirituality at work: A conceptualization and measure. *Journal of Management Inquiry*, *9*(2), 134–145. https://doi.org/10.1177/105649260092008

Barnett, J. E., et al. (2007). *In case of ethical dilemma, break glass: Commentary on ethical decision making in practice*. Retrieved from: https://www.researchgate.net/publication/232507221_In_Case_of_Ethical_Dilemma_Break_Glass_Commentary_on_Ethical_Decision_Making_in_Practice

Bass, B., and Steidlmeier, P. (1999). Ethics, character, and authentic transformational leadership behavior. *Leadership Quarterly*, *10*(2), 181–217.

Caldwell, C., Hayes, L., Karri, R., and Bernal, P. (2008). Ethical stewardship The role of leadership behavior and perceived trustworthiness. *Journal of Business Ethics*, *78*(2), 153–164.

Caldwell, C., Hayes, L. A., and Long, D. T. (2010). Leadership, trustworthiness, and ethical stewardship. *Journal of Business Ethics*, *96*(1), 497–512.

Caldwell, C., Ichiho, R., and Anderson, V. (2017). Understanding level 5 leaders: The ethical perspectives of leadership humility. *Journal of Management Development*, *36*(5), 724–732. https://doi.org/10.1108/JMD-09-2016-0184

Chmielewski, C. (2004). *The importance of values and culture in ethical decision making*. NACADA Clearinghouse of Academic Advising. https://nacada.ksu.edu/Resources/Clearinghouse/View-Articles/Values-and-culture-in-ethical-decision-making.aspx.

Collins, J. (2005). Level 5 leadership: The triumph of humility and fierce resolve. *Harvard Business Review*, *83*(7), 136–143.

Dean, K. W. (2008). Values-based leadership: How our personal values impact the workplace. *Journal of Values-Based Leadership*, *1*(1), 1–8.

Enciso, S. Millkin, C., and O'Rourke, J. S. (2017). Corporate culture and ethics: From words to actions. *Journal of Business Strategy*, *38*(6), 69–79.

Ethical Advocate (2018, April 13). Biggest 2017 corporate scandals. www.ethicaladvocate.com/biggest-2017-corporate-scandals.

Giacalone, R., and Jurkiewicz, C. (2003). *Handbook of Workplace Spirituality and Organizational Performance*. New York: Spring Books.

Johnson, C. E. (2009). Spirituality and ethical leadership: Moral persons and moral managers. *Faculty Publications–School of Business*. Paper 79.

Kanungo, R. N., and Mendonca, M. (1998). Ethical leadership in three dimensions. *Journal of Human Values*, *4*(2), 133–147.

Kumar, V., and Kumar, S. (2014). Workplace spirituality as a moderator in relation between stress and health: An exploratory empirical assessment, *26*(3), 344–351. https://doi.org/10.3109/09540261.2014.924909

Kumar, V., and Vij, S. (2014, November 24). The role of spirituality and ethics in transformational leadership. *International Conference on Spirituality*.

Ling, T. J., and Hauck, J. M. (2016). The ethics model: Comprehensive, ethical decision-making. *Ideas and Research You Can Use. VISTA2017*.

Marschke, E., Preziosi, R., and Harrington, W. (2009). Professionals and executives support a relationship between organizational commitment and spirituality in the workplace. *Journal of Business & Economics Research*, 7(8), 33.

McCormick, D. W. (1994). Spirituality and management. *Spirituality and Ethics in Management*, *9*(6), 5–7.

McGhee, P., and Grant, P. (2016). The transcendent influence of spirituality on ethical action in organizations. *Journal of Management Spirituality & Religion*, *14*(2), 1–19. https://doi.org/10.1080/14766086.2016.1268539

Mendonca, M. (2009). Preparing for ethical leadership in organizations. *Canadian Journal of Administrative Sciences*, *18*(4), 266–276.

Roland, N. (June 23, 2008). Low odds for NYSE effort to ease SarbOx: Big board wants law relaxed for small, mid-size players. *Financial Week*.

Sekerka, L. E., Corner, D. R., and Godwin, L. N. (2014). Positive organizational ethics: Cultivating and sustaining moral performance. *Journal of Business Ethics*, *119*(4), 435–444.

Subramaniam, M., and Panchanatham, N. (2016). *Influence of personality on workplace spirituality*. Retrieved from: https://ictactjournals.in/paper/IJMS_V_2_I_3_Paper_4_357_361.pdf

Tsai, Y. (2011). Relationship between organizational culture, leadership behavior and job satisfaction. *BMC Health Services Research*, *11*, 98.

Weber, D. P. (2018). The largest corporate scandals of 2018. *The Hill*. https://thehill.com/opinion/finance/423238-the-largest-corporate-scandals-of-2018.

29
RISK AND INNOVATION

Kevin Meredith

Introduction

Enhancing the understanding of risks and opportunities today will help better prepare for the ever-changing realities of tomorrow. If leaders are not actively trying to understand and managing the most significant risks and promising opportunities of tomorrow, they are leaving the future hanging by the thread of chance alone. For example, the Fourth Sector Innovations team just helped a start-up, Dirass Inc. (Direct-Assimilation Incorporated), launch and commercialize a unique technology that has the power to transform learning and knowledge. Using the latest brain-machine-interface (BMI) techniques, Dirass developed an approach that allows anyone to walk into any participating library or bookstore with their platform and service to immediately assimilate all of the content for a single collection with complete and instant recall. Think of it like plugging your brain into the internet, but better.

Their team has not only been obsessed with bringing this technology to life, but they did so with the highest degrees of passion for providing the ultimate user experience. This product far exceeds and disrupts antiquated paradigms of knowledge sharing, like storytelling, reading books, scouring the web, listening to podcasts and watching YouTube videos.

> *Exercise*: Take a few minutes to think about what section of books you would choose. Why did you choose that?

The company is seeking customers to help make this technology scale and change the world. Some people are very comfortable being early adopters, and it would take very little convincing to get them to sign up for the service. Even for those tech pioneers, the team thinks it is important for customers to know that this process is so intense that it (1) can only performed once, (2) is not reversible and (3) requires a monthly service subscription to access the books and data. In other words, each subscriber only gets one chance to pick a section, and they have to keep all of the acquired data in their brain for the remainder of their life, and they can only access the data if they stay current on their membership.

> What questions do you think are the most important before you become a customer? Why are those the most important questions for you to ask?

DOI: 10.4324/9781351107242-35

What are the consequences are if something goes wrong? How about the benefits if it goes as planned? How likely are these things to occur? What things do you have immediate control over? And what is beyond your control? Who else might be impacted? How much complexity is involved with this?

All of those questions and many, many more, should be considered by Dirass Inc., its founders, its investors, board members and every other conceivable internal stakeholder. It cannot stop there, either. The family members of employees, academic researchers and society at large should have an opportunity to not simply be an afterthought of the inevitability of innovation, technology and the next unicorn (a start-up with billion-dollar valuation).

One of the most studied yet still misunderstood parts of the human body is the brain. Specialist that spend their entire careers studying the brain are far from completely understanding this amazing organ. According to Dr. Michio Kaku, an internationally recognized theoretical physicist and scientist specializing in popularizing scientific principles: "The human brain has 100 billion neurons, each neuron connected to 10 thousand other neurons. Sitting on your shoulders is the most complicated object in the known universe." Kaku said "we've learned more about the human brain in the last 10 to 15 years than in all of human history combined."[1]

Furthermore, there is this amazing complement to the brain; a body to supply the nutrients and execute automatic and decided actions. There is an undeniably complex and intricate system that we have been collectively trying to understand for tens of thousands of years, with great intensity over the last few thousand years and exponential learning over the previous few hundred years.

There is more data-driving resulting from research and development and applied life sciences than ever before, and it is growing at an exponential rate. Medical research and applied healthcare are at all-time high levels as well. Millions of people get insights into their DNA every year simply by submitting a dose of saliva through the mail! Has it ever been easier to access and understand information about your personal genetics?

So there are incredibly focused and intelligent people studying something we use every millisecond of every day. There is deep system-level understanding of the core components and functionality. And there people and computers constantly exploring new insights and generating all data be produced and analyzed. All of these incredible resources are brought to bear and yet there is so much that is still not understood or able to be completely controlled.

People are living longer, and that trend is expected to continue. But is a longer life really the right measure? Is the benefit of living ten years longer really an improvement if a significant percentage of that time will be bedridden with a failing memory and less body control? And even when all of that is considered, there are still additional factors that may end it completely. There are excellent and healthy people that die every day.

People have not mastered risk across the entirety of their lifetime, nor in their daily lives. Not with respect to health and longevity. Not in the work performed. And certainly not in the opportunities sought to advance collective existence in a more satisfying way.

Collectively, people still have much to learn and incorporate when it comes to risk.

If nothing else, this chapter aspires to challenge your assumptions about the relationship between innovation, entrepreneurship and risk. If successful, it will provide a boost to the reader to achieve their greatest contribution and inspire those around them to achieve their full potential.

This is not an abstract or academic approach to risk and opportunity management. This is also not a place to go deep on every specific methodology, to pontificate about the tool du jour or cutting-edge practices and techniques for risk management. This uses established practices in a pragmatic way to ensure that innovations and entrepreneurial efforts yield their desired impact.

1. See generally, "The Most Complicated Object in the Universe: UConn Health Journal: UConn Health pioneers explore new frontiers to better understand one of humankind's perpetual mysteries." March 16, 2018 | Julie (Stagis) Bartucca, University of Connecticut.

It is hard to identify another time in history in which innovation and entrepreneurship can impact as many people with as few resources at lower individual risk than the present. At the same time the existing paradigms are not sufficiently demonstrating the composite and cumulative risks are being optimally managed.

There is no doubt that the future will see amazing advances in risk and opportunity management in the days and years to come. Scientific discoveries will initiate new paths of understanding. Technology will become more ubiquitous in people's lives. Computers will get smaller and faster. Models will get more powerful and accurate. Applications will be more accessible and user-friendly.

All that said, today's leading organizations are a long way from collectively mastering the foundational principles and management techniques surrounding risks, opportunities, innovations and entrepreneurial pursuits that can exponentially improve the overall progress that can result from delivering on the promise of the future. The question is: whether the complexity and vast oceans of data available and being generated are fully being considered actually results in greater decision making and performance.

Innovation and Risk

This section is agnostic to industry, economic sector (for profit, government, nonprofit), scale of deployment, regulatory stringency and organization attributes such as age, growth stage, size and the maturity of innovation capability. The topics covered in this section have the ability to inform and enhance any, and all, innovation efforts. Period.

This work is the result of hard work and experience developing, implementing and scaling a comprehensive yet easily understood approach to help people and the organizations they support make innovation real.

More specifically, this is accomplished by assisting in the establishment and or enhancement of their innovation capability. This approach comprises three primary components: (1) a comprehensive system model, (2) powerful principles and (3) robust operations and resource kit. While we progress through these elements, we will explicitly demonstrate how to pursue all types of innovations while simultaneously pursuing strategic objectives with correlated risk profiles.

Each year since 2005, the Boston Consulting Group (BCG) has surveyed and assessed companies all over the world to understand and share insights about leading innovators. In their most recent conclusions, they state that

> Nearly 75% of companies say innovation is one of their top three management priorities, and 35% rank it above all others. That's not surprising. After all, a winning innovation strategy—paired with the right innovation system—can make a big difference. Since 2005, the businesses in BCG's annual ranking of the world's 50 most innovative companies have delivered a total shareholder return two percentage points higher than that of the global market. But innovation is hard. Only about 30% of companies think they are good at it. And it's only getting more challenging.[2]

One does not have to be CEO or even in the C-suite to obtain value from this work. The worst outcome is that one will become informed on a topic that leadership persistently cares about. Or perhaps it will inspire someone to translate the information from this section into actions that propel organizational efforts forward with confidence.

It is helpful to start with some background on the origins of innovation.

2. See, e.g., Overcoming the Innovation Readiness Gap, Boston Consulting Group, available at: https://www.bcg.com/publications/2021/most-innovative-companies-overview (2021.)

Why "New" Is Not Enough

In a lot of ways, the 1500s represent some of the most transformational years in our collective human history. At this time, humankind is moving from the middle ages to the modern age. Regional and transregional interactions begin to form into global networks. The Ottoman Empire is reaching its pinnacle. The Ming dynasty in China and the Renaissance of Europe are heading into their concluding years.

This is a great confluence for intellectual, scientific and cultural bounty that provides the momentum required for the Enlightenment. This period is marked by lasting progress and the establishment of massively harmful foundations that are still being reckoned with today. The 16th century saw the steep rise of Anglo-European global colonialism, the annihilation of entire civilizations (the Aztecs, among many others) and the first slaves from Africa being transported to the New World.

On the other hand, science, reason, and exploration are opening unimaginable paths for progress. Ideas, inventions and goods are being transferred further and faster than ever before because of trade routes that stretch from Europe to Africa and Asia.

There are also significant breakthroughs introducing paradigm shifting realities about Earth and its place in the cosmos. It was in 1512 that Copernicus proposes the heliocentric universe by establishing the sun as the center of the solar system. A few years later in 1519, Ferdinand Magellan initiated a three-year journey to lead the first circumnavigation of the globe.

The middle of the century provides us with the first time that the word *innover* is introduced into language by the French, with origins from two Latin words *in* and *novus* meaning "into new." And from this point forward, the word "innovation" has been overly reliant on the notion of "new."

Yet, how much has the world changed since the mid-1500s? More accurately, how much more are we collectively endowed with experience, data, information, knowledge and wisdom today?

Besides the great emerging shifts outlined above, it also known in hindsight that countless minor and significant advances were yet to come.

It can be argued that business is presently the greatest driver of innovation, yet in the mid-16th century we are still waiting another 50 years before the first publicly traded company was formed, the Dutch East India Company (VOC). The invention of the decimal point was not yet invented. Darwin and Wallace were yet to formulate their principles of evolutionary biology. Newton was yet to throw his weight behind calculus and physics, and Adam Smith was yet to inject new thoughts about economics and capitalism. It would even be over 200 years until the roots of democracy embodied in the great experiment called America would take root.

As one zooms through the Enlightenment and Industrial Revolution and pauses to think about the present day, it is hard not to observe unimaginable progress.

And because science, technology and innovation are not yet powerful enough to produce the elusive "time machine," we are forced to simulate one with a thought experiment.

What do you think one of your relatives from the 1500s would think about a world as you describe your everyday life? Would they even have the ability to comprehend what you are saying in any meaningful way? Would they bow down to your wealth of knowledge? Would they just run away? Or even worse for you, would they go straight to the authorities to have you detained and burned at the stake?

Now let's try to explore that thought from a slightly different perspective. How many of the principles and technologies that you were trying to describe about life in the 21st century to your distant relative would exist today if the prevailing "knowledge" of that period were available today?

The world today would be nearly unrecognizable in many ways to a vast amount of people. The understanding of the world (and beyond) and countless things affiliated with it have enabled humans to pursue and achieve unimaginable outcomes. And until that elusive time machine from above becomes real, it is not possible to go back and rerun the last 500 years with such constraints in place. And we don't have to.

Is there any meaningful argument that could compel one to conclude that the way people understood the world in the mid-14th century should be the basis used today?

When the word innovation was first coined, there was little need to distinguish its meaning from ideas and invention in any substantial way. They could be used in a pretty interchangeable way. However, progressing to the present day from over the last half millennium, it is clear that today, more than ever, that there is a need to make very deliberate distinctions between innovation and other terms. Furthermore, it becomes clear that the definitions and expectations of innovation have not kept up the advances which innovation is often attributed to.

For as long as I have been studying innovation, the definition has been persistently dependent on "new." While it is impossible and undesirable to disconnect "new" from the origins of innovation, one really must ask if it is a defining characteristic today. Does it suffice to equate "new" with innovation? Is the bar so low that all we need is "new"? Or is it time to evolve the definition of innovation in a way that honors the origins without being overly emphasized by it in today's world?

After studying and searching for a more appropriate definition of innovation that was not overly reliant on new, a determination was made to create one that was better suited for today's realities.

Innovation—The Conversion of Creativity for Stakeholders

It is helpful to explore the definition in more detail, starting at the beginning.

Conversion. This is a recognition that innovation is a process. Just like any well-designed process, there are inputs that are acted on to produce a desired outcome. And just like any process, innovation can be learned, improved, become more capable and yield greater impact over time.

> **The Bell and the Cat**[3]
>
> A family of mice was constantly living in fear because of a cat. At their wit's end they pulled everyone together for a half-day workshop to discuss ideas to defeat their nemesis. At some point late in the workshop, one mouse gets up to suggest an idea. She suggests that a bell be placed around the cat's neck, so they can hear it whenever it is moving nearby. All the other mice agree and excitement builds. It is at this point that interjects with a dash of reality and says, "Who will put the bell on the cat?"
>
> This fable shows four important aspects affiliated with ideas and innovation: (1) action and execution differentiate innovation and ideas through value created; (2) ideas on their own are not enough and they are relatively cheap; (3) there is no meaningful path for innovation without creativity and ideas (see lottery analogy below); and (4) some solutions create more or bigger problems and risks than the original problem.

The second key word in the definition is creativity. The broader use of creativity here allows us to capture the traditional paradigm of "new" as being connected to innovation while expanding the range of inputs that can be employed to produce meaningful outcomes.

That leads us to most important word of the entire definition, value—and ironically enough, the word that is missing from the classic definitions. We could be creative all day long, but if we don't produce value for the stakeholders that need it most, then we are not able to legitimately consider something innovative.

And finally, stakeholders. In order to talk about creating value, we need to know who we are creating value for. We must understand, engage and honor the commitments being made to the people

3. See, Aesop's Fables, Belling the Cat, available at: https://read.gov/aesop/003.html.

that buy, use and are otherwise impacted by innovation efforts. *Stakeholders are the ultimate controllers of value.* It is the innovator's responsibility to understand and translate the ever-changing stakeholder needs and value assertions into compelling solutions.

This is not an abstract discourse on semantics. It is only with a comprehensive and relevant definition of innovation, that one can meaningfully talk about the relationship between innovation and risk. If one were to simply focus on "new" as the driver of innovation, they would never consider using the full complement of resources available to pursue and realize innovation. Such a narrow viewpoint produces blind spots in the ability to understand, mitigate and eliminate significant risks associated with any effort attempting to deliver meaningful value to stakeholders.

Just as the aperture was opened on how innovation is defined, it is important to have holistic ways to understand innovation, develop innovation capability and realize innovative solutions for stakeholders. Each one of these is related to the other and when done properly, they provide dynamic input to elevate the expectations and performance. Any innovation effort that does this effectively will inherently carry lower cumulative realized risks. In essence, we are building our entire innovation capability to continuously identify and reduce risk.

Understanding Innovation Better

Understanding innovation and how to employ it most effectively seems like a no-brainer, but there are countless examples of teams being all amped-up on the idea starting an "innovation program" without fully understanding what they are about to initiate. While the push for action can certainly be a great sign for engagement, it can embed long-term and devastating risks that ultimately prevent the program from achieving its objectives.

As stated above, innovation is the conversion of creativity into value for stakeholders.

Additional insights are revealed about the unique benefits and limitations of innovation's role in understanding if the elevation of perspective is shifted to a higher vantage point. This location allows one to more appropriately observe an opportunity's maximum value potential, and more importantly, optimal value realization. From there, it becomes ever more clear where innovation plays its strongest role.

To explore this relationship, it is helpful to think about the cumulative value realization curve. To produce the curve, place "value" on the *y*-axis and "time" on the *x*-axis and then plot the value added over time. This allows one to see how a series of activities contribute to the ultimate value realized. The properties of the curve created allow us to then calculate the cumulative value realized using the area under the curve.

For a small project or one that does not scale incredibly well, there is a good chance that the complete curve can be defined with a straight line over its entire life cycle. The more scalable the offering, the more logarithmic the curve. This means incrementally more resources can produce exponentially more value. Most tech start-ups and investors focus their efforts in this paradigm.

To start, refer look back to the definition and see that creativity is the input to the "conversion" process, and value for stakeholders is the output.

The front end is really focused on the early stage of a value realization process, everything from creativity to ideas and inventions to innovation to commercialization to widespread internal adoption. Creativity enables ideas and inventions, ideas enable in innovations, and innovations enable commercialization and adoption.

Beyond innovation is commercialization. This is the location of a potentially huge tail that typically makes up most of the time-based contribution to the life cycle and is where most of the value is ultimately realized.

Creativity

Whether someone believes they are "creative" or not does not matter. Everyone is creative. It is hardwired into human existence.

> *Self-reflection*: Right now, select neurons are firing across synapses in your brain and you are searching for patterns and opportunities to connect with the words on the page. Recognizing and expressing patterns. As soon as one is processed with a relationship to some other piece of data, an opportunity for creativity is presented. It happens so fast and frequently that most of the time we are not even aware that it is happening. But it is!
>
> If this book is functioning properly, then you are creatively connecting the words with your experiences and heuristics are constantly seeking opportunities to connect. If we have done a poor job at holding your attention, your brain is thinking about something else that is more deserving of your thoughts. Once that switch occurs, you have redirected the pathways for creativity. Either way, the point is the same: you possess an innate and amazing capacity for creativity, and you exercise it countless times every day. Your brain is one of the most successful creativity generators yet to be discovered and, in terms of volume, creativity holds the most prolific tally of inputs for value.

The average person will have an opportunity for creativity to occur 20 trillion times a second. The human brain has about 100 billion neurons, and each one fires about 200 times per second. Not every one of those is used explicitly for creativity, but they all support the human that produces the creative output. But to be conservative, let's say that just 1% are explicitly for what we consider creativity. That means that there are still 200 billion chances a second for creativity to occur. Multiply that by 7.4 billion people and you have 1.48e+21 chances per second in the world for creativity to occur.

> And this is just a human centric tally. There is more and more evidence supporting the notion that creativity is not a distinct human ability. We don't necessarily need to include non-human creativity in our analysis, but if we ignore billions of other sources for creativity to inspire humans to have a larger positive impact, we must account for the opportunity cost of doing so.

Unfortunately, these high quantities of creative stimuli are not necessarily the most meaningful measure of value contribution. Most of them are filtered out and never become ideas. This effectively means that creativity alone has virtually zero contribution in value realization. If just one creative idea comes out per minute, there is still a bunch of zeros trailing behind a decimal point before you get to anther digit. Effectively zero contribution in action taken to fully realize the ultimate potential of an idea or new business.

"OK, then why even include creativity this book if it does not significantly add value?"

Because, by definition, innovation cannot occur without it.

It is in many ways like the lottery. The odds of winning the lottery are virtually the same if you play or not (effectively zero). Most lotteries in the United States require the player to choose five or six numbers and one additional bonus number. According to Allstate Insurance, the odds of winning the Powerball jackpot are 1 in 292,201,338 (0.000000342%), and the odds of winning Mega Millions are 1 in 258,890,850 (0.000000386%).[4]

4. "Here are your odds of winning both Powerball and Mega Millions," Chris Isidore, CNN Money, August 10, 2017, available at: https://money.cnn.com/2017/08/09/news/economy/mega-millions-powerball-odds/index.html

But someone can only win if a ticket is purchased to play the game. If creativity is not recognized at the front end of the value delivery process, innovation does not ensue.

It's like lotto: you gotta be in it to win it.

Please note that it is the application of creativity that drives the most value. Creativity is not the outcome.

Unlike buying a ticket for the lottery, creativity is not a binary activity. Creativity can be continuously applied throughout all key stages of value accumulation. It provides an ongoing benefit as additional value contributions are explored. Creativity has to occur at least once for innovation to occur; however, in the most robust implementations it is reapplied to support even greater levels of value realization throughout the entire life cycle.

Creativity is a dot connector, so, one must have context (education), intent and awareness of some point to connect the dots. Otherwise, they are just filtered out as noise. Human mental models can be honed and the brains heuristics enhanced. Much more research will continue to be done here and hopefully provide key breakthroughs in the understanding for even more creative impulses for innovation to do amazing things.

In conclusion, creativity is a crucial component of innovation, but each individual creative output provides a tiny contribution. That being said, a nearly infinitesimally small creative spark is all that it takes to ignite the sequence of value realizations that alters the trajectory of humankind.

Ideas/Inventions

Ideas

Even though it takes creative stimuli to initiate innovations, it is insufficient in helping innovation realize its full potential.

Ideas are a manifestation of creativity. Ideas reconstruct and organize creativity into a more valuable output, however ideas are not worth much, either. All the ideas in the world will not assure additional value is realized. Even if the greatest solutions to the greatest challenges did exist, they still would be essentially worthless. It takes action to produce an innovation that actually provides value. (Remember the bell and the cat.)

Ideas represent the articulation of creativity. Committing the creative output to memory or writing it down provides incrementally more value than those creative impulses that are filtered out. The problem is that ideas are not really worth that much. That might hurt the ego of many readers, potential founders and product developers, but the idea for the next big thing is worth about the same as an nearly infinitesimally small improvement. This is because if the originator does not do anything with an idea (but effort into making it a reality), they are living in a fantasy world in which a little sprinkle of magical "value realization dust" means all ideas become innovations. Everything is easy and awesome in fantasy land. Unfortunately, just like magic "value creation dust," the notion that "ideas = innovation = optimal value realized" also exists in fantasy land only.

IDEA ECONOMICS AT PAUL'S BOUTIQUE

Ideas without action are fantasy. It takes effort to test ideas against conditions of reality. The truth is, ideas are not even close to as valuable (as a discrete measure) as the old saying that suggests 12 of them are worth ten cents. And just like "Suckers, they come a dime a dozen," it is "suckers" that believe their ideas are worth as much as "a dime a dozen." The market value of an idea in this scenario is $0.83 (10 cents/12 ideas).

How about "If I had a penny for my thoughts, I'd be a millionaire"? If one assumes that a "thought" in this equivalent to an "idea," then it would take a prolific idea generator just 100 million thoughts to reach millionaire-hood. No math is required for the unit value of an "idea," as it is defined as $0.01.

Exercise

Let's do a thought experiment:

> Come up with 12 ideas in one minute. As much as possible, do not filter your thoughts of it will be difficult to make it. They call this stream of consciousness.
>
> DON'T PEEK!
> These are ideas that just popped into my head with minimal filtering:

1. Purple reading socks
2. Batteries for business cards
3. Wooden electrical tape
4. Seeds for crustacean homes
5. Rocks that talk
6. Flight instruments that are invisible
7. The Beatles, Beck and Metallica doing a mash-up
8. Foam door hinges
9. Talking clouds
10. Self-repairing screens
11. Artificial coral
12. Self-solving Rubik's Cube

So, with these two economic benchmarks from Paul's Boutique, one can clearly see ideas command a market value of between $0.01 and $0.83 each. Now this is quite a spread, so to be conservative, the economic forecasters have decided to use a unit value for each "idea" to be one penny.

Now suppose that employees at Paul's Boutique are asked to spend every minute of their working day coming up with ideas because each one is so valuable. It is generally accepted that the average worker really performs only three hours[5] of productive work per day. This corresponds to about 2,160 ideas per day and a value of $21.60 per day. Over the course of a work-year that equates to about $56,000 in "idea" income. Over a 30-year career that would have an accumulated worth of almost $17 million dollars! What a great world.

This would eliminate the poverty of today's standard in the United States—just with ideas! How awesome! So powerful are ideas in the land of fantasy!

But that is not reality. There are many factors ignored in fantasy land that would surely exist in the "idea" market of the real world. Things such as supply side economics and the time value of money, taxes, measures of quality.

Let's look at the latter. With all those ideas proliferating there would be no way to realize the expected market value of nearly $17 million over the next 30 years. There is no market system ever observed over a 30-year period that saw that level of supply dramatically increase (as the "idea income" would certainly create) without impacting the resulting price. As supply increases without changes to demand, prices fall, which has an effect of reducing the incremental value of each idea produced.

Note: If there really was a market for ideas it would likely would not eliminate poverty. We would simply move the bar for poverty to around $50,000, slightly below the amount that a majority of the population could achieve simply by creating infinite lists of ideas.

5. www.inc.com/melanie-curtin/in-an-8-hour-day-the-average-worker-is-productive-for-this-many-hours.html.

Last, there has been no mention of quality of ideas. Even if Paul's Boutique and the rest of the world could maintain a flat value of $0.01 per idea, that does not mean that all ideas are really worth the same amount. Part of the real value of ideas in the real world is contextual. Does the idea align with existing conditions or predicted outcomes? Does it build off an established lineage of previously demonstrated results? Does it violate physics or other established scientific discipline? Referring to the list in the exercise above, as absurd as that list may be, there are actually some kernels of value potential that could be explored and others that should be immediately dismissed. In the real world, an attempt is made to strengthen the value provided of ideas through action.

Ideas do have value in their ability to be communicated and to inspire others to do the hard work. This should not be seen as some great contribution to value realization but more like a hand-off from idea generator to idea executor. Just like track and field, a lot can go wrong on the hand-off in a relay race. The difference between gold and disqualification is a fraction of time. However, that is a very small contribution, a nearly imperceptible contribution to the ultimate pull potential of value. Much of the early weight falls on innovation. Before moving along the value realization curve to innovation, it is important to talk about inventions.

Inventions

Inventions are a little better than ideas at contributing to the accumulation of value, but only marginally. Just like the reality of creativity and ideas, people are inventing all the time. It is unclear why there is such a mysterious cloud that prevents people from recognizing and realizing their inventiveness.

One definition of invention offered up "a unique or novel device, method, composition or process."[6] Invention is really the articulation of an idea. An invention does not have to exist in physical form or actually have to demonstrate that it will work the way that it claims. This means that the value realized is only slightly more for an invention than idea. It is also why innovation is a relevant and distinguished component of any early-stage value realization activity.

Humans have been inventing tools and new ways to accomplish a given task for tens of thousands of years (possibly hundreds of thousands). In fact, it is not even a defining human characteristic. Birds build nests with whatever they can. They do not make the same nest every time. They are inventing a new home with materials best suited within proximity to their desired location. While they might use a similar approach each time a nest is constructed, they certainly do not follow a full kit, like an IKEA bedroom set.

Anyone can invent something, and most people are inventive on a daily basis whenever a problem is solved without the optimal conditions. People make use of what is around them create an inventive solution. *Note*: This is not innovation nor necessarily being innovative!

Also of note is that inventiveness is not necessarily the same as what is widely understood in the term "invention."

Most people who understand inventions in their professional lives automatically associate them with intellectual property protection. In most situations this is through patents.

A patent is essentially an authorization from an agency to grant the patent holder(s) with a monopoly with certain restrictions (e.g., types of use, time frames).

Most inventions are not patented. A vast majority are never formally requested for protection. There is far from a one-to-one relationship between inventions and patents. Think of all the paths of inventiveness that are never formally captured, from family recipes handed down from generation to

6. https://en.wikipedia.org/wiki/Invention#:~:text=An%20invention%20is%20a%20unique,an%20object%20or%20a%20result.

generation to watching a parent invent some new character, voice and story to avert the meltdown of a toddler.

A little less than half of all the formal applications that are submitted to the US Patent and Trademark Office (USPTO) are rejected. Since 1963, the USPTO has an average rate of patent acceptance of 57%.[7] Furthermore, an inventor does not necessarily stake a commercial claim or set an expectation of commercialization for an invention. There are millions of inventions and patents that are not realizing commercial or monetary benefit to their owners.

Patents: There is a seemingly endless number of innovation assessments published each year that continue to disproportionately weight patents or as complete proxy for "innovative" a given company or industry. Patents are poor measures of innovation. At best they are a minor indicator.

One of the biggest drivers of this confluence is that it can very hard to find consistent and objective measures of innovation that are meaningful. Innovation as a discipline has not even reached the embryonic stage of development and understanding. Furthermore, about 20 years ago a significant trend started to emerge with respect to patents. It was at this time that the term "patent trolls" was first observed and companies started gobbling up patents (primarily by acquiring individual patents or entire companies) as a strategic resource. This became offensive and defensive action primarily deployed in the courts. Are companies that amass thousands of patents in this manor instantly more innovative? It is hard to sufficiently make this argument in a comprehensive manner at scale. There are many remedies for all of these concerns that extend beyond this chapter. The reader should take warning and proceed with caution; the risks that are present whenever innovation efforts are conflated with invention.

Innovation

For continuity, innovation is placed here; however, this being the main focus of the chapter, it will be skipped until commercialization. For now, what is most important is to highlight the keystone position of innovation between the previous portions of the value realization curve and the next stop at commercialization and widescale adoption.

Commercialization/Adoption

Most of the value that can be expected, the "fat" or "long" tail, occurs beyond innovation on the value realization curve. Commercialization is the process of managing or running something principally for financial gain. Here is a more detailed definition:

> Commercialization is the process by which a new product or service is introduced into the general market. The process of commercialization is broken into phases, from the initial introduction of the product through its mass production and adoption. It takes into account the production, distribution, marketing, sales and customer support required to achieve commercial success.[8]

Commercialization is where most of the value is realized. We will not spend too much on this; however, it is important that commercialization is one of the ultimate tests for innovation and where many "innovations" die.

7. www.uspto.gov/web/offices/ac/ido/oeip/taf/us_stat.htm.
8. www.investopedia.com/terms/c/commercialization.asp#ixzz4pmh0axge.

Just because you have something innovative does not mean that it will be commercially successful. When done a certain way (one might suggest the "right" way), innovation can help increase the likelihood of producing an offering that will achieve commercial success.

Consequentially, it should be observed that this section is commercialization and adoption. Not every innovation desires to be or needs to be commercialized in order to ultimately deliver its maximum accumulated value. The widespread adoption of anything that produces value for stakeholders is eligible to be considered in this section.

Regardless of how slow the acceptance of these new forms are realized, it is ultimately their accumulated value that matters.

Find the leaders of any defined style of painting and there are defining examples. Da Vinci and Rembrandt portraits, Monet and Degas Impressionist scenery, van Gogh and Gauguin Post-impressionism, Picasso and Matisse on modern art, and so forth. They pushed the boundaries of expectation, and oftentimes they pulled along art critics and connoisseurs kicking and screaming. Innovation is not clean and pretty. More often than not, it is difficult and requires extreme effort to realize the cumulative value and praise received by the masses. And while it may not entail bodily harm, as with van Gogh's self-inflicted lopping of his earlobe, it is clear that it there is more than simply doing something new that matters. How many more artists have tried something innovative, or even just new, that are neglected by fame and history books?

It also important that we use a broad of definition of commercialization to include adoption by stakeholders. In many companies there are a lot of innovations that primarily serve internal stakeholders. These innovations are demonstrated through impact to internal operations rather than commercial success in the marketplace. These should not be perceived as "second-rate" innovations in the big picture. To the contrary, companies like Amazon and Google are prime examples of finding important operational advantages that not only led to widespread adoption within their organizations but also proved themselves in the marketplace. They were willing to eat the dogfood (see "Eating Your Own Dog Food" below) and ultimately create thriving revenue streams that produce more economic value than entire countries.

While working with a company with $100 billion in annual revenue and 170,000 employees, there was no shortage of internal opportunities to test ideas prior to developing potential innovation for or in support external market offerings. And not just the marquee products, but many other products, services, and processes as well. There were literally millions of opportunities per day to engage with stakeholders and test critical innovations and integrate them into practice. Every day that innovators are not using all the resources available, there are opportunities being missed, and the deadweight of opportunity cost weighs down innovation performance.

Key Concept

Will the dog eat the dog food? There is a saying in business about the dog eating dog food or "dog fooding it." This is a really important principle to actively reduce innovation risk with respect to commercialization and widespread adoption.

You could make the greatest dog food on the planet that provides more nutrition per bite than anything ever previously produced, but if the dog will not eat it, it is essentially worthless. Your dog will not get healthier; it will become malnourished and weak. The same is true with commercialization. If people will not adopt, buy or use your product or service (aka "eat the dog food"), it will be very difficult to achieve maximal value from any potential innovation.

Eating Your Own Dog Food

This can also be applied to internal testing and adoption of potential innovations. Will the employees, teams and groups in your organization eat the dog food that they produce? Will they really use it if it is simply mandated from executive leadership? Will they pay for implementation and continued use? Are they clamoring for access to the dog dish to try the new food? Each of these, and many more, can be great litmus tests and risk mitigation strategies to test the value of innovations, provided that the conditions of use are similar to that of your intended external customers and markets.

Often there is an effective strategy is to develop capability for internal business needs that can ultimately be vetted inside the company to receive the initial value benefit. If successful internally and the major parameters of use are consistent to the broader market(s), then it is possible that even more value can be derived. This is the example of Amazon Web Services (AWS). It was a necessity for its own operations to establish a new internal platform that could scale along with Amazon's growth. This led to creating an internal cloud. After several years, they got so good at it that they decided to open it up to the market, where they have dominated.

Eating the dog food can be a strong indicator to potential external customers as well.

Just about every product and service imaginable falls under this paradigm, as do internal process improvements and capabilities that ultimately support the development of a market-facing offering.

How do you test out innovations that serve internal and external stakeholders?

1. Top down
   Executive leadership and decision makers—this is what they are chartered to do in most companies. But this seems to be made into a more complicated endeavor than it needs to be. There are opportunities. Positive is the ability to see big picture that helps convert internal adoption to external market opportunities. Chart the path for risk mitigation. Sometime there are big investments that are required in order to rapidly respond to changing conditions.
2. Organic adoption
   Employees pull ideas along with them and demonstrate local benefit prior to expanding implementation to more of the organization.
3. Artificial markets
   Artificial markets are created to by distributing "idea" or "innovation" currency to employees throughout the organization. Most often this system is tied to an innovation management or employee crowdsourcing platform. Employees use their currency to demonstrate their support of a given project and in return receive early access when it is deployed.

   While we have seen attempts to create artificial markets to drive "commercialization" within the company, it seems unnecessary in many situations and almost always increases the overhead required to achieve this adoption. This in turn means that the types of ideas that get converted into value must require additional justification and pressure. This is the start of a vicious cycle—a principle that is discussed in more detail when we explore the "process" component of the integrated innovation system.

There are lots of ways to dog-food ideas. Be honest. Be creative. Be savvy.

The exact shape and proportion that innovations contribute to the full range of these curves is not absolute. It depends on the life cycle of the product or service that is provided. For example, the Romans built structures over a span of decades that are still standing today. A commercial aircraft is historically developed in nine years and then has a useful life of 30 years, whereas an app can be developed in a matter of weeks or days and may have a useful life of just a few months.

Innovation Is the Keystone

Innovation is not a silver bullet or magic pill. Those who see it as such or as an isolated or singular outcome are typically the same people that are most disappointed in the outcomes. Just to reiterate: innovation is part of a broader value realization system.

Innovation requires the appropriate mix of components applied to your specific situation to realize the intended results.

Arches are one of the most efficient ways to distribute loads in architecture, engineering, and construction (AEC). In fact, the "A" in EAC contains the word "arch."

It can be informative to better understand a classical arch. There are many pieces in an archway, and every single voussoir (piece of the archway) supports in the fight against gravity. In fact, there can be a nearly infinite set of options for how the specific components in the arch are configured, yet every single one will require at least one common and defining trait. Every imaginable formulation requires a keystone. There is only one keystone, and it must fit just right or the entire structure will fail.

Innovation is crucial because of its position in value realization.

It is innovation that holds the keystone position for value realization. The critical component that connects creativity and ideas/inventions with commercialization and widespread adoption.

Interestingly, it is one primary force that allows a keystone to successfully execute its unique responsibility in the archway and its critical role of uniting all subsequent elements of the arch in a coherent functional structure. It is not some exquisite mechanism using the latest technology. It is not highly skilled workers with the most exquisite craftsmanship. It is not advanced construction methods. It is not even about the materials the arch or keystone are made of. It is even more encompassing, relentless and universal.

It is gravity.

Value is the equivalent of gravity. Without value, innovation is pointless. Without gravity, so too is the keystone rendered useless (as well as the entire eloquence of the arch). Again, this is why value is foundational for innovation to occur.

Additionally, each classical arch was not absolutely the same. Each one required a complete set of components that fit together just right to have a structure that will last.

> Note: A keystone is also known as a capstone. In academia, the terms are often interchangeable. While this is not technically correct, the concept is consistent (see below if you care to split hairs). A lot of academic programs evaluate the totality of learning through a culminating course or project, often called a capstone. In order to successfully complete the capstone a student must be able to pull together a bunch of relevant pieces of learning to demonstrate the totality of their learning.
>
> A capstone is technically any stone in a coping. In practice the main function is simply to protect the structure that rests upon. This is most commonly seen a solid flat or beveled piece of concrete or stone. While this is an important functional role, one could argue there are many approaches to achieve the same outcome. There is only one keystone. An arch will not stand with integrity without it. A wall can stand for extended durations without a capstone.

There are four major drivers of innovation's keystone position on the value realization curve: regulate the interface between ideas and the market, increase the quality of opportunities pursued, reduce risk with iterations and diversification, and demand a total life cycle perspective of value.

To see this, a few additional components are added to the basic value realization curve.

The zoom is closer to the value realization curve compared to the previous illustration. Instead of showing creativity, ideas/inventions, innovation and commercialization/adoption, this version focuses in on innovation and shows the asymptotic barrier where commercialization/widespread adoption reside.

As the zoom occurred, it was able to show specific process elements for innovation. The components illustrated are presented to show the types of activities that occur in a comprehensive innovation system designed to reduce common risks of innovation success. The specific steps are not a gold standard or the only way for innovation to deployed. They do, however, represent decades of research, testing and implementation around the world.

> The composite risk of any innovation being pursued decreases as it moves from the left of the illustration to the right. This risk reduction can been approached on two levels simultaneously:
>
> 1. Iterative cycles of rapid validation with real stakeholders throughout all phases of the development and innovation process steps.
> 2. Composite innovation portfolio risk reduction in which the administrators of innovation for a given organization coordinate with company leadership and strategic intent to ensure the composite risk profile of a collection of innovations being pursued is aligned with the needs of the organization. For example, an organization that is more desperate may rely on a more aggressive portfolio that puts all of its eggs in one basket with large moonshot-type bets. This would be contrasted with an organization that is performing will and looking to utilize a more balanced portfolio that values incremental innovations and a smaller reliance on breakthrough innovations.

Value is subjective and must be considered from the eye of the stakeholder and not solely of those pursuing its creation. Value is constantly changing, most of the time in little ways, but sometimes in very significant ways.

We now have the requisite framework to understand how innovation is just a single element of a broader value realization curve, and we hold insights about the critical role it plays in pursuits to accumulate value. This provides us with what we need to begin exploring how a systems engineering approach to innovation can further reduce risk.

Develop Innovation Capability

Experience would also suggest that nine of ten readers:

- Have heard leadership talk about innovation as top priority within their organization;
- Cannot locate a documented innovation plan that is connected to strategy;
- Do not have a defined process for innovation that is delivering intended results;
- Contain important building blocks that can be immediately used to drive innovation;
- Believe people throughout the organization are underutilized;
- Can identify significant missed opportunities to create value for stakeholders;
- Have not had direct conversations about innovation with suppliers and customers.

An effective way to minimize such risks is to approach innovation across three layers: (1) a systems approach, (2) driving principles and (3) operational resources. A common thread across all three is the importance of developing innovation capability over time so that the organization can constantly achieve near and long-term objectives.

The concerns of such findings are reinforced when we ask clients about deliberately applying systems engineering principles for innovation capability development. And when we see where they are struggling with innovation, we see a direct linkage to increased risk occurrence because of a lack of foundational elements from a comprehensive systems approach to innovation.

Note we are not saying that the following systems model for innovation is the only or even the best systems approach for innovation. If you have another comprehensive model, feel free to use that. The important part is that innovation capability development is being approached from a systems perspective. For the purposes of illustration in this chapter, we are going to use the model we have the most experience with, the Fourth Sector Innovations Integrated Innovation System.

There are seven major elements required for an integrated innovation system to deliver maximum value: purpose, people, places, processes, methods, measures and meta (Table 29.1).

Realize Innovative Outcomes

The system provides the framework for comprehensive innovation efforts that reduce the risk of the opportunities being pursued. But just as ideas are insufficient to have real innovation, the system model alone is insufficient. It is everything that makes up the model that distinguishes innovation theatre and those that are able to achieve meaningful innovation outcomes.

Table 29.1 Fourth Sector Innovations Integrated Innovation System

Purpose	Sets the tenor for your innovation quest. Everything else stems from here. Purpose simultaneously serves as the touchstone for consistency and the rallying cry for realizing a desired future. The rest of the system is built upon this element, so be sure to communicate and use its artifacts effectively.
People	The real heroes of the system, who should be treated with great reverence. When aligned with purpose, the collaboration between those providing grassroots action, executive leadership and key stakeholder (internal and external) insights provide the connections where innovation can thrive.
Places	Where people primarily engage (physically and virtually) with the innovation system. The best spaces are designed, nurtured and aligned with a desired purpose and outcome. Optimally this includes designated spaces (internal and external) explicitly used to get the most value from creative action.
Processes	Perhaps the least respected element and disparaged by the uninformed. It holds a seminal role in defining how to best execute the most important activities associated with the innovation system. The ability to establish the right balance between structure, speed and established practices is key.
Methods	Crucial linkage between people, processes and measures. Having a full kit of techniques, templates, tools, and training (TTTN'T) comprising best practices from around the world. Instant digital access to the most appropriate resource to support gives more time for outcomes.
Measures	When properly implemented, they serve as the gateway for truth and are the sworn enemy of poor decision-making. They should be focused on providing insights into the realities around achieving desired outcomes. It is important to apply to both the macro system and the endeavors that it supports.
Meta	Provides the nutrients that flow throughout every aspect of the system. The most important elements are culture, data, interfaces and resources. They are vital to the system because of the magnitude, persistence and dynamic nature their influence has on realizing maximum total benefits.

One of the major ways a systems approach to innovation helps comprehensively reduce risk is the expectation that innovation capability and performance are persistently pursued in maturity. The maturity exists within individual elements of the system and for the system as a whole.

One of the most important aspects of this approach is that determination of maturity is not measured against some arbitrary standard but rather against the stated objectives and realities of each organization pursuing innovation outcomes. It also drives transparency and accountability by internal and external stakeholders.

Part of that accountability, and ultimately improved innovation capability, requires the organization to clearly define what it is trying to accomplish. It is with this purpose identified that the rest of the system can be tuned. Among many other things, it is purpose that helps identify and manage critical measures of performance and reinforce the cultural elements that deepen innovation outcomes.

Innovation Errors, Defects, and Failures

In Chapter 5 of this text there is a section about errors, defects and failures (EDF). At a gross level there is consistency in the macro application of these terms for innovation, as they were defined more broadly for risk. In practice, however, it is important to be reminded of innovation's unique role in the cumulative value realization curve. Innovation is simultaneously a litmus test on value and a mechanism to improve organizational performance with decreased risk. While errors and defects certainly need to be considered in any meaningful evaluation of performance, it is the notion of failure that requires the largest degree of contextualization, so we will start there.

It is important to recognize that what a failure is, and is not, changes depending on different contexts. The ideas of failure are different when exploring technology or early-stage ventures compared to legal and statutory failures. One of the defining differences is around the normative strength of obligation.

In the context of innovation, the expectations of failure are different than other settings. Failure in a learning organization deploying innovation is only realized in five scenarios: (1) not trying at all; (2) not attempting to fully understand, reflect and share when a desired outcome is not achieved (big or small); (3) sharing is influenced beyond the confines of truth and facts (political or otherwise); (4) repeating a previously experienced failure; and (5) directly refusing to accept and apply learning.

A decision to mitigate or eliminate a particular risk is not the same as actually mitigating or eliminating that risk. This is forgotten far too frequently in risk management and innovation. The management makes the decision. That fire is "out" because they gave the direction, and their attention must shift to the next fire.

This mindset is more akin to containment than it is corrective action or organizational learning. Perhaps it is a nuanced difference, but one that is important.

For example, when a fire is burning, the immediate goals are to ensure safety, stop the fire from spreading and put out the fire. This is the unifying focus of the team. This is not the right time to determine what caused the fire (outside of the immediate need to know if the source of the fire is still actively feeding the flames).

Once everyone is safe, the fire is out and there is assurance that there is no additional threat (e.g., a potential for the remaining structure to fail), the investigation begins in earnest. At this point the collective efforts of the team move to investigating how the fire started and the path by which it spread.

With respect to any high-performing team/organization and innovation, keeping everyone out of the fire and danger is equivalent to ensure the psychological safety of all participants in the innovation system. According to Dr. Frederik G. Pferdt, Google's chief innovation evangelist, the number-one predictor of innovation success is psychological safety.[9]

Psychological safety can be defined as the collective comfort of individuals in a team or organization to take risks without feeling intimidated or threatened. One of the leading experts of this

9. See, e.g., https://www.bigspeak.com/innovation-speaker-alert-introducing-dr-frederik-g-pferdt-googles-former-chief-innovation-evangelist-adjunct-professor-stanford-university/

emerging field of study is Dr. Amy Edmondson of Harvard University. In her book *The Fearless Organization: Creating Psychological Safety in the Workplace for Learning, Innovation, and Growth*, she provides strong examples about the different ways organizations have successfully been challenged to achieve psychological safety. The basis of her work is the relationship between psychological safety and accountability for meeting demanding goals. She also explicitly discusses how important it is for individuals and teams to be united in purpose, solve problems collectively and learn together.

Two major institutional risks that exist in too many innovation programs are the risk of trying and not succeeding and the risk of not trying. Both of these are relatively easy to correct with the proper implementation of systems, mindset and operational resources. Another institution risk was discussed in Chapter 5 under Secret 6 ("Risk and Opportunity Are Collectively Boundless"). When common traps like ignorance and hubris get in the decision-making loops, very bad outcomes can result.

One of the most devastating and acute examples of many important aspects of psychological safety going awry was found within NASA.

It is generally agreed that the NASA Space Orbiter, the core of the iconic space shuttle, is the most complex machine ever designed and built. It is a shining example of innovation with the ability to inspire an entire generation to dream about space.

According to NASA the shuttle had more than 2.5 million parts, including almost 370 kilometers (230 miles) of wire, more than 1,060 plumbing valves and connections, over 1,440 circuit breakers, and more than 27,000 insulating tiles and thermal blankets. This machine was designed and developed in the 1960s and '70s, flew over 100 missions in the 1980s and '90s, and flew its last mission (STS 135, the 135th mission) in 2013. The remaining fleet is permanently on view at five museums around the United States.

In 1986 the space shuttle suffered a catastrophic failure and NASA's first fatalities of a "manned" mission to space. Much of the complexity is driven by doubly and triply redundant systems that help ensure safety and continued operations after many failures.

Culture at NASA was driven by an era in which there was a seemingly unlimited budget to put US astronauts on the moon. The realities of the shuttle program were much different. Haggai Cohen, who during the Apollo days was NASA's deputy chief engineer, NASA contracted with General Electric Co. in Daytona Beach, Fla., to do a "full numerical PRA [probabilistic risk assessment]" to assess the likelihood of success in landing a man on the moon and returning him safely to earth. The GE study indicated the chance of success was "less than 5 percent." When the NASA Administrator was presented with the results, he felt that if made public, "the numbers could do irreparable harm, and he disbanded the effort," Cohen said. "We studiously stayed away from [numerical risk assessment] as a result. 'That's when we threw all that garbage out and got down to work,' Willoughby agreed."[10]

> Amid such political unpopularity, which threatened the program's very existence, "some NASA people began to confuse desire with reality," said Adelbert Tischler, retired NASA director of launch vehicles and propulsion. "One result was to assess risk in terms of what was thought acceptable without regard for verifying the assessment." He added: "Note that under such circumstances real risk management is shut out."

> **"Disregarding data"**

> By the early 1980s, many figures were being quoted for the overall risk to the shuttle, with estimates of a catastrophic failure ranging from less than 1 chance in 100 to 1 chance in 100 000.

10. "The Challenger Disaster: A Case of Subjective Engineering," IEEE Spectrum, Trudy E. Bell and Karl Esch, January 28, 2016, available at: https://spectrum.ieee.org/the-space-shuttle-a-case-of-subjective-engineering

> "The higher figures [1 in 100] come from working engineers, and the very low figures [1 in 100 000] from management," wrote physicist Richard P. Feynman in his appendix "Personal Observations on Reliability of Shuttle" to the 1986 Report of the Presidential Commission on the Space Shuttle Challenger Accident.
>
> The disintegration of the vehicle began after a joint in its right solid rocket booster (SRB) failed at liftoff. The failure was caused by the failure of O-ring seals used in the joint that were not designed to handle the unusually cold conditions that existed at this launch. The seals' failure caused a breach in the SRB joint, allowing pressurized burning gas from within the solid rocket motor to reach the outside and impinge upon the adjacent SRB aft field joint attachment hardware and external fuel tank. This led to the separation of the right-hand SRB's aft field joint attachment and the structural failure of the external tank. Aerodynamic forces broke up the orbiter.

At the cold launch temperature experienced, the O-ring would be very slow in returning to its normal rounded shape. It would not follow the opening of the tang-to-clevis gap. It would remain in its compressed position in the O-ring channel and not provide a space between itself and the upstream channel wall. Thus, it is probable the O-ring would not be pressure actuated to seal the gap in time to preclude joint failure due to blow-by and erosion from hot combustion gases.

Richard Feynman

"The Challenger disaster cost the nation $3.2 billion and rocket seals suspected of triggering the explosion should be redesigned before shuttles fly again even if they are absolved of blame," the head of NASA is attributed as saying.

This O-ring was a known concern and the component cost a fraction of a penny ($6,000–8,000 per flight) compared to the total cost of the Orbiter ($3.2 billion) and the economic impact of shutting down the manned space program to investigate the disaster. The engineers that raised the concern prior to launch were placed in a near impossible situation, as seen next:

> Special thanks to Allan J. McDonald, "Only Person in U.S. History Restored to His Job by Congress" for his generous support in helping shed new light on this important incident. We use the Challenger tragedy in many ways for our innovation work. Most frequently it is about the critical, and often overlooked, role that interfaces play in innovation and risk. According to McDonald "I believe that the SRB O-ring costs you were quoted are probably in the ballpark, because I vaguely remember that the O-rings were slightly less than $1,000 each before the *Challenger* accident." This was the first time that we were able to find first-hand knowledge from someone who was directly involved on the program to help narrow the component cost of the O-rings. As the text above states, these critical interfaces failed and contributed to the incident at an interface. An interface that was known to be a concern and insufficient leadership, ultimately one of the single worst days in NASA and US history ensued.[11]

At this point, the basics of innovation, the role of risk on and in innovation efforts, and important mechanisms to get more out of innovation efforts have been laid out. It is now time to move onward to one of innovation's most trusted companions: entrepreneurship.

11. Ibid.

Table 29.2 NASA Risk and Opportunity Criteria (for Reference)

Level	*Characteristics*	*Complexity*
5 Near Certainty	Planned approach and processes cannot mitigate this type of risk; no known processes or workarounds are available	Extremely complex
4 Highly likely	Planned approach and processes may mitigate this risk, but a different approach might	Significant increase in complexity
3 Likely	Planned approach and processes may mitigate this risk, but workarounds will be required	Moderate increase in complexity
2 Low likelihood	Planned approach and processes have usually mitigated this type of risk with minimal oversight in similar cases	Minor increase in complexity
1 Not likely	Planned approach and processes will effectively avoid or mitigate this risk based on standard practices	Simple design

Levels (1–5)	*1* *Minimal*	*2* *Minor*	*3* *Moderate*	*4* *Significant*	*5* *Severe*
Technical	Minimal or no impact	Minor performance shortfall, same approach retained	Moderate performance shortfall, but workarounds available	Unacceptable, but workarounds available	Unacceptable; no alternatives exist
Schedule	Minimal or no impact	Additional activities required; able to meet key dates	Minor schedule slip; will miss need date	Program critical path affected	Cannot achieve key program milestone
Cost	Minimal or no impact	Budget increase or unit production cost increase <1%	Budget increase or unit production cost increase <5%	Budget increase or unit production cost increase <10%	Budget increase or unit production cost increase >10%

Opportunities

Level	*Probability*	*Maturity*
5 Near certainty	90% or more probability of occurrence under current plan	Existing design or processes
4 Highly likely	65% to 90% probability of occurrence under current plan	Technology available in similar application or process
3 Likely	35% to 65% probability of occurrence under current plan	Redesign or adaptation of existing design or process
2 Low likelihood	10% to 35% probability of occurrence under current plan	Major redesign of existing design or process
1 Not likely	Less than 10% probability of occurrence under current plan	New design or process

Level	*1* *Minimal*	*2* *Minor*	*3* *Moderate*	*4* *Significant*	*5* *Substantial*
Technical	Minimal or no impact to achieved TPM performance	Achieved TPM performance improves as much as 5%	Achieved TPM performance improves as much as 15%	Achieved TPM performance improves as much as 35%	Achieved TPM performance improves more than 35%

Level	*1 Minimal*	*2 Minor*	*3 Moderate*	*4 Significant*	*5 Substantial*
Schedule	Minimal or no impact on schedule	Major milestone(s) met up to 3 weeks early	Major milestone(s) met up to 7 weeks early	Major milestone(s) met up to 13 weeks early	Major milestone(s) met more than 13 weeks early
Cost	Minimal or no impact on program cost	Reduction in ETC of up to 1%	Reduction in ETC of up to 3%	Reduction in ETC of up to 5%	ETC reduction exceeds 5%
Producibility	Minimal improvement in flow, tooling, or resources	Minor improvement in flow, tooling, or resources	Medium improvement in flow, tooling, or resources	Significant improvement in flow, tooling, or resources	Producibility goals exceeded in multiple areas

Entrepreneurship and Risk

After scouring the planet for best definition of entrepreneurship, the one that stands out is Howard Stevenson's "The Pursuit of Opportunity Beyond Resources Controlled."

There are lots of reasons why this definition rises above the rest.

The most significant is that there is an advantage to any leader that enables and encourages every member of their organization to not settle for what they have and push the boundaries of what is possible; to have every single person achieve more than they are supposed to! How much more would every organization achieve if this form of entrepreneurship were fully embraced and integrated into the fabric of daily activities?

This definition is equally powerful when perspective shifts from individuals within the organization to the organization as a whole.

Most organizations seek to continuously grow in defined directions. For some it is profit. For others it is constituents served. For others it is impact. While this is only a tiny sampling of total growth motivations for an organization, they all would benefit from being able to achieve their greatest potential by pursuing external opportunities beyond the resources controlled and further elevate their ability to deliver more desired outcomes.

Pursuing new opportunities beyond resources controlled opens small and large pathways to achieve more. This could be a new product line within an existing customer base. A new customer segment using an existing or new product. Strategic partnerships that have mutually beneficial outcomes. Or even a merger or acquisition aimed at moving the needle in a big way.

While an organization can surely take any of these actions through executive action alone, unmatched benefit can be achieved when employees and leadership fully embrace entrepreneurship as a core value and component of their culture.

It also allows everyone to avoid having to create new, and by some unnecessary, words and distinctions. An example would be the difference between an entrepreneur and an intrapreneur. This is an artificial distinction that falls into oblivion when entrepreneurship is pursued with Stevenson's intent.

Another false categorization that this definition allows us to avoid is that entrepreneurship is solely applicable in the domain of for-profit, private-sector endeavors and organizations. By artificially isolating major contributors and organizations that are obsessed with value creation, the entire endeavor is cheapened.

Last, the definition does not overly emphasize where the pursuit of opportunity to be specifically affiliated with a limited part of a life cycle. An organization does not need to be a start-up to reap great benefits from entrepreneurship and possessing an entrepreneurial mindset.

Furthermore, this definition overcomes limitations of applicability that more commonly used definitions promote. Let's start by looking at a few of the most widely accessible definitions and why they might hinder an organization from realizing its greatest impact.

The Oxford English Dictionary defines entrepreneurship as "the activity of setting up a business or businesses, taking on financial risks in the hope of profit."

Merriam-Webster utilizes a similar framework to define an entrepreneur as "one who organizes, manages, and assumes the risks of a business or enterprise."

While not intended, these definitions even include "risk" in their very definition. Perhaps a bit surprising in a book about "risk" this inclusion is a bit troubling. Why?

First, over the last seven decades have seen exponential growth in the use of the word "entrepreneurship." This means that more people than any other point in history are exposed to entrepreneurship than any other point in history (we have more people using the word more frequently). This alone is not the problem. The problem lies in that most popular definitions are introducing an unnecessary bias into the discussions about entrepreneurship. The core of that bias is that entrepreneurship is by definition directly associated with "risk."

It is quite common for people to immediately be transported to the beautiful campuses of tech giants in Silicon Valley whenever the word entrepreneurship is spoken. If they are not whisked away to where the magic happens, they are reminded of the devices and applications that they spend most of their waking hours using. The technology industry and the leading companies within it some of the most ubiquitous with success in the world.

And why shouldn't they be? The Big Five (Amazon, Apple, Alphabet [the parent company of Google], Microsoft, and Facebook) took in about $900 billion in revenue in 2019. This is up a staggering $100 billion from 2018. Their combined market capitalization is $6.24 trillion dollars! Their valuation is equivalent to approximately 14% of global GDP.

The oldest of these five companies are Microsoft (1975) and Apple (1976), which are pushing 50 years; all the rest are less than 30 years old! Evidence shows that the average age of publicly traded companies is shrinking.

The mantra of Silicon Valley is roughly summarized as "spend big, grow/spend fast and break things." The extended version of that is throwing in the word "disruption" someplace. And with more unicorns (start-ups with a $1 billion valuation) simultaneously frolicking around the planet than ever before, it is hard to deny some amazing outcomes.

When most people talk about startups and risk, especially how "risky" they are, the conversation is almost always skewed using language from the investor's perspective.

This is not to say that entrepreneurship, running a small business or hatching a start-up is easy. But difficulty and risk should not be conflated. For instance:

90% A staggering nine out of every ten start-ups will fail;
0.05% Only 1 out of 2,000 start-ups ever receives venture capital (VC) funding;
94% More than $9 out of $10 invested by VCs goes to start-ups that are no longer considered early stage;
0.015% Just 3 out of 20,000 start-ups have a successful exit or harvest event.[12]

Even with such daunting stats in mind, from the entrepreneur's perspective—there has never been a lower-risk way to start a company that can reach billions of people and achieves the once mythical "unicorn" status of a billion-dollar valuation.

12. See, for example: Startup Failure Rate, available at: https://www.failory.com/blog/startup-failure-rate.

Some of the reasons that the statistics and facts above are not overly worrisome is because there are some equally promising facts to counterbalance the other side of the equation.

1. X as a service—There are platforms and services that other people have developed and require relatively low overhead to access. This is in sharp contrast to previous generations of companies that are beholden to larger organizations or had to invest in developing the capability in-house. It is hard to find a business function that does not have a platform or service that can be subscribed to in monthly and annual increments. Cloud services are the most ubiquitous and flexible currently available. The ability to scale up and down with only incremental investment is an incredibly agile and powerful leverage point.

> *Note*: Silicon Valley got its name because sand is one of the first ingredients of the computer chips used in the emerging semiconductor industry in the early 1970s. It is a little bit ironic that the namesake is still one of the most capital intense forms of tech investment yet the dominant economic drivers are companies that use silicon instead of produce it.

2. Customer discovery and rapid cycles of validation—today there are more resources available to start-ups to de-risk the acute risks to their venture than ever before. The inclusion of key stakeholders in short validation cycles that are focused on rapidly testing and validating/invalidating the most critical assumptions first is one of the most powerful risk reduction capabilities available. Learn as much as possible with the precious resources available to establish the culture and product/service that stakeholders are compelled to buy and use. This includes formal and informal programs focused on these principles. Formal programs like incubators and accelerators have demonstrated their value around the world when properly executed and applied. Data suggests that start-ups that go through a formal incubator or accelerator program have a survival rate of 92%. This is significantly higher than the typical failure rate of start-ups in the 90% range!

3. Founders come with experience—One of the most common misconceptions about start-ups is the average age of company founders. The media and general population see stories like the founders of Facebook working tirelessly in the dorms to hatch overnight billion-dollar success stories. The reality is that the average age of successful start-up founders in the United States is in her or his early- to mid-forties. While this may be surprising to some, it shouldn't be. This is aligned with a common crossroad in an individual's life and career. It is a time to decide "Am I going to keep doing what I have been doing for the last 15 years since receiving my college degree?" or "Am I going to try giving a start-up a shot?"

4. Bridges and safety nets—While there are lots reasons why founders choose to start a company, there are many conditions in which the founders make the transfer from a position of choice over necessity. The number-one way in which founders operate with a safety net is to continue to work their day job and moonlight to launch their start-up. Crucially, and perhaps counterintuitively, it is vital for founders like this to ensure they maintain performance of their work in the day job and disclose any potential conflicts of interest with their employer. This can help make sure there is minimal or no risk of wrongdoing post-departure. It is also important that professional and personal relationships are not negatively affected. Many employers can see it as a badge of honor when an employee leaves to run a start-up. Even if they don't go that far, it is important that the founder does not burn bridges. Last, another form of safety can be severance packages and accumulated personal savings. Such resources can be a vital safety net—just by virtue of knowing it is there.

5. Shift risk profiles for investors—Even the VC (and other types of venture financiers) are de-risking acute risk from a portfolio perspective. VC funds typically operate in eight-year cycles that are broken down into three stages: (1) raising the fund (~1 year); (2) sourcing deals and making initial investments (2–3 years); and (3) managing prior investments, reserve, and a support any new surprise opportunities.

While this basic model has not shifted a whole lot over the last couple of decades, other trends have:

1. Deals are getting bigger—Venture capital investments are typically aligned to company life cycle through a series of funding stages or "series" The most common are pre-seed, seed, Series A, Series B, Series C, and so on. The size of the investment is typically directly correlated to the number

of rounds. In the last five to ten years there has been a trend where what used to be a Series A round is the average value of a seed round. Each round continues to get bigger. Similarly, deals that used to be the sole domain of VC are now being supported by angel investors and family offices. Things have gotten so big that VCs are now butting up against private equity in terms of deal size.

2. New risk mix—As the deals get bigger, there is more capital at stake and increased impact when investments don't make their expected return. That being said, they are spreading some of that additional risk back to the start-ups by requiring them to have de-risked much of the market risk in advance of doling out funding. So while the entire industry is moving to bigger risk per deal, the cumulative risk for an investment portfolio decreases.

Note: Another potential way that VCs and investors are helping de-risk a venture is to encourage founding teams instead of sole founders. While this increases managerial burden and the potential risk of interpersonal differences and capabilities gaps enlarge, it decreases the risk of "single point failures."

It is also hard to ignore the significant fissures that are cracking the bedrock of these notions apart.

There are actually signs of systemic risk in the Silicon Valley approach. The days of Silicon Valley being defined by companies like Apple, HP, and others launching from a garage are harder to imagine.

There are countless stories about large groups of software engineers and developers cramped in too small of dwellings just to balance affordability and geographic proximity to work. Most of them will not work for a start-up that goes public or has a major harvest event. What happens when the support staff for the buildings can no longer afford to live in the area? What happens more broadly when the cost of living increases and the quality of life decreases? These are not the conditions where people and businesses thrive, and there is some evidence that people are seeking alternatives.

While most of the biggest companies in the world are tech companies based in the United States (and all of them have operations in Silicon Valley). There is no doubt that they have enormous influence, but it is also hard to ignore the fact that they represent about 8% of total market value of all the publicly traded companies on earth. The composite influence of the other 92% cannot be ignored. Furthermore, it is also these organizations within established companies that undertake actions every single day that have more collective risk to the global economy than if all of the institutional start-up investors (angel and VC) suddenly investing the world combined (a mere $300 billion compared to global market cap of $88 trillion). This is systemic risk. The notion of "too big to fail" is the type of risk that should be keeping people up and relentlessly de-risking.

As it was laid out in the earlier part of this handbook, risk is contextual, meaning that all risk is not created equal and that it can only be purely understood and managed from the proper perspective.

Entrepreneurship, innovation and risk seem to be as inseparable in the everyday parlance of business and government as just about any other three related topics, the foundational stool legs of any modern organization. And this is not a convenient construct defined over half of a millennium of business activity or few thousand years of social organization and governance. It cannot even be bound in exclusivity as a strictly human experience. The history of life on this planet can be characterized as an endless tension between cause and effect on the direct and indirect influence of these constructs. A journey of constant exploration whose path is scouted by survival down to the most foundational unit of generational lineage. And this is done upon a sea whose conditions require navigators to constantly evaluate and adjust based on the dynamic drivers of change.

These same factors have had an influence on the speed and scale that humans are best suited to study and understand. Humans are good at linear thinking at relatively slow speeds in spatial references. We have a hard time dealing with understand the really slow and really fast. We cannot intuitively grasp the vastness of the universe, the speed of light or the seemingly large epochs of time in which life on earth has evolved.

There are countless quotes on the internet about how important it is to take risks. Many of them boil down to something like "If you don't take risks, you will never . . .

> be your best self."
> know how far you can go."
> get the reward you want."

How about:

> "Go big! Or go home!"
> "You miss 100% of the shots you don't take."
> "If you want it, go for it. Take a risk. Don't always play it safe or you'll die wondering."

These slogans proliferate on quote lists as pithy overlays to some compelling picture and internet fodder more broadly but are not really sound advice. Many of them, especially the last one, are biologically flawed. They flow counter the logic and evidence of evolution. There is so much to learn from nature when only hubris and elitism don't blind understanding and progress.

There are very few examples in which taking a risk, just for the sake of the rush of risk, is able to yield sustainable value. Success depends on previous preparation, and without such preparation there is sure to be failure. While it is not as catchy, a more informative takeaway from dramatic motivational quote posters is "Be skilled at evaluating risks and take reasonable steps to be prepared when risks appear." This is sound advice for work and life.

Final Bonus

Regardless of which term is preferred, global warming and climate change are prime examples of systemic influences that are affecting business and entrepreneurial pursuits that culminate in risk. One of the largest capital management firms on the planet is BlackRock. In 2020, their CEO, Larry Fink, provided a detailed letter to fellow CEOs outlining what he called "A Fundamental Reshaping of Finance." This letter is so important to this book and the future of entrepreneurship that we highly recommend you look it up as complementary reading.[13]

13. See also: Mandatory ESG Reporting Gains Momentum, https://www.blackrock.com/corporate/investor-relations/larry-fink-ceo-letter?cid=ppc:blk:ll:na:ol:goog:na:v1:bhv:tl&gclid=3cc7673bf3fb15edb3e806cba9056a96&gclsrc=3p.ds, explaining that, for instance, in early 2022, the CEO of BlackRock, Larry Fink, published a letter delineating the greater importance of ESG in its investment strategy, reflecting greater demands of ESG inclusion in overall business strategy. These points are also further analyzed in Chapters 2 and 3 of this handbook.

30
UNCERTAINTY MANAGEMENT

Chris Guzelian

I spent much of the last decade as a law professor teaching US constitutional law in the classrooms of a stand-alone law school ranked in the fourth tier (i.e., the lowest), while also heavily embroiled in volunteer committee and community organizing work at the local San Diego branch of the Armenian Apostolic church, a relatively small and infrequently recognized sect of Eastern Christianity. Previously, I held various roles in government settings, including military intelligence, bankruptcy courts, and state criminal prosecution. I have dipped a toe in the for-profit world as a bookseller and donut shop proprietor. And now I am, as I write this, transitioning to a business school professorship at a premier university in Texas.

So much for my work resume. Why does this history qualify me to write about the topic of "uncertainty management"? Because I am unable to discern semantic threads to my professional existence. It has been goalless, and I have been tossed about by the streams of life. When you customarily meander without specific goals, you gain a lot of experience interfacing with *uncertainty*.

Uncertainty is a word fraught with meaning. To most, it is scary and to be avoided. A few thrive on it. Some seek answers to make uncertainties certain, while others strive for a Zen-like mentality to radically accept uncertainty—surrendering up any hope or idea to change it. What I want to do in this chapter is talk about uncertainty and then give some suggestions about how to *manage* uncertainty—not to eliminate it, control it, ignore it, radically embrace it, or fight it.

In other words, this chapter is a *compass* to help you sail as safely and enjoyably as can be in the ocean of uncertainty that you—and every businessperson, whether they admit it or not—find yourselves in every day. It is your choice, however, to accept and use my offered compass, along with your own capacity to sail your ship, whatever condition it may be in.

Mine is not the only compass for sale. Plenty of people sell compasses for uncertainty management. (As a starting place, just check the self-help or pop psychology section of your local bookstore.) Which compass you use—or don't use—will determine the results you get. I happen to think mine is right. Some people who sell compasses do so fraudulently to acquire dishonest profit. I'm not defrauding you. I'm a teacher, not a profiteer. Alternately, some compasses are billed as uncertainty *management* tools, when really they are uncertainty *removal* tools. I'm not going to remove your uncertainty. It's actually impossible to do. That is because you are on a ship in the ocean of uncertainty. You will never reach a shore of certainty in this mortal life. Before you ever started in business, you were born on the ocean of uncertainty. You will die on the sea of uncertainty after your business career finishes, or your business career will finish when you die in the sea of uncertainty. So I reject

DOI: 10.4324/9781351107242-36

any compass—and I think you should too—that suggests a way *out* of uncertainty or a way to *suppress* the uncertainty over the long haul.

Briefly summarized, what my compass does is reorient your attitude about business uncertainty. It gives you a new *posture* to take toward uncertainty, if you don't already have the same posture I do (and you might). It's important to describe what this posture does for you and what it doesn't do for you. The posture does *not* guarantee business results. It won't necessarily make you rich; it won't necessarily make you wiser; it won't necessarily make you famous, promoted, or respected. It may not help you avoid shareholder strike suits, hostile takeovers, layoffs, criminal prosecution, employment discrimination, or other business calamities.

Then again, this posture toward uncertainty *will make you more you*. It will help you express the true, authentic nature of yourself in the marketplace. It will allow your true market character to shine. And modern marketplaces are often dark indeed—groping for light. Markets worldwide desperately need more of you to be *you*. We don't need any more fake yous that feel compelled to make a quick buck or prop up a quarterly earnings report.

Why do people need to be their authentic selves in the marketplace? I contend it is because—like all things—honesty, authenticity, and truth about yourself and what you are selling or buying are the indispensable pillars upon which any business can be conducted. They are the background values—neglected too often (or flouted)—that ensure orderly, predictable, fair, meritocratic, and nonviolent markets. Markets don't work without people being themselves. If you are selling products or services you don't believe in, or that you know won't work well, to whose benefit is that? I firmly believe no one in their deep soul truly wants to be a liar or swindler at heart, and yet, how many merchants are willing to say, make, or do things that they would not want done to them? I read an article recently about a chair that is intentionally architected to break after it is sat in a certain number of times. One commentator described this as "diabolical genius," but it's not really that "genius" in my opinion. Entire industries have fallen into habits of building things whose covert design is to fall apart just like self-destructing chairs. These businesses' products have life cycles that usually end shortly after warranties are up, in an effort to produce more sales. Is this good practice? One could argue the consumer gets what they pay for, but aren't businesses playing off the consumer's usual hope and expectation (regardless of what the legal language in his warranty may say) that his dishwasher, computer program, car, and video game console will last "a really long time" without a need for updates as long as he cares for them reasonably well? Is anyone (or the environment) served well by products that conform far more reliably to legal requirements tilted in the insider's favor than they are to practical durability?

There are countless such examples how inauthenticity clambers into the marketplace. No one at heart wants to be the swindler. And yet, many become that, often in small incremental stages that they rationalize as just inevitable parts of doing business.

There is a link between uncertainty and authenticity. People facing uncertainty are often uncomfortable, if not outright afraid. And when people are afraid, they do unethical, immoral, or illegal things that they might not do if they were in a better frame of mind. By adopting a correct posture toward uncertainty, you can find your true self in the marketplace. You won't do bad things—or at least not as commonly as you would if you remained so afraid or uncomfortable about business success in the face of uncertainty. Adopting a bad posture toward uncertainty (and remember, you will always be swimming in a sea of uncertainty) will leave you in discomfort or fear. You will stay prone to making ethical errors and misrepresenting your true self to the market. And with enough false people operating, it guarantees swindler markets, crony capitalism, and kleptocracy. And in corrupt markets, even the people who can manage uncertainty well suffer. No one can escape the pain entirely when the market collectively becomes inauthentic.

The key, then, is to identify why uncertainty management strategies typically mislead people into bad business practices. Once we understand that, we will then be better positioned to ask how we can improve uncertainty management.

Let's start with the core tension at the root of business uncertainty. Consider two principles:

1. Most business rewards growth and punishes failure.
2. Sooner or later, everyone and everything fails—and the ultimate, unavoidable failure is death.

The unpleasant ultimate certainty behind all uncertainty is death. People die—every one of us. So do companies—every one of them. Yes, the legal fiction is that corporations live in perpetuity. And granted, some companies like JP Morgan (established 1871) have lived long. Yet no company truly lives in perpetuity, even those that we adamantly believe cannot fail on our watch.[1] And some entire industries are intent on living about as long as fruit flies, such as plumbing or heating/air conditioning companies that routinely shut down within the first few years of operations.

Business, on the other hand, wants to postpone the inevitable, and it rewards those who can grow a company's profitability, or sustain profitability when it is threatened with decline. This business fetish for growth can cause "short-termerism," as investors or shareholders impatiently demand immediate results. Executives who hit quarterly earnings targets are frequently rewarded with vast bonuses. This leads to business decision-making that fuels hypergrowth in the short term but can make a business less sustainable over the long term and hasten the company's ultimate demise (usually after the culpable executives have left the company's employ with generous severance packages).

Uncertainty arises because despite promises, hopes, aspirations, and forward-looking statements, executives truly cannot guarantee the future. And thus, there becomes personal and corporate pressure to match expectations that may not match reality.

Businesspeople adopt different business ethical approaches when faced with the challenge of the uncertain prolonging and growing of a corporation ultimately facing certain death. The most common of these is to begin by identifying the goals one wishes to achieve and then employing means to achieve those goals. For instance, a CEO might say, "we want to achieve 4% growth in profits by the end of the third quarter." If that goal is adopted, then the company adjusts its current course to strive toward that end.

Ends matter. Life is a good thing, whether for people or for corporations. Growing and extending life are good things. But only some means have any hope—yet no guarantee—of achieving corporate life. Paradoxically, when one sets out a certain corporate goal (e.g., 4% quarterly growth), one creates a great deal of pressured uncertainty whether the goal can be met. It is not unlike that problem of driving: when one looks at the obstacle near the side of the road, one tends to steer unhelpfully toward it, not away from it. And so, aspiring to hit a 4% growth target might lead to actions and consequences harmful to the corporation's growth and longevity. (Such as the short-termerism I have already mentioned, or other untoward consequences such as layoffs, mergers and acquisitions, outsourcing, stock buybacks, or otherwise). By defining the goal so concretely, the life of the corporation is shaped to meet the goal. One can prune a bonsai tree to conform to the dimensions of a specific planter box, but then the bonsai is defined by that box. And ultimately, that decision of conformity may limit the life or health of the tree (or to extend the analogy, the corporation).

Therefore, goal-directed thinking—which is the bulk of what passes for executive action—may actually be what is stifling so much corporate innovation these days. Indeed, my current university

1. I say this as someone who witnessed the first-ever law school in American history to be stripped of American Bar Association (ABA) accreditation (i.e., given a death sentence). Law as a reliable profession stretches back to ancient times. The idea that American law schools could be closed down by the ABA was simply never contemplated until 2018.

has set out its annual mission to be "innovation" (as if we did not want to intellectually innovate prior to this, or that by placing pressure on the creative process will induce further innovation).

I want to persuade you to endorse an alternative way of thinking about how to prolong growth and life of corporations. This proposal will seem a paradox: it calls upon us to stop thinking about the growth and life of the corporation. It calls upon us to lift the burden from our own shoulders of being responsible for the life and growth of the corporation. Various people of different traditions and cultures have referred to this concept alternatively as "flow," "calm," "mindfulness," "zen," "contemplative thinking," "alchemy," "meditation," "the zone," or "wisdom." The concept calls upon us to stop thinking about corporate goals when fashioning our daily thoughts and activities. Indeed, only by doing so can any worthwhile goals related to growth and life be sustainably achieved.

Instead of thinking constantly of goals and then reacting to those thoughts, we seek to experience life fully. What does it mean to experience life? It means to be present with the *reality* of what is happening *presently*, rather than living in regrets of the past or anticipation of the future. It is to recognize that thoughts are constantly passing through our head without *judging* those thoughts with a valence of "good" or "bad" (a process which leads to self-criticism and ineffective performance). It is to embrace something other than a hyper-efficient internal compulsion to seek and meet goals.

What can or should we embrace other than goals, if we are to seek the good welfare of our corporation, its executives, its shareholders, its customers and partners? *What fills the void that is created when we abandon the goal-seeking, competitive striving for corporate growth?* This is a question debated by many, and there are many different answers. I want to firmly suggest that the *only* answer is found in faith traditions, rather than in bourgeois or materialist values. There simply has to be a transcendent quality to one's thoughts, actions, and contemplation in order to serve effectively the mundane materialist goods and services of corporations. Steve Jobs understood that in creating computers, he was not simply providing products and utility—he was creating an art that appealed to our universal sense of beauty and awe. Even the packages that Apple products are shipped in and the stores that they are sold in are works of art, refined in their contours, lines, harmonies, and colors. One might well compare a museum-quality sculpture to one of Jobs' products. Jobs understood the transcendent. And he succeeded wildly where many fail. Jobs understood the journeying, pilgrimage-like nature of a corporate life—that it is not a matter of planning or seeking stop-off points but a fluid, turbulent, dynamic wandering that can be shaped a bit here or there by the travelers, but whose path is inherent to the corporation's own nature in the greater economy of the world at large.

Sergei Bulgakov was a Russian monk who wrote on economics. In his book *Philosophy of Economy*, Bulgakov described the world as a "household." The metaphor is apt. Corporations are collectives of people expressing their unique natures through the goods and services they sell. And the world writ large is a massive collective of people—the superset—that comprises all the smaller collectives. Thus, one can think of humankind as a household—a group of beings all seeking to be in harmony with what Bulgakov called "Sophia." Sophia is a divine wisdom, Bulgakov explained, that penetrates and innervates all humankind. It blows gently and constantly across our minds, as a cool wind might do for cypress or willow trees at the banks of babbling river. Sophia provides the inspiration, the hopes, the support, the nurturing of life. It motivates our actions if we let it, and shapes our thoughts if we accept it.

Most of all, Sophia is inherently *good*. It is life sustaining, life supporting, growth endorsing, peaceable, beautiful, inspiring, sustainable, responsible, organic, and all the other healthy adjectives we invoke to describe the best of corporate life. To embrace being in the presence of Sophia is to embrace the wisdom of the heavens. And the heavenly wisdom is the only wisdom that can help corporations to avoid destruction of the people and environment that they impact. Goal setting not in line with Sophia's desires will only wreck things, even if it might seem otherwise in our competitive way of living in the short term.

How then shall we access Sophia, know its thoughts, embrace its ways, and rid ourselves of the false and arbitrary goals that we might establish in our earthly mindsets? One way endorsed by nearly every faith tradition with which I am familiar is to allow for contemplation. Contemplation could mean sitting in lotus position, humming chakras, or chanting, for hours on end. Some faith traditions do actually endorse such, and I do not discount that such practices can help one to clear one's mind and activities of the clutter that fills us daily. Others suggest that listening to or playing inspiring music lifts our souls above the mundane and spans the gap between the tangible and the intangible in life. This too is seen in many faith traditions. Dancing is sometimes seen as the moving inspiration of Sophia. Whether participating with whirling dervishes in Turkey or flamenco dancers in Spain, one can see the fleeting presence of Sophia in the particularly inspired dancer's movements. Yoga practitioners insist that the stretching and tightening of one's body in concert with breath allows the divine to pierce one's being and to bring one into harmony with the great world. One might see it in the vagabond wanderings of the peripatetic Bilbo Baggins in *The Lord of the Rings*. Not quite knowing where he is going, or how to get there, he seeks the Ring. He does not fret that he has no plan to acquire it; he simply trusts Sophia will lead him to it.

But all of these to me are temporary elicitations of Sophia, corporeal attempts through self-fashioning activities to "summon" it through chant, dance, stretch, sit, or walk. What about for those of us who do not seem to have the apparent luxury, under the pressures of our time, to chant, dance, stretch, sit, or walk when our boss is yelling that we have not met weekly sales figures, or that the department will be shutting down and we have no discernible way forward to meeting our mortgage and kids' school payments next week? How can this gobbledygook about a divine Sophia relate to me practically when I am suffering from the decline and anxiety of a corporation under goal-driven pressure? How can I be freed from the stress of life under the uncertainties facing a corporation bound to die some day or another? Is Sophia some gift for the rich and spoiled and time-pampered elites of the world, or can it still talk to me as the local manager of a beleaguered franchise?

In his book, *The Gifts of the Jews*, Thomas Cahill describes the Israelite response to Sophia. Avram was a man from Sumeria, a region of richest culture and commerce in ancient times. And by any account, Avram was a very rich merchant. He had prospered and had hundreds of servants, countless livestock, and much abundance. One thing he lacked was children. Sumeria at the time was representative of much of the ancient world. The universal Sumerian "wisdom" was the Wheel, not Sophia. The Wheel was the omnipresent belief that life was entirely cyclical—things are born, they procreate or produce, and then they die. The sun goes up, it reaches its midpoint, and it sets. The moon begins, it waxes, and then it wanes. The tides come in and go out. The seasons change from spring to winter and back again. And on to infinity. From this understanding of reality, any attempt to strive in some direction not in conformity with these three things—birth, procreation, and death—is fruitless, stupid, and bound for failure. Much of Sumerian religion centered on worship of procreation and the life circle. There were temple prostitutes engaged in sex acts with priests, there were ritual sacrifices of children to appease the gods and stave off famine or disaster from striking a civilization causing premature mass death, and there were routine planting and harvest festivals celebrating the seasons of the year (and life).

It was in this setting, in his middle age, that Avram heard a whisper from Sophia. It told him to go west, to leave behind all he knew and had experienced to find a Promised Land, and that this voice would make him a father of people so countless that there were not that many stars in the sky. To a childless rich man, this sounded like the fulfillment of the hopes that Avram had always had. One problem: the *method* to achieve children was totally out of sorts with what Sumerian culture prescribed. One did *not under any circumstances* abandon one's lot in life in pursuit of a hope or dream. Granted, procreation was very much at the core of the Wheel, and in that sense, Sophia was appealing to Avram's desire to embrace the Wheel. But in another sense, Sophia was asking Avram to simultaneously reject the Wheel.

This a good Sumerian should not do, particularly one as wealthy and established as Avram, who had life relatively good. Ask any Sumerian whether walking out of town into the desert in pursuit of procreating and having lots of children because of some voice in your head would be a good idea and they would have laughed hysterically. Avram was embracing the height of folly. He was rejecting the station he was born into in life and seeking something outside of the obvious. To Sumerians and followers of the Wheel, Avram was simply suicidal and not in his right mind.

And yet, Avram did so walk. He wasn't rash and heedless in following Sophia, throwing off all of the attributes of his Sumerian upbringing. Some of the Wheel came with him (as it must for anyone steeped for his entire life in a certain philosophy). He brought all his servants and livestock with him. A good itinerant merchant doesn't become a mendicant by virtue of his travels. But he left Sumeria. The Wheel was being broken.

Avram journeyed to his Promised Land. Sophia told him along the way he would now be called Abraham ("The Father of Many Nations"). Abraham was gaining a new identity, one provided for him by Sophia and not the lot in life he was born into.

Fast-forward hundreds of years to another man, descended from Abraham, raised in absolute luxury who would hear again from Sophia after many centuries when mankind did not hear Sophia's voice, but rather kept on serving the Wheel. A man named Moses saw a bush burning in a desert place. Moses had been raised as a son of the Pharaoh, the most powerful man on Earth and a fervent believer in the Wheel. And from this encounter with a talking, burning bush, Moses abandoned his powerful station in life and became a Bedouin desert wanderer for 40 years, leading a ragtag group of former Israelite slaves through scorching deserts in search of the Promised Land that Abraham had been given by Sophia centuries earlier.

Moses never entered his Promised Land. He died in that desert. And so, to anyone who ascribes to the Wheel, his folly was evident. He left behind the certainty of the circle for the ashes of the scorching desert. And thus, his was a life wasted.

But to someone listening to Sophia, Moses' striving and pain was hardly a waste. The Wheel says there is nothing new under the sun. It is all about birth, procreation, and death, and everything that happens follows that pattern. But Moses created something brand new in the life of the world—the Law. The Law was whispered down on high from Jehovah, the God who claimed he was more powerful than any gods who serviced the Wheel (such as the Sumerian fertility gods). And this God, Jehovah, said he was the voice that was whispering in the ears of Moses and Abraham and many other people. Jehovah was the Sophia. Jehovah was offering Moses by his desert wanderings the opportunity to create something *new* that the Wheel had overlooked.

What was the Law? It was a pattern of righteous living. It said that sacrifice of children to appease unseen fertility gods was wrong, as were temple prostitutes. It said that there was immeasurable value to life in doing things that did not conform to the pattern of the Wheel, such as leaving behind certain places when Sophia said to, or forfeiting wealth when it was a hinderance. It said that all creation was disordered and the Wheel was an illusion and the Law would help it to become reordered. Most importantly, the Law showed that there were goals to aim for apart from birth, procreation, and death. That things that might seem frivolous or wasteful were in fact very good, and that in seeking those ends, time would travel *in a direction*. Life was not a circle, it was a *journey* with a definite beginning and destination—one that potentially transcended the mortal life.

The Israelites had upended the Wheel. Time had a direction, and that direction was not a circle. Once time has a direction with a beginning and end, then making choices about how to use that time becomes important. And so, wandering into the desert to create the Law doesn't seem so stupid after all. Nor does anything that endorses "progress."

I am aware that this brief, glossy recount of the Hebrew Bible may seem rather strange to this audience. And I am also aware that most of us take for granted that there is law and order and that time goes in a certain direction, rather than around and around in circles. (These are taken for granted, however, only because Abraham and Moses and countless others defied the Wheel and did something radically different than what the prevailing culture said to do.)

But in another light, many people today still follow the Wheel whether they know it or not. Yes, we "know" there is law and that it should be followed. But how many corporate executives today are willing to take a fine and pay it if it means exorbitant profits for breaking the law? (According to one California deputy attorney general I recently met, most major corporations are willing to do so.) The Law means something only if it benefits us? If the Law and the Wheel are co-existent? Or is there something good that comes of following the Law to spite the Wheel, or when following the Law has an immediate disadvantage for us.

The Israelites, and later the Jews, extolled that following the Law, regardless of the apparent consequences, had immeasurable value and was the only good life that there is. It is not a matter of chanting, yoga bending, dancing, or summoning the Gods. Sophia has spoken. It has told us the hidden wisdom of the world. All we have to do is meditate upon that wisdom, and seek to resist conforming to the Wheel, and we will live the good life (and so will the corporations that we pilot). Yes, our corporation may die in a desert as Moses did, but we will have created something beautiful, good, and true in creating a lawful corporation, a humane corporation, something that defied the Wheel.

And so, for many corporate executives today, it is little surprise that a study of law can enhance their lives, careers, and corporate well-being. Doing so will not make your corporation necessarily live longer or grow faster, but Sophia—the wisdom that created the world—will be pleased with our efforts and they will radiate to all mankind a goodness that causes a restoration of the disorder in the world. I teach business law to business students, and I begin by telling them that studying the law will not make them necessarily rich or famous, but it will make them good and beautiful, which are far more important in the light of eternity.

But I want to conclude this dialogue by talking a little about Sophia itself because Sophia, as it turns out, ultimately revealed something more to mankind than the Law through Moses. It revealed its own true character. It revealed to people at different times and places, stretching over hundreds of years, that *Sophia is a human being—one of us*. This was a radical concept. *A God who is human.* Nowhere in the mythologies of the Sumerians, the Greeks or Romans, or even the Israelites themselves, had this revelation taken place. (The Greeks did acknowledge there was an "unknown God" but had not heard Sophia say that it was a human.)

I am a Christian. And Christians believe that Sophia, as a human, speaks *in our language* today and always to every human on earth. Quietly, patiently, taking us as we are, in whatever state of consciousness we are, moving from a disciple of the Wheel to a friend journeying toward Sophia. In many ways, Sophia is curing us all from a distorted belief that life is just one uninspired roundabout with the final silent grave awaiting us (or our corporation). Instead, life is a grand journey from birth on walking back to our Creator, Sophia. Our corporations may die, but their lives and deaths were not in vain. They taught us lessons, brought restoration, and sharpened our vision to keep always in mind the only goal of this life: to reconnect with someone other than ourselves someday. Someone who *loves* us. And that, through all our boardroom goals and stockholder meetings, is what we are really craving: Sophia's love.

Uncertainty management, therefore, converges with the Christian faith, which teaches us that life is not a circle but a path (often winding) toward *home*. Many of us on that path toward home end up working in corporate enterprises, but always by remembering that our experiences, pains, and loves are leading us back to Sophia, who is the person we really want to be with at the bottom of our hearts, re-centers us to realize that we don't need to set goals or make plans. We just need to have a conversation with Sophia, who will stroll with us and talk to us day by day counseling us on the journey, regardless of whether or not we are doing yoga pretzels or meditation seminars.

To sum this all up, I am reminded by a mentor of mine that there are really two stages of life: stages when we ask questions and stages when we answer them. To some of you reading this chapter, you are in the question phase of life. You are asking why bad things are happening to you: why you are suffering, why your corporation is facing bankruptcy, why you had to lay off your best friend or why your best friend just laid you off, or whether you will be able to make the rent next week. The period of asking questions, "Why? Why? Why?" is often a painful one because the answers sometimes—even often—don't come when you want them to.

But here is what my experience (and the experiences of countless billions) with Sophia tells me: someday the answers *do* come. And when they do, they are good and true answers. They are fantastic answers. And those answers reaffirm that this life is not a Wheel, not simply a matter of getting up, shuffling through another painful meaningless day in the middle of our helpless lot in life, and eventually dying. Instead, those answers tell us that no experience, however painful, was wasted. No corporation, however humble, that sought to abide by Sophia's counsel, was ineffective. No uncertainty, however deep, cannot be forded. And that we will journey to a safe and loving home one day, where we will see that the moment by moment living has been preparing us, progressing us, on our journey home. This is the essence of uncertainty management: to embrace Sophia's counsel that defies what seems certain doom before your corporation.

Enjoy the journey home. Trust that Sophia voice. It is already within you.

31 A VIEW FROM THE TOP

Cynthia Patton

Values and Mission Statements

Thoughtful Creation

The foundation of every corporate entity, big or small, is its values and mission statement. For most, however, these statements are merely words on paper. They are usually drafted over days or weeks of "strategy" meetings by senior management teams, often with the assistance of highly paid consultants. These drafting sessions are just one of a few tasks to be completed during the meeting, and the results read like "mom and apple pie". They are neither inspiring nor controversial. What most senior management teams do not realize, however, is that the values and mission statement are crucial to the development of a culture of integrity and compliance.

When developing a mission statement, a company should include as many stakeholders as possible. The goal is to have every employee and board member know, understand and be inspired and guided by the company's values.[1] Consultants can be used to obtain feedback and assist in utilizing the feedback to develop the values and mission statement—feedback via focus groups and surveys. In this way, the enterprise will own the mission. Once complete, the vision and mission serve as the north star for the organization and can be referred to when looking for direction on strategy.

Take for example Amazon's vision statement: "To be the Earth's most customer-centric company, where customers can find and discover anything they might want to buy on line".[2] This statement is effective from a compliance perspective because it drives a customer focus, as well as a motivational or aspirational focus for the company and its employees. Similarly, the Amazon values create a strong customer centric message: "We strive to offer our customers the lowest possible prices, the best available selection, and the utmost convenience."[3] Once again, note the emphasis on the customer. The company's values stress that every team member is an "Amazon leader" and must be guided by their core principles which include:

1. Customer obsession
2. Ownership

1. See, for example, Ford's Governance and Policies, https://corporate.ford.com/operations/governance-and-policies.html
2. https://www.aboutamazon.com/about-us
3. *Ibid.*

DOI: 10.4324/9781351107242-37

3. Insist on the highest standard
4. Earn trust of others
5. Have backbone; disagree and commit.

Amazon's success as a company can be closely tied to its adherence to these principles and like Ford, part of the company success is making sure its core values are part of every employees' DNA from the beginning.

How to Live the Values

The Compliance Program

While values are a driver to developing corporate culture, they must be lived to be successful. It is important that staff see their corporate senior management live the values and set the example for the company. The compliance office is one source to assist senior leaders as they consistently demonstrate their adherence to and belief in the values. The compliance officer and her team develop the policies and procedures, the reward systems and the consequences for values and policy violations. Generally, the compliance office performs their duties by being integrated into the business of the organization and assisting the business on how to accomplish the company mission while following applicable laws, regulations, ethical standards and company policies. Effective compliance programs help the company identify and mitigate corporate and reputational risk while assisting smooth operations by eliminating uncertainty and confusion on how to work compliantly. It also can protect the company from regulatory enforcement actions by documenting company adherence to laws and compliance culture.

There is no one way to establish and structure an effective compliance program. There are, however, several sources for guidance on building a program. In 2003, the US Office of Inspector General (OIG), Department of Health and Human Services, developed the OIG Compliance Program Guidance for Pharmaceutical Manufacturers.[4] The OIGs guidance includes seven elements that it deems important in establishing an effective compliance program. Similar guidance has been developed by the OIG for other industries. In addition, the US Department of Justice has created a checklist for evaluating corporate compliance programs. All of these guidance documents have substantially similar characteristics. The majority of pharmaceutical manufacturers have adopted most if not all of these elements. In addition, the International Organization for Standardization (ISO), based in Europe, has also developed relevant compliance standards including ISO 37001:2016, Antibribery management systems,[5] which attempts to provide a model of standards to "fight bribery and promote an ethical business culture." There are pros and cons to each, and they are not mutually exclusive. They both give a company a guide to developing a compliance program, however, if a company is operated in the United States the OIG guidance should be followed. While all elements are important, we will focus on the key elements that help to foster a culture of integrity and enforce a company's values.

Compliance Officer

A compliance program cannot be successful without an effective chief compliance officer. The CCO should be independent and have access to the board of directors. There is consistently a question as

4. https://www.hhs.gov/guidance/document/oig-compliance-program-guidance-pharmaceutical-manufacturers
5. https://www.iso.org/standard/65034.html

to whether the CCO should be a lawyer and report to the general counsel (GC), CFO, or CEO. Perhaps the biggest debate revolves around departmentalization of the CCO's office from the legal department, often citing the loss of privilege as a reason to primarily keep the role reporting to the GC and not CEO and independence as the reason to separate the roles. The emphasis should, however, be on what are the organizations primary needs from the CCO. The CCO's role is to help organizations understand what they can do, what they should do and the difference between the two. The missing element in law departments is often what "we should do". This does not mean that the compliance officer has a "lock" on ethics. However, many CCOs have been in the position of having to be the member of the C-suite to point out ethical fading or blind spots characterizing ethical decisions as business decisions.

Any compliance structure can work with the right people in place. However, the OIG has consistently made clear that it prefers for the CCO to report to the CEO and has required that reporting structure in all of its CIAs to date. In addition, in its *Measuring Compliance Program Effectiveness: A Resource Guide*, the OIG lists as one factor to look at when determining the effectiveness of a compliance program is whether the CCO reports to the CEO/Board and not the CFO or legal. Finally, while it is not a requirement that the CCO be a lawyer, an understanding of the law and the ability to interpret laws and regulations is necessary. Non-lawyers should surround themselves with a stellar legal team.

Policies and Procedures

All compliance programs need to have policies and procedures that guide the organization on how to follow applicable laws, rules, regulations and company standards. Every program should have a code of conduct that serves as the corner stone of the company policies. There is often confusion about what is a policy and what is a standard operating procedure (SOP). Policies are formal statements that are reflections of corporate objectives. These policies reflect the foundation of a company's values and are designed to last and resist change or erosion overtime.

Procedures are detailed step by step instructions to achieve a given goal or mandate. They often act as the "cookbook" for staff to consult to accomplish a repeatable process, and they are reviewed on a defined review schedule.

Policies and procedures need to be understandable and drafted in a manner that is easy for the organization to follow. As the program develops and matures the procedures can move from rules-based to principle-based policies.

Rules-Based Policies

Rules-based policies are relatively easy to establish. They consist of telling employees what they can and cannot do. Rules- based policies are not by their nature, however, grounded in corporate values; they are prescriptive and often lead to a "how do we get around the rules" or "it does not say we can't do this" mentality. Employees spend more time trying to figure out the limits of the rules as opposed to the spirit of the rules.

While not perfect, rules-based compliance policies are a good place to begin the development of a compliance program because they create a set of norms that an organization can follow. Take the example of protection of privacy rights. All companies have policies that guide the use of personal information. Such policies set up rules that make it a violation to transfer identifiable information regarding, for example, a customer's medical or financial status. Those policies most likely justify the rules by citing various laws such as HIPAA and GDPR. Every employee knows that they cannot share the information but they do not know why because the laws are too complicated for employees to understand and the policies don't explain them. The problem with not knowing why will cause employees to second guess the policy when there is a gray area, such as when personal information is needed to market to customers who have purchased other products. That's where principle-based policies come into play.

Principle-Based Policies

Principle-based policies help clarify the "why" behind policies. In the example above regarding privacy laws, if the company starts with its own values to develop its policies the employees can make the right decisions without specific "dos and don'ts". For example, instead of starting with the laws the company could start its policies with a reflection on its values. If we go back to the values and mission statement in the earlier Amazon example, a company with similar values could draft a privacy policy by stating something such as the following:

> At company X we are customer obsessed and strive for the highest standards in everything we do, therefore, protecting our clients' privacy advances our mission and everyone in our company has a role to play in protecting our customers. Violation of our policies and the laws related to personal information could subject our customers to harm and put our corporate reputation at risk. When in doubt, we err on the side of our customers.

The policy should also then state what laws apply and give a few examples of the policy in action.

The above sets up a principle that all employees can understand and gives them a mechanism to make the right or values-based choice without understanding the nuances of the law or a laundry list of dos and don'ts.

Training

No matter what type of policies a company has, they will only be successful if they are effective. Companies must demonstrate that their code of conduct and policies are understood and followed by their employees. In other words, the policies cannot be binders sitting on a literal or virtual shelf. One vital compliance tool is training. Successful training can serve as a method to show company and employee commitment to compliance. Training on policies should be:

1. Risk based

   Training should be tailored to the function and role that a staff member performs. It should be fit for purpose and not "one size fits all."
2. Accessible

   The training and the policies themselves should be accessible. They should be easily located on a company website or portal. Training should take a variety of formats, including live, web-based, and in multiple languages to accommodate staff needs. And staff must know where to go to seek guidance when they have questions.
3. Documented

   The company should keep records of training taken by all employees and also regularly update and document enhancements to its policies and training. In addition, periodic assessments of the effectiveness of the training will help the CCO enhance the program, and these records will serve as evidence of an effective compliance program.

Tone at the Top

Staff need to see that senior management live the values. A successful compliance program will have senior leaders who not only understand the company values but also demonstrate their commitment on a daily basis. Compliance programs will fail only if the compliance team doesn't enforce the values. The compliance program can and should assist the leadership in how to model compliance. Examples include promoting compliance at all staff and other meetings, including compliance incentives in performance reviews and acknowledging employees who demonstrate compliant behavior.

Another powerful tool is a senior leader certification process. The purpose of such certification is to assist leaders in developing their ethical leadership capabilities in order to maintain a consistent culture of integrity across the company. To complete the certification process, leaders should be asked to confirm annually that they are aware of and are fulfilling their responsibilities as a leader in the areas of ethics and compliance. This includes developing an ethics and compliance leadership engagement plan at the beginning of the year and executing that plan over the course of the year.

Speaking Up

Finally, creating an ethical culture means that employees feel comfortable speaking up when they suspect ethical violations without fear of retaliation. Through this open communication, the company becomes more efficient, more collaborative and innovative. When it comes to speaking up, compliance programs want all staff to know they have a voice and should provide multiple channels for speaking up when employees are faced with ethical and compliance dilemmas or concerns.

Even though speaking up is encouraged, fear and uncertainty can create barriers. Here are a few myths surrounding speaking up and the facts on how compliance encourages staff to share their concerns.

1. *Myth*: I'll face retaliation if I speak up or disagree with someone at work.
   Fact: Compliance programs have anti-retaliation programs and do not tolerate retaliation against staff members who report concerns in good faith or participate in good faith in any investigation or other proceeding. The company's stance on retaliation should be clearly outlined in a compliance reporting and non-retaliation policy and should apply to any reports made through any source, including a business conduct hotline.
2. *Myth*: I don't think I have enough information, or I'm not senior enough to say something.
   Fact: Employees should be encouraged to report any potential misconduct they see or hear about, even if they believe they only have partial information. Everyone, regardless of level, has a responsibility to report suspected misconduct.
3. *Myth*: I don't think the company will do anything.
   Fact: The company must take all reports seriously and look into every issue reported through any channel, including the business conduct hotline and human resources. The ability to thoroughly investigate an issue sometimes depends on the completeness of the information provided. Therefore, anyone making a report must be encouraged to provide as much information and detail as possible so the concern may be investigated and addressed. It may not be possible for the company to provide specific details on the outcome of a report, however, once a case has closed, to the extent possible, the reporting employee should be notified the case was appropriately resolved.
4. *Myth*: I assumed someone else would say something.
   Fact: The "bystander effect"—a phenomenon where the presence of others discourages an individual from intervening, or in this case, reporting—does exist. Employees must be encouraged not to fall into apathy when faced with wrongdoing. They must understand that when they

see or learn of something that concerns them, they must take responsibility to report what they know.

5. *Myth*: If I report something, it won't be kept anonymous
   Fact: Unless prohibited by local law, an employee reporting a concern may remain anonymous. Employees should be informed of this and the company should remind employees of the methods they use to keep information and identity of reporters anonymous (such as encryption and caller ID disabling) (footnote).

A culture of compliance is not easy to create and sustain. It starts with a foundation of values and a mission that every employee can understand and embrace. The compliance program is critical to helping to sustain the company's culture and to reinforce it. But culture does not thrive with the work of compliance alone; it is the job of every senior leader.

INDEX

Note: Page numbers in *italics* indicates figures and page numbers in **bold** indicates tables on the corresponding page.